Good _____ Guide 1996

To Jeys

With best wishes
and Sincere gratitude
· for your exceptional skill.

Arthur Reeves

Dec 95

In memory of our good friend and colleague, Lucy Dicker, who was
a contributor to the Guide and who died tragically on 6 April 1995 in a fall
on La Meije above the French resort of La Grave.

THE
Good Skiing Guide 1996

The 400 best winter sports resorts
in Europe and America

**Edited by Peter Hardy
and Felice Eyston**

in association with the
Ski Club of Great Britain

CONSUMERS' ASSOCIATION

Which? Books are commissioned by Consumers' Association
and published by Which? Ltd, 2 Marylebone Road, London NW1 4DF

E-mail address for readers' reports: guidereports@which.co.uk

Distributed by The Penguin Group:
Penguin Books Ltd, 27 Wrights Lane, London W8 5TZ

First edition of The Good Skiing Guide: 1985

This edition August 1995

The Guide has been prepared with the help of the Ski Club of
Great Britain, which is gratefully acknowledged. But the views expressed
herein are those of the Editors, and not necessarily those of the Club.

Editors	Peter Hardy and Felice Eyston
Sub-editor and	
researcher	Caroline Ellerby
US consultant	Nicky Holford
Contributors	Minty Clinch, Lucy Dicker, Graham Duffill, Elisabeth Hussey,
	Lloyd Rogers, Doug Sager, Patrick Thorne, Arnie Wilson
Design	Editorial Design Partnership
Cover design	Paul Saunders
Cover photo	John Pakington for Skishoot
Maps	Holmes Linnette

British Library Cataloguing-in-Publication Data:
A catalogue record for this book is available from the British Library

ISBN 0 85202 580 7

Typeset by	Editorial Design Partnership, Albion Courtyard,
	Greenhills Rents, London EC1M 6BN
Printed & bound	
in Great Britain by	Scotprint Ltd, Musselburgh

Contents

Which ski resort?

Reference

Introduction

What should have been the greatest season for a generation began with dry green fields at resort level in December and ended in wet ones, as the greatest snowfall in living memory was finally washed away in torrential spring rain.

When the snow did arrive, not in sufficient quantity in most European resorts for Christmas but in copious amounts for New Year, it just went on falling. In Austria's great January storm two metres fell in two days. Val d'Isère was briefly marooned and snow-clearance teams throughout the main alpine countries worked around the clock during much of the winter to keep the traffic rolling.

The higher slopes in the French Alps, when we left them in April, looked set to hold their cover into mid-summer. The Rockies had a good, if not spectacular, winter and California excelled. Mammoth Mountain in California, just keeping its head above an astonishing five-metre base at the end of March, was confidently hoping (at the time of going to press) to stay open well into July.

Norway, steadily increasing in popularity and no longer outrageously expensive in comparison to the main alpine countries, had a more than adequate covering. Both sides of the Pyrenees had a similarly satisfactory winter and the only real casualty was Sierra Nevada, in southern Spain, which suffered the ignominy of having its World Alpine Championships cancelled owing to lack of snow.

The amount and quality of snow should have been exceptionally good news to the skier, who, when the sun did emerge between storms, found conditions hovering between perfection and heaven. So it was, but harsh economic reality struck viciously home and cast continuing blight on an industry beset by woes in recent years.

Exchange rates

The inescapable fact is that the cruel exchange rate exacted against sterling on its sick bed is, like some virulent form of cancer, slowly killing off the possibility of Britons skiing in what traditionally are considered the main alpine countries. If the trend continues, there will come a time when the high-speed lifts of Austria, Switzerland and, to a lesser extent, France will be devoid of British skiers.

Tour operators, busy selling holidays for next season, are keen to point out that they have held prices down to the same as, or even less than, last season's rates (although this claim rarely stands up to detailed analysis). But the basic price of a ski holiday is only a part of the total cost. The extra money you need for meals, lift pass, equipment hire and après-ski entertainment is of crucial importance. National tourist boards fight a valiant rearguard action, spiced with statistical analyses of opposition country prices and the inevitable phrase 'value for money'. Well-meaning they may be, but exchange rates are beyond everyone's control.

British skiers have for years complained that the pound in their pocket had, to put it mildly, limited flexibility in most resorts; but what we have now is a crisis. In ten years (1 May 1985–1 May 1995) the number of Austrian schillings to the pound has fallen from ÖS26.30 to ÖS15.31, the number of Swiss francs from SF3.15 to SF1.80 and French francs from 11.50FF to 7.71FF. Frighteningly, the value of the pound to these three main alpine countries plunged again during the course of the season.

Currency	1 Dec 1994	1 May 1995	Change (%)
Austrian schilling	16.77	15.31	8.76
Swiss franc	2.03	1.80	11.30
French franc	8.16	7.71	5.51

(figures compiled by Thomas Cook)

At New Year in the Swiss part of the Portes du Soleil, we came across cheese-on-toast costing £10 in a mountain restaurant, and a bottle of indifferent wine for £20. The blanket imposition of 6.5 per cent VAT, coupled with domestic inflation, had pushed prices in Switzerland to an all-time high. By the time of our return in April, the further collapse of the pound had added nearly 11 per cent more to these prices.

A family skiing holiday in Switzerland is now viable only for the rich and the super-rich. The single-figure percentage of the British ski market to which Switzerland has managed to cling, through the charm of its resorts and undoubted quality of its skiing, will be squeezed still further in 1995–6.

Austria is similarly affected. Once upon a time (only ten years ago) it attracted over 60 per cent of all British skiers. Few Germans skied anywhere else and, with the added bonus of Dutch and Scandinavian visitors, the friendly slopes of the Tyrol and Salzburgerland, plus the much tougher terrain of the Arlberg, annually played host to the most buoyant ski market in Europe.

Times have changed. Austria now accounts for only 30 per cent of the British market. Recession in Germany has shattered the pattern of German visits; Swedes and Norwegians have defected to less expensive pastures. Only the Dutch remain stalwart supporters, supplanting the British in such former strongholds as Saalbach-Hinterglemm and the Ski-Welt.

France takes a marginally less painful third place in this roll-call of economic misery, although more British skiers now go here than anywhere else. There are still a large number of wistful skiers who mentally divide by ten to convert francs to pounds.

In contrast, the pound has fared considerably better against the US dollar, going from $1.183 in May 1985 to $1.574 at the end of last season. The Canadian dollar rate has changed for the better from CDN$1.647 to a much more comfortable CDN$2.310.

The number of Spanish pesetas to the pound has fallen only marginally from Pta213 to Pta193. The number of Italian lira to the pound has risen from L2,421 to L2,629. The course of the winter presented few unwelcome surprises.

Currency	1 Dec 1994	1 May 1995	Change (%)
US dollar	1.53	1.57	-2.67
Canadian dollar	2.10	2.13	-1.43
Spanish peseta	198	193	2.52
Italian lira	2,462	2,629	-6.78

(figures compiled by Thomas Cook)

You don't have to be a financial genius to understand why North America and Italy proved to be two of the most sought-after ski destinations last season, and why we can expect to see further huge increases in their popularity against the more traditional European resorts.

Lifts

It is satisfying to note that the four resorts we have most criticised in the past two editions of the Guide for their lack of reinvestment in the mountains from which they make their living have now found the money for expensive new lifts. Kitzbühel is at last to retire the old Hahnenkamm cable car and replace it with a jumbo gondola in time for the 1996–7 season. Mayrhofen will be transformed this winter with a new lift to replace the old sardine-cans of the Penken cable car. Even Verbier has introduced a 30-person gondola from Ruinettes to Attelas (although this does not address the worst bottlenecks). Zell am See is building a 10km tunnel to ease the traffic that clogs the resort and is to construct two further stages of the Schüttdorf gondola.

Ski schools

We continue to receive a distressing amount of correspondence on the inadequacies of ski schools in the Alps (in marked contrast to the US, where the standard of teaching is consistently praised) and now seriously question whether most group classes after the first week serve any useful function at all beyond piste-guiding. 'We played follow-my-leader' and 'the instructor seemed more interested in showing off his skills than imparting them to others' are the kinds of comment that make up a large proportion of our postbag.

The attitude among too many instructors is that group lessons are a necessary evil to be got out of the way, so that the main part of the day can be devoted to more lucrative private tuition. One consequence of this is that, in too many resorts, the gap between morning and afternoon sessions is now an annoying three to four hours, instead of the far more satisfactory two. Some schools come in for considerably more criticism than others. Indeed, the Swiss Ski School (SSS) in Zermatt wins our special award for once again attracting more adverse comments on its shortcomings than any other school in the Alps.

The advent in other resorts of an increasing number of rival ski schools to the state institution must be of benefit to skiers who can now shop around for the best and the cheapest tuition, although the variation in price tends to be minimal. However, the number of such schools is now reaching epidemic proportions in some resorts: Saalbach Hinterglemm has 9 and Val d'Isère/Tignes has 12.

Ski lessons are universally expensive, and skiers on a budget should seriously question whether they are getting value for money or spending large sums on an unnecessary holiday extra. The dramatic increase in the number of ski schools comes at a time when the number of skiers is static, if not falling, and the process of learning to ski is easier than ever.

Naturally, complete beginners need intensive tuition. However, huge technical advances in equipment, coupled with modern teaching techniques, mean that any reasonably co-ordinated and fit person aged 20-30 can learn to ski parallel within two weeks. Such skiers can, in a fortnight, attain a standard that used to take five years of ski holidays. What you then need is experience and whether you gain this by skiing behind an expensive instructor or a tour operator's free ski-guide is a matter for serious thought.

The next stage of instruction is to get off what is known as the intermediate plateau. While further group lessons may benefit some skiers, one-to-one tuition or a specialist course with only a handful of pupils and run by an instructor who is a fluent English speaker is eminently preferable. 'I learned more in two days than in five years of group lessons', enthused one correspondent.

There is no doubt that instruction in your own tongue is of great benefit and speeds up the learning process. A number of the more go-ahead ski schools in the most popular resorts do employ British instructors. The ski-instructor war, led by the French against the intrusion of foreign teachers, has now largely been settled. Last season saw the welcome emergence of the British European Ski Teachers (BEST), an association of professional British ski instructors who have the highest qualification (BASI 1) and are licensed to teach in Europe. Members based in France have all passed their *équivalence*, the tough international ski exam set by the French, and can work in harmony with the local ski school.

Beginners' tickets

The meanness of many ski resorts in charging beginners, even children, for the use of all nursery-slope lifts strikes a harsh chord with most readers. However, this is exceeded by a handful of the greediest who demand that complete novices buy a full-area lift pass.

Pas de la Casa in Andorra, which is hardly the smartest of European resorts and one that prides itself on its low prices (it has precious little else going for it), leads the field in this respect. On the last day of the half-term holiday we wanted to take our three-year-old once, perhaps twice, up the baby rope-tow in the nursery area while our confident seven-year-old amused himself on the same slope. To achieve this necessitated a walk of half a mile to the main ticket office for a free under-fives lift pass and the investment of Pta3,050 (£15.25) for the older child and Pta3,600 (£18) for one adult: a total cost of Pta6,650 (£33.25) for a few runs down a 50m slope. We declined.

Interestingly, some of the major French resorts, otherwise not necessarily famed for their magnanimity, offer the best deals. Courchevel, Val d'Isère, Flaine and Les Arcs all have three or more free lifts along with Courmayeur in Italy. Risoul, La Plagne, Crans Montana and Snowbird have at least one. Most Austrian and Swiss resorts operate a points-ticket system for beginners, which is at least preferable to buying a full lift pass before you have discovered whether or not you actually like skiing.

Accident

Our season ended suddenly and tragically in April with a fall in a couloir above the French Dauphiné resort of La Grave. Lucy Dicker, an important contributor to *The Good Skiing Guide* who had just spent a whole year skiing around the world, was killed, and Peter Hardy, co-editor of the Guide, was seriously hurt in the 250m fall and is still recovering from his injuries.

One consequence of the accident and Peter Hardy's subsequent stays in French and British hospitals was to give us an insight into the performance of ski insurance in the event of a major claim, and to emphasise the importance of having sufficient cover. Advanced skiers in particular should check whether their policy covers off-piste skiing with or without a mountain guide, and all skiers should ensure that it covers the full cost of medical repatriation for themselves and their family.

Peter Hardy was skiing off-piste with a guide, which satisfied the terms of his American Express Centurion Assistance scheme. Amex use Europ Assistance, Europe's largest travel insurance company, which swung smoothly into action after one telephone call. Peter spent ten uncomfortable days in hospital in Briançon before he was strong enough to be flown home on a stretcher. The cost of operations and all medical care was handled directly by the insurance company. It also paid for his wife's basic accommodation, as well as taxi transfers and flights home for his two children and a guardian. A nurse was arranged to accompany Peter from hospital to hospital on the stretcher journey home.

Mountain guides

The accident also raised the question of the area of responsibility of a mountain guide hired by a skier to take him or her off-piste for what, in this case, should have been a relaxed day in the sunshine for a party of mixed-ability skiers. The accident happened at 4pm in the notorious Couloir des Trifides above La Grave. Peter Hardy was aware that two skiers had already been killed in previous days in that same couloir. He said afterwards: 'Hindsight is easy, but had I known the name of the couloir we were skiing I most certainly would not have gone into it.

'The rescue helicopter guide later told me that he would have taken a single expert skier down it in the morning only. The thought of taking a party of seven, which included two less experienced skiers, down the couloir in the icier afternoon conditions did not, in his opinion, bear contemplation.

'In the final analysis, all of us who go into mountains must accept responsibility for our own safety. That is not in dispute. We didn't have to ski that couloir, the guide gave us a choice, but there is a natural tendency to stay with your friends and put your total trust in the judgement of the accompanying expert. It never occurs to most skiers that this judgement could be flawed.'

Snow Rangers

A technical innovation looks set to reshape the way we ski in the future. It started with the introduction of Fat Boys, a range of super-wide skis led by Atomic Powder Plus, that have become the rage in North America and the large French resorts, but mysteriously have yet to return to Austria where they were invented. Once mounted on these uglies, which resemble shrunken water-skis rather than snow skis, anyone who can ski on piste will be able to ski in deep snow with much pleasure and little effort. However, their performance is limited on a hard-packed piste.

The problem is that, at least in Europe, you are liable to encounter all kinds of snow conditions in one day. Völkl, which produces the Explosiv, a Fat Boy with 40 per cent more lift than a conventional ski, set about building a hybrid that could be used as an all-rounder. What Völkl came up with was the Snow Ranger. This looks like a Fat Boy in its second month at Weight Watchers, still a third wider than a conventional ski but no longer obese. You ski it at your usual length or 10cm shorter. It gives 30 per cent more lift off-piste and carves like a dream on hardpack. A cult following developed so rapidly last season that it became more and more difficult to find them. Völkl has increased production for this season and other companies are anxiously trying to emulate the Snow Ranger. Unlike Fat Boys, the ski has been accepted unequivocally by experts. Ski gurus like the Zimmer brothers, who run the Top Ski guiding company in Val d'Isère, now use nothing else.

Finally, we cannot emphasise enough the importance of contributions from readers. We need your help to compile the Guide. With the aid of our small team of researchers we inspect each season all the major and as many of the minor resorts as we can. However, in a single working visit it is sometimes difficult to dig far beneath the surface. Instead, we rely upon our discerning army of reporters to tell us what is new and what is false. Without your help *The Good Skiing Guide* would not have earned and maintained the respect it has over the past decade as 'the bible of the ski industry'. Do please keep sending us details of your experiences. There is now an e-mail address for report forms (see page 571).

Choosing your resort

When to go skiing is almost as important a factor to consider as where to go, but both are just part of the equation that makes a successful skiing holiday. Companions, accommodation and travel arrangements are also crucial factors. You do, of course, also need snow and sunshine; too little of each results in disappointment. The level of occupancy of the resort is also a major consideration: too many skiers means overcrowded lifts and pistes.

Most European ski resorts open in mid-December but will not necessarily run their entire lift system until the weekend before Christmas. American ski resorts traditionally open for Thanksgiving, which falls on the third Thursday of November. At this time of year it is essential to choose a resort with a high top lift-station where at least some skiing is guaranteed. 'Safe' resorts in Europe include Val d'Isère/Tignes, Val Thorens, Les Deux Alpes, Saas-Fee, Zermatt and Obergurgl.

Prices and crowds peak over Christmas and New Year, with the second week being the busier of the two. Again, it is important to go for altitude. Pretty Christmas-card resorts such as Alpbach, Kitzbühel, Megève, Mürren and Grindelwald do not look quite so festive in a surrounding of green fields.

The low-season begins in the second week of January. This is often the best time to visit the big-name resorts like Verbier, Chamonix, Zermatt and Kitzbühel. Both North American and European slopes should be at their best in February. Unfortunately, the normal peak conditions are invariably coupled with peak crowds, which coincide with school holidays. March and April bring longer, sunnier days and provide some of the best skiing of the winter. Bear in mind that by the end of March, in an average winter, the best snow will be above 1800m.

For the past decade skiing in April has been outstanding, with fresh snowfalls and warm sunshine. As the cover transforms into spring snow, the off-piste opportunities can be exceptional. By Easter the best snow is likely to be above 2000m.

The French school holidays are now staggered by geographical zones to avoid the overcrowding of the main French resorts. Nevertheless, it is worth choosing alternative dates, if you can, to the Paris, Lyon and Grenoble holidays. Visitors to the French Pyrenees and Andorra should note the holiday dates for Toulouse. French school holiday dates to avoid in 1996 are: 24 Feb–11 March and 13–29 April (Grenoble, Lyon, Toulouse) and 2–18 March and 17 April–2 May (Paris).

After deciding *when* to go you then have to decide *where* you want to take your holiday. This depends on your individual preferences and requirements. The choice is influenced by the budget you have available, your skiing ability and experience.

Complete beginners face the hardest task of all, not helped by the inundation of advice from well-meaning friends. A course of lessons on a dry ski slope will save some of the time wasted getting to grips with the basics during the first days of the holiday. Do not be put off by how difficult it all seems; a real slope is much easier than an artificial one.

Modern equipment and teaching methods mean the novice outgrows the nursery slopes within a couple of days. You therefore need to choose a resort with plenty of easy runs for the next stage of progress; large resorts with extensive ski areas and consequently expensive lift passes are generally not suitable. It is also advisable to take a budget holiday instead of spending a fortune, only to discover you do not like it.

Intermediates make up the vast majority of skiers and can find plenty of runs that are suitable for their ability in most resorts. Advanced skiers will need to choose a resort with a large and varied ski area, which has plenty of black (difficult) slopes and off-piste opportunities. In this guide we have endeavoured to indicate the resorts, the ski areas and the runs that are of major interest to each standard.

The final choice of resort should be dependent on the type of holiday you want, the importance of the ski area versus the village and off-slope activities. We feel that most intermediates (and therefore most skiers) should choose the country first and the resort second.

Where you stay within a chosen resort is largely dictated by your budget. In Austria, Italy and Switzerland most accommodation is in hotels. France leads the field in self-catering apartments, but the American condominium is an altogether more luxurious affair. The chalet is a uniquely British and increasingly popular concept with its origins in Switzerland, but is now found in most alpine resorts. You can take over the entire chalet as a group or join a chalet party as an individual or a couple. The standard is now generally high, with more and more operators offering 'luxury' or 'gourmet' weeks.

The all-inclusive staffed-chalet formula is ideal for families, particularly those with young children. A growing number of operators employ their own qualified nannies, who look after pre-skiing children and babies and will often collect older children from ski school while their parents are still on the slopes. The standard and type of hotel or chalet nanny-service can vary, so it is wise to decide whether you prefer a crèche that is run from a well-equipped playroom in the building or a mobile one where the nanny comes to you.

Night-time entertainment traditionally centres around bars of varying degrees of rowdiness or sophistication. As a rule of thumb Austria has the liveliest nightlife and the warmest atmosphere, Italy follows, with Switzerland just behind, while France takes up the rear. Late-night revellers should seek out the major resorts like St Anton, Kitzbühel, Verbier, Zermatt and Cortina d'Ampezzo.

Whichever way you look at it, skiing is an expensive holiday — and is becoming more so. Eastern Europe and Andorra are by far the cheapest destinations. Of the main alpine countries Italy provides the best value because of currency rates. North America, with Canada in particular, is becoming increasingly competitive.

Using the Guide

The tables on the following pages record our verdicts on the advantages and disadvantages of the European and North American resorts that we have covered in detail in the Guide. This year we have listed resorts in alphabetical order by country to aid comparisons; research shows that most readers first choose a country, followed by a resort. Having made an initial selection from the tables on the following pages, we advise you to compare the appropriate sections in the chapters of your choice. For most aspects of a resort we use a simple measure of good or bad (a tick or a cross). Where it is average we have left a blank.

Most headings are self-explanatory but a few need further clarification. **Snow probability** is based on the likelihood of skiing being possible in or around the resort, especially at the beginning of the season. Some resorts receive snow not because of high altitude but because of their own micro-climates. **Tree-level skiing** denotes those resorts that offer sheltered skiing on bad-weather days, with the subsequent improvement in visibility.

Ugly mountain scenery does not exist, so we have only used the affirmative tick for particularly **beautiful scenery**, such as in the Dolomites. **Resort charm** applies to villages that either have beautiful architecture, like Kitzbühel, or are rich in atmosphere like Alpbach or Jackson Hole. Aesthetically unpleasing resorts and busy towns with particularly heavy traffic receive a cross.

Big vertical drop applies to resorts that have a difference of at least 1500m from the top to the bottom of the ski area. In assessing how good or bad a resort is for **tough runs**, we have concentrated on whether a resort as a whole is likely to appeal to skiers who relish a challenge.

Après-ski receives a tick not only for a lively nightlife, but also for a large choice of restaurants, as in Aspen. **Family skiing** refers to a family with a mixture of ages. **Children's facilities** refers to whether or not a resort has ski and non-ski kindergarten as well as babysitting facilities. Resorts rated highly for **resort access** are those that present no local difficulties for drivers or are close to an airport.

We have introduced new colour piste maps of resorts. The key (right) shows types of lifts and grading of runs.

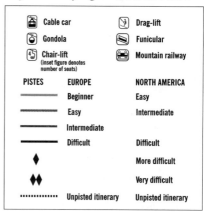

Cable car		Drag-lift
Gondola		Funicular
Chair-lift (inset figure denotes number of seats)		Mountain railway

PISTES	EUROPE	NORTH AMERICA
	Beginner	Easy
	Easy	Intermediate
	Intermediate	
	Difficult	Difficult
♦		More difficult
♦♦		Very difficult
··········	Unpisted itinerary	Unpisted itinerary

RESORT VERDICTS

	Large ski area	Tough runs	Intermediate skiing	Easy runs	Nursery slopes	Off-piste	Summer skiing	Cross-country	Snowboarding	Lift queues
AUSTRIA										
Alpbach	✗	✗		✔					✗	✔
Badgastein	✔	✔	✔							
Innsbruck			✔	✔			✔			✗
Ischgl	✔	✗	✔	✔		✔				
Kitzbühel	✔	✗	✔	✔				✔		✗
Lech/Zürs			✔	✔		✔			✔	✗
Mayrhofen		✗	✔	✔	✔		✔			
Niederau	✗	✗		✔	✔					
Obergurgl	✗	✗		✔	✔		✔			
Obertauern			✔	✔	✔	✔			✔	✔
Saalbach/Hinterglemm	✔		✔	✔	✔				✔	✗
Schladming	✔	✗	✔	✔	✔			✔	✔	
Sölden			✔	✔			✔			
Söll and the Ski-Welt	✔		✔	✔				✔	✔	
St Anton	✔	✔		✗		✔				✗
St Johann im Pongau	✔	✗	✔	✔	✔			✔	✔	✔
St Johann in Tirol	✗	✗		✔	✔			✔		

Long runs	Tree-level skiing	Big vertical drop	Skiing convenience	Snow probability	Non-skiing	Mountain restaurants	Beautiful scenery	Resort charm	Compact village	Traffic	Resort access	Late holidays	Low prices	Après-ski	Family skiing	Children's facilities
			✗		✔		✔				✔	✗			✔	
	✔		✗					✗	✗		✔		✔	✔		✗
			✗	✔	✔		✔				✔			✔		
				✔	✗	✔	✔							✗	✔	
			✗	✗	✔		✔		✗		✔	✗		✔		
				✔		✗	✔				✗		✗	✔		
			✗								✔			✔	✔	✔
✗	✔										✗	✔	✔	✔		
			✔	✔	✗	✔	✔	✔			✔			✔	✔	
			✔	✔	✗			✗			✔			✗	✔	✔
								✗	✔	✔	✗	✗			✔	✔
	✔		✗	✗	✔		✔				✔	✗		✔		
			✔					✗	✗		✔			✔		✗
	✔		✗	✗		✔	✗				✔			✗	✗	
✔			✔	✗			✗							✔	✗	
	✔			✗	✔		✗	✗			✔				✔	✔
	✔		✗	✗		✔		✗		✗	✔	✗		✔	✔	

	Large ski area	Tough runs	Intermediate skiing	Easy runs	Nursery slopes	Off-piste	Summer skiing	Cross-country	Snowboarding	Lift queues	
Zell am See/Kaprun		✗		✓		✗	✓	✓		✗	

FRANCE

	Large ski area	Tough runs	Intermediate skiing	Easy runs	Nursery slopes	Off-piste	Summer skiing	Cross-country	Snowboarding	Lift queues	
Alpe d'Huez	✓	✓	✓		✓	✓	✓		✓	✓	
Les Arcs	✓		✓			✓			✓		
Avoriaz	✓	✓	✓	✓	✓				✓		
Barèges	✓	✗	✓	✓							
Chamonix	✓	✓		✗		✓			✓	✗	
Châtel	✓		✓	✓							
La Clusaz		✗	✓	✓				✓			
Courchevel	✓	✓	✓	✓	✓	✓		✓			
Les Deux Alpes			✓		✓	✓	✓		✓		
Flaine	✓		✓	✓	✓	✓			✓		
Megève	✓	✗	✓	✓	✓			✓			
Les Menuires	✓	✓	✓	✓		✓					
Méribel	✓	✓	✓	✓	✓	✓		✓			
Montgenèvre	✓	✗	✓	✓		✓					
Morzine	✓		✓	✓					✓	✓	✓
La Plagne	✓	✗	✓	✓	✓	✓	✓				

Long runs	Tree-level skiing	Big vertical drop	Skiing convenience	Snow probability	Non-skiing	Mountain restaurants	Beautiful scenery	Resort charm	Compact village	Traffic	Resort access	Late holidays	Low prices	Après-ski	Family skiing	Children's facilities
			✘	✔	✔		✔	✔		✘	✔	✔		✔		
✔	✘	✔		✔		✔	✔	✘				✔		✘	✔	✔
		✔	✔	✔	✘	✘	✔	✘		✔		✔		✘	✔	✔
		✔		✘						✔	✔				✔	✔
			✘	✘				✔		✔	✘	✔				
✔		✔	✘	✔	✔	✘	✔			✘	✔	✔		✔	✘	✘
			✘	✘		✔		✘	✘	✔	✘			✘		
		✘	✘		✔	✔		✘	✘	✔	✘				✔	✔
✔	✔		✔	✔	✘	✔					✔	✘	✔	✔	✔	✔
	✘	✔	✘	✔	✘	✘	✔	✘	✘	✘		✔		✔	✔	✔
		✔	✔	✘			✘		✔	✔		✔	✘	✔	✔	✔
✔	✔			✘	✔	✔		✔	✘	✘	✔	✘		✔	✔	✔
✔	✘		✔		✘		✔	✘	✘	✘			✔	✘	✔	✔
✔				✔					✘	✘				✘	✔	✔
	✔		✔	✘	✘	✘		✔		✘	✔	✘		✘		
✔			✘	✘	✔			✔		✘	✔	✘			✔	✔
		✔	✔	✔	✘					✔	✔	✔		✘	✔	✔

	Large ski area	Tough runs	Intermediate skiing	Easy runs	Nursery slopes	Off-piste	Summer skiing	Cross-country	Snowboarding	Lift queues
Risoul/Vars	✔	✘	✔	✔						✔
La Rosière	✔	✘	✔	✔	✔	✔				✔
Serre Chevalier	✔		✔	✔		✔		✔	✔	✔
Tignes	✔		✔			✔	✔		✔	
Val d'Isère	✔	✔	✔	✘	✘	✔	✔		✔	
Valmorel		✘	✔	✔	✔	✔			✔	✔
Val Thorens	✔		✔			✔	✔			
ITALY										
Bormio		✘	✔				✔			✔
Canazei	✔		✔							
Cervinia	✔	✘	✔	✔	✔		✔			✘
Cortina d\Ampezzo	✔		✔	✔	✔	✔		✔		
Courmayeur		✘	✔		✘	✔	✔			
Livigno		✘		✔	✔					
Sauze d'Oulx	✔	✘	✔			✔				✘
Selva	✔		✔	✔	✔	✔		✔		
Sestriere	✔	✔	✔			✔				✘
La Thuile	✔		✔	✔	✔	✔				

Long runs	Tree-level skiing	Big vertical drop	Skiing convenience	Snow probability	Non-skiing	Mountain restaurants	Beautiful scenery	Resort charm	Compact village	Traffic	Resort access	Late holidays	Low prices	Après-ski	Family skiing	Children's facilities
	✔		✔	✔	✘	✘			✔	✔	✘		✔	✘	✔	✔
			✘		✘			✘					✔	✘	✔	
✔	✔		✘					✘	✘	✘	✘	✘	✔		✔	✔
✔	✘	✔	✔	✔	✘	✘		✘				✔		✘	✔	
		✔	✘	✔	✘	✘		✘				✔		✔		✘
			✔	✘				✔	✔	✔					✔	✔
	✘		✔	✔	✘				✔			✔		✘		✔
✔		✔		✔	✔	✔	✔			✘	✔	✔			✔	✘
			✘	✔	✔	✔	✔		✘	✘		✘	✔		✔	
✔	✘	✔		✔	✘			✘	✘	✘	✔	✔	✔		✔	
✔	✔	✔	✘		✔	✔	✔	✔		✘		✘		✔		✔
	✔	✔	✘		✔	✔	✔	✔	✘		✔		✔	✔		
			✔	✘	✘				✘	✘	✔	✔			✘	✘
	✔		✘	✘	✘	✔		✘			✔	✘	✔	✔		✔
✔		✔	✘	✔	✔	✔		✘			✘		✔		✔	✔
✔			✔	✘				✘								
	✔		✔	✘				✘	✔	✔			✔	✘		✘

	Large ski area	Tough runs	Intermediate skiing	Easy runs	Nursery slopes	Off-piste	Summer skiing	Cross-country	Snowboarding	Lift queues
SWITZERLAND										
Champéry	✔		✔	✔						
Crans Montana			✔	✔	✔	✔	✔	✔	✔	
Davos	✔		✔		✗	✔		✔	✔	
Flims	✔	✗	✔	✔				✔		✔
Gstaad	✔	✗		✔			✔		✔	✔
The Jungfrau	✔	✗	✔	✔		✔				
Klosters	✔	✔	✔		✗	✔		✔		
Saas-Fee	✗		✔		✔		✔		✔	
St Moritz	✔		✔	✔	✗	✔	✔	✔	✔	✗
Verbier	✔	✔	✔			✔	✔		✔	✗
Villars		✗	✔	✔	✔			✔		
Zermatt	✔	✔	✔	✗	✗	✔	✔			
NORTH AMERICA										
Aspen	✔	✔	✔	✔	✔	✔		✔	✔	
Banff/Lake Louise		✗	✔	✔					✔	
Jackson Hole		✔			✗	✔	✔			
Lake Tahoe	✔		✔	✔		✔				

	Long runs	Tree-level skiing	Big vertical drop	Skiing convenience	Snow probability	Non-skiing	Mountain restaurants	Beautiful scenery	Resort charm	Compact village	Traffic	Resort access	Late holidays	Low prices	Après-ski	Family skiing	Children's facilities
	✔				✗	✗	✔		✔	✔		✔	✗	✗	✗		
		✔	✔		✔			✔	✗	✗	✗	✔		✗			✔
	✔	✔	✔	✗	✗	✔	✔		✗	✗	✗		✗	✗	✗		
	✔	✔		✗	✗	✔	✔	✔		✗	✗		✗		✗		
				✗	✗	✔			✔		✗	✔		✗			
				✗	✗			✔			✔		✗	✗			
	✔	✔	✔	✗	✗		✔		✔		✗		✗	✗	✗		
		✗		✗	✔	✔		✔	✔		✔	✗	✔	✗		✔	✔
	✔		✔	✗	✔	✔	✔	✔	✗	✗	✗	✗	✔	✗	✔		
	✔		✔		✔			✔			✗	✔	✔	✗	✔	✔	✔
								✔				✔		✗	✗	✔	✔
	✔	✔	✔	✗	✔	✔	✔	✔	✔	✔	✗	✔	✗	✔	✗	✔	✗
		✔		✗	✔	✔	✔		✔		✗	✗		✗	✔	✔	✔
				✗	✔		✔		✗				✔	✔		✔	✔
	✔	✔		✗	✔	✗	✔	✔				✗	✔	✔			✔
		✔			✗		✔	✗							✔	✔	✔

	Large ski area	Tough runs	Intermediate skiing	Easy runs	Nursery slopes	Off-piste	Summer skiing	Cross-country	Snowboarding	Lift queues
Mammoth Mountain	✔	✔	✔	✔	✔	✔			✔	✘
Park City			✔	✔	✔			✔	✘	
Ski The Summit	✔	✔	✔	✔	✔	✔				✘
Snowbird		✔	✔	✘	✘	✔				✔
Steamboat	✘	✘	✔						✔	✔
Vail/Beaver Creek	✔		✔	✔	✔	✔		✔	✔	
Whistler/Blackcomb	✔	✔	✔	✔	✔	✔	✔		✔	✘
OTHERS										
Andorra	✘	✘	✔	✔	✔					✘
Eastern Europe	✘	✘		✔	✔	✘				✘
Norway	✘	✘	✔	✔				✔		✔
Scotland	✘			✔	✔					✘
Spain	✘		✔							

	Long runs	Tree-level skiing	Big vertical drop	Skiing convenience	Snow probability	Non-skiing	Mountain restaurants	Beautiful scenery	Resort charm	Compact village	Traffic	Resort access	Late holidays	Low prices	Après-ski	Family skiing	Children's facilities
					✔	✔	✗		✗	✗		✗	✔		✗		✔
		✔		✗	✔							✔			✔	✔	✔
		✔		✔	✔							✔	✔		✔	✔	✔
				✔	✔	✗	✗	✔	✗			✔	✔		✗		✔
		✔			✔				✗				✔			✔	
		✔		✔	✔	✗	✗		✔	✔		✔	✔	✗		✔	✔
	✔	✔	✔	✔				✔		✔		✔	✔	✔		✔	✔

	Long runs	Tree-level skiing	Big vertical drop	Skiing convenience	Snow probability	Non-skiing	Mountain restaurants	Beautiful scenery	Resort charm	Compact village	Traffic	Resort access	Late holidays	Low prices	Après-ski	Family skiing	Children's facilities
				✔		✗	✗	✗				✗	✔	✔	✔	✔	✔
				✔		✔	✗	✗				✗	✔			✔	
	✗	✔			✔			✔				✔	✗			✔	
	✗			✗		✔	✗	✗				✔				✔	
								✗					✔		✔	✔	✔

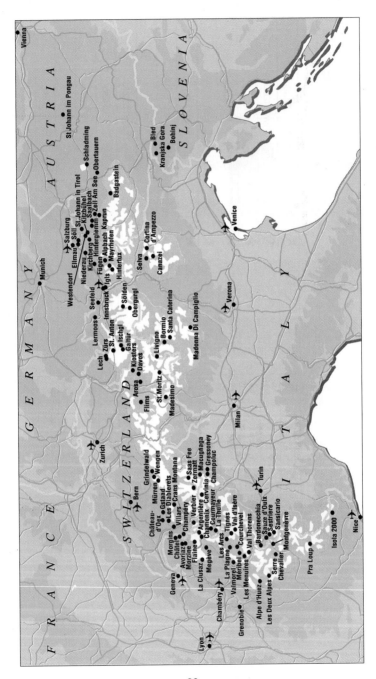

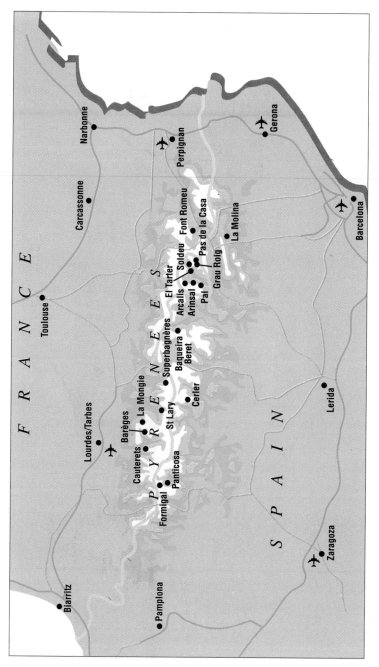

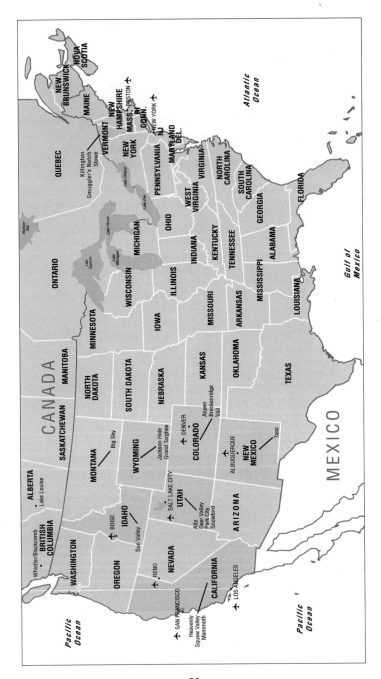

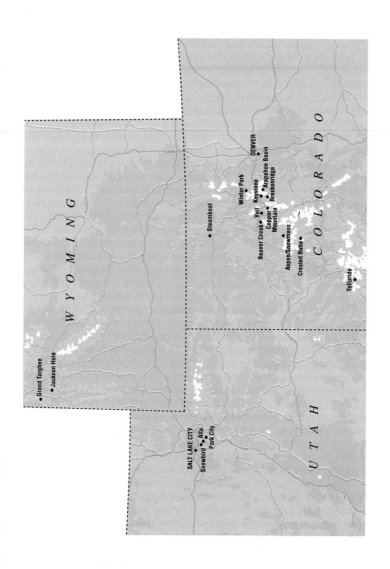

Austria

Poor old Austria suffers from bad press. Cruel currency exchange rates have knocked the stuffing out of the tourist industry on which the economy is largely dependent. Nevertheless, budget apart, Austria remains one of the most attractive of all ski destinations.

To most holidaymakers, mountain village atmosphere is almost as important as the quality of the skiing itself. Ambience, or *Gemütlichkeit*, is what Austria has in abundance. With few exceptions, Austrian resorts are alpine farming villages that have absorbed the demands of tourism while still maintaining their traditional way of life.

The upgrading of Innsbruck Airport to accept charter as well as scheduled flights has greatly eased access to the popular Tyrolean resorts. Most others are reached from Salzburg, while the Arlberg end of Austria is closest to Zurich. Munich Airport, in its new location, is now 45 minutes further from the Austrian border than it was previously.

While the average resort altitude is much lower than in France, this does not necessarily mean that Austria receives less snow. However, to be sure of adequate cover for early or late skiing, it is prudent to pick one of the higher or glacial resorts; these include Obergurgl, Sölden, Obertauern, Kaprun, Ischgl, Zürs and St Anton. Kitzbühel and other famous Tyrolean resorts are notable absentees from this list.

The skiing in general lacks both challenge and variety. While the low and gentle pastures of the Tyrol are scenically beautiful and ideally suited to beginners and wobbly intermediates, more advanced skiers will quickly tire of this benign terrain in any but the best of powder conditions.

Certainly, today's skier does demand considerably more than his or her predecessor of the 1950s and 1960s. This may in part explain the defection in large numbers to the far greater challenges and ski circuses of France. Austria does, however, offer a number of linked or semi-linked complexes covered by one lift pass. These include Ski-Welt (Söll) in the Tyrol, plus Sportwelt Amadé (St Johann im Pongau) and the Glemmtal (Saalbach-Hinterglemm) in Salzburgerland. St Anton in the Arlberg is the exception. It stands alone as Austria's only resort and ski area that offers truly world-class slopes for advanced skiers.

Skiers will find the standard of accommodation higher than any-where else in Europe. Unfortunately, the same cannot always be said for the food. While Austrian mountain-cooking has improved dramatically over the years, the diet of *Wienerschnitzel*, *Gulaschsuppe* and endless dumplings does begin to pall by the end of a holiday.

You can still find the occasional *Tirolerabend*, complete with *Lederhosen*, thigh-slapping and musical wood-chopping, but the empha-sis here is on lively bars and discos. Importantly, there is normally no entry fee into an Austrian nightclub. However, reporters have found worrying examples of doorstep charges creeping in.

Alpbach

ALTITUDE 1000m (3,280ft)

Alpbach is one of the most traditional and charming villages in Austria, with an array of national prizes to prove it. Unlike many of its more commercially minded neighbours, new building has been strictly limited and the resort has retained its original character, while at the same time still catering for the needs of families who have been returning here winter after winter, generation after generation, for the past 65 years.

Certainly the skiing is of secondary importance to the attraction of Alpbach. The ski area is limited both in size and in variety of terrain and is best suited to beginners and less adventurous intermediates who are happy to ski the same runs over and over again. As well as this, there is the

inconvenience of having to take a free ski-bus from the village to the main mountain and back again each day. However, a number of reporters have commented on the efficiency of the service, including: 'Never have I done less walking in a ski resort'. A car is useful for day trips to other resorts such as Mayrhofen, Söll or Kitzbühel for variety. Parking in the village can, however, be a problem.

Alpbach is neither the place for intermediates who are trying to clock up the kilometres, nor is it for advanced skiers searching for new challenges. Unlike many of its lowland Tyrolean rivals, however, it does provide adequate scope (for a week) for the full spectrum of skier, from beginner to expert. Consequently, it deserves its reputation as a pretty family resort ideal for a Christmas holiday, although snow in the village cannot be guaranteed.

On the mountain
top 2000m (6,560ft) bottom 830m (2,722ft)

Apart from the nursery slopes next to the village and the Böglerlift with its south-facing red (intermediate) run (rarely open), all of Alpbach's skiing is on the slopes of the **Wiedersberger Horn**, a five-minute bus ride from the village. One reporter comments: 'It's a great resort if you don't mind doing the same run over and over again.' Mountain access from Alpbach is on the two-stage six-seater Achenwirt gondola across the wooded north-facing slopes to **Hornboden** at 1850m. Queuing is not a problem here, although the number of skiers increases at weekends.

Alpbach has a large vertical drop compared to other Austrian resorts of a similar altitude, and there are a number of long runs. It is interesting to note that although it has always had the reputation of being a beginners' resort, all but a couple of the runs on the mountain are marked red and only one, the Familienabfahrt, is blue (easy). Mountain access is also possible by chair-lift from **Inneralpbach** along the valley. Here the lifts join up with the skiing above Hornboden, and a long, easy red run takes you from Gmahkopf back down to Inneralpbach. The top lift here, Hornlift 2000, opens up some higher altitude and more challenging intermediate skiing.

Beginners
Complete novices need not stray far from the village. Easy nursery runs are served by two drag-lifts in **Alpbach Dorf** itself, and a third drag-lift, the Dorferlift, provides greater challenge. Once the basics have been assimilated or if poor snow conditions exist at this low altitude, skiers progress to the Familienabfahrt on the Hornboden, reached via the gondola.

■ **WHAT'S NEW**

The swimming-pool complex has been renovated

This is a long path from Gmahbahn to Kriegalm, which reporters claim is often icy. The views around Hornboden are superb, and the terrain open and gentle with several short drag-lifts also suitable for near-intermediates

With the exception of a couple of moderately challenging black (difficult) runs, the whole mountain is given over to intermediate skiing. The small number of pistes (ten) marked on the local piste map does not do full justice to the actual size of the groomed area; the pistes are extremely wide and an equivalent US resort would manage to triple the number and give them more appealing names. The standard of piste preparation is very high.

Advanced
From Hornboden a couple of wide pistes run back down to the **Kriegalm** halfway-station, including an FIS racecourse, which is one of the two black runs on the mountain; the other is Brandegg. From here, a red run carries on down to the bottom, creating a good, fast course of over 1000m vertical, which is used by British racing clubs for their competitions.

Off-piste
Alpbach is said to be ideal for 'lazy powder skiers'. According to one reporter you can lie in bed after a night of snowfall until 10.30am and still cut fresh tracks. The long red itinerary route from Gmahkopf down to Inneralpbach is not pisted, though it is usually well skied, and conditions are not generally difficult. There is some interesting off-piste skiing around the Wiedersberger Horn, and the ski school runs special tours for this on Saturdays.

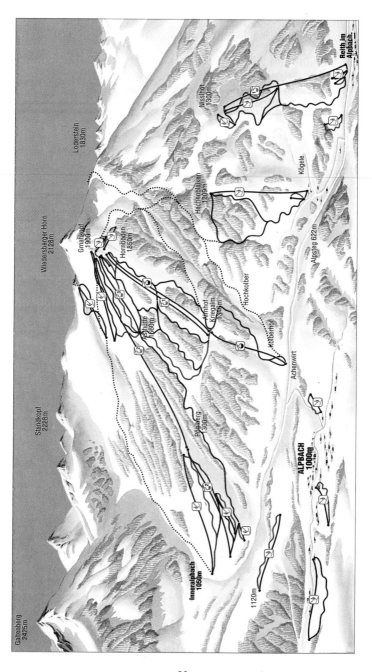

Snowboarding
Both the Alpbach and Innertal ski schools offer snowboarding courses.

Ski schools and guiding
We have favourable reports of the Alpbach Ski School. It is said to be 'well organised' and 'the instructors spoke good English'. One reporter commented: 'The standard of instruction was about the best I have had anywhere.' Guided powder-tours can be arranged through the schools.

Mountain restaurants
Hornboden is a self-service and à la carte restaurant at the top-station of the gondola and is also easily reached by non-skiers. Reporters describe it as 'crowded and expensive'. Rossmoos is above the village and offers typical Tyrolean food. The Gmahstuben is recommended by one reporter for 'very good food', but, as can be expected up the mountain, it is 'not cheap'. The Gasthof Wiedersberger Horn at Inneralpbach is said to be one of the best lunch spots in the region.

Off the mountain
Alpbach is a small, sunny village set on a steep hillside. The compact resort has a pretty green-and-white church at its centre, which is sur-rounded by old wooden chalets. A few new buildings have recently been added, though all new additions have to be built in the traditional style. Many of Alpbach's regulars are British, and there is a British ski club, the Alpbach Visitors, based here since 1968 for children's race training. Shopping is limited to just two sports shops, two boutiques and three souvenir shops.

■ OTHER SPORTS
Swimming, sleigh rides, parapente, tobogganing, indoor tennis at Kramsach (12km away)

Accommodation
Most of Alpbach's accommodation is in hotels, ranging from basic bed-and-breakfast to the very comfortable. The three most luxurious hotels, all with pools, are the Böglerhof, the Alphof and the Alpbacherhof. The latter is centrally placed, and several reporters found the food and service to be excellent here. The Alphof is for the more energetic skiers as it is reached by a 15-minute uphill walk from the village. Its restaurant is warmly recommended. Less expensive hotels include the Post, Haus Angelika, Haus Elisabeth, Haus Erna and Haus Max. The keenest skiers may find the Galtenberg and the Gasthof Achenwirt well-positioned for the gondola, and **Inneralpbach**, 4km along the valley, is another option for finding a convenient and quiet place to stay.

Eating in and out
The restaurants do not offer much variety, although the recommended ones include the Gasthof Jakober, Alpbacher Taverne, the Reblaus for

Skiing facts: **Alpbach**

TOURIST OFFICE
Postfach 31, A-6236 Alpbach
Tel 43 5336 5211
Fax 43 5336 5012

THE RESORT
By road Calais 1080km
By rail Brixlegg 10km
By air Innsbruck 1 hr, Munich 2 hrs
Visitor beds 2,400
Transport free ski-bus between village and gondola runs every 15 mins

THE SKIING
Linked or nearby resorts Reith (n)
Longest run Kafner, 3km (red)
Number of lifts 21
Total of trails/pistes 45km (22% easy, 56% intermediate, 22% difficult)
Nursery slopes 7 lifts (5 at Alpbach, others at Inneralpbach and Reith)
Summer skiing none
Snowmaking 20km covered

LIFT PASSES
Area pass (covers Alpbach and Reith) ÖS1,280 for 6 days
Day pass ÖS295
Beginners no free lifts
Pensioners reduction for 65 yrs and over
Credit cards accepted no

SKI SCHOOLS
Adults Alpbach Ski School and Innertal Ski School, 10am-midday and 1.30-3.30pm, ÖS1,250 for 6 days
Private lessons both ski schools, ÖS1,900 per day
Snowboarding both ski schools, by appointment, prices and times on request
Cross-country Alpbach Ski School ÖS1,100 for 6 half-days, Innertal Ski School ÖS900 for 5 half-days
Other courses ski-touring, off-piste, monoski
Guiding companies through ski schools

CHILDREN
Lift pass (covers Alpbach and Reith), 6-14 yrs, ÖS820 for 6 days, free for 5 yrs and under if accompanied by a parent
Ski kindergarten Alpbach Ski School, ÖS1,850 and Innertal Ski School ÖS1,760, both for 6 days including lunch
Ski school Alpbach Ski School ÖS1,250 and Innertal Ski School ÖS1,220, both for 6 days (4 hrs per day)
Non-ski kindergarten 3-5 yrs, Mon-Fri 9.15am-4pm and Sat 9.15am-midday, ÖS900, extra ÖS60 per day for lunch

FOOD AND DRINK PRICES
Coffee ÖS25, glass of wine ÖS18, small beer ÖS25, dish of the day ÖS130

pizzas and the Gasthof Wiedersberger Horn. The most luxurious is the restaurant in the four-star Hotel Böglerhof. Rossmoos and Zottahof, both up the mountain, are popular in the evening.

There are two Spar supermarkets in Alpbach and one in Inneralpbach, which sell self-catering basics. One reporter points out that all Austrian supermarkets are closed on Sunday. Self-caterers are strongly advised to bring enough basic supplies for the weekend.

Après-ski
The nightlife in Alpbach is not too expensive, according to our reporters.

You will find typical Tyrolean evenings; sleigh rides, skating, curling and bowling are the main post-skiing pastimes. The public swimming-pool and sauna are about five minutes' walk from the village centre and there is a long toboggan run at **Reith**.

The Jakober Bar is the focal point of the village, and the Hotel Messnerwirt is also lively. The Hornbeisl, next to the lifts in Inneralpbach, is always busy, the Waschkuch'l is a good place for a quiet drink and Birdies Pub in the village centre for a noisy one. The Schneeloch disco in the basement of the Hotel Böglerhof is recommended as 'remarkably sophisticated'. The less popular Weinstadl disco is 400m from the village centre. One reporter recommends the horse-drawn sleigh rides up to a 300-year-old inn at the head of the valley.

Childcare
Alpbach has both a ski kindergarten and non-ski kindergarten.

Linked or nearby resorts
There is more skiing at Reith, 7km down the valley from Alpbach, which includes mainly red runs and some beginners' skiing served by several more nursery slope lifts.

Badgastein

ALTITUDE 1100m (3,608ft)

The Gasteinertal has five ski areas: Badgastein, Bad Hofgastein, Graukogel, Dorfgastein and their modern neighbour, Sportgastein. Between them they offer 250km of bus- and mountain-linked skiing in a magnificent winter-sports setting. **Badgastein**, dramatically stacked on a steep hillside, is the best-known centre of the quintet. It is no alpine charmer, but a town of that slightly faded grandeur associated with spas, with impressive-looking and rather formal hotels looming above the River Ache. With a smart casino and many first-class hotels, it still attracts a well-heeled clientèle, but that does not mean it is a resort purely for wealthy gamblers.

■ GOOD POINTS

Large intermediate ski area, tough runs, tree-line skiing, variety of après-ski, easy rail access, reasonable prices

■ BAD POINTS

Lack of skiing convenience, awkward for families with small children, heavy traffic

Its sister, **Bad Hofgastein**, is a spacious and comfortable spa without any grandiose pretensions in a more peaceful and traditional Austrian village setting, which makes it particularly popular with families.

Similarly **Dorfgastein**, situated just inside the narrow gateway to the valley, is an unspoilt rustic village with direct access to plenty of easy and intermediate skiing. **Graukogel** is simply a ski area on the outskirts of Badgastein. **Sportgastein**, at the head of this narrow endless valley, remains largely undeveloped beyond a couple of restaurants and because of its high altitude it can be cold and bleak. It does, however, come into its own when snow is poor elsewhere in the valley.

Gold and silver were mined in the Gasteiner Valley a century before Christ, and the rich ore of the Tauern mountains continued to be the major source of revenue for the area until the sixteenth century. Apart from recent fame as a conference centre and ski destination, its reputation as a resort is founded on its curative thermal baths. Schubert composed his D Major Piano Sonata Deutsch 850 here while taking the cure in the summer of 1825. By coincidence, Mozart's widow and mother were here at the same time.

On the mountain

top 2686m (8,810ft) bottom 850m (2,788ft)

The main mountain access from **Badgastein** is via a two-stage gondola, which climbs from above the station to the Stubnerkogel at 2246m, a tangled junction of lift arrivals at the top of a long ridge. The east-facing runs to Badgastein provide good, tough skiing, with a mixture of open ground above halfway and woods below, which are mostly graded red (intermediate), but difficult when conditions are poor. The blue (easy) run winds down the mountain and is usually crowded and often icy. The wide top-half of the slope gives plenty of opportunity for off-piste variations.

In addition to the main ski area between Badgastein and Bad Hofgastein, there are three other separate areas, all with differing attractions. The Graukogel runs above Badgastein on the far side of the valley are few in number, but long and satisfying descents for good skiers. The friendly skiing shared by Dorfgastein and Grossarl is a confidence-building, but at times challenging, small area for beginners and intermediates.

Sportgastein, at the head of the valley, can get icy when the weather closes in. On a fine day, however, the piste skiing is varied enough to be challenging and the off-piste can be quite exceptional. If snow conditions are poor elsewhere in the valley, Sportgastein can become crowded. However, the bottleneck has been dramatically alleviated by the installation of a smart new gondola to replace the old chair, which provides main mountain access.

Beginners

The area has five nursery slopes served by baby drag-lifts, but overall cannot be recommended as ideal for beginners or even second-week skiers. From Badgastein, the novice slopes are an inconvenient ten minutes away at **Angertal**. Most blue runs are a pinkish-red in comparison with Austrian resorts of a similar size and the whole Gasteinertal is better geared towards more accomplished skiers.

Intermediates

The entire valley is better suited to confident intermediates looking for a combination of mileage and challenge. Graukogel has superb tree-level skiing and is the place where the locals go on a snowy day. Confident skiers will be mainly interested in the long run around the back of the mountain, which is reached either from Höhe Scharte at 2300m or from Kleine Scharte at 2050m. In good snow conditions it is possible to ski 1450m vertical over 8km all the way to the bottom of the railway. Skiing is possible with only a minimum of snow cover, as most of it is on pastureland with few rocks and stones.

Advanced

The north-facing runs down into the Angertal provide some of the best skiing in the region. From Jungeralm a long, undulating black (difficult) run drops directly through the woods.

Off-piste

Untracked opportunities abound above the Schlossalm next to Höhe Scharte. Both the north and south faces of Sportgastein can provide excellent, long powder runs after a snowfall.

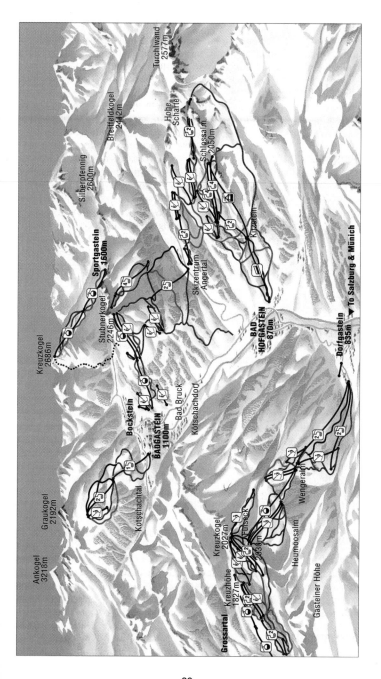

Tuchlwand 2571m

Breitfeldkogel 2442m

Hohe Scharte

Silberpfennig 2600m

Schlossalm 2050m

Kötzstein

Sportgastein 1600m

Kreuzkogel 2686m

Stubnerkogel 2246m

Skizentrum Angertal

Bockstein

BADGASTEIN 1100m

Bad Bruck

Kötschachdorf

BAD HOFGASTEIN 870m

Dorfgastein 835m

▼ To Salzburg & München

Graukogel 2192m

Ankogel 3218m

Kötschachtal

Wengeralm

Heumoosalm

Kreuzkogel 2027m Fulseck 2050m

Kreuzhöhe 1827m

Grossartal

Gasteiner Höhe

Snowboarding

Badgastein and Dorfgastein have man-made half-pipes, but the most highly recommended is the natural half-pipe at Sportgastein. Both Badgastein's ski schools offer snowboard tuition.

Ski schools and guiding

We have good reports of both the Skischule Pflaum and the Skischule Luigi. Class size seems to vary between four and twelve. The standard of English is high — 'the instructor even understood our jokes'.

Mountain restaurants

The area is plentifully served with pleasant huts on the slopes as well as self-service cafeterias at the lift stations. Prices appear to be no higher than in the valley, and there they are low by Austrian standards, which is surprising in a resort of this standing. Reporters particularly recommend the Wengeralm above Dorfgastein for its 'very good traditional fried-potato pancakes'. The Jungerstube on the far side of the Stubnerkogel is praised for its 'wicked hot chocolate'. Sportgastein has two new restaurants to go with its refurbished image, one at the bottom and the other at the halfway gondola station. Both are said to provide decent food with good service.

Off the mountain

Badgastein is built in a cramped, claustrophobic position on the steep, wooded slopes, which abruptly close the southern end of the **Gastein Valley**. The main road and railway bypass the resort centre, which is more simply negotiated by the steep footpaths and stairways than by car.

The focus of the resort is a smart complex including a hotel, shopping precinct, casino and conference hall projecting from the hillside beside the waterfall. The resort's upper level, a steep but short climb away, is a rather ordinary collection of unfashionable spa hotels, which attract skiers in winter because of their convenient location, and newer accommodation, which has sprung up here for the same reason.

Badgastein has an annoyingly complicated one-way system; traffic is heavy and parking can be difficult. Because of the steepness of Badgastein itself, transport within the resort is preferable to walking. The bus service between the resorts is efficient but 'hideously overcrowded' during high season and confusing, with both city- and ski-bus lines to different destinations: 'bus-stops within the resort are not always marked, and timetables can be hard to find'. Taxis are plentiful and rates negotiable. Reporters say a car is handy for visits to the Graukogel ski area on the other side of the valley, Bad Hofgastein and Dorfgastein. A growing number of reporters enthuse about the region and as one put it: 'There is nothing you can find that is bad about Badgastein'.

Accommodation

Most of the accommodation is in hotels, of which there are quite literally hundreds in the valley, some with hot and cold thermal water. Among the hotels at the top of the resort within easy walking distance of the Stubnerkogel lifts is the Bärenhof, which is the most comfortable and expensive. The Krone and Goethehof are ideally placed, but rather uninspiring middle-range hotels. Much more charming and in a quieter position is the simple Fischerwirt. Hotel Mozart is recommended as comfortable and spacious, and 'well-positioned for the skiing and the nightlife'. The Tannenburg is in an excellent location and has been completely refurbished to a high standard of comfort. The renovated Salzburgerhof is a luxurious five-star, which is recommended for its 'exceptional attention to detail'. At the foot of the Graukogel lift is the Schillerhof, recommended for its 'splendid views, clean and comfortable rooms'.

Eating in and out

The choice of restaurants is mainly limited to the hotels, but the Bahnhof restaurant is particularly recommended as good value for money. The Mozart on Mozartplatz is praised for its fondues. The Restaurant am Wasserfall is 'inexpensive and cheerful', as is the Felsenbad swimming-pool restaurant. The Chinarestaurant on Kaiser-Franz-Joseph 'makes a pleasant change from *Wienerschnitzel*'.

> **■ OTHER SPORTS**
>
> Skating, curling, indoor tennis and golf, squash, swimming, sleigh rides, tobogganing, rifle shooting, parapente, snow-shoeing

The Villa Hiss is said to offer 'outstanding gourmet fare at a price', and the Restaurant Rader in Böckstein provides 'a great evening out for those who care about their food'. The Prälatur and the Brasserie are both recommended for discerning diners, as are the Leimböck Fischerstube and Evianquelle.

Après-ski

Badgastein used to suffer severely from the 'Scandinavian Disease', personified in the annual influx of mainly drunken and mainly Swedish visitors who did much to enliven to nightly saturation point what was otherwise a quiet resort in the after-dinner hours. We are officially assured that the upward spiralling prices of this and indeed all Austrian resorts have put the bung in this barrel. Certainly reporters provide supporting evidence.

The Gatz Music Club is recommended at tea-time and again much later in the evening. Eden's Pub is said to be usually crowded, 'not least because a giant moose head takes up most of the room.' For night owls the Blockhäusl Club near Mozartplatz begins to liven up after 1am. The Salzburgerhof Hotel bar has live music: 'everything from UB40 to Glenn Miller'.

Manfreda and Kir Royal bars are ever popular. Other late bars to check out include the Belmondo, Filou, Gasteiner Stamperl, Hexn-Häsl, Weinfassl, Pub am Wasserfall and the Zirbenstube. The bar of the Hotel

Tannenburg is said to have 'the cheapest beer in town'. The thermal baths are reputed to be 'the best cure ever for aching limbs and a bruised body and ego', but they are not cheap.

Childcare

Like all resorts with a disparate ski area of this nature it is difficult to recommend Badgastein for children. All the villages have ski kindergarten, which take children from three years old, but finding someone to care for younger ones is more difficult. Hotel Grüner Baum in Badgastein does run a crèche, although we have no reports about it. The nursery slopes are ten minutes from the centre.

Linked or nearby resorts

Bad Hofgastein 870m (2,854ft)

Bad Hofgastein has neither the inconveniently steep and dark setting, nor the faded grandeur of its neighbour. It is smaller, but is still a sizeable resort with 18 hotels spread along the broadest part of the valley. The Kitzstein funicular is a long walk or a bus-ride away. It is a good base for the valley's walks and cross-country trails, and busy skating and curling rinks complete the winter scene. There is an outdoor, naturally heated swimming-pool as well as a modern sports centre with tennis and squash. The kindergarten takes children from three years old.

Accommodation is mainly in hotels. The Gasthof zum Boten is described as an 'excellent old post-house with big, clean comfortable rooms'. The Kaiser Franz and the more expensive Hotel Norica both receive good reports, as do the Hotel Moser and the Salzburgerhof. The Tennis Treff, opposite the funicular station, attracts the main crowds as they come off the slopes with its 'good atmosphere, occasional live music and reasonably priced drinks'. Later on the action moves to Francky's Kneipe along with Sonia's Pub. C'est La Vie is a quiet bar where locals and visitors mix. The one disco is not usually busy.

TOURIST OFFICE
Tel 43 6432 7110-0
Fax 43 6432 7110-31

Dorfgastein 835m (2,739ft)

Dorfgastein is the first of the settlements you come to on entering the Gasteinertal. Too many visitors to the area drive through without stopping. What they miss is a delightful little village with a charming main street lined with arcades. It remains untouched by the slightly depressing health-conscious image of its bigger sisters. Horses and carts clatter along the narrow street past the old church, more often taking local folk about their business than taking tourists for joy rides.

There are several well-kept, friendly and comfortable hotels in the centre. The Steindlwirt and Kirchenwirt are two of the larger ones. The

Skiing facts: **Badgastein**

TOURIST OFFICE
Haus Austria, Kaiser Franz Josefs 1, A-5640 Badgastein, Salzburgerland
Tel 43 6434 25310
Fax 43 6434 253137

THE RESORT
By road Calais 1200km
By rail station in resort
By air Salzburg 1½ hrs
Visitor beds 6,500
Transport free ski-bus with lift pass

THE SKIING
Linked or nearby resorts Bad Hofgastein (l), Dorfgastein (n), Sportgastein (n), Grossarl (n)
Longest run Angertal at Graukogel, 11km (red/blue)
Number of lifts 53
Total of trails/pistes 250km (30% easy, 30% intermediate, 40% difficult)
Nursery slopes 5 lifts and trails
Summer skiing none
Snowmaking 40km covered, 150km in area

LIFT PASSES
Area pass Gastein Super Ski (covers Schlossalm-Angertal-Stubnerkogel-Graukogel-Grossarl and all Gastein resorts), ÖS1,580-1,860 for 6 days

Day pass ÖS330-390
Beginners points tickets
Pensioners 10% reduction for women 60 yrs and over and men 65 yrs and over
Credit cards accepted yes

SKI SCHOOLS
Adults Pflaum and Luigi, ÖS1,650 for 6 days
Private lessons ÖS450 per hr
Snowboarding ÖS1,360 for 3 days, or ÖS450 per hr
Cross-country private lessons ÖS450 per hr or 3 days (2 hrs per day) with Paul Lederer, ÖS600. Loipe 18km
Other courses off-piste
Guiding companies Pflaum and Luigi ski schools, ÖS2,700 per day

CHILDREN
Lift pass 7-15 yrs, ÖS1,120 for 6 days, free for 6 yrs and under
Ski kindergarten 3-5 yrs, ÖS2,400 for 6 days including lunch and some skiing
Ski school Pflaum and Luigi, 3 yrs and over, ÖS2,600 for 6 days including lunch
Non-ski kindergarten 3-5 yrs, ÖS2,400 for 6 days including lunch

FOOD AND DRINK PRICES
Coffee ÖS25, glass of wine ÖS36, small beer ÖS22, dish of the day ÖS90

---

skiing begins at least a five-minute walk from the village. The Gasthof Schihäusl stands at the foot of the slopes. Evenings are said to be livelier than you might expect in a village of this size.

TOURIST OFFICE
Tel 43 6433 277
Fax 43 6463 737

Innsbruck

ALTITUDE 575m (1,886ft)

RESORTS COVERED Axamer Lizum, Fulpmes,
Igls, Neustift, Seefeld,

The third most important city in Austria is not only a minor ski resort in its own right, but is strategically placed to give easy access to some of the best skiing in the Tyrol and even in the Arlberg. It has twice hosted the Winter Olympics and has the advantage of having its own international airport (dramatically enclosed by towering mountain ranges on either side of the Inn Valley). Its geographical situation used to carry serious restrictions to size of aircraft and weather conditions. However, the installation of state-of-the-art air traffic control technology means the airport can now accept charter flights as well as regular scheduled services. The transfer time to most resorts has now been cut by half.

A variety of good local skiing with attractive lift-ticket arrangements is to be found within short commuting distance of this beautiful and historic city. The most important resorts are also accessible for the day by bus, or even more conveniently by car. Innsbruck stands at the crossroads of Western Austria and is well served by a network of motorways fanning out towards the Arlberg, through the Inn Valley towards the German border, as well as up towards the Brenner Pass and Italy beyond.

The Ötztal and the snow-sure skiing of **Obergurgl** and **Sölden** can be reached in under 90 minutes. The journey to **Kitzbühel** and the **Ski-Welt** takes an hour. To add to the incentive of staying in the city, a single ski-pass called the Innsbruck Gletscherskipass covers the six main local areas including **Igls**, **Axamer Lizum** and the **Stubai Glacier**; it gives access to a total of 52 lifts serving 112km of piste.

The two permutations of the more expensive Innsbruck Superskipass also allow you to ski Kitzbühel and/or the **Arlberg** for a day, thus providing 200 lifts and 500km of piste for your money. Bus travel is included in the price, and anyone staying for more than three days is entitled to a Club Innsbruck discount card, giving a reduction on the passes. Free ski-buses depart from the Landestheater and the Hauptbahnhof each morning and bring skiers back at the end of the day. Reporters are impressed with the service.

Pleisen 2236m

Hoadl 2343m

To Kühtal ▲

KALKKOGEL

Gschwandtkopf 1500m

Seefeld 1200m

Härmelekopf 2050m

Axamer Lizum

Axams

Seefelder Spitze 2220m

Seefelder Joch 2100m

Stubaier Wildspitze 3340m

Nockspitze 2406m

Birgitzkopf 2098m

Schaufelspitze 3333m

Pfarmeskopf 1800m

Götzens

Solstein

Haflekar 2334m

Schlick

Mutterer Alm 1610m

Mutters

Seegrube 1905m

Stubaier Gletscher

Neustift 1000m

Fulpmes

Schönberg

Patsch

IGLS 893m

INNSBRUCK 575m

Hungerburg

Habicht

To Brenner Pass ▲ & Italy

Heiligwasser

Lans

Serles

Aldrans

Sistrans

Patscherkofel 2247m

Rinn

Hall in Tirol

Tulfes

To Vienna, München ▲ & Salzburg

Glungezer 2677m

2059m

Halsmarter 1643m

Compared with what one might call a conventional ski resort, the cost of staying in the city is considerably lower. The choice of restaurants is wide and nightlife is both lively and varied. One reporter comments that 'not many places can include *Die Fledermaus* at the opera as après-ski on New Year's Eve'.

Innsbruck's 'own' skiing is to be found just outside the city across the River Inn in the Seegrube-Nordkette area above **Hungerburg** on the south-facing slopes of the Hafelekar. The black (difficult) Karrine and the red (intermediate) Langes Tal runs are both particularly challenging. The Glungezer area above **Tulfes** on the other side of the valley consists of two blues (easy) and two reds on the slopes beneath the 2677m Glungezer.

Axamer Lizum 1600m (5,248ft)

This is a somewhat characterless ski station. It has four hotels and a huge car-park set in the heart of the largest and most appealing all-round ski area beneath the peaks of the Hoadl and Pleisen mountains. Weekend lift queues, as in all the Innsbruck ski areas, can be a problem, but the ten lifts provide piste possibilities, which are both extensive and varied. The 6.5km Axamer, graded black, but red by most resorts' standards, takes you all the way down to the quiet village of Axams at 874m.

Across the narrow valley, a long chair serves either the black Riesenslalom Herren run back to Axamer Lizum or it gives access to the sunny and easy pistes above **Mutters**, the sixth and smallest of Innsbruck's own ski areas. Expectations of an improved link to form a ski circus here have not yet been met; and they now seem likely to have evaporated in the light of the growing environmentalist lobby in the Tyrol.

TOURIST OFFICE
Tel 43 5234 8178
Fax 43 5234 7158

Fulpmes 937m (3,073ft)

Slightly further away, but still within easy post-bus travel, the **Stubaital** offers some of the best skiing in the area. **Mieders**, **Telfes**, **Fulpmes** and Neustift all share a lift pass. Above Fulpmes, but not directly accessible from it, there is good skiing in a sheltered bowl now branded as Schlick 2000 Skizentrum. Lifts include a four-seater chair going up to 2200m. Some of the runs are tough and unpisted, but the majority are easy and confidence-building, and good for lower intermediates. The small, sunny nursery area receives favourable reports and Innsbruck can be reached by a scenic train/tram ride.

The Hotel Stubaierhof and the Hotel Alte Post are both recommended. Restaurants include the Leonardo Da Vinci ('very popular and good value'), and the Gasthaus Hofer, which serves 'simple, plain Austrian farmhouse fare'. The Café Corso, the Ossi-Keller, Platzwirt and Dorfalm discos make it a lively place by night.

TOURIST OFFICE
Tel 43 5225 2235/2892
Fax 43 5225 3843

Igls 893m (2,929ft)

Igls, five kilometres up towards the Europabrücke and the Italian border, has the best skiing in the immediate area and is a fine example of a traditional Tyrolean village. The skiing goes up to 2247m and is served by a cable car, a chair-lift and four T-bars. The ski area consists of four runs cut through the trees. The red Olympic downhill presents a challenge on the front face of the mountain. It was here that Franz Klammer threw caution to the wind and hurled himself down the mountain to win the greatest Winter Olympics gold of all time. The blue Familienabfahrt follows a less direct route. There are off-piste opportunities from the top of the Gipfel lift.

Igls has four mountain restaurants, most of them criticised for their high prices, although the restaurant at the top of the cable car receives considerable praise.

The resort manages to support two ski schools, Igls 2000 and Schigls; instructors at both speak good English. The two nursery slopes are covered by snow-cannon and are a five-minute walk from the village centre. A non-ski kindergarten operates from 9am to 5pm. Ski-age children are catered for all day, between 10am and 4pm, with lunch in the kindergarten.

The village is small and uncommercialised. It has sedate hotels and coffee houses, excellent walks for non-skiers and the Olympic bob-run, which is open to the public and according to one reporter is 'totally brilliant'. The Astoria is a sound family hotel, the Sporthotel and the Schlosshotel together with the Kurzentrum are upmarket and expensive, while the Gasthof Stern is more middle-of-the-road. The Pension Gstrein is 'a simple, but good guesthouse'. Two main supermarkets look after the needs of self-caterers.

Après-ski is not the strongest point of Igls, but the bars at the Bon Alpina and the Astoria are the livelier spots. The Sporthotel disco is for the later crowd.

TOURIST OFFICE
Tel 43 5123 377101
Fax 43 5123 378965

Neustift 1000m (3,280ft)

The main community and the centre of the broad and lush Stubaital, Neustift is a large, spread-out village, which has seen great expansion in recent years. Nevertheless, it remains very much at heart a traditional Tyrolean village centred around one of the more magnificent and ornately decorated churches in this corner of Austria.

Recommended hotels include the Tirolerhof ('excellent food and a warm welcome') and the budget-priced and quaint Hotel Angelika in the centre of town. Nightlife is noisy in the Romansstuben with 'strange music, but a great, fun atmosphere'. The Sumpflöchl in the Hotel Stubaierhof is also popular. Neustift has its own gentle ski area on wooded north-facing slopes but it is also the hotel base for the more important skiing on the **Stubai Glacier**, 20 minutes away at the end of the valley. A free ski-bus operates regularly.

The skiing here is year-round at a top altitude of 3200m and is one of the most extensive summer ski areas in Europe. The old four-seater gondola from the base-station at **Mutterbergalm** has been supplemented by a six-person gondola running in parallel to the first stage at Fernau. From here you can either continue by gondola or chair-lift to a network of drags, which take you up to the top of the ski area. When snow is short elsewhere, the slopes can become unbelievably crowded and, out of season, German bank holidays are to be avoided. The glacial ski area is also extremely well-equipped and efficiently run. The ski shop at the top-station is highly recommended for repairs, as most of its customers outside the winter months are international racing teams.

Keen skiers will stay in the Alpensporthotel Mutterberg, a comfortable establishment right at the base of the lifts. It has its own swimming-pool, disco and bowling alley, which is just as well as it is particularly isolated. Separate ski schools operate in both Neustift and on the glacier and each has a kindergarten. The Stubai Superskipass covers a small area at **Milders** and all the assorted lifts in the valley.

TOURIST OFFICE
Tel 43 5226 2228
Fax 43 5226 2529

Seefeld 1200m (3,936ft)

Seefeld is a tiny version of Salzburg, Innsbruck, Kitzbühel and the other beautiful towns of Austria, with its frescoed houses and medieval architecture. Everything about the village exudes style and sophistication: the six luxury hotels, a casino, an extensive health centre with a Hollywood-style grotto and waterfalls, horse-drawn sleighs and a pedestrianised village centre complete with exclusive jewellery shops, sports shops and boutiques.

It does not, however, justify its reputation as an alpine ski resort in its own right, which explains its downgrading in this edition of *The Good Skiing Guide* to another satellite, albeit a large and outstandingly attractive one, of the mother city of Innsbruck.

Seefeld's main winter activity is cross-country skiing. There are also three small pisted ski-areas for those who want to try their hand at alpine skiing in beautiful surroundings, and a variety of other activities.

Geigenbühel is the nursery slope area, **Gschwandtkopf**, a low peak used mainly by the ski school, and **Rosshütte** the more extensive with the slightly steeper runs. All three areas are reached from the village centre by the free bus-service.

Rosshütte is the main eating place in the area of the same name. It has a large sun terrace filled with a throng of skiers and non-skiers at lunchtime. The restaurant on the Gschwandtkopf mountain is recommended as is the Café Christina, which is waiter-service only.

Seefeld boasts some unusual and exotic hotels, including the five-star Klosterbräu, a former sixteenth-century monastery complete with indoor and outdoor pools and a Roman sauna with steam grotto. On a more reasonable price scale the family-run Hotel Bergland and Hotel Haymon are in a quiet location on the edge of the pedestrian zone. The Kaltschmidt has 'palatial apartments' and is 'very handy for the nursery slope with a nice pool on the fourth floor'. The two-star Krinserhof is reported as being 'small and friendly with good food but a long walk from the village'. The Gartenhotel Tümmlerhof is set in its own park and offers all-day childcare. The resort kindergarten is based in the Olympia Sport and Congress Centre.

Gourmets can try the Alte Stube in the Hotel Karwendelhof, and the many alternative eating places include Beim Jörg, the Diana Stüberl and the Seefelderstuben. A handful of pizzerias are available for those who do not appreciate Austrian food, including Da Pino's, Pizzeria Angelo and Pizzeria Don Camillo.

Café Nanni and Café Moccamühleis are popular after-skiing places for a drink or snack. The Big Ben bar is as English as you would expect, complete with an old red telephone box, and the Britannia Inn is another popular English pub. Monroe's disco-bar attracts the late-night crowd along with the Miramare and the Postbar in the Hotel Post. The Kanne in the Hotel Klosterbräu, the centre of the village's social life, has live music at night as well as tea-dancing. Reporters also recommend the Lamm and the Siglu. The bar Fledermaus has live jazz in the evenings. The casino is worth a visit if only to watch the punters.

Cross-country

Seefeld is a year-round resort, and in winter cross-country skiing is its *raison d'être*. It has twice hosted the Winter Olympics cross-country events, in 1964 and 1976, and in 1985 the Nordic World Championships were held here for the first time. Seefeld also has some excellent facilities for the recreational cross-country skier with the Nordic ski school, including a team of specialist cross-country instructors, at the Olympia Centre. The 200km of loipe is mechanically prepared and a special cross-country trail map is available from the tourist office.

TOURIST OFFICE
Tel 43 5212 2313
Fax 43 5212 3355

Ischgl

ALTITUDE 1400m (4,592ft)

Ischgl is Austria's most unsung resort. Geographically, it is a near neighbour of awesome St Anton, it has somehow managed to remain largely unknown internationally, except to the thousands of Germans who regard it as one of the most important ski destinations of all. If

■ **GOOD POINTS**

Reliable snow cover, variety of easy runs, extensive ski area, beautiful scenery, alpine charm, ski-touring possibilities, sunny slopes

■ **BAD POINTS**

Lack of challenging runs, high prices even for Austria, little for non-skiers

Hannes Schneider, founder of the Arlberg Ski School, had happened to have been born in the remote and beautiful Paznaun Valley instead of Stuben in the St Anton ski area, history might have smiled more favourably on this smart and delightful resort. As it was, Ernest Hemingway was about the only celebrity to root for Ischgl. He dropped in here one afternoon in 1925 and became so entranced with the region that he stayed for the season.

An increasing number of skiers are now discovering that Ischgl and neighbouring Galtür provide the near perfect mix of skiing and snow reliability together with alpine charm, an extensive ski area and some of the liveliest nightlife in Austria. As if that were not enough, the duty-free resort of Samnaun is linked across the Swiss border. Apart from bargain shopping, the Swiss side of the mountain also has excellent mountain restaurants and some of the best skiing in the area. We continue to receive reports from satisfied customers.

On the mountain
top 2864m (9,394ft) bottom 1377m (4,517ft)

The skiing principally consists of open slopes above Ischgl; long descents through woods to the village and a series of high, rocky bowls above with plenty of open, easy pistes. A long mountain crest, which forms the Austro-Swiss border, is reached by lift and easily breached on skis in a number of places, opening up a less extensive but delightful area on the Swiss side, above the resort of Samnaun. The slopes on the Ischgl side face north-west and west, while on the Samnaun face they are mainly south and east.

Mountain access from Ischgl is from both ends of the village: one gondola takes you up to **Idalp**, a broad and sunny, open plateau with a ski school, restaurants, hotel and nursery slopes. A second ascends to **Pardatschgrat**, 300m higher, where there are runs back down to Ischgl or an easy connection with the rest of the lift system via Idalp.

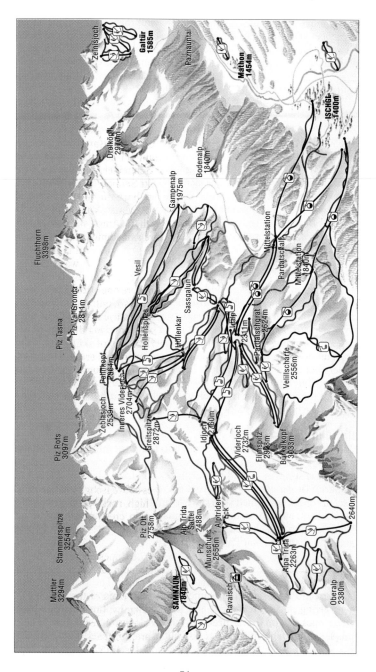

In the past Ischgl has suffered from terrible queues; this came about largely because the Austrian side of the frontier ridge had almost twice the uphill capacity of the Swiss side. On the first sunny day of each week all Ischgl-based skiers took a day trip to Samnaun with disastrous queuing consequences when they tried to return home.

However, last season a quad-chair from Alp Trida to Idjoch was installed, with beneficial results. Even more importantly, we are promised that the new revolutionary double-decker cable car from Samnaun to Alp Trida will be operating for 1995–6. With a capacity of 180 it is the first double-decker as well as being the world's largest cable car. The Velill parallel drag is being upgraded to a six-person chair to carry the traffic back to Idalp and the home run to Ischgl. It is also encouraging to see that one by one the old-time T-bars are being recycled in this environmentally conscious corner of Austria.

> ■ **WHAT'S NEW**
>
> Double-decker cable car from
> Samnaun to Alp Trida
> 6-person chair-lift
> Ski-kindergarten at Idalp

Beginners

A short tow at the northern end of the village can be used by novices if snow conditions permit. Otherwise, beginners head up to the plateau at Idalp, where there is an extensive variety of blue (easy) runs. No 8 is usually busy with ski school classes but it is a good run for finding your ski legs. After gaining a little confidence skiers should be able to tackle the long run down from Inneres Viderjoch on the border ridge. However, readers point out that most blues here have the occasionally vicious red (intermediate) patch, and you should explore with caution. It seems a pity that there is no blue run back to the village. Beginners have no sensible choice but to return by gondola.

Intermediates

Many of the red runs are long enough to test most intermediates to the full. A long and enclosed chair-lift, which provides necessary protection against the weather in mid-winter, takes you from Gampen Alp up to Palinkopf. It is relatively little-used and No 40 is a scenically beautiful descent for accomplished skiers, while on the other side of the ridge No 80 takes you all the way down to Samnaun. No 20, from the top of the Palinkopfbahn, is a challenging run, which leads on into blue No 24 and takes you to the Höllkar Parallellifte.

Advanced

Ischgl's skiing contains few really difficult runs. The pistes down to Ischgl from Pardatschgrat are among the best for good skiers, some of them giving an uninterrupted and demanding 1200m vertical across open slopes and on down through swathes cut through the trees. These runs are graded intermediate or difficult. Black 4, down to the mid-station, seems more worthy of red classification. In the late afternoon these runs become crowded with skiers who cannot always handle the terrain, making it hazardous for themselves and for those skiers who can. Elsewhere in the resort piste-grading seems mixed.

Off-piste
The off-piste and more exacting touring possibilities in the region are extensive and, importantly, because Ischgl does not have the fashionable cachet of St Anton, it does not immediately become 'skied out' after a proper snowfall. Piz Val Gronda at the top of the Fimbatal has been ear-marked as a potential projection of the lift system, with long runs down the back past the Heidelberger Hütte as well as down the front face to link into No 40. However, for the moment powder enthusiasts hoof it to the top on skins for their own private descents.

Snowboarding
Both Ischgl and Samnaun have their own permanent half-pipes for snowboarders.

Ski schools and guiding
The Ischgl Ski School has had a solid reputation over many years, how-ever, according to some reports, the lack of competition can lead to com-placency. One reporter encountered an English-speaking instructor who insisted on conducting the class in German. Another spoke of 'chaos and time loss' as the classes were organised at the beginning of the week. In fact most instructors speak good English. The average size of classes is as high as 10 to 12 pupils. Off-piste tours can be arranged through the ski school in what is exceptional touring terrain, particularly late in the season.

Mountain restaurants
The Paznauer Taja is recommended for its 'truly wonderful panoramic views' and it sometimes has a live band on the terrace. Nearby Bodenalp ('hard to reach, but worth it'), is an attractive alternative as well as the pleasant hut at the bottom of the Höllenkar. The restaurant at the foot of the baby slope in Alp Trida is reportedly good, provided you avoid peak hours.

All reporters found a noticeably higher standard of cuisine on the Swiss side ('try the *Rösti*'). The absence of duty is not noticeable in restaurant prices, which are in Swiss francs, although Austrian schillings are accepted everywhere.

Off the mountain
Ischgl is an old village, which has developed in a smart and harmonious way with a high standard of new buildings and accommodation and a high price level to go with it; what the 50 working farmers lose on EC cheese prices they recoup in winter lets. More recent building is said to be less, rather than more, environmentally conscious in conception, and

some hotels are in danger of losing their traditional character with the addition of charmless modern extensions. The centre, bypassed by the main road, positively bustles with activity and excitement in the early evening. The remainder of the village sprawls along the valley in the shadow of the steep, wooded mountainside, which makes up the ski slopes. Parts of the village are hilly with several staircases and steep paths, which can become dangerously icy.

■ **OTHER SPORTS**

Ice-driving, parapente, skating, curling, indoor tennis, indoor climbing, swimming, tobogganing at Kappl

A free ski-bus service links Ischgl, **Kappl** and Galtür infrequently during the day and not in the evening. For non-skiers there are good walks, both in the valley and up the mountain to the restaurants at Bodenalp. The Silvretta Sports Centre houses a swimming-pool and a bowling alley. The farming museum at Mathon on the bus route to Galtür is also reportedly worth a visit.

Accommodation
Much of the accommodation is centred around the two lift departure points at either end of the village. Although Ischgl has grown in recent years, it takes only a few minutes to walk from one end to the other, and therefore location is not a priority in choosing where to stay. The Goldener Adler, near the Silvretta gondola, receives good reports: 'a fine example of a proper Austrian hostelry in the old style.' The Post is centrally positioned. The Antony, on a hillside opposite the village, is 'very pleasant, with spacious rooms and excellent food'. The Pension Paznaunhof is said to be 'very clean with a good breakfast in a pleasant atmosphere'.

The Albona is situated far enough from the centre to be quiet, but still conveniently accessible for the gondola. It is recommended for its 'outstanding food'. One guest complained that British guests were housed in the basement, while Germans had rooms on the upper floors: 'handy for the sauna, but lacking in views'. The Hotel Verwall has 'comfortable family rooms, friendly staff, and a predominance of German guests'. Hotel Elizabeth is said to be 'excellent, with very good food and service, a pool and sauna'. Hotel Solaria has reportedly improved, having been considerably criticised in the past for the attitude problem of the staff. Some of the outlying Gasthofs operate a courtesy mini-bus service.

Eating in and out
Most of the restaurants are in the hotels, and one reporter comments on the 'sameness' of both menus and prices. The best eating places are tucked away off the main street. The Trofana Alm bar-restaurant has a warm atmosphere and 'delicious pizza cooked on a wood-burning stove, with a good salad table'. The Golderner Adler is recommended for delicious fresh trout and other gourmet food in its wonderful traditional setting. The Niki's Stadl in the Piz Buin Hotel and the restaurant at the Hotel Tyrol are also worthy of note. The Sports Centre is suggested for

good-value food and 'the lack of atmosphere was compensated for by the lack of cigarette smoke'. Popular fondue expeditions to the Heidelberger Hütte by snow cat or horse-drawn sleigh are organised most evenings.

Après-ski
Ischgl becomes extremely lively when the lifts are closed for the night. Action starts at the outside bar of the Hotel Elizabeth. One reporter claimed the village square was virtually taken over from 4pm to 6pm by Scandinavians. 'The Trofana Alm is the place to go if you are up to it. Dancing on the tables, loud music and much alcohol flowing — but no loutish behaviour.' Later on the Tenne is popular. Niki's Stadl and the Kitzloch are recommended for 'real early-evening Austrian après-ski'. Tea-dancing, that ancient Austrian courtship ritual, flourishes in Ischgl. There is also plenty of traditional entertainment of the *yodel-und-Schuhplatte* variety complete with log-chopping.

For a more tranquil coffee and cake, reporters recommend the Konditorei Salner and the Dorfcafé. Thommy's Bar is suggested for those who want to enjoy a quiet drink. The Madlein Wunderbar has a reputation for being the hot spot in town with live action including strip shows ('come and meet 300 of the Tyrol's prettiest girls'), which one reader found 'pretty offensive'.

Another commented on the '60s and '70s evening: 'whatever Austrians were listening to in these two decades, it never reached England, thank God.'

Childcare
The main nursery slopes are a 20-minute cable car ride up the mountain, but there is also a baby-drag near the village. Three hotels have crèches as well as the Gästekindergarten at Idalp, which takes potty-trained children and, although inconveniently situated up the mountain, is warmly recommended by reporters. One reporter commented: 'don't be put off by the primitive nursery conditions, the staff are charming and make up for the lack of amenities.'

Linked or nearby resorts

Galtür 1585m (5,200ft)
This pleasing Austrian village is only a few minutes' drive from Ischgl, but offers an altogether more relaxing, crowd-free environment coupled with limited but varied skiing. It is small, but with a total capacity of 3,500 visitor beds, it is certainly not tiny. It enjoys a sunnier position than Ischgl at the widening head of the valley. The lifts are a bus-ride away at **Wirl**. Buses are reliable and frequent, but only during peak hours. Given the energy, you can pole your way home at the end of the day. Avalanche slopes on both sides of the village mean that it can be completely isolated for short periods after a major storm.

The main access to the slopes is by a covered chair and the skiing

Skiing facts: **Ischgl**

TOURIST OFFICE
Postfach 24, A-6561 Ischgl, Tyrol
Tel 43 5444 5266
Fax 43 5444 5636

THE RESORT
By road Calais 1017km
By rail Landeck 30km, frequent buses from station
By air Innsbruck 1½ hrs
Visitor beds 7,920
Transport free bus service (with guest card) links Ischgl, Kappl and Galtür

THE SKIING
Linked or nearby resorts Samnaun (l), Galtür (n), Kappl (n)
Longest run Idjoch–Ischgl, 7km (red)
Number of lifts 41
Total of trails/pistes 200km (27% easy, 63% intermediate, 10% difficult)
Nursery slopes 3 lifts
Summer skiing none
Snowmaking 40 hectares covered

LIFT PASSES
Area pass Silvretta Ski Pass (covers Ischgl, Samnaun, Galtür, Kappl and See) ÖS2,340 for 6 days, VIP pass ÖS1,800 for 6 days
Day pass ÖS360 (Ischgl/Samnaun)

Beginners books of tickets
Pensioners ÖS1,320 for 60 yrs and over
Credit cards accepted no

SKI SCHOOLS
Adults Silvretta Ski School, 9am-midday and 1.30-3.30pm, ÖS1,330-1,400 for 6 days
Private lessons ÖS2,000 per day
Snowboarding ÖS1,200 for 3 half-days. Permanent half-pipe
Cross-country prices as regular ski school. Loipe 28km
Other courses telemark
Guiding companies Stefan Wolf

CHILDREN
Lift pass ÖS1,115 for 6 days
Ski kindergarten 3-5 yrs, ÖS575 per day including lunch, or ÖS1,850 for 6 days
Ski school 4 yrs and over, ÖS1,780-1,850 for 6 days including lunch
Non-ski kindergarten Children's Room at the Idalp, 4 yrs and under, 10am-4pm, ÖS170 per day, extra ÖS75 per day for lunch

FOOD AND DRINK PRICES
Coffee ÖS25, glass of wine ÖS15-18, small beer ÖS25, dish of the day ÖS70

---

goes up to 2464m at Saggrat with a series of red and black (difficult) runs down a wide, undulating bowl. The skiing immediately above Wirl is of a more intermediate nature, with a couple of long blues giving nearly 600m vertical and an assortment of easy reds. Lift queues are non-existent, and one reporter describes the skiing as 'the perfect example of how skiing should be everywhere: no queues, well organised, pretty and reasonably varied for a small resort'.

The two mountain restaurants are said to be adequate, with the one near the main chair-lift offering the best food and prices.

The ski school is recommended for 'friendly and competent teaching'. The kindergarten takes children aged three years and over, and we have glowing reports of the standard of child instruction.

The nightlife is much quieter here, but there are a number of cheerful bars, some with live music and tea-dancing, including the popular La Tschuetta. The Hotel Rössle is recommended for its comfortable rooms and is described as 'the best restaurant in the village'.

The Hotel Post and the Fluchthorn are centrally located. The Ballunspitze is slightly further out but an equally sound choice. The family-run Alpenrose is 'quiet, very welcoming, and offers excellent food'. We have good reports of the Alp Aren apartments: 'very luxurious with colour television, coffee machine, and dishwasher.' The hotels at Wirl are isolated but have their own excellent facilities. The Almhof is said to serve good, cheap lunches and has a swimming-pool. The Wirlerhof is recommended as a place to stay with children.

Other activities here include skating and curling, floodlit tobogganing, and the smart sports centre has a swimming-pool, squash, tennis and bowling.

TOURIST OFFICE
Tel 43 5443 521
Fax 43 5443 52176

Samnaun 1840m (6,035ft)

Samnaun is one of those anomalous communities in high, cul-de-sac corners of the Alps, which has stayed alive thanks to its duty-free status coupled with its existence as a ski resort. This Swiss village is not exactly booming; it is little more than a large cluster of shops, hotels and supermarkets. Unless the price of spirits and electrical goods is your primary consideration, it is not outstanding as a winter holiday centre. Petrol is also very cheap, but ski equipment and perfume are not such great bargains. The shops thoughtfully sell backpacks.

Its attraction is enormously enhanced this season by the inauguration of the world's largest and only double-decker cable car. The village also has a 10km cross-country track plus a ski school, which specialises in organising ski-tours, and a kindergarten at Alp Trida. Access by car is from the Inn Valley south of Landeck, not far from **Serfaus** and **Nauders**.

TOURIST OFFICE
Tel 41 8186 85858
Fax 41 8186 85652

Kitzbühel

ALTITUDE 760m (2,493ft)

K itzbühel remains the most attractive ski town in Europe. It is a walled medieval settlement of heavily buttressed buildings painted with delicate frescoes, which survives the relentless battering of a nine-month tourist season with measured aplomb. Only in April and May and again in November, when the snow has either just gone or is about to arrive, is Kitzbühel devoid of visitors.

In winter it is the one destination in the Tyrol really suitable for skiers and non-skiers alike. This contributes strongly to its international status as one of the smartest European resorts. At the heart of its world popularity is the Hahnenkamm, the toughest downhill on the World Cup calendar. With the understandable exception of World War II and the odd failure of nature to provide snow, it has been held here annually since 1931. In fact, the Hahnenkamm is not the race, but the name of the steepest of Kitzbühel's two separate mountains; locals call it the Streif.

■ GOOD POINTS

Large ski area, beautiful architecture, alpine charm, lively après-ski, wide range of activities for non-skiers, short airport transfer, extensive cross-country skiing

■ BAD POINTS

Lack of tough runs, lift queues, poor snow record, heavy traffic outside pedestrian centre

Racers, who negotiate its tortuous twists and mighty jumps at speeds of up to 85mph, say that every survivor is a winner. So great is the G-force on the first left-hander of the course that Austrian superhero Franz Klammer once stripped the thread from the screws holding his binding to his ski. Konrad Bartelski has aptly described the start as 'the six most difficult seconds of skiing in the world'. However, the aura surrounding this annual event gives an entirely erroneous impression that Kitzbühel's skiing is for experts only.

When not prepared for racing, most of the Streif course is given over to a pleasant red Familienabfahrt (family run), which meanders down through the trees and rolling summer pastureland to the nursery slopes on the edge of town. The notorious Mausfalle, the nastiest and most technical section, is roped strictly out-of-bounds, and the recreational skier not present on race day might well wonder what the fuss is all about.

Kitzbühel's early wealth came from its key position on the trade route between Bavaria and Italy as well as its success as a copper- and silver-mining centre in the sixteenth century, but its winter popularity has centred around skiing for over 100 years. In January 1893 local lad Franz Reisch obtained a pair of skis by mail order from Norway, thereby introducing the sport to the Tyrol and changing the face of retail shopping.

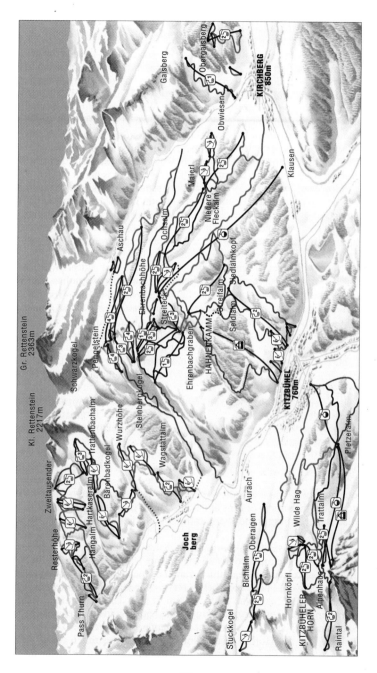

On the mountain

top 2000m (6,562ft) bottom 760m (2,493ft)

The main skiing is divided between two mountains: the **Kitzbüheler Horn** and the far more challenging **Hahnenkamm**. For an international resort of its standing, the Kitzbühel lift system has long been a disgrace. The Hahnenkamm cable car was built in 1928 and looks like it; two-hour morning queues are not uncommon. When you do finally reach the front, the car, which carries 48 skiers compared to 160 in its modern equivalent in France or Italy, only takes you up 870 vertical metres. Plans to replace it have been on the drawing board for 20 years but have met with continued opposition from locals who regard the old lift as an integral part of Kitzbühel's charm.

However, in March 1995 a compromise was finally reached, and it will be replaced by a £13-million six-person gondola, which will be in operation by 1996–7. The old mountain station will become a museum, and the new gondola will dock in a restaurant complex slightly higher up the mountain. The new lift will increase uphill capacity from 400 to what may in the future prove to be a still inadequate 2,000 an hour.

Meanwhile, for at least another full season, wise skiers who have failed to finish breakfast by 8am when the crowds start to gather, should go for the less frustrating option of a 3km ski-bus ride to the hamlet of Klausen on the road to Kirchberg. From here the Fleckalm gondola takes you swiftly up into the system.

Alternatively, you can plod across the nursery slopes to the two-stage Streifalm chair, which deposits you at a slightly higher point than the cable car. From here a network of mainly red (intermediate) and blue (easy) cruising runs spread out down three faces of the mountain and surrounding 'peaklets' over undulating terrain to form the largest and most challenging of Kitzbühel's two main ski areas.

■ WHAT'S NEW

Four-star Hotel Astron
Extended snowmaking
Hahnenkamm cable car to be
replaced by six-person gondola
for 1996–7

Lift connections are not all they should be, and a couple of notorious bottlenecks can result in annoying queues during high-season weeks. However, even though the area is confined, the variety of runs and scenery give you a pleasant impression that you are going somewhere, rather than skiing the same slopes over and over again.

Kitzbühel's second ski area is the Kitzbüheler Horn to the east of town, across the main road and the railway tracks. It towers above the resort, a distorted but beautiful pyramid of rock and ice. A newish cable car, which would have been better serving the majority of skiers on the Hahnenkamm, takes you up to 1996m. It rises 1200m from the valley floor, and the views from the top of the rocky Wilde Kaiser peaks are spectacular. The skiing is pleasant and gentle, but experienced skiers will quickly find the Horn a disappointment with pistes much easier than they are graded. Only when conditions are bad do the runs become more difficult, which towards the bottom of the mountain is quite often since they mostly face south-west.

Aurach, a 10-minute ski-bus ride away from Kitzbühel, is a third and minor separate area served by a single chair and a couple of drag-lifts. They provide access to three gentle blue runs and a marginally steeper reddish alternative. It is an area that is hardly skied and, if there has been a fresh fall or you just cannot face the queue for the Hahnenkamm, it is worthy of a morning's skiing.

Much is finally being done to improve its lift system – the Silberstube drag-lift has been replaced by a quad-chair – but Kitzbühel's insuperable problem is its lack of altitude. Outside the middle winter weeks you must be prepared to contend with slushy conditions as the norm, at least at lower levels, and be grateful if they are otherwise. Snowmaking was introduced three years ago on the Streif and this is to be extended to the Ehrenbachgraben, Steinbergkogel, Talsen and Bärenbadkogel runs.

Beginners

Kitzbühel has four good nursery slopes near the town and plenty of easy skiing for wobbly second-weekers. The blue Pengelstein run from the top of the chair of the same name all the way down to Kirchberg is one of the best in the resort.

Over on the Kitzbüheler Horn, the long Hagstein blue run (marked 3 on the piste map) is a gentle cruise all the way from top to bottom. However, nervous skiers should beware of the Pletzerwald variation through the trees, which turns into a choice between an awkward red and the steep black (difficult) Horn Standard.

Intermediates

Kitzbühel is essentially for cruisers. Pengelstein-Süd is a long, flowing red, which starts at the top of the Pengelstein double-chair and is the gateway into the Ski Safari (see below). It brings you down to the hamlet of Trampelpfad. The Hochsaukaser red at Pengelstein is a wide, fast piste with wonderful lips and rolls; one side is usually left unprepared and becomes a challenging mogul field.

The celebrated Ski Safari, marked by elephant signposts, is an enjoyable pisted itinerary, which takes you from the Hahnenkamm up the Kitzbühel Valley to **Jochberg** and **Pass Thurn**. Anyone with a couple of weeks of ski experience can manage the outing, which consists of a series of blue and gentle red runs linked by lifts up the east-facing slopes of the valley. The wooded skiing on the Wurzhöhe above Jochberg is always uncrowded and it is certainly worth spending some time here before moving on.

Pass Thurn is an isolated ski area in its own right at the southern end of the valley, overlooking the town of Mittersill, home of Blizzard skis. Wrap up well in mid-winter as it can be extremely cold. But the broad band of runs, accessed by a sole double-chair from the roadside, holds the best snow in the region. The downside is that the Safari is no circuit – it can be fully skied only in one direction. To return to Kitzbühel you have to queue for a bus for the 19km road journey from Pass Thurn. You can ski back to Jochberg, which is only 9km from home, but you may wait much longer for a bus here because most seats have already been filled by skiers joining at the Pass.

Advanced
The best of the steep skiing is reached via a network of lifts in the Ehrenbach sector of the Hahnenkamm. Try the Sedlboden and Ochsenboden. The black variation of Oxalm-Nord is part of the otherwise long intermediate run down to Kirchberg. Rettenstein at Pass Thurn is a short, sharp black, which ends up at the bottom of the Zweitausender double-chair.

Off-piste
Those who are new to off-piste skiing can find plenty of easy powder skiing close to the pistes in the Hahnenkamm area after a new snowfall. Pass Thurn is particularly recommended, and Bichlalm is another good area for enjoying the powder. Kitzbühel now has a specialist off-piste ski school called Ski Alpin Kitz.

Snowboarding
There is a special half-pipe for snowboarders on the Kitzbüheler Horn, and all the ski schools offer lessons.

Ski schools and guiding
Kitzbühel has four separate ski schools including the famous Red Devils. All have a generally good reputation and the resulting competition between them is healthy indeed. However, we have mixed reports of the Red Devils. One reporter in a class of 13 notes that 'the instructor was a gloomy soul, older than usual, and his English was pretty basic'. There are a number of complaints regarding oversized classes and instruction that amounted to little more than guiding, with no individual tuition.

Mountain restaurants
The Alpenrose at the top of the Kitzbüheler Horn is noted for its *Germknödel*. The Hagstein, also on the Horn, is said to be 'very small, but reasonably priced and overflowing with charm'. The Ochsalm on the Hahnenkamm is renowned for its *Apfelstrudel*. Trattenbergalm, between Jochberg and Pass Thurn, has some of the best simple food in the region. Panorama-Alm above Pass Thurn has a glass-walled bar outside to keep out the wind and a roaring log-fire and cheerful service within. The Pengelstein restaurant has been expensively extended, but still tends to be crowded. One reporter recommends the Ehrenbach at the bottom of the Steinbergkogel summit chair for its good food and because 'it is always empty, but don't tell anybody!' The Brandseit, which is described as 'cheap and uncrowded', is situated near the bottom of the Fleckalm gondola.

Off the mountain

The town centre is mercifully traffic-free, but the one-way ring road is usually heavily congested. Reporters consistently remark on improvements in the free ski-bus service, which ferries skiers to and from both the Hahnenkamm and the easier slopes of the Kitzbüheler Horn. However, the buses to surrounding villages are seriously oversubscribed at peak times. For skiing convenience Kitzbühel gets a heavy minus mark, but the overwhelmingly elegant architectural beauty of the pedestrian Vorderstadt with its backdrop of snowy mountains, makes up for all its detractions. Serious shoppers will, however, be disappointed. Apart from Louis Vuitton, the local Sportalm fashion outlet, and a scattering of ski shops and boutiques, Kitzbühel lacks the designer retailers you might expect in what was once the most upmarket resort in Austria.

Accommodation

For both comfort and service the Goldener Greif and the Jägerwirt head an impressive list of 16 four-star hotels. The once grand Maria Theresia is criticised for the quality of its food on half-board rates. The converted hunting lodge of Schloss Lebensberg, on the outskirts, offers a hedonistic level of pampering; this includes a pool, solarium, massage and Turkish bath as well as free babysitting on weekdays. The Tiefenbrunner has a loyal following. The Weisses Rössl, once the town's prominent coaching inn, is a picture of faded splendour, slightly ragged around the edges but still enormously popular. The more reasonably priced three-star Haselsberger and the Montana, near the Hahnenkamm lift, are recommended. Two regular visitors recommend the family-run Mühlberghof, on the edge of town. Schloss Münichau in the village of Reith on the far side of the Schwarzsee is a 500-year-old castle, which is said to be 'delightfully quiet, with good prices and superb food'. It can be reached by ski-bus, but you do really need a car to stay here.

Eating in and out

Austrian alpine food wins few gastronomic prizes, but you can eat better and with more variety in Kitzbühel than in most resorts. The Goldener Greif is renowned for its *Salzburgerknockerl*, a kind of hot meringue soufflé. The chef in the Hotel zur Tenne in the Vorderstadt specialises in an unusual variety of ways of cooking fresh trout. The Huberbräu Stuberl serves excellent *Wienerschnitzel* in an intimate atmosphere. Chinarestaurant Peking in the Kirchplatz rings the culinary changes. The existence of a McDonald's seems a shame in such beautiful surroundings but its presence is muted.

Après-ski

Life after skiing focuses almost entirely on the pedestrian-only streets in the centre. Praxmair, in the Vorderstadt, is the original coffee house and

Skiing facts: **Kitzbühel**

TOURIST OFFICE
A-6370 Kitzbühel, Tyrol
Tel 43 5356 21550
Fax 43 5356 2307

THE RESORT
By road Calais 1130km
By rail station in resort
By air Salzburg 1½ hrs, Munich 2½ hrs, Innsbruck 2 hrs
Visitor beds 7,074
Transport free ski-bus

THE SKIING
Linked or nearby resorts Kirchberg (l), Jochberg (l), Pass Thurn (l), St Johann in Tyrol (n)
Longest run Pengelstein Süd, 6.8km (red)
Number of lifts 28 in Kitzbühel, 64 in linked area
Total of trails/pistes 60km in Kitzbühel, 160km in linked area (39% easy, 46% intermediate, 15% difficult)
Nursery slopes 4 lifts in Kitzbühel, 7 in linked area
Summer skiing none
Snowmaking 10.5km covered in Kitzbühel, 12.5km covered in linked area

LIFT PASSES
Area pass (covers Kitzbühel, Kirchberg, Jochberg, Pass Thurn and includes ski-bus, swimming-pool and reduction for sauna) ÖS1,640 for 6 days
Day pass ÖS370
Beginners points cards
Pensioners 20% reduction for women 60 yrs and over and men 65 yrs and over
Credit cards accepted no

SKI SCHOOLS
Adults Red Devils, ÖS1,350 for 6 days, Total ÖS1,300 for 6 days, Kitzbüheler Horn ÖS1,259 for 5 days, Hahnenkamm ÖS1,200 for 5 days, all 9am-4pm
Private lessons Red Devils, ÖS2,200 per day, Total ÖS2,100 per day, Kitzbüheler Horn prices on demand, Hahnenkamm ÖS1,900 per day
Snowboarding Red Devils, ÖS2,100 for 6 days, prices of other ski schools on demand
Cross-country Red Devils, ÖS1,500 for 6 days. Loipe 30km in Kitzbühel, 120km in area
Other courses telemark
Guiding companies Ski Alpin-Kir and through ski schools

CHILDREN
Lift pass ÖS910 for 6 days
Ski kindergarten Total, ÖS1,400 for 6 days, Hahnenkamm ÖS1,800 for 6 days, Kitzbüheler Horn ÖS1,250 for 5 days. All 3-14 yrs and extra ÖS80 per day for lunch, times as adults
Ski school Red Devils, ÖS1,350 for 6 days, Total ÖS1,250 for 6 days, Kitzbüheler Horn ÖS1,250 for 5 days, Hahnenkamm ÖS1,200 for 6 days. All 3-15 yrs, 9am-4pm and ÖS80 extra per day for lunch
Non-ski kindergarten Anita Halder, prices on demand, or Herta Hechenberger, ÖS80 per hour or ÖS400 per day, including meals

FOOD AND DRINK PRICES
Coffee ÖS23, glass of wine ÖS30, small beer ÖS30, dish of the day ÖS95

brasserie where you will find more locals than tourists. The Goldener Gams in the Vorderstadt is a modest restaurant and bar with live music and a sophisticated Tyrolean atmosphere, which attracts all ages. 'S Lichtl, in the same road, is a bar with a warm atmosphere. Big Ben and The Londoner are noisy pubs, which act as a magnet for every young party-goer in town. Seppi's Pub is where Austria meets London's Old Kent Road. One reporter recommends La Fonda, opposite the casino, for a quiet drink. Biwak, in Bichlstrasse, is a small and trendy drinking spot. The Happy Horse, at the back of the Hotel Postkutsch, is a cheap and cheerful disco-bar, which closes at midnight. The late-night crowd move on to Royal Dancing and the Graffiti Club, both in the Hinterstadt. The Aquarena is free to those with a ski pass.

Childcare
Five lifts make up what is an extensive nursery slope on the golf course at the foot of the Hahnenkamm. There is a ski kindergarten in the resort, which has recently been joined by two non-ski kindergartens run by Anita Halder and by Herta Hechenberger.

Linked or nearby resorts

Kirchberg 850m (2,788ft)
Once upon a time Kirchberg was the back door into this ski area, the no-frills dormitory village that gave you Kitzbühel's skiing at knockdown prices, but without its medieval charm. This once poor relation, only a couple of kilometres around the shoulder of the Hahnenkamm at the head of the Brixental, still gives alternative access to Kitzbühel's main ski area, but its personal circumstances have changed.

What was once a pretty little farming village now boasts an astonishing 25 three- and four-star hotels in its sprawling extension.

Kirchberg has its own small beginner and intermediate lifts on the **Gaisberg**, as well as access to the Hahnenkamm by a two-stage chair and the Klausen gondola. It has a kindergarten and two ski schools. The town's layout is not designed for ski convenience. Distances are considerable and the ski-bus service is seriously oversubscribed. Choose where you stay with care in relation to both price and where you want to ski.

The Tiroler Adler Schlössl, run by the Egger family, is neither particularly convenient nor cheap but is one of the best in town. The less expensive Landhaus Brauns looks not just towards the West but also to Austria's new ski market; owner Gabriele Schmolz and her staff speak Polish, Russian and Czech. Nightlife is just as busy as in Kitzbühel, if less sophisticated. Charlie's Club and Le Moustache are among the main centres of action.

TOURIST OFFICE
Tel 43 5357 2309
Fax 43 5357 3732

Lech

ALTITUDE 1450m (4,756ft)

Every skiing nation has at least one ultra-smart resort which lures the Beautiful People to its manicured slopes and the pampered luxury of its hotels. Austria has Lech, with Princess Diana as its star annual visitor, and the higher neighbouring village of **Zürs**, much patronised by Princess Caroline of Monaco. Back in the 1920s, Zürs — then no more than a tiny hamlet of huts and an inn at the top of the Flexenpass around the shoulder of the Valluga from St Anton — was one of the cradles of modern alpine skiing. The great Hannes Schneider was born around the corner in Stuben, and Victor Sohm gave the first ski lesson in Zürs as long ago as 1906. Visitors in the 1920s were an eclectic blend of stolid Swiss Burger and upper-class British, drawn by the open slopes of the Trittkopf and Hexenboden, as well as the towering Madloch on the far side of the frozen Zürsersee.

■ GOOD POINTS

Alpine charm, sunny slopes, plenty of easy skiing, no T-bars, varied off-piste skiing, good artificial snow cover, high standard of hotels, facilities for family holidays

■ BAD POINTS

Difficult road and rail access, lack of mountain restaurants, high prices

Today Zürs is still little more than a cluster of buildings astride the pass, although the huts have been replaced by four- and five-star hotels and an assortment of marginally less exotic establishments. Lech, which nestles beside the river of the same name in what in winter is a closed valley beyond, has grown into the larger and more cosmopolitan resort of the two. It is the text-book example of the charming Austrian village, a farming community centred around its onion-domed church, which, despite major expansion into a complete dependency on tourism over 35 years, has still managed to retain its rural character. In 1964 Egon Zimmerman, then a hotel chef, became Olympic downhill champion. In 1992 the church bells rang out to celebrate the surprise Olympic downhill gold medal of Patrick Ortlieb, born and raised in **Oberlech**, a satellite on the open pastureland above. Once the summer home of herdsmen and shepherds, Oberlech is reached by cable car from Lech. Its collection of chalets and hotels are ideally placed for the skiing and provide an attractive car-free centre for families with small children. It has more accommodation but similar rural charm to **Zug**, three kilometres away through the woods from Lech up a pretty valley. Zug was once accessible only in winter by horse-drawn sleigh from Lech. This method of transport still provides a delightful evening excursion to the old village inn, which is now a major hotel, but Zug is now well-linked into the lift system which joins Zürs with Lech.

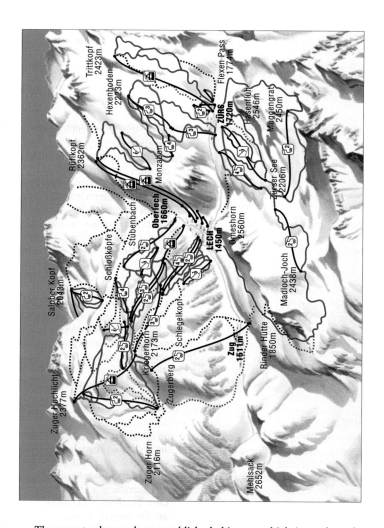

The resorts share a long-established ski area, which is moderately extensive but lacks serious challenge. Advanced skiers will be more interested in the off-piste and touring opportunities which abound in the area. St Anton, with its larger choice of expert piste terrain, is included in the same Arlberg ski pass but annoyingly the bus service is not. Reporters complain that if you plan to ski only Lech and Zürs the lift pass is extremely expensive.

Lech and Zürs lie close to the major road and rail link between Austria and Switzerland, but the journey is an awkward one. The Flexenpass can be blocked for hours or, on rare occasions, days after a major storm. Parking in both villages is restricted and ruthlessly policed.

On the mountain
top 2450m (8,036ft) bottom 1445m (4,740ft)

Lech and Zürs share a ski-circus spread over three mountains, which can be skied only in a clockwise direction. This results in crowds of people all heading for the same lifts at the same time, with resultant high-season queues. However, a steady upgrading of the lifts — the resort is now entirely T-bar free — has done much to alleviate the problem. Although the valleys are not wide, the connections across them are not perfect. Zürs is high, with all its skiing above the tree-line, while Lech has a more attractive arrangement of gentle lower slopes among the trees.

■ WHAT'S NEW

Snowboarding Fun Park

Mountain access to the circus is via the Rüfikopf cable car, which scales an impressive wall from the centre of Lech, too steep to be skied directly (except in springtime by experts) but with long, difficult and spectacular unprepared runs off the shoulder, which are often closed after heavy snowfall. These lead down in either direction through the woods to the road by Zürs, or back to Lech via a scenic itinerary through the Wöstertäli. Alternatively, you can take the lengthy and beautiful pistes towards Zürs.

Lech's main skiing area, on the other side of the valley, is contrastingly open and mostly gentle, although the slopes immediately above the village are quite steep. Four types of lifts, including a detachable quad-chair, provide mountain access on this side from different points in or near the village. Above Oberlech, lifts and pistes are scattered about a wide, fragmented basin below the peaks of the Kriegerhorn and the Zuger Hochlicht. The two are linked by a cable car, from which there are spectacular views.

Beginners

First-timers can get by with a points card or a daily beginner's ticket; they should not buy the expensive Arlberg Ski Pass until advised to do so by their instructor. Lech has excellent nursery slopes behind the church as well as at Oberlech. Combined with Zürs the area has 13 novice runs served by 9 lifts. Beginners should quickly progress to a whole range of blue (easy) runs on the Oberlech side of the valley. One of the attractions of the resort for second-week skiers is that they should be able to negotiate the blue Rüfikopf run from the top of the cable car, which in turn links into the Familienabfahrt to take them all the way to Zürs with an ego-boosting sense of achievement.

Intermediates

Confident red (intermediate) run skiers can head up the Rüfikopf cable car for a choice of pistes down the Hexenboden and Trittkopf. Follow the local lift map with care: appropriately coloured circles indicate pisted runs, while ungroomed ski routes are marked by diamonds. It is easy to think that a red diamond with a thin black border is a hard intermediate run. In fact it is an extreme ski route.

From Zürs take either the scenic Zürsertäli or one of the more direct routes down to the Zürsersee and on via the Madloch towards Lech.

Advanced

Zürs has a couple of short, sharp black (difficult) runs, notably the Hexenboden Direkte, but in hard-packed conditions advanced skiers will want to head for the greater challenges of St Anton.

Off-piste

When fresh snow falls, both Lech and Zürs are a delight. The ski-routes marked on the lift map offer considerable challenges and experts will be interested mainly in the various descents of the 2173m Kriegerhorn and the Zuger Hochlicht beyond it. The long run down from the top to the village of Zug via the narrow Zuger Tobel can be spectacular in the right snow conditions. Langezug and Tannegg around the shoulder of the Rüfikopf are dramatic in the extreme.

Snowboarding

Lech has created a snowboard training area called the Fun Park, an enclosed zone 300m long and 100m wide. It contains a half-pipe and obstacles such as Funboxes (humps which are accessible from four sides), Gaps (jumps over a trench) and a quarter-pipe. Both Lech and Oberlech offer snowboarding lessons at their ski schools.

Ski schools and guiding

The Austrian Ski School in Lech, Oberlech and Zürs has a particularly fine reputation and we have received no adverse reports. Most instructors speak good English. However, one reporter said that because the majority of guests are German, the instructors have to be reminded to translate into English.

Mountain restaurants

The choice of mountain eating-places is extremely limited, surprisingly so in an area that attracts so many potentially discerning lunchers. Most are concentrated around Oberlech. The Mohnenfluh is criticised for its 'excruciatingly slow service'. Hotel Burg in Oberlech is consistently praised. The Rüfikopf restaurant (not to be confused with the burger bar) is acclaimed for 'fine fare and the price you must expect'. The Seekopf at Zürs is also recommended. The Palmenalpe above Zug is one of the better self-service restaurants, provided you avoid peak hours, and the Sonnenburg is another reasonable self-service.

Off the mountain

Lech is a delightful village. Originally it was called Tannberg im Lech after the fir trees (*Tanne*), which grow in the valley. It was first settled by Swiss immigrants in the fourteenth century and this corner of the region still looks more towards Switzerland, its nearest neighbour, than to the main part of Austria. The modern expansion of the resort has been unobtrusive and Lech retains a real village feel to it, despite the presence of luxury hotels and designer boutiques. Regular, but infrequent, post-buses connect Lech, Zug, Zürs, Stuben and St Anton, as well as the rail-head at Langen.

Reporters complain of overcrowding and that public transport comes to a halt in the early evening. A car is almost mandatory if you want to ski St Anton. Taxis in the area are expensive, weekend traffic jams are hideous, and parking is difficult, although hotels have their own private spaces.

There is rather more scope of entertainment here than in most other Austrian resorts, but the toboggan run and the curling rink are both liable to closure in warm weather or snow. Non-skiers can buy return tickets on the Rüfikopf and Oberlech cable cars and can therefore join skiing friends for lunch.

Accommodation

Accommodation is mostly in comfortable and expensive hotels, plus some apartments and the odd tour-operator chalet. The village is fairly com-pact, and location of the accommodation is not particularly important (although we recommend families with small children stay in Oberlech). The smartest hotel — indeed, one of the most celebrated five-stars in

> **■ OTHER SPORTS**
> Skating, curling, swimming, helicopter rides, indoor tennis and squash, tobogganing, sleigh rides, winter walks

Austria — is the ornately frescoed Post. But it has only 40 rooms, and you need to book a year in advance. The Arlberg and the Almhof Schneider are both warmly recommended by regu-lars. The Tannbergerhof is popular with the British and is the centre of Lech's social life. Less formal hotels are numerous and there are plenty of *Fremdenzimmern* (bed-and-break-fasts), but nowhere is cheap. In high season rooms can be extremely hard to find at any level on the scale. It is worth noting that even the smartest hotels do not generally accept credit cards.

Oberlech has several comfortable hotels near the cable car station and chalets spread widely around the hillside. The main attraction of staying here is to avoid ski school crowds on the Schlegelkopf lifts out of Lech itself, and to holiday in a car-free environment. The Sporthotel Petersboden is known for its piste-side Red Umbrella bar. In Zug the original inn, the Rote Wand, is now a luxury four-star hotel. Hotel Elizabeth is also recommended.

Eating in and out

Good restaurants abound, as you might expect in a resort of this charac-ter, but none of them is cheap. The Brunnenhof is strongly recom-mended, as is the Bistro s'Caserole. The Käsknöpfle's food is described as 'a bit too Austrian, but the restaurant is good fun and friendly'. Pizzeria Charly is consistently popular with reporters for 'sound Italian

Skiing facts: **Lech**

TOURIST OFFICE
A-6764 Lech, Arlberg
Tel 43 5583 21610
Fax 43 5583 3155

THE RESORT
By road Calais 1100km
By rail Langen 17km, frequent buses daily
By air Innsbruck 2 hrs, Zurich $3\frac{1}{2}$ hrs
Visitor beds 6,751
Transport buses to resorts in linked area
not included in lift pass

THE SKIING
Linked or nearby resorts Zürs (l), St Anton
(n), Stuben (n), St Christoph (n), Zug (l)
Longest run Madloch-Lech, 5.2km (red)
Number of lifts 88 in linked area
Total of trails/pistes 110km in Lech (40%
easy, 40% intermediate, 20% difficult).
220km in linked area (30% easy, 40%
intermediate, 30% difficult)
Nursery slopes 13 runs and 9 lifts in Lech,
Oberlech and Zürs
Summer skiing none
Snowmaking 60 hectares covered

LIFT PASSES
Area pass Arlberg pass (covers Lech,
Oberlech, Zürs, Rauz, St Christoph, St
Anton, Stuben, Sonnenkopf-Klösterle)
ÖS2,140 for 6 days
Day pass ÖS445 (Arlberg)
Beginners points tickets
Pensioners Senior ticket for women 60 yrs

and over, and men 65 yrs and over, ÖS400
per day. Snowman ticket for seniors 80 yrs
and over, ÖS100 for whole season
Credit cards accepted no

SKI SCHOOLS
Adults Lech and Oberlech, 9am-midday
and 1.30-5pm, ÖS1,510 for 6 days
Private lessons Lech and Oberlech,
ÖS2,100 per day
Snowboarding Lech and Oberlech ski
schools, times and prices as ski lessons
Cross-country private lessons only,
ÖS2,100 per day. Loipe 17km
Other courses telemark, slalom, race
training
Guiding companies through Lech and
Oberlech ski schools

CHILDREN
Lift pass (covers resort and linked area)
6-15 yrs, ÖS1,280 for 6 days. Snowman
ticket for 5 yrs and under, ÖS100
for season
Ski kindergarten Oberlech, $3\frac{1}{2}$ yrs and
over, 9am-4pm, ÖS1,390 for 6 days, extra
ÖS80 per day for lunch
Ski school Lech, 12 yrs and under, 10am-
3pm, ÖS1,390 for 6 days
Non-ski kindergarten not available,
babysitting service through tourist office

FOOD AND DRINK PRICES
Coffee ÖS30, glass of wine ÖS50, small
beer ÖS30, dish of the day ÖS250

fare served with a smile, not as schilling-snatching as others.' In
Oberlech the Ilga Kellerstübli and the Goldener Berg are famous for fondues. A couple of small supermarkets sell basic foods and there is one
expensive butcher.

Après-ski
In Lech, après-skiers prefer to put their hair up, rather than let it down.

The Tannbergerhof is where it all begins at the ice-bar on the pavement outside (weather permitting). Guests filter inside to join in the tea-dancing, which begins as the lifts close. There is live music later in the evening here and at a number of other hotels. Both the Krone and the Tannbergerhof have discos, but the Rote Wand in Zug is renowned for having the liveliest one. The Rüfikopf cable car transforms into a moving cocktail bar at dusk. Sleigh rides to Zug for dinner are popular, and you can take the cable car up to Oberlech and toboggan down afterwards (the cable car closes at 1am). s'Pfefferkörndl is a lively bar with inexpensive food. Café Fritz is recommended for tea.

Childcare

The area lends itself well to family skiing, particularly at Oberlech where the main nursery slopes are situated. A number of hotels run their own crèches and we have good reports of the ski kindergarten, which has a mainly English-speaking staff and a sympathetic attitude. Children under six ski for ÖS100 for the whole season. A photograph is required; to avoid long weekend queues at the photo booth you are strongly advised to bring one with you.

The ski school takes children all day and supervises lunch, though parents must remember to provide lunch money each day.

Linked or nearby resorts

Zürs 1720m (5,642ft)

Zürs stands in an isolated position above the tree-line astride the Flexenpass and lacks much of the charm of Lech, although resort-level snow is guaranteed for most of the season. It is little more than a collection of extremely smart hotels. While it may completely lack the showy gaudiness of St Moritz or Gstaad, the degree of opulence of its clientèle is often greater — it just wears the wealth more discreetly. The Zürserhof is strongly recommended, both for its facilities and its restaurant. The Alpenrose Post and the Arlberhaus, marginally less expensive, both receive glowing reports. The kindergarten takes children from three years old and provides ski instruction for children four years old and upwards.

TOURIST OFFICE
Tel 43 55 83 22 45
Fax 43 55 83 29 82

Mayrhofen

ALTITUDE 630m (2,066ft)

Mayrhofen has earned a strong reputation over many years as one of the foremost learning centres for skiing in the Alps and maintains its place in the top five most popular resorts in Austria. Given that the skiing is neither convenient for beginners nor challenging enough for experts, it is not always clear why this should be so.

However, a fundamental and much-needed improvement in the infrastructure of the resort will dramatically upgrade its image this winter. For decades Mayrhofen has suffered from completely unacceptable queues during the main weeks of the year, creating a situation that led one experienced reporter to comment 'I would frankly rather be at home in Stoke'.

■ GOOD POINTS

Reputable ski school, improved lift system, lively après-ski, short airport transfer, sunny slopes, varied skiing in area, extensive family facilities, snow-sure glacier at Hintertux

■ BAD POINTS

Little challenging skiing, lack of skiing convenience

At the root of the problem was the ancient 50-person capacity Penkenbahn cable car, which provided the only access from the resort itself to the main ski area. Queues of 90 minutes or more for this uncomfortable sardine-can were the frustrating norm. The agony was further exacerbated by the need to take it down again at the end of the day (the topography does not enable you to ski back to the resort).

At last, after years of broken promises, work began in March 1995 on its replacement, a 15-person jumbo gondola, which will increase uphill capacity from 600 to 2,000 skiers per hour.

Mayrhofen's setting in the heart of the **Zillertal** is certainly a beautiful one: a long and steeply wooded offshoot of the Inn Valley and the Munich–Innsbruck *Autobahn*. Its hotels are numerous, clean and comfortable. Away from the slopes there is much to do, and the nightlife in Dutch- and British-dominated bars and discos is both raucous and energetic. The ski school has the finest of reputations for coping with beginners who do not speak German. The whole valley, of which Mayrhofen is the unchallenged capital, is geared towards families, with a particular emphasis on childcare.

On the mountain
top 2250m (5,355ft) bottom 630m (1,499ft)

The skiing takes place on both sides of the valley. The main area is the **Penken**, which can also be reached by gondola from the village of

Schwendau, a bus-ride away to the north and from Finkenberg, an inconvenient journey of equal length further up the **Zillertal**. The new Penkenbahn gondola will provide a swift and convenient means of access from the edge of town.

■ **WHAT'S NEW**

Penkenbahn cable car replaced by a
15-person jumbo gondola

The secondary area is the **Ahorn**, reached by ancient cable car from a parking lot, which is a long walk from most of the accommodation. For all these lifts (with the exception of the Finkenberg gondola) there is a free bus service, which is often disastrously overcrowded. In particular, it cannot cope with the influx of visitors who want to return in the afternoon from the Horbergstal gondola at Schwendau. However, it seems likely that the new lift will equalise the pressure on the bus system.

The 2095m Penkenjoch provides Mayrhofen's main skiing. The new gondola climbs over an unskiable, wooded mountainside to the sunny Penken balcony just above the tree-line. Two awkwardly linked chair-lifts then take you to the top of this rounded mountain, which naturally lends itself to varied bowl-skiing.

Beginners

The gentle slopes of the Ahorn at 2000m make an excellent beginner and lower-intermediate area surrounded by outstanding views down the Zillertal. Wide confidence-building pistes are served by five short drag-lifts and a chair-lift. An intermediate trail goes down through the woods to the Wiesenhof restaurant and it is possible to ski on down from here to the bottom of the Ahornbahn on the bank of the Ziller.

Intermediates

Most skiers head for the Penken, which consists of a relatively narrow band of open and lightly wooded skiing on the north and south sides of the Penkenjoch. The runs are short, generally more red (intermediate) than blue (easy), with the easiest ones back along the ridge towards Penken. However, accomplished intermediates will soon tire of the limited scope here and should explore the wider range of skiing reached by bus elsewhere in the Zillertal.

Advanced

From the bottom of the Penken chair-lifts it is possible to ski all the way down to the Horbergbahn gondola station via an interesting and ungraded route through the trees, which is steep and awkward in places. In good snow conditions this is one of the best runs in the resort for accomplished skiers.

Off-piste

From just below the Horberg gondola top-station, a double-chair climbs up to 2250m on the sunny Gerent side of the Horberg Valley. The unpisted run down beneath the lift is long and steep with pitches of

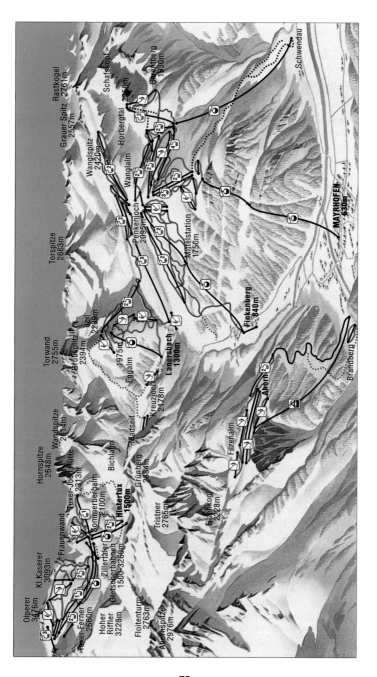

75

around 27 degrees, which can become heavily mogulled.

Snowboarding

All the five ski schools teach snowboarding, although group lessons last for only two hours each day. Private tuition is also available.

Ski schools and guiding

Generations of British have mastered the basics here on the gentle nursery slopes of the Ahorn and Finken before moving on to other resorts, which offer more of a challenge. Mayrhofen now has five schools, which provide a healthy level of competition. The standard of all is said to be high, and we also still have particularly warm reports of the original Uli Spiess school, which seems to thrive under the challenge. Large classes at all schools remain a drawback in high season.

Mountain restaurants

Vroni's Skialm at Penkenjoch receives the most favourable reports out of a cluster of eating places all offering much the same standard of Austrian fare. The Almstüberl by the mid-station of the Finkenberg gondola is recommended for its *Gulaschsuppe* and home-made bread. Hilde's Schitenne, a third of the way down the Tappenalm chair on Piste 8, is praised for its cosy atmosphere. Crowds are again a problem and one reporter suggests that you 'eat early or not at all if you want to ski in the afternoon and beat the lift queues down before supper time'. The Ahorn now has three restaurants as well as the Weisenhof on the way down.

Off the mountain

Mayrhofen is a large, traditional village with chalet-style buildings and ornately frescoed walls. Despite the village's huge expansion into a major tourist centre, it still manages to retain its charm. It is a lively place, full of young people, and this 'fun resort' atmosphere is the enduring reason for its popularity. The valley road bypasses the main part, and, although traffic can be heavy around the outskirts and parking is a problem, congestion in the streets is not a major drawback. Action centres on the long, wide main street, between the market place near the station and the Penken gondola, which is busy and bustling by day and night. There is no public transport in the evening.

Mayrhofen has a modern health centre with swimming-pools, sauna, solarium and a restaurant within the complex. There are plenty of attractive excursions to Innsbruck and Salzburg.

Accommodation

Most accommodation is in traditional hotels, Gasthofs and small pensions with the usual high standards of service and cleanliness, if not necessarily of haute cuisine. We have favourable reports of the Hotel Neuhaus and the Landhaus annexe opposite it ('everything you expect of a fine Austrian hotel'). Hotel Strass has lively après-ski. The interconnecting and more expensive Sporthotel has its own squash courts. One reporter praised the Strass Chalets (family-run guesthouses at various locations throughout the village) as 'the best value I have ever found in Austria'. Hotel Pramstraller is also strongly recommended, 'although rather inconveniently situated a long walk from either lift'.

Eating in and out

The 400-year-old Wirtshaus zum Griena, an old beamed farmhouse, is recommended for its traditional Austrian food and 'marvellous atmosphere'. The Neuhaus and the Alpenhotel Kramerwirt restaurants serve good four-course dinners, and Die Gute Stube is a gourmet restaurant. Pizzerias include Mamma Mia, Pizzeria Manni, Pizza and Strudl, and the pizzeria at the Hotel Rose. Other recommendations are the Edelweiss, Mount Everest and The Sporthotel. The restaurant in Hotel Strolz caters for special diets.

Après-ski

Evening entertainment is lively by any standard, with the full range on offer, from tobogganing and sleigh rides to Tyrolean evenings of thigh-slapping and yodelling, through to late-night discos. The Sporthotel bar is most popular with the British ('not exactly dripping in atmosphere, but a nice crowd'). Scotland Yard is more of a pub and usually heavily packed throughout the evening. The Aven and Schlössel discos are less British-orientated and are popular late in the

> ■ **OTHER SPORTS**
>
> Parapente, swimming, skating, curling, indoor tennis, squash, tobogganing, sleigh rides, winter walks

evening. The Hotel Kramerwirt's Andreas Keller has a live band for more sedate dancing. The Elizabeth has an expensive, but stylish nightclub where you can drink and hear yourself talk.

Childcare

Because of the severe queuing problems until now in getting both up and down the Penken, the crèche operates for longer than normal hours: Wuppy's Kinderland opens at 8am and parents do not have to return until 6pm. All three ski schools run their own all-day ski kindergarten.

Linked or nearby resorts

The Ski-Zell-Superski pass covers the entire valley and opens up the possibility of an enormous range of skiing. South of Mayrhofen the Zillertal splits into three smaller valleys, one of which leads on into the Tuxertal along a narrow, steeply wooded passage between the mountains, at the end of which is the **Tuxer Glacier**. Just above Mayrhofen, the compact little village of **Finkenberg**, home of former Olympic downhill champion Leonard Stock, shares Mayrhofen's main Penken ski area. Further on, Vorderlanersbach and Lanersbach have their own ski areas, which are tentatively planned to link into the system. For keen skiers who

Skiing facts: **Mayrhofen**

TOURIST OFFICE
Postfach 21, A-6290 Mayrhofen, Zillertal
Tel 43 5285 2305
Fax 43 5285 411633

THE RESORT
By road Calais 1000km
By rail station in resort
By air Innsbruck 1 hr, Munich 2 hrs
Visitor beds 7,921
Transport free bus service around Zillertal included in lift pass

THE SKIING
Linked or nearby resorts Finkenberg (l), Fügen (n), Gerlos (n), Hintertux (n), Kramsach (n), Lanersbach (n), Ramsau (n), Schwendau (n), Kaltenbach (n), Vorderlanersbach (n), Zell am Ziller (n)
Longest run Ahorn–Abfahrt, 4.5km (black)
Number of lifts 30 in Mayrhofen, 154 in the Zillertal
Total of trails/pistes 91km in Mayrhofen (23% easy, 61% intermediate, 16% difficult), 450km in the Zillertal
Nursery slopes 3 runs and lifts
Summer skiing 18km of runs and 7 lifts on Hintertux Glacier
Snowmaking 4.5km covered in Mayrhofen

LIFT PASSES
Area pass Zillertal (covers whole Zillertal Valley) ÖS1,965 including Glacier, or ÖS1,500 not including Glacier, both for 6 days

Day pass ÖS330
Beginners no free lifts
Pensioners no reduction
Credit cards accepted no

SKI SCHOOLS
Adults Uli Spiess, Manfred Gager, Max Rahm, Peter Habeler, Hannes Brandner, ÖS1,500 for 6 days (4 hrs per day)
Private lessons all ski schools, ÖS470 per hr
Snowboarding all ski schools, ÖS350 for 2 hrs, private lessons ÖS470 per hr
Cross-country all ski schools, ÖS840 per day. Loipe 20km
Other courses ski-touring
Guiding companies Peter Habeler

CHILDREN
Lift pass Zillertal, ÖS1,180 including Glacier, or ÖS900 not including Glacier, both for 6 days
Ski kindergarten 4 yrs and over, 9am - 4pm ÖS720 per day including lunch
Ski school all ski schools, 4-14 yrs, ÖS600 per day (4 hrs) not including lunch
Non-ski kindergarten Wuppy's Kinderland, 3 mths-7 yrs, 8am-6pm, ÖS320 per day or ÖS1,500 for 5 days, extra ÖS50 per day for lunch

FOOD AND DRINK PRICES
Coffee ÖS23, glass of wine ÖS20, small beer ÖS27, dish of the day ÖS130

are happy with little or no après-ski these resorts have the advantage of easy access to the snow-sure skiing on the glacier. A regular, but over-subscribed bus service operates from Mayrhofen to Hintertux.

To the north of Mayrhofen, back towards the river Inn and along the banks of the Ziller, which flows into it, lies an assortment of small resorts with their own ski areas. **Zell am Ziller** (not to be confused with Zell am See in Salzburgerland) is the most important of these, followed by **Kaltenbach** and **Fügenberg**. All of them can be reached easily by bus.

The Tuxer Glacier 1500m (4,920ft)

This provides Austria's steepest year-round skiing and for that reason is much favoured by national team downhill trainers. There is no village of Tux as such; the community is made up of Lanersbach, Juns, Madseit and Hintertux. **Lanersbach** has 20km of interesting open skiing on the 2300m Eggalm slopes of the Beilspitz, as well as a further 13km of generally easier skiing on the sunny Lämmerbichl plateau. A free shuttle-bus runs every 30 minutes to and from Vorderlanersbach to the bottom of the Tuxer.

The glacier is a cold and forbidding place on a harsh winter's day, but snow cover is guaranteed here when much of the rest of the Tyrol is green. A rather tired gondola and parallel double-chair start a kilometre beyond the small village of Hintertux. They climb over steep wooded slopes to the summer pastureland of Sommerbergalm, a sunny platform with restaurants beneath the Tuxerjoch and an easy, east-facing ski area served by two drag-lifts and a quad-chair. The main glacier area is separated from here by a narrow gorge.

The second stage of the gondola and a cold parallel chair take you up to the Tuxerfernerhaus restaurant at 2660m, the bottom of the summer ski area. Two more slow and bitterly cold chairs take you on up to 3250m just below the top of the aptly named Gefrorene Wand (frozen wall). The broad, open slopes here are served by a number of T-bars and a central chair-lift, and a triple-chair off the back has opened up access to 350m of vertical sunny skiing at the top of the Schlegeisgletscher.

While the runs on both sides are generally easy, the glaciers are considerably steeper than most. On the western side, in particular on the long runs both above and below glacier level, there are more demanding stretches than you might expect. A short T-bar returns you to Sommerbergalm from which point you can take either a tricky ungraded route, which is steep and narrow in places, or a red (intermediate) route down the western flank of the mountain through the trees. A more attractive alternative for experienced skiers is to take the Tuxerjoch chair-lift and then traverse an unnervingly steep slope to reach a delightful run down the bowl of the Schwarze Pfanne. It is all off-piste, but an extremely popular and by no means difficult run.

TOURIST OFFICE
Tel 43 5287 6060
Fax 43 5287 60629

Zell am Ziller 600m (1,428ft)

Zell is a large and not particularly remarkable village downstream from Mayrhofen and has long been a popular summer resort. It has gained considerable popularity in winter, due more to the desire of tour operators to maintain favourable two-season contracts with hoteliers than from any particular merit as a ski centre. Neither the main **Kreuzjoch** ski area, which opened in 1978, nor the minor Gerlosstein/Sonnalm is conveniently situated and both have to be reached by ski-bus. The Kreuzjoch gondola, which starts from a large car-park on the Zillertal highway, takes you up the Wiesenalm. It is not possible to ski back down to the bottom. A chair-lift takes you on up to Rosenalm at 1744m. From here a choice of lifts fan out across a sunny bowl up to Kreuzjoch, which, at 2559m, is the top of the ski area. The runs down are a mixture of blues and satisfying reds. The Sportbahn Karspitz double-chair from Wiesenalm serves a more challenging black (difficult) run, which takes you back to Wiesenalm.

The **Gerlosstein** area, five kilometres (three miles) away from the centre, is accessed via a cable car. Runs down are a mixture of mainly undemanding reds and easy blues. One mostly north-facing red offers a pleasant cruise of 1000m vertical all the way to the base-station. This area can also be reached from the village of **Ramsau** via a chair, which takes you up to Sonnalm halfway down this road. A double-chair from Sonnalm takes you on up to Arbiskogel.

TOURIST OFFICE
Tel 43 5282 2281
Fax 43 5282 228180

Niederau

ALTITUDE 830m (2,722ft)

Niederau is the capital of a small group of Tyrolean resorts south of the Inn Valley between Alpbach and Söll; they are collectively known and marketed as the **Wildschönau**. Despite this savage-sounding name, the skiing here is extremely gentle and ideal for the beginner and early-intermediate visitors, many of whom return year after year before finally moving on to larger ski areas, which offer a greater challenge. The resort has easy nursery slopes where, as one reporter put it, 'you are not constantly bombarded by experienced skiers swishing past to the lifts at the end of a long run, and skiers of different standards can easily meet for lunch'.

Prices are five per cent lower than in other resorts in the region, and you will find a considerable proportion of skiers are English-speaking. The skiing is such that if it were not for this latter consideration the Wildschönau would not feature in this book on its merits alone.

■ **GOOD POINTS**

Easy runs, gentle and extensive nursery slopes, excellent for beginners, tree-level skiing

■ **BAD POINTS**

Limited skiing, lack of challenging skiing, short runs, not suitable for late holidays

On the mountain
top 1900m (6,232ft) bottom 830m (2,722ft)

The skiing above Niederau is in two small linked areas, reached by the Lanerköpfl lift and by a new eight-person gondola, which this season has replaced the old Markbachjoch chair and improved mountain access. The network of mainly blue (easy) and red (intermediate) runs provides few challenges but is beautifully set out, and the views are spectacular.

Oberau and neighbouring **Roggenboden** are a short bus-ride away along the valley floor. They are served by eight short drag-lifts offering nothing more than nursery slopes. The one exception is the red run down from the Riedlberg lift, which one reporter argues is not as difficult to cope with as the rutted track of the actual T-bar itself.

Auffach, further along the valley, has a gondola rising up from a busy car-park to the south of the village, which offers more, although not necessarily more interesting, skiing including one long red run from Schatzberg at 1903m providing over 1000m vertical.

Beginners

Essentially, this is a resort for beginners. Easy nursery slopes situated sensibly away from the bustle of the main mountain runs provide ideal novice terrain. When snow conditions in the valley are poor, novices start on the easy runs at the top of the Markbachjoch, which are now less effort to reach via the new gondola.

Intermediates

The two runs down from the top of the Lanerköpfl lift are both long reds. The more westerly one is given the status of 'ski-route', which means that while it is not groomed it should still be periodically checked by the ski-patrol. Both runs are sound intermediate trails cut between the trees and offer plenty of confidence-building terrain and no surprises. The short run above them from the summit of Lanerköpfl is graded black (difficult) but is not discernibly steeper.

> **■ WHAT'S NEW**
>
> Eight-person jumbo gondola has replaced the Markbachjoch chair-lift
> Half-pipe at Auffach

Intermediates will also enjoy the longer, but no more difficult, descents from the 1903m summit of the Schatzberg above Auffach.

Advanced

This is not a place for advanced skiers. A couple of ski-routes, including one directly beneath the new Niederau gondola, are graded black but are by no means difficult in average snow conditions.

Off-piste

Given good powder conditions and the services of a local guide it is always possible to find interesting terrain, even in an area that concentrates on beginners, and the Wildschönau is no exception. The Auffach gondola gives access to some long off-piste variations down to the valley, which are not marked on the lift map.

Snowboarding

A dedicated snowboarding piste with a new half-pipe has been set aside at **Auffach.**

Ski schools and guiding

Good instruction from both the Skischule Wildschönau and the Skischule Aktiv is what has given Niederau its reputation, and we continue to receive enthusiastic reports. As one correspondent says: 'The care taken in bringing on the starters was excellent, but really ambitious up-and-coming intermediates would not choose Niederau as it lacks the ability to stretch this level of skier'. Another reporter commented: 'All of the instructors I met were particularly likeable'.

English is widely and well spoken, and a number of the instructors are native English-speakers.

Mountain restaurants

Overcrowding is a problem in the limited choice of mountain eating-places. Most reporters choose to eat in the easily accessible restaurants

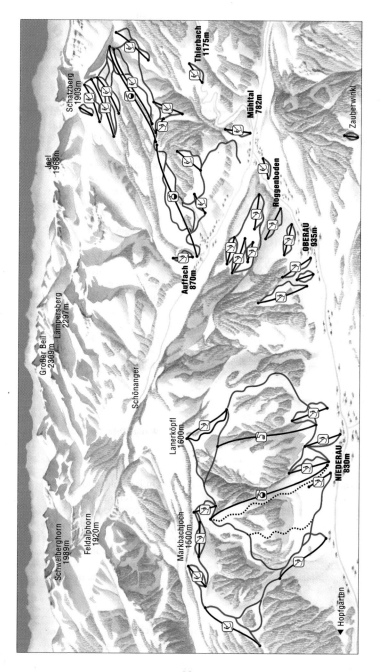

Schatzberg 1903m

Joel 1968m

Großer Beil 2309m

Lämpersberg 2297m

Schweiberghorn 1989m

Feldalphorn 1920m

Thierbach 1175m

Mühltal 782m

Zauberwinkl

Roggenboden

OBERAU 935m

Auffach 870m

Schönanger

Lanerköpfl 1600m

Markbachjoch 1500m

NIEDERAU 830m

▼ Hopfgarten

at the bottom of the lifts in Niederau. We have, however, good reports of the 'elderly establishment' above the Hotelhanglift. The restaurant at the Auffach gondola mid-station is said to be 'reasonably priced, not crowded, and clean'.

Off the mountain

The village, which sprawls away from the foot of the two main ski areas, has modern hotels and Gasthofs built in traditional style, as well as a village square. However, it somehow seems to lack the real heart of so many similar villages in this part of Austria. While it is not particularly charming, the skiing is certainly convenient to the point of being door-to-door from some hotels. Non-skiers who are not content to potter along gentle paths between the villages will find activities in the Wildschönau extremely limited. A few local craft shops and the usual sports outfitters are the extent of the shopping.

Accommodation

The most convenient hotels are the four-star Austria and the Alpenland, situated at the base of the nursery slopes and close to the main mountain-access gondola. The Hotel Staffler is nearby and is 'basic, but efficiently run'. However, a couple of reporters complain that 'the dining-room doubles as the main sitting area, so if you dislike eating in a smoky atmosphere, avoid it'. Pension Jägerrast is said to have larger than usual bedrooms and separate dining- and living-rooms. The Hotel Vicky remains popular with the British and is one of the focal points of the resort's nightlife. The four-star Sonnschein, a few minutes' walk from the centre, is said to shine above the others ('excellent, quiet, elegant service, and the food is good'). It has an indoor swimming-pool, a children's playroom, and caters for vegetarians. The friendly Pension Diane is run by an Englishwoman and her Austrian husband. For those who prefer to self-cater, the Jägerhof has four-star apartments.

■ **OTHER SPORTS**

Parapente, skating, curling, swimming, tobogganing, sleigh rides, night-skiing

Eating in and out

As is usual in most of Austria, the restaurants are mainly in the hotels, and these can vary from more formal dining-rooms serving typical Austrian dishes to those specialising in pizzas and pasta. Hotel Austria has an à la carte restaurant, the hotels Wastlhof and Harfenwirt are among the best value, and the pizzas in the Café Lois are said to be substantial.

Après-ski

There is a kind of Niederau fan club, which is made up of skiers who return here annually because, apart from knowing every inch of every run, they are also on first-name terms with every village barman. As well

Skiing facts: **Niederau**

TOURIST OFFICE
A-6311 Niederau, Wildschönau
Tel 43 5339 8255
Fax 43 5339 2433

THE RESORT
By road Calais 1114km
By rail Wörgl 10km
By air Innsbruck 1½ hrs, Salzburg 2 hrs
Visitor beds 8,290
Transport ski-bus to Oberau and Auffach, free with lift pass

THE SKIING
Linked or nearby resorts Oberau (n), Auffach (n), Mühltal (n), Roggenboden (n), Thierbach (n)
Longest run Schatzberg, 7.5km (red)
Number of lifts 37 in area
Total of trails/pistes 42km (6% beginner, 56% easy, 32% intermediate, 6% difficult)
Nursery slopes 3 lifts in Niederau, 2 in Oberau
Summer skiing none
Snowmaking none

LIFT PASSES
Area pass Wildschönau (covers Niederau, Oberau, Auffach) ÖS1,430 for 6 days
Day pass ÖS300
Beginners points tickets
Pensioners 60 yrs and over, as children

Credit cards accepted yes

SKI SCHOOLS
Adults Wildschönau, 10am-midday and 2-4pm, Aktiv, 10am-midday and 1-3pm, both ÖS1,280 for 6 days
Private lessons both ski schools, ÖS400 per hr
Snowboarding both ski schools, ÖS900 for 3 half-days, ÖS1,100 for 4 half-days
Cross-country both ski schools, ÖS1,050 for 6 half-days. Loipe 38km in the valley
Other courses ski-touring
Guiding companies Wildschönau ski school or Bernd Opperer mountain guiding

CHILDREN
Lift pass 6-15 yrs, ÖS860 for 6 days, free for 5 yrs and under if accompanied by an adult
Ski kindergarten Wildschönau, 9.30am-4.30pm, ÖS800 for 6 days, not including lunch
Ski school Wildschönau and Aktiv, times as adults, ÖS1,240 for 6 days
Non-ski kindergarten Wildschönau, 2-6 yrs, 9.30am-4.30pm, ÖS800 for 6 days, not including lunch

FOOD AND DRINK PRICES
Coffee ÖS24-26, glass of wine ÖS20-22, small beer ÖS23, dish of the day ÖS65-120

as a friendly atmosphere, Niederau has a lively choice of entertainment after the lifts close for the night. Swimming is available at some of the hotels including the Austria and the Sonnschein, and the Hotel Sportklause has a bowling alley. The Vicky is popular with British visitors and has live music two nights a week ('go early if you want a seat'). The Dorfstuben Café and the Cave Bar beneath the Staffler are for latenight drinkers. The latter also has a disco, as does Gasthof Schneeberger. The Alm Pub is a more traditional nightspot. Sleigh rides are popular and Oberau has floodlit skiing.

Childcare

The children's ski school here has a formidable reputation and takes children from four years old for the entire day. Younger non-skiers, from two years old, are cared for in the Gästekindergarten. The nursery slopes are gentle and convenient. More extensive baby slopes can be found at Oberau.

Linked or nearby resorts

Oberau 935m (3,067ft)

Oberau is an attractive and friendly little village with its own nursery slopes, but no access to the main skiing. A free ski-bus runs every 15 to 20 minutes to and from Niederau. It is a resort strictly for beginners with its own ski school. Hotel Tirolerhof, in the centre by the beginner's lift and the ski school, is said to be extremely comfortable with live entertainment most evenings. The hotel's Sno'Blau Bar is the centre of what limited nightlife there is. The attractive Gasthof Kellerwirt, which was once a monastery, has a popular Bauernstube restaurant, a busy Kellerbar and organises harp-music evenings.

TOURIST OFFICE
Tel 43 5339 82 55/22
Fax 43 5339 24 33

Auffach 870m (2,854ft)

Auffach has developed relatively little as a resort. It consists mostly of a gathering of chalets around the church as well as a line of hotels and gasthofs along the road beyond the gondola station. Hotel Bernauerhof, the Weissbacher and Gasthof Platzl are all recommended. The Schönangeralm restaurant is also praised for its 'great local venison and cheerful staff'. The Avalanche Pub is the main après-ski gathering point.

TOURIST OFFICE
Tel 43 5339 82 55/20
Fax 43 5339 24 33

Obergurgl

ALTITUDE 1930m (6,330ft)

Obergurgl has a reputation as the most snow-sure family resort in Austria, a high-altitude village close to the Italian border at the head of the remote and beautiful Ötztal. Its wealth of four-star hotels (18 at the last count) attract an upmarket, but by no means aloof clientèle, predominantly from Germany but traditionally bolstered by British families. The old village, centred around the traditional church and the original hotel, the Edelweiss und Gurgl, manages to maintain its character despite the lashings of luxurious, modern accommodation that has sprung up around it. Development has remained largely in the hands of three families who have neither sought nor needed outside investment and, sensibly, they have largely limited the number of beds in proportion to the capacity of the lift system.

> ■ **GOOD POINTS**
>
> Excellent for beginners and children, extensive ski-touring, ideal for families, reliable snow record, late-season skiing, resort atmosphere
>
> ■ **BAD POINTS**
>
> Lack of tough runs, limited for non-skiers, small ski area

Obergurgl's position discourages day-trippers and keeps its beautifully unspoilt terrain exclusive for its paying guests. It is almost as if there is a sign on the final approach road saying: 'keep out (unless you can afford it) — exclusive family ski area'. It is interesting to note that the resort is devoid of coach parking facilities.

The resort is hugely popular, particularly at Christmas and Easter, with the same families returning annually for virtually guaranteed snow conditions. Guests confess to being bowled over by the natural unspoilt beauty of the resort, which exerts an unfailing loyalty. As one reader put it: 'I almost didn't want to send in this report in case too many others discover this lovely resort.'

It therefore comes as a surprise to discover that the size of the ski area and the challenge offered by it are limited to the point of inadequacy in comparison to other European resorts of such formidable reputation.

Hochgurgl, just a few kilometres away by regular free ski-bus, is seen, at least by Obergurgl, as part of the same resort. In reality it is an entirely separate destination with a different character and a different clientèle, but it has the same lift pass. While Obergurgl draws families like a moth to a searchlight, Hochgurgl has a more serious ski image perhaps because there is little else to do here. Only limited **Vent** and mass-market **Sölden** are within easy reach for a day out. Lift passes are not compatible, and most Obergurgl visitors are more than content to remain secure in their elegant eyrie at the head of the valley.

Obergurgl made its mark on the European map of skiing on 27 May 1931, when Swiss aviation pioneer Professor Auguste Piccard force-landed his hot air balloon on the Gurgler-Ferner Glacier. What he had just achieved was the world altitude record of 16000m, what he was about to achieve was world recognition for one of Austria's most exclusive ski resorts. Local mountain guide Hans Falkner spotted the balloon landing in the last light of the day. The following morning he carried out a triumphant rescue of the explorers, leading them between the crevasses to Obergurgl and glory for the village and all concerned.

On the mountain
top 3080m (10,104ft) bottom 1793m (5,881ft)
The slopes of Obergurgl and Hochgurgl occupy a north-west-facing area at the southern end of the **Ötztal** on the Italian border. Most of the skiing is above the tree-line and runs are intermediate. Not all of the handful of black (difficult) runs justify their gradings, and expert skiers, unless they are interested in ski-touring, for which the area is outstanding, will tire of the limited pistes within hours. However, there is plenty to keep less adventurous skiers and families occupied in what are truly magnificent surroundings.

The skiing takes place over three small areas, naturally divided by the

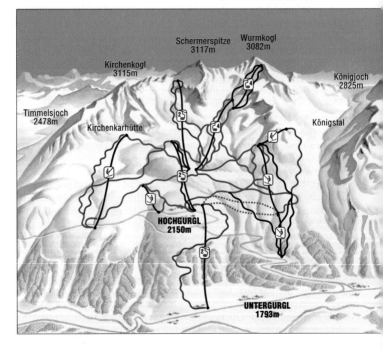

contours of the terrain. Hochgurgl offers the greatest vertical drop off the glacier and adds the variety of a wide, wooded hillside down to Untergurgl, little more than a roadside lift-station and car-park. Obergurgl's two sectors, linked in one direction only, generally comprise more interesting terrain with the steeper runs at the top and some good off-piste alternatives. Access to the Festkogl area is via a modern gondola on the outskirts of Obergurgl, while Gaisberg is reached by a chair-lift, which rises lazily over gentle slopes from the village centre.

Beginners

Complete novices start on nursery slopes set well away from the village near the cross-country track. While Obergurgl has easy skiing in both its main sectors, Hochgurgl has a far more comprehensive selection of blue (easy) pistes. The top of the long glacier is served by two chairs, one a high-speed covered quad-chair, which affords some protection against the elements, often severe at this altitude. Even on a sunny day in February extremely low temperatures can be the price you pay for high-quality snow.

Intermediates

The Festkogl gondola rises steeply to a sunny plateau with a restaurant and a couple of drag-lifts. The area of mainly red (but not difficult) inter-

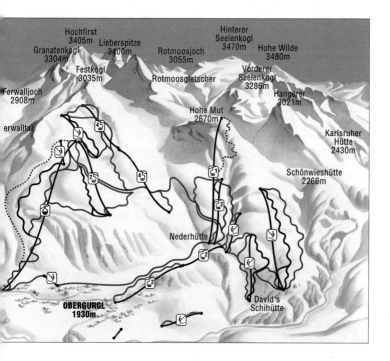

mediate skiing is served by a modern quad-chair, which takes you up to the highest point of the skiing at 3035m. Less confident skiers will enjoy the blue run down from the gondola station to the bottom of the Rosskar double-chair.

While Hochgurgl's skiing is generally less challenging, the Schermer-Spitz chair with conveyor-belt entry gives access to a wide and easy red piste, the start of nearly 1500m vertical all the way down to Untergurgl. A two-stage covered quad-chair now takes you up to the summit of the Wurmkogl, which offers an exciting descent for strong intermediates.

The drag-lift on the southern side of the ski area, with a short, steep second section to it, serves an interestingly long and varied red run with moguls on the bottom half. One reporter describes the bottom half as 'much more difficult than any other red runs in the resort'.

> ■ **WHAT'S NEW**
>
> Wurmkogl II quad-chair on last section up to the Wurmkogl

Advanced

The piste skiing offers little serious challenge or scope. In the **Gaisberg** sector a long, antique single-chair takes you up to the Hohe Mut at 2670m. The first part of the only official run down is graded as a ski-route, which in turn becomes a black piste, but the 1.8km descent is not difficult when snow cover is good, and you cannot but suspect that the grading is designed to reduce traffic and avoid bottlenecks at the outdated lift.

Accomplished skiers will enjoy the black itinerary down the Ferwalltal from the top of the Festkogl gondola. However, the run is prone to avalanche danger and great care should be taken. In Hochgurgl, a black variation from halfway down the red run, served by the Vorderer Wurmkogllift, dips into the scenic Königstal and ends up in the same place.

Off-piste

The head of the Ötztal, with its 21 glaciers, is one of the great ski-touring centres of Europe. More limited opportunities also exist for those who prefer to take their powder by lift rather than on skins. An off-piste run off the back of the **Hohe Mut** takes you down through what in good powder conditions is a glorious descent and ends up near the Schönwieshütte.

Snowboarding

There is a half-pipe in the ski area, and riders are allowed on all the lifts. Special lessons are taught in the ski schools.

Ski schools and guiding

Obergurgl is one of the homes of the Austrian Instructors Ski School; it is, therefore, not surprising that the standard of instruction and organisation here is among the highest in the country. We have generally favourable reports of the Austrian Ski School in Obergurgl. However, some reporters have complained that classes, in theory restricted to 12 pupils, can have as many as 15 during high season and division into language groups is not always well organised.

In contrast the Austrian Ski School in Hochgurgl comes in for considerable criticism. Gripes include lack of English-speaking instructors, poor group selection and 'almost non-existent tuition skills'.

Mountain restaurants

The Hohe Mut Hütte, at the top of the single-chair at Gaisberg, provides magnificent views of the Ötztal and the Dolomites. You can make the return journey by chair, but the alternative post-prandial prospect of the black ski-route down acts as a deterrent and means that the old wooden chalet is the least crowded restaurant in the area. On fine days there is an ice-bar and barbecue on the terrace. The Schönwieshütte, a 15-minute walk from the Sattellift piste, is a touring refuge that serves simple meals ('best *Gulaschsuppe* and *Kaiserschmarren* ever'). David's Schihütte at the bottom of the Steinmannlift is recommended particularly for its *Tirolergröstl*. The Festkogl mountain restaurant is described by a number of reporters as 'indifferent'.

In **Hochgurgl**, the Wurmkogl by the top of the Wurmkogl quad-chair is the best of the three altitude restaurants. Reporters warn that restaurants in Hochgurgl itself are nearly all attached to the smart hotels and are considerably more expensive. Toni's Almhütte is a rustic wooden hut attached to the Hotel Olymp and is highly praised. The sun terrace of the Hotel Riml has 'the best views on the mountain'.

Off the mountain

Building in Obergurgl has reached capacity within the avalanche-safe area. Despite the large number of luxury hotels it remains a small village set on the lower level around the church and a handful of shops, and on the upper area around an open-air ice rink. At the heart of it all is the Edelweiss und Gurgl Hotel, once the local inn and now the focal four-star around which much of the village life revolves. A free bus-service operates from the centre to Untergurgl and Hochgurgl. Post-buses run to Sölden and beyond. Cars are banned from the village between 11pm and 6am and parking is not easy.

OTHER SPORTS

Snow-shoeing, skating, billiards, curling, squash, swimming, shooting range

Accommodation

Most of the accommodation is in smart hotels and, to a lesser extent, in Gasthofs and pensions. It is also possible to rent attractive and spacious apartments by contacting the resort direct. Hotel Crystal is a monster of a building, completely out of keeping with resort character but extremely comfortable inside.

The second group of hotels is clustered around the ice rink on high ground above the centre. The Bergwelt ('art deco furniture and a great pool') and the Austria are both warmly recommended. Hotel Gotthard is also praised. In the centre, the Edelweiss und Gurgl is highly thought of, although its bedrooms are not as large or as well equipped as those in the new four-stars. The Jenewein is also praised for its friendly service and 'quite exceptional demi-pension food'. Hotel Alpina is described as 'outstanding, with wonderful hospitality from the owners'.

Eating in and out

Dining is largely confined to the main hotels, most of which have separate à la carte restaurants. Pizzeria Romantika in the Hotel Madeleine provides some respite from the ubiquitous rounds of *Wienerschnitzel*. The Edelweiss has a comfortable candlelit Stübli, which offers 'relaxed elegance'. The Bergwelt is recommended for its nouvelle cuisine. Pizzeria Belmonte in Haus Gurgl has 'the best pizzas in town'. Restaurant Pic-Nic is also recommended. One reporter speaks warmly of fondue evenings organised at the Nederhütte.

Après-ski

Obergurgl is surprisingly active in the evenings. The Nederhütte, at the top of the Gaisberg lift, becomes crowded as the lifts close for the day. Tea-dancing and copious measures of Glühwein prepare you for the gentle run down to the village. The outdoor bar of the Edelweiss at the foot of the Gaisberg lift continues to attract customers until darkness falls. The Joslkeller has a cosy atmosphere and good music, which gets louder with dancing as the evening progresses. You find the odd person in ski suit and ski boots still here in the early hours. The Krump'n'Stadl is noisy, with yodelling on alternate nights. Hexenkuch'l has live music along with Toni Almhütte in the Hotel Olymp in **Hochgurgl**. The Edelweiss's cellar disco is said, by most reporters, to be the best in town .

Childcare

The Gästekindergarten takes non-skiing children aged between three and five years old. A number of hotels operate their own crèches, usually free of charge, and the minimum age accepted varies between hotels. These include the Alpina, Austria, Bellevue, Bergwelt, Crystal, Hochfirst, Hochgurgl and Mühle.

Linked or nearby resorts

Hochgurgl 2150m (7,052ft)

Hochgurgl is little more than a collection of modern hotels perched by the side of the road leading up to the Timmelsjoch Pass, which is closed in winter. It has a loyal following among reporters who admit they return here 'to ski, and only to ski'. We have good reports of the Hotel Riml and the less expensive Hotel Ideal ('it is, as the name implies!'). The three-star Alpenhotel Laurin is highly recommended for its excellent food.

TOURIST OFFICE
Tel as Obergurgl

Skiing facts: **Obergurgl**

TOURIST OFFICE
A-6456 Obergurgl, Ötztal
Tel 43 5256 258
Fax 43 5256 353

THE RESORT
By road Calais 1200km
By rail Ötztal 54km, regular buses from station
By air Innsbruck 1½ hrs
Visitor beds 3,900
Transport free ski-bus between Obergurgl and Untergurgl

THE SKIING
Linked or nearby resorts Hochgurgl (n), Sölden (n), Untergurgl (n), Vent (n)
Longest run Wurmkogl-Untergurgl, 8.5km (black/blue/red)
Number of lifts 22
Total of trails/pistes 110km (32% easy, 50% intermediate, 18% difficult)
Nursery slopes 4 runs and lifts
Summer skiing none
Snowmaking 1km covered

LIFT PASSES
Area pass Gurgl (covers Obergurgl, Untergurgl, Hochgurgl) ÖS2,090 for 6 days
Day pass ÖS420
Beginners coupons ÖS140 for 10 runs
Pensioners 60 yrs and over, as children
Credit cards accepted no

SKI SCHOOLS
Adults Obergurgl ÖS1,520 for 6 days, Hochgurgl ÖS1,970 for 6 days, Hochgurgl/Untergurgl ÖS1,490 for 5 days, all 10am-midday and 2-4pm
Private lessons Obergurgl ÖS1,400 and Hochgurgl/Untergurgl ÖS1,350 per 2hr lesson
Snowboarding Obergurgl, ÖS900 for 3 half-days or ÖS1,700 for 6 half-days, private lessons through Obergurgl and Hochgurgl/Untergurgl ski schools
Cross-country Obergurgl, ÖS300 per half-day, private lessons through Obergurgl and Hochgurgl/Untergurgl ski schools. Loipe 13km
Other courses snow-shoeing, telemark, monoski
Guiding companies through Obergurgl ski school

CHILDREN
Lift pass 6-15 yrs, ÖS1,280 for 6 days, free for 5 yrs and under if accompanied by an adult
Ski kindergarten as ski school
Ski school Obergurgl, 5-14 yrs, ÖS1,420 for 6 days. Hochgurgl/Untergurgl, 3 yrs and over, ÖS1,490 for 6 days, times as adults
Non-ski kindergarten Obergurgl Ski School, 3 yrs and over, 9.30am-12.30pm and 1.30-4.30pm, ÖS1,420 for 6 days, extra ÖS200 per day for lunch

FOOD AND DRINK PRICES
Coffee ÖS24-26, glass of wine ÖS20-22, small beer ÖS23, dish of the day ÖS65-120

Obertauern

ALTITUDE 1740m (5,707ft)

If there is snow in Austria, then you will find it in Obertauern. What is Austria's best, or indeed only, shot at a purpose-built resort lies on a high pass in the Niedere Tauern mountains, 90km south of Salzburg. When other resorts are struggling to cope with a lack of cover during lean winters, Obertauern is usually rolling in metres of the stuff. It was for this reason that 60 years ago a group of local enthusiasts built a stone refuge here at the highest point of the pass. In the 1930s this developed into a handful of huts, which in turn evolved into what today is one of Austria's top five tourist centres, with a predominance of German and Dutch visitors.

■ **GOOD POINTS**

Excellent snow record, reliable resort-level snow, sunny slopes, skiing convenience, extensive nursery slopes, varied off-piste skiing, variety of easy runs

■ **BAD POINTS**

Late-season queues, limited activities for non-skiers, quiet après-ski, spread-out village

Thanks to a motorway tunnel, the Tauern Pass (once an important Roman trade route at the only point in the range where altitude falls below 2000m) — is now a quiet backwater. The impressive peaks of the **Niedere Tauern** surround the road around the resort, allowing the construction of lifts from a central point to fan out into a natural ski circus. It is possible to ski the arena in either direction and, unlike most Austrian ski resorts, it is also possible to ski to and from the doorsteps of nearly all the accommodation.

Although the village is far higher than most Austrian resorts, the skiing only rises a further 573m and pistes extend 100m below village altitude. The area is not particularly extensive, but provides a variety of gradient and terrain.

A car is not necessary for getting about the village but it is an advantage for making use of some of the other skiing in the area. **Schladming** and a host of other resorts are included in the Top-Tauern Skischeck lift pass. Obertauern's favourable micro-climate has one disadvantage: when other resorts are suffering from lack of snow its easy accessibility means a large daily influx of coaches and cars, particularly at weekends. Late in the season, when the cows are out on the lower pistes of the Tyrol, serious queues are reported.

On the mountain
top 2313m (7,587ft) bottom 1640m (5,379ft)
The circus can be skied in both directions, but the skiing is concentrated

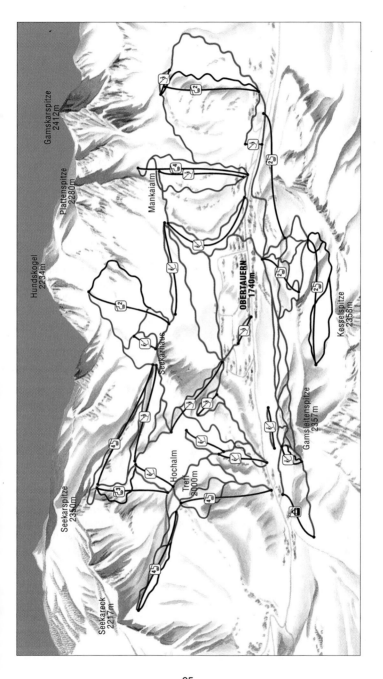

on the north side of the resort, spread around a broad, undulating and mainly treeless bowl ringed by rocky peaks. Four main lifts rise from around the bowl to points near the rim. Two of them ascend to approximately 2000m from almost the same point at **Hochalm** (1940m); the Seekareckbahn quad-chair takes you up over a steep east-facing slope, and the Panorama triple-chair over a more varied south-facing one.

The Hundskogel chair serves a slightly longer slope offering a choice of routes down, with a moderately steep piste away from the lift on the north side as well as off-piste routes more directly down on the south side. A little further down the pass the Schaidberg double chair-lift serves the steepest run on the north side of the resort. It also gives access to a short drag, which is gentle enough to be used as a high-altitude beginner slope. There is an easy run back to the village from here.

■ **WHAT'S NEW**

Achenrainbahn double chair-lift

A clockwise circuit of this northern part of the area need not involve any of the higher, more difficult runs. However, the pistes that are most appealing to timid skiers are the easy, open runs across the middle of the bowl, served by drag-lifts including the long Zentral lift from just below the village.

On the south side of the resort the mountains rise more immediately, keeping the village in shade for much of the day in mid-winter. The major lift is the Zehnerkar cable car, climbing over 500m from the western extremity of the village and giving access to a long, moderately testing run branching to various points along the pass. One reporter comments that the cable car continues to be a major bottleneck ('still long queues for most of the day').

The local lift map fails to show either piste names or numbers, but signposting of the clockwise and anticlockwise circuits is generally good. Thanks to the fact that no less than seven different lift companies share the ski area, the quality of grooming brought about by competition between them is unsurpassed anywhere in Austria. There is substantial artificial snowmaking.

Beginners

The nursery slopes are excellent with a short, gentle drag-lift in the heart of the village, just north of the road, and another longer one on the lower slopes at the east end. Another runs parallel to and just south of the road, although it is out of the sun for much of the day in mid-winter. The high Gamskarlift, at the top of the steep Schaidberg chair, also provides gentle skiing.

Intermediates

The entire circuit is geared towards intermediates with some truly excellent, long, but not over demanding, descents from the rim of the bowl. Some of the best are accessed from the Panorama Sesselbahn and Hundskogel lifts. The top of the Plattenkarbahn quad-chair is the starting point for a challenging run of over 400m vertical.

Advanced

In most snow conditions there is enough to keep most advanced skiers happy for a week, although the more adventurous will want to explore other resorts in the region. Pistes can become heavily mogulled around the rim of the bowl, and a couple of runs are positively steep. The upper Gamsleiten 2 chair serves a seriously steep, unprepared run from the high point of the system. When snow is in short supply, this rocky slope may lack adequate cover despite its north-east orientation.

Off-piste

In powder conditions the off-piste is spectacular with long runs both above and below the tree-line. To find the best safe runs you really do need the services of a local guide.

Snowboarding

All ski schools give snowboarding lessons. Christian and Werner Schmidt run their Snowwave snowboard school and snowboard camps from the Hotel Solaria.

Ski schools and guiding

Obertauern now has four ski schools including the Krallinger (Süd), which has a higher than average number of female instructors and is much favoured by tour operators. The others are: Schischule Koch (Nord); CSA, known as Ski On Grillitsch (Nord); and the new Ski School Top in the village centre. We have satisfactory reports of the CSA ('good use of time and a maximum of ten to a class').

Mountain restaurants

Because of the ski-in ski-out nature of Obertauern it is quite easy to ski back to the village for lunch, nevertheless, the supply of mountain restaurants is more than adequate. The Seekarhaus at Kringsalm is a cosy spot with good food, but it can become crowded. Similarly, the Sonnhof is overcrowded at peak times and has a 'busy and chaotic self-service system that entails a scrum and a long wait'. The Schaidberg Liftstube has an extensive menu. The Achenrainhütte at Gamsleiten is 'very pleasant, but small'. The open-air grill at the top of the Grünwaldkopbahn serves four kinds of sausage with tarragon mustard and 'a wonderful garlicky dish in a frying-pan that you could smell halfway down the red run at the back of the restaurant'.

Off the mountain

The resort itself is no classic beauty. If you are expecting a chocolate-box Austrian village with an onion-domed church, frescoes and ornately fret-worked balconies you will be disappointed. Under its usual blanket of snow the long straggle of roadside hotels and bars looks more like a Wild West town. It is by no means devoid of charm, but we have disturbing reports that its growth in recent years has not always been absorbed with

Skiing facts: **Obertauern**

TOURIST OFFICE
A-5562 Obertauern, Salzburgerland
Tel 43 6456 252
Fax 43 6456 515

THE RESORT
By road Calais 1222km
By rail Radstadt 20km
By air Salzburg $1\frac{1}{2}$ hrs
Visitor beds 6,200
Transport no bus system

THE SKIING
Linked or nearby resorts Schladming (n)
Longest run Seekarspitz-Bahn, 1.5km (red)
Number of lifts 26
Total of trails/pistes 120 km (20% easy, 60% intermediate, 20% difficult)
Nursery slopes 6 runs
Summer skiing none
Snowmaking 45 hectares covered

LIFT PASSES
Area pass ÖS1,645 for 6 days
Day pass ÖS360
Beginners points tickets
Pensioners no reduction
Credit cards accepted no

SKI SCHOOLS
Adults Krallinger ÖS1,400 for 4 days, Koch ÖS1,400 for 5 days, CSA ÖS1,580 for 6 days, TOP ÖS1,450 for 4 days
Private lessons all ski schools, ÖS450 per hr
Snowboarding Snowwave, ÖS900 for 3 days (8 hrs), or through ski schools
Cross-country all ski schools, times and prices as regular ski schools. Loipe 17km
Other courses off-piste
Guiding companies through ski schools

CHILDREN
Lift pass 15 yrs and under, ÖS1,035 for 6 days
Ski kindergarten all ski schools, 3 yrs and over, 10am-midday and 2-4pm, ÖS1,450 for 6 days, extra ÖS120 per day for lunch
Ski school all ski schools, 6-15 yrs, 10am-midday and 2-4pm, ÖS1,400-1,580 for 6 days
Non-ski kindergarten Hotel Alpina, up to 2 yrs, ÖS400 per day including lunch

FOOD AND DRINK PRICES
Coffee ÖS25, glass of wine ÖS40, small beer ÖS30, dish of the day ÖS110

---

grace ('expanding rapidly from an isolated village at the top of a remote pass to a large and less attractive holiday town'). The range of non-skiing activities is limited, although the building of a sports centre has gone some way towards rectifying this.

Three large car- and coach-parks at either end of the resort cope with most of the weekend traffic. It takes around 20 minutes to walk from one end to the other. The main cluster of buildings, which constitutes the centre, is around the village nursery slope and the tourist office.

Accommodation
Nearly all the accommodation is in hotels and guesthouses, few of them cheap. Location is not particularly critical unless you have small children (choose a hotel within easy walking distance of one of the kindergarten).

Hotel Krallinger, across the road from the Gamsleiten chair and close to the Kurven lift, is recommended as a good ski-in ski-out base with satellite television in the rooms. Haus Kärntnerland is said to be 'clean, comfortable, and friendly with exceptional food'.

The four-star Hotel Rigele is praised for its food. The Alpenrose apartments in the village centre are said to be 'cosy and well-appointed'.

> **■ OTHER SPORTS**
>
> Swimming, indoor tennis, squash, badminton

The lavish Sporthotel Marietta remains a favourite with reporters. Hotel Enzian is also mentioned for its excellent skiing location. Petersbühel Sporthotel is 'owner-run and it shows, with the best rooms we have seen in years – clean as a whistle'. Pension Sailer and Gästehaus Weinberger are also praised.

Eating in and out

Most of the restaurants are in hotels. The Stüberl restaurant in the Hotel Regina is reported to be extremely good value ('quiet, candlelit, and serves enormous portions'). The Lurzeralm requires reservations and serves 'well-presented, good food, although the service is slightly on the sniffy side'. The Latsch'n'Stüberl has friendly service and well-prepared food. Café Samson is recommended along with the Lurzeralm and Da Giorgio's, a new Italian restaurant. Two supermarkets have the basics for self-caterers.

Après-ski

This is centred on the main hotel bars, of which more than 15 offer music and dancing. The Edelweisshütte is the place to go at the end of the skiing day, along with the Gamsmilch Bar. Later on the action moves to La Bar and Premillos, next to the Hotel Steiner. The Gasthof Taverne reportedly has the most lively disco later in the evening. Hotel Enzian has a popular bar.

Childcare

Non-skiing children can be left all day in the Hotel Alpina crèche, and all four ski schools run ski kindergarten with lunch provided on request.

Saalbach-Hinterglemm

ALTITUDE 1000m (3,280ft)

Saalbach-Hinterglemm is the collective marketing name of two once separate villages in the pretty Glemmtal near **Zell am See**. The narrow valley, with uniform 2000m peaks on either side, lends itself to a natural ski circus, which can be skied as happily in one direction as in the other.

It was justly chosen to host the 1991 Alpine World Championships and it provides some of the best intermediate and advanced skiing in Austria, second only to the Arlberg's.

The two villages, a ten-minute drive apart, have grown so much over the years that they now stretch along the valley, almost meeting. Those looking for two cheap and cosy little Austrian villages will be disappointed. Both are expensive, even by Austrian standards. Saalbach is the larger and brasher of the two, while Hinterglemm is marginally more family-orientated. A third village, **Leogang**, provides a back door into the ski area and is a quieter and more attractive alternative.

On the mountain
top 2096m (6,875ft) bottom 1000m (3,280ft)

Both sides of the valley are lined with a network of 64 lifts, which is also linked to neighbouring Leogang. Much of the system has been upgraded to provide an easy traffic flow around the 200km circuit of prepared pistes; this can be skied in either direction, although the anti-clockwise route is longer. The resort was previously criticised for its annoying surfeit of T-bars, and many of these have now been superannuated.

From the bottom of Saalbach, the Schattberg-Ost cable car gives direct and easy access, in good snow conditions, to the southern half of the circuit. The 100-person lift is prone to serious queues when the opposite and sunny side of the valley has scarce snow cover. From the top end of the village a triple-chair is the starting point for the northern half.

From **Vorderglemm**, which is a ski-bus ride down the valley towards Zell am See, the two-stage Schönleitenbahn gondola takes you up to **Wildenkarkogel** and into the Leogang ski area. You can also find your way here from Saalbach via a cluster-gondola, which feeds a network of gentle south-facing runs.

Beginners

Both villages have their own nursery slopes, and the north side of the valley is dotted with seven T-bars serving an unusual variety of beginner terrain. When you feel capable of graduating to the main circus you can start on the gentler southern side, which offers a vast area of gentle blue (easy) runs. When snow conditions are not all they could be, take either gondola to the 1984m Zwölfer. The long Familienabfahrt back to the valley usually holds the snow well. From **Schattberg-Ost** the 7km Jausernabfahrt is a gentle cruise down to Vorderglemm, from where you can take the Wildenkarkogel gondola up the other side of the valley for the easiest of cruises back to Saalbach.

Intermediates

Anyone who can ski parallel will enjoy skiing the full circuit, although it is possible to shorten the outing by cutting across the valley at four separate points. Timid skiers seeking confidence-building slopes will have a field day here as most of the southern side of the valley is devoted to an easy blue playground. The principal and more challenging exceptions to this are the Schönleiten Talstation from beneath the Brundlkopf, the thigh-tingling women's downhill from Kohlmaiskopf and a few shorter red (intermediate) runs above Hinterglemm. The Leogang sector has some interesting and usually uncrowded terrain that is well worth exploring at weekends when the main slopes are at their busiest.

> ■ **WHAT'S NEW**
>
> Limberg quad-chair
> Snow-cannon at Jausern

Advanced

Schattberg-Ost, **Schattberg-West** and **Zwölferkogel** are the north-facing slopes, which group together to make up the area's most challenging skiing. The north face of the Zwölfer is a classic harsh black (difficult) run, which can be heavily mogulled down its entire 3km. The home run from Schattberg-Ost can be extremely icy and desperately crowded. A far more enjoyable route begins with the Westgipfel triple-chair to Schattberg-West, from where you can take one run down the steep black to the bottom and, after the repeat chair ride, follow the challenging, unpisted itinerary down to Bergstadl.

Off-piste

The north side of the valley offers some exceptional powder runs, but you do need a local guide to discover which slopes are safe.

Snowboarding

Saalbach has devoted 13km of slopes for riders of all levels. The snowboard park includes two half-pipes and all nine ski schools give lessons.

Ski schools and guiding

Since deregulation permitted the establishment of alternative ski schools in Austria, no less than nine now compete for the big business that this resort clearly generates. Schischule Wolf ('wonderful off-piste guide'), based in Hinterglemm, attracts a disproportionate number of Anglo-Saxon guests. The smaller Mitterlengau, also in Hinterglemm, is praised for 'excellent instruction, with clear and precise analysis of bad habits and practical help in correcting them'. At Zink in Saalbach, one reporter experienced between six and ten to a class, the instructor had a very good command of English and lessons were well explained. He described it as one of the best classes he had attended.

Mountain restaurants

Saalbach-Hinterglemm has a wide selection of mountain eating-establishments. As one reporter put it: 'Almost as many restaurants and delightful huts as there are runs. The Pfefferalm above Hinterglemm is the most picturesque old farmhouse we have ever encountered — don't be startled by the huge rabbits jumping about in the snow outside, you haven't had too much to drink, they live here!' The Goatssalm is equally rustic in nature and is recommended for its Glühwein. Rosswaldhütte, beside the Rosswald lift in the Hochalmspitze area, is an attractive chalet where the friendly staff serve good value food and wear traditional Austrian costumes. The rather twee Wildenkarkogel Hütte, at the top of the Vorderglemm gondola, is also accessible for non-skiers. It offers good pasta, as well as a special children's menu. The Stockalm self-service at the Leogang gondola mid-station is complimented on its high standard of service. Barnalm is a small, attractive restaurant at Bernkogel; dishes include the Austrian speciality of *Kaiserschmarren* (pancakes accompanied by stewed plums and sugar). The Panorama Alm on the Kohlmais is much praised and its Lederhosen-clad owner, Alex, is prone to dispensing free Schnapps. The Gondelstube at the foot of Zwölferkogel is 'not the usual self-service nightmare, but is well-decorated with a good choice of snacks'. Nearby Hotel Gunau is renowned for its Glühwein.

Off the mountain

The steep and now thankfully pedestrianised main street of Saalbach, with its smart hotels and high-priced fashion boutiques, gives one the distinctive feeling of having strayed on to the set of a Hollywood studio preparing to

> ■ **OTHER SPORTS**
> Indoor tennis, swimming, skating, curling, hang-gliding, sleigh rides, tobogganing, ice hockey, squash, parapente

shoot some twenty-first-century sequel to *The Sound of Music*. The 'authentic' Alpine charm is intact but positively Disneyesque in depth. Old it may appear but most of the village dates from the 1980s. Hinterglemm is little more than a collection of stolid Austrian hotels, which act as an alternative base at the far end of the ski system.

The atmosphere is lively and friendly. Both villages used to suffer from a surfeit of drunken and overly boisterous Scandinavians; however, like the Brits (who once claimed this delightful valley for their own), the Scandinavians have dwindled in number due to rotten exchange rates. The nationality of the clientèle here has changed as a result. Their mainly Dutch replacements party almost as loudly but with more charm and less high-octane input.

Accommodation

Alpen Hotel Hechenberg is a 'very comfortable and welcoming' four-star. The Karlshof is praised for its buffet breakfast. Hotel Hasenauer in Hinterglemm is convenient for the lifts, but one reporter comments: 'rooms, water and staff were all rather too cool for comfort'. Hotel Glemmtalerhof is described as 'pleasant enough, but German-orientated, and we could well have done without the Mexican evening'. Haus

Wolf is said to be 'clean and very friendly'. The Hotel Ingonda in Saalbach is among the most luxurious. More than 30 four-star hotels and nearly as many three-stars indicate the high calibre of the average clientèle here, and shops and restaurants reflect this in their high prices. However, the resort does have a wide selection of pensions, private rooms and 50 youth hostels at budget prices.

Eating in and out

Bäckstättstall is the most exclusive restaurant in town. The Hotel Bauer is said to be 'good value, with a much more varied menu than you expect in Austria'. Hotel Hasenauer in Hinterglemm is 'cheaper than anywhere else, with nice people and nice fish in a sauce'. The Bärenbachhof is 'not as expensive and better than most.' The Hubertushof in Hinterglemm has 'great pizza and the locals come here, so it must be well-priced'. Del Rossi is Italian and expensive. Two reporters spoke warmly of the Gollinger Hof 'dumplings of every possible variety'.

Après-ski

The endearing feature of Saalbach is that the basic jolly Austrian formula is immutable. True, the folk dancers now save their thigh-slapping and yodels for the more appreciative lakes-and-mountains clientèle in the summer, but the waitresses still wear their *Dirndl* dresses and genuine smiles of welcome as they pocket your money in the same bulging leather wallets.

The Schirmbar is recommended. Hinterhagalm has a huge copper pot of Glühwein over the bar, and Bauer's Schialm, by the church in Saalbach, has it on draft. The Siglu in Hinterglemm has low prices and wall-to-wall Dutchmen after the slopes close. The snow-bar of the Glemmtalerhof is always crowded. Lumpi's Bla Bla in Hinterglemm has a good atmosphere. The Pfeiffenmuseum Café in the Glemmtalerhof houses a quite enormous collection of pipes and smoking paraphernalia. Later on, 15 discos come to life: King's is popular with teenagers. The Londoner is the hot-spot for all age groups in Hinterglemm.

Childcare

The Schischule Wolf operates a ski kindergarten every day except Sunday for children aged from three years old, provided they are out of nappies. Lunch is provided on request. Hotels including the Partners, Gartenhotel Theresia, Lengauerhof and Egger care for non-skiing children from 2½ or 3 years.

Linked or nearby resorts

Leogang 800m (2,625ft)

Leogang is a spread-out farming community, which claims with some justification, the title of the longest village in Europe. A smart modern gondola takes skiers up to **Sitzhütte** at 1758m. A short run down there is a quad-chair and three subsequent T-bars, which bring you into the

Skiing facts: **Saalbach-Hinterglemm**

TOURIST OFFICE
A-5753, Saalbach, Salzburgerland
Tel 43 6541 72720
Fax 43 6541 7900

THE RESORT
By road Calais 1193km
By rail Zell am See 19km
By air Salzburg 1½ hrs
Visitor beds 17,130
Transport free ski-bus with lift pass

THE SKIING
Linked or nearby resorts Badgastein (n),
Bad Hofgastein (n), Grossarl (n), Kaprun
(n), Leogang (l), Zell am See (n)
Longest run Jausernabfahrt, 7km (blue)
Number of lifts 64
Total of trails/pistes 200km (45% easy,
47% intermediate, 8% difficult)
Nursery slopes 9 lifts
Summer skiing none
Snowmaking 65 hectares covered

LIFT PASSES
Area pass (covers Saalbach-Hinterglemm
and Leogang) ÖS1,510-1,895
Day pass ÖS370-390
Beginners points tickets
Pensioners reductions for women 60 yrs
and over, men 65 yrs and over
Credit cards accepted yes

SKI SCHOOLS
Adults Fritzenwallner, Fürstauer,
Heugenhauser, Hinterholzer, Zink,
Gensbichler, Lechner, Mitterlengau
and Wolf ski schools, all 10am-
midday and 2-4pm, ÖS1,500 for
6 days
Private lessons ÖS500 per hr (2 people)
Snowboarding as regular ski lessons
Cross-country as regular ski lessons
Other courses telemark, ski-touring, race
training
Guiding companies through ski schools

CHILDREN
Lift pass 6-10 yrs ÖS830, 11-15 yrs
ÖS930-1,130, both for 6 days, free for 5 yrs
and under
Ski kindergarten Ski School Wolf, 4 yrs and
over, 10am-4pm, ÖS1,400 for 6 days
including lunch
Ski school as ski kindergarten
Non-ski kindergarten Gartenhotel
Theresia, Hotel Lengauerhof and Hotel
Egger, all 3 yrs and over, and Partner
Hotels, 2½ yrs and over, all 10am-4pm,
ÖS450 per day including lunch

FOOD AND DRINK PRICES
Coffee ÖS25, glass of wine ÖS25-28,
small beer ÖS25-27, dish of the
day ÖS130

Glemmtal and the ski circus. Accommodation is in a mixture of hotels and
chalets. We have excellent reports of the Chalet Thurnhaus, an eight-
minute walk from the gondola. Readers recommend both the Skischule
Gerhard Altenberger and Skischule Franz Deisenberger. The five cross-
country loipes total over 40km, and snow-rafting is also available. The
kindergarten in Hotel Krallerhof takes children from two years old.

TOURIST OFFICE
Tel 43 6583 234
Fax 43 6583 7302

Schladming

ALTITUDE 745m (2,444ft)

Schladming is an attractive town that lies at the heart of the area that is marketed under one lift pass as **Skiparadies**, 140km and 78 lifts in the province of Styria. It all sounds pretty impressive until you appreciate that it is made up of half-a-dozen quite separate mountains, none of which are linked.

Most of the skiing takes place in the wooded foothills of the Tauern mountain range, which offers a series of long, broad runs through the woods from a top altitude of 2000m down to the valley floor at 745m. The remainder includes the snow-sure, but limited, alpine pistes of the **Dachstein Glacier**. Large this area may be, but unfortunately there is a pronounced lack of variety in the intermediate skiing, and a number of readers commented that it did not live up to their expectations and left them with a vague feeling of dissatisfaction. However, one veteran reporter describes it as 'an intermediate paradise groomed to perfection'.

■ **GOOD POINTS**

Large ski area, lively après-ski, extensive nursery slopes, alpine charm, tree-level skiing, excellent cross-country facilities, short airport transfer, easy road and rail access, variety of mountain restaurants

■ **BAD POINTS**

Unreliable resort-level snow, few tough runs, lack of skiing convenience

With the one exception, where two lifts fan out to adjoining mountains from the same valley station, you have to transfer tediously from one to the other by free ski-bus. Much talk has gone on over too many years about providing on-mountain links between the five main ones. However, nothing has ever materialised, and we must now presume that it never will. Schladming would otherwise be considered as an important intermediate playground in a not particularly well known corner of Austria. However, the strength of the local 'green' lobby is such that state planning permission is unlikely.

Schladming claimed international fame as a ski resort when it hosted the World Championships in 1982. Its FIS downhill course still takes its turn on the World Cup circuit, and the town and surrounding mountains are therefore familiar to thousands of armchair skiers as well as holidaymakers. The town is situated on a main east-west road and rail route. To the north are the spectacular rocky peaks of the Dachstein, with summer skiing (both alpine and cross-country) on its extremely gentle glacial slopes.

Further substantial ski areas, including **Obertauern** and the **St Johann im Pongau** ski circus, are within easy driving distance. In fact, several reporters have commented that a car is advisable, even for the local skiing.

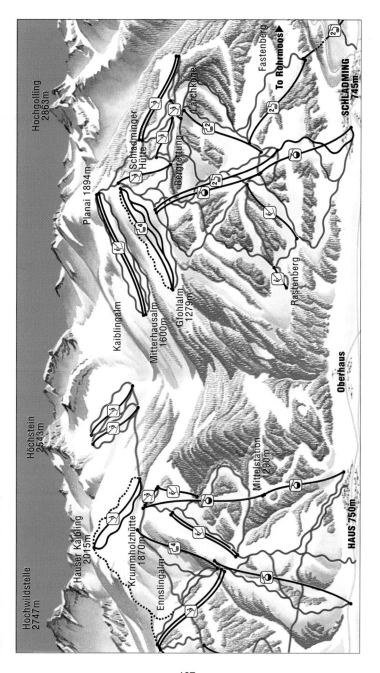

Hochwildstelle 2747m

Hochgolling 2863m

Höchstein 2543m

Planai 1894m

Schladminger Hütte

Lärchkogel

Fastenberg

To Rohrmoos ▶

SCHLADMING 745m

Kaiblingalm

Mitterhausalm 1600m

Gfohlalm 1279m

Bergfreitung

Rastenberg

Oberhaus

Hauser Kaibling 2015m

Krummholzhütte 1870m

Ennslingalm

Mittelstation 1290m

HAUS 750m

On the mountain
top 2015m (6,609ft) bottom 750m (2,460ft)

Schladming lies in the centre of a long and beautiful valley with the main slopes of the Skiparadies spread disparately across half-a-dozen mountains on the southern side. **Planai** 1894m and **Hochwurzen** 1850m are the mountains closest to Schladming and are linked by a two-stage chair-lift at valley level, a long walk or a short bus-ride from the town. Easier access to Planai is via a two-stage gondola from the edge of Schladming, a comfortable walk from the centre. The Kessleralm mid-station of the gondola can also be reached by car. A new quad-chair from here up to Larchkogel, and a triple-chair running parallel with the second stage of the gondola ease congestion at the height of the season. Hochwurzen offers several long red (intermediate) runs (and a toboggan run) from 1850m, which are served by two steep drags, a jumbo gondola and a double-chair.

> ■ **WHAT'S NEW**
> Larchkogel quad-chair on Planai
> Increased snowmaking

Hauser Kaibling at 2115m towers over the pretty village of Haus in Ennstal. Mountain access is via a gondola, which starts from a large car-park, a long walk east of the village. This terminates at the mid-station, which can also be reached by bus. Motorists can drive up to Knappl at 1100m on the eastern side of the mountain and avoid queues by working their way into the system via two drag-lifts. The Krummholzhütte summit can also be reached directly from the western end of Haus via a small, inefficient cable car.

Still further along the valley, the **Galsterbergalm** at 1976m offers a few mainly gentle slopes reached by cable car from the village of **Pruggern** at 680m. This, in turn, gives access to a couple of T-bars for some open skiing above the tree-line.

At the western end of the valley the slopes of the **Reiteralm** at 1860m offer a variety of red and blue (easy) tree-lined runs down to the villages of Pichl and Gleiming on the banks of the River Enns. Access is either by gondola from the edge of **Gleiming** or by a double-chair from an isolated riverside lift station across the valley from **Pichl**.

Most of these slopes are north-facing and gentle. Indeed, such is the lack of variety in the terrain that it is often difficult to tell one run from another. At higher altitudes there is skiing above the tree-line on the west- and east-facing flanks of Planai and Hauser Kaibling. An efficient network of snow-cannon covers the main runs.

On the other side of the valley from Schladming, the commune of **Ramsau Ort** at 1200m has no less than 19 lifts scattered around the hills on either side of the village. All are short beginner and easy slopes with 100-580m in vertical.

Turlwand, outside Ramsau, is the starting point for the cable car up to the Dachstein Glacier, which has limited year-round skiing that is too gentle to be of much more than scenic interest for alpine skiers. It is served by a chair- and three drag-lifts.

Beginners
The area is as inconvenient for beginners as it is for everyone else. The functioning of the 15 listed nursery slopes depends on the weather at this altitude. The gentle Rohrmoos meadows on the lower slopes of Hochwurzen are ideal for first turns when snow cover permits, with plenty of easy alternatives on the higher slopes of the main mountains.

Intermediates
Despite the lack of variety, there is enough red and blue cruising terrain here to keep most skiers busy for a week. The World Cup racecourses on both Planai and Hauser Kaibling should please fast intermediates, and the long downhill course on Hochwurzen is thigh-burning. The usually uncrowded Reiteralm also gives plenty of opportunity for high-speed cruising. Less confident skiers will enjoy the two short drag-lifts that serve a remote, uncrowded area of gentle skiing at Kaiblingalm, which has a friendly restaurant and good snow conditions.

Advanced
This is not a place for advanced piste-skiers, who will quickly tire of the limited variety of terrain.

Off-piste
Off-piste skiing is discouraged on the main mountains except on marked ski-routes. In the right snow conditions the north face of Hauser Kaibling offers plenty of scope, and the runs through the trees from Bergstallalm on Planai are recommended. There are plenty of opportunities for ski-touring in the region.

Snowboarding
Snowboarding is big business in Schladming, not least because it is the home of former European champion Gerfried Schuller, who runs his own school here together with the Blue Tomato snowboard shop. He also operates Kids On Board, Europe's first children's snowboard school, which takes *jungen Shreddern* from five years old. The school also organises various camps for riders throughout the season. Group and private lessons are also offered by the local ski schools.

Ski schools and guiding
The Weltmeister Keinprecht Kahr ski school, owned by veteran Austrian team trainer Charley Kahr, has an outstanding reputation and Arnold Schwarzenegger is among its annual pupils. The Franz Tritscher school is also recommended ('good English, good teaching, good fun').

Mountain restaurants
'Never', said one reporter, 'have I been to a resort with so many mountain restaurants.' Indeed, they are so numerous that they are not all featured on the piste map. 'Food and service vary, but at their best they are excellent', commented another. The Krümmelholze at Haus received

particular recommendation. On Planai the Mitterhausalm and Schladmingerhütte are praised, along with Onkel Willy's Hütte ('buzzing with atmosphere and serves great ham and eggs in an individual frying pan') for live music and a sunny terrace. The Eiskarhütte on Reiteralm, the Seiterhütte and the Hochwurzenhütte on Hochwurzen are all recommended.

Off the mountain

Schladming, an ordinary Austrian town with a life of its own outside tourism, 'gives an overriding impression of friendliness'. As well as wooden chalets with painted shutters, there are sober, old stone buildings, including the remains of the town walls, which date back to 1629. It is fairly compact, with most of the shops and a good many of the hotels, restaurants and bars concentrated around

■ OTHER SPORTS

Curling, skating, hot air ballooning, sleigh rides, parapente, indoor tennis, swimming, squash, tobogganing

the broad and attractive main square, the Hauptplatz, which is now pedestrianised. Visitors to the resort looking for *Lederhosen-und-oompah Gemütlichkeit* will discover that it still thrives here.

Accommodation

Most guests stay in hotels and guesthouses around the **Enns Valley**. Without a car location is crucial, and many reporters found themselves staying too far from the town centre or the lifts, or both. The Sporthotel Royer receives rave reviews, as do both the Neue Post and the Alte Post ('small bedroom, but good food with Strauss, Mozart and Haydn in the background'), which are in the main square. Haus Stangl, a simple bed-and-breakfast place, is also recommended.

Eating in and out

The restaurants are mainly in the hotels. We have good reports of the Rôtisserie Royer Grill in the Sporthotel Royer and of the Restaurant Bachler, described as having 'friendly staff and good food at not ridiculous prices'. The Neue Post has two recommended à la carte restaurants, the Jägerstüberl and the Poststüberl. The French restaurant, Le Jardin, is warmly commended. The Gasthof Kirchenwirt is 'unmatched for quality of food, price, atmosphere and service'.

Après-ski

Most of the après-ski centres around the numerous bars. The Siglu in the Hauptplatz attracts the biggest crowd after skiing and is said to be 'very lively, but reasonably priced compared to similar establishments in other resorts'. The Planaistub'n, also known as Charly's Treff, draws large crowds. Café-Konditorei Langland and Niedal are both praised. One reporter favoured Ferry's Pub in the Steirergasse, and another the Hanglbar. The bowling alley behind the latter is said to offer a good night

Skiing facts: **Schladming**

TOURIST OFFICE
Postfach 1, A-8970 Schladming, Styria
Tel 43 3687 22268
Fax 43 3687 24138

THE RESORT
By road Calais 1235km
By rail station in resort
By air Salzburg 1hr, Munich 2½ hrs
Visitor beds 3,500
Transport free ski-bus with lift pass

THE SKIING
Linked or nearby resorts Haus (n),
Obertauern (n), Rohrmoos (n),
Ramsau/Dachstein (n), St Johann im
Pongau (n)
Longest run Hochwurzen, 7.7km (red/blue)
Number of lifts 78
Total of trails/pistes 140km (28% easy,
61% intermediate, 11% difficult)
Nursery slopes 15 lifts in area
Summer skiing nearest on Dachstein
Glacier
Snowmaking 48km covered

LIFT PASSES
Area pass (covers Dachstein-Tauern
region) ÖS1,645-1,770 for 6 days
Day pass ÖS290-355
Beginners reductions available
Pensioners reductions for women 60 yrs
and over and men 65 yrs and over

Credit cards accepted yes

SKI SCHOOLS
Adults WM-Skischule Planai and Skischule
Tritscher, ÖS1,300 for 6 days, times on
application
Private lessons both ski schools, ÖS450
per hr
Snowboarding Dachstein-Tauern
Snowboardschule and Snowboardschule
Tritscher, ÖS1,700 for 5 half-days
Cross-country both ski schools, ÖS760 for
3 half-days. Loipe 250km
Other courses off-piste, race training,
moguls (all dependent on
demand)
Guiding companies Alpinschule
Schladming-Rohrmoos

CHILDREN
Lift pass 16 yrs and under ÖS885
Ski kindergarten Tritscher and Planai, 4
yrs and over, 9am-5pm, ÖS1,800 for 5 days
including lessons and lunch
Ski school both ski schools, 4 yrs and over,
ÖS1,800 for 5 days including lunch
Non-ski kindergarten Ma Petite Ecole, 2-6
yrs, 7am-4pm, ÖS1,100 for 5 days
including lunch

FOOD AND DRINK PRICES
Coffee ÖS23, glass of wine ÖS25, small
beer ÖS25, dish of the day ÖS120

out and there is a disco at the Sonderbar. The Beisl bar is 'intimate and lively with good music'. La Porta is 'small and crowded, with a great atmosphere'. The toboggan run from top to bottom of Hochwurzen down the hairpin road is only open at night (when the road is closed) and is claimed to be the longest in Austria; it offers great entertainment.

Childcare

Few resorts receive such glowing reviews for both their non-ski and ski kindergarten. 'Outstanding facilities for very young children', commented one reader, and '40 small children in the ski kindergarten and facilities were brilliant — this is definitely the area to bring small children to be looked after well and to learn to ski', said another.

Linked or nearby resorts

Rohrmoos 870m (2,854ft)

This diffuse satellite-suburb has easy skiing to and from many of its hotel doorsteps. Among the choice of good-value hotels and guesthouses is the Austria, well-placed at the point where the lower, gentle slopes of Rohrmoos meet the steeper slopes of Hochwurzen. The smarter Schwaigerhof has a good position on the edge of the pistes and is one of the few places with a swimming-pool. The après-ski is informal and centres around hotel bars. The café at the Tannerhof is a tea-time favourite. Barbara's and the Alm Bar are busy later on.

TOURIST OFFICE
Tel 43 3687 61147
Fax 43 3687 6114718

Haus in Ennstal 750m (2,460ft)

Haus is a quiet village with its farming origins still in evidence, although it has a considerable amount of holiday accommodation in guesthouses and apartments. There are a couple of shops and cafés, one of which has jazz nights. The upmarket Hauser Kaibling has a swimming-pool and is recommended for its good food. Gasthof Kirchenwirt is a traditional hotel in the village centre, the Gasthof Reiter is a fine old chalet and is much cheaper than most, and the Gürtl is a quiet family-run hotel well situated for the cable car. Hotel Schlosserwirt is said to have a service which varies between 'cheerful and friendly and offensive and arrogant'. Its food is of 'poor school-dinner standard'. There is a gentle, open nursery slope between the village and the gondola station.

TOURIST OFFICE
Tel 43 3686 2234
Fax 43 3686 22344

Sölden

ALTITUDE 1380m (4,526ft)

Sölden, a high-altitude, and therefore snow-sure resort, has long been a popular destination with mass-market tour operators due to the high number of available tourist-beds in this spread-out village, near the end of the isolated Ötz Valley. Two developed glaciers, which are separate from the main ski area, come into play when snow conditions on the main mountain are poor and they add to Sölden's security as a ski destination.

The vertical drop is substantial by Austrian standards and, at least in high season, the après-ski entertainment is lively to the point of being raucous. The off-piste and touring opportunities are extensive, but the piste skiing itself is limited and lacks variety, although not to the extent of that at Obergurgl, its more upmarket neighbour. Complacency, the worst enemy of Austrian resorts, took a strong hold of Sölden at the end of the 1980s.

> ■ **GOOD POINTS**
> Late-season holidays, glacier skiing, modern lift system, lively après-ski
>
> ■ **BAD POINTS**
> Lack of skiing variety, heavy traffic, few facilities for small children, spread-out village

Like Verbier, Sölden has a partisan following, and any mention of its basic drawbacks produces a torrent of protest. The skiers who really enjoy the resort are the intermediates who seek more challenge from the nightlife than the mountain. They are joined by weekend crowds from Innsbruck, which is 90 minutes away by car.

Hochsölden is a collection of hotels, set on a shelf with dramatic views of the Ötztal, 700m up the mountainside; it gives easy access to the slopes at the busier and more mundane side of the mountain.

On the mountain
top 3058m (10,030ft) bottom 1377m (4,517ft)

Sölden's ski area is in two sections, linked by chairs up both walls of the narrow Rettenbachtal, which provides the toll road up to the two glaciers. Both sectors are reached by gondolas at either end of the village, which are in turn linked by a ski-bus that runs efficiently every nine minutes. The skiing is extensive, with a drop of nearly 1700m vertical, half above and half below the tree-line, but less varied in difficulty than the piste map suggests.

The main mountain access is via the Gaislachkogl 24-person gondola at the far end of the resort. The main run down through the trees from the mid-station can be icy and overcrowded, especially at the end of the day, and should be skied with caution.

The top stage of the gondola rises steeply over 850m to the craggy peak of the **Gaislachkogl** at 3058m. The Hochsölden ski area can be reached via a flat traverse from the gondola mid-station or via a continuation of the red (intermediate) run from Gaislachkogl, which starts at the top of the Stabele double-chair, at the bottom of the Rettenbachtal.

Alternative mountain access to Hochsölden is via a 20-minute chairlift from the other end of Sölden or a gondola up to **Giggijoch** above it. Above this gondola is a wide, open expanse of gentle mountainside served by a variety of lifts. This part of the mountain used to be prone to the worst congestion, but new lifts, including a quad-chair to the top of the Hainbachjoch, have greatly relieved the pressure, at least for good skiers who will enjoy the small mogul field at the top and the overgraded black (difficult) run down.

The **Rettenbach** and **Tiefenbach** glaciers are reached by toll road and separated by a dramatic tunnel through the mountain. A total of ten lifts serve a selection of mainly blue (easy) runs, which are more enjoyable for their panoramic views than the actual challenge of their skiing.

Beginners

The best nursery slopes and easy beginners' runs are found above the gondola at Giggijoch. A short button-lift, which has been installed adjacent to the Hainbachkar lift, is a welcome addition. Novices do not have to buy area lift passes, which is a major holiday saving; first-week skiers can use points tickets on the nursery lifts. Wobbly second-weekers will find themselves largely confined to the same area, apart from tackling the stiff blue down to Hochsölden.

Intermediates

Open slopes around the Gaislachkoglbahn mid-station provide easy intermediate skiing served by a couple of chair-lifts, one of which gives access to a long red run down to Gaislachalm at 1982m, where the sunny terraces of the restaurants prove popular lunching places. A long path takes you back on to the lower pistes of Sölden at Innerwald. Run 1 on the piste map, from the top of Gaislachkogl all the way to the gondola base-station, gives a substantial vertical drop of 1700m and is the most enjoyable cruise in the resort. The Silberbrünnl blue is an easy and enjoyable first run of the day.

Advanced

The front face directly beneath and to the south of the Gaislachkogl gondola top-station is an exciting expert descent on which enormous care should be taken. It can look like a piste at the top, due to the many who choose to ski it, but there are no markers and considerable expertise is required in hard-packed or icy conditions. The top is deceptively easy, but after a couple of hundred metres the bowl divides into two. The

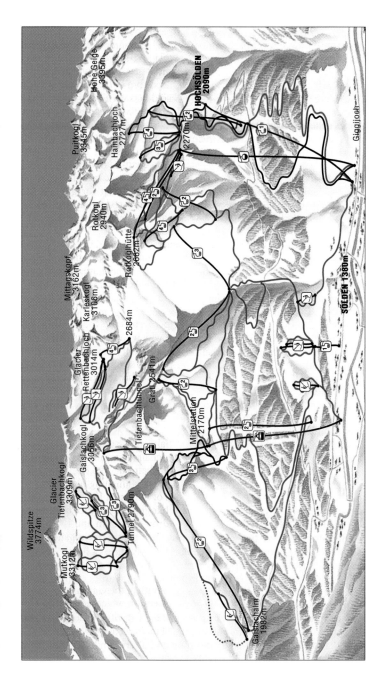

southern couloir (to the right as you descend) is the wider and therefore easier of the two. It is not dauntingly steep, 33 degrees at its worst, but the length is such that any fall would be serious.

Off-piste
There are considerable off-piste opportunities from the top of the Stabele double-chair and, given good snow conditions, on the sunny slopes accessed by the Langegg I chair and the Silberbrünnl chair on the other side of the valley. Return in both cases is along paths at the edge of the road to the chair-lifts.

Snowboarding
The Sölden/Hochsölden Ski School, Ski School Ötztal 2000 and Ski School Vacancia all offer group and private snowboarding lessons. A new half-pipe will open in the Giggijoch ski area this season (1995–6).

Ski schools and guiding
Instruction in Sölden benefits from the competition between the three ski schools: the Sölden/Hochsölden, Total Vacancia and the new Ötztal 2000. We have good reports of the Sölden/Hochsölden ('our middle-aged instructor spoke fluent English, he was very sound on technique with lots of useful feedback; as a result our skiing improved tremendously in just four half-day lessons').

One reporter who used the alternative school, Total Vacancia, said she was 'very impressed with their attitude'. We have no news as yet of Ötztal 2000.

Mountain restaurants
The ski area has a larger than usual choice of mountain restaurants. The Gampe Alm, Eugen's Obstlerhütte and Löple Alm are all authentic huts with plenty of atmosphere. The Giggijoch is a large modern complex with a sun terrace ('lots of choice, but it should be avoided during peak hours'). The Rotkoglhütte has 'sound Austrian fare' and is 'not overcrowded or overpriced'. Both the Gaislachalm and the Silbertal at Gaislachalm have sun terraces, a wide variety of food and live accordion music.

Off the mountain
Sölden stretches over two kilometres on either side of the road and river along the valley floor. It is an unmemorable collection of hotels, restaurants and bars that lacks alpine charm. Nevertheless, it would be uncharitable to dismiss the whole as unattractive. Most visitors come here by car, and traffic is a real hazard throughout the day. Once in the resort a car is neither necessary nor desirable, except for visits to **Vent**, the glaciers and the **Gurgls**, and parking is extremely difficult. Ski-buses run regularly around the resort, and the post-bus service in the valley is efficient. Hochsölden is served by morning and afternoon buses, but there is no service after dark and taxis are expensive.

Accommodation

Location is moderately important here; better skiers should base themselves in the southern end of town within easy reach of the Gaislachkogl gondola, while less experienced visitors will need to access Giggijoch from the other. As one reporter put it: 'A hotel near one of the two main lift stations is a must'. The Hotel Regina, right by the Gaislachkoglbahn, is strongly recommended ('good-sized rooms, friendly staff, ample good food'). Gästehaus Sonneheim, in the same area, is praised for being 'extremely cheap and reasonably sited — we shall come here again'.

Hotel Stefan, by the Giggijoch gondola station 'could not be more conveniently placed and the restaurant is superb'. Gästehaus Paul Grüner continues to receive praise as a 'more than adequate' bed-and-breakfast establishment.

Eating in and out

Most of the restaurants are in the hotels and serve traditional Austrian food. Dominic is said to be the best eating place in the village ('friendly, beautifully furnished and decorated, with excellent and well-presented food – try the *Filettopf*'). The Kupferpfanne in the Hotel Tirolerhof is famed for its venison and steaks. The à la carte restaurants in the Alpina, Stefan and Hubertus hotels are also recommended. Hotel Tyrol and Hotel Alpenland are cheaper alternatives, although one reporter complained about the small portions of meat. La Tavola is said to be excellent value. Hotel Sonne has a Stüberl with a cosy atmosphere.

> ### ■ OTHER SPORTS
> Parapente, skating, curling, indoor tennis and badminton, indoor rifle shooting, swimming, tobogganing

Self-caterers are warned that here, as elsewhere in Austria, all supermarkets and grocery stores are closed on Sundays, which makes for a hungry start to the week for those who do not come prepared.

Après-ski

Once the lifts close Sölden swings into life. Café Philip at Innerwald, reached via an often rocky run down, has a lively atmosphere and is a focal gathering point for young people. The single-chair down from here runs until 6pm for those whose legs are wobbly from the skiing or otherwise. The Hinterer, Dominic Bla-Bla and Café Heiner near the Giggijoch gondola are always crowded. The Park Hotel and the Nanu Bar are recommended for a quieter drink. Later in the evening, Jakob's Weinfassl attracts a 30-something clientèle in 'beautiful decor and surroundings'. The Piano Bar in the Hotel Central is a sophisticated disco with free entry but double-price drinks.

Childcare

Apart from private babysitting, Sölden has no special facilities for small, non-skiing children. The Sölden/Hochsölden Ski School runs a ski kindergarten with a play area for skiers aged three years old and above.

Skiing facts: **Sölden**

TOURIST OFFICE
Postfach 80, A-6450 Sölden, Tyrol
Tel 43 5254 22120
Fax 43 5254 3131

THE RESORT
By road Calais 1000km
By rail Ötztal-Bahnhof 30km, Innsbruck 88km
By air Innsbruck $1\frac{1}{2}$ hrs
Visitor beds 9,312
Transport free ski-bus runs through village every 9 mins

THE SKIING
Linked or nearby resorts Hochsölden (n), Untergurgl (n), Hochgurgl (n), Obergurgl (n), Vent (n), Zwieselstein (n)
Longest run Gaislachkogl, 10km (red)
Number of lifts 22 (excluding Glacier)
Total of trails/pistes 101km (42% easy, 43% intermediate, 15% difficult)
Nursery slopes 3 lifts and trails
Summer skiing 10 lifts on Rettenbach and Tiefenbach glaciers
Snowmaking 50 hectares covered

LIFT PASSES
Area pass (including Glacier) ÖS1,920 for 6 days
Day pass ÖS430
Beginners points tickets
Pensioners reduction for women 60 yrs and over and men 65 yrs and over
Credit cards accepted no

SKI SCHOOLS
Adults Sölden/Hochsölden, ÖS1,600 for 6 days (4 hrs per day). Total Vacancia, ÖS1,000 for 6 days ($2\frac{1}{2}$ hrs per day).
Ötztal 2000, ÖS2,400 for 6 days ($4\frac{1}{2}$ hrs per day)
Private lessons Sölden/Hochsölden, ÖS1,400 per 2hr lesson, Total Vacancia, ÖS1,400 per $2\frac{1}{2}$ lesson, Ötztal 2000, ÖS1,200-1,400 per 2hr lesson
Snowboarding Sölden/Hochsölden, ÖS1,910 per 4hr lesson, Total Vacancia ÖS1,320 per $2\frac{1}{2}$hr lesson, Ötztal 2000 ÖS2,400 per $4\frac{1}{2}$ hr lesson. Private lessons: Sölden/Hochsölden ÖS1,600 for 2 hrs, Total Vacancia ÖS1,400 for $2\frac{1}{2}$ hrs, Ötztal 2000 ÖS1,200 for 2 hrs
Cross-country Sölden/Hochsölden ÖS1,600 for 4 hrs, Total Vacancia ÖS1,240 for $2\frac{1}{2}$ hrs, Ötztal 2000 ÖS2,400 for $4\frac{1}{2}$ hrs. Private lessons also available. Loipe 3km near Sölden and 5km at Zwieselstein
Other courses telemark, monoski
Guiding companies through ski schools

CHILDREN
Lift pass 6-14 yrs, ÖS1,130 for 6 days, free for 5 yrs and under
Ski kindergarten Sölden/Hochsölden, 3 yrs and over, 9.30am-4pm, ÖS1,600 for 6 days including lunch
Ski school Total Vacancia, 4 yrs and over, 9.30am-midday and 1-3.30pm, ÖS1,460 for 6 days, extra ÖS100 per day for lunch. Ötztal 2000, 4 yrs and over, 10am-midday and 1-3.30pm, ÖS2,300 for 6 days, extra ÖS50 per day for lunch
Non-ski kindergarten not available, private babysitting on request

FOOD AND DRINK PRICES
Coffee ÖS25, glass of wine ÖS35, small beer ÖS30, dish of the day ÖS120-250

Söll and the Ski-Welt

ALTITUDE 703m (2,306ft)

Söll has an unfair and unfounded reputation as the lager-lout capital of skiing, a resort better known for its uninhibited partying than the challenge of its pistes. In fact, this rather unmemorable village is positively staid in comparison with many other destinations in Austria, and its skiing offers much more than its après-ski. It lies at the heart of a vast ski circus, made up of a total of 9 resorts, with 90 lifts and 250km of skiing (almost all of which is interlinked) on one lift pass. It is best suited to intermediates, but the area, which is now unendearingly known as **Ski-Welt**, has enough on- and off-piste skiing to keep the most adventurous skier happy for a week.

Söll does attract the budget-end of the market (if 'budget' skiers can possibly afford to ski in Austria at present) and is considerably more attractive to singles and groups than it is to families. However, anyone looking for a wild time here is in for a disappointment. The resort seems mournfully quiet in comparison with the flesh-pots of **Kitzbühel** a few kilometres down the road. You have to wonder whether, in the lurid minds of sensational tabloid news editors, Söll sometimes becomes confused with Sölden or even with Soldeu. Both the latter, elsewhere in Austria and in Andorra, are considerably more prone to the 'ere-we-go, 'ere-we-go school of skier who is no more prominent in Söll than anywhere else.

Söll aims itself, with not inconsiderable success, at a clientèle mainly in their twenties, and, according to reporters, it is not ideal for those in search of 'a quiet drink after a long day's skiing'. The one popular disco may thump away through the night, and the main three bars are full until the early hours, but the majority of their clients are Dutch rather than British. For non-skiers the resort offers good alternative sporting activities but the shops are disappointing and the village is deserted during skiing hours.

■ GOOD POINTS
Large linked ski area, attractive scenery, efficient lift system, short airport transfer, tree-level skiing, extensive cross-country trails

■ BAD POINTS
Limited après-ski, unreliable bus service, limited facilities for families, lack of activities for non-skiers, low altitude

On the mountain
top 1829m (5,999ft) bottom 622m (2,040ft)
The skiing is some of the most underrated in the whole of the Alps. Kilometre upon kilometre of varied piste will take an average intermedi-

ate from one typically Tyrolean village to another, with the chance to stop en route at a number of pleasant little mountain restaurants, many of them with panoramic views over the pretty valley.

The whole Ski-Welt area ranges from 622m at **Hopfgarten** to 1829m. Söll's skiing takes place on north-facing slopes on the far side of the main road, a testing walk from the village or free ski-bus ride away. The distance is an annoying inconvenience that makes Söll unsuitable as a base for families with small children. A car is useful and means you can join the Ski-Welt system from other nearby resorts.

■ WHAT'S NEW

Mini Club kindergarten at the gondola base
Extended snowmaking at Hochsöll

Mountain access is by the fast and efficient Hochsöll gondola. At the top is Salvenmoos, the hub of Söll's ski area from where a cluster of lifts fan out. A single chair takes you up to Hohe Salve at 1829m, the high point of the system.

Access to **Westendorf** from Söll is via the covered bubble-chair from the mid-station (thereby avoiding Hohe Salve), then skiing the excellent runs down to **Brixen** (via **Hoch Brixen**), and a bus-ride to the Westendorf gondola station. Apart from having to make the short bus-connection to Westendorf or another to the much smaller area of **Kelchsau**, the rest of the huge circus can be reached on skis.

The lift system is, on the whole, fairly modern by Austrian standards. The Ski-Welt lift companies insist that their policy is only to build new and larger lifts when they are quite sure about the safety of allowing extra skiers in that part of the ski area. More realistically it is the local government's 'green' policy that forbids further expansion.

The lack of piste hazard-warning signs is a persistent complaint, especially at those times when snow cover is insufficient; reporters are continually coming across bare pistes and one reader commented: 'I lost count of the number of runs I came down, only to find that halfway down I had to negotiate mud for about 200m'.

Beginners

The nursery slopes are in the open fields between the village and the bottom of the mountain. The low altitude means snow here is uncertain and in the event of poor cover, beginners are taken up to Salvenmoos. A scenic blue (easy) run leads back down to the base-station of the gondola when snow conditions permit. For much of the winter it is wiser to download.

Intermediates

Ski-Welt was designed for intermediates; it is an interlocking network of runs spread over low but varied mountains from **Going** at one end to Westendorf and Kelchsau at the other. This is excellent cruising terrain, both above and below the tree-line, with plenty of steep and usually undergraded pitches to keep the adrenalin running.

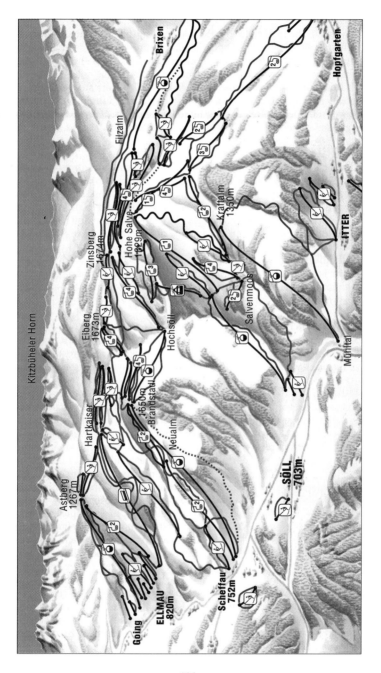

Advanced

Advanced skiers should try the challenging black (difficult) run at Scheffau, which is marked with a skull-and-crossbones sign at the starting point. Westendorf has a black mogul field from the top of the Alpenrose chair and a run to Santenbach and Kandler.

Many of the red (intermediate) runs in the area are steep enough to qualify as blacks elsewhere, including the Abfahrt in **Ellmau** and the runs down from the four-seater chair in Söll. From Hohe Salve, Grundried is a good black mogul-slope back down to the Salvenmoos area.

Off-piste

Good off-piste skiing can be found under the single-chair from Hohe Salve. The small bowl here usually holds its snow in good conditions for longer than any of the neighbouring pistes. The unpisted run down through the trees at Kasbichl, between Rigi and Salvenmoos at Hopfgarten, can also be challenging. Innere Keat above Söll has a number of off-piste opportunities, including an itinerary route to Brixen.

Snowboarding

There is a half-pipe on the Salvenmoos slope and a fun park, complete with jumps and a landing area, on the Stöckl piste. Both of Söll's regular ski schools offer group lessons.

Ski schools and guiding

Söll's two ski schools are Söll-Hochsöll and Austria Söll. Reports for both are of friendly instructors, but 'too many classes in the first few days of the week were crowded on to the limited nursery area'.

Mountain restaurants

In the Söll area mountain-restaurant queues of up to half an hour are not uncommon during busy weeks. However, most of the eating places are reported to be comfortable, reasonably priced and serve a wide variety of food. The Rigi restaurant at the top of the Kasbichl chair above Hopfgarten has a wonderful view of the valley and some of the neighbouring resorts ('you can smell the barbecued chicken from a mountain away. It is not to be missed').

Similarly, from the Gipfel self-service restaurant above Hopfgarten you can soak up the sunshine and the awesome panorama of the **Wilder Kaiser**. Owner Georg Arger, a former professional ski champion, uses the restaurant walls as a showcase for his cups and medals. All grades of skier can meet up here as it is easily reached by the gondola and chair-lift from Söll. Kraftalm, at the top of the **Itter** gondola, is one of the area's original restaurants and remains the most popular stop-off point at the end of the skiing day. Fitzalm, in Brixen, is an attractive old hut run by an elderly farmer whose specialities are home-

■ OTHER SPORTS

Skating, curling, sleigh rides, tobogganing, swimming, rifle range, squash, hang-gliding, parapente, winter walks

made bread and home-cooked food. Jochstube, at the top of Zinzberg in Scheffau, is another old hut, with a large open fireplace and several tiny rooms.

Off the mountain

Söll has a small traffic-free centre based around the church and original village-inn. The local council is particularly keen on entering competitions and has won all kinds of prizes, not least one for being the best 'pedestrian and bicycle village in Austria'. It even won the European 'Village Improvement Project' award, but for all that it is no great charmer. Hotels, chalets and guesthouses fan out from the middle of town in an untidy sprawl. The proximity of a major trunk road makes Söll ideal for easy transfers to Innsbruck and Munich but otherwise cuts an unpleasant swathe across the pastures. Although there is a lack of the typical Tyrolean atmosphere found in nearby resorts such as Kitzbühel, the local inhabitants have a sensible cosmopolitan attitude towards tourism.

Accommodation

The main hotel in the pedestrian zone is the Postwirt; a comfortable modern annexe has now been added to the old traditionally furnished hotel. We have good reports of both the Greil and the Austria, also in the town centre. The Hotel Tyrol is recommended with 'rooms not exactly large, but comfortable and clean'. Another reporter comments: 'Meals were excellent and well worth the cost'. Hotel Maria, at the northern end of the resort, is 'fairly basic, but it offers friendly and helpful personal service and superb food'. Sporthotel Modlinger is commended for its 'excellent, polite and quick service, but the portions of food were on the small side'. Hotel Teresa is said to be 'small, but with good food and a friendly atmosphere'. The Alpenschlössl is a new luxury four-star hotel.

Eating in and out

The majority of Söll's skiers tend to eat at their hotels on half-board terms. The choice of restaurants is limited, but the cost of eating out is by no means as prohibitive as in some resorts. The Schindlhaus and the Greil are renowned for their Austrian nouvelle cuisine, and the Postwirt restaurant is also recommended. At the cheaper end of the scale, the Venezia Pizzeria and the Gasthof Christophorus offer value for money. The Hotel Tenne is reported as 'basic, but good value', while the Dorfstube offers traditional Austrian cooking. The hotels Postwirt and Gänsleit serve vegetarian meals on request. The Elbow Bar Pizzeria is 'excellent'. The three supermarkets are 'cheap, spotlessly clean and well-stocked with all you could need'.

Après-ski

The upstairs bar of the Hotel Austria is said to have 'excellent '60s and '70s evenings, which invariably end up as a hugely enjoyable sing-song. Do not expect a chair after 8pm'. For a quiet evening in more traditional

Tyrolean surroundings, the Dorfstube is recommended. The après-ski starts at 4pm with the focus on the village's three main bars. Pub 15 is now under new management and is not as 'loud and horrible' as it used to be.

Whisky Mühle, housed inside a giant beer barrel in the pedestrian zone, has established itself as a Söll landmark over the years. It was beginning to fall apart from years of manic misuse but has finally been refurbished. Pub Austria and the Elbow Room are said to be 'more civilised'. The Gasthof Christophorus has live music.

Childcare

The much-needed new Mini Club is situated next to the gondola base-station and takes children from three to five years old, either all day or mornings-only, six days a week. The emphasis is on play, with a chance to take first steps on skis within the safe confines of the club. The ski schools take children from five years old, however, the distance from the village to the gondola makes this an inconvenient resort for families with young children.

Linked or nearby resorts

Ellmau 820m (2,690ft)

Ellmau's once compact centre has, over recent years, been expanding and now straggles the whole 400m up to the ski area. It has more shops, bars and general après-ski facilities than the other Ski-Welt resorts and is a livelier place to stay than Söll. In terms of location, where you stay is no longer of any real importance as the maximum walk to the centre or the lifts is ten minutes. There is a nursery slope T-bar in the village centre and five other nursery slope lifts in the main ski area. The resort supports three ski schools.

Mountain eating-places include the self-service Bergrestaurant Hartkaiser ('over-busy at peak times, but great *Gulaschsuppe*'). The Alte Post is one of the more comfortable hotels. Après-ski venues include Café Widauer, the Helden bar, Café Breit, Café Kaiserman, Café Monica and the Memory Pub. Recommended restaurants include Pizzeria Sojer, Renate's Bistro and Café Restaurant Hermann. Late-night revellers gather at the Rendezvous, Ellmauer Tenne and Helden discos.

TOURIST OFFICE
Tel 43 5358 2301
Fax 43 5358 3443

Going 800m (2,624ft)

A quainter place than most of the others in the Ski-Welt, Going is a village of attractive, old wooden chalets at the far end of the valley towards **St Johann in Tirol**. The north-facing slopes, although they start at a low 800m, hold their snow longer than some of the neighbouring resorts.

TOURIST OFFICE
Tel 43 5358 2438
Fax 43 5358 3501

Hopfgarten 622m (2,040ft)

The mainly south-facing and sunny slopes here do not hold their snow well, and if you are planning to use the resort as a base it is advisable to book during the first half of the season. The village, which is placed between Westendorf and Itter, has an ancient appearance with its steep, cobbled streets and compact centre. For no known reason it attracts a disproportionate number of South Africans, Australians and New Zealanders giving the village an unexpected international air. Café Mayer and the Old English Pub are popular, and the restaurant Brixental is recommended.

TOURIST OFFICE
Tel 43 5335 2322
Fax 43 5335 2630

Scheffau 750m (2,460ft)

Scheffau is not as well placed for skiing as some of its neighbours. The actual village is a short bus-ride away from the slopes on the far side of the main road. However, the rustic solitude of the village, with hotels dotted around the pastures and a pretty green-and-white church, more than makes up for this inconvenience. Reporters speak warmly of it: 'Small, quiet and friendly, ideal access point for the Ski-Welt'. The free bus to and from the slopes runs regularly. The slopes are reached by gondola or chair-lift, and the runs back down to the base-station are open and wide. The chair-lifts at Eiberg are fast and usually uncrowded. The only queues are for the gondola in the morning and the Brandstadl chair at lunchtime and in the evening.

Scheffau is known for holding its snow better than any of the other Ski-World villages, and access into Ellmau and Söll's skiing, on either side of Scheffau, is straightforward. Hotel Alpin serves 'four-course dinners and plenty of it' and has a swimming-pool. The Gasthof Weberbauer, in the village centre, is recommended for its 'excellent bedrooms and bathrooms and very good evening meal'. Pub Royal, the main nightspot, is a friendly place with live music, the Kaiseralm disco is expensive, and Conny's Corner attracts mainly locals.

TOURIST OFFICE
Tel 43 5358 8137
Fax 43 5358 8539

Westendorf 800m (2,624ft)

Westendorf is next in line along the valley from Brixen and joins into the whole ski area by a free-bus link. An efficient six-person gondola starts in the village, and beside it is an immense beginner's ski area, well covered by snow-cannon, at the foot of the principal slopes. The main runs are generally more demanding than elsewhere in the region. One reporter comments: 'They were steeper, icier and more difficult than we expected'. Much, of course, depends on snow conditions. The only lift queues of more than a few minutes seem to be for the nursery-slope drag, an indication of the immense popularity of this resort for beginners. The tourist office claims that more British have learned to ski here than anywhere else in the Alps. Recommended mountain eating-places include the Alpenrose and Breckhornhaus. The Talkaiser at the top of the gondola is said to lack charm.

Westendorf is one of the most compact and attractive of all the Ski-Welt villages and has a genuine Tyrolean atmosphere coupled with a liveliness, which is lacking in resorts such as Scheffau and Going. The general standard of accommodation appears to be high, with the most expensive hotels also being the most conveniently placed. Hotel Jakobwirt is recommended for its 'friendly staff, good food, good facilities and central location'. The Schermerhof apartments are described as suitable for families.

The après-ski has plenty of variety and is very lively. The Cow Shed at the bottom of the gondola is recommended, and Café Angerer is a popular meeting place. Skiers dine early here with restaurants filling up by 7pm; reservations are recommended. Chez Yves is good for pizza and steaks, the Schermer for fresh farm-produce and local venison, and Pizzeria Toscana is also recommended. The Bichlingerhof and the Jakobwirt restaurant are more expensive. Gerry's Inn attracts the young disco crowd.

Westendorf has all the makings of a good family resort. It is traffic-free, the slopes are a five-minute walk from the centre of the village (a free bus is available), and both ski schools (Ski School Westendorf and Ski School Top) have non-ski and ski kindergarten catering for children from two years old. We have mixed reports of Ski School Westendorf, which is the larger of the two. One reporter complains that 'the sole playing point consisted of a mountain of ice made from previously piled-up snow. No sledges, toys or other such useful items were available'. Reporters said that the smaller Ski School Top appears to offer a more personal service for adults and children alike.

TOURIST OFFICE
Tel 43 5334 6230
Fax 43 5334 2390

The remaining Ski-Welt resorts are **Brixen im Thale** at 800m (the bus connection-point for Westendorf), **Itter** at 730m between Söll and Hopfgarten, and **Kelchsau**, a small, unconnected farming village between Hopfgarten and the **Wildschönau** area.

Skiing facts: **Söll**

TOURIST OFFICE
Postfach 21, A-6306 Söll, Tyrol
Tel 43 5333 5216
Fax 43 5333 6180

THE RESORT
By road Calais 1114km
By rail Kufstein 12km, St Johann 17km,
Wörgl 2 hrs from Munich or Salzburg
By air Innsbruck 45 mins, Salzburg $1\frac{1}{2}$ hrs
Visitor beds 4,000
Transport free bus between village and ski
area

THE SKIING
Linked or nearby resorts Brixen (l),
Ellmau (l), Going (l), Hopfgarten (l), Itter (l),
Kelchsau (n), Kirchberg (n), Kitzbühel (n),
Scheffau (l), Westendorf (n)
Longest run Hohe Salve-Kraftalm-Söll,
7.5km (red)
Number of lifts 12 in Söll, 90 in Ski-Welt
Total of trails/pistes 250km in Ski-Welt
(43% easy, 49% intermediate, 8% difficult)
Nursery slopes 3 lifts and runs
Summer skiing none
Snowmaking 125 hectares covered

LIFT PASSES
Area pass Ski-Welt (covers all lifts in area)
ÖS1,560 for 6 days
Day pass Söll ÖS300, Ski-Welt ÖS330
Beginners points tickets
Pensioners no reduction
Credit cards accepted no

SKI SCHOOLS
Adults Söll-Hochsöll, ÖS1,230 for 5 days.
Austria Söll, ÖS1,280 for 6 days, both
9.30am-4.15pm
Private lessons both ski schools, ÖS430
per hr
Snowboarding both ski schools, ÖS360 per
day
Cross-country both ski schools, ÖS360 per
day, private instruction on request. Loipe
30km
Other courses telemark, race training,
moguls
Guiding companies through ski schools

CHILDREN
Lift pass 6-15 yrs, ÖS860 for 6 days, free
for 5 yrs and under if accompanied by an
adult
Ski kindergarten Söll-Hochsöll, 3-5 yrs,
9.30am-4.30pm, ÖS300 per day including
lunch
Ski school Söll-Hochsöll, 5-14 yrs,
9.30am-4.15pm, ÖS1,170 for 5 days (extra
ÖS100 per day for lunch). Austria Söll, 5-14
yrs, ÖS1,220 for 6 days (4 hrs per day)
including lunch
Non-ski kindergarten Mini Club, 3-5 yrs,
9.30am-4.30pm, ÖS290 per day including
lunch

FOOD AND DRINK PRICES
Coffee ÖS22-25, glass of wine ÖS18-27,
small beer ÖS22-25, dish of the day
ÖS125-140

St Anton

St Anton is to skiing what St Andrews is to golf. The **Arlberg** region, of which St Anton is the capital, is the birthplace of modern technique and in part responsible for the way in which we ski today. The neighbouring hamlet of **St Christoph** is the seat of the Bundessportheim, Austria's Ski Academy and the highest teaching body in the land.

For those who love skiing and its accompanying traditions, St Anton is the best resort in Austria. When it comes to variety and degree of difficulty, its slopes are world-class, on a par with those in Val d'Isère, Verbier and Chamonix.

■ **GOOD POINTS**

Expert ski terrain, extensive off-piste, large ski area, ski-touring opportunities, efficient lift system, lively après-ski

■ **BAD POINTS**

Little for beginners, limited for non-skiers, not ideal for families, crowded pistes

Skiing came to the Arlberg in the late 1800s: the Pastor of Lech visited his parishioners on skis as early as 1895. In 1921 Hannes Schneider opened the Arlberg Ski School, which proved to be the father of all ski schools. Generations of Europeans grew up with the distinctive Arlberg technique — skis clamped together, shoulders facing down the hill — a contrived yet elegant style that dominated the sport until the French, with Jean-Claude Killy their greatest exponent, declared technical war in the 1960s.

Piste preparation, courtesy of two men and a roller, was pioneered in the resort in 1949. Today, 38 snow-cannon, 22 drivers and 16 snow cats work for up to 9 hours a night to ensure good coverage right down to the town.

The price of such fame is the presence of 'ski bums' — notably Scandinavians drawn by the challenge of its radical slopes. For years St Anton has suffered from extremes of raucous, drunken behaviour, which begins before the lifts close for the day and escalates through the evening and into the early hours. Steps to curb these excesses have included closing the bars and nightclubs at 2am instead of 3am but with little effect. Closing times have now been restored to the later hour. However, nothing has been as successful as the strong rise of the Deutschmark-linked Schilling against other European currencies. Even ski bums have to pay for drinks.

St Anton lies barely within the Tyrol on the border of the Vorarlberg, Austria's most westerly province. It is geographically closer to Geneva than Vienna, and it is as easy to get there from Switzerland as from Munich or Innsbruck. The main east-west railway through Austria runs

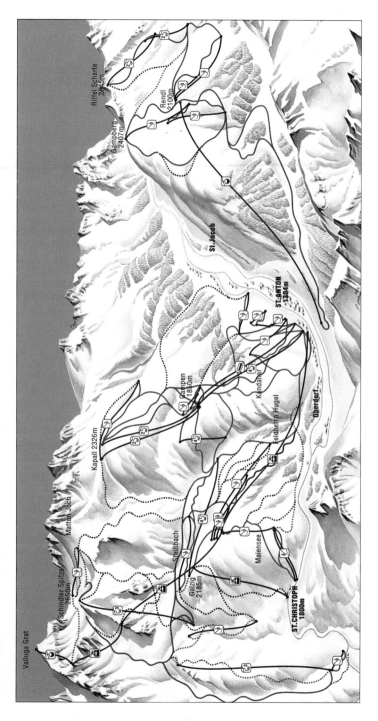

Valluga Grat

Riffel Scharte 2645m

Rendl 2100m

Gampberg 2407m

St. Jacob

ST. ANTON 1304m

Rauhen 1650m

Kindamer

Kapall 2326m

Feldherrn Hügel

Oberdorf

Schindler Spitze 2660m

Matttun Joch

Steißbach

Maiensee

Galzig 2185m

ST. CHRISTOPH 1800m

straight through the middle of town, and in March you can even travel to the snow aboard the Orient Express, which stops here at the start of its nine-month season.

On the mountain
top 2811m (9,222ft) bottom 1304m (4,278ft)

The Arlberg ski pass covers the linked area of St Anton, St Christoph and **Stuben** as well as adjoining **Lech** and **Zürs**. It provides excellent value for skiers based in **St Anton**, but is wildly expensive for the Princess of Wales and others who base themselves in the much smaller separate region.

St Anton's skiing takes place on both sides of the valley, but the main area of challenge is on the northern slopes dominated by the 2811m Valluga.

A gradual upgrading of the lift system has done much to improve mountain access, and the high-speed quad chair-lift to **Gampen** takes the morning strain off the Kandahar funicular railway and the Galzig cable car. They all take you to the skiing, so you simply choose the shortest queue.

As you rise up to mid-mountain level, the ski area splits into two, separated by a valley. Gampen at 1850m, has a children's ski enclosure, and is a sunny plateau with two chair-lifts rising to its higher slopes of Kapall at 2326m. Galzig is the focal point of the serious skiing in St Anton.

From **Galzig** you can ski down to St Christoph at 1800m, a small hamlet crowned by the Hotel Arlberg-Hospiz. Above Galzig lie the more sublime challenges of the Valluga and the Schindlergrat at 2605m.

The **Valluga** is reached by a second and over-subscribed cable car from Galzig, which is operated with a confusing and unsatisfactory numbered ticket system. You take a ticket and ask the lift attendant to translate it into time so that you know when to return.

The alternative is to ski down into the valley behind Galzig and take the quad chair-lift up to the Schindlergrat.

The **Rendl** at 2100m is a separate ski area on the other side of the St Anton Valley and is reached by the Rendlbahn gondola, a short ski-bus ride from town. It offers interesting and often uncrowded skiing and catches so much sun its local nickname is Rendl Beach.

Beginners
St Anton is not a beginner's ski resort and anyone less than a confident intermediate would be well advised to avoid it. The few blue (easy) slopes that exist would nearly all be classified as intermediate elsewhere. Even the crowded main run back into the village is seen as a challenging red (intermediate) run by most skiers. There are three learner T-bars spread between Nasserein and the funicular railway. The Gampen has a children's ski area and the gentle Gampenlift T-bar. St Christoph has its own Maiensee beginner lift. Beginners with a little experience may also find some of the runs on the Rendl negotiable.

Intermediates

Confident intermediates head for Galzig. The sunny slopes below are served by the newly installed Ostbahn high-speed quad and the main runs are sufficiently self-contained to encourage confidence, but vary dramatically in degree of difficulty. A delightful and easy blue run takes you down into St Christoph and a new quad-chair has been built to replace the old cable car for the return journey. The Osthang, a fearsome bump run with a hostile camber, takes you back down towards St Anton, but there are less extreme alternatives.

> **■ WHAT'S NEW**
>
> Quad-chair replaces St Christoph's old cable car
>
> Ostbahn high-speed quad at Galzig

Timid skiers should note with care that St Anton has dispensed with black (difficult) runs in favour of unpisted ski-routes, which appear on the map as either plain red or black-bordered diamonds. For red read black, for black-border read double black.

Advanced

Depending on the snow conditions almost all of St Anton's skiing can be considered expert. From the Vallugagrat, three of St Anton's finest long runs lead back to the broad flat valley of the Steissbachtal, a corridor between the Valluga runs and those on the adjoining Kapall.

The toughest of the three is the Schindlerkar, a wide 30-degree mogul marathon that seems to go on forever. Strong skiers can repeat it continually by riding the Schindlergratbahn high-speed quad, but its south-facing aspect makes it vulnerable to early-morning ice and late-afternoon slush. The Mattun is a series of mogulled bowls linked by traverses, less steep in pitch but with a wider variety of challenges. The third, much easier option, the long dog-leg via the Ulmerhütte, opens up the Valluga to confident intermediates. It is also the starting point for the run to the high, cold outpost of Stuben.

Off-piste

The off-piste possibilities are almost limitless, and a guide can find fresh powder a week after the last fall. An experienced skier wanting to enjoy St Anton to the full should view the services of a local guide as part of the basic cost of the holiday. In some resorts guides can effectively do little more than find a bit of untracked snow beside a piste, but in St Anton they can open up whole hidden valleys.

The patio-sized top of the Valluga is accessed by a final six-person cable car confined to sightseers or skiers accompanied by a qualified guide. It is possible to ski down the Pazieltal into Zürs and Lech. The valley itself is not difficult to ski, but the first few metres of the north face of the Valluga are terrifying, with a cliff ready to take away anyone who falls.

The Malfon Valley over the back of the Rendl is a wide, enjoyable off-piste run which, when there is sufficient snow, ends on a road at the base of the lift. Above Stuben, a 20-minute walk up the Maroi Kopfe gives entry to the Maroital Valley.

Snowboarding

Snowboarders were once few in this traditional alpine ski resort. Today the off-piste attracts increasing numbers of riders, although relatively few are attracted to the main runs. The Rendl is popular with snowboarders because of its wide and uncrowded runs, and its half-pipe.

Ski schools and guiding

The Arlberg Ski School has 180 instructors, half of whom teach ski school classes while the other half are hired out as private guides. The rival St Anton school run by Franz Klimmer has 30 instructors. Competition between the two is fierce, which helps to maintain standards. Class sizes are usually restricted to ten. We have excellent reports of both: 'The patient instructor spoke good English because he was English' (St Anton), and 'excellent instruction in private lesson' (Arlberg).

Mountain restaurants

Reporters found most restaurants here offer reasonable fare at high-altitude prices. The bleak self-service at Galzig has panoramic views over the slopes and inevitably gets overcrowded, but it does have an adjoining waiter-service restaurant. Stopp's at St Christoph is popular. The Sennehütte and S'Grabli are both recommended. The Taps, below Kapall, is also praised. The terrace of the Arlberg-Hospiz is also popular with 'attentive service from traditionally dressed waiters — Prince Edward has eaten here, but prices are not outrageous'.

Off the mountain

The setting of St Anton is hardly seductive, a meandering valley along the main railway line between Zurich and Vienna. There is not much that is distinguished about the architecture, a blend of old and new that owes little to planning and a lot to those who had an eye to the main chance before the current strict zoning regulations came into force. A fierce policy of no outside ownership, no holiday homes and no expansion in the number of guest beds has saved it from otherwise inevitable blight.

The opening of St Anton to the outside world began in 1884 when the railway tunnel under the Arlberg Pass was completed. What had been little more than a hamlet grew steadily into a village, with its narrow main street running parallel to the tracks. In the days before the road tunnel under the Arlberg Pass and the St Anton bypass were opened in 1977, the street was a traffic nightmare. Today it is a relatively peaceful pedestrian zone lined with shops, cafés and St Anton's most handsome traditional hotels.

The rest of the town straggles along the road in both directions, towards Mooserkreuz at the top of the resort to the west, and towards the satellite villages of **Nasserein** and **St Jakob** to the east. British clients without their own transport should beware of package holidays in low-budget Nasserein, frequently featured in the St Anton section in brochures. Access to the ski area was greatly improved by the opening of the Mulden chair-lift but, as the shuttle-bus does not run in the evening, the nightlife is limited to local bars unless you are prepared for a 30-minute walk.

Accommodation

The area has two five-star hotels – the historic and expensive Arlberg-Hospiz at St Christoph and the modern St Antoner Hof near the bypass. The four-star options are headed by the

■ OTHER SPORTS
Curling, swimming, indoor tennis, squash, sleigh rides, tobogganing, skating

Post ('accommodation excellent, but staff snotty'), the Alte Post and the Schwarzer Adler ('comfortable and convenient'), all much richer in tradition and much closer to the lifts. With a strong British tradition and presence here it comes as no surprise that St Anton has an abundance of chalets, as well as a large number of pensions and apartments.

One reporter strongly recommends Haus Lina for 'fabulous breakfasts, en-suite baths, Austrian decor and few Brits'. Hotel Arlberg is recommended and has 'excellent food and rooms and friendly, helpful English-speaking staff'. The Goldenes Kreuz is a family-run three-star hotel described as 'clean, friendly, and very good value'.

Eating in and out

With the exception of the Arlberg-Hospiz and its sister restaurant, the Hospiz-Alm, dining out is not a strong feature of St Anton. Elsewhere, the emphasis is on substantial rather than sophisticated fare. Austrian alpine food has improved dramatically in a generation, but boiled meats, dumplings and rich desserts still feature strongly. The restaurants in the Post and the Alte Post do these things rather better than more contemporary rivals. Café Sailer is a reasonably priced establishment. Fondue is also popular, especially at the family-run Montjola. So too are the candle-lit dinners at the Ferwall, and never more so than when they are reached by a brisk 45-minute sleigh ride along one of the most beautiful valleys in the Alps. Most guests eat in their hotels or chalets, and the freelance diner strolling the town is a comparatively rare sight.

Après-ski

St Anton's undeniably vibrant après-ski starts to warm up from lunchtime onwards in the Sennehütte before sliding down to the Krazy Kangaruh just above the final descent to the resort. This bustling Australian-inspired bar remains packed to bursting point long after the lifts close. Most guests, after dancing in their ski boots and consuming copious amounts of drink, still manage to negotiate on skis in the dark the final 800m home past a battery of active snow-cannon. The Moosewirt ('absolutely rocking'), situated below the KK, continues to provide serious competition, and one reporter feels it may have finally stolen its mantle last season.

Down in the resort the Postkeller disco begins its quaint '5 o'clock tea-dance' with some not so quaint music and the cavernous Piccadilly buzzes until the early hours. The Underground, a giant wine bar with piano music, houses the noisy and expensive Stanton and Drop Inn subterranean discos ('high techno music for trendies'). The Hazienda is a recommended bar and the Platz'l Après is a wooden barn next to the Alte Post with live piano music.

Childcare

St Anton is not recommended for children. It can, for reasons explained above, be noisy at night and has very restricted easy skiing. The main children's area, with cut-out figures to ski through, is on the Gampen. It is accessible either by chair-lift or more conveniently by the funicular railway. There are baby slopes at the base of the mountain, but the valley is so deep at this point that the sun does not penetrate to its base for much of the day.

Linked or nearby resorts

Stuben 1407m (4,616ft)

The village was named after the warm parlour (Stube) of a solitary house on the Arlberg Pass where pilgrims used to shelter 200 years ago. Only 32 houses have been added since then and Stuben has a mere 104 residents and 650 guest beds. The Post Inn, now a four-star hotel, was where mail-coach drivers changed horses for the steep journey up the pass. With its small collection of hotels and restaurants, Stuben is seen by some as an ideal way to enjoy the Arlberg without any of the bustle of the major resorts.

TOURIST OFFICE
Tel 43 5582 761
Fax 43 5582 7626

St Christoph 1800m (5,906ft)

Further up the Arlberg Pass, St Christoph was the last stop for the pilgrim making his way between the mountains. In 1386 a shepherd called Heinrich Findelkind von Kempten built a hospice on the pass with his own savings and manned it in the winter with two servants. The Brotherhood of St Christoph, a charitable foundation of locals inspired by von Kempten, still exists but the hospice burned down in 1957. The five-star Arlberg-Hospiz hotel was built on the site. St Christoph has five other hotels, the Bundessportheim Ski Academy and very little else.

TOURIST OFFICE
Tel as St Anton

Skiing facts: **St Anton**

TOURIST OFFICE
A-6580 St Anton, Arlberg
Tel 43 5446 22690
Fax 43 5446 2532

THE RESORT
By road Calais 1092km
By rail station in resort
By air Innsbruck 75 mins, Zurich 3-4 hrs,
Munich 3-4 hrs
Visitor beds 8,000
Transport free ski-bus

THE SKIING
Linked or nearby resorts St Christoph (l),
Lech (n), Pettneu (n), Stuben (l), Zürs (n),
Klösterle (n)
Longest run 8km, from the top of the
Vallugagrat via the Ulmerhütte and
Steissbachtal to the resort (black/blue)
Number of lifts 44 (88 on the Arlberg Ski
Pass, including Lech and Zürs)
Total of trails/pistes 260km of prepared
pistes and 180km of off-piste runs in linked
area (30% easy, 40% intermediate, 30%
difficult)
Nursery slopes 2 lifts
Summer skiing none
Snowmaking 18km covered

LIFT PASSES
Area pass Arlberg Ski Pass (covers St
Anton, St Christoph, Stuben, Lech, Zürs,
Klösterle) ÖS1,980 for 6 days
Day pass ÖS445
Beginners no free lifts, ÖS335 per day

(valid only for beginner lifts)
Pensioners reduction for women 60 yrs
and over and men 65 yrs and over
Credit cards accepted no

SKI SCHOOLS
Adults Arlberg ÖS1,420, St Anton ÖS1,300,
both for 6 days (4 hrs per day)
Private lessons Arlberg ÖS1,370 and
St Anton ÖS1,250, both per 2hr
lesson
Snowboarding Arlberg ÖS1,100 for 3 half-
days, St Anton prices on request
Cross-country Arlberg and St Anton, as
regular ski school prices. Loipe 40km
Other courses telemark, off-piste,
heli-skiing, ski-touring
Guiding companies Alpine Faszination, or
through ski schools

CHILDREN
Lift pass Arlberg Ski Pass, 6-15 yrs,
ÖS1,190 for 6 days, 5 yrs and under, ÖS100
for whole season
Ski kindergarten Arlberg, 4 yrs and over
ÖS2,210 for 6 days (4 hrs per day) including
lunch
Ski school 5-14 yrs, 9am-4.30pm,
prices as adults
Non-ski kindergarten Jugendcenter, $2\frac{1}{2}$
yrs and over, 8.30am-4pm, ÖS1,050 for 6
days including lunch

FOOD AND DRINK PRICES
Coffee ÖS24, glass of wine ÖS21, small
beer ÖS25, dish of the day ÖS80

St Johann in Tirol

ALTITUDE 650m (2,132ft)

St Johann in Tirol is a large, busy town with a small ski area, which has attracted generations of beginners and timid intermediates to its benign and sunny slopes. The expansion of St Johann (not to be confused with St Johann im Pongau) from a pretty Tyrolean village to a sprawling light-industrial centre has done little for its charm. Nevertheless, the centre, with its ornately frescoed buildings and fine old coaching inns, remains largely unspoilt and the traffic is neatly confined to the outskirts.

■ GOOD POINTS

Undemanding pistes, ample mountain restaurants, lively après-ski, short airport transfer, easy resort access, extensive cross-country trails, facilities for family holidays, variety of tree-line runs, extensive snowmaking

■ BAD POINTS

Poor resort-level snow record, lack of skiing convenience, limited tough runs

The resort lies off a busy road junction only ten minutes by car or train over the hill from **Kitzbühel** — but there the similarity ends. The hill is the Kitzbüheler Horn, Kitzbühel's second ski area and St Johann's only one. An on-mountain link between the two is technically feasible and not particularly costly, but fashionable Kitzbühel has no desire for any closer contact with its more mundane neighbour and its unsophisticated clientèle.

Like its skiing, which best suits beginners and early intermediates, St Johann's appeal is much more basic. Away from the industrial-estate suburbs, it offers a pleasant, chalet-style setting for a lively and quite varied winter holiday at prices that, by Austrian standards, are reasonable.

On the mountain
top 1700m (5,576ft) bottom 680m (2,230ft)

A two-stage gondola goes up from the edge of the resort all the way to **Harschbichl** at 1700m. From this point, runs fan out down three gentle rounded ridges, separated by wooded glades; some of them split and link up further down the mountain. Practically all the skiing on the top half of the mountain is graded red (intermediate), and properly so. The terrain is both varied and occasionally challenging. Most runs go all the way down to the valley, snow permitting, but plentiful drag-lifts and chairs allow you to stay at a high altitude. The lower half of the mountain is generally easier and more suited to less confident intermediates.

In general queues are not a problem, either at village level or up the mountain, but the balance can be upset by weekend visitors from Innsbruck and Munich when conditions are good. The resort has a reputation for being a snow-trap, although not as good as neighbouring

Fieberbrunn. The main gondola has a 'singles' lane where skiers travelling alone can join others to ensure all cars leave full. This minimises the potential problem of queues building up due to gondolas travelling up half empty, so waits of more than ten minutes are uncommon. There is artificial snow on the main piste down from above Angereralm to the town, and on the piste of the short Hochfeld chair nearby. This, combined with the northward orientation of the slopes and good grooming, generally keeps slopes in fine condition.

> ■ **WHAT'S NEW**
> Jodlalm double-chair

Beginners
St Johann is particularly geared towards beginners, with six nursery-slope lifts rather inconveniently scattered between the town and the hamlet of **Eichenhof**, which is a served by a regular ski-bus. The rolling lower pastures are ideal novice terrain, with a choice of blue (easy) runs higher up to which novices can progress after a few days of intensive tuition.

Intermediates
St Johann is ideally suited to red-run intermediates looking for immaculately groomed pistes on which to hone their technique. The area is limited in size and lacks any real challenge, but some of the reds are superb. Try the long Lacknerabfahrt, which links with Eichenhofabfahrt II to provide a scenic descent from Jodlalm to Eichenhof.

Advanced
The Penzing quad-chair gives access to a long and attractive black (difficult) run, the Saureggabfahrt. This has a FIS downhill-course rating, but should not deter reasonable skiers. Like all downhill courses, it becomes truly testing only when prepared for a race. In normal conditions, with the exception of one steep pitch halfway down that can provide a few problems in poor snow, the run can be managed by any intermediate.

Off-piste
While there is little here to interest the advanced skier, St Johann is famed for the quality of snow on its north-facing slopes, which harbour excellent powder long after a major snowfall. The *cognoscenti* from Kitzbühel know this, and when this international playground is absurdly overcrowded during key winter weeks, they come here.

Snowboarding
Both ski schools offer half-day group snowboarding lessons.

Ski schools and guiding
The two established ski schools, St Johann ('excellent and friendly') and the Schischule Eichenhof ('sympathetic and expert tuition'), have much experience in teaching foreign visitors to ski. The standard of English spoken at both is said to be good and Eichenhof has a policy of including

native English-speaking instructors among its staff. Every Sunday there is free ski guiding around the area.

Mountain restaurants

A choice of 18 mountain restaurants is way above average for a resort of this size. Practically every piste has a welcoming hut at the top, bottom or part-way down. On the main run down it is possible to stop off at no less than eight bars or restaurants — if you have the stamina. One reporter waxed lyrically about Hochfeld, halfway down the gondola mid-station ('popular with instructors, less quaint, but good food').

Off the mountain

St Johann stands at a junction of valleys, rivers and roads, and has a railway line running through it. The attractive centre is a triangle, neatly defined by the railway on the south side and by the confluence of two rivers to the north. The ski slopes are on the far side of the railway line, and the sprawl of suburbs in the remaining two directions are grim. Eichenhof, the eastern satellite, is conveniently situated for the lifts but is 'an unattractive 15- to 20-minute walk from the town centre along a busy, dusty road'.

> **■ OTHER SPORTS**
>
> Parapente, hot air ballooning, skating, curling, floodlit tobogganing, indoor tennis, swimming, sleigh rides, winter walks

Accommodation

Most guests stay in hotels, no-frills pensions and private rooms. Hotel Gasthof Post, which dates from 1225, is the beautifully frescoed central feature of St Johann; it is recommended for its breakfast buffet and three-course dinners. The Hotel Park, near the gondola, is one of the four-star establishments. We have good reports of the Hotel Moser ('pleasant family owners who know how to cook'), and the Hotel Fischer. The Goldener Löwe is strongly recommended for families with children: 'the staff seemed genuinely fond of them, and were unfazed by head-butts at groin level'. The Pension Kaiserblick is quietly located off the main street. Pension Schwaiger is 'within 100m of the main lift and less to the ski school: clean, simple and more than adequate'.

Eating in and out

The Speckbacherstub'n and the Rettenbachstüberl are both said to offer value for money. The Pizzeria Masianco and Pizzeria Rialto prove popular with the generally young skiers here. One reporter speaks warmly of the Löwengrill on Speckbacherstrasse. Dinner at the Hotel Park is also recommended.

Après-ski

It is noisy and plentiful, but aimed at the younger crowd. After skiing the action starts at the Café Rainer, Max's Pub near the station and in

Bunny's Pub nearby. Later on, the scene moves to Holzschuh, Schickeria and the Tatoo and Caprice discos. Thigh-slapping evenings can be enjoyed at the Huberbrau Stalle.

Childcare

St Johann is a suitable resort for families, apart from the major drawback of the distance across town to the lifts. There is a non-ski kindergarten as well as an efficient babysitting service organised by the tourist office. Older children can have lunch as well as lessons with their ski school class.

Linked or nearby resorts

Fieberbrunn 800m (2,624ft)

The sprawling village of Fieberbrunn lies ten kilometres up the road from St Johann, along the Pillerseetal. The centre is set back from the road and has typically Tyrolean hotels and guesthouses, a pretty church, and a lively après-ski atmosphere. The resort overall is inconveniently strung-out for nearly 2km along the road, and is not close to the skiing.

The small but attractive ski area is north-facing, and prides itself on being the eastern Tyrol's *Schneewinkel* (snowpocket); indeed the snowfalls here are generally heavier than those in St Johann and Kitzbühel. The main skiing is at tree level and goes up to Lärchfilzkogel at 1655m. There are several long and easy runs, some varied off-piste skiing including treks over to Kitzbühel (the ski school specialises in powder skiing), and steeper slopes down to a broad and empty valley. The only black run is Reckmoos, which is steep and narrow with moguls.

TOURIST OFFICE
Tel 43 5354 6304
Fax 43 5354 2606

Waidring 780m (2,558ft)

This unspoilt village is less than 20km from St Johann in Tirol. Situated in the same snowpocket as Fieberbrunn, Waidring is known for its family skiing, with the **Hausberg** nursery slopes right in the village. The rest of the skiing is at Steinplatte, 4km from the village, which rises to 1860m offering mainly beginner to intermediate skiing. There are five mountain restaurants on the slopes. The best hotel is the Waidringerhof, which has a swimming-pool, a cosy dining-room, and live music on some evenings. Hotel Tiroler Adler is also in the village centre. The nightlife is relaxed and informal, with the Schniedermann bar and the Alte Schmiede both popular venues.

TOURIST OFFICE
Tel 43 5353 5242
Fax 43 5353 52424

Skiing facts: **St Johann in Tirol**

TOURIST OFFICE
Poststrasse 2, A-6380 St Johann in Tirol
Tel 43 5352 2218
Fax 43 5352 5200

THE RESORT
By road Calais 1133km
By rail station in resort
By air Salzburg 1½hrs, Innsbruck 45 mins, Munich 1½ hrs
Visitor beds 5,172
Transport free ski-bus

THE SKIING
Linked or nearby resorts Fieberbrunn (n), Kitzbühel (n), Oberndorf (l), St Jakob (n), St Ulrich (n), Waidring (n)
Longest run Harschbichl-Abfahrt, 5km (red/blue)
Number of lifts 18 in St Johann in Tirol, 51 in *Schneewinkel*
Total of trails/pistes 60km (41% easy, 47% intermediate, 12% difficult)
Nursery slopes 6 lifts
Summer skiing none
Snowmaking 40 hectares covered

LIFT PASSES
Area pass Schneewinkel (covers St Johann in Tirol, Oberndorf, Fieberbrunn, St Ulrich, Waidring) ÖS1,650 for 6 days
Day pass ÖS320

Beginners points tickets, half-day card for beginner lift
Pensioners no reductions
Credit cards accepted no

SKI SCHOOLS
Adults Schischule St Johann and Schischule Eichenhof, ÖS1,280 for 6 days
Private lessons both ski schools, ÖS450 per hr
Snowboarding both ski schools, ÖS360 per half-day, ÖS880 for 3 half-days
Cross-country Schischule St Johann, ÖS1,280 for 6 days, private lessons ÖS450 per hr. Loipe 75km on east and west side of town
Other courses off-piste, slalom
Guiding companies through tourist office

CHILDREN
Lift pass 6-16 yrs, ÖS795 for 6 days
Ski kindergarten both ski schools, 2 yrs and over, ÖS1,280 for 6 days
Ski school both ski schools, ÖS1,280 for 6 days
Non-ski kindergarten Schischule St Johann, 0-10 yrs, ÖS260 per day, extra ÖS90 per day for lunch

FOOD AND DRINK PRICES
Coffee ÖS25, glass of wine ÖS18, small beer ÖS23, dish of the day ÖS150

Zell am See

ALTITUDE 750m (2,460ft)

Zell am See is one of the prettiest lakeside towns in Austria and caters for more visitors in summer than it does in winter. Its huge international popularity rests on its hard-to-beat geographical setting at the foot of the 2000m Schmittenhöhe. The mountain provides an ample amount of easy intermediate skiing, and the towering presence of the Kitzsteinhorn above neighbouring **Kaprun** ensures that snow is guaranteed. Kaprun has the best developed glacier in Austria, with year-round skiing on the upper slopes. In times of poor snow cover it becomes a daily point of pilgrimage for thousands of tourists from other resorts in Salzburgerland, and overcrowding here can be unacceptable. The two resorts have joined forces and market themselves under the unoriginal name of **Europa Sport Region**. The shared lift pass covers a total of 130km of skiing and access to 55 lifts.

■ **GOOD POINTS**

Variety of easy runs, convenient road and rail access, many facilities for non-skiers, short airport transfer, extensive cross-country skiing, pleasant town, lively nightlife, resort charm

■ **BAD POINTS**

Heavy traffic, poor skiing convenience, peak season lift queues, lack of challenging skiing

Zell is a pretty town with a pedestrian precinct, exceptional panorama and a nightlife that is both loud and lively. However, we have severely criticised it in the past for skiing inconvenience and lift queues. The town is dangerously bisected by a traffic-clogged trunk road, which, pollution apart, makes even reaching the slopes a hazardous business. The mountain itself suffers from an inadequate lift system with severe queues. However, all that is to change as Zell am See undergoes the most dramatic refurbishment of any resort in Austria.

A 10km tunnel due to open in 1996 will take traffic coming from the village of Schüttdorf beneath the town, hopefully restoring Zell to the pleasant and peaceful backwater it used to be. At the same time, the focus on uphill transport to the Schmittenhöhe will switch from the slow and overcrowded Schmittenhöhebahn at Schmittental to Schüttdorf. The Areitbahn gondola from here is to be extended for 1996–7 by two further stages so that the summit of the mountain can be reached in just 20 minutes.

Skiers based in Zell-am-See will take the Zeller Bergbahn gondola to the mid-station. The Hirschkogelbahn double-chair from here is to be upgraded to a quad, which will link into the third stage of the Areitbahn. Hopefully, these ambitious plans will eliminate the two major bottlenecks on the mountain at the Hirschskogel lift and the Schmittenhöhe cable car.

The new lifts alone are expected to cost the equivalent of £8.1 million.

Sceptics argue that this huge investment will simply replace the traditional lift queues with equally overcrowded pistes. Zell prides itself on its 'green' image and has vowed to replace old lifts but not to build any entirely new ones.

On the mountain
top 1965m (6,445ft) bottom 750m (2,460ft)

The Schmittenhöhe looks like a *Germknödl*, the rounded sweet dumpling to be found in mountain restaurants. Its gentle slopes provide long, gentle red (intermediate) runs both back down to the village itself and along the southern flank to the satellite of Schüttdorf. Steeper slopes drop down from a bowl and provide the most challenging skiing, and off-piste if it were allowed.

Until the improvements are completed the main mountain access where the Zeller Bergbahn gondola rises to the mid-station at 1320m, is on the 'wrong' side of the road. From Schmittental, 2km from the centre of Zell, the old Schmittenhöhe cable car whisks you to the summit, or a second cable car takes you into the Sonnalm area on the sunny south-facing side of the bowl, which is served by two more chairs and a drag-lift.

A small area of blue (easy) and red runs behind the summit is served by a chair and a couple of drag-lifts. None of the skiing could be classified as difficult in good snow conditions, although a steepish pitch down the black (difficult) run below Sonnalm can present problems when it is worn and icy.

The Ebernberglift, above the road between Zell and Schüttdorf, is mainly used for slalom practice. The run down is short and fairly steep, offering panoramic views of the town. There is artificial snow on the black runs down into the pit of the bowl (which without snow can be become dangerously icy) as well as on the nursery slopes.

Thumersbach, on the other side of the lake, has a chair-lift and three short drags that provide a couple of gentle, uncrowded runs back down the wooded slopes with wonderful views of Zell am See.

■ WHAT'S NEW

Probable construction of new half-pipe on the Schmittenhöhe
Additional snowmaking on the Areitalm
Extension of Areitbahn cable car
Road tunnel beneath town

The pretty village of Kaprun, a five-minute journey on the ski-bus, also has its own larger ski area above the village, with mainly blue runs. However, the best of its skiing is on the Kitzsteinhorn Glacier, 20 minutes from Zell. A choice of gondola followed by quad-chair or the original underground funicular takes you up to the Alpincenter at 2450m, from where lifts take you on up to the top of the ski area at 3029m.

The Alpincenter includes a modest hotel, restaurants and a first-class ski shop. The glacier offers good but exposed blue and red runs, most of

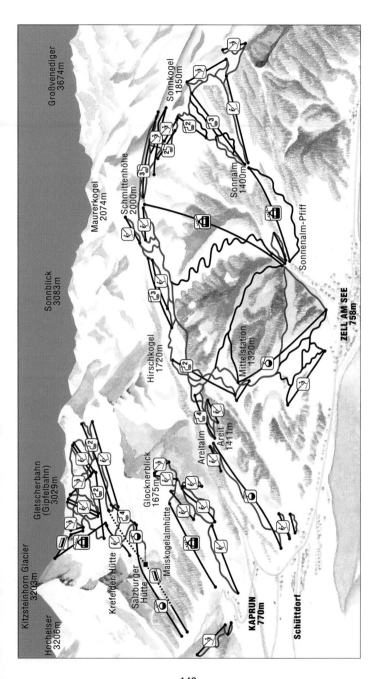

which are open nearly all year round (August skiing is usually limited to a couple of T-bars). A cable car takes you to the Aussichtsrestaurant at the top and gives access to the only difficult run: a short, steep mogul field. There is also a year-round cross-country circuit below the ridge at the top of the bowl. In winter a long red run takes you down to the mid-station of the funicular and ends in a push along the plastic floor of a long tunnel. The construction of a gondola up to the glacier has done much to reduce queuing, but when snow cover is poor in this part of Austria the extensive car-parks fill up with coaches at first light.

Beginners

At present, the ski school meets at the bottom of the Schmittenhöhebahn, although no doubt this will change as the lift's importance is downgraded. The main novice slopes are on the top of the mountain, and you will need to take the lift down again at the end of the day. There are also nursery slopes at the bottom of the cable car and at Schüttdorf.

Intermediates

Intermediates will enjoy all the skiing here, which presents few real challenges. South of Schmittenhöhe a succession of gentle, broad and sunny pistes descend along the ridge and on down to Schüttdorf. A right fork takes you to Areitalm, arrival point for the first stage of the Schüttdorf gondola; the cruising piste down to the bottom does not keep its snow in warm weather. The left fork brings you down to the Zell am See mid-station. The Sonnalm area also provides plenty of easy cruising.

Advanced

The two black runs that branch off over the southern lip of the bowl provide the best advanced terrain. These soon steepen into testing, but not intimidating, long runs with the occasional pitch of almost 30 degrees. The other two runs to the base-station are less severe but get more sun.

Off-piste

Zell's strong environmental policy means that off-piste skiing is severely restricted to the point of almost being forbidden. After a fresh fall a number of tree-line runs look particularly enticing but protection of saplings is a priority, and you risk confiscation of your lift pass.

Snowboarding

Plans are afoot to build a new half-pipe on the Schmittenhöhe in time for the 1995–6 season. Kaprun already has one in operation, snow permitting, all year round. Snowboarders should note that what little off-piste is available on the Schmittenhöhe is not available for them: snowboarding is forbidden outside the marked runs.

Ski schools and guiding

Ski schools in the valley seem to vary in quality, and we have mixed reports of the eight schools in the region. None of them has priority in the lift lines so it is not worth taking lessons just to jump the queues. The Wallner Prenner in Zell am See is the most recommended with 'excellent instructors, all of whom speak good English'. The Zell am See/Schmittenhöhe has a number of Australian teachers and also receives considerable praise. The Kitzsteinhorn Ski School operates year-round and has a high standard of instruction, particularly for advanced skiers.

Mountain restaurants

Zell am See has a good choice of eating places on the mountain, although these are crowded during busy weeks; prices are reasonable. The black run down from Sonnalm has a pleasant hut for those who can get to it. The Sonnenalm-Pfiff is praised for its 'delicious hot chocolate'. Schmiedhofalm has amazing views from its sunny terrace. The mid-station restaurant serves 'huge and excellent *Kaiserschmarren*'. Glocknerhaus, on the way down to Schüttdorf, is also popular. The Berghotel terrace bar has loud music and attracts a young crowd.

Off the mountain

Zell am See, at the gateway to Austria's highest mountain, the **Gross Glockner**, is an established town first settled by a monastic order in the eighth century. In recent years it has done much to smarten up its image. The whole of the centre has been pedestrianised, and the investment in hotels has been mighty. It has an altogether more upmarket feel to it as it strives to be a kind of mini-Kitzbühel in Salzburgerland (with its nucleus of medieval buildings), rather than the chocolate-box Austrian village that it is not.

The range of shops is wide, as you would expect in a market town of this size. It has an even larger summer trade, centred on water-sports, than it does in winter. Buses run every 15 minutes to the lifts and regularly to Kaprun and the Kitzsteinhorn. There is also a regular bus service to Thumersbach, but you can also walk across the lake in mid-winter. Reporters complain that the buses tend to become very crowded, and if snow conditions confine skiing to the Kitzsteinhorn then a car is more of a necessity than a luxury. The cross-country skiing is extensive, and non-skiers will find plenty of attractions in and around the town.

Accommodation

The luxurious Grand Hotel, jutting out over the lake, receives much acclaim, although even by five-star standards prices are said to be very high. The duplex rooms with private sauna and hot tub are described as 'the last word in hedonism'. Other four-stars are the Alpin, Fischerwirt and the Alpenblick. Hotel Bellevue is a recommended three-star. The Tirolerhof is highly recommended ('friendly staff with good English, and the four-course meals were excellent with individual attention to a vegetarian in our party'). One reporter stayed in Thumersbach: 'Apartment

Skiing facts: **Zell am See**

TOURIST OFFICE
Kurverwaltung, Brucker Bundesstrasse,
A-5700 Zell am See, Salzburgerland
Tel 43 6542 2600
Fax 43 6542 2032

THE RESORT
By road Calais 1296km
By rail station in resort
By air Salzburg 1½ hrs
Visitor beds 14,380
Transport free ski-bus with lift pass

THE SKIING
Linked or nearby resorts Kaprun (l),
Saalbach-Hinterglemm (n)
Longest run Nordabfahrt, 6.1km (blue)
Number of lifts 27 in Zell am See, 55 in
Europa Sport Region
Total of trails/pistes 80km in Zell am See
(38% easy, 50% intermediate, 12% diffi-
cult), 130km in Europa Sport Region
Nursery slopes 5 lifts
Summer skiing 15 lifts on Kitzsteinhorn
Glacier (open all year)
Snowmaking 20km covered

LIFT PASSES
Area pass Europa Sport Region (covers Zell
am See, Kaprun, Saalbach-Hinterglemm)
ÖS1,880 for 6 days
Day pass Zell am See only or Kitzsteinhorn
only, ÖS390
Beginners special price of ÖS10-20 per
ride for lower drag-lifts
Pensioners 10% reduction for women 60
yrs and over and men 65 yrs and over
Credit cards accepted no

SKI SCHOOLS
Adults Wallner Prenner (9.30am-4pm),
Schmittenhöhe (9.30am-4pm), Areitbahn
(10am-4pm), all ÖS1,500 for 6 days.
Thumersbach, ÖS850 for 6 half-days
Private lessons all ski schools, ÖS500
per hr
Snowboarding Wallner Prenner,
Schmittehöhe and Areitbahn ÖS990 for 6
half-days, Thumersbach ÖS460
for 3 half-days. Private lessons
ÖS550 per hr
Cross-country Markus Werth/Schüttdorf,
ÖS900 for 5 days, private lessons ÖS370
per hr. Harald Nicka/Schüttdorf, ÖS870 for
5 days, private lessons ÖS400 per hr
Other courses telemark, monoski
Guiding companies Ludwig Kranabeller,
Helmut Göllner, Mont Alpini

CHILDREN
Lift pass 6-15 yrs, ÖS1,170 for 6 days,
free for 6 yrs and under if skiing
with parents
Ski kindergarten all ski schools, times as
adults, ÖS1,650 for 6 days
Ski school as ski kindergarten
Non-ski kindergarten Areitbahn, 3 yrs and
over, 9am-4.30pm, ÖS1,650 for 6 days.
Feriendorf Hagleitner, 12 mths and over,
10am-4pm, ÖS1,200 for 5 days. Ursula
Zink, 2 yrs and over, 9.30am-3.30pm,
ÖS1,500 for 6 days

FOOD AND DRINK PRICES
Coffee ÖS25-27, glass of wine ÖS40-42,
small beer ÖS21-23, dish of the day
ÖS112-120

comfortable, but taxis were necessary to enjoy the nightlife.'

Pension Daxer, at the top end of the village and close to the cable car stations, is said to be convenient for the skiing but not for the après-ski, otherwise it is 'small, friendly and highly recommended'. Also well positioned for the lifts are the Schwebebahn and the Waldhof St Georg. The three-star Traube in the pedestrian zone is small and comfortable. The Neue Post, Hotel zum Hirschen and the expensive Salzburgerhof are also praised. For those who stay in hotels with television sets in the bedrooms, fixed weather-cameras on both the Kitzsteinhorn and the Schmittenhöhe allow you to check the weather on top before you get out of bed in the morning. There is a good range of comfortable apartments in all sizes in the Zell am See area, including Hagleitner, Sulzer, and Skiner. A comprehensive list is available from the tourist office.

Eating in and out

The Neue Post is praised for its 'amazing fresh trout'. The Alpenkönig, Steinerwirt and Chataprunium are considered the best value for money along with the Kupferkessel and the Saustall. Waldhof St Georg, the Ampere, Landhotel Erlhof and the Salzburgerhof are all recommended for their high standards of cuisine. The Pizza House is said to be great value, and the ubiquitous McDonald's in the town centre has prices that are much the same as in the UK.

Après-ski

Zell am See is lively by any standards. Once the lifts have closed for the day the zither music starts, *Schuhplatte* commences and the beer flows. Tea-dancing still exists, and a number of reporters have enjoyed watching major-league ice-hockey matches. Action begins at 4pm in the Kellerbar of the Hotel Schwebebahn near the lifts. The Feinschmeck and the Mösshammer in the main square both have good coffee and cakes, but away from the traditional Austrian entertainment there are bars and discos to suit all pockets. Crazy Daisy is a focal point for Anglo-Saxon visitors but said by one reporter to be 'very expensive and unpleasantly crowded'.

> **■ OTHER SPORTS**
>
> Parapente, hang-gliding, luge-ing, hot air ballooning, sleigh rides, skating, curling, indoor tennis and squash, swimming, shooting range, climbing wall, tobogganing, snow rafting, helicopter rides

Another commented that the local Austrian bar-game, which involves driving nails into logs, enlivened many an evening. Other haunts include the Bierstadl, Insider and Idefix-Pub.

The Pinzgauer Diele has a seemingly endless happy-hour and is popular with the British. The Kellerbar of the Hotel zum Hirschen is lively, and the main bar of the Tirolerhof is a good place to relax and drink and hear yourself think at the same time. The Wunderbar, a glass conservatory on the roof of the Grand Hotel, has views of the lake and mountains. Sugar Shake and the Schnelle Bier are popular. Late-night action switches to the Pinzgauer Diele, Viva and the Baum-Bar among half-a-dozen discos in the valley.

Childcare

Facilities for children are generally good, with a kindergarten taking them from 12 months old. Ski lessons are given from the age of three. One parent described it as better than the adult ski school he attended: 'We have no complaints about the standard of tuition or care of the children'. The Grand Hotel and the Feriendorf Hagleitner both run crèches.

Linked or nearby resorts

Kaprun 770m (2,526ft)

Kaprun is a delightful, typical Austrian holiday village a few kilometres back into the mountains from the lakeside. It has seen considerable expansion in recent years as it has developed into a year-round ski resort. However, despite new hotel and apartment developments Kaprun has managed to retain its essential village atmosphere based around the church and stream. It has a handful of sports and gift shops, the odd tea-room and has made a good attempt at providing a nightlife for its visitors, who range from lakes-and-mountain walkers to winter-holiday skiers and the professionals who use the glacier as their workbench during the summer months. The Baum Bar, on the edge of town, is worthy of special mention as the liveliest nightclub in the valley. The more culturally minded will enjoy a visit to the castle ruins on the outskirts.

The four-star Orgler has comfortable accommodation and one of the best restaurants. The Barbarahof and the Sportkristall are both recommended. The Sonnblick and the Kaprunserhof cater specially for families. We have good reports of the Pension Salzburgerhof ('pleasant, spacious bedrooms'), and Hotel Toni has some of the best food and friendly staff.

TOURIST OFFICE
Tel 43 6547 8643
Fax 43 6547 8192

Round-up

Bad Kleinkirchheim
top 2000m (6,560ft) bottom 1080m (3,543ft)

BKK is the home resort of Austrian super-hero Franz Klammer, and as one reporter put it: 'What is good enough for Franz is good enough for me.' These days the greatest of all downhill champions spends more time in Colorado than in Carinthia, but the old spa town (and thriving summer resort) continues to develop its skiing in his absence. The ski area is linked to the neighbouring village of **St Oswald** and together the two provide 85km of mainly intermediate pistes served by 32 lifts. BKK is quite spread out and has a good choice of hotels, but après-ski is limited. There are a few bars, one disco and some good-value restaurants. There are also excellent spa facilities, including indoor and outdoor thermal pools.

The ski area is low with the top lifts only reaching 2000m; snow conditions are consequently unreliable both early and late in the season. The World Cup downhill course was designed by Klammer himself and includes a sequence of jumps, which even when prepared as a recreational run requires considerable concentration. However, most runs are wide and gentle. Lift queues during high season are reported.

TOURIST OFFICE
Tel 43 4240 8212
Fax 43 4240 8537

Lermoos
top 2200m (7,216ft) bottom 1004m (3,293ft)

Lermoos and nearby **Ehrwald**, at the foot of the impressive Zugspitze, are typical Tyrolean working villages. The two are linked by bus and lift and are in an attractive area to the north-west of Innsbruck near the German border. Both villages are unspoilt and have plenty of bars and reasonably priced restaurants.

The skiing is divided into four small separate sections all covered by the Happy Ski Card lift pass. Beginners can try the nursery slopes at the Lermoos base and graduate to a longer gentle run by taking the gondola up Ehrwalder Alm. Intermediates will find good wide pistes and a series of easy red (intermediate) runs in the Zugspitze Bowl, which lead over the border into Germany. Advanced skiers will find the area limited; there is one black (difficult) run on the Grubigstein above Lermoos. However, in good snow conditions you can ski down from the **Zugspitze Glacier**. This is an excellent area for cross-country with more than 100km of prepared tracks.

149

TOURIST OFFICE
Tel 43 5673 2401
Fax 43 5673 2694

St Johann im Pongau
top 2188m (7,177ft) bottom 650m (2,132ft)

The four valleys of St Johann, Wagrain, Flachau and Zauchensee lie only 45 minutes from Salzburg and provide an intermediate playground offering some impressive statistics: a dozen resorts with 350km of linked (albeit not always on the mountain) skiing, served by 120 lifts all covered by one ski pass. St Johann itself (not to be confused with St Johann in Tirol) is a cathedral town with little charm. It has its own small, separate ski area, but the action starts at the hamlet of **Alpendorf**, a 4km ski-bus ride away.

The area, which is known as the **Sportwelt Amadé**, is popular with almost every nationality apart from the British. This is partly because few British tour operators come here as they cannot contract enough hotel beds to make the area's inclusion in the brochures a commercial viability. Attractive Wagrain is the central resort of the system, from which it is easy to access both ends. Flachau is an almost equally attractive alternative. The area offers one of the best-value ski passes in Austria.

Gasthof Taxenbacher, Sporthotel Alpenland, Hotel Wielander and Hotel Tennerhof are all recommended.The après-ski here is strictly limited to a few lively bars.The inconvenient bus journey to Alpendorf means that St Johann is not ideal for families.

The busy little village of **Wagrain** has fortunately been able to develop away from the minor road from St Johann to Flachau and Radstadt. Hotel Grafenwirt is discreetly upmarket, although some of the rooms are small. The Hotel Enzian and the Wagrainerhof are both recommended. There is a ski kindergarten, which takes children from three years old.

Neighbouring **Flachau** has undergone considerable expansion in recent years. The main accommodation is in large chalet-style hotels and inns, as well as apartment blocks. There is a non-ski kindergarten, and the Griessenkar Ski School takes children from three years old. Cross-country skiers are well served by the 160km of trails along the valley.

The attractive market town of **Altenmarkt** is a centre for the local sportswear and ski-equipment industries where Atomic skis, Schneider ski-wear and Steffner sweaters are manufactured. A modest ski area is linked to neighbouring Radstadt, but the main skiing is a bus-ride away at **Zauchensee** (or Flachau). The kindergarten cares for children from three years old. Hotel Schartner is one of the main village rendezvous points.

Filzmoos is a small village, which dates from Edwardian times when it was a popular holiday spot for the wealthy Viennese. Today it has its own ski area, shared with neighbouring **Neuberg**, of 17 lifts. The kindergarten takes children from three years old and has English-speaking staff. The Alpenkrone is one of the most popular hotels. The smart restaurant in the Hotel Hubertus is recommended. Après-ski centres around the Happy Filzmoos and the Mühlradl.

France

M ore British skiers holiday in France than in any other country. The Savoie, Haute Savoie and Dauphiné mountains offer more of a challenge than their counterparts in Austria, as well as a better chance of early- and late-season snow cover. A myriad of resorts have been developed at enormous expense over the past 30 years and are far better equipped than their Swiss or Italian equivalents.

France now offers the largest and most sophisticated lift-systems in the world. The size of some is truly staggering; Méribel has 16 gondolas, and the Trois Vallées has 200 lifts linking 600km of piste.

However, in spite of this all is not well in the France camp. A disastrous downturn in the domestic ski market over the past four years has seen a number of resorts fall into serious financial trouble. Valfréjus and Les Arcs have both been rescued by state intervention. Observers believe it is only a question of time before some relatively well-known ski destination in the French Alps will be forced to close its lifts.

The main players such as Courchevel 1850, Megève and Val d'Isère remain completely unaffected by this recession. In fact, they attract even more international visitors than ever in what is billed as a survival battle of the fittest and the richest.

Unlike their alpine neighbours, most French resorts are purpose-built *stations de ski*, which provide ski-in ski-out convenience but often at the cost of ambience. However, the French have learned their lesson from the original architectural follies of the 1960s, such as Tignes, Flaine and the earlier villages of La Plagne. Valmorel, Risoul and other more recent developments have been constructed with far more consideration for their natural mountain-environment.

In all resorts there is more accommodation in apartments than in hotels, and the earlier concrete *résidences* were constructed with rooms that are far too small for the demands of today's tourist.

Many readers complain that French resorts lack the atmosphere of their Austrian cousins. Certainly the welcome can be muted to the point of rudeness, although competition for custom and the growth of international business has done much to improve matters.

The nightlife does not compare. With a few notable exceptions like Chamonix and Les Deux Alpes, après-ski struggles to survive in the land that invented the word. In the main purpose-built resorts visitors find themselves forced to make their own entertainment in apartments or prop up the neighbourhood bar. Discos are often grossly overpriced, underfrequented and play unrecognisable *Euromusak*.

However, none of these shortcomings seriously detracts from what the French Alps have to offer. The reason why more British now ski here than anywhere else is inescapable: the skiing, taking every factor into consideration, is better than anywhere else in Europe.

Alpe d'Huez

ALTITUDE 1860m (6,100ft)

A lpe d'Huez is a hotch-potch of a resort perched on a sunny balcony above the original hamlet of Huez, 90 minutes' drive from Grenoble and the centre of **Les Grandes-Rousses**, the fifth largest ski area in France. It was chosen as a venue for the Killy Winter Olympics in 1968 and for a while nurtured the notion of joining that exclusive club of fashionable French resorts led by Megève and Courchevel 1850. However, as the resort developed, it traded exclusivity for the mass market. The clientèle is predominantly French and its proximity to Grenoble means that it also attracts weekenders. In recent years it has become increasingly popular with British families who benefit from its truly all-round skiing.

Its lift system dates from 1934 when a young engineer called Pomagalski tied a tractor engine to a rope and invented the drag-lift just a few days ahead of a rival in Davos. Today, what is one of the most sophisticated and modern systems in the Alps serves a total of 220km of linked piste served by 82 lifts. The satellites of **Auris**, **Oz**, **Vaujany**, and **Villard-Reculas** have emerged as resorts in their own right and, to some extent, are in danger of eclipsing their grizzled old master.

On the mountain
top 3330m (10,922ft) bottom 1100m (3,608ft)

Alpe d'Huez is a genuine all-round resort with excellent nursery slopes, good intermediate runs, long black (difficult) runs, and extremely serious off-piste opportunities. Mountain access is multiple. Two main modern gondolas feed traffic out of the village into the Pic Blanc sector and there are alternatives at peak times. Such is the efficiency of the lift system, capable of shifting 90,000 people an hour, that Alpe d'Huez claims to have dispensed with the lift queue. With the exception of the older cable car up to the highest point of the ski area this is largely true. Even on peak days you will not have to wait for more than a few minutes for access to the main gondolas. The downside of this is that the pistes immediately above the village (Les Chamois, Le Signal and Le Lac Blanc) are prone to overcrowding.

First glances can be deceptive and none more so than here. The

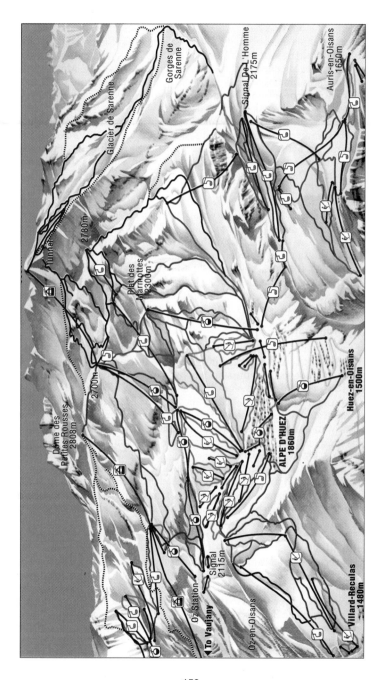

Gorges de Sarenne

Glacier de Sarenne

Signal De L'Homme 2175m

Auris-en-Oisans 1650m

2780m

Tunnel

Pic Blanc 3300m

2700m

Dôme des Petites Rousses 2808m

Huez-en-Oisans 1500m

ALPE D'HUEZ 1860m

O: Station

◄ To Vaujany

Signal 2115m

Oz-en-Oisans

Villard-Reculas 1480m

skiing as seen from Les Bergers lift station looks disarmingly mild; an open mountainside served by an array of gondolas, chair- and drag-lifts. However, skiers who have cut their teeth on the gentle pastures of the Tyrol will be shocked by the hidden severity of the skiing. Much of the Pic Blanc is hidden from sight by the lie of the land. From its 3330m summit it is possible to ski over 2000m vertical in good snow conditions down to well below Alpe d'Huez itself.

The area divides naturally into four main sectors: **Pic Blanc**, **Signal de l'Homme/Auris**, **Signal/Villard-Reculas**, and **Oz/Vaujany**. The central part of the skiing takes place immediately north-east of the resort on sunny slopes, served by the impressively efficient two stages of the 25-person DMC jumbo gondola.

Beginners

The first stage of the DMC serves an enormous area of green (beginner) runs close to the resort. The green Rif Nel piste is the gentlest of the long beginner runs from the base of the DMC back down to Les Bergers.

All the satellites have nursery slopes, some of them more novice-friendly than others. Vaujany's ski area really starts from **Montfrais**, a sunny balcony above the resort, which is reached by gondola. A series of short drag-lifts here give access to green and gentle blue (easy) runs, which are ideal débutant terrain.

Intermediates

From the mid-station of the DMC, the Lièvre Blanc chair gives access to a lot of good, challenging skiing. It serves its own red (intermediate) piste, but also leads to the satisfyingly secluded red Balme, which takes you all the way down to Alpe d'Huez.

From the top of the DMC try the long red Les Rousses (110 on the local piste map). Take the usually mogulled and crowded first 100m slowly so as not to miss the path, which cuts north-west beneath the cableway into the Vaujany sector. From here you can ski all the way down to Oz or to Vaujany.

Signal is the second mountain of Alpe d'Huez, a rounded snow-covered peak adjacent to the resort itself. This provides open, easy, inter-mediate runs covered by snow-cannon, which are easily accessible from the heart of the village. Behind Signal, longer runs drop down the open west-facing slopes above the satellite of Villard-Reculas.

Advanced

The top of the Clocher de Mâcle chair is the starting point for a choice of black runs. These include the beautiful Combe Charbonnière, past Europe's highest disused coal mine and from there either down into the Sarenne Gorge or round to the resort. The short run down from Clocher de Mâcle to Lac Blanc is steep, but the snow is usually good.

From the top of Pic Blanc two black runs, the Sarenne and the Château Noir, take you all the way down into the Sarenne Gorge and are claimed, at 16km, to be the longest black runs in the Alps. However, it should be pointed out that they accrue most of their length from the long run-out along the bottom of the gorge. Only some pitches of the Sarenne are really black, but it is long and tiring. Both runs are narrow in places and can produce bottlenecks.

The front face of Pic Blanc is accessed via a tunnel through the rock 200m below the summit, with an awkward path at the end of it. The steep and usually icy Tunnel mogul field that awaits you can be extremely daunting when no snow has fallen for some weeks.

Off-piste

Opportunities for *ski sauvage* from the top of Pic Blanc are superb. Variations include the Grand Sablat, the Combe du Loup and a long and tricky descent via the Couloir de Fiole. A 20-minute climb from the cable car station takes you to the top of La Pyramide, off-piste starting point for more than 2000m of vertical bringing you down through a range of gulleys and open snowfields all the way to Vaujany or Oz. The top can be very icy, and ropes may be needed to negotiate the steeper couloirs in packed snow conditions.

> **■ WHAT'S NEW**
>
> 50% off lift pass for second child under 20 in family of 4
> Chemin du Pâtre blue run to Villard-Reculas
> Fontbelle four-seater chair-lift at Bergers
> ESF instruction for handicapped skiers
> Indoor swimming-pool at sports centre
> Enlarged three-storey crèche at Vaujany

The off-piste variation from the ridge separating Oz from Alpe d'Huez is a gloriously steep powder field, which filters into the tree-studded gorge at the bottom. It is prone to avalanche and should only be attempted in the morning. There are seven itineraries in the area, which are marked on the piste map.

Snowboarding

Planète Surf is the major snowboarding school here. The International Ski School (ESI) holds *nouvelle glisse* courses, which include snowboarding as one of the options, and the French Ski School (ESF) offers snowboard tuition. As in all major French resorts, the sport has really taken off here. Fun Evasion is said to be the best place from which to hire snowboards.

Ski schools and guiding

The ESF has 300 instructors based in Alpe d'Huez, Auris, Oz and Vaujany. Reports of the schools are improving, with more English-speaking instructors than in the past. One reporter remarks that, although the initial impression of the ski school was one of 'total chaos, with hundreds of instructors and students jostling together', the instructors were 'excellent, always cheerful and friendly with excellent English' Beginners are taught using the *ski évolutif* method. The ESI offers English-speaking classes restricted to eight, however, we have no reports, favourable or otherwise.

A new independent ski school, Force 10 Adventure, has recently been set up by British instructor Steve Scott, who runs both group and individual courses in English for all standards. One reporter claimed he received 'the best instruction I have ever had'.

Mountain restaurants

The ski area is dotted with mountain restaurants. The Poutran in Oz offers quality and good-value food. Auberge de l'Alpette, a stone hut below the top of the **Alpette** gondola on the Oz piste, offers simple farmhouse fare and homemade cheeses at reasonable prices but has recently been criticised for its poor service. Les Airelles is a delightful restaurant built into the rock at the top of Les Airelles nursery drag-lift. It has a rustic atmosphere with roaring log fire and classical music, is good value for money and is popular with the mountain workers. La Cabane du Poutat, above the resort, has the rare distinction for a mountain restaurant of being awarded a knife-and-fork in the current Michelin Guide.

La Bergerie, on the red run down to **Villard-Reculas**, is an alpine museum that doubles as a restaurant. It has been run by the same family for over a quarter of a century, and the food and service are as good as ever. The setting, complete with open fire and cow bells, is particularly attractive. The Chalet du Lac Besson, on the cross-country trail between the DMC and Alpette, is another cosy place with good food.

Le Tetras in **Auris** serves fine pizzas and has a good wine list, but reporters have recently found the service slow. We also have glowing reports of the Forêt de Maronne below Auris, which is a cosy place serving local cuisine. Combe Haute in the Sarenne Gorge has a welcoming feel to it. La Perce Neige, on the red run down to **Oz**, is also recommended. Reporters give an overwhelming thumbs down to Les Marmottons and the Combe Haute. Descriptions of Les Marmottons include: 'all the charm of a warehouse', 'hangar-like' and 'like a cattle market'.

Off the mountain

Alpe d'Huez first opened as a resort in 1931 with a handful of beds. At the time of the 1968 Olympics it was little more than a one-street alpine village dominated by a futuristic modern church. The massive, apparently uncontrolled, building surge that followed saw the resort spread out in all directions in a profusion of architectural styles.

Traffic remains a problem, although it must be pointed out that as there are no through-roads from the resort to anywhere else, it is more a question of overcrowded parking than busy main roads. A bucket lift acts as the primary people-mover. A shuttle-bus takes skiers up to the slopes from the lower reaches of what is a steep resort for pedestrians, but several reporters say there was no sign of a bus during their entire stay in the resort. Shops are limited to a few boutiques and tacky T-shirt and souvenir establishments. The ski shops are generally good, particularly in the Bergers area 'where a mini price-war seemed to be in operation'.

Alpe d'Huez is one of the few resorts that can be reached directly by aircraft into its own altiport. **Les Deux Alpes** is a few minutes away by helicopter or 45 minutes by road.

Accommodation

Accommodation in Alpe d'Huez is split between a wide range of self-catering apartments, a few tour-operator chalets and a number of medium-priced hotels. Basically, the higher up the hill you are, the easier it is to get to and from the skiing. The hardcore of one four-star (The Royal Ours Blanc) and eight three-star hotels is supported by numerous family establishments.

Le Petit Prince is a small, family-run hotel, which guests found relaxing but a little quiet 'with an excellent standard of service'. The Christina is friendly and charming and one of the few attractive chalet-style buildings at the top of the resort. The Chamois d'Or is a bright and comfortable hotel with a highly regarded restaurant. L'Ourson is a family-run hotel. The best apartments include those in the Rocher Soleil, which has its own outdoor heated swimming-pool and optional catering. Maeva's Les Bergers apartments are recommended by our reporters.

Eating in and out

Dining is an important business in Alpe d'Huez, perhaps a legacy from its more exclusive days. There are over 50 restaurants in the resort itself. Le Petit Creux, Le Chamois d'Or, Le Lyonnais and L'Outa all vie with each other as the best centres for *haute cuisine* in town. La Cordée, La Pomme de Pin, Génépi, La Crémaillère and Caribou all offer mountain specialities. Pizza Origan is 'friendly and serves a good range of pizzas and pasta'. The restaurant in **Vaujany**'s Hotel Rissiou is open to non-residents and has excellent cuisine and wines.

Supermarkets in Alpe d'Huez are adequate, and reporters recommend Les Bergers in the Centre Commercial as convenient and well-stocked. Serious food shoppers drive down to the Rallye supermarket in **Bourg d'Oisans**.

■ OTHER SPORTS

Ice-driving, snowmobiling, snow-shoeing, aeroclub, parapente, hang-gliding, swimming, helicopter rides, skating, curling, frozen waterfall-climbing, indoor tennis, climbing wall

Après-ski

Charley's Bar, with its pool tables and table football, is popular and has a friendly owner. The Cactus Bar has a live band most nights and reasonably priced beer. Le Petit Bar has live blues every night. The Lincoln Pub and the Avalanche Bar are 'lacking in atmosphere' with 'music and loud holidaymakers'. The Sporting Bar, which overlooks the skating rink, has live music. Le Chalet has a smarter image. Etoile des Neiges is a typical French café. Alpe d'Huez sports four discos, including the Igloo and Crystal where an entry fee of 50FF includes your first drink.

Childcare

The ESF Club des Oursons takes children from four years old at **Grandes-Rousses** and **Bergers**. Both have playgrounds and their own drag-lifts. The ESI runs The Club des Mickeys et des Papotines, which starts at three-and-a-half years, and the Club des Marmottes for 5- to 12-year-olds. The Club des Eterlous, next to the Club Med building, takes children from 6 months to 14 years. The crèche in **Vaujany** is one of the best equipped we have come across in the Alps and, if you have small children, almost a reason in itself for choosing the resort. It takes children from three months up to three years and has an English nanny provided by Ski Peak. There is a garderie in **Oz**.

Linked or nearby resorts

Auris-en-Oisans 1600m (5,249ft)

Auris consists mainly of apartment blocks. The Beau Site hotel attracts predominantly French guests. It is somewhat isolated from the bulk of the skiing in Les Grandes-Rousses but well positioned for outings to Les Deux Alpes, Briançon/Serre Chevalier, and **La Grave**. Down the hillside in the old village are the more traditional Auberge de la Forêt and Les Emeranches hotels, as well as chalets and *gîtes* to rent. Over the hill behind the resort and served by pistes and a lift is the Forêt de Maronne hotel.

TOURIST OFFICE
Tel 33 76 80 13 52
Fax 33 76 80 20 16

Oz Station 1350m (4,428ft)

This small, purpose-built village lies above the old village of Oz-en-Oisans. It is reached by a fast all-weather road from the valley in only 20 minutes and thereby provides an excellent back-door into the lift system. The resort consists of some large apartment blocks built of stone and wood in pleasing harmony with the environment. Two gondolas branch upwards in different directions: one to **L'Alpette** above Vaujany and the other in two stages to the mid-station of the DMC gondola above Alpe d'Huez. The shopping and nightlife are both limited here.

TOURIST OFFICE
Tel 33 76 80 78 01
Fax 33 76 80 78 04

Vaujany 1250m (4,101ft)

Vaujany is a sleepy farming community, which, but for a quirk of fate, would have slowly crumbled into agricultural oblivion. However, compensation in the 1980s for a valley hydroelectric scheme made the village rich beyond its residents' wildest dreams. Oz benefited to a lesser extent from the scheme and the two villages plunged their millions into the winter-sports industry. This explains why, in the case of Vaujany, an apparently impoverished mountain village manages to own a state-of-the-art 160-person cable car, which ranks among the top three in the world. No one has yet to see a queue here, but who is complaining? Considerable, but considered, development is taking place and a number of new chalets and apartments have been built, however, the community retains its rural atmosphere.

There are four simple hotels in the village centre. The Etendard, closest to the lift station, is the après-ski hub. The Rissiou is under British winter management and produces a much higher standard of food and accommodation than you might expect in a village of this size. The Hotel Cimes, across the road, is a friendly little hostelry. The Grandes-Rousses Hotel is less central. The Voltige disco is crowded with mainly Belgians in their teens and twenties and positively swings. The Sabot is the more sophisticated alternative. Shopping is limited to a single grocery store and a ski shop.

TOURIST OFFICE
Tel 33 76 80 79 40
Fax 33 76 80 79 52

Skiers based in Vaujany or Oz can also join the Pic Blanc sector via the second stage of the Vaujany cable car to the Dôme des Petites Rousses at 2808m, slightly above the starting point for the Pic Blanc cable car and linked by an easy red piste. The hamlet of La Villette is linked by gondola to Vaujany and the home run is served by a battery of snow-cannon.

Villard-Reculas 1500m (4,921ft)
The rustic old village is linked into the ski area by chair- and drag-lift. Much has been done in recent years to renovate the village, including a number of apartments to add to the single hotel and the converted cow-sheds and barns. Sustenance is provided by one small supermarket and a couple of small bars and restaurants including the Bergerie (*see Mountain restaurants*). A new blue piste from the bottom of the Petit Prince runs to the village, offering an alternative route to the steeper runs. The road to Allemont on the valley floor is wide and easily accessible in winter, but the one-track road to Huez is normally closed during the season.

TOURIST OFFICE
Tel 33 76 80 45 69

Skiing facts: **Alpe d'Huez**

TOURIST OFFICE
BP 28, F-38750 Alpe d'Huez, Dauphiné
Tel 33 76 80 35 41
Fax 33 76 80 69 54

THE RESORT
By road Calais 934km
By rail Grenoble 62km
By air Lyon 2 hrs, Grenoble 1½ hrs
Visitor beds 32,000
Transport free ski-bus

THE SKIING
Linked or nearby resorts Auris (l),
Oz-en-Oisans (l), Vaujany (l),
Villard-Reculas (l), Les Deux Alpes (n),
La Grave (n)
Longest run Sarenne, 16km (black)
Number of lifts 82
Total of trails/pistes 220km
(36% beginner, 28% easy,
25% intermediate, 11% difficult)
Nursery slopes 8 including extensive
nursery runs immediately above Alpe
d'Huez
Summer skiing Sarenne Glacier (July only)
Snowmaking 100 hectares covered by
385 snow-cannon

LIFT PASSES
Area pass (covers whole Grandes Rousses
area) 935FF for 6 days, includes entry to
sports centre
Day pass 195FF weekdays, 165-175FF
weekends
Beginners 2 free lifts at Alpe d'Huez and
Visalp Initiation Pass, 1,325FF for 6 days
including 6 morning lessons
Pensioners free for 70 yrs and over
Credit cards accepted yes

SKI SCHOOLS
Adults ESF, 850FF for 6 days, 5 hrs per day.
ESI, 9.30am-midday, 640FF for 6 mornings,
or 3-5pm, 505FF for 6 afternoons
Private lessons ESF and ESI, 160FF per hr
Snowboarding Planéte Surf, 800FF for 6
days, private lessons 160FF per hr. ESI,
private lessons 160FF per hr
Cross-country ESF, 850FF for 6 days, 5 hrs
per day. Loipe 50km
Other courses monoski, moguls, freestyle,
slalom, off-piste, competition, couloir skiing, Stuart Adamson's Ski Academy
Guiding companies La Compagnie de
l'Oisans

CHILDREN
Lift pass 13 yrs and under 655FF,
18 yrs and under 842FF, free for 5 yrs
and under Visalp Initiation Pass,
1,080FF for 6 days including
6 morning lessons
Ski kindergarten ESF Club des Oursons
at Bergers and at Grandes-Rousses,
4 yrs and over, 9.45am-12.45pm and
2.30pm-5pm, 60FF per hr. ESI Club des
Mickeys et des Papotines, 3 yrs and over,
9.30am-midday, 580FF for 6 mornings, or
3-5pm, 505FF for 6 afternoons. Les
Eterlous, 2-14 yrs, 9am-5.45pm,
1,290FF for 6 days
Ski school ESF, 4-13 yrs, 700FF for
6 days, 5½ hrs per day. ESI, Club des
Marmottes, 4-13 yrs, 9.30am-midday,
580FF for 6 mornings, or 3-5pm, 460FF
for 6 afternoons
Non-ski kindergarten Les Eterlous,
6 mths and over, 9am-5.45pm, 1,290FF
for 6 days including lunch. Crèche Vaujany,
3 mths-3 yrs, 9am-5pm, 650FF for 6 days
including lunch

FOOD AND DRINK PRICES
Coffee 10FF, glass of wine 6-15FF, small
beer 12-20FF, dish of the day 40-60FF

Les Arcs

ALTITUDE 1600-2000m (5,248- 6,560ft)

More than any other third-generation French resort, Les Arcs epitomises a high-altitude, modern, snow-sure *station de ski* — an arena built specifically for the purpose of skiing. Critics of purpose-built French-resort architecture generally concede that Les Arcs is not unpleasing and that it is certainly innovative, both off and on the slopes. With its proven graduated ski-length teaching method (*ski évolutif*) and particularly good nursery slopes, those interested in learning quickly and enjoying the process will find Les Arcs a pleasant and even exciting ski college.

Les Arcs comprises three separate, predominantly self-catering, resorts (**1600**, **1800** and **2000**) sharing 150km of skiing and 79 lifts.

On the mountain
top 3226m (10,581ft) bottom 850m (2,788ft)

With so much variety skiers are unlikely to find their enthusiasm flagging, no matter what their ability. Strong skiers have a wealth of choice from unusually long runs that start way above the tree-line and progress down through the woods to traditional villages like **Le Pré** and **Villaroger**, to extensive off-piste opportunities. Intermediates can cruise forever, and beginners are specially catered for. The greatest concentration of lifts, slopes, and therefore skiers is above Arc 1800, where sunny and gentle slopes attract intermediates and family groups. The skiing above Arc 1600 is steeper and more wooded, with some good off-piste opportunities.

Another of Les Arcs' claims to fame is its Olympic Flying Kilometre (speed-skiing track) on the lower face of the Aiguille Rouge, which can be tested by members of the public. With typical Les Arcs panache, the course has recently been used to establish 'Flying K' records for motorbikes and even mountain bikes.

■ GOOD POINTS
Large ski area, modern lift system, range of child facilities, skiing convenience, extensive off-piste skiing, beautiful scenery

■ BAD POINTS
Lack of alpine charm, few activities for non-skiers, limited après-ski

Lift queues are not generally a problem, although there are a few exceptions. At Carreley 20 and Chantel 21 reporters came across 'huge queues until 10am and again at the end of the day'. Some reporters found mid-afternoon crowds for the Vallandry 74 lift. The piste map is said to be 'accurate and well marked; it was easy to find our way around even in poor visibility'.

Beginners

Les Arcs is the home of *ski évolutif*, where absolute beginners start with very short skis of one metre and change to a slightly longer pair each day. This concept produces a fast learning curve, enabling most beginners to manage embryonic parallel turns by the end of the week, when they can choose from 24 green (beginner) runs. Each of the three villages has nursery slopes close by, with the most extensive just above Arc 1800 around the Altiport and Le Chantel area, and in the bowl above Arc 2000. Above Arc 1600 strong beginners and timid intermediates can enjoy the long blue (easy) run from Les Deux Têtes.

Intermediates

As a rule, the bigger the ski area the more scope there is for intermediates, and Les Arcs is certainly no exception. Of the resort's 112 runs, 70 are divided equally between blue and red (intermediate), and many of the red runs are not difficult. The slopes above Arc 1800 are packed with relatively easy intermediate slopes. The classic black (difficult) bump-run down Comborcières to Pré-St-Esprit is a good test for strong intermediates. There are good cruising runs between Le Grand Col, L'Aiguille Grive and L'Arpette. Much of the skiing above Peisey-Nancroix and Vallandry provides classic intermediate terrain. The Aigle and L'Ours reds are particularly recommended by reporters as 'nice, not too testing runs down through the trees'. Malgovert, down to Arc 1600, is described as 'quite narrow — it felt like an off-piste run but without the worry, and hazards were marked; it leads down to the wonderfully wide and flattering Mont Blanc blue run'.

Advanced

The classic run here is the 7km descent from the top of the Aiguille Rouge all the way down to Le Pré and Villaroger, with a vertical drop of more than 2000m. Of the total of 18 black runs, the Piste de l'Ours from Arpette is one of the most exciting. Varet, a long, steep run from the top of the Aiguille Rouge is a real challenge, especially in deep snow. The Robert Blanc, named after the man who helped found Les Arcs, is an excellent run off the north face. Drosets, down to St-Esprit, is another testing run from the Aiguille Rouge. The Dou de l'Homme chair accesses several long black runs.

Off-piste

There are so many off-piste opportunities in Les Arcs that it really does pay, in terms of both safety and finding the best terrain, to hire a guide. In good snow conditions the steepest and most exhilarating powder skiing is below the Aiguille Rouge. There is good steep bowl-skiing beneath the Crête de L'Homme, accessed by a traverse to the right as you exit the Aiguille Rouge cable car. Other good off-piste is behind the Aiguille Grive and the Aiguille Rousse at the south-western edge of Arc 1800's ski area. Exciting off-piste descents start from the Grand Col to Villaroger, with the route going behind the Aiguille Rouge, and from the

Aiguille Grive down to Peisey-Nancroix. The Comborcières slopes offer a number of good off-piste opportunities.

Really serious off-piste experts can try a whole cluster of couloirs over the back of the Aiguille Rouge on the East Face, but special permission has to be obtained from the Vanoise Park authorities, who charge for access to these slopes.

> ■ **WHAT'S NEW**
>
> Grand Col drag at Arc 2000 replaced by a quad-chair, with part of the old lift resurrected nearby

Snowboarding

Les Arcs, with its innovative *nouvelles glisses* concept of trying anything that slides on snow, now accepts that the love-affair it once had with the mono-board is over and that the snowboard, or 'surf' as they prefer to call it, has dethroned it. As well as the French Ski School (ESF) and International Ski School (ESI) snowboard courses there are two surf specialists — Tip Top and In Extremis — which also run special courses for children over seven years of age.

Ski schools and guiding

Les Arcs has the ESF (in all three villages). ESI/Arc Aventures, Virages and Henalu are all based in Arc 1800.

Mountain restaurants

Mountain eating-places are not a particular strength of Les Arcs ('we were not too impressed and the selection was limited'), but there are some quite attractive, rustic-style establishments. The restaurants on the rather bleak terrace at the base of Arc 2000 (Le Red Rock and Le St Jacques) are cheerful when the sun is shining. There are two popular lunch spots at Pré St-Esprit below Arc 2000. Of these, the rustic Bélliou la Fumée is the smaller and more attractive, with waitress service and better food. L'Arpette, above Arc 1800, is a busy mainstream restaurant. La Crèche, at the top of the Transarc gondola, is a self-service restaurant, which also has a dining-room with table service.

There are good reports of the cosy Solliet restaurant on the way down to Villaroger, and in nearby Le Pré the Aiguille Rouge and La Ferme attract lunchtime skiers when the long run down is open. In nearby Le Planay, Chez Léa provides good, wholesome food in an old farmhouse; bookings are recommended.

Off the mountain

There is little in the resort for non-skiers ('I wouldn't like to be a non-skier stuck here'). Of the three distinct villages that make up Les Arcs, Arc 1600 is the lowest. Arc 1800 has three sub-sections of its own: Charvet, Villards and Charmettoger, and is the heart of the resort with most of the accommodation, shops, après-ski and wonderful views across to Mont Blanc in the north-west.

The highest and bleakest village is Arc 2000 (opened in 1979), which sits in its own secluded bowl at the foot of Les Arcs' theme mountain, the

Aiguille Rouge at 3226m, and is close to some of the best skiing. One reporter dubs it 'a totally characterless garage in the sky'. All three villages are served by a road that comes up from **Bourg-St-Maurice**, but there is also a funicular, Arc en Ciel ('rainbow'), which takes just seven minutes to reach Arc 1600. Although Les Arcs is largely car-free and the resorts are linked by a bus service, a car is useful to reach the other resorts available on the same lift pass.

Accommodation

About two-thirds of the skiers visiting Les Arcs stay in apartments, and of these the majority find themselves in Arc 1800, where the best reports come from those in the sub-villages of Charmettoger and·Villards. Les Arcs has now sold off virtually all its accommodation to outside property companies, the lion's share to Pierre et Vacances and others to Maeva. Few chalets are available.

The best of the hotels include the Gran Paradiso, which opened a few years ago at Charmettoger in Arc 1800. The Golf is the largest and most central, and its Arc 1800 stablemate, Latitudes, is also a three-star. The Cachette at Arc 1600, renowned for its all-day crèche and good food, is being completely renovated for the 1995–6 season. Also at 1600, the old Winston Hotel has been modernised and renamed L'Explorer's. The Trois Arcs, also in 1600, is a small and friendly three-star hotel, but reports suggest it does not merit its third star. At Arc 2000, the two-star Aiguille Rouge remains popular. We have no reports on the Mélèzes, formerly the Eldorador, which has been elevated to three stars. There is a Club Med and a Club Aquarius at Arc 2000.

Les Lauziers apartments in 1800 are convenient for the slopes and popular with young people ('a functional building with strange sloping floors; we didn't like the cramped and spartan interiors').

Eating in and out

Self-catering rules in Les Arcs, but no one wants to cook every night of the week. The best choice of restaurants is at Arc 1800, with L'Equipe the biggest but not necessarily the best ('for a posh meal, with Savoyard dishes and a good-value fixed-price menu'). Last winter, visitors spoke highly of the fondue, raclette and *pierrade* at Le Choucas. Casa Mia specialises in Italian food ('basically a pasta and pizza place, decor rustic — after a fashion — and the service was friendly and informal'). L'Onglet and Le Coq Hardy are also recommended. For good-value family fare the Laurus is worth visiting. At Arc 2000 Le Red Rock is popular and informal with live music, and Le St Jacques is more intimate with higher prices. Self-caterers will find a wider selection and lower prices in Bourg-St-Maurice, with its two hypermarkets on the outskirts of town. In 1800 there are 'some good bakeries, an expensive butcher and a small supermarket with limited fresh supplies'.

Visitors considering an outing to traditional restaurants in outlying villages between Les Arcs and Bourg-St-Maurice can try the Bois de Lune at Montvenix. Booking is recommended here, and the restaurant will collect you by arrangement and take you back. Chez Mimi at Vallandry, L'Ancolie at Nancroix and Chez Léa at Le Planay are other options.

Après-ski
When the lifts close in Arc 1800, skiers and instructors tend to divide themselves between two bars at Le Charvet (Le Gabotte and Le Thuria). At nearby Les Villards much of the action is at the Pub Russel and the Saloon Bar, which features live music. At 2000 the Red Rock is the in-place for a *vin chaud*. The Hotel Du Golf has live jazz and Le Fairway disco in the basement. All three resorts have discos, including the Arcelle in 1600 and Rock Hill in Le Charvet, while snowboarders prefer the Carré Blanc in Les Villards. The music at KL 92 in Arc 2000 is said to be sufficiently 'sympa' to allow conversation.

■ OTHER SPORTS
Ice-driving, snowmobiling, snow-shoeing, aeroclub, parapente, hang-gliding, swimming (Bourg-St-Maurice), skating

Childcare
Les Arcs has a 'three-kids' grading (the highest) of the 'Label Kid' stamp of approval from the Ministry of Tourism, denoting that the resort offers children a safe environment with plenty of entertainment, toys and equipment. Toddlers aged one year and over are welcome in the day nurseries at Bourg-St-Maurice, Arc 1600 and Arc 1800. The nursery at Arc 2000 accepts children for skiing and non-skiing activities. Babies from three months old are welcome at crèches in Bourg (Garderie Pomme d'Api) and at the Hotel de la Cachette in Arc 1600. The ESF organises courses for children aged three years old and over in the Pommes du Pin Club. Older children can enrol in Ski Nature courses to explore the mountain environment and study animal tracks in the snow.

Linked or nearby resorts

Peisey-Nancroix-Vallandry 1350-1600m (4,428-5,248ft)
Skiers in Les Arcs tend to regard this cluster of villages at the south-western end of the ski area as a useful tree-line bolt-hole in bad weather. French families, who have been coming here since the Second World War, prefer to think of it as a peaceful, undemanding ski area that is occasionally invaded by Johnny-Come-Latelys from Les Arcs. The area offers a more rural setting and a cheaper accommodation base for the region. Peisey is a traditional farming community, and Nancroix is the starting point for 40km of cross-country trails. The small ski resorts of **Plan Peisey** and **Vallandry** are linked by gondola to Peisey in the valley below. Three lifts serve the nursery slope area.

TOURIST OFFICE
Tel 33 79 07 94 28
Fax 33 79 07 95 34

Skiing facts: **Les Arcs**

TOURIST OFFICE
F-73706 Arc 1800, Savoie
Tel 33 79 07 12 57
Fax 33 79 07 45 96

THE RESORT
By road Calais 937km
By rail Bourg-St-Maurice 15km, buses and direct funicular to Arc 1600
By air Lyon 2½ hrs, Chambery 2 hrs, Geneva 2½ hrs
Visitor beds 31,807
Transport free shuttle-bus between Arc 1600, 1800 and 2000. Also bus to Bourg-St-Maurice 48FF

THE SKIING
Linked or nearby resorts Bourg-St-Maurice (l), Peisey-Nancroix (l), La Plagne (n), Le Pré (l), Vallandry (l)
Longest run Aiguille Rouge, 7km (black)
Number of lifts 79
Total of trails/pistes 150km (22% beginner, 31% easy, 31% intermediate, 16% difficult)
Nursery slopes 11 runs
Summer skiing none
Snowmaking 20 hectares covered

LIFT PASSES
Area pass (covers Les Arcs, Villaroger, Peisey and Vallandry and includes skiing in La Plagne and 1 day in La Rosière/Trois Vallées/Tignes and Val d'Isère), 940FF for 6 days
Day pass 205FF
Beginners 3 free lifts
Pensioners no reduction
Credit cards accepted yes

SKI SCHOOLS
Adults ESF, 600FF for 6 days, ESI/Arc Aventures 780FF for 6 days, Virages 800FF for 6 days, Henalu in 1800, details on request
Private lessons ESF 165FF per hr, ESI 170FF per hr, Virages 185FF per hr
Snowboarding In Extremis, 350FF per day (2 hrs), Tip Top, 660FF for 3 days (3 hrs per day), ESF, 620FF for 6 days (2 hrs per day), ESI/Arc Aventures, 580FF for 5 days (2½ hrs per day), Virages, prices on request
Cross-country ESF, 600FF for 6 days (3 hrs per day). Loipe 15km in Arc 1800, 1600 and 2000
Other courses monoski, *ski évolutif*
Guiding companies ESF or ESI/Arc Aventures

CHILDREN
Lift pass 7 yrs and over, 940FF for 6 days, free for 6 yrs and under
Ski kindergarten ESF Pommes du Pin Club, 3 yrs and over, 8.30am-6pm, 890FF for 6 days. Arc 1600, 3-7 yrs 1,710FF, 7-12 yrs 1,960FF for 6 days, both including lunch
Ski school ESF and ESI/Arc Aventures, 3-7 yrs, 780FF for 6 x 5 hrs, Virages 880FF for 6 days, details on request
Non-ski kindergarten Arc 1600, 3 mths-3 yrs, 1,290FF for 6 days. Arc 1800, 1-3 yrs, 770FF for 6 days, 4-6 yrs, 850FF for 6 days. Arc 2000, 3 yrs and over, 770-850FF for 6 days. All 8.30am-6pm

FOOD AND DRINK PRICES
Coffee 7FF, glass of wine 10FF, small beer 12FF, dish of the day 50FF

Barèges/La Mongie

ALTITUDE 1250-1800m (4,092-5,904ft)

Skiers who have tired of the characterless and overcrowded ski circuses of the French Alps with their ever-rising prices should look westwards towards the Pyrenees for a quiet and unspoilt alternative. Here it is still possible to find that elusive combination of an unspoilt French country village with reasonable prices, a short transfer time from an international airport and, to cap it all, the varied runs of a large ski area.

Barèges fulfills all these requirements. Another major attraction of the resort (indeed also of **La Mongie** and the rest of the French Pyrenees) are the people, who seem to be genuinely friendly and welcoming — a rare occurrence in some of the more popular resorts in the Alps. The locals have managed to retain their traditional way of life and at the same time adapt to the needs of tourism without the compulsion to milk their visitors dry.

At first sight, Barèges is a down-at-heel grey spa town near the head of a narrow valley, however, it has a friendly atmosphere, largely due to

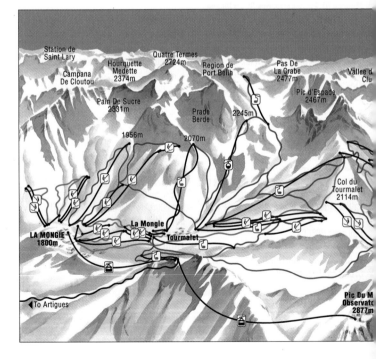

its small size, and is not at all claustrophobic. Prices are low by French standards but there is little to do after skiing except soak up the sulphur waters of the thermal spa.

Barèges was one of the original ski resorts of the Pyrenees. The village also comes into the spotlight in the summer months when it becomes part of the Tour de France route. It has a lift system that follows the course of the road, which (in summer only) leads over the Col du Tourmalet to the more modern resort of La Mongie. Although hardly the Trois Vallées, the area offers a variety of terrain and skiing for all standards, and while the mountains may not be as awe-inspiring as the Alps, the views are pleasant, in particular from the ridge beside the Col du Tourmalet.

■ **GOOD POINTS**

Large intermediate ski area, short airport transfer, sunny slopes, low prices, variety of easy skiing, small and unspoilt village of Barèges

■ **BAD POINTS**

Weekend lift queues, limited tough runs, lack of resort-level snow, not suitable for late-season holidays, few activities for non-skiers, bleak village of La Mongie

La Mongie is the larger, higher, but considerably less charming resort of the two. It offers no more facilities than Barèges and is set in the blander half of the ski area. It is, however, the better place for complete beginners or nervous second-weekers, with

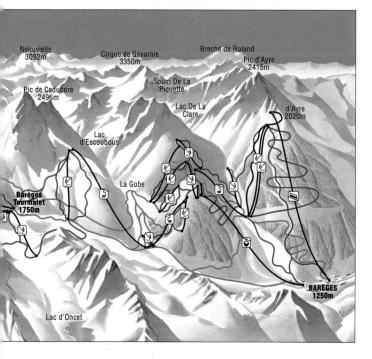

easy slopes around the resort that keep their snow relatively well. The lifts linking the two resorts sometimes close in bad weather.

On the mountain
top 2350m (7,708ft) bottom 1250m (4,100ft)

Snowfall in the Pyrenees is a subject that always causes disagreement. There is little substantiation in the idea that the mountains receive less precipitation in winter than the Alps; the trouble is that it does not always fall as snow. Because the mountains are further west and closer to the warm Atlantic, the winter is shorter, but the advantage is the high number of sunny days.

Barèges and La Mongie form the largest ski area in the Pyrenees, sharing 100km of wide, mainly intermediate pistes served by 53 lifts. The area's upper slopes are open and sunny, while the lower ones above Barèges offer sheltered tree-line skiing. The slopes are reached from Barèges by either of two mountain-access lifts. The village fathers have now finally found the money to rebuild the track of the old Ayré funicular, which climbs steeply from the village centre through the woods to serve red (intermediate) and black (difficult) runs down to a clearing at **Lienz**. This is some of the best skiing in the area when conditions are favourable.

La Laquette gondola is the alternative access lift from the resort and provides the direct route towards La Mongie, as well as the way up to the ski school meeting place. At Tournaboup, from the top of the lift, an easy link-run leads on to **Super Barèges**, which is little more than a restaurant. A development to the north of Super Barèges, below the Lac d'Oncet, has in recent years added to the size of the whole ski area.

Queues can be a serious problem at weekends, especially on Sundays; as Barèges cannot cope with many cars, the lifts from the top of the village and from Tournaboup are crowded, and the Col du Tourmalet can be a bottleneck in both directions.

Beginners

Barèges itself has no nursery slope; the main one is at the top of La Laquette gondola. Of the two resorts, La Mongie is the better place for first-timers to learn; a large area of nursery slopes around the resort keeps its snow relatively well but suffers from being a popular thoroughfare. Tournaboup, just outside Barèges, has a small nursery slope beside the car-park and there is also a baby-lift at **La Mongie-Tourmalet**. At Barèges, second- and third-week skiers can make their way across to Lienz from the mid-station of the Ayré funicular. Of the two runs from there down to Barèges, the green (beginner) run is a path that starts with an uphill section.

Intermediates

A variety of short intermediate pistes covers the sides of the hill at the top of La Laquette gondola, to Lienz on one side and to Tournaboup on the other. Above La Mongie the runs are mainly wide and easy. A gondola is the main lift on the north-facing side, serving a long and shaded blue gully. The slopes beneath the Sud chair-lift are not particularly gentle, and the blue run contains a narrow section. On this sunny side of the mountain the most interesting runs are reached from the top of the Coume Lounque drag and chair where there are a couple of reds. One trail follows a valley down to La Mongie, the other leads down to Super Barèges. Part of the run is steep enough to be graded black (difficult) and can be icy in the morning.

Advanced

Ayré at 2020m has some of the area's steepest skiing, and there is no easy way down from the top of the funicular. There are some fairly sheer west-facing slopes below the Col du Tourmalet, including a selection of short mogul fields. The rocky slopes bordering La Mongie and the road are steep and although there are lifts, the terrain does not give much scope for pistes. The most challenging run around La Mongie is the black under the Prade Berde chair-lift.

Off-piste

The itinerary round to the Lac d'Oncet is a good place for spring snow, even in mid-winter. At Tournaboup there is a long chair-lift over a wide and fairly steep, west-facing mountainside, which is left unpisted although it is much skied in good conditions.

At the top of the Coume de Pourteilh gondola above La Mongie, the 4 Termes chair has added to the overall length of the run and gives access to an off-piste itinerary down the Aygues Cluses Valley, ending at Tournaboup.

Snowboarding

Both the French Ski School (ESF) and Ecoloski give snowboarding lessons but there are no special facilities on the mountain for riders.

Ski schools and guiding

French Pyrenean resorts have made considerable efforts to improve the standard of their ski schools in recent years, and the number of English-speaking instructors has risen. Ecoloski in Barèges offers, among other classes, tuition in off-piste skiing and moguls, although we have reports of the school being 'disappointing, I was in much too difficult a group; when I asked to change groups I was told to "have courage"'. The ESF also operates in Barèges, however, we have no reports on it. Henri Nogué is a high-mountain guide who organises off-piste courses and ski-touring in the area. There are ski schools at both La Mongie and La Mongie-Tourmalet.

Mountain restaurants

The mountain restaurants are inexpensive by alpine standards but are few and far between. Chez Louisette is popular, Auberge La Couquelle is a small and friendly place with the highlight 'a delicious warm goat's cheese salad with honey dressing'. There is a restaurant at the Col du Tourmalet, and Le Yeti in La Mongie is recommended.

Off the mountain

Barèges is little more than a single street climbing steeply beside a river, enclosed by tree-lined mountainsides. There is no natural site for a village and none would have appeared had it not been for the sulphur springs, which became famous in the seventeenth century. However, it was only relatively recently that avalanche barriers allowed the construction of permanent dwellings, which stand today as a grey and unmemorable (except for the spa itself) mixture of renovated and grand old buildings at the top of the narrow village. Parking spaces are restricted, and the ski-bus, covered by the lift pass, cannot cope when runs to the village are closed and too many skiers have ended up at Tournaboup.

■ OTHER SPORTS

Winter walks, snowmobiling, 4-wheel motorbiking circuit, swimming, tobogganing, ice climbing, snow-shoeing, parapente, spa treatments

La Mongie is divided into two parts. The lower village is the main one, a bleak and charmless place with a crescent of restaurants, shops and hotels, plus a car-park in the middle. The upper village of La Mongie-Tourmalet is a long and jagged complex with a single hotel, a restaurant and apartments. The two sections of the resort are linked by a day-time bucket lift.

The road up to La Mongie from **Bagnères-de-Bigorre** is extremely busy at weekends and can be closed when the resort is full. The nearest airport to the area is Lourdes, 25km away.

Accommodation

Those in search of luxury will be disappointed as Barèges has nothing more superior than the simple two-star hotel. The family-run Richelieu is a friendly little place just below the funicular station. L'Igloo is run by a former ski champion and is close to La Laquette gondola. Some reporters found the Hotel Central 'unfriendly'. The one-star Poste and Modern hotels are moderately priced at 100FF and 80FF per room per night respectively. The British-run Les Sorbiers is a popular small hotel: 'It provides simple, attractively furnished, clean accommodation. The bedrooms were warm, but the public area rather chilly. The vegetarian options were superb.' Shops are confined to a good chemist and the most simplistic of ski-hire and souvenir shops. A single supermarket is stocked for the needs of self-caterers.

La Mongie has one three-star hotel, Le Pourteilh, plus three two-stars and two other smaller hotels. La Mongie-Tourmalet has just one three-star hotel, Lamandia.

Eating in and out

The restaurants include La Rozeli for fondues and pizzas. The Toscane is a pizzeria/takeaway. Le Pichounet serves a delicious *fondue au choco-lat noir*. La Couquelle, with a welcoming open fireplace, is close to Tournaboup and is open in the evenings as well as at lunchtime. The main event of the week is an evening at Chez Louisette, organised by the ski school, which culminates in a torch-light descent. You can also reach the restaurant by snowmobile, snow cat or on foot. The staple diet of the region appears to be *magret de canard* and *confit de canard*, not to men-tion *foie gras*; as one reporter put it: 'I never want to see or taste another duck as long as I live'.

Après-ski

After-skiing entertainment centres on a few bars, a handful of restau-rants and two discos. The liveliest places are Pub l'Oncet, L'Isba and the Café Richelieu. The discos open at 11pm and do not fill up until 1am; Le Club Jonathan is the most popular. Many of Barèges' visitors come here for the spa, which dates from the seventeenth century. Today, the treat-ments take place in an austere building at the top of the high street. Facilities include whirlpools, saunas, thermal baths and showers, an aqua-gym and aqua massage, all of which use Barèges' special healing waters — great for relaxing after a hard day on the slopes. There are cross-country skiing and scenic walks in the woods around Lienz, but otherwise the resort is not recommended for non-skiers.

Apart from a few restaurants and bars, La Mongie has nothing for the non-skier.

Childcare

The ESF and Ecoloski both have a ski kindergarten, and Les Marmottes non-ski kindergarten takes children from three to six years old. Ecoloski's Jardin des Enfants is based at the Tournaboup car-park. There is also a kindergarten at La Mongie.

Linked or nearby resorts

Cauterets 1000m (3,280ft)

This attractive thermal resort became a ski station in 1962 and today it has more than 22,000 visitor beds in a large selection of hotels. The nearest airport is Tarbes, 40km away. The skiing is in the open and often very exposed **Cirque du Lys** bowl, accessed by a two-stage cable car, which also brings skiers back to the resort at the end of the day. The ter-rain is best suited to beginners and intermediates. There are 20 runs, including one black, with the rest equally divided between reds, blues and greens. The 29km of pistes are served by 13 lifts. There is another small but developing ski area nearby at **Pont d'Espagne**, renowned for its cross-country trails.

The ski school offers instruction in freestyle, snowboarding, para-pente, off-piste, as well as ordinary group and private lessons. Les Marmottes non-ski kindergarten takes children from 3 months to 6 years old. Children from 4 to 10 years old are taught in the ski school.

The extensive choice of accommodation ranges from *gîtes*, chalets and hotels of the *Belle Epoque*. Hotel Bordeaux is recommended as a comfortable three-star with a good restaurant and a pool table. The Hotel Club Aladin has a fitness centre with a swimming-pool, squash courts and sauna among its facilities. The Astérides is the other three-star, and Etche-Ona is a two-star near the scenic Pont d'Espagne. The Royalty pub is popular, as is the St Trop video bar. Other resort facilities include a theatre, cinema, casino, two discos, a swimming-pool and a large indoor skating rink, as well as the thermal spa.

TOURIST OFFICE
Tel 33 62 92 50 27
Fax 33 62 92 59 12

Font-Romeu 1800m (5,906ft)

The resort, 19km from Perpignan and 200km from Toulouse, is set on a sunny plateau known for its mild climate, making it unreliable for snow at the beginning and end of the season. The skiing is 4km from the village and is linked by a bus service. The 52km of piste and 32 lifts, which rise to a top height of 2204m at Roc de la Calme, suit beginners to intermediates as well as families. Weekend queues are a problem as the resort is popular with both French and Spanish skiers. Fifty per cent of the total skiing terrain is covered by snow-cannon.

There are two-dozen hotels and pensions, over a dozen youth hostels and various self-catering apartments. Après-ski activities include 25 restaurants, a casino, cinemas, 3 discos and 10 bars. Other sports include tobogganing, dog-sledding, skating and ski-jumping. Cross-country skiing is very important here, with two specialist schools, Pyrénées Ski Nordique and ANCEF. There is also a snowboarding park.

TOURIST OFFICE
Tel 33 68 30 68 30
Fax 33 68 30 29 70

St-Lary 830m (2,722ft)

St-Lary-Soulan, 80km from Lourdes, is a typically Pyrenean village of stone-built houses and one main, rather narrow street. The skiing is suitable for beginners to intermediates. It begins a four-minute walk from the village centre at the cable car to **St Lary Pla d'Adret** (1680m), itself a small, but dull, modern ski station with some accommodation. From here a bus runs to two other small centres, **St Lary La Cabane** and **St Lary-Espiaube**. The ski area is served by a chain of 31 lifts, but is mainly treeless and lacks variety. There are six nursery slopes and three ski schools. Two mountain guiding companies arrange ski-tours, which are popular here.

Hotel Mir is recommended, as well as the Altéa Cristal Parc and the Chalets de la Cabane. The Andredena Hotel is in a quiet position and has

Skiing facts: **Barèges**

TOURIST OFFICE
F-65120 Barèges, Hautes-Pyrénées
Tel 33 62 92 68 19
Fax 33 62 92 66 60

THE RESORT
By road Calais 1135km
By rail Lourdes 25km (TGV from Paris)
By air Tarbes 50 mins, Toulouse 2 hrs
Visitor beds 4,200
Transport free ski-bus with lift pass

THE SKIING
Linked or nearby resorts La Mongie (l), Cauterets (n), Font-Romeu (n), Luz-Ardiden (n), Gavarnie (n), St-Lary (n), Piau Engaly (n), Superbagnères (n)
Longest run Tourmalet-Barèges, 7km (green)
Number of lifts 53
Total of trails/pistes 100km (65% easy, 29% intermediate, 6% difficult)
Nursery slopes 6 lifts
Summer skiing none
Snowmaking 1 snow-cannon

LIFT PASSES
Area pass (covers Barèges and La Mongie) 675FF for 6 days
Day pass 135FF
Beginners no reductions
Pensioners 60 yrs and over, 472FF for 6 days
Credit cards accepted yes

SKI SCHOOLS
Adults ESF, 10.30am-12.30pm or 2-5pm, 378FF for 6 x 2hr lessons or 504FF for 6 x 3hr lessons. Ecoloski, 9.30am-12.30pm, 500FF for 6 lessons
Private lessons ESF, 152-168FF per hr. Ecoloski, 150FF per hr
Snowboarding ESF, private lessons only, prices on request. Ecoloski, 150FF for 3hrs
Cross-country ESF, prices on request. Ecoloski, 150FF for 3hrs. Loipe 18km at Lienz
Other courses monoski, ski-touring, telemark, off-piste, moguls
Guiding companies Henri Nogué

CHILDREN
Lift pass 6-11 yrs, 400FF for 6 days, 12-17 yrs, 405FF for 6 days, free for 5 yrs and under
Ski kindergarten ESF Jardin d'Enfants, 4-8 yrs, 10.30am-12.30pm and 2-5pm, 94FF for 3hrs. Ecoloski Jardin d'Enfants, 4-8 yrs, 10am-midday and 2-5pm, 900FF for 6 days
Ski school ESF, 12 yrs and under, 504FF for 6 x 3hr lessons. Ecoloski, 12 yrs and under, 450FF for 6 x 3hr lessons
Non-ski kindergarten Les Oursons, 2-6 yrs, 9.30am-12.30pm and 2-5.30pm, 26FF per hr, extra 30FF per day for lunch. ESF, 2-6 yrs, 9.30am-12.30pm and 2-5.30pm, 130FF per half-day including lunch

FOOD AND DRINK PRICES
Coffee 4FF, glass of wine 10FF, small beer 15FF, dish of the day 50FF

a swimming-pool. At Espiaube there is La Sapinière hotel.

TOURIST OFFICE
Tel 33 62 39 50 81
Fax 33 62 39 50 06

Chamonix

ALTITUDE 1035m (3,396ft)

From a skier's point of view, Chamonix is not so much a resort as a chain of unconnected areas set along both sides of the valley dominated by **Mont Blanc**. On stormy days, of which there are many, it is a brooding place, menaced by razor-sharp peaks and tumbling walls of ice. On sunny days, it is glitteringly beautiful and deceptively tranquil. Its focus is the town of Chamonix, a core of hotels and villas built around the turn of the century and subsequently hemmed in by the new brutalist architecture of post-war tourism. A morning stroll through the bustling streets on the banks of the Arve makes it easy to believe that less than half of the winter visitors are skiers.

- **GOOD POINTS**

Unsurpassed alpine scenery, big vertical drop, extensive off-piste skiing, excellent mountain guides, short airport transfer, wide choice of non-skiing activities, cosmopolitan atmosphere, vibrant nightlife

- **BAD POINTS**

Poorly linked ski areas, unsuitable for families and mixed-ability groups, unpredictable weather patterns, decrepit lift system

The name Chamonix first appeared in the history books in 1091 in connection with the foundation of the monastery of St-Michel-de-la-Cluse. The coming of the monks marked the start of farming in the valley, a dour form of subsistence agriculture practised by people who were known for their resistance to outside authority, especially when it came to paying taxes. Such rugged individualism stood them in good stead when Chamonix's peaks became a magnet for climbers from all over the world: locals joined the Compagnie des Guides, the oldest mountain guiding service in the world and generally rated the best.

As in many other parts of the Alps, the pioneering climbers were British. The celebrated Middle Eastern explorer Richard Pococke and his companion William Windham arrived in the Chamonix Valley from Geneva in 1741. Their party of 13 had expected to encounter 'savages' along the way and was consequently heavily armed. Pococke, further to confuse the peasants they actually encountered along what is now the Autoroute Blanche was, for reasons best known to himself, dressed as an Arab.

Forty-five years later, the locally born doctor, Michel-Gabriel Paccard, and his reclusive partner, Jacques Balmat, conquered Mont Blanc, the most famous of many first ascents that have made Chamonix pre-eminent among climbers everywhere.

Over the past 30 years, it has acquired a comparable status among skiers because of the first descents made by radical extremists like Jean-

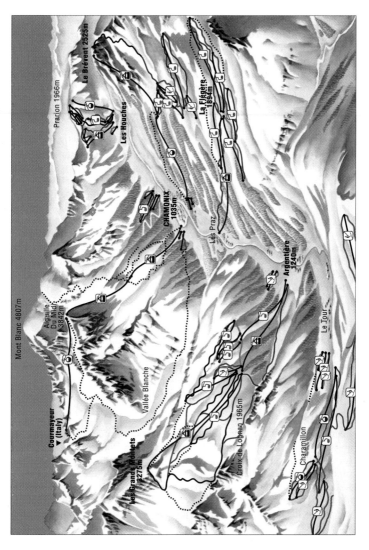

Marc Boivin and Patrick Vallençant, who now lie buried in the local churchyard. Today, the torch is carried by the one-time Chamonix bank clerk Pierre Tardivel, whose first descents include Everest.

On the mountain
top 3842m (12,605ft) bottom 1035m (3,396ft)
The skiing in the Chamonix Valley caters for all levels, but not in the

same place, which makes it difficult for mixed-ability groups to ski on the same mountain. There are six main base-stations, none within easy walking distance of the town centre. The closest are **Le Brévent** and **La Flégère**, both restricted intermediate areas, and the **Aiguille du Midi**, which takes skiers up on to the shoulder of Mont Blanc. The toughest and easiest skiing lies further up the valley, at Argentière and Le Tour respectively, while on the other side of town there are extensive slopes, a number of them below the tree-line, which makes them popular when visibility is poor.

For many years the area has relied on reputation rather than renewal to bring in the customers, a policy that has resulted in antiquated lift systems, a lack of snowmaking equipment and a general feeling of inertia. Chamonix's legions of enthusiasts — most of them ski fanatics — love it unreservedly, but the authorities now believe that the time is ripe for investment if the resort is to hold its position in the twenty-first century.

In the mid-nineties, Les Houches is leading the way, with the installation of the Kandahar and Crozat high-speed quads for the 1994–5 season. By 1996 there will be snowmaking from both Prarion and Bellevue, Les Houches' twin peaks, down to the village. Permission has also been obtained for a cable car link to **Megève** through **St-Gervais** or **St-Nicholas**. When this opens in 1996–7, Les Houches will be part of a 350km linked ski circus.

In Chamonix itself, work has finally begun on the long-awaited Le Brévent–La Flegère link, planned as an eight-person gondola and due for completion for the 1996–7 season. Also in the pipeline is a much-needed replacement for the ancient Bochard chair at Argentière, either with a funitel (an extremely wind-resistant, but expensive double mono-cable lift) or a 12- to 16-person gondola. The adjacent Herse chair will also be replaced with a high-speed quad when funds permit.

Beginners

Learn to ski in Chamonix if you must, but don't necessarily expect to enjoy it. The town has small training areas at **Les Planards** and **Le Savoy** for absolute beginners, but once you have grasped the basics the best practice slopes are in **Le Tour**, the most far-flung of the valley's outposts. As it is tree-free, the light is often hostile, but on a clear day the comfortable gondola access to Charamillon and the wide, empty slopes that fan out across the Col de Balme above it are very user-friendly. The best bad-weather cover is the small network of blue (easy) runs at the top of Prarion in **Les Houches**.

Intermediates

Chamonix may be short of motorway pistes, but there is more than adequate compensation in the diversity of the pistes on offer. Skiers with the skills to tackle a red (intermediate) run with confidence can spend a week in the valley without going to the same place twice. The most convenient starting point is Le Brévent where the six-seater gondola to Planpraz gives access to a choice of inviting blue runs down to the Col

Cornu chair. This, in its turn, opens up several moderately challenging reds, the longest of which goes to the bottom of La Charlanon drag-lift. Planpraz is also the launch point for the dramatic cable car ride up to Le Brévent itself, a 2525m crag with unsurpassed views of Mont Blanc. From this high point, the return to the mid-station is via a sweeping red piste or a bumpy black (difficult) one. Only genuinely confident intermediates should attempt the return to Chamonix down the black run from the bottom of La Parsa chair.

La Flégère is reached from the suburb of **Les Praz**, a ten-minute bus-ride from the town centre. The terrain is similar to Le Brévent, with long red and blue runs from the top of L'Index to the mid-station and a black descent back to the base. When the link with Le Brévent is finished, it will create a viable ski area out of two scrappy ones.

No visit to Chamonix is complete without a ride up the two-stage Aiguille du Midi cable car, the highest in Europe. This is the departure point for the 20km glacier run down the **Vallée Blanche**, a gentle cruise through some of the most grandiose mountain scenery in the world. As it can readily be tackled by low intermediates, it provides thousands of skiers with their first unforgettable taste of high-mountain off-piste adventure. Such terrors as there are come early in the day in the shape of the infamous steps cut into the spine of the ridge from the cable car station to the start of the skiing.

> **■ WHAT'S NEW**
>
> The Kandahar and Crozat high-speed quads in Les Houches
> Extensive snowmaking at Les Houches

Experienced mountaineers ignore both the safety rope and the vertical drop-offs on either side as they trot down as effortlessly as if they were in Chamonix's main street, but first-timers, burdened with skis on their backs, can freeze with the horror of it all. Some guides prefer to rope their clients together, a precaution that can increase the feeling of danger if several people slip at once, but the reality is that everyone gets down safely in the end.

This is not true of the Vallée Blanche itself, a minefield of death-trap crevasses that should never be skied without a guide. It can also be accessed from the **Courmayeur** side via Punta Helbronner, a route that eliminates the ridge hazard altogether. Until 1992, the return to Chamonix included a 30-minute uphill trek, which can now be avoided by taking the refurbished Montenvers railway.

The golden rule for Chamonix is to ski the Vallée Blanche when the sun shines and Les Houches when the weather closes in. Following it can make for congestion in both places, but there is no doubt that the glades of Bellevue and Prarion are the best places to be in a blizzard. By comparison with its neighbours, Les Houches is very low, and this severely restricts skiing in bad snow years. Access is via the Bellevue cable car or the Prarion gondola, both of which connect with the extensive network of red and blue runs on the Col de Voza. The one black run, the international downhill Noire des Houches, starts below Prarion and ends almost in the village.

Advanced

When enthusiasts talk of Chamonix, they really mean the **Grands Montets** at Argentière. This is a truly magnificent expert mountain, so steep, complex and dramatic that there seems to be no end to its possibilities. It is reached either by the 80-person cable car to Lognan or the high-speed quad-chair to Plan Joran, both of which run out at the Argentière base-station. When the *cognoscenti* arrive at Lognan, they join the rush — and almost inevitably the queue — for the Grands Montets cable car.

The huge popularity of this lift is undiminished either by the supplement payable on top of the Mont Blanc lift pass or the 200 slippery metal steps leading from the top-station to the start of skiing. This is then revealed as a bumpy defile that divides into two black runs, Les Pylones under the cable car and the awkwardly cambered Point de Vue which, as its name suggests, provides stunning views of the glacier as it tracks down its edge. The Bochard lift opens up another huge section of the mountain, including the tough 4.5km Chamois descent to the Le Lavancher chair.

Off-piste

On a powder morning, the rush for the Grands Montets is fierce and fearsome, but the area is so enormous that skiing it out in a hurry is even beyond the powers of Europe's most dedicated first-track pack. Although there are plenty of open snow fields, bowls and gullies between the marked pistes, maximising the experience means hiring a guide to safely negotiate the glacier, a web of crevasses and seracs that change position from season to season.

Although the more macho of the temporary residents claim to know the mountain well enough to ski it alone, the truth is that to go without a qualified guide is to court death. From a skiing point of view, the most challenging descent is the Pas de Chèvre, a run from the top of Bochard via one of several extreme couloirs down the Mer de Glace to the bottom of the Vallée Blanche. Another classic is the Envers route down the Vallée Blanche, reached from the top of the Aiguille du Midi cable car, but far removed from the regular run when it comes to degree of difficulty.

Snowboarding

Most of Chamonix's snowboarders are powder surfers who shred the Grands Montets in hot competition with regular skiers. The tiny minority who prefer to practise tricks can be found at the surf park at **Charamillon**, the mid-station at Le Tour, and the half-pipe near the Kandahar chair in Les Houches. Lessons in Nouvelle Glisse (snowboarding, monoski and telemark) are available from the French Ski School (ESF).

Ski schools and guiding

The Chamonix branch of the ESF and the Compagnie des Guides share an office in the downtown area, but the less traditional Ski Sensation takes a 'wilder' approach to the learning curve that is said to be popular with British clients. The Association of Independent Guides is one of several alternative guiding services, but British adventurers are advised to contact fluent English-speakers like Roland Stieger and Fred Harper directly. The ESF also has an office in Argentière, while Les Houches is served both by the ESF and the International Ski School (ESI).

Mountain restaurants

The Chamonix Valley is not recommended for skiers who lunch on the mountain in any serious way. Le Brévent and La Flégère have crowded self-service cafeterias while Le Tour's Hotel Olympique is acclaimed for its sunseeker's terrace, but less so for food, which is dismissed as 'so so' and service as 'the worst in the valley'. Those who ski the Vallée Blanche have little choice but to eat at the spectacularly sited Requin refuge, now under new ownership and recommended for its fruit tarts. Ironically, the best restaurants are on the Grands Montets, the place where skiers are least likely to stop to enjoy them. Nevertheless it is necessary to book in advance for La Chavanne, a tin hut under the Bochard lift station that is decidedly more promising inside than out. The spacious Plan Joran has an extensive self-service area, with decent, reasonably priced hot and cold food, and a small waiter-service restaurant offering more sophisticated fare.

Off the mountain

Chamonix's current concerns are mostly with traffic management in a town that took shape before the cars took over. Most visitors to the Valley rightly consider a car to be essential, the alternative being the local bus service that links the base-stations with moderate efficiency but little comfort, especially at peak hours.

Chamonix's original village square is fully pedestrianised and the main street is closed to traffic during daylight hours. This allows for the free flow of shoppers at the cost of considerable congestion on the outskirts, especially the ever-expanding new township of Chamonix Sud. The problem has not been improved as much as was hoped by the new 300-space car-park at St-Michel. The shopping facilities are so comprehensive here that one reporter comments: 'Almost a range of shops that one would expect to find in any British town.'

A subsidiary worry is the proposed second tunnel under Mont Blanc, a scheme that is rigorously opposed by the majority of Chamonix's 10,000 permanent inhabitants on the grounds of massive pollution. As it is favoured by Brussels due to fears that the existing tunnel will become a bottleneck as soon as the four-lane access roads on the Italian and French sides are completed, most residents fear the worst.

Accommodation

Chamonix offers the full spectrum from dormitory-style youth hostels to four-star hotels, plus a wide choice of chalets and rental apartments managed by British tour operators. The seven privately owned Les Autannes apartments in a former old stone-built hotel near **Le Tour** are some of the best-appointed here.

The most luxurious hotels are the Albert 1er and Auberge du Bois Prin, owned by brothers Denis and Pierre Carrier. In the three-star category, the Sapinière, run in true family style by Jeannie and Patrick Cachet, recalls the heyday of the British Empire, both in its furnishings and its clientèle. The Richemond also trades on the faded glories of yesteryear, and from a more central location. The Alpina is a good quality three-star close to the town centre.

Eating in and out

No one denies that the Michelin-rated Albert 1er has the best food in Chamonix, but prices have risen to a point at which even the rich hesitate to go there except on special occasions. The Auberge du Bois follows it closely in both quality and price and the food at the Hotel Eden in **Les Praz** is also recommended.

In a more accessible bracket, the once reliable National and Atmosphère restaurants have suffered from changes of ownership. La Bergerie serves Savoyard specialities, while the Bistro de la Gare is known for its cheap daily special. The friendly Le Sarpein Les Bois is praised for quality combined with good value. L'Impossible, the ancient barn in **Chamonix Sud** converted by Sylvain Saudain, is a winner as far as atmosphere is concerned. Other recommendations include La Cantina for Mexican cuisine and Le Cafeteria, which is said to provide 'very reasonably priced wholesome food.'

> ■ **OTHER SPORTS**
> Indoor tennis and squash, ice-driving, snow-shoeing, hang-gliding, heli-skiing, curling, indoor and outdoor skating, swimming

Self-caterers are well served by specialist food shops and branches of popular French supermarket chains.

Après-ski

The ski-mad early evening trade may concentrate on the fashionable video bars of Le Choucas and Driver, but there is no shortage of alternative entertainment. Last year floodlit skiing was introduced at Les Bossons and a bowling alley and billiard school in Chamonix Sud. After dinner, the action focuses on Arbat, which has the best live music in town. Wild Wallabies, inspired by St Anton's Krazy Kangaruh, is another top choice, while real late-nighters end up at the Blue Night, which stays open till 5am.

The Bumble Bee and the Mill Street Bar in Chamonix are both recommended, as is The Office Bar in Argentière. Jekyll and Hyde and the Ice Rock Café in Chamonix Sud are both popular; the latter is a large basement bar incorporating half a truck and various motorcycles and is packed until the early hours.

Skiing facts: **Chamonix**

TOURIST OFFICE
85 Place du Triangle de L'Amitié, F-74400
Chamonix Mont Blanc, Haute Savoie
Tel 33 50 53 00 24
Fax 33 50 53 58 90

THE RESORT
By road Calais 900km
By rail station in resort
By air Geneva 1½ hrs
Visitor beds 56,000
Transport free bus service from Le Tour to
Les Houches included in lift pass

THE SKIING
Linked or nearby resorts Argentière (n),
Courmayeur (n), Les Houches (n), Megève
(n), St-Gervais (n)
Longest run Les Grands Montets, 8km
(black)
Total of trails/pistes 140km (52% easy,
36% intermediate, 12% difficult)
Nursery slopes 17 beginner runs
Summer skiing none
Snowmaking 47 snow-cannon

LIFT PASSES
Area pass Mont Blanc Skipass (covers 13
resorts in Mont Blanc region), 900FF for 6
days
Day pass 75FF, or 173FF for Grands
Montets
Beginners no free lifts
Pensioners 20% reduction for 60 yrs
and over

Credit cards accepted yes

SKI SCHOOLS
Adults ESF, 700FF for 6 days (2 hrs per
day)
Private lessons ESF, beginners only, 180FF
per hour, 2hr lesson 480FF
Snowboarding ESF, 660FF for 3 after-
noons, private lessons, 480FF for 2 hrs
Cross-country ESF, prices as regular ski
lessons. Loipe 43km around Chamonix and
Argentière
Other courses heli-skiing
Guiding companies Compagnie des Guides
de Chamonix, Association Independante des
Guides

CHILDREN
Lift pass Mont Blanc Skipass, 4-11 yrs,
645FF for 6 days, free for 3 yrs and under
Ski kindergarten ESF, 9.30am-5.30pm,
1,200FF for 6 days including lessons and
lunch. Panda Ski, 8.30am-5.30pm,
1,350FF for 6 days
Ski school ESF, 4-6 yrs, 620FF for 6 days.
6-12 yrs, 580FF for 6 days
Non-ski kindergarten Halte-Garderie, 18
mths-6 yrs, 8am-6.15pm, 220FF per day,
extra 19FF per day for lunch. Panda Club, 3
mths-3 yrs, 8.30am-5.30pm, 1,400FF for
6 days including lunch

FOOD AND DRINK
Coffee 6-10FF, glass of wine 10FF, small
beer 15-20FF, dish of the day 45-55FF

Childcare
The ESF in Chamonix and Argentière have classes for children between
4 and 12 years of age. Alternatively, the Panda Club in Argentière provides care for children aged three months to three years, seven days a
week. For three- and four-year-olds, Panda Ski offers daily sessions in
the Jardin des Neiges near the Lognan lift station. In addition, there is a

municipal crèche, which provides entertainment including sledging, games and ski fun for children aged 18 months to 6 years.

Linked or nearby resorts

Argentière 1240m (4,067ft)

In winter Argentière's main street becomes ski bum alley, with a large proportion of its rooms let out cheaply for the season. After dark the bars fill up with macho talk of the day's derring-do. The Office, now relocated to larger premises, is the favoured British watering hole. The Rusticana has a more cosmopolitan flavour, while the Savoie dares to remain resolutely French. The Dahu Hotel, a prominent landmark in this predominantly Savoyard village on the congested road from Chamonix to Martigny, is recommended both for comfort and food.

TOURIST OFFICE
as Chamonix

La Clusaz

La Clusaz is a large, spread-out resort off the Autoroute Blanche on the way to Chamonix, less than two hours from Geneva Airport. Consequently, it is extremely attractive to skiers from Britain and Holland who have bought apartments here and visit for weekends. It is also popular with Geneva-based skiers and, when snow conditions are good, weekend crowds can be a problem. La Clusaz has none of the exclusive cachet of Megève, its sophisticated neighbour; the atmosphere is no-frills provincial French in what has been a ski and summer resort since 1898. Municipal records show that La Clusaz received a substantial 4,000 tourists in 1908.

■ GOOD POINTS
Variety of skiing for beginners, easy road access, short airport transfer, beautiful scenery, numerous mountain restaurants

■ BAD POINTS
Unreliable snow cover, heavy traffic, lack of skiing convenience, unsuitable for late holidays, weekend crowds, lack of tough runs

The layout of the resort is annoyingly inconvenient and to avoid long walks in ski boots it is advisable to choose your accommodation with care. However, its real drawback is its lack of altitude. The village itself is only 1100m, which is extremely low by Haute Savoie standards, and the skiing only goes up to 2600m. This means there is usually little or no snow at resort level for much of the winter, and the danger is always that some precipitation will fall as rain over most of the ski area. Its proximity to Geneva means that it is prone to some weekend overcrowding, although serious city skiers tend to drive on by down the Autoroute Blanche heading for the more diverse attractions of the Chamonix Valley.

Reblochon, one of the greatest cheeses of France comes from here. During the madness of the French Revolution, La Clusaz attained fame similar to that of Gretna Green; marriages were declared legal if the happy couple walked three times around the designated tree of liberty in the village square. Divorce was as easily accommodated — in reverse.

More recently, La Clusaz became famous for its Flying Kilometre course on the top-half of the Vraille run in the Balme sector, where a number of world records were set in the 1980s. It has now fallen into disuse because it is simply not steep enough to match the records being set in Les Arcs.

The 40 lifts of nearby **Le Grand-Bornand** are included in the regional lift pass. A car is useful for access to the different sectors of what is an inconveniently arranged ski area or for excursions further afield into the **Chamonix Valley**.

On the mountain
top 2600m (8,528ft) bottom 1100m (3,608ft)

La Clusaz has five ski areas spread around the sides of a number of neighbouring valleys facing north, east and west. Mountain access to **Beauregard** and **L'Aiguille** is by lifts from the resort centre. The other three are reached from various points along the valleys via a satisfactory ski-bus network. Despite roads and rivers all five are linked by lift or piste, although some of these connections are long green (beginner) pistes that involve a plod; another is a trans-valley cable-car shuttle.

■ **WHAT'S NEW**

Extended snowmaking facilities
Quad chair-lift on Col de Balme

Beauregard, served by a single cable car from the bottom of the resort, is a 1690m flat-topped, wooded mountain, with attractive and easy skiing in pastoral surroundings at the top.

L'Etale is an enjoyable area of short, gentle runs through the trees, spread over a knoll between the cols of La Croix-Fry and Merdassier. It is mainly served by a single cable car, which takes you up to the top at 2200m. Skiing is limited to the north-west-facing flank of the mountain, which is open and fairly steep on the upper half, with a network of drag-lifts serving the gentler and more spacious slopes at the bottom and giving access to an easy run across to the Merdassier sector, which offers considerable variety.

There are steeper and more open runs on the other side of Merdassier, as well as a gentle run across to L'Etale, which provide the return link. Apart from the attraction of the extra skiing, the area is well supplied with restaurants beside the two cols.

L'Aiguille is the largest of the sectors and is directly accessible from the village by efficient chair- and drag-lifts. The Crêt du Merle mid-station has a small nursery slope, ski school assembly area and restaurants. None of the runs down from here offer any degree of difficulty. From the next stage the Crêt du Loup, the long west-facing run to the valley, offers more than 600m vertical.

The north-west-facing slopes of the **Massif de Balme** provide La Clusaz's highest and most challenging pistes, with enjoyable long runs down the Combe de la Balme and the Combe de la Torchère, providing over 1200m vertical with plenty of scope for off-piste variations. Two long, flat green runs lead back to the resort; the lower one requires a lot of poling.

Beginners
There are small but good nursery slopes close to the village centre and at the bottom of each sector, but snow cover may not be satisfactory at this low altitude. The best novice slopes are at Crêt du Merle in L'Aiguille sector and on the top of Beauregard. Two long blue (easy) and two green runs take a line around both shoulders of Beauregard back to the resort. Beauregard also has a cross-country loipe and pleasant trails for walkers.

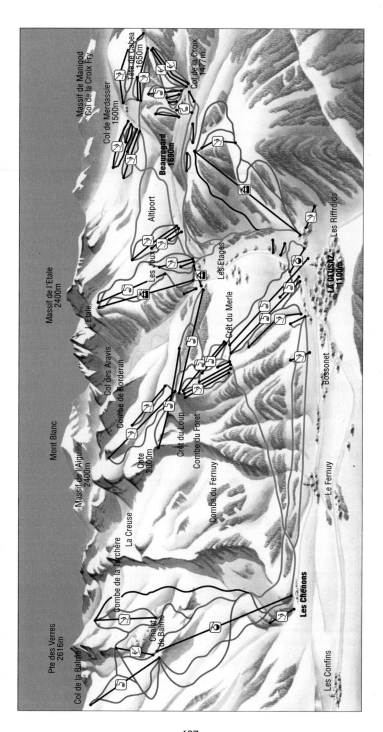

Pte des Verres
2616m

Col de la Balme

Mont Blanc

Massif de l'Etale
2400m

Massif de Manigod
Col de la Croix Fry

Massif de l'Aiguille
2400m

Col des Aravis

Col de Merdassier
1500m

Tête de Cabeau
1650m

Col de la Croix
1477 m

Beauregard
1690m

Altiport

Les Joux

Etale

Les Etages

Crêt du Merle

Les Riffrôids

LA CLUSAZ
1100m

Combe de Borderan

Crêt du Loup

Oste
2000m

Combe du Foret

Bossonet

Combe du Fernuy

Combe de la Torchère

La Creuse

Le Fernuy

Chalet de Balme

Les Chenons

Les Confins

187

Intermediates

All the areas offer plenty of scope for confident parallel skiers, although the longer runs in the Balme area are the most enjoyable. Moderate red (intermediate) runs descend from both top-stations here, and a long blue winds its way down more sedately from the top of the Bergerie chair. Try also L'Aiguille run from the top of the drag-lift of the same name and Tétras from the top of L'Etale.

Advanced

The pistes of La Clusaz are of limited appeal to truly advanced skiers. La Noire, one the resort's three black (difficult) pistes follows the fall-line down the front face of Beauregard. The run starts gently but becomes steeper with a couple of awkward pitches. Le Vraille, down the Combe de la Torchère in the Balme sector, may no longer be steep enough for speed-skiing records, but the gradient is sufficient to test anyone's skills.

Off-piste

In deep snow the area beneath the Crêt du Loup chair-lifts in L'Aiguille sector, as well as in the bowl above them, provide good opportunities for off-piste skiing. Itineraries include the Combe de Borderan and the Combe du Fernuy; both are long, steep gullies in the wall of the Chaîne des Aravis. Ski-touring is available with the Ski Académie.

Snowboarding

Only the French Ski School (ESF) and the Ski Académie at the International Ski School (ESI) teach snowboarding.

Ski schools and guiding

La Clusaz has three ski schools: the ESF, Aravis Evasion and the ESI Ski Académie. We have reports of over-subscribed classes run by the ESF ('our instructor just could not remember 15 names'). We have no reports of either of the other schools.

Mountain restaurants

La Clusaz has a surprisingly high number of good mountain eating-places. The disadvantage is that some of the better ones are on the lower pistes and are not always accessible because of scant snow cover. They are mainly attractively old-fashioned and inexpensive in comparison with those in other French ski areas, especially at La Croix-Fry/Merdassier. Le Vieux Ferme at Merdassier is lavishly praised by all reporters who have stopped there ('outstanding cuisine in a wonderful setting'). The Beauregard, beside the cross-country track, has 'good food, a wonderful sun terrace and spectacular views'. Chez Arthur at Crêt du Merle is praised for its welcoming atmosphere ('good food at reasonable prices — the perfect place for a rainy afternoon'). Le Bercail on the Crêt du Merle piste is an old Savoie farmhouse with a log fire. Balme does not offer such a high standard, with both restaurants at the top and bottom of the gondola being 'disappointing and expensive'.

Off the mountain

The resort has considerable charm, not least because it functions as a year-round farming community, and its economy is not solely dependent on the seasonal influx of skiers. While the village centre, with its limited choice of shops but wider range of restaurants, remains relatively compact, buildings have burst out of the natural setting along the steep sides of the wooded valleys that surround it.

The village, nevertheless, remains attractive, and as one reporter enthuses: 'The scenery is as impressive from the town as it is from the slopes'. The newer suburbs are complicated by a series of road junctions

> ■ **OTHER SPORTS**
> Curling, swimming, indoor tennis at the Raiffeisen Tennis Centre, squash, sleigh rides, tobogganing, skating

and roundabouts. It is a confusing place to find your way around, and traffic can be a serious problem during the late afternoon and at weekends. Parking is difficult, and the village is well policed, however, there is an underground car-park.

The heart of the village is pleasantly traditional, built around a large church, with a stylish modern shopping precinct beside it and a fast-flowing stream below. The shops are few in number but varied, and you can still find the ordinary French café of the lowland villages, not normally so apparent in a ski resort. The spread-out nature of the skiing makes La Clusaz dependent on an efficient bus service, which it has by and large, although reporters complain of long waits on some routes. The hourly service to Col de Merdassier seems hopelessly inadequate, and the heavy traffic does not contribute to its smooth operation.

Its identity as a real village, rather than just a *station de ski,* makes La Clusaz a reasonable choice for non-skiers. Activities here include swimming and skating, along with snow-shoe excursions to fill the daytime and evening hours. The scenic cross-country tracks around **Lac des Confins** reportedly hold the snow well and they are served by a regular bus service. The area on top of Beauregard is well laid out and signposted but it is busy and there is more chance of conflict with downhill skiers.

Accommodation

Accommodation is divided between tour operator chalets and a number of hotels of markedly varying quality. We have exceptionally glowing reports of the three-star Hotel Beauregard, close to L'Aiguille lifts ('extremely well-fitted, modern pine interior, the food is excellent and it really deserves a four-star rating'). Another reporter commented: 'It is rare and delightful to find a hotel of this quality at a price you can afford.'

It is important to find out where the lifts are in relation to where you are staying and to discover whether there is a bus-stop nearby. The skiing convenience factor here is one of the lowest in this guide, and any visit involves considerable trudging about in ski boots. In the centre of the resort are lots of simple, reasonably priced hotels. The Alpenroc (formerly the Vita) is strongly recommended ('really good rooms with satellite television, splendid and varied food with a local accent'). Hotel Nouvel is also praised, and the two-star Hotel Christiania and Hotel Floralp receive favourable reports. The three-star Panorama has no restaurant and is 'reasonably priced, but in serious need of complete renovation'.

We have particularly good reports of the Résidence du Centre apartments, which are close to the church and ideally situated 100m from the Praz chair-lift to L'Aiguille.

Eating in and out

La Clusaz has a much wider choice of restaurants than you would expect in a resort of its size. Le Foly is a particularly attractive and expensive log-cabin in the **Confins Valley**. The Symphonie in the Hotel Beauregard offers 'excellent cuisine with a cheerful service in warm surroundings'. The Coin du Feu is recommended for its 'delicious *crêpe sucré*'. Restaurant St Joseph is praised for its grilled steaks. The Cremaillère specialises in fondue and raclette. One reporter raved about the chilli and burgers at the Tex-Mex Café. Other popular choices are the Calèche, L'Ourson and L'Outa.

Après-ski

Most of the muted action centres around a few bars. Le Pressoir is the 'in' place for snowboarders, the Tex-Mex Café is always busy, and the Angelus is suitable for a quiet drink. Resort workers meet in the Lion d'Or. L'Ecluse is said to be the best of the discos, with a glass dance-floor over the river, while Le Club 18 attracts the locals and an older clientèle. Après-ski is quiet during the week (some would say too quiet) but can become extremely lively during weekends.

Childcare

Le Clusaz has a 'three-kids' rating as one of the better equipped French resorts for children. The Club des Mouflets crèche takes youngsters from eight months old up to four-and-a-half years and the Club des Champions ski kindergarten gives lessons for children aged three-and-a-half to six years.

Skiing facts: **La Clusaz**

TOURIST OFFICE
F-74220 La Clusaz, Haute Savoie
Tel 33 50 32 65 00
Fax 33 50 32 65 01

THE RESORT
By road Calais 820km
By rail Annecy 30km, frequent bus service to the resort
By air Geneva 1 hr 50 mins
Visitor beds 19,500
Transport free ski-bus with lift pass of 4 days or more

THE SKIING
Linked or nearby resorts Chamonix (n), Le Grand-Bornand (n), Megève (n)
Longest run La Motte, 4km (green)
Number of lifts 56
Total of trails/pistes 130km (70% easy, 26% intermediate, 4% difficult)
Nursery slopes 10 lifts
Summer skiing none
Snowmaking 13 hectares covered

LIFT PASSES
Area pass Aravis (covers La Clusaz and Le Grand-Bornand), 720FF for 6 days. La Clusaz (covers La Croix-Fry/Merdassier), 680FF for 6 days
Day pass La Clusaz 135FF
Beginners points tickets
Pensioners no reduction
Credit cards accepted yes

SKI SCHOOLS
Adults ESF, 730FF for 6 days, Aravis Evasion, 420FF for 6 half-days, ESI Ski Académie, 340FF for 4 days (2 hrs per day)
Private lessons ESF and Aravis Evasion, both 170FF per hr, ESI Ski Académie 175FF per hr
Snowboarding ESF, 430FF for 4 days (3 hrs per day), ESI Ski Académie, 340FF for 4 days (2 hrs per day)
Cross-country ESF, 656FF per day ($4\frac{1}{2}$ hrs), 150FF per hr. Centre Ecole Ski de Fond, 610FF per day ($4\frac{1}{2}$ hrs), 125FF per hr. Loipe 70km around Beauregard and in Les Confins Valley
Other courses telemark, race training, moguls, monoski, slalom, off-piste
Guiding companies ESF and ESI

CHILDREN
Lift pass 4-12 yrs 530FF for 6 days, 13 yrs and over 680FF for 6 days, free for 3 yrs and under
Ski kindergarten Le Club des Champions, $3\frac{1}{2}$-6 yrs, 8.30am-6pm, 960FF for 6 days including lunch
Ski school as ski kindergarten
Non-ski kindergarten Club des Mouflets, 8 mths-$4\frac{1}{2}$ yrs, 8.30am-6pm, 960FF for 6 days including lunch

FOOD AND DRINK PRICES
Coffee 5-10FF, glass of wine 12FF, small beer 20-30FF, dish of the day 40-70FF

Les Deux Alpes

ALTITUDE 1650m (5,412ft)

When Monsieur Rudolphe Tessa built a tiny hunting lodge at the Alpe de Mont de Lans in 1934 and opened it to visitors that winter, he sowed some of the early seeds of this international ski resort. Shortly afterwards, he announced that he would buy any car capable of climbing the mule track to his premises. Several manufacturers attempted this challenge, but a Peugeot with a special mountain axle accomplished it best. 'However,' the archives inform us, 'it was necessary to carry the car on the bends'.

One Easter just before the outbreak of World War II, a Heath-Robinson-style rope-tow was opened with great ceremony, but it fell down 15 minutes later. It was not until the late 1950s that a new gondola and one of

<table>
<tr><td>■ GOOD POINTS</td></tr>
<tr><td>Extensive beginner terrain, snow-sure slopes, modern lift system, excellent off-piste, beautiful scenery, lively après-ski, glacier skiing</td></tr>
<tr><td>■ BAD POINTS</td></tr>
<tr><td>Inconvenient for beginners, large and spread-out village, heavy traffic, lack of tree-line skiing, crowded pistes</td></tr>
</table>

France's first ski passes — costing 2.50FF per day — paved the way for Les Deux Alpes to develop into a proper ski area. Today, this efficient and only partly purpose-built resort between Grenoble and Briançon has 63 lifts, which distribute a potential 61,000 skiers an hour to every conceivable point on the mountain. It is a large ski factory, but with fresh air and impressive scenery. Both village and ski area are long and narrow, and there is less skiing terrain than one would imagine for such a high vertical drop. However, the skiing links with **La Grave**, one of the most dramatic off-piste ski areas in Europe.

On the mountain
top 3600m (11,808ft) bottom 1300m (4,264ft)

The chamois hunters and old shepherds who once roamed what are now the ski slopes would scarcely recognise their traditional haunts today. Indeed, it is easy for skiers to be confused by such a multitude of lifts and 200km of piste within a relatively confined area. Apart from a smaller uncrowded area to the west of the village, between Pied Moutet at 2100m and the Alpe du Mont de Lans, the bulk of the skiing is between the village and La Toura at 2600m to the east. Reporters criticise the 'sameness' of the pistes: 'a huge array of blue and green runs, all of which are rather dull' and 'it seems to be something of a damning indictment that a resort which claims 200km of piste has so few runs of any real interest'.

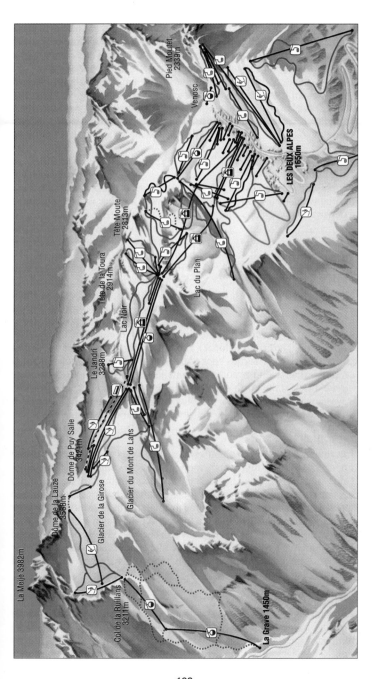

La Meille 3982m

Dôme de la Lauze 3568m

Dôme de Puy Salie 3421m

Glacier de la Girose

Col de la Ruillans 3211m

Glacier du Mont de Lahs

La Grave 1450m

Le Jandri 3288m

Lac Noir

Tête de la Toura 2914m

Tête Moute 2813m

Lac du Plan

Pied Moutet 2339m

Venosc

LES DEUX ALPES 1650m

Of the numerous lifts, the principal bulk-carrier is the Jandri Express jumbo gondola, which deposits skiers on the Glacier du Mont de Lans in 20 minutes. Above La Toura, the terrain narrows down to something of a bottleneck, where it can sometimes be difficult to thread your way through skiers and pylons, until the Col de Jandri at 3200m. Here, it widens again to include some good intermediate cruising before reaching the broader glacier plateau. This sector offers easy slopes and even a sub-glacial funicular for novice skiers who find wind-blown T-bars daunting. There is also some skiing below the village when conditions are good.

Beginners

People who learn to ski at Les Deux Alpes will be surprised at how easy and convenient it is when they move on to another resort. The most extensive nursery slopes are at the top of the ski area on the Glacier du Mont de Lans, while the lower slopes just above the village are too steep for beginners. This combination is the reverse of what most resorts have to offer. However, the excitement of being able to ski high on the mountain with magnificent views of the Oisans mountain range more than compensates for having to download to the resort by lift at the end of the day. There are 22 green (beginner) runs, including some nursery slopes beside the village. The runs back to the village are not suitable for novices or timid skiers; one reporter comments: 'It is not worth taking the 'green' track at the north end of the village more than once per holiday, it was icy, ill-defined in poor visibility, and very crowded. It is a lot safer and more pleasurable to take the gondolas back to the village'.

> ### ■ WHAT'S NEW
>
> Additional snowmaking
> Chair-lift replaces Belle Etoile drag
> from the resort
> Quad-chair replaces Les Crêtes drag

Intermediates

Intermediates can enjoy themselves at Les Deux Alpes on most of the upper slopes, although less experienced skiers may find themselves somewhat overwhelmed by the steep homeward-bound runs, which can become crowded at the end of the day. One way to escape from the mainstream skiing is to try the runs through the trees, which are a rarity in Les Deux Alpes. There is an enjoyable piste down to the village of Bons at 1300m, while Mont de Lans can be reached from both ski areas. Les Gours, the new run down to La Voute quad-chair, opened last year and has converted a celebrated off-piste itinerary into an easy red (intermediate) run.

Advanced

Advanced skiers inevitably gravitate towards the Tête Moute area, which provides some of the steepest terrain on the mountain. They will be tempted to go straight from the Alpe de Venosc end of the village by gondola to Le Diable at 2400m, which can also be reached by a more roundabout route via the Télésiège du Thuit. From Le Diable, the Grand Diable chair reaches the Tête Moute itself where there are steep, north-facing runs to Lac du Plan and onwards towards the Thuit chair. Le Diable run offers a challenging and often mogulled 1200m descent to the village. There are seven other black (difficult) runs.

Off-piste

Les Deux Alpes has enclosed bowl-skiing, which is ideal for those want-ing to try off-piste for the first time. For seasoned deep-snow skiers there are a number of easily accessible but not so easily skiable couloirs. However, Les Deux Alpes also has one of the most exciting and scenic off-piste ski areas on its doorstep: La Grave. There is an 'over-the-top' link from Les Deux Alpes via the Glacier du Mont de Lans, which involves a 20-minute walk. The ancient resort, at 1450m, has a steep, unpisted and glacial area with phenomenal opportunities for deep-snow and couloir skiing in the course of its 2134m vertical drop. But skiers should be careful before venturing into this remarkable arena: it is dan-gerous as well as splendid and should only be contemplated if you engage the services of a local mountain guide.

Snowboarding

Each October, snowboarding takes pride of place here as an *apéritif* to the ski season. This year, for the sixth year running, the resort held its World Snowboard Meeting and Grand Prix des Deux Alpes, which claims to be 'the highest and biggest exhibition of snowboarding on the planet'. The events are held on the glacier at 3200m and include slalom, giant slalom and half-pipe competitions; it attracts some 15,000 visitors. Three organisations — Stage Babi Pourtier, Stage Snowboard Luc Pelisson and Yellow Cab Surfing — offer snowboarding courses.

Ski schools and guiding

There are two rival ski schools: the main French Ski School (ESF) at Les Deux Alpes and the International Ski School (ESI) at St-Christophe. Both offer group and private lessons and special courses for snowboard-ing, telemark, monoski and cross-country. A new ski school, Ski 3000 is Anglo-Italian-run and is praised: 'I cannot speak highly enough of the teachers, who explained everything fully and taught with a high degree of understanding and patience. This was backed by video analysis. By the second day I was turning properly on the easy runs. My wife had five in her class and I had three in mine!'

Mountain restaurants

Les Deux Alpes does not receive many bouquets for its six mountain restaurants, and if it were not so inconvenient more skiers might con-sider lunching in town. 'Uninviting' and 'overpriced' are among com-ments expressed by reporters. La Pastorale, at the top of the Diable gondola, is generally regarded as one of the better ones, with reasonable prices ('alpine charm and a pleasant atmosphere'). The Panoramic is reportedly 'friendly but a bit crowded at peak hours'. The highest restaurant, Les Glaciers, is as its name suggests, on the glacier. The other mountain restaurants are La Patache at Les Crêtes, and La Troika. La Meije has a 'friendly, efficient service with local specialities at very reasonable prices'. La Petite Marmite is also recommended.

Off the mountain
Les Deux Alpes is a narrow, rather higgledy-piggledy and bustling small town that has developed in a somewhat haphazard way from the two separate farming communities of Mont de Lans and Alpe de Venosc. Although the town itself is not attractive, it is by no means the worst example of modern French architecture. The resort links with the quaint old hamlet of Venosc with its cobbled streets via a new six-person gondola. Les Deux Alpes scores high for après-ski — for those who like lively, noisy bars and discos and do not mind bumping into lots of other British. (More than 25 per cent of non-French visitors are British.)

Accommodation
Most of the accommodation is in apartments, with the remainder in the resort's 40 hotels and pensions. At the top end of the market are three four-star establishments, of which the Bérangère is particularly praised. There are nine three-star hotels and 21 two-stars. The Edelweiss is warmly recommended for its 'wonderful gourmet dinners, with local produce properly cooked and well presented; the staff were patient and helpful and the bedrooms large, with furnishings OK, if a little spartan'. The Brunerie is described as 'welcoming'.

■ **OTHER SPORTS**

Parapente, bungee-jumping, swimming, skating, curling, helicopter flights, ice-climbing, indoor tennis and squash

Ten rental agencies deal with self-catering apartments and there is 'a good range of supermarkets, plus a good spread of *boulangerie*, *boucherie* and *pâtisserie* shops; self-catering is definitely a possibility.

Eating in and out
The 45 restaurants range from pizzerias such as L'Apri and pasta houses like La Spaghetteria, to more sophisticated establishments including Restaurant de la Bérangère, which has a Michelin star. Gourmets will also enjoy the Chalet Mounier. La Patate is good for mountain-style raclette and fondue, Les Crêpes à Gogo is singled out for its ambience and the Paellou Brasserade Grill is also well spoken of. Meilleurs Voeux (serving crêpes and pizzas) is described as having 'a fabulous log fire and a bar made from old Scotch whisky cases'.

Après-ski
Les Deux Alpes fairly teems with après-ski opportunities: Mike's Bar, near the Jandri lift, Smokey Joe's and Le Windsor are all popular haunts.

The Rodeo, at the Venosc end of town, has a bizarre mechanical bull, which inevitably attracts the wilder element of après-skiers. The Asterix Bar, in the hotel of the same name, is 'not very pretty, but has a good and friendly service'. Le Pressoir and Le Tonic are described as 'useful watering-holes'. A watering-hole of a different kind, the Tanking Centre provides a therapeutic sensory deprivation experience whereby you float in warm water in total darkness. Sensory deprivation is far from absent at the four discos of La Casa, Le Club 92, L'Avalanche and L'Opéra.

Childcare

Children under four can use the ski lifts, swimming-pool and skating rink free of charge. Among the bridges, tunnels and animal characters at the Espace Loisirs (leisure centre) there is a trampoline, a small slalom course, toboggan run, ski-biking, inner-tubing and an inflatable bob-run, with organised races most days. Qualified staff welcome children from six months to two years old at a slope-side crèche, and the Snowman's Kindergarten (La Garderie du Bonhomme de Neige) caters for two- to six-year-olds.

The ESF operates a kindergarten slope in the centre of town close to the Jandri Express and the ESI has its own kindergarten. Both ski schools offer half- or full-day courses for children over four years of age who wish to ski, snowboard or monoski. Yellow Cab Surfing has created a snow garden, Papoose Valley, which has snowboarding courses for children over four years old.

We have mixed reports of the ESF children's ski school: 'The French instructors spoke adequate English and even in the worst of the weather they took the wee souls out for at least part of the three-hour lesson. When they got cold, wet and fed up they returned to the ESF chalet to dry out and watch videos'. However, another reporter says: 'Frankly, we were not impressed with the ESF ski kindergarten. On the first day we found our four-year-old son alone in the kindergarten hut — crying.

Linked or nearby resorts

Venosc 950m (3,116ft)

This attractive village in the valley below Les Deux Alpes is well worth a visit, with its cobbled streets and three 'extremely pleasant, atmospheric and inexpensive' restaurants. This is also a good place to stay if you pre-fer the rustic charms of a 'real' village, yet still want to be able to ski. The village can be reached either by gondola or on foot (40-minutes down and a 90-minute walk back up again). You cannot ski back to the resort. More than half-a-dozen craft shops sell a range of high-quality goods.

TOURIST OFFICE
Tel 33 76 80 06 82
Fax 33 76 80 18 95

Skiing facts: **Les Deux Alpes**

TOURIST OFFICE
BP 7, F-38860 Les Deux Alpes, Dauphiné
Tel 33 76 79 22 00
Fax 33 76 79 01 38

THE RESORT
By road Calais 953km
By rail Grenoble 70km
By air Grenoble 1½ hrs, Lyon 2 hrs
Visitor beds 27,425
Transport free ski-bus

THE SKIING
Linked or nearby resorts La Grave (l),
Alpe d'Huez (n), Serre Chevalier/Briançon
(n), St-Christophe-en-Oisans (l), Venosc (l)
Longest run Mont de Lans, 10km
(red/blue)
Number of lifts 63
Total of trails/pistes 200km (62% easy,
28% intermediate, 10% difficult)
Nursery slopes 2 free lifts and 2 runs
Summer skiing mid-June to Sept, 16 lifts
covering 200 hectares of skiable glacial terrain
Snowmaking 14 hectares covered

LIFT PASSES
Area pass 870FF for 6 days (includes 1 free
day in Alpe d'Huez, Serre Chevalier, Puy-St-
Vincent or the Milky Way)
Day pass 174FF
Beginners 2 free lifts
Pensioners reduction for 60 yrs and over
Credit cards accepted yes

SKI SCHOOLS
Adults ESF, 675FF for 6 mornings (9.15am-
12.15pm), 580FF for 6 afternoons (2.30-
5pm). ESI, 9.30am-midday and 2.30-5pm,
1,150FF for 6 days
Private lessons ESF 170FF per hr, ESI
180FF per hr
Snowboarding ESF 1,050FF for 6 days, ESI
900FF for 6 days, Yellow Cab Surfing
1,200FF for 6 days, Stages Babi Pourtier
1,300FF for 6 days, Stages Snowboard Luc
Pelisson 1,200FF for 6 days
Cross-country ESF, 9.15am-12.15pm,
675FF for 6 mornings. ESI, 130FF for one
afternoon. Loipe 20km
Other courses ski-touring, monoski,
telemark, slalom
Guiding companies Altro Ski, Aventures
Verticales, ESF Bureau des Guides

CHILDREN
Lift pass 4-13 yrs, 653FF for 6 days, free
for 3 yrs and under
Ski kindergarten Le Bonhomme de Neige,
2 mths-6 yrs, 645FF for 6 days including
lunch
Ski school ESF, 6-12 yrs, 900FF for 6 days.
ESI, 13 yrs and under, 1,150FF for 6 days
Non-ski kindergarten La Crèche du Clos
des Fonds, 6mths-2 yrs, 170FF per day
including lunch

FOOD AND DRINK PRICES
Coffee 5-10FF, glass of wine 6-10FF, small
beer 12-16FF, dish of the day 40-70FF

Flaine

ALTITUDE 1600m (5,248ft)

Flaine is a wholly functional resort within easy reach of Geneva via the Autoroute Blanche. It has a surprisingly large international following of skiers, a fair proportion of which is British. Visitors come to this resort for the skiing not for the ambience which, as one reporter put it, 'simply doesn't exist'.

Apart from purists who see Flaine as an interesting example of the Bauhaus school of design, most visitors to the resort view it as an architectural disaster area created in the 1960s at the same time as Les Menuires, Chamrousse and other French resorts of its generation.

The liberal use of grey, unfinished concrete is depressing enough even when the resort is cloaked under a blanket of fresh snow. In the springtime, when the white fades and the rains come, it defies description. One

> ### ■ GOOD POINTS
>
> Large ski area, excellent family facilities, skiing convenience, short airport transfer, car-free resort, wide range of easy and intermediate runs, reliable resort-level snow, suitable for skiing on a budget, variety of off-piste skiing
>
> ### ■ BAD POINTS
>
> Ugly architecture, lack of alpine charm, limited après-ski

reporter, however, commented that: 'Compared with the area of east London where I work, Flaine is quite pretty'.

Unfortunately, the compact no-walking convenience of the original concept no longer exists for much of the village due to expansion; the original aim was to provide doorstep-skiing at affordable prices but with no regard for appearance and little for the other qualities that give the older (and more recently, the more modern) resorts their broader appeal.

Despite all this Flaine's good points outnumber the bad, making it not an entirely unattractive proposition. It benefits from having good-value accommodation, excellent nursery slopes and few queues, and from being car-free. Add to these ingredients a short transfer from Geneva Airport, and the resulting popularity with British families and budget-conscious skiers is easy to understand.

Flaine's bowl-skiing connects with the three lower and more traditional resorts of **Samoëns**, **Morillon** and **Les Carroz**, and a piste has now been established down the Combe de Gers to the charming village of **Sixt**. These areas greatly add to Flaine's skiing and replace some of its missing vital ingredients such as sheltered tree-line skiing, long runs and atmospheric mountain eating-places. Unfortunately the lift links can sometimes close down in bad weather or due to poor snow cover for several days at a time, severely limiting the extent of the skiing to the Flaine bowl alone.

On the mountain
top 2480m (8,134ft) bottom 690m (2,263ft)

Flaine is the core of the large, linked ski area of **Le Grand Massif**, which comprises around 260km of linked skiing served by 80 lifts. It divides naturally into separate segments. Flaine's own skiing is arranged around the north-facing part of its home bowl, with lifts soaring to nearly 2500m around the rim. Most of the skiing is open and unsheltered above the tree-line. The main mountain-access point from the village centre is a huge gondola up to Grandes Platières, a high and wide plateau with panoramic views. A large number of runs go from here down to the resort. Most of them are graded red (intermediate) and blue (easy) with exotic names such as Lucifer, Faust and Belzebuth.

In general, the skiing in the enclosed Flaine bowl itself is somewhat limited, and its real attraction as a destination relies on its link with the remainder of Le Grand Massif area. This is via the Grand Vans chair-lift, which, because of its exposed top-station, is usually the first to close in bad weather.

The Tête du Pré des Saix is the central point of the whole Grand Massif system. From here north-facing runs drop down steep mogul slopes towards Samoëns. Halfway down, the descent is broken by the lifts that go up a short distance to **Samoëns 1600**. Next is a further 800m drop down to **Vercland** on the outskirts of Samoëns itself; the steeper black (difficult) option goes through the trees but unfortunately it does not hold its snow well and quickly becomes patchy.

On the other side of the valley the easier pistes towards Morillon run in parallel, comprising long and gentle trails in the tree-line, with a couple of restaurants along them. There is an efficient gondola from Morillon village to Morillon Grand Massif.

The runs to Les Carroz are short but give a wide variety of tree-line trails, including some more difficult sections at the top of the reds and some good off-piste. The blue run to the village is often crowded and bare. We have received complaints that L'Airon chair-lift, which provides the best link to Flaine, is often closed; without it a long traverse or a 180m uphill walk are necessary. Access to the slopes is on Le Kédeuse gondola, which is reported to have queues in the morning.

Sixt, along the road from Samoëns, has its own small ski area and a cross-country track linking with Samoëns and Morillon. The village has now been directly linked into the Grand Massif via a new piste down the Combe de Gers. This begins with the Styx black run, which is served by its own drag-lift, and then continues with a 6km blue run. One reporter complains that narrow, plunging pitches alternate with uphill sections, 'where we encountered cross-country skiers coming towards us'. A bus connects skiers with Samoëns. The Flaine bowl in particular still has too many ancient drag-lifts with alarming take-off speeds, and reporters continue to complain that it is hard to avoid becoming airborne on them.

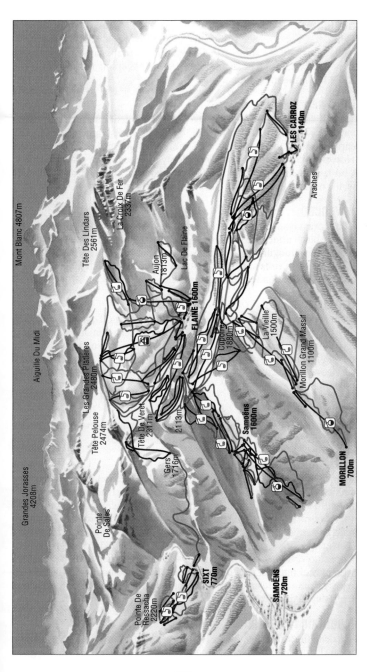

Beginners

Flaine has good novice slopes in the middle of the village. For quasi-beginners there are some wide, snaking blues to the bowl's west-facing slopes. Crystal and Serpentine are long, sweeping runs around the shoulder of the mountain.

Intermediates

The whole area is essentially designed for confident intermediates. Day-long forays into the far corners of the Grand Massif are well within the capabilities of most skiers with more than four weeks experience. However, it is important to allow plenty of time for the return journey. The Tourmaline blue from Les Grands Vans down to Le Forêt is usually well-groomed and is one of the classic runs of the resort.

Advanced

The more advanced skiing sections of the Flaine bowl are in the middle, graded black under the gondola and red to each side. The black Diamant Noir is a fun mogul slope. Unlike some other large linked areas, there are plenty of steep runs and a good variety of terrain, which makes Flaine a suitable destination for advanced skiers.

Off-piste

Flaine and the Grand Massif area have outstanding off-piste possibilities. The proximity to Mont Blanc creates its own micro-climate, and the area has a much better snow record than its altitude might suggest. The rocky terrain means that powder hunts can all too easily end on a cliff, and the services of a local guide who really knows the region are absolutely essential.

Snowboarding

The resort has its own snowboard park in the main Flaine bowl. Lessons can be taken with the International Ski School (ESI).

Ski schools and guiding

Flaine has two ski schools. We have a couple of reasonable reports of the French Ski School (ESF): 'Large class, but the instructor was extremely helpful'. However, we continue to receive disastrous criticism of the ESI ('little or no teaching; little more than two pieces of advice in 12 hours of teaching might be described as frugal'). Another reporter comments: 'Never, in 30 years of skiing, have I seen such disorganisation. Communication between the rude staff in the office and the teachers who may or may not turn up for lessons simply did not exist. My children hardly ever got the same teacher from morning to afternoon, let alone from day to day.'

Mountain restaurants

Those in the immediate Flaine vicinity are limited, especially in the Aujon area. The Blanchot is recommended, and Chalet Bissac has 'a good selection of salads, adequate loo provision, and a jolly, smiling lady at the till, so unusual for France'. La Combe, in the Morillon area, has 'terrific ambience'. Bar L'Eloge, by the Flaine gondola, has a simple choice of food and friendly service. The Oréade, at the top of La Kédeuse gondola, is recommended for its good food and large, sunny terrace. The restaurant on the Chariande piste at Samoëns has reasonable prices and an excellent view from the terrace. Le Pativerdans at Vercland, near the foot of the gondola, is reported to be good value, with English hosts who have immersed themselves in the local community. The Chalet Les Molliets is said to be cheaper than most, and the bar at the Tête du Pré des Saix sells 'the biggest and hottest hot chocolate in the resort'.

Off the mountain

The first view down into Flaine is a surprising one; it nestles in an isolated bowl where you would not expect to find any centre of habitation at all. The grey concrete matches the grey rock formation in what some would call an ugly, at best inoffensive, purpose-built village. Reporters' opinions of Flaine vary from 'no soul' and 'a ski ghetto, which does not give one the feeling of being in France' to 'a pleasant atmosphere because it is so compact'. In contrast to this grey image Flaine has recently developed a reputation as a centre for fine art. Works by Picasso, Dubuffet and Vasarely are dotted around the village streets and also housed in the resort's arts centre.

Two people-mover enclosed lifts operate day and night between the higher and lower villages. The Hameau area is served by a free bus, which runs from the chalets to the nursery slopes every 15 minutes during the day but is apparently not reliable at night.

Accommodation

Flaine Forum is the heart of the resort with the main shops, restaurants and the school meeting place. The Hotel Totem, with Picasso's statue of the same name standing outside, is the main piste-side hotel. Reporters' views range alarmingly from 'expensive with clinical, modern decor' and 'still living on its old reputation' to 'a truly grand establishment'. The food is praised by most ('quite exceptional cuisine every night' and 'very acceptable vegetarian menu for two provided with no fuss').

Les Lindars, Flaine's most famous family-orientated hotel, is expected to become a Club Aquarius this season; no deal had been signed at the time of writing, but the hotel was not accepting tour-operator contract bookings. The two-star Aujon is conveniently located. It has undergone some refurbishment and according to one regular visitor 'the standard of the half-board food has improved out of all recognition — it is now some of the best in the resort'.

Flaine Fôret, on a shelf above **Flaine Forum**, has mainly self-catering accommodation and its own shops and bars. Most of the rental apartments in the resort were bought in Spring 1995 by property giant Pierre et Vacances, and some much-needed refurbishment is expected to take place in time for the 1995–6 season. The apartments are small, even by French standards ('thank goodness we had booked an apartment for eight for the six of us'). The **Hameau de Flaine** on the mountain at 1800m is the latest development of attractive Scandinavian-style chalets inconveniently situated for the ski area. It has its own sports shop, bar, restaurant and supermarket.

Eating in and out

Chez La Jeanne is 'small and friendly with excellent pizzas and good house wine'. La Perdrix Noire has a good early-evening family menu ('brasserie and fine food in a warm atmosphere'). The rustic Chalet du Michet is one of the few original buildings in the valley; it was converted from a cow shed into an excellent restaurant specialising in fondue and raclette. La Pizzeria is ever popular, and La Trattoria has a 'pleasant, almost Italian atmosphere and good wine'.

Après-ski

Skiers who want a riotous nightlife do not holiday in France and in particular they do not holiday in Flaine. Most visitors – especially those with small children – tend to opt for quiet evenings in their apartments. A few bars provide the alternative to making your own entertainment. The Diamant Noir bar attracts the locals, the Cîmes Rock Café has pool tables and a giant video screen. The White Grouse Pub, that little piece of Scotland that is forever France, has raised its standards and is reported to have fought its way back as one of the main meeting places of the resort. The Bodega is the main disco.

Childcare

Flaine has a long-established reputation as one of the best resorts in the Alps for families with young children. Certainly it is car-free and safe, with a large central playground and good nursery slopes and it has a short airport transfer. Much of its reputation has, however, been based on the remarkable and ever-popular Hotel Les Lindars, which is entirely geared towards young children. The hotel runs its own crèche, serves organised children's meals and has an electronic baby-listening service.

> **■ OTHER SPORTS**
>
> Parapente, hang-gliding, snowmobiling, ice-driving, climbing wall, swimming

However, at the time of writing it looked as if the hotel was to be taken over by Club Aquarius. Assurances have been given that it will continue to operate along much the same lines as ever.

The Green Mouse Club (Souris Verte) at the ESI is recommended by several reporters, with staff speaking reasonable English and 'happy to accommodate children's wishes to ski or not'. The staff were also praised for 'playing with the children, rather than sticking them in front of the video'. Both the ESF Rabbit Club and the Green Mouse will collect children from their accommodation each morning and return them at the end of the day.

Skiing facts: **Flaine**

TOURIST OFFICE
F-74300 Flaine, Haute Savoie
Tel 33 50 90 80 01
Fax 33 50 90 86 26

LONDON AGENT
Erna Low Consultants, 9 Reece Mews,
London SW7 7HE
Tel 0171-584 2841
Fax 0171-589 9531

THE RESORT
By road Calais 890km
By rail Cluses 25km, frequent bus service
to resort
By air Geneva 1½ hrs
Visitor beds 5,620
Transport free ski-bus between Flaine and
Hameau de Flaine

THE SKIING
Linked or nearby resorts Les Carroz (l),
Morillon (l), Samoëns (l), Sixt (n)
Longest run Serpentine, 4.5km (blue)
Number of lifts 31 in Flaine, 80 in Grand
Massif
Total of trails/pistes 150km in Flaine
(35% easy, 50% intermediate, 15%
difficult). 260km in Grand Massif
Nursery slopes 2 slopes and 3 free lifts
Summer skiing none
Snowmaking 3km covered

LIFT PASSES
Area pass Grand Massif (covers Flaine, Les
Carroz, Morillon, Samoëns and Sixt), 760FF
for 6 days
Day pass Flaine 140FF, Grand

Massif 160FF
Beginners 4 free lifts in area and special
beginner pass at 80FF per day for adults,
65FF per day for children
Pensioners 60 yrs and over, as children
Credit cards accepted yes

SKI SCHOOLS
Adults ESF 440FF and ESI 460FF, both for 6
days (2 hrs per day)
Private lessons ESF 185FF per hr, ESI
170FF per hr
Snowboarding ESI, 695FF for 6 days (3 hrs
per day)
Cross-country ESI and ESF, prices and
times on application. Two tracks of 4km at
L'Arbaron and a 700m beginners' circuit
Other courses off-piste
Guiding companies through ski schools

CHILDREN
Lift pass 5-16 yrs, 540FF for 6 days (Grand
Massif), free for 4 yrs and under
Ski kindergarten ESF Rabbit Club, 3-12
yrs, 9am-5pm, 1,150FF for 6 days including
lunch. ESI Green Mouse Club, 4-12 yrs,
9am-5pm, 1,100FF for 6 days including
lunch
Ski school as ski kindergarten
Non-ski kindergarten Garderie des Petits
Loups, 6 mths-4 yrs, 9am-5pm, 150FF per
day, not including lunch. Nursery at hotel
Les Lindars, 3 mths-2 yrs, 9am-5pm,
245FF per day including lunch

FOOD AND DRINK PRICES
Coffee 9FF, glass of wine 7.50-14FF, small
beer 13-18FF, dish of the day 50-70FF

Linked or nearby resorts

Les Carroz 1140m (3,739ft)

Les Carroz is large and, in the view of most correspondents, more pleasing to the eye than Flaine. However, its drawback as an alternative base
is its low altitude. It spreads across a broad, sunny slope on the road to
Flaine and attracts many families and weekend visitors who use it as an
access point for this substantial ski area. The gondola and chair-lift are a
steep walk from the centre of the village but within easy reach of some
attractive, simple old hotels including Les Airelles and the Croix de
Savoie. The well-located Hotel des Belles Pistes, run by an English couple, is said to be decorated 'Cotswolds-style with little local character;
however, the chef is French and very good'. The Front de Neige is said
to cope well with the needs of small children.

Most of the self-catering accommodation is much less conveniently
placed. The cross-country skiing is good here. The bus is not included in
the lift pass, and there are only three services per day to Flaine; late-night
taxis between the two resorts are hard to find.

TOURIST OFFICE
Tel 33 50 90 00 04
Fax 33 50 90 07 00

Samoëns 720m (2,362ft)

The beautiful old town of Samoëns in the Giffre Valley has been a ski
resort since 1912 and is the only one in France to be listed as a historical
monument. It was once a thriving stone-cutting centre, and twice a week
the tourist office organises guided tours around the town's architectural
sites. In the centre of town is a botanical alpine garden with over 4,000
species of mountain plants from all around the world. Traditional-style
bars and restaurants abound in what is a resort largely undiscovered by
other nationalities, in particular the British. The hotels Neige et Roc, Les
Sept Monts and Les Drugères are recommended. One reporter speaks
highly of Le Pierrot Gourmet restaurant.

Samoëns has its own ski school, a crèche for children from six
months old, and a ski kindergarten for children aged three to six years.
It also has a cross-country ski school.

TOURIST OFFICE
Tel 33 50 34 40 28
Fax 33 50 34 95 82

Megève

Megève remains one of the two most fashionable resorts in the French Alps (the other is Courchevel 1850) and, despite major growth in recent years, it still manages to retain the charm and elegance that made it France's smartest resort in the early days of skiing. In 1914 Baroness de Rothschild built the Palace Hotel Mont d'Arbois, which was to become the cornerstone of the resort during the first few years. Later on, Megève boasted that, at the height of the season, it was home to more crowned heads of state than any other ski resort in Europe.

■ GOOD POINTS

Long and easy runs, wide range of activities for non-skiers, large choice of restaurants, ideal for beginners and children, lively après-ski, short airport transfer, tree-level skiing, attractive village centre

■ BAD POINTS

Lack of skiing for experts, low altitude, unreliable resort-level snow, heavy traffic outside pedestrian area

Today, more modestly, royalty extends no further than the Saudi royal family, who own a large chalet above the town at Rochebrune. However, Megève is still unsurpassed throughout the French Alps in both atmosphere and après-ski. The continued patronage of families like the Rothschilds, Benettons, Taittingers and Citroëns has much to do with the resort's upmarket image, but its exclusivity is largely due to keeping prices high in the wide choice of restaurants and nightclubs.

However, most of Megève's visitors are families; 70 per cent of them are well-heeled French, who choose to stay here because of the unique mixture of extensive, yet mainly easy, skiing combined with the possibility of day-trips to the Chamonix Valley and to a collection of small, separate resorts all on the same lift pass.

The rest of Megève's clientèle is made up of non-skiers, who wear designer creations never likely to touch the snow. They spend their days shopping in town, taking health treatments at one of the many 'beauty farms', commuting by centrally-heated snow cat to the mountain top for gourmet lunches, and frequenting the casino or one of the numerous nightclubs after dark.

The village is built around a fine medieval church and carefully restored old buildings. The streets are colourful with designer boutiques and 32 brightly painted sleighs, owned and driven by the local farmers out of season. The disadvantage is that 'you have to watch where you are treading as the streets are littered with horse manure'. There are no noticeable architectural eyesores, and recent additions have been built in a sympathetic chalet-style.

On the mountain
top 2350m (7,708ft) bottom 850m (2,788ft)

The skiing takes place on pistes as smooth and well-groomed as their skiers. Two of the three areas, **Mont d'Arbois** and **Rochebrune**, are connected at their bases by cable car. Mont d'Arbois is the most extensive and it in turn is accessed by separate gondolas from La Princesse outside **Combloux**, **Le Bettex** above St-Gervais, and **St-Nicolas-de-Véroce**. The skiing around Mont d'Arbois is predominantly on the gentle side, although there are some more challenging runs higher up on Mont Joux.

The **Rochebrune** area was, until recently, served by Megève's oldest cable car, built in 1933, which begins on the outskirts of town, and the gondola from the centre. However, we are assured that it will be replaced by a swift 12-person gondola this season. Rochebrune is also connected to Mont d'Arbois by cable car. The area offers arguably the most attractive runs in delightful tree-lined settings. Reporters also claim that it is less crowded than Mont d'Arbois.

Megève's third skiing area is **Le Jaillet**, completely self-contained and reached by gondola only after a lengthy walk or ski-bus ride from the middle of town. Its runs are mainly gentle but do not hold their snow well.

Beginners

The nursery slopes at Mont d'Arbois are easily accessible by cable car or ski-bus. The resort also abounds in green (beginner) and gentle blue (easy) runs for the next stage of learning. From Mont Joux, long easy runs descend to Les Communailles near Le Bettex, with drag-lifts back up to the ridge. The runs into Megève itself are mostly wide and easy, including a long green piste. There is a drag-lift amidst the trees at the top-station of Jaillet for novices, and the runs in this area are both gentle and pleasant, mainly suited to beginners and early intermediates.

Intermediates

The scope of skiing at Mont d'Arbois has been greatly increased by the chair-lift, rising over an open slope of more than 30 degrees in places, to the high point of the area at 2350m. A choice of long and fairly gentle red (intermediate) runs takes you down into the attractive little village of St-Nicolas-de-Véroce. The large ski area is well suited to intermediates, although lack of snow cover makes the season a short one.

Advanced

Megève is not recommended for advanced skiers although this is the most pleasant resort in the Mont Blanc area in which to base yourself to enjoy the 13 resorts (including **Chamonix** and **Argentière**) covered by the Mont Blanc lift pass. Mont Joux, the next peak along from Mont d'Arbois, on the ridge which climbs towards Mont Joly, has some of the

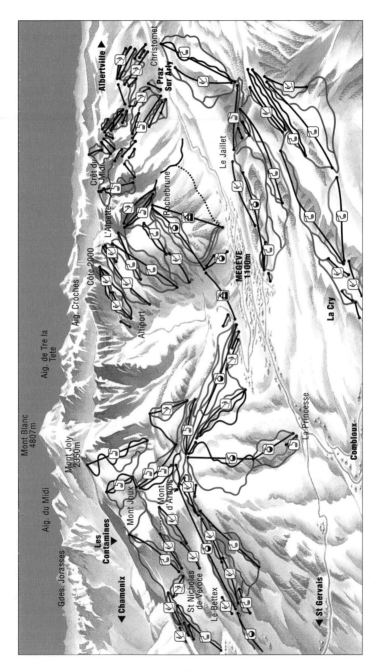

Mont Blanc 4807m
Aig. du Midi
Gdes. Jorasses
Aig. de Tre la Tete
Aig. Croches
Côte 2000
Mont Joly 2350m
Les Contamines
▲ Chamonix
Mont Joux
Mont d'Arbois
St Nicholas de Veroce
Le Bettex
▲ St Gervais
Comblouz
La Princesse
La Cry
MEGÈVE 1100m
Le Jaillet
Rochebrune
L'Alpette
Crêt du Midi
Altiport
Christomet
Praz Sur Arly
▲ Albertville

steeper slopes around its bowl. Those on the north-facing La Princesse side of the mountain are wooded and more challenging than most in the area, but the black (difficult) grading is not altogether justified.

Off-piste
The area through the trees towards La Princesse provides excellent powder skiing after a fresh snowfall, as does Côte 2000. The off-piste is skied far less than in most of the other Mont Blanc resorts and is therefore likely to remain untracked for much longer. You can also ski from the top of Mont Joly, after a 20-minute uphill walk, over to the resort of **Les Contamines**.

Snowboarding
Both the French (ESF) and International (ESI) ski schools offer group courses for all standards of snowboarder. The ESF also runs special snowboarding classes for children.

Ski schools and guiding
Megève's ski schools have fine reputations, particularly for beginners who progress speedily from the nursery areas to the rest of the resort's long and flattering slopes. The resort has its own guiding company, Bureau des Guides de Megève, which is heartily recommended. It employs 16 mountain guides who take skiers off-piste and organise ski-tours.

Mountain restaurants
Megève certainly has no shortage of lunch venues. Some 30 restaurants in the ski area (there is a special walker/cross-country skier lift map, which clearly marks most of them) add to the resort's gourmet attraction. Reporters do, however, note that mountain eating is expensive. L'Alpette, on the crest of the same name, offers a unique view of the surrounding area. A snow cat takes non-skiers from the top of the Rochebrune gondola up to the restaurant for lunch at regular intervals. L'Auberge Grenand, also in the Rochebrune area towards **Praz-sur-Arly**, offers typically French cuisine and local specialities. La Côte 2000 restaurant is recommended for 'fresh, well-cooked food'. Lower down at Rochebrune, the self-service La Caboche is good value by local standards.

Off the mountain
Megève has become one of France's largest ski towns, with a mass of suburbs stretching out in all directions. The attractive medieval heart is made up of a traffic-free main square with four streets branching off it, all teeming with an 'abundance of fur coats and matching dogs'. Reporters praise the town as 'a window-shopper's paradise'; this includes jewellers, perfumeries, delicatessen, antique shops, chocolate-makers, children's clothing shops, designer boutiques and popular fashion outlets like Poivre Blanc and Benetton, as well as sports equipment retailers.

However, traffic is a major problem here, particularly during the main shopping hours of between 4 and 7pm; a main road runs through the town, although the actual centre is bypassed. Ski-buses link the mid-town with the lifts, and coaches run to other nearby resorts covered on the Mont Blanc lift pass. Megève is one of the easiest ski resorts to reach. Not only is it close to Geneva (70km) but it also has two motorail termini close by at Sallanches and at St-Gervais.

Accommodation

Megève has a wide range of more than 50 hotels, as well as sumptuous and more utilitarian private chalets. The standard of its six four-stars and some of its 15 three-stars is outstanding. The Parc des Loges has *art deco* rooms, each with its own fire-place. The Chalet du Mont d'Arbois is owned by Baron Edmond de Rothschild and is located some distance from the town near the Mont d'Arbois cable car. Hotel Mont Blanc is the town's showpiece. At the bottom of La Princesse ski area is the four-star Hotel Princesse de Megève,

> **■ OTHER SPORTS**
> Parapente, hang-gliding, skating, curling, indoor tennis, climbing wall, swimming, ice climbing, snowmobiling, snow-shoeing, winter walks

which has only 11 rooms. At the top of Mont d'Arbois and reached by gondola is L'Igloo, again with only 11 rooms.

Les Fermes de Marie is a smart, modern hotel built in traditional style with a fitness room and swimming-pool. Much recommended in the three-star category is the charming Fer à Cheval, a central chalet-style hotel, which has all the comforts of a four-star but without the prices to match. On the other side of town, Au Coin de Feu is recommended and La Chauminé is a good-value place to stay.

Eating in and out

A reporter comments on the 'extensive quantity and variety of eating places to suit all budgets'. This is certainly true; Megève has more than 70 restaurants and is, along with Courchevel 1850, one of the gourmet dining resorts of the French Alps. However, it also offers a good choice of less exotic places. The Chamois is a lively bistro with good local white wines and fondues. At the Piano à Bretelles you can eat and dance the night away. Good-value restaurants include Les Griottes, which has à la carte specialities, and the Michel Gaudin, which combines Mediterranean and alpine cooking. The Sapinière is an unpretentious bistro with some of the best food in town and comes highly recommended. La Maisonette is also popular.

At the top of the range, the Hotel Mont Blanc's Les Enfants Terribles, with interior design by Jean Cocteau, has delicious but expensive food. La Rotonde serves Lyonnais cuisine in 1930s surroundings. The Chalet du Mont d'Arbois used to be the Rothschild family home and is now a high-quality restaurant with a particularly interesting wine cellar. Les Fermes de Marie offers good Savoyard cooking, and Le Fer à Cheval serves a fine dinner but is also recommended for its English breakfast.

Après-ski

Après-ski is taken almost more seriously here than the skiing and the choice of venues is enormous, ranging from the simplest of bars to the most exotic of nightspots. Le Prieuré and the Milady are recommended for tea and cakes at 5pm. The Milady has 'delectable apple tart'. Le Chamois is a traditional place with a warm atmosphere. The Village Rock Café is popular with teenagers.

Later on, the nightlife is not cheap and largely revolves around Megève's nine nightclubs and piano bars. Club de Jazz des 5 Rues is one of the most popular evening venues, set in cosy surroundings complete with open fire; during the season it attracts some of the big international names in jazz. Les Enfants Terribles is a popular bar in the heart of the village. The most popular nightclubs include L'Esquinade, which is also a casino with Sacha Distel and Charles Aznavour among its regulars. Le Rols Club is the place for those who like their evening entertainment on the decadent side. The Glamour is half piano-bar and half disco. Les Caves de Megève has a young atmosphere. The Pallas and Harri's bar keep going until dawn.

Childcare

Megève is extremely well served with facilities for children. It has four ski kindergarten, each one conveniently placed next to a main lift station. The non-ski kindergarten, Meg'Loisirs, is housed in a well-equipped two-storey building next to the Palais de Sports.

Linked or nearby resorts

Les Contamines-Montjoie 1164m (3,818ft)

This unspoilt Savoyard village is near the head of the narrow Montjoie Valley, just over the hill from Megève. It has a keen following, despite the fact that the whole set-up is badly planned: the long village is on one side of the river and the ski area on the other, and **Le Lay** base-station is a long uphill walk from the centre. Prices are, on the whole, below average for this area of France, and the accommodation is modest.

The east-facing bowl, which makes up the ski area, tends to hold its snow well and offers a good alternative when neighbouring resorts like Megève have none. Two efficient gondolas take skiers up to a plateau at 1500m where the sole gondola can cause a bottleneck to Le Signal and the start of the main skiing. Reporters recommend the Pontet alternative to the Auberge-du-Télé lift, which is quieter as it is further down the valley. There is a small nursery lift at Le Signal at 1900m, which can often be busy when snow is poor lower down.

There is little challenging skiing, although we have experienced some excellent and virtually untouched powder all over the area after a fresh snowfall. On-piste, the higher runs towards Mont Joly are steeper, test-

Skiing facts: **Megève**

TOURIST OFFICE
BP 24, F-74120 Megève, Haute Savoie
Tel 33 50 21 27 28
Fax 33 50 93 03 09

THE RESORT
By road Calais 890km
By rail Sallanches 12km, regular bus service to resort
By air Geneva $1\frac{1}{2}$ hrs
Visitor beds 13,860
Transport free ski-bus with lift pass (links centre with access lifts). Coach shuttles run between the 13 ski resorts in the Mont Blanc region

THE SKIING
Linked or nearby resorts Chamonix (n), Combloux (l), Flumet (n), Le Bettex (l), Les Contamines (n), Les Saisies (n), Nôtre-Dame-de-Bellecombe (n), Praz-sur-Arly (n), St-Gervais (l), St-Nicolas-de-Véroce (l)
Longest run Milloz, 3.6km (red)
Number of lifts 82 in Megève, 190 in Mont Blanc ski area
Total of trails/pistes 300km in Megève (49% easy, 36% intermediate, 15% difficult). 700km in Mont Blanc ski area
Nursery slopes 3 runs and 3 lifts
Summer skiing none
Snowmaking 3 hectares covered

LIFT PASSES
Area pass Mont Blanc (covers 13 resorts including Chamonix and Argentière and a free day at Courmayeur), 900FF for 6 days
Day pass Megève only 148FF, Evasion Mont Blanc (covers Megève, St-Gervais, St-Nicolas-de-Véroce, Combloux) 155FF
Beginners single lift tickets available
Credit cards accepted yes

SKI SCHOOLS
Adults ESF (5 centres), 9.30-11.30am and 3-5pm, 750FF for 6 days. ESI, 10am-midday, 550FF for 6 half-days
Private lessons ESF 170FF, ESI 185FF, both per hr
Pensioners 60 yrs and over, as children
Snowboarding ESF 780FF, ESI 650-780FF, both 1-3pm for 6 half-days
Cross-country ESF (Mont d'Arbois), times and prices as regular ski school. Loipe 75km in Megève area
Other courses telemark, monoski, race training, artistic/acrobatic skiing, off-piste, heli-skiing
Guiding companies Bureau des Guides de Megève, and through ESI

CHILDREN
Lift pass Evasion Mont Blanc, 12 yrs and over, 540-634FF for 6 days. Skipass Mont Blanc, 12 yrs and over, 580-645FF for 6 days. Free for 4 yrs and under with pass required only on cable cars
Ski kindergarten Alpage, 3-6 yrs, 9.15am-5.30pm, 365FF per day. Princesse, 3-6 yrs, 9am-5pm, 250FF per day. Caboche, 3-10 yrs, 9am-5.30pm, 275FF per day. (All prices include lunch). ESI, as regular ski school
Ski school ESF, 5-12 yrs, 9.30-11.30am and 3-5pm, 690FF for 6 days. ESI, 5-12 yrs, 10am-midday and 3-5pm, 850FF for 6 days. ESI Club 7 (maximum of 7 children), 1-3pm, 780FF for 5 days
Non-ski kindergarten Meg'Loisirs, 1-6 yrs, 8am-6pm, 170FF per day including lunch

FOOD AND DRINK PRICES
Coffee 8.50FF, glass of wine 10-14FF, small beer 16-21FF, dish of the day 61FF

ing blacks, which will keep good skiers occupied.

The village runs along a single street and has an old church, old-fashioned hotels and a few shops and cafés. The best location is on the east side of the river near the gondola.

TOURIST OFFICE
Tel 33 50 47 01 58
Fax 33 50 47 09 54

St-Gervais Mont Blanc 850m (2,788ft)

As a spa, St-Gervais has attracted tourists since 1806. The town is an informal, if busy, one ('full of traffic, even during the night') on two sides of a river gorge. It is popular with families wanting a cheaper alternative to Megève. A reporter recommends it as an ideal base for visiting other resorts in France, Italy and Switzerland. Nearby, **Le Bettex** is a quieter village with a few comfortable hotels and some cross-country skiing.

The main ski area of St-Gervais is on the slopes of Mont d'Arbois and is linked with that of Megève. It is accessed by a fast, 20-person gondola from the edge of the resort to Le Bettex at 1400m. The second stage goes up to what is known on this side of the mountain as St-Gervais 1850. This is a popular and often crowded entrance to Megève's ski area. Skiing on the Mont Blanc side of St-Gervais is served by the Tramway funicular, which climbs slowly to the Col de Voza at 1653m, where it links with the skiing above **Les Houches**. The only run back to St-Gervais is off-piste and sometimes unskiable.

St-Gervais has three nursery-slope lifts and its own kindergarten, which takes children between six months and six years old. The ESF St-Gervais and ESI at Le Bettex both teach snowboarding, monoskiing, telemark, slalom and off-piste, as well as the usual group classes. There is also a local guiding organisation, St-Gervais Val Montjoie Mountain Guides.

Hotels here include the Carlina with a swimming-pool, the Val d'Este, L'Adret (without a restaurant) and the Edelweiss. A reporter recommends the Regina with its simple rooms, reasonable prices and friendly staff. At Le Bettex, the quiet Arbois-Bettex has a heated outdoor swimming-pool, and the Flèche d'Or is also recommended. Hotel-Restaurant L'Igloo and the Terminus in Le Fayet both have good reputations for their cuisine.

St-Gervais has a moderate range of restaurants with three of particularly good value: L'Eventail and the Dômes de Miage, plus L'Eterle pizzeria. Le Four and Le Robinson are popular eating places serving a variety of local specialities. La Tanière and La Chalette at Le Fayet are traditional. Après-ski is said to be 'extremely limited'. The only disco is La Nuit des Temps, although the Chardon Bleu restaurant in Le Fayet has a dance floor.

TOURIST OFFICE
Tel 33 50 78 22 43
Fax 33 50 47 76 08

La Plagne

ALTITUDE 1250m (4,100ft)-2100m (6,889ft)

It may be hard to imagine it today but in 1960 the huge snow bowl above the town of Aime in the Tarentaise Valley was a natural mountain wilderness. Thirty-five years later, it is the heart of the ten-village complex that makes up the resort of La Plagne. Ski convenience is so superior that it regularly heads the popularity charts in the French domestic market. For this, the world can thank the then Mayor of Aime, Dr Borrione, who noticed both that the area was a developer's dream waiting to happen and that the Tarentaise was becoming depopulated at an alarming rate as young people left for the cities. When he formed an association with three neighbouring towns to build **Plagne Centre** on their joint common land, his prime purpose was to provide jobs. Such was his success that the

■ GOOD POINTS

Huge integrated ski area, convenient facilities for skiers of all levels, extensive off-piste skiing, choice of centres, geared to family skiing, uncongested roads

■ BAD POINTS

Limited hotel accommodation, lack of challenging pistes, shortage of non-skiing activities, restricted nightlife

building was still going on 20 years later. The original architect was the celebrated skier, Emile Allais, who was employed to design the layout of the slopes.

La Plagne's six high villages lie in this central area, at altitudes ranging from 1800m to 2100m. In the order in which they were built, they are **Plagne Centre** (1961–2), **Aime La Plagne** (1969–70), **Plagne Villages/Plagne Soleil** (1971), **Bellecôte** (1974), **Belle Plagne** (1980) and **Plagne 1800** (1981). Its four low villages lie on different access roads in far-flung parts of the mountain but all are connected by lift with the central complex.

Although the farming village of **Montchavin** was adapted to become a satellite ski resort in 1972, the smell of manure from winter cowsheds still lingers in the air. In 1995 the opening of two chair-lifts, the four-seater Dos Rond and the innovative six-seater Pierre Blanches, to replace three ancient drag-lifts, revolutionised its accessibility. It has a gondola link to neighbouring **Les Coches**, a modern ski complex with its own wooded slopes that opened in 1981.

Champagny-en-Vanoise, at the base of the back of the mountain (south-facing), is a series of hamlets in a quiet valley linked to the ski area by an efficient gondola. **Plagne Montalbert** and its satellite holiday centre at **Longefoy** have inferior snow conditions on west-facing slopes in the immediate vicinity and less convenient connections into the main bowl.

On the mountain
top 3250m (10,660ft) bottom 1250m (4,100ft)

La Plagne represents the ultimate in ski-in ski-out convenience. To point your skis in any direction from the nexus in Plagne Centre is to lock into the network of lifts on the shallow gradients of La Grande Rochette, Les Verdons and Le Biolley. The Bellecôte gondola provides the most efficient connection with Roche de Mio, a steeper mountain with more challenging terrain. It, in its turn, is the gateway to the lift to the Bellecôte Glacier, the highest point in the resort.

The Montchavin/Les Coches area is connected to the central arena through Arpette, a direct quad-chair ride from Bellecôte. The predominantly wooded Plagne Montalbert-Longefoy pistes lie the other side of the resort below Aime La Plagne. Access to Champagny-en-Vanoise is via Les Verdons, the midway point on the rim of the main bowl, or **Roche de Mio**.

With over 100 lifts catering for 114,000 skiers per hour, La Plagne has few queues in good weather, but the links to the outlying areas close down rapidly as soon as the storms move in, causing congestion in the centre.

■ **WHAT'S NEW**

Chalet/Hotel Les Montagnettes in Belle Plagne

3 drags replaced by 2 chairs in Montchavin/Les Coches

Additional snow-cannon at Montchavin/Les Coches

Beginners' lift at Champagny

Child's lift pass rate now extended to under 16 yrs

Beginners
With the exception of Champagny-en-Vanoise, all parts of the mountain have extensive beginner slopes. Those in the other three low-altitude villages gain in visibility by being below the tree-line, but this is balanced by less reliable snow conditions, especially in spring when the slopes are icy in the morning. Aesthetics aside, there can be no more encouraging place to learn to ski than La Plagne's central area in fine weather. The pistes on either side of the Arpette ridge above Bellecôte offer gradients so gentle that even the most fearful novice should gain in confidence while the web of blue (easy) runs between Belle Plagne and Plagne Centre makes for a natural second-week progression.

Intermediates
As befits a state-of-the-art ski area, La Plagne offers most to skiers dedicated to racking up kilometres. This can be done most readily on the red (intermediate) runs on the eastern side of the bowl above Aime La Plagne. However, Roche de Mio has more varied terrain, with the run back to Belle Plagne via a long tunnel particularly recommended. An adventurous alternative is the Crozats piste down to **Les Bauches 1800**, which has a link back to the main circus via two chair-lifts. The summer ski drag-lifts at the top of the glacier are not usually open in winter, but La Combe and Le Chiaupe runs to the Bellecôte gondola base-station hold no terrors for committed motorway cruisers.

Enterprising intermediates will enjoy the exhilarating Mont de la

Guerre run from Les Verdons to Champagny-en-Vanoise, but check conditions first because the descent is extremely rocky when snow is sparse. The same applies to the more wooded route from the Roche de Mio, via Les Borseliers.

Advanced

In the main, glaciers are not known for steep skiing, but La Plagne's is one of the exceptions. The disadvantage is the 45-minute trek to the top from the centre of the resort. However, once in place advanced skiers will find plenty to test them on the Bellecôte and especially Les Rochu runs to the bottom of the Chalet du Bellecôte chair. The other steep area is off Le Biolley ridge above **Aime La Plagne**. When conditions are good (which they often are not) the Morbleu piste is a compellingly direct drop to Le Fornelet cross-country area, with return access via the Coqs chair. On the east-facing side of the ridge, the Emile Allais descent to the bottom of the outlying Charmettes chair at the side of the Olympic bob-run is the longest black (difficult) run in the resort.

Off-piste

If La Plagne is not a favourite among dedicated powder skiers, this is more because of lack of ambience than lack of opportunity. As with the expert pistes, the best areas are on the fringes of the resort, with the long sweeping descent from the top of the glacier down to Les Bauches high on most people's list. From here, the choice lies between an easy blue piste to Montchavin, a return to Arpette via the Bauches chair or, more dramatically, an itinerary down to **Peisey-Nancroix** in the adjacent valley.

The second prime off-piste area lies on the western slopes of Le Biolley, especially towards the end of the season when spring snow is at its best. The back of the Bellecôte Glacier offers the demanding Col du Nant run into the remote valley of **Champagny-le-Haut**, followed by a return to Champagny-en-Vanoise by shuttle-bus. The woods above Montchavin and Les Coches provide exciting powder skiing in the trees, but access is often restricted, at least as far as downtown La Plagne is concerned, by the closure of the link through Arpette.

Snowboarding

The French Ski School (ESF), Oxygène and Elpro offer tuition, both privately and in groups, but the resort has no special facilities for snowboarders. On powder mornings, the wide open spaces between the network of groomed runs in the central bowl offer exhaustive opportunities for practice.

Ski schools and guiding

Clients have a choice between the ESF, which has eight offices spread throughout the resort, Oxygène and Elpro. The numbers are so great that the ESF has been able to introduce six-day teenage ski classes for greater peer-group pleasure. It also has six-day guided off-piste courses for alpine and cross-country skiers and snowboarders in La Plagne and the surrounding outposts of the Tarentaise Valley.

Mountain restaurants

In an area that is not known for its mountain restaurants, there are two outstanding choices. The Au Bon Vieux Temps, just below Aime La Plagne, is recommended for its sunny terrace, traditional Savoyard dishes and efficient service. The Petit Chaperon Rouge, just above Plagne 1800, has equally good food and waitress-service, and on a snowy day, is the wiser choice because of its open fires. The Lincoln pub in **Plagne Soleil** serves generous portions and English beer, while the self-service restaurant at the Roche de Mio scores for its fast food (the chips with everything variety). The restaurant at Les Bauches is a sun-trap with reasonable self-service food. Good value is represented by the Dou au Praz above Plagne Villages (its varied menu features a popular *plat du jour*), and the Crêperie at the top of the Champagny gondola.

Off the mountain

La Plagne's success lies in its diversity, which reinforces the conviction that whatever visitors want, they will be sure to find it somewhere. As far as modern architecture is concerned, later is better: Belle Plagne's attractive village centre, with its integrated arcs of apartment buildings, is a fine example of imaginative design, while the low-rise wood-clad complexes at Plagne 1800 and Plagne Villages are inspired by Savoyard tradition. These are a far cry from the monolithic 'battleship' at Aime La Plagne or the square slabs at Plagne Centre. Some British visitors like Bellecôte's semi-circle of high-rise reddish blocks, but Belle Plagne is the firm favourite. Inevitably, the complexities of the area are confusing at first; this may explain why regulars prefer to book the same apartment in the same block every year rather than take a chance on unknown territory.

> ### ■ OTHER SPORTS
> Snowmobiling, snow-shoeing, night-skiing, parapente, swimming, skating, bob-rafting, taxi-bob, Olympic bob-sleigh run, squash, hang-gliding, paragliding, climbing wall

All ten villages are self-sufficient, with their own selection of shops, bars and restaurants. The six high villages are connected by bus or covered lifts from 8am to 1am. As its name suggests, Plagne Centre has the lion's share of essential services, banks, post office, police and doctors, in the environs of its bleak subterranean commercial precinct. Aesthetic it is not but it scores highly for convenience as does Bellecôte, which also has banks and a post office.

Accommodation

Of La Plagne's 45,000 beds, two-thirds are in the high-altitude villages and one-third in the satellites down the valley. Only eight per cent of all accommodation is in hotels, therefore the vast majority of visitors opt for self-catering apartments. Many are owned by Maeva or Pierre et Vacances, which means that they are studio-style rabbit hutches with bunks in the passage and sofas that convert into beds in the only living area; the French do not mind this but the British do. It is best to remember this when deciding how many apartments your group needs. As with the architecture, newer tends to be better (and more spacious), which gives the edge to Plagne Soleil and 1800.

The recently opened Chalet/Hotel Les Montagnettes in **Belle Plagne** represents a welcome wind of change with comfortable six- to eight-person apartments and up to 12-person chalets. Built out of natural stone and wood they can be rented for self-catering or with full hotel services.

Eating in and out

Gourmet dining is guaranteed in La Soupe au Schuss in Aime La Plagne, an expensive restaurant serving Périgordian regional specialities. Alain Cressend's Le Matafan in **Belle Plagne** stays closer to home, with a range of medium-priced Savoyard dishes including raclette and fondue. Le Loup Garou, a short sleigh ride (or walk) down the path from **Plagne Centre** to 1800, serves similar dishes in a festive atmosphere. The Cheyenne Café in Belle Plagne provides a cheap, cheerful and substantial mixture of Tex-Mex and French. All the villages have supermarkets for the self-catering brigades, but there is a shortage of specialist food shops.

Après-ski

By comparison with its Tarentaise neighbours, Val d'Isère and Courchevel, La Plagne's nightlife is decidedly low profile, with such clubs as there are confined to Centre and Bellecôte. The current favourites in Centre are the King Café, which has live music most nights, and Le Must disco. The Jet 73 disco in Bellecôte is also popular. The Hotel Eldorador often has jazz groups playing until 10pm, followed by a disco in the bar. Mat's, under the same ownership as Le Matafan, is a faithful re-creation of a British pub, making it a winner among Brits staying in Belle Plagne. Currently, the favourite watering hole in Bellecôte is the Showtime Café, while the Lincoln is the winner in Plagne Soleil.

The most exhilarating non-skiing activity in La Plagne is the Olympic bob-run, which is open to the public whenever conditions permit. The softer option is the Bob-Raft, a four-man foam-rubber cocoon that hurtles down in gravity-propelled mode in 90 seconds at a cost of 160FF per person. The Taxi-Bob is the more genuine experience, with two rookies paying 430FF each to be sandwiched between a professional driver and a brakeman for a breathtaking 50-second descent at speeds of up to 105km an hour.

For those with energy to spare after skiing, the Winform fitness centre in Belle Plagne has a 10-pin bowling alley and an electric golf clinic as well as a gym, sauna and Turkish bath. Bellecôte has an ice rink and a swimming-pool and there are cinemas in Plagne Centre, Aime La Plagne and Bellecôte.

Childcare

The ESF has learn-to-ski programmes for children aged three to seven years in specially designed snow gardens in several of the villages. The Montchavin/Les Coches nursery has a mixed programme of skiing and other learning activities for children aged three years and upwards.

La Plagne has ten nurseries where children aged 18 months to 6 years are looked after for a half-day or whole day, with meals if required. Hotel Eldorador has a children's mini club from 9am to 5pm, and babysitting by arrangement in the evening. The nurseries in Montchavin/Les Coches, Belle Plagne and Plagne Centre accept children from 9 or 18 months.

Skiing facts: **La Plagne**

TOURIST OFFICE
Le Chalet, BP 62, F-73214, Aime Cedex
Tel 33 79 09 79 79
Fax 33 79 09 70 10

UK Agent:
Erna Low, 9 Reece Mews, London SW7 3HE
Tel 0171-584 2841
Fax 0171-589 9531

THE RESORT
By road Calais 930km
By rail Aime 18km
By air Lyon or Geneva 3 hrs
Visitor beds 45,000
Transport inter-resort link by télébus, télémetro and télécabine (15FF return). Free ski-bus between Plagne 1800, Centre and Bellecôte

THE SKIING
Linked or nearby resorts Les Arcs (n), Peisey (n), Vallandry (n), Trois Vallées (n), Val d'Isère (n), Tignes (n)
Longest run Roche de Mio to Montchavin, 10km (red)
Number of lifts 113
Total of trails/pistes 210km (66% easy, 28% intermediate, 6% difficult)
Nursery slopes 1 lift in each centre
Summer skiing 4 lifts and 2 runs on Bellecôte Glacier open July and August
Snowmaking 3km covered in Montchavin, also at Belle Plagne

LIFT PASSES
Area pass 940FF for 6 days (covers Les Arcs and 1 day in L'Espace Killy or Trois Vallées)
Day pass 205FF
Beginners free lift in each centre
Pensioners 705FF for 60 yrs and over

Credit cards accepted yes

SKI SCHOOLS
Adults ESF in all centres, 5-6 hrs per day, 710-940FF for 6 days. Oxygène at La Plagne Centre, Elpro at Belle Plange, details on request
Private lessons 150-180FF per hr
Snowboarding ESF in all centres, 1,300-1,450FF for 6-day Multiglisse course including equipment. Oxygène at La Plagne Centre, Elpro at Belle Plagne, details on request
Cross-country ESF group and private lessons as regular ski school. Loipe 79km in area
Other courses off-piste, speed skiing, ski-touring, teenager group lessons (including lift pass), freestyle, heli-skiing, monoski, disabled skiing
Guiding companies through ESF

CHILDREN
Lift pass 7-16 yrs, 705FF for 6 days, free for 6 yrs and under
Ski kindergarten in all 10 villages, times, prices and ages vary, example: ESF Belle Plagne, 3 yrs and over, 1,175FF for 6 days including lunch
Ski school ESF all centres, 6-16 yrs, times as adults, 1,200-1,300FF for 6 days including lunch. Oxygène at La Plagne Centre, Elpro at Belle Plagne, details on request
Non-ski kindergarten in all 10 villages, times, prices and ages vary, example: ESF Belle Plagne, 18 mths-6 yrs, 1,070FF for 6 days including lunch

FOOD AND DRINK PRICES
Coffee 6-7FF, glass of wine 10FF, small beer 10-12FF, dish of the day 60FF

Portes du Soleil

ALTITUDE Avoriaz 1800m (5,904ft), Champéry 1055m (3,460ft), Châtel 1200m (3,936ft), Morzine 1000m (3,280ft)

Les Portes du Soleil is one of Europe's three largest ski areas. It straddles the French-Swiss border close to Geneva and is an uneasy marketing consortium of a baker's dozen of ski villages; these range from large, internationally recognised resorts to the tiniest of unspoilt hamlets.

The published statistics talk about 650km of piste served by 228 lifts, a well-linked circus covering vast tracts of land bordered by Lac Léman; the reality is that Les Portes du Soleil consists of a series of naturally separate ski areas. Most are joined by awkward and often confusing mountain links, while a few like **St-Jean d'Aulps/La Grande Terche** and **Abondance** are entirely independent resorts, which include themselves in the association for promotional reasons.

While it is possible to complete a circuit of the main resorts in one day, this actually involves limited enjoyable skiing and a considerable amount of time spent on lifts and in lift queues. To explore the region fully you need four weeks, at least two different bases and a car.

Les Portes du Soleil might be considered one of Europe's greatest overall ski areas were it not for one major fault: it is far too low. With a top height of only 2350m and the villages mostly below 1200m, snow cover is by no means guaranteed at any stage of the season, and the links are liable to rupture at any time. Out of all 13 resorts only **Avoriaz** can be recommended as a snow-sure base and, when cover is poor or non-existent elsewhere, the overcrowding here becomes a complete misery. However, keen skiers will want to base themselves at this end of the circuit, where the slopes are far more challenging.

Sign-posting has been vastly improved, as has the overall Portes du Soleil piste map; it indicates the links from area to area, as well as a rather over-optimistic figure for the suggested time it takes. Skiers who want to explore more than the main circuit still, infuriatingly, have to obtain separate piste maps on arrival in each resort. Seven hundred slope-markers should tell you where you are, the difficulty of the run and where it is taking you.

When the snow is good there are few better playgrounds in Europe for intermediate skiers who enjoy fast cruising and want to feel that they

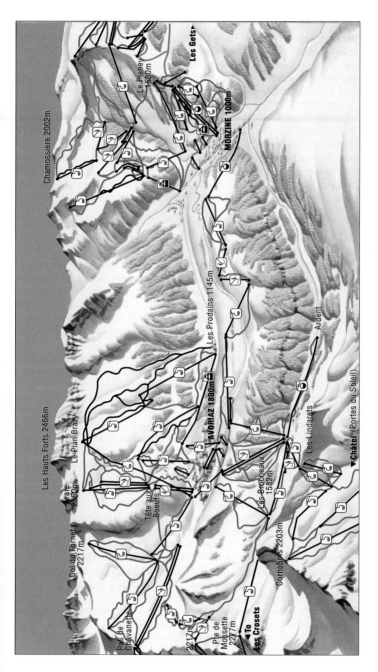

are actually going somewhere each day. There are no border controls, but skiers are advised to carry passports as well as two sets of currency; both countries accept both types of franc but not always at an advantageous rate. Customs controls do exist with border patrols on the snow, and in the countryside where smuggling is a centuries-old profession, we have heard tales of rucksacked skiers being chased by excise men.

Les Portes du Soleil takes its name from a 2000m col, which separates the French Haute Savoie from the Swiss Valais above the small Swiss resort of **Les Crosets**. Much credit is due to Jean Vuarnet (founder of Avoriaz) in establishing the mainly successful *entente cordiale* between the two 'tribal' groups of mountain folk on both sides of the border. Remembered by the French for his heroic Olympic gold medal at Squaw Valley in 1960 and immortalised elsewhere for his sunglasses, he persuaded the different resorts to band together.

On the mountain
top 2350m (7,708ft) bottom 1100m (3,608ft)
The skiing around **Avoriaz** itself can be divided into four main areas. Above the village is an extension of the main nursery slopes (Le Plateau), with a variety of drag-lifts serving a series of confidence-building green (beginner) runs, which link with the series of lifts coming up from **Morzine**. In the opposite direction are pistes down to **Les Marmottes**, from where lifts branch off towards **Châtel**; these runs are by no means always easy and are often crowded. From Les Marmottes a satisfyingly easy red (intermediate) run goes on down a beautiful gorge to **Ardent**, from where you can take a jumbo gondola back up. This also provides a useful access point into the best skiing for those staying in Châtel, **Torgon** and the other lower resorts at this end of the system.

At the bottom of Avoriaz you are faced with three choices. Directly to the south is the main **Arare** sector, which looks steeper than it really is from Avoriaz. The skiing here is mainly above the tree-line. Such is the volume of traffic that the separate marked runs amalgamate to form a whole pisted face to the mountain. The runs are mainly easy, with a few more difficult pitches towards the bottom. This sector is much frequented by the ski school, parts are often closed for slalom practice and it does become seriously congested. A long chair-lift from the same area at the bottom of the village takes you up to Hauts Forts, which offers the most challenging skiing in Avoriaz.

Several routes take you down all or part of the way to **Les Prodains**, 650m below Avoriaz and a full 1300m vertical from Hauts Forts. The often heavily mogulled pistes here narrow considerably as you descend into the trees, and are prone to ice. The blacks are genuinely black (difficult), and the main red run from the Arare sector has an extremely difficult pitch, which causes major problems for otherwise confident intermediates. The lower runs are usually congested in the late afternoon and very popular when visibility is poor above the tree-line.

The third direction is by chair- and drag-lift to the north-west-facing

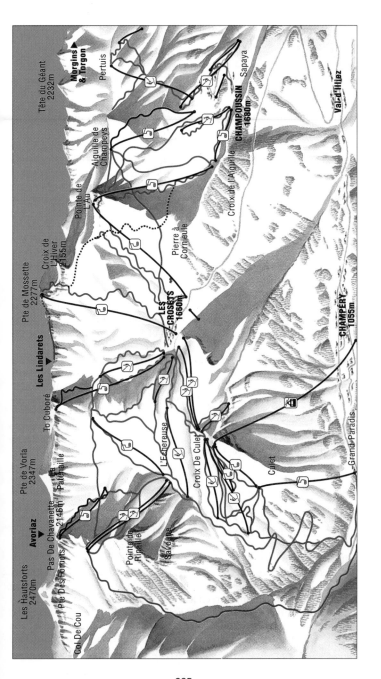

bowl between **Pas de Chavanette** and the Col du Fornet. This is another area of wide, open intermediate skiing above the tree-line. More adventurous skiers can return from Chavanette through the next valley; after an initial mogul field a pleasant run takes you down to Les Marmottes.

The border point, where the skiing of Avoriaz meets the big, open pastures of the three Swiss resorts, starts with the Chavanette (also known as the Swiss Wall or the Wall of Death); it is the most notorious black run in Europe but the hype is considerably greater than the degree of difficulty. The faint-hearted or the plain sensible can take the chair down during icy conditions. Below the Wall, acres of open snowfield are served by the lifts on either side of the Chavanette chair-lift, connecting with the slopes of Planachaux above **Champéry** and with the adjacent bowl of Les Crosets. Planachaux is reached from Champéry by cable car or by chair-lift from Grand-Paradis. The run down at the valley end is a delightful one, winding its way gently down through sleepy hamlets and across the river against the dramatic backdrop of the Dents du Midi; snow disappears early in the season here. Annoyingly irregular and crowded buses connect Grand-Paradis with Champéry.

Les Crosets sits above the tree-line surrounded by abundant wide pistes, some of them north-facing but most of them sunny. There are lifts up to the French border. The connection with **Champoussin** and **Morgins** is via the Pointe de l'Au, a series of linked drags and easy to intermediate pistes. The mountainside above Champoussin is wide but with little variety of terrain; the addition of a quad-chair from above the resort to the ridge has greatly improved the skiing. The pistes here are ideal for intermediates who need to build up their confidence.

Morgins has little skiing on the approach side from Champoussin, but it includes an excellent north-facing intermediate run cut through the woods above the village. Those who wish to continue skiing the circuit must walk across the village or take a short bus-ride to the nursery slopes and the lifts for Super-Châtel and France. In strong contrast to the sometimes bleak ski-fields of Avoriaz and Planachaux, the pistes here wind through the trees and are connected by a series of short drag-lifts.

The Morclan chair from **Super-Châtel** up to 1970m serves the most challenging slope, a moderately difficult mogul field. The black piste down to the village presents no real problems provided snow cover is reasonable. The top of this chair is the departure point for Torgon, one of the further extremities of Les Portes du Soleil, back across the border in Switzerland. The remainder of the skiing around Super-Châtel is mostly blue (easy) and red, on wide areas both above and below the lift station. The valley runs can be tricky in poor snow conditions.

Les Portes du Soleil circuit breaks down at **Châtel**, and whichever way you are travelling, the link cannot be made on skis. If you are going in a clockwise direction, a green traverse from the Linga lift delivers you to Châtel's nursery slopes, leaving you with a walk across the village to the jumbo gondola for Super-Châtel. If travelling anti-clockwise, you take a bus from Châtel to the ten-person gondola up to Linga; this is the first of a long chain of lifts and pistes towards Avoriaz and to the chair

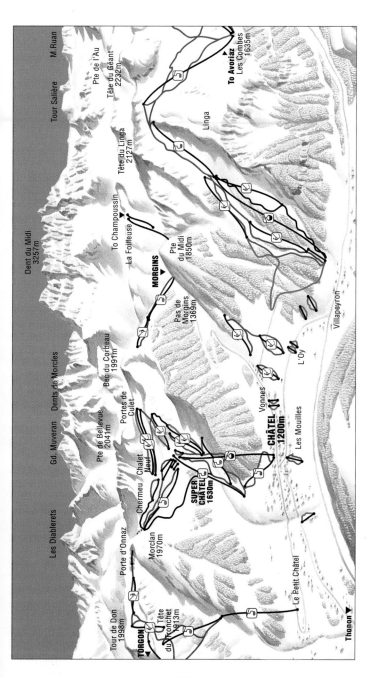

M.Ruan

Tour Salière

Pte de l'Au

Tête du Géant
2232m

To Avoriaz
Les Combes
1635m

Linga

Tête du Linga
2127m

Dent du Midi
3257m

To Champoussin

La Foilleuse

Pte
du Midi
1850m

MORGINS

Pas de
Morgins
1369m

Bec du Corbeau
1991m

Dents de Morcles

Gd. Muveran

Pte de
Bellevue
2041m

Portes de
Culet

Villapeyron

L'Oy

Vonnes

**CHÂTEL
1200m**

Les Mouilles

Les Diablerets

Chermeu Chalet
Neuf

Chalet
Neuf

**SUPER
CHÂTEL
1630m**

Porte d'Onnaz

Morclan
1970m

Le Petit Châtel

Tour de Don
1998m

Tête
du Tronchet
1913m

TORGON

Thonon

from Pré-La-Joux. The skiing in this sector offers more variety than other major legs of the circuit and includes a long, challenging black beside the Linga gondola for clockwise skiers or those with time to play en route.

The fairly steep slope above the gondola, served by a chair-lift, has a blue traverse cut into it, as well as the red and black routes shown on the local piste map. The run down by the Combes chair-lift towards Avoriaz is a satisfying red; the Cornebois chair, which goes up from the same point, has good intermediate pistes of its own and also connects with the top of the Chaux des Rosées chair-lift from Plaine Dranse; the runs down this chair are seriously challenging. One more lift and one easy run bring you down to Les Marmottes for the return to Avoriaz.

A cable car from the satellite of Les Prodains connects Morzine with Avoriaz, and on the other side of Morzine, a gondola and a cable car climb steeply to **Le Pleney** (1500m), which is more of a sunny ridge than a peak. From the lifts you look down on the less enticing sections of the direct black run from Le Pleney, which is fairly steep and often scraped to an icy glaze by too many skiers. Easy skiing can be found on the north-west side of the mountain, including a long blue down to the resort. An attractive area on the eastern side provides a series of mainly red runs complicated only by a number of piste crossroads.

From Les Fys at the eastern end of this area, a quad-chair gives access to **Plateau de Nyon**. The Fys chair climbs back to the top of the ridge (Belvedere), where easy link-runs go down both wooded flanks of the ridge; south-westward runs take you to the village of Les Gets, south-eastward pistes to the junction of Le Grand Pré, where a chair and a drag-lift link with Nyon, and the long Charniaz chair climbs gently up to the Tête des Crêts. This lift is the usual access route to **Les Gets** ski area and the runs beneath it: a red, which is mostly a schuss, followed by a green along the road are the only ways back to Morzine.

The Plateau de Nyon can be reached by cable car from just outside Morzine. Its appeal is mainly for good skiers: the Pointe and Chamossière chairs reach the high points of the system and serve its most challenging summits — shadowy north-facing ridges beneath the sharp peaks, which tower over Morzine's ski area and keep the early sun off much of it. The wide bowl below the Chamossière lift offers plenty of off-piste opportunities. Behind Chamossière there is a pleasant red run, which offers interesting off-piste alternatives before following a road through the woods to Le Grand Pré. From the Plateau de Nyon you can either ski down to the bottom of the cable car or the whole 11.5km directly back to Morzine via a flimsy-looking, but well-protected, bridge over a gaping river gorge.

The Tête des Crêts is near the top of the north-facing half of the Les Gets ski area. This is gentle, with long runs over lightly wooded slopes to the resort. These pistes pass through **Les Chavannes**, a cluster of restaurants and hotel buildings with a nursery-slope area, walking trails and cross-country loipes that link up with Le Pleney. It is accessible by road as well as by lift from Les Gets. Only one of Les Chavannes drags climbs to Tête des Crêts, for access not only to Morzine but also to a broad, upper bowl. The direct blue run to Les Gets is not obvious from here; the piste down La Turche drag to the edge of the village is an equally gentle alternative.

The south-facing skiing of Les Gets is on **Mont Chéry** and is reached by a six-seater gondola; its base-station is a short walk across the road from the Chavannes lifts and runs. Good snow on the lower red and black runs is a rarity for much of the winter. The top half of the mountain has easier, open skiing with magnificent views to the south of the Mont Blanc massif. The fairly steep, open slope behind Mont Chéry has good black and red runs to the Col de L'Encrenaz.

Most queuing problems in Les Portes du Soleil are in the Avoriaz area, largely because of the greater volume of skiers than any major deficiencies of the lift system in this quarter. Reporters suggest heading out towards Châtel and **Les Lindarets** on Sundays to avoid the crush. The Swiss resorts also tend to be less busy.

Beginners

Given acceptable snow conditions, it does not really matter which end of the circus you choose. Châtel and Morgins both have good ski schools, easy nursery slopes and plenty of tree-line skiing to which novices can graduate after a few days. Morzine, and in particular the runs around **Super-Morzine**, are ideally suited to learners.

Intermediates

The whole of Les Portes du Soleil is ideal cruising territory. Less confident skiers will prefer the long, sweeping runs at the Châtel end of the circuit. Stronger skiers will look towards the greater challenges of Champéry and Avoriaz. Les Gets is also an ideal base from which to explore some of the best intermediate skiing. Little resorts like St Jean d'Aulps/La Grande Terche, Abondance and **La Chapelle d'Abondance** can also provide excellent skiing when the region is crowded.

Advanced

Ideally, advanced skiers should base themselves at the **Avoriaz** end of the circuit, although **Champéry** is a delightful alternative with easy access to the Avoriaz area. The Swiss Wall is the most notorious run in the area; a sign at the top warns that it is only to be attempted by experts, and certainly the initial angle of descent is such that you cannot see what lies ahead. However, the wall itself is wide and, after the first 50m, it flattens out considerably but still maintains an average gradient of 34 degrees. Like all black runs, the degree of difficulty depends on snow conditions; it is normally heavily mogulled within hours of a major dump of snow. Great care should be taken, not least because of the volume of less competent skiers who attempt it. This run certainly has to be skied, but there are plenty of other equally challenging pistes in the region, including the World Cup run from Le Plan Brazy above Avoriaz all the way down to Les Prodains.

Off-piste

Again, the best powder runs are to be found above Avoriaz on both sides of the Swiss border. After a fresh snowfall various itineraries parallel to the Swiss Wall can be far more exhilarating than the actual run itself. The area is prone to considerable avalanche danger, and the services of a qualified guide are essential.

Snowboarding

Avoriaz was the first resort in Europe to realise the importance of the new sport in the early stages of its development and was the first to build a half-pipe. It is now recognised as the world's snowboard capital. Morzine shares in this glory, and the percentage of snowboarders to be at this end of the circuit is higher than in any other ski area in Europe.

Ski schools and guiding

Views on the French Ski School (ESF) in Avoriaz and Morzine range from 'miserable' to 'superb'. Regardless of the questionable attitude of instructors, the standard of teaching, particularly for beginners, seems high at both. The ESF at Châtel also has a solid reputation, and we have positive reports of the Swiss Ski School (ESS) in Champéry and in Morgins. However, the establishment that has received the rave reviews of the season is the British Alpine Ski School in Morzine and Avoriaz. This enterprise, set up by a couple of BASI instructors (who have passed the tough *équivalence* ski exam that allows them to teach legally in France), is described by one reporter as 'everything the ESF is not — small classes and good technical advice in one's mother tongue. Highly recommended and deserves a gold medal'.

Mountain restaurants

Les Portes du Soleil has a variety of restaurants ranging from over-crowded self-service establishments to wonderful old huts off the beaten track. Prices are generally high on both sides of the border, and all our reporters are agreed on one point: there are simply not enough restaurants. Coquoz at Planachaux has a circular open fire and offers wonderful local Swiss specialities. Les Lindarets, the hamlet just north of Avoriaz, has the best concentration of eating places with competitive prices. La Cremaillère is considered to be outstanding ('delicious *chanterelle* omelettes and wild *myrtilles* tart'), and Les Marmottes and the Pomme de Pin are also praised.

Les Prodains, at the bottom of the Vuarnet run from Avoriaz, is much praised, not least for its reasonable prices. The restaurants at Plaine Dranse are singled out as 'inexpensive and good'. Two restaurants at the top of Le Pleney are said to be always busy, 'but the wait is worth it'. The one at the top of the Super Morzine gondola is highly recommended for its 'good food and prices and spectacular view'. Les Raverettes at Les Gets is a handy stop before skiing back to Morzine. There is a good eating-place halfway down the blue piste from Le Pleney to Morzine. The Perdrix Blanche at Pré-de-la-Joux is recommended for its warm atmosphere and good-value food. Chez Gaby in Champoussin is highly praised ('we were ecstatic about the tomato fondue, but get here early or you won't find a free table'). Le Corbeau above Morgins is said to be 'a rustic, family-run affair with thoroughly reasonable prices'.

Off the mountain

Avoriaz is mainly a collection of apartment blocks perched on the edge of a cliff far above Morzine and built in what for the 1960s was a truly futuristic style. Unfortunately, many of the older blocks are showing their age, and no amount of face-lifts can improve the lack of space in their interiors. The resort is reached from the valley either by a narrow, winding road or by cable car from Les Prodains. You are strongly advised to leave your car 'downstairs', or indeed to leave it at home. One reporter comments: 'There are too many cars already in Morzine, so don't spoil the environment even further by bringing one.' Certainly it has no useful application in car-free Avoriaz, and the charges in either car-park are iniquitous. It is apparently legal to leave your car on the roadside on the outskirts of the resort, but you run the risk of it being buried or damaged by a snowplough.

Transport to your apartment block or hotel is via expensive horse-drawn sleigh, piste machine or on foot. Between snowfalls the amount of horse manure combined with dog-dirt deposited on the resort 'roads' does little to improve the ambience. When not on skis, moving around is made easier by public lifts within the apartment blocks to different levels of this steep resort. The busiest part is the middle section, around the foot of the nursery slopes; there are lots of bars and restaurants linking the slopes, and shops for ski gear, fashion and food. The best supermarket is, by consensus, the Codec near the tourist office.

Champéry is an attractive and traditional Swiss village set in dramatic surroundings at the foot of the Dents du Midi. The one-way main street is lined with wooden chalets, most of the hotels, shops and restaurants. However, the focus of development has moved down the hill to the valley road that skirts the village. The sports centre is here, as is the 125-person cable car up to **Planachaux**. The lift is served by a free mini-bus that circles the village.

Châtel is still a farming village, but caring for livestock and tilling the fields take second place behind the more lucrative business of tourism. Precious little planning has gone into the development of the village, a huge, ungainly straggle of buildings up towards the Morgins Pass and Switzerland, as well as down the hillside and along the valley towards the Linga lift, which is its connection with the skiing at Avoriaz. One reporter describes it as 'an excellent resort for a couple not too worried about après-ski, but who want to ski gently in breathtaking scenery'.

The valley lift departures are linked by free buses, which are crowded in the afternoon and have to fight their way through a village centre, which is often choked with traffic. Despite this, the disparate nature of the resort makes a car an advantage for reaching the out-of-town lift stations and for travel to the other unlinked resorts on the circuit. The resort has a small market on Tuesdays.

Morzine is a market town and long-established resort with a Gallic atmosphere at the foot of the road up to Avoriaz. It has all the appeal of an old-style chalet resort set in charming, wooded surroundings. Its biggest fault is its lack of altitude (1000m), which means that resort-level snow is scarce. The town covers a large area on both sides of a river gorge and on several levels. It has a serious traffic problem, but a high footbridge over the river makes getting around less torturous for pedestrians than for motorists. The main congested shopping street climbs from the old village centre beside the river to more open ground at the foot of Le Pleney, where the resort has developed with hotels and shops around the tourist office.

> ■ **OTHER SPORTS**
>
> **Avoriaz**: parapente, hang-gliding, sleigh rides, snowmobiling, skating, swimming, squash
> **Champéry**: parapente, skating, curling, swimming
> **Châtel**: parapente, snow-shoeing, skating
> **Morzine**: hang-gliding, parapente, dog-sledding, snow-shoeing, ski-jumping, ice-hockey, skating, curling, climbing wall, swimming

Such is the diffuse nature of the resort that the free buses are an essential form of transport. Horse-drawn taxis are an alternative means of transport, although one reporter said he felt guilty when the horse ran out of steam on the steep hills. As Morzine is a real town, the range of shops is far above the standard of most ski resorts; it has a large sports centre with an indoor ice rink.

Accommodation

The **Avoriaz** accommodation is nearly all in apartment blocks that vary in quality according to their age. Alpage I apartments are said to be 'clean, but fairly cramped', La Falaise units are similarly well-scrubbed but 'seriously short of storage space and maybe a bit cramped', and La Thuya apartments are 'rather dilapidated'. In general, it seems prudent to halve the number of advertised bed spaces. Hotel des Hauts Forts is recommended as 'surprisingly cheap'. Location within the resort is of no importance for skiing purposes, although some of the village streets, which are also pistes, may prove difficult for novices.

Champéry's accommodation is in hotels and chalets. The four-star Hotel Suisse is described as 'very Swiss, with large bathrooms and a formal dining-room, and the old-fashioned bedrooms lack hanging space'. Pension Souvenir is well located in the resort centre ('average, with no en-suite showers or baths, but cheap'). The Hotel de la Paix is said to be 'rather expensive and rooms slightly cramped for the price, but it serves a good breakfast'. Hotel de Champéry is centrally located and 'very comfortable, with all the facilities you would expect of a four-star, plus the bonus of friendly staff'.

Châtel has a wide choice of hotels, most of them chalet-style and simple. Location is important, and it is well worth checking out the distance from a main lift before booking. The Améthyste is said to be 'excellent and cheap', the Résidence Yeti is recommended, and Hotel Fleur de Neige is praised for its 'wonderful food' and 'homely atmosphere', but is expensive. The Flèche d'Or apartments are 'clean and comfortable, provided you halve the recommended occupancy figure'. Hotel Les Rhododendrons is 'perfectly located and typically French'.

Morzine has a plentiful supply of hotels in each price bracket; most are chalet-style and none is luxurious. In the central area, Les Airelles is one of the more comfortable, while Hotel Concorde is family-run and has a relaxed atmosphere. We continue to receive favourable reports of the Hotel Dahu ('excellent and friendly, with lovely rooms — the children loved the pool'). In the Hotel Sporting 'staff could not do enough for us, even buying our 15-month-old son a new high-chair'.

Eating in and out

Avoriaz has a choice of around 30 restaurants, most of which are rather overpriced as you would expect in a *station de ski* of this type. Reporters comment favourably on Les Intrets for its raclette, fondue and *pierrade*. Le Petit Vatel serves rustic fare including fresh trout, frogs' legs and snails. The Bistro opposite the Children's Village is 'good, but expensive'. Les Fontaines Blanches is 'reasonably priced, with a wide range of excellent food, a good French atmosphere and occasional live music'. US One serves Tex-Mex, and Le Savoyard has plenty of local flavour.

Grand-Paradis, two kilometres away from **Champéry** at the foot of the slopes, has a friendly atmosphere and wooden interior. It has a separate raclette and fondue restaurant. Le Vieux Chalet is 'reasonably priced by Swiss standards and has a warm atmosphere', and Restaurant de la Paix is extremely popular. Other choices include the Farinet, the Café du Centre, Le Levant and Le Pub ('great pizzas'). Grill Le Mazot in the Hotel Champéry has the best and most expensive steaks in town.

In **Châtel** La Bonne Menagère is popular, as is the Vieux-Four ('slow service but food is good, basic French)'. The Fleur de Neige has some of the best cuisine. Le Kitchen, out of town, is recommended for raclette and has 'a great atmosphere created by its English owner'.

In **Morzine** Le Dahu is again recommended for its 'mouth-watering dinners, night after night'. The Neige Roc at Les Prodains and Le Tremplin are also rated highly by reporters. L'Etale serves regional specialities in a 'wonderful, authentic mountain atmosphere'.

Après-ski

In **Avoriaz** broomball on the ice rink is a popular form of après-ski. The Place has live non-French music and an 'excellent atmosphere'. Le Choucas is recommended; it has live music and is usually not too crowded. Le Tavaillon is described by one reporter who spent five weeks here as 'the nerve centre of Avoriaz'. The nightclubs are said to be generally overpriced and empty, except on striptease nights when audience participation is invited. The discos, Le Festival and Le Roc Club, both have entrance fees, while the Midnight Express has a free 'bucking bronco'. All three hold sponsored evenings; at Le Roc, where the seats are covered in animal skins, one reporter was bemused to find his evening commercially endorsed by a condom company: 'Buckets-full were thrown at us. As a result there were probably two-dozen packets on our small table at any one time and the dance floor was covered in them.'

Champéry is not famous for its nightlife. Le Pub bar and restaurant is often the liveliest place in town and much patronised by the locals. Reporters also recommend the Farinet bar ('quiet, friendly atmosphere and not expensive'); its nightclub can be crowded at weekends, but entry is free and drinks are said to be not too exorbitant. The basement nightclub of the Hotel Suisse is 'smart and a bit boring'. One reporter recommends Charly's Bar in Val d'Illiez as the best in the area ('very comfortable with pool and videos').

Châtel has a bowling alley and an ice-rink, but otherwise the après-ski activity is mainly limited to a handful of bars including the popular l'Isba, which has a lively atmosphere and shows ski videos. One reporter claimed: 'There was nothing to do and nowhere to go after 2.30am.' The Slalom bar is British-owned. **Morzine** abounds with civilised tea-rooms and bars. The Wallington complex houses a bowling alley, pool hall, bar and disco. Le Pacha is another popular disco.

Childcare

The Children's Village in **Avoriaz** has a justified reputation as one of the better childcare establishments in France. Children from three years old are taught in the village, using methods developed by French ski champion, Annie Famose. Younger children are looked after in Les P'tits Loups day nursery of which we have good reports.

Champéry has a gentle baby slope with a simple rope-tow right in the middle of the village; snow permitting, this provides an ideal beginners' area for small children. Parents should, however, be warned that there is no barrier to prevent over-enthusiastic youngsters on skis or toboggans crashing out into the road, or even the railway line beyond. The ESS Mini Club takes children up the mountain for the whole day.

Châtel has the Village des Marmottons for children as young as 14 months, with a mixture of games and skiing for the older ones. The ESF operates classes for five-year-olds and upwards.

The **Morzine** crèche takes infants of two months to four years old, with one-hour ski lessons for children of three and over. However, 'the instructor did not speak English, the location was awkward, and the attitude was unsympathetic to slow starters.'

Linked or nearby resorts

Abondance 930m (3,050ft)

This tiny historic village lies 7km from La Chapelle and is not linked into the main Portes du Soleil system. It has a small ski area on the slopes beneath the Col de l'Ecuelle, served by a gondola and a series of drags.

TOURIST OFFICE
Tel 33 50 73 02 90
Fax 33 50 73 04 76

Les Crosets 1660m (5,445ft)

Les Crosets is a ski station in the heart of the open slopes on the Swiss side of Les Portes du Soleil. It is a tiny place with some modern chalets, a couple of hotels and a handful of restaurants and has no obvious appeal to anyone but serious skiers who want an early night. The walk into Champéry takes around two hours. There are four daily buses to Val d'Illiez, which is one train stop from Champéry. Main uphill transport from here is a new detachable quad-chair, which replaces the old gondola. The Hotel Télécabine is simple, British-run and serves excellent food.

TOURIST OFFICE
Tel 41 25 772077
Fax 41 25 773773

Champoussin 1680m (5,182ft)

Champoussin represents more of an attempt to create a mini-resort than Les Crosets. Its new buildings, in rustic style, are almost all apartments. Reports of the main hotel, the Alpage Ambassador, range from 'highly impressive' to 'the management of the hotel was dreadful'. It has a sauna, a pool and a disco. The Alpage Ambassador apartments are highly recommended. The hotel runs its own kindergarten and mini-club and has a parapente school. Après-ski, which is limited to the hotel and Le Poussin bar/restaurant is 'soporific' and 'almost non-existent'.

The resort is dominated by Dutch visitors. The small ski school does not receive impressive ratings ('in six days our Dutch instructor never asked us our names'). Two of our reporters have violently opposing views on the resort. One writes 'great for family holidays, but singles and extreme skiers should look elsewhere'. The other says: 'Champoussin is so small and remote that just looking at it could give you cabin fever.' The one supermarket is said to be inadequate.

TOURIST OFFICE
as Les Crosets

La Chapelle d'Abondance 1010m (3,313ft)

This little resort lies 6km down the valley from Châtel. It is an old farming community straddling both sides of the road without any defined centre. On one side, two long chairs take you up to Crêt Béni at 1650m from where a series of drags serve a choice of mainly easy runs. On the other side of the road a recently built gondola and chair-lift link into Torgon, Châtel and the main Portes du Soleil system. La Chapelle also has 22km of loipe, which offer some of the best cross-country skiing in the region. Les Cornettes du Bis and the Alti Mille hotels each have a swimming-pool and fitness centre. The Cornettes restaurant provides

Skiing facts: **Avoriaz**

TOURIST OFFICE
Place Central, F-74110 Avoriaz, Haute
Savoie
Tel 33 50 74 02 11
Fax 33 50 74 18 25

THE RESORT
By road Calais 889km
By rail Thonon les Bains 43km, Cluses
40km
By air Geneva 2 hrs
Visitor beds 16,000
Transport traffic-free resort

THE SKIING
Linked or nearby resorts Abondance (n),
Champoussin (l), Champéry (l), La Chapelle
d'Abondance (l), Châtel (l), Les Crosets (l),
Les Gets (l), Montriond (l), Morgins (l),
Morzine (l), Saint Jean d'Aulps/La Grande
Terche (n), Torgon (l)
Longest run Crozats, 4km (black)
Number of lifts 42 in Avoriaz, 228 in Portes
du Soleil
Total of trails/pistes Avoriaz 150km (8%
beginner, 55% easy, 27% intermediate,
10% difficult), 650km in Portes du Soleil
Nursery slopes 7 lifts
Summer skiing none
Snowmaking 18 mobile snow-cannon

LIFT PASSES
Area pass Portes du Soleil (covers 13
resorts), 885FF for 6 days
Day pass Avoriaz 150FF, Portes du Soleil
190FF

Beginners 380FF for 6 days
Pensioners reductions for 60 yrs and over
Credit cards accepted yes

SKI SCHOOLS
Adults ESF, 780FF for 6 days, Ecole de
Glisse, 400FF for 5 days (2 hrs per day)
British Alpine Ski School, details on request
Private lessons ESF 160FF per hr, Ecole de
Glisse 150FF per hr
Snowboarding ESF, 1,130FF for 6 days,
Ecole de Glisse, 480FF for 6 days (2 hrs per
day)
Cross-country ESF 75FF for 2 hrs (morn-
ing), or 115FF for 3 hrs (afternoon). Loipe
45km at Super Morzine
Other courses telemark
Guiding companies through ski schools

CHILDREN
Lift pass 5-16 yrs, Avoriaz 108FF per day,
Portes du Soleil 570FF for 6 days, free for 4
yrs and under
Ski kindergarten as ski school
Ski school ESF Village des Enfants,
3-16 yrs, 1,070FF for 6 days
including lunch
Non-ski kindergarten 3 mths-5 yrs: Halte
Garderie, 9am-5.30pm, 200FF per day; Les
P'tits Loups, 9am-6pm, 1,000FF for 6 days
including lunch

FOOD AND DRINK PRICES
Coffee 6FF, glass of wine 12FF, small beer
18FF, dish of the day 60FF

one of the best gastronomic experiences in the Abondance Valley.

TOURIST OFFICE
Tel 33 50 73 51 41
Fax 33 50 73 56 04

Les Gets 1175m (3,854ft)

Les Gets straddles a low mountain-pass 6km from Morzine, with lifts and pistes on both sides and good nursery slopes on the edge of the village and higher up at Les Chavannes (1490m), which is reached by road or gondola. This attractive village, an old farming community which has expanded almost out of recognition, also has a large and under-used floodlit piste. Parts of the ski area and many of the restaurants within it are accessible on foot. There is a bus service to Morzine for access to Avoriaz but it starts late in the morning and is infrequent.

Les Gets has three ski schools, and we have favourable reports of them all. Ski Plus has 'excellent private tuition in English' and there is a choice of kindergarten; Ski Espace ('lots of fun, they don't take the skiing too seriously') receives better comments than the ESF. The non-ski Bébé Club takes children from three months to two years old.

Much of the accommodation is in tour-operator chalets. Hotel l'Ours Blanc is 'comfortable, with good service, and we would go back there again'. The Régina is well placed in the quieter part of the village, and the Labrador and the Alissandre are both said to offer a high standard of service. Le Meridien, La Cachette and the Clé des Champs chalets are recommended, along with the Soleil and La Bouillandire apartments. Restaurants include Le Tyrol and Le Gallichou.

Most of the nightlife centres around hotel bars, but there are also three discos. The English-run Pring's and the piano bar in the Hotel Régina are popular. There is an open-air skating rink in the centre, a motor-tricycle circuit, a mechanical museum and two cinemas.

TOURIST OFFICE
Tel 33 50 75 80 80
Fax 33 50 79 76 90

Montriond 950m (3,116ft)

Montriond is little more than a suburb of Morzine and a number of simple and reasonably priced hotels. A bus links you to the resort's gondola, which provides direct access into the main lift system.

TOURIST OFFICE
Tel 33 50 79 12 81
Fax 33 50 79 04 06

Morgins 1350m (4,428ft)

Morgins is situated a few kilometres from Châtel just over the pass of the same name and is the border post with Switzerland. It is a spacious, res-

idential resort spread across a broad valley, but it is not the ideal base for
keen skiers because, quite simply, the best of Les Portes du Soleil skiing
is elsewhere. A car is an asset for visiting other resorts in the region, but
traffic is a problem at the beginning and end of the day due to day-trippers from other parts of Les Portes du Soleil.

Most of the accommodation is in chalets and apartments. We have
received poor reports of the once popular Hostellerie Bellevue, which is
described as 'rather tatty' with 'dinners uninspiring at best'. The resort is
relaxed but short of any real character. It has a crèche, of which we have
extremely positive reports. The large nursery slope in the centre of the
village is prone to overcrowding.

Après-ski is limited to a natural skating rink, indoor tennis courts and
a few bars. The Hotel Bellevue's disco provides some measure of lively
late-night entertainment in season, and its swimming-pool is open to the
public. Several reporters have enjoyed the thermal baths at Val d'Illiez.
The three cross-country loipe total 15km, and there is a long, marked
but unprepared route to Champoussin.

TOURIST OFFICE
Tel 41 25 772361
Fax 41 25 773708

St Jean d'Aulps/La Grande Terche 900m (2,952ft)

St Jean is the village, while La Grande Terche is the name given to a tiny
development of apartments at the foot of the lifts, which are a 15-minute
drive from Morzine. The skiing is not as yet fully linked into the system,
but it is surprisingly good and well worth the visit if staying elsewhere in
the area. It has a combined ski area with **Bellevaux**.

TOURIST OFFICE
Tel 33 50 79 65 09
Fax 33 50 79 67 95

Torgon 1100m (3,608ft)

Torgon is perched above the Rhône close to Lac Léman on the outer
edge of Les Portes du Soleil. Although it is in Switzerland it is linked in
one direction with La Chapelle and in the other with Châtel, both of
which are in France. Access is only possible by road from the French side
of the lake, which makes it somewhat isolated. The distinctive and none-
too-pleasing A-frame architecture houses comfortable apartments. Last
season the resort's two lift companies went into receivership, a fact that
emphasises the uneasy relationship between the member resorts of Les
Portes du Soleil. However, we are assured that the links will remain in
operation. There is little else to do here but ski.

TOURIST OFFICE
Tel 41 25 813131
Fax 41 25 814620

Skiing facts: **Champéry**

TOURIST OFFICE
CH-1874 Champéry, Valais
Tel 41 25 791141
Fax 41 25 791847

THE RESORT
By road Calais 900km
By rail station in resort
By air Geneva 2 hrs
Visitor beds 7,300
Transport free ski-bus

THE SKIING
Linked or nearby resorts Abondance (n), Avoriaz (l), Champoussin (l), La Chapelle d'Abondance (l), Châtel (l), Les Crosets (l), Les Gets (l), Montriond (l), Morgins (l), Morzine (l), Saint Jean d'Aulps/La Grande Terche (n), Torgon (l)
Longest run Ripaille-Grand-Paradis, 6km (red)
Number of lifts 17 in Champéry, 228 in Portes du Soleil
Total of trails/pistes 80km in Champéry/Les Crosets (47% easy, 47% intermediate, 6% difficult), 650km in Portes du Soleil
Nursery slopes 2 lifts
Summer skiing none
Snowmaking 4 mobile snow-cannon

LIFT PASSES
Area pass Portes du Soleil (covers 13 resorts), SF210 for 6 days

Day pass Champéry SF35, Portes du Soleil SF46
Beginners no free lifts, reductions
Pensioners reductions for 60 yrs and over
Credit cards accepted yes

SKI SCHOOLS
Adults ESS, 9.30am-12.30pm, 120FF for 5 days
Private lessons ESS, SF45 per hr
Snowboarding ESS, 2-4pm, SF120 for 5 days
Cross-country through ESS. Loipe 7km at Grand-Paradis
Other courses heli-skiing, ski-touring, telemark
Guiding companies Bureau des Guides

CHILDREN
Lift pass Champéry SF24 per day, Portes du Soleil SF31 per day or SF135 for 6 days
Ski kindergarten ESS Mini Club, 3-6 yrs, 9.30am-4.30pm, SF240 for 5 days including lunch
Ski school ESS, 5-12 yrs, 9.30am-12.30pm, SF120 for 5 half-days
Non-ski kindergarten La Maison des Schtroumpfs, 6 mths-5 yrs, SF40 per day

FOOD AND DRINK PRICES
Coffee SF2.50-3.00, glass of wine SF2.80-3.00, small beer SF3.10-3.50, dish of the day SF14-20

Skiing facts: **Châtel**

TOURIST OFFICE
F-74390 Châtel, Haute Savoie
Tel 33 50 73 22 44
Fax 33 50 73 22 87

THE RESORT
By road Calais 900km
By rail Thonon les Bains 45 mins, regular bus service to resort
By air Geneva 2 hrs
Visitor beds 17,924
Transport free bus between village and Pré-la-Joux lift and around resort

THE SKIING
Linked or nearby resorts Abondance (n), Avoriaz (l), Champéry-Planachauz (l), Champoussin (l), La Chapelle d'Abondance (l), Les Crosets (l), Les Gets (l), Montriond (l), Morgins (l), Morzine (l), Saint Jean d'Aulps/La Grande Terche (n), Torgon (l)
Longest run Linga, 1km (red/black)
Number of lifts 50 in Châtel, 228 in Portes du Soleil
Total of trails/pistes 82km in Châtel (22% beginner, 27% easy, 39% intermediate, 12% difficult), 650km in Portes du Soleil
Nursery slopes 13 runs
Summer skiing none
Snowmaking 10 mobile snow-cannon

LIFT PASSES
Area pass Portes du Soleil (covers 13 resorts), 885FF for 6 days. Châtel only 660FF for 6 days
Day pass Châtel 150FF, Portes du Soleil 195FF
Beginners no free lifts
Pensioners 60 yrs and over, Châtel 491FF for 6 days, Portes du Soleil 584FF for 6 days

Credit cards accepted yes

SKI SCHOOLS
Adults ESF, 510FF for 6 days (2 hrs per day), ESI, 9am-midday, 610FF for 6 days, Stages Henri Gonon, 600FF for 5 days (3 hrs per day) with video
Private lessons ESF 168FF per hr, ESI 175FF per hr, Stages Henri Gonan, prices on request
Cross-country ESF, 9.30am-midday, 510FF for 6 days. Loipe 24km (largest loipe 5km at Super-Châtel)
Snowboarding ESF, 2.30-5pm, 740FF for 6 days. ESI, 2-5pm, 550FF for 5 afternoons
Other courses telemark, monoski, slalom, moguls, skwal
Guiding companies through ski schools

CHILDREN
Lift pass Châtel, 5-16 yrs, 491FF for 6 days, Portes du Soleil 584FF for 6 days, free for 4 yrs and over
Ski kindergarten Le Village des Marmottons, 14 mths-10 yrs, 9.30am-4pm, 1,020FF for 6 days including lunch
Ski school ESF, 5-14 yrs, 390-460FF for 6 days (2 hrs per day). ESI, 8 yrs and over, 610FF for 6 afternoons or ESI Juniors Club, 9am-5pm, 1,490FF for 5 days including lunch
Non-ski kindergarten Le Village des Marmottons, 14 mths-3 yrs, 8.30am-5.30pm, 670FF for 6 days including lunch

Food and drink prices
Coffee 6FF, glass of wine 3.50FF, small beer 6FF, dish of the day 65FF

Skiing facts: **Morzine**

TOURIST OFFICE
BP 23, F-74110 Morzine, Haute Savoie
Tel 33 50 74 72 72
Fax 33 50 79 03 48

THE RESORT
By road Calais 880km
By rail Cluses or Thonon les Bains 30km
By air Geneva 1½ hrs
Visitor beds 16,000
Transport free bus service runs throughout Morzine and to Avoriaz (Les Prodains)

THE SKIING
Linked or nearby resorts Abondance (n), Avoriaz (l), Champéry-Planachauz (l), Champoussin (l), La Chapelle d'Abondance (l), Châtel (l), Les Crosets (l), Les Gets (l), Montriond (l), Morgins (l), Saint Jean d'Aulps/La Grande Terche (n), Torgon (l)
Longest run Piste Chamossière, 11km (red)
Number of lifts 66 in Morzine, 228 in Portes du Soleil
Total of trails/pistes 133km in Morzine (13% beginner, 37% easy, 37% intermediate, 13% difficult), 650km in Portes du Soleil
Nursery slopes 2 lifts
Summer skiing none
Snowmaking 85 hectares covered

LIFT PASSES
Area pass Pleney-Nyon/Les Gets, 695FF for 6 days. Portes du Soleil (covers 13 resorts)

885FF for 6 days
Day pass Pleney-Nyon/Les Gets 135FF, Portes du Soleil 190FF
Beginners special prices for some lifts
Pensioners as children
Credit cards accepted yes

SKI SCHOOLS
Adults ESF, 520FF for 6 half-days, British Alpine Ski School, details on request
Private lessons ESF, 160FF per hr
Snowboarding ESF private lessons 165FF per hr, group lessons as regular ski school
Cross-country ESF private lessons 165FF per hr. Loipe 97km in Vallée de la Manche, Super-Morzine, Pleney and around Lac de Montriond
Other courses race training
Guiding companies through ski school

CHILDREN
Lift pass 5-16 yrs, Morzine only 450FF for 6 days, Portes du Soleil 584FF for 6 days, free for 4 yrs and under
Ski kindergarten ESF, 4-12 yrs, 8.30am-6pm, 520FF for 6 days (2½ hrs per day). Leisure Centre OUTA, 8.30am-6pm, 1,257FF for 6 days
Ski school as ski kindergarten
Non-ski kindergarten Halte Garderie, 2 mths-4 yrs, 8.30am-6pm, 865FF for 6 days

FOOD AND DRINK PRICES
Coffee 6FF, glass of wine 3.50FF, small beer 6FF, dish of the day 65FF

Risoul/Vars

ALTITUDE 1850m (6,068ft)

Risoul and Vars share the same ski area 35km from Briançon and are two of the more remote resorts, with transfer times from any French airport of between three and five hours. However, devotees are quick to point out that their isolation and good snow record means that pleasant, uncrowded skiing can always be enjoyed here even when other resorts are having a lean time. However, the remoteness of the area is not conducive to the daily 'busing in' of frustrated holidaymakers from elsewhere.

The combined ski area, marketed as the **Domaine de la Forêt Blanche**, is one of the largest in the Southern Alps. **Risoul 1850** is a compact resort of large wood-and-stone buildings. It is a purpose-built yet attractive place constructed on the lines of a real village with a main street, and the cars to go with it. It is situated above the original village of Risoul.

Reasonable prices have led to the resort growing in popularity with British tour operators. When one of our reporters first visited about 12 years ago Risoul 1850 was 'a quiet resort with nothing to offer except skiing: no mountain restaurants and no lift queues'. It has not changed much according to current reports. There is still nothing for non-skiers, and the après-ski is limited, but the area does now support half-a-dozen mountain restaurants. Queuing only appears to be a problem during the peak French holiday weeks and during the British half-term. Last season one reporter summed up Risoul as 'suitable for families and mixed-ability groups, but not for youngsters looking for a good time'.

On the mountain
top 2750m (9,020ft) bottom 1650m (5,412ft)

The open, bowl-shaped ski area around Risoul 1850 also has some wooded areas that are good for bad-weather skiing. The runs are mainly short and present few challenges. Several of the higher slopes are steeper, as are some of the slopes around Vars, but generally the skiing is perfect for intermediates.

A new four-person chair-lift was installed during the 1994–5 season, giving an additional access point from the resort towards La Platte de la Nonne at 2200m. There are also several drag-lifts from the ski area base, which give a choice of mountain access.

Access to Vars is on a short, slow drag on the Pointe de Razis, followed by a long, gentle blue (easy) run. Mountain access from Vars to the slopes is on the Chabrières gondola as well as on three alternative drags from different points in town. Runs back to Risoul 1850 start on a narrow and windy ledge with steep drops on either side. It is important to start heading back to Risoul by 3pm; if you miss the last lift it is an expensive taxi ride around the mountain to get home again. It is also worth noting that links to and from Risoul/Vars are sometimes closed due to high winds.

On the Crête de Chabrières, the highest point of the area, is the speed skiing slope – well worth a look when the racers are in action.

Reporters continue to criticise the area's piste-marking as being inconsistent, with 'blues more difficult than some of the red (intermediate) runs', 'some blue runs could have been green (beginner)', and 'some of the red runs easier than the blues'. Piste-grooming is reported to have greatly improved in recent seasons.

Beginners

Risoul has good, centrally located nursery slopes with a total of six lifts (one is free). Second-week skiers should be able to progress comfortably to runs such as Le Clos du Vallon and the Liaison Cezier-Alpet.

Intermediates

This is an area for intermediates, the more confident of whom will relish the long cruising pistes in this large and mainly well-linked ski area. Some of the best runs are on the Crête de Chabrières at the highest point of the ski area. From the top of L'Homme de Pierre at 2361m, what starts as a wide red schuss gradually becomes a steeper run as you enter the trees. The top of Mélezet links on to a path into Risoul with access to a steeper red route down. Pinatiaux Superior, from the top of Platte de la Nonne, is a long red run combining schusses, moguls and some steeper narrow sections and is voted one of the best runs here by our reporters, as well as 'an ideal last run of the day'.

Advanced

This is not a resort for advanced skiers, but there is sufficient variety to keep most experts happy for a week. The steeper skiing of the area is immediately above Vars on the 'wall' of the Grand Ubac and also on La Casse above Sainte-Marie.

Off-piste

In the right conditions any resort can produce deep powder fun. Risoul is no exception, with plenty of tree-line skiing, particularly from the Pointe de Razis. A guide is essential as the best runs do not end up in the resort and involve a pre-arranged taxi transfer home. The area is also prone to avalanche danger, and the greatest care should be taken.

Snowboarding
Both the French Ski School (ESF) and the International Ski School (ESI) offer group and private snowboarding tuition. There is a half-pipe at the base of the ski area.

Ski schools and guiding
We have a mixed bag of reports on the ESF and none at all on the ESI. Comments are mainly favourable, but a number of people complain at the large size of classes (up to 15) and protest about the follow-my-leader style of teaching and lack of individual tutoring ('I often found the instructors acted more as guides than as teachers'). However, one reader comments: 'Through patient instruction I regained my confidence and came on in leaps and bounds.' One criticism is that lessons only take place for two hours in the morning ('instructors tend to abandon their classes wherever they are on the mountain as soon as noon strikes').

The children's ski school is 'excellent, with small classes and good instructors; there was no English-speaking class, but my son didn't find this a hardship and the exposure to French will have benefited him'.

Mountain restaurants
There are half-a-dozen of them, which is more than are shown on the rather confusing lift map. Three are in Risoul's ski area: Le Vallon, Le Prarond and the Refuge Valbelle. Chez Plumot in Vars is recommended for lunch and has a good atmosphere but is not cheap by the area's standard. La Licorne, next to the pistes, is a good place for lunchtime pizzas, salads and crêpes.

Off the mountain
Risoul 1850 is a relatively new resort and has the advantage of sympathetic wood-and-stone architecture. It is set in an open position in attractive surroundings. At the top of the village, next to the slopes, is a crescent of apartments and cafés. Shopping is limited to 'some dreadfully expensive and nasty souvenirs and not much else apart from sports shops'.

Accommodation
Le Dahu is Risoul 1850's only hotel; it is well located towards the centre of the resort. **Risoul Village**, lower down the valley with a bus running to Risoul 1850, has three more hotels: Le Rochasson I, Le Rochasson II and La Bonne Auberge. **Vars** has three recommended hotels: Les Escondus, Le Caribou (in the best location) and L'Ecureuil (without a restaurant). Village Leo Lagrange holiday centre in Risoul has 500 beds.

Over 90 per cent of Risoul's visitors stay in self-catering accommodation. Les Mélèzes apartments are well located for the slopes but have the disadvantage of a ten-minute uphill walk back from the village centre. Reporters note the lack of space in the four- to six-person apartments, with only enough seating for three ('you couldn't go to the loo with the door shut'). The Belvedere apartments, also reached after a long uphill trudge, are more spacious: 'The decor is unusual. It helps if you like strawberries because the curtains, tablecloth, pillows and bed-linen are covered in them.' The Christiana studios for two are reported as being convenient, quite spacious and well-equipped but poorly maintained.

■ OTHER SPORTS

Snow-shoeing, parapente, skating, squash, tobogganing

Eating in and out

Hotel Dahu is endorsed by reporters for its half-board food. La Licorne is a lively meeting place in the evenings, and the Bergerie is praised by several reporters for its good value food, although its menu is limited. L'Assiette Gourmande has good quality and good value food but tends to be very crowded in the evenings. L'Ecureuil is also recommended.

The main shopping area includes two supermarkets, and there is another near the Mélèzes apartments, which stays open until 10pm. Reporters found that the wine and beer was cheap and the food of a high quality, although they noted a shortage of meat at reasonable prices. There is also a take-away pizza establishment.

Après-ski

Le Pick-Up and Le Dahu are the two discos, but other après-ski revolves around bars such as La Licorne and the Bar Rock Café. Non-sporting activities are limited.

Childcare

Risoul 1850 has extensive kindergarten facilities as it is a truly family-orientated resort. Les Pitchous is for non-skiing children from six months, and both the ESF and the ESI have mini-clubs for children three years old and upwards.

Linked or nearby resorts

Vars 1850m (6,068ft)

Vars is a mainly wooden-built, though not particularly attractive, resort situated above the town of Vars-Sainte-Marie, where the skiing goes down to 1650m. It attracts a largely French clientèle and is connected to Risoul by a windy ridge. Hotels include the Caribou, which has a swimming-pool, Les Escondus, and L'Ecureuil at Vars 1850, as well as Le Vallon, Le Mayt and the Edelweiss at Vars-Sainte-Marie. Chez Plumot, also at Vars-Sainte-Marie, is a restaurant worth visiting.

TOURIST OFFICE
Tel 33 92 46 51 31
Fax 33 92 46 51 31

Skiing facts: **Risoul**

TOURIST OFFICE
Risoul 1850, F-05600 Guillestre,
Hautes-Alpes
Tel 33 92 46 02 60
Fax 33 92 46 01 23

THE RESORT
By road Calais 1024km
By rail Montdauphin 30 mins, bus
connection with Risoul
By air Grenoble 3 hrs, Marseille 3 hrs
Visitor beds 12,500
Transport none

THE SKIING
Linked or nearby resorts Vars (l), Vars-
Sainte-Marie (l)
Longest run Côte Belle, 2.4km (blue)
Number of lifts 58
Total of trails/pistes 170km (56% easy,
40% intermediate, 4% difficult)
Nursery slopes 6 lifts
Summer skiing none
Snowmaking 29 hectares covered in Risoul
and Vars

LIFT PASSES
Area pass (covers Risoul and Vars) 770FF
for 6 days
Day pass 140FF
Beginners 80FF per day and 1 free lift
Pensioners reductions for 60 yrs and over,
free for 70 yrs and over
Credit cards accepted yes

SKI SCHOOLS
Adults ESF 390FF and ESI 540FF, both for 6
x 2 hrs
Private lessons ESF 160FF per hr, ESI
175FF per hr
Snowboarding ESF, 390FF for 6 x 2 hrs, ESI
540FF for 6 x 2 hrs
Cross-country ESF, 85FF for 2 hrs. ESI,
prices on request. Loipe 30km
Other courses monoski, telemark, slalom
Guiding companies through ESF and ESI

CHILDREN
Lift pass 5-11 yrs, 655FF for 6 days, free
for 4 yrs and under
Ski kindergarten ESF Mini-Club, 5-12 yrs,
3,070FF for 6 x 2 hrs. ESI, 4-12 yrs, 65FF
for 2 hrs
Ski school ESF, 3 yrs and over, 370FF for 6
x 2 hrs. ESI, 2 yrs and over, 635FF for 6 x 2
hrs including refreshments
Non-ski kindergarten tourist office
crèche, 6 mths-6 yrs, 8.45am-
5.15pm, 600FF for 6 days not including
lunch

FOOD AND DRINK PRICES
Coffee 6FF, glass of wine 7FF, small beer
12FF, dish of the day 50FF

Serre Chevalier/Briançon

ALTITUDE 1200-1500m (3,936-4,920ft)

Serre Chevalier is not one but three separate villages grouped along a valley between the Col du Lautaret and Briançon. Ten other hamlets share the ski area, and more recently the ancient garrison town of Briançon, just five minutes' drive away, has built a gondola linking it with the ski area.

Of the three main villages, **Villeneuve/Le Bez** (marketed as Serre Chevalier 1400) is the most central and lively, while **Monêtier-Les-Bains** (Serre Chevalier 1500) is both the sleepiest and prettiest. **Chantemerle** (Serre Chevalier 1350) and Villeneuve share most of the visitor accommodation and have the best après-ski facilities. All three are hamlets, which over the years have been added to with a hotch-potch of newer architecture mainly along the busy Grenoble-Briançon road, which cuts through their centres. **Briançon** is an attractive town in a beautiful setting, with the added attraction of hill-top fortifications built by Napoleon's military engineer, Marquis de Vauban. These enclose a maze of delightful streets and alleyways reminiscent of a miniature Carcassone.

■ GOOD POINTS

Large ski area, good artificial snow cover, varied off-piste, tree-line skiing, minimal queues, extensive cross-country trails, many children's facilities, good-value holidays

■ BAD POINTS

Heavy traffic along main highway, strung-out resort, unreliable resort-level snow

A car is a definite bonus when staying here; take advantage of the off-slope facilities in both Serre Chevalier and Briançon, and the Grande Galaxie lift pass, which covers five nearby resorts including **Montgenèvre** in the Milky Way area, 15 minutes down the road. The skiing is for all standards, but is particularly well suited to the good intermediate who will enjoy the 250km of cruising and the well-linked, albeit now rather old-fashioned, lift system.

Reporters are unanimous in their praise of the resort and its skiing: 'Serre Chevalier is one of France's best-kept skiing secrets. I loved being here and would unhesitatingly come again and bring all my friends.' Friendly locals are another plus: 'The ski-lift attendants, instructors and bus drivers are noticeably more cheerful than in established international resorts such as Méribel. A very helpful and unspoilt lot.'

The skiing
top 2800m (9,184ft) bottom 1326m (4,351ft)

The three main mountain access-points are by gondola and cable car from Villeneuve/Le Bez, Chantemerle and Briançon, with most of the

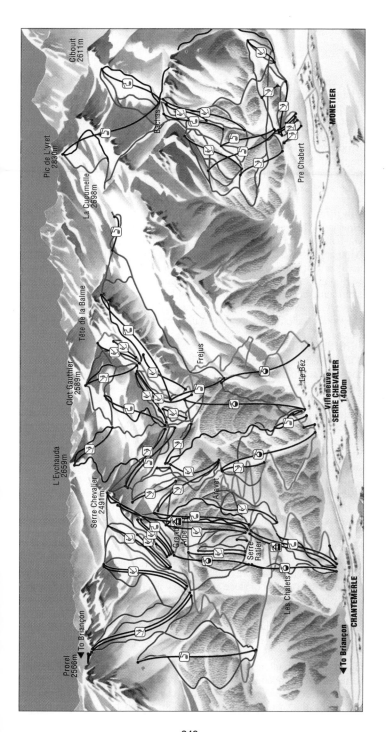

Cibouit
2611m

Pic de L'yret
2830m

La Cucumelle
2698m

Tête de la Balme

Clot Gauthier
2589m

L'Eychauda
2659m

Serre Chevalier
2491m

Prorel
2566m

Bachas

Frejus

Grand
Alpe

Aravet

Serre
Ratier

Les Chalets

◄To Briançon

◄To Briançon

Pre Chabert

Le Bez

MONETIER

Villeneuve
SERRE CHEVALIER
1400m

CHANTEMERLE

lifts and pistes concentrated in the area above Villeneuve and Chantemerle. The Monêtier section also has its own lifts starting from the base and is the most appealing sector of the whole area, although the least accessible. Serre Chevalier's upper slopes are open and rather exposed to the weather, but the lower slopes are well protected by trees. Briançon has a floodlit piste for night-skiing. Snowmaking is extensive on the lower runs, and a good bus system links all the villages. According to reporters 'the piste-marking leaves a lot to be desired', however, the area is praised for its lack of queues.

Beginners

Novice skiers are well catered for with a choice of ten nursery slopes, and ski schools offering beginner-tuition in all the main villages. **Le Grand Alpe** area above Chantemerle has a good but sometimes busy nursery area, and Briançon has a beginner area of its own at the 1625m gondola mid-station. Both Monêtier and Villeneuve have commendable nursery slopes and beginner lifts at their bases. For those who have mastered the nursery slopes, a long green (beginner) run from Col Méa at the top of the ski area, all the way down to Villeneuve/Le Bez is the next step.

Intermediates

This area is best suited to intermediate-level skiers ('for an average skier there are few better places'). Monêtier has some enjoyable red (intermediate) pistes through the woods. The Vallon de la Cucumelle above Fréjus is a good red run but can become icy in spring: 'Varied from being wide and treeless at the top to narrow and mogulled in a few places, although nothing a three- to four-week skier could not cope with.' From Bachas at 2180m down to the valley at Monêtier there is a wide choice of intermediate runs through the woods. Le Bois is a short, but fun, tree-lined red piste, which is also pleasant in fresh powder.

Advanced

Overall, Monêtier is the best area of the mountain for advanced skiers, although the high and exposed link with Villeneuve can sometimes be closed, both in harsh weather conditions and at the end of the season when the slopes quickly lose their snow. Isolée is an exciting black (difficult) run, which starts on the ridge from L'Eychauda at 2659m and plunges down towards Echaillon. Tabuc is a long black through the woods with a couple of steep and narrow pitches. The Casse du Boeuf, a sweeping ridge through the trees back to Villeneuve, is 'outstanding' and 'the best black run we have ever skied'. Its natural snow is supplemented by snow-cannon when necessary.

Off-piste

The Fréjus-Echaillon section above Villeneuve provides some of the best runs for experienced skiers, with short and unprepared trails beneath the mountain crest. L'Yret chair-lift gives easy access to some off-piste runs including the testing face under the lift, which has a gradient of 35 degrees at its steepest point and often becomes mogulled. The Serre Chevalier lift map includes a separate map of off-piste itineraries.

Ski schools and guiding

We have generally favourable reports of the ESF in both Serre Chevalier and Briançon, although good spoken English is not always high on the list of the instructors' qualities. There are five ski schools in Serre Chevalier and six mountain-guiding companies for off-piste skiing. The Buisonnière Ski School is 'excellent, with small groups, the instructor spoke good English, had a sense of humour and the tuition was clear'. Both the ESF and Buisonnière's private lessons are recommended, although we have no reports of the International Ski School (ESI) in Villeneuve/Le Bez and Chantemerle.

Snowboarding

All the ski schools offer snowboarding lessons for all ages. First Tracks is a specialist school in Villeneuve and is run by the French Ski School (ESF). Its snowboarding camps include half-board accommodation, lift passes and video tuition for beginners through to advanced-level. There is a half-pipe at the bottom of L' Yret chair.

Mountain restaurants

The choice of eating places is small for an area of this size, although the quality is generally high. Pï Mai, at the foot of the Vallon de la Cucumelle run in Fréjus, is highly praised for its 'excellent food and good atmosphere; the *Croûte* is especially good'. La Bachas is recommended, and Jacques A is 'crowded, but the place to go to at 4.40pm every day as it has the best atmosphere'. L'Echaillon is said to be 'pretty and off the beaten track, with friendly staff', but is also said to be the 'poorest value for money'. Le Grand Alpe serves 'big portions', and Aravet 2000, at the top of the Aravet gondola, is criticised as 'mediocre, with bland food and casual service'. Père et Noèlle, at the bottom of the same gondola, has 'large, beautiful salads'.

Off the mountain

Monêtier (1500) is the furthest resort from Briançon and is the quietest and least-affected by modern architecture. It is a charming rural spa village, which attracts fewer tourists than its neighbours. Next along the valley is Villeneuve, with its oldest section, Le Bez, at the top of the village and closest to the slopes. At the bottom of the village, beside the river, is an attractive narrow street with bars and restaurants. In the centre and above the main road is Villeneuve itself, a collection of modern apartment buildings including a small shopping centre. Chantemerle is the closest village to Briançon and acts as a base-station for commuters staying elsewhere in the valley. It has a good shopping centre.

The old town of Briançon became a ski resort when the Prorel gondola was built just a few years ago. It is the main commercial centre of the region and the last major town before the Italian border. It does not have the atmosphere of a typical ski resort. However, the advantages of staying in a real town like this are many, including the large choice of shops and restaurants, a hypermarket, and favourably priced hotels.

Accommodation

Most of Serre Chevalier's accommodation is in apartments, some 40 hotels throughout the three main villages and more than 20 in Briançon. The Altea, Vauban and Parc hotels are the town's three-stars. The Pension des Ramparts is a small and simple hotel with a loyal following. Le Clos de Chantemerle is a popular two-star with good food. L'Alliey in Monêtier is a charming and central hotel with a fine menu. L'Auberge du Choucas, also in Monêtier, is known for its gastronomic cuisine. The Christiania in Villeneuve is on the main road, so make sure you ask for a room overlooking the river rather than the traffic. The Lièvre Blanc, also in Villeneuve, is British-owned.

Eating in and out

A car is great for visiting the many restaurants along the valley. Le Petit Duc is a friendly crêperie beside the river in the lower part of Villeneuve/Le Bez. Pastelli in Le Bez has been criticised for its 'unimaginative food'. Le Bidule, also in Le Bez, has a friendly ambience and specialises in fresh fish and seafood ('excellent, with a huge choice'). L'Auberge du Choucas in Monêtier serves fine regional cuisine, and La Brasera, in the same village, has delicious pizzas. L'Aigle Fin in Chantemerle's new commercial centre is recommended. Le Passé Simple in Briançon has a historic Vauban menu with recipes from the seventeenth century. The Rallye hypermarket in Briançon is the best place for food shopping.

■ OTHER SPORTS

Ice-driving, snow-shoeing, aeroclub, parapente, hang-gliding, swimming, helicopter rides, skating, dog sledding, winter walks, night-skiing, sleigh rides

Après-ski

All three villages are quiet places after dusk, with nightlife mainly confined to the bars, although Le Frog and L'Iceberg discos in Villeneuve are both recommended. Others include Le Serre Che in Chantemerle, La Baita in Villeneuve/Le Bez and Le Sous Sol in Monêtier. The old fortified town of Briançon is well worth a visit; as well as its steep cobblestone streets and range of shops and restaurants, the views from the ramparts are breathtaking. Both Briançon and Monêtier have extensive health and fitness facilities.

Childcare

Each village has its own crèche and children's ski school. Kids de l'Aventure in Monêtier is for children aged between 10 and 15 years old, and includes ski tuition and a variety of other activities. Le Petit Train, a toy train on road-wheels, transports skiers and non-skiers around Villeneuve and is extremely popular with small children.

Skiing facts: **Serre Chevalier**

TOURIST OFFICE
BP 20, F-05240 La Salle Les Alpes, Hautes-Alpes
Tel: 33 92 24 71 88
Fax: 33 92 24 76 18

THE RESORT
By road Calais 1159km
By rail Briançon 6km, regular bus service to resort
By air Lyon 3 hrs, Turin 2 hrs, Grenoble 2½ hrs
Visitor beds 30,000
Transport free ski-bus with lift pass and regular bus service between all centres

THE SKIING
Linked or nearby resorts Briançon (l), Montgenèvre (n), La Grave (n), Les Deux Alpes (n), Puy-St-Vincent (n)
Longest run L'Yret, 1.3km (red)
Number of lifts 72 in Grand Serre Chevalier area
Total of trails/pistes 250km in linked area
Nursery slopes 10 runs
Summer skiing none
Snowmaking 13km covered

LIFT PASSES
Area pass Grand Serre Chevalier (covers all centres) 805FF for 6 days including 1 day in each of Les Deux Alpes, La Grave, Montgenèvre, Puy-St-Vincent and Alpe D'Huez
Day pass 160FF
Beginners no free lifts
Pensioners 60 yrs and over as juniors
Credit cards accepted yes

SKI SCHOOLS
Adults ESF (1350, 1400, 1500) and ESI (1350, 1400), 610-780FF for 6 days
Private lessons 155-165FF per hr
Snowboarding ESF (1350, 1400, 1500) and ESI (1350, 1400), prices as regular ski lessons. First Tracks, 2,700-3,400FF for 6 days, including video tuition, lift pass and half-board accommodation
Cross-country ESF (1350, 1400, 1500) and ESI (1350, 1400), 160FF for 3 hrs, licence 130FF per wk. Loipe 45km
Other courses telemark, monoski, skwal, race training
Guiding companies Bureau des Guides du Serre d'Aigle, Compagnie des Guides de L'Oisans, Ecole Buissonnière, Montagne et Ski, Montagne à la Carte, Ecole de l'Aventure

CHILDREN
Lift pass children (4-8 yrs) 425FF for 6 days, juniors (9-16 yrs) 635FF for 6 days, free for 3 yrs and under
Ski kindergarten Kids Club (1500), 9am-7pm, 1,450FF for 5 days including lunch
Ski school ESF (1350, 1400, 1500) 505FF for 6 days, ESI (1350, 1400) 780FF for 6 days
Non-ski kindergarten Les Poussins, 8 mths and over, 9am-5pm, 195FF per day including lunch. Les Schtroumpfs, 6 mths and over, 9am-5pm, 6 mths and over, 165FF per day not including lunch. Halte de Pré Chabert, 18 mths and over, 180FF per day not including lunch, 1,000FF for 6 full days

FOOD AND DRINK PRICES
Coffee 6FF, glass of wine 18FF, small beer 15FF, dish of the day 35FF

The Trois Vallées

ALTITUDE Méribel 1450-1700m (4,756-5,576ft), Courchevel 1300-1850m
(4,264-6,068ft), Val Thorens 2300m (7,544ft), Les Menuires 1850m (6,068ft)

The French, who rarely venture beyond their own mountains, claim the Trois Vallées, with dubious justification, is the largest ski area in the world. While the true winner in this category is almost certainly the Sella Ronda in the Dolomites, the Trois Vallées team takes top step on the international podium for best all-rounder.

At one end, above the Bozel Valley, sits chic **Courchevel 1850** with its not-so-chic satellites beneath it. At the other, the pastoral Vallée de Belleville is dominated by functional **Val Thorens** and the *bête noire* **Les Menuires**. In the middle sits cosmopolitan **Méribel** in Les Allues Valley, with its British bulldog over-tones. The skiing is reached by two winding mountain roads from Moûtiers, or by an under-used gondola from **Brides-Les-Bains**.

MERIBEL
■ GOOD POINTS

Large ski area, widest choice of luxury chalets in the Alps, resort-level snow, extensive nursery slopes, suitable for all standards of skier

■ BAD POINTS

Heavy traffic and limited parking, no free ski-bus, skiing inconvenience from much of accommodation, limited nightlife

What puts the Trois Vallées ski-lengths ahead of its rivals in the super-circus league is the range and sophistication of its resorts, coupled with the variety of the skiing on offer. An ideal topography means that the links between each valley are serious runs in their own right.

Its critics claim that 90 per cent of the skiing is geared towards inter-mediates, but then 90 per cent of skiers are intermediates, and it still provides more than adequate scope for those of greater or lesser ability. This substantial chunk of the French Alps is covered by what is considered the most efficient overall lift system in any country.

The annually improving combination of cable cars, gondolas, detachable chairs and tows is of gargantuan proportions. Mammoth, the largest US resort, has 30 lifts; the Trois Vallées has 200, all of them linked by a mighty 600km of prepared slopes and uncounted hectares of off-piste. Méribel alone has an extraordinary 16 gondolas.

Given a single week's holiday, a competent skier will barely scratch the surface. It takes an entire 20-week season based in at least two different resorts to get to grips with it. However, the area is not without fault. The mountains are managed by an uneasy alliance of seven separate lift companies, each of which looks after itself extremely well and pays lip service to its agreement with the others. The result is a series of exasperating shortfalls. Ski passes are checked on almost every lift and

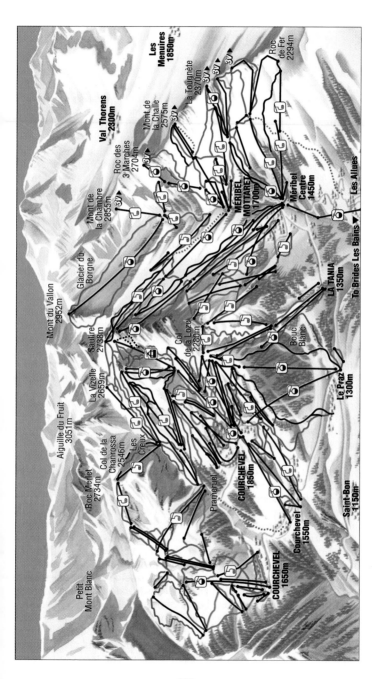

an unnecessarily complicated ticket structure does not include half-day Trois Vallées area passes.

The French regard it as their premier destination. At peak holiday times all 115,000 beds will be taken, but even at New Year it passes the acid test of a good ski area: when the whole area is operational you will struggle to find a queue of 15 minutes anywhere on the mountain.

COURCHEVEL
■ GOOD POINTS

Large ski area, big vertical drop, excellent nursery slopes, suitable for all standards of skier, long cruising runs, tree-line skiing, resort-level snow, gourmet restaurants, wide choice of luxury accommodation, skiing convenience

■ BAD POINTS

Limited activities for non-skiers, high prices in Courchevel 1850

Each resort has its own character, as well as its individual ski area aside from the hundreds of kilometres they share. Méribel has such a strong British chalet-holiday tradition, that in some bars French is either the second language or not spoken at all. Courchevel is ultra-chic and international, at least at 1850, where designer ski suits outnumber their brasher chain-store counterparts. Les Menuires could not be a bigger contrast, a budget resort where the main evening entertainment for the hardcore of bourgeois French who make up its winter inhabitants is watching the rented television in their rented apartment, or walking the dog, which accompanied them on holiday. Val Thorens, architecturally slightly more pleasing, is for skiers who want to be as sure of finding snow in early December as in late April. Brides-Les-Bains in the valley below Méribel is connected by a 25-minute gondola ride and provides a budget base and useful back door into the system.

On the mountain
top 3300m (10,825ft) bottom 1300m (4,264ft)

Each resort has its own large ski area, which is covered by a single-valley local pass. Less than confident intermediates are strongly advised to take stock of what is on offer before buying the more expensive Trois Vallées pass. The links between the three valleys are liable to be suspended when snow cover is insufficient or when stormy conditions prevail. You should also note that the standard Trois Vallées lift map is printed back to front and **Courchevel 1650**, which appears to be the most westerly resort in the complex, is in fact the most easterly. What appear to be south-facing slopes are in fact north-facing and consequently hold the snow well.

The Les Allues Valley, dominated by **Méribel** and its higher satellite of Mottaret, lies in the middle and provides the ideal jumping-off point for exploring the whole area, but does not necessarily give the easiest access to the most rewarding of the skiing.

Both sides of the open valley are networked with modern lifts for all standards. The western side culminates in a long skiable ridge, which separates it from the beautiful Belleville Valley and the resorts of **Val**

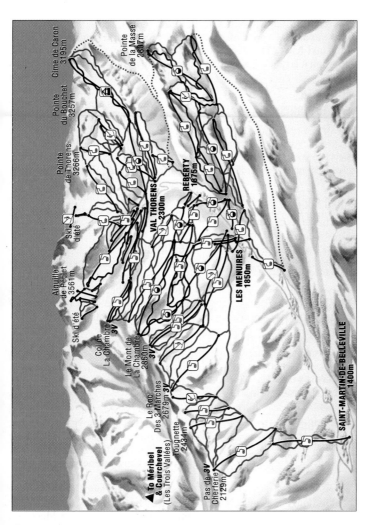

Thorens, **Les Menuires** and **St-Martin-de-Belleville**.

The eastern side rises to the rocky 2738m summit of Saulire and the Col de la Loze at 2274m. Beyond lies the Bozel Valley and Courchevel — not one but four separate resorts at different altitudes — as well as the modern purpose-built addition of **La Tania**. At the head of the Les Allues Valley lies the 2952m Mont du Vallon, the most easterly of the horseshoe of 3000m peaks accessed from Méribel and Val Thorens, which provide some of the most scenic and demanding off-piste in the region.

The ski area has now been extended over the back, beyond Val

Thorens and the Cime de Caron, into a fourth valley, the Maurienne. This was always a great off-piste itinerary involving a long climb or a very long taxi back. The red (intermediate) run down is still not pisted, although it is quickly packed by skiers. A run of 660 vertical metres takes you down to the Chalet Refuge de Plan Bouchet mountain hut and restaurant. A fast chair takes you back up to the Col de Rosaël. Expansion plans here include a series of chairs and a huge valley car-park designated not so much for the inhabitants of the Maurienne, but for the thousands of Italians from Turin who can reach this link to the Trois Vallées through the Fréjus Tunnel. The overcrowding does not bear contemplation.

Beginners

Facilities for beginners are good in all the major resorts of the Trois Vallées, although the sheer volume of visitors here is bound to lead to a level of impersonal instruction, which is not conducive to the early learning process. The runs surrounding the altiports at both Courchevel and Méribel are excellent beginner areas with enough length to help build confidence. The green (beginner) Truite run connects Mottaret with Méribel and is popular with novice ski classes, but for more proficient skiers taking the whole run 'in the tuck' on their way to lunch it can be unnerving.

Once the basics have been conquered the area lends itself to easy exploration. Les Teppes Noires followed by Le Gros Tougne and L'Allée take you from Méribel via the Tougnette gondola down to Les Menuires. It is an ideal chance for a second-week skier to feel he or she is really going somewhere.

Intermediates

The Trois Vallées constitutes what many skiers rightly regard as the greatest intermediate playground in the world, a seemingly endless network of moderately graded runs, which challenge all levels of skiers. The Combe de Vallon is a magnificent cruise of 1100 vertical metres from the top of Mont Vallon all the way down to Méribel Mottaret. The Cime de Caron above Val Thorens is more famous for its Combe du Caron black

---

VAL THORENS
■ GOOD POINTS

Large ski area, resort-level snow, long skiing season, glacier skiing, ski-in ski-out convenience at its best, variety of off-piste skiing, freedom from cars

■ BAD POINTS

Lack of tree-level skiing, exposed and cold in mid-winter, limited for non-skiers, lack of après-ski, late-season lift queues

---

LES MENUIRES
■ GOOD POINTS

Large ski area, suitable for all standards of skier, long cruising runs, sunny slopes, off-piste skiing, well-run children's village, budget prices, extensive snowmaking, skiing convenience

■ BAD POINTS

Ugly architecture in centre, heavy traffic, limited après-ski, lack of tree-line runs, limited for non-skiers

---

(difficult) descent, but there is also a red (intermediate) variation around the shoulder, as well as the long and scenic Itinéraire du Lou.

The blue (easy) Arondiaz run from the top of Courchevel 1650 back down to the resort is a great last run of the day and its north-facing nature means usually excellent conditions.

Advanced

With a maximum gradient of around 38 per cent, the couloirs of Courchevel are among the most radical black runs marked on any piste map in the world. Take the 150-person cable car up from the Courchevel side of Saulire and take extra care on the entry route, which can be dangerously icy. In most conditions, they are not as radical as they look from below.

The Courchevel side of Saulire is the starting point for a magnificent descent of 1400 vertical metres down to Le Praz. It is more tiring than technically difficult, apart from the black Jockeys piste on the final section, which is shaded for most of the winter and consequently icy. La Masse above Les Menuires boasts Les Enverses and the usually icy La Dame Blanche.

Off-piste

The guided off-piste opportunities are outstanding and one of the great charms of the Trois Vallées is that after a major dump the best powder runs are some of the most accessible. The long runs down to Les Menuires from the Méribel ridge are outstanding.

The summit of La Masse on the far side of the Belleville Valley is also the starting point for long itineraries towards St-Martin and into the Vallon du Lou. Roc Merlet, above Courchevel 1650, is the jump-off point for a glorious descent around the shoulder into the Avals Valley, which brings you back, after a short walk, to 1650. Mont Vallon and the Col du Fruit offer further excitement.

Snowboarding

There is a new half-pipe for snowboarders at the top of Les Plattières gondola in Méribel. In Courchevel 1850, the Gansen slope is especially for boarders. Neither Val Thorens nor Les Menuires have any special facilities.

Ski schools and guiding

Courchevel has Ski Masterclass, its own British ski school, run by Alan Hole and Kenny and Sue Dickson. It is staffed by eight BASI instructors all of whom have passed the rigorous *équivalence* test, which allows them to work legally as instructors in France. We also have positive reports of Ski Academy at Courchevel 1850, where class size is restricted to seven and instructors are described as 'patient and sympathetic'. Ski Cocktail in Méribel has overcome initial expansion problems to provide a more than viable alternative to the French Ski School (ESF) in the resort; instructors are praised for their sympathetic attitude, although the standard of English is not always as high as would be expected of a school set up primarily for the Anglo-Saxon market. The International Ski School (ESI) is the only real competition. Magic in Motion in Méribel maintains a lower profile ('somewhat disorganised with no central office, but friendly instruction').

Mountain restaurants

The majority of mountain restaurants in the Trois Vallées serve bland fast-food at truly shocking prices and regular visitors tend to head down into the resorts at lunchtime. Pierre Plat at the top of the Saulire gondola wins a special award for overpriced fare and sullen service. Staff refuse to supply tap water for free.

Try Bel-Air at the top of the Courchevel 1650 bubble and La Soucoupe above Courchevel 1850. Le Bouc Blanc at the top of La Tania bubble, is always welcoming. Chez Jacques is an old hut just off the piste above Les Menuires. Jacques doesn't always cook, but when the mood takes him, his are the finest and cheapest *steak frites* on the mountain.

The French Connection (Méribel) serves toasted sandwiches. Les Castors (Méribel), at the foot of the Truite run, has great spaghetti with each serving cooked in individual copper pans. Roc des Trois Marches offers consistently good value. Chalet de Pierres above Courchevel 1850, with liveried waiters hovering on the edge of the piste, is a gastronomic delight, but you'll need a bulging wallet. Le Kalico at Courchevel 1850 is recommended. Plein Soleil at Mottaret is 'perfect for a sunny-day lunch'.

L'Ours Blanc is the smartest hotel in Les Menuires and also serves 'excellent value lunches'. Quatres Vents above Les Bruyères has a strong following. Pub Le Ski Lodge down in La Tania is said to offer 'the cheapest lunches in the Trois Vallées'.

Off the mountain

Méribel alone attracts more British skiers than anywhere in the Alps, except for Val d'Isère, which explains why half the legally bonded British tour operators now offer holidays here. Indeed, so many British holiday or work in the resort during the winter months that any attempt to order a drink or a meal in French is met with a look of blank incomprehension.

It is a smart, expensive resort, which offers more luxury chalets and apartments with en-suite bathrooms than any other ski destination. Méribel was founded by an Englishman; dedicated pre-war skier Colonel Peter Lindsay built the first lift here in 1938. Amazingly, the resort has stayed faithful to his original concept of a traditional chalet village, with every building constructed in local stone-and-wood in harmony with the mountain setting. Today, it has stretched, with little or no long-term planning, into a hotch-potch of confusingly named hamlets at different altitudes. Their convenience for skiing, shopping and nightlife varies considerably.

'The Heart of The Trois Vallées' is its marketing slogan, but because of its diffuse layout, Méribel is devoid of a single heart and its atmosphere is muted accordingly. Méribel Centre (1450m) is now known generally as Méribel and is the commercial core, a one-street village with the tourist office 'square' as its focal point. It has a number of boutiques and souvenir shops beyond the usual sports shops and one main supermarket. The bi-weekly street-market provides colour and the occasional clothing bargain.

Méribel Mottaret (1700-1800m) is a separate satellite further up the valley, which itself is now divided into separate hamlets. It is 22 years old and should really be accorded its own resort status. The higher altitude of Mottaret ensures good snow cover and is the starting grid for the best motorway skiing. This may explain why Alain Prost built his winter home here, but it has few other obvious temptations.

The different sectors of Méribel are all connected by a bus service, which is supposed to run every 20 minutes but often fails to do so. Disgracefully, the bus is not included in the lift pass. Traffic, parking and pollution from petrol fumes are serious problems, which are not adequately addressed.

Courchevel is not one, but four quite separate resorts at different altitudes, which are linked on-piste, but have nothing else in common. Before booking a holiday here it is crucial to discover exactly where you will be staying. Courchevel 1850 is the international resort with the jet-set image and most tour operators are happy for you to think that their accommodation is here, even when it is not.

Courchevel 1850 is the most fashionable of all French ski destinations. Like its rival Megève, a high proportion of its designer-clad visitors come here to see and to be seen. The only exercise they take is centred around the ferrying of gastronomic delights from plate to mouth at the resort's clutch of fine restaurants.

Unlike Megève, the other Parisian playground, 1850 offers seriously challenging skiing, which is some of the best and most accessible in the whole of the Trois Vallées, and its high altitude ensures early- and late-season snow cover. For all that, it is not a particularly charming resort in aspect; a sprawl of chalet-style wooden buildings over four serpentine bends in the road leading to the central lift station.

A covered mall houses expensive boutiques, and a couple of supermarkets cater for the more mundane needs of self-caterers. The Beautiful People live above the resort in the secluded Jardin des Alpins sector. This Millionaire's Row of sumptuous chalets and shockingly expensive hotels, tucked discreetly away in the trees, provides at least an illusion of privacy.

Courchevel 1650 is 200 vertical metres lower down the mountain and the social scale. Many would argue that this is 'le vrai Courchevel' with its year-round population and feel of the farming community it once was. The intermediate skiing here is extensive and is isolated from the main Trois Vallées thoroughfares; as a consequence it is wonderfully uncrowded even at peak times.

Courchevel 1550 is off the beaten track away from the heart of the skiing. It is little more than a cluster of apartment buildings and a few hotels. It is popular with self-catering French families.

Le Praz (sometimes known as Courchevel 1300) is an old and still functional farming village at the foot of the lift system, which is becoming an increasingly popular and cheap base for Courchevel's skiing. Snow cover is by no means guaranteed in the hamlet, however, it is served by two gondolas, which swiftly take you up towards the Col de la Loze or into 1850.

Val Thorens, at 2300m, used to be the highest ski resort in Europe while Obergurgl, which has a church, claimed to be the highest ski parish. After 22 years Val Thorens has established itself as the place for late-season skiing and has also built its own little church to sneak away with both titles.

It is one of the only resorts in Europe where you are virtually guaranteed snow at resort level over both Christmas and Easter. On a sunny day its functional, purpose-built architecture is positively attractive compared with its nearest neighbour, Les Menuires. You can ski into the centre of the car-free village and view the dramatic horseshoe of surrounding peaks.

In bad weather, this far above the tree-line you may be forgiven for thinking you have been stranded amid the mountains of the moon. Few places in the Alps are colder and a white-out is just that.

Poor **Les Menuires** down the valley from here at 1850m has a joke reputation as the ugliest resort in the Alps. Certainly the original centre **La Croisette** is a prime example of the alpine architectural vandalism of the 1960s. Minuscule apartments are housed in anonymous box-like buildings clad in unpainted concrete. However, a small fortune was spent cleaning up the place for the 1992 Winter Olympics. No longer do you get the feeling that you might be mugged while wandering around here at night.

The more modern satellites of **Reberty** and **Les Bruyères** are far more appealing and you can holiday in comfort without hardly ever venturing into La Croisette. Both are on the piste and have their own hotels and restaurants, as well as all the shops you might need, apart from a chemist (there is one in La Croisette).

The main skiing here is exceptionally sunny. A bank of snow-cannon installed for the Olympic slalom keeps the home run in good condition until late into the season.

Accommodation

In **Méribel** the lavish Aspen Park is now a Club Med, but other four-star hotels include L'Antarès, Le Chalet and the ever popular Grand Coeur. However, Méribel began as a chalet resort and so it remains. In the short summer months the village rings to the sounds of saw and hammer as new luxury establishments sprout in response to demand. Hotel Saulire, operated by Snowtime, is much praised for the quality of its food, although accommodation is 'simple'. Meriski has the widest portfolio of luxury chalets here.

Mottaret has five hotels including the three-star Les Arolles and La Tarentaise, but most guests stay in apartments. These vary from the compact Pierre et Vacances studios for four to the unashamed indulgence of The Ski Company's Olympie III chalet.

Courchevel 1850 has a host of four-star de luxe hotels (there are no five-stars in France), which pamper their exotically wealthy guests. The Byblos de Neige is the star. Les Airelles, owned and managed by the redoubtable Raymonde Fenestraz, the property princess of Courchevel, is more discreet. The three-star La Sivolière provides four-star comfort. The reasonably priced two-star Courcheneige is situated on the edge of the piste near the altiport and caters for families. The quality of some of the luxury catered chalets here ranks alongside the smartest hotels. The Forum apartment complex is much praised by reporters ('nice, modern and in a good location').

Accommodation in **Val Thorens** is divided between the standard French apartments and mainly unremarkable hotels; the four-star Fitz-Roy is the exception. Readers report that the apartments in the Naska block of the Temples du Soleil complex are 'surprisingly spacious with enormous bathrooms'. Résidence Altineige is said to be 'extremely noisy', thanks to the Ski Rock Café next to the reception area. Hotel Trois Vallées in the centre of Val Thorens is praised as 'comfortable, convenient and friendly'. Le Bel Horizon and Le Sherpa ('best hotel in town, very friendly') are reporters' favourites, along with Le Val Chavière where 'staff are actually pleased to see you'.

Les Menuires is again apartment territory: the older ones in La Croisette are cramped and largely to be avoided. Their more modern counterparts in Les Bruyères are already showing signs of exhaustion. However, reporters praise the Necou apartments at Reberty 2000 as being a 'high quality, well-designed ski-in ski-out complex'. The Hotel Les Latitudes in Les Bruyères offers some of the best-value accommodation and five-course dinners in the region ('quite exceptional food, pleasant rooms, and ideally situated on the edge of the piste – don't tell anyone else').

Eating in and out

Méribel has a surprisingly limited choice of good restaurants for a resort of its size, mainly because such a large proportion of the clientèle self-cater. La Cava is good for fondue and Le Jardin d'Hiver has fresh seafood. Refurbished La Taverne offers pizzas and Savoyard dishes and has, in a season, become one of the main off-piste focal points of the Méribel Centre. Chez Kiki specialises in charcoal grills in appealing surroundings. Santa Marina is praised for 'excellent pizza and pasta'. Bibi

Crêperie in the main street is said to be good value.

In **Mottaret**, Ty Sable is recommended. Hotel Tarentaise, on the edge of the piste, is British-managed but popular with the French for its food. The central Côte Brune restaurant has changed hands but is still a culinary mainstay. Pizzeria du Mottaret is the bar/restaurant with the best atmosphere and has reasonable prices. There is a small supermarket at Le Hameau and a larger one in Mottaret.

■ OTHER SPORTS

Méribel: skating on Olympic ice rink, snow-shoeing, parapente, hang-gliding, tobogganing, swimming
Courchevel: parapente, tobogganing, aeroclub, skating, luge-ing, ice-climbing, squash, swimming, snow-shoeing, snowmobiling
Val Thorens: micro-lighting, car-racing on ice, swimming, indoor tennis and squash, indoor golf, volleyball, climbing wall
Les Menuires: parapente, skating, swimming, snowmobiling, hang-gliding, snow-shoeing

Courchevel 1850 abounds in fine restaurants. The Chabichou Hotel has two coveted Michelin stars, as does Le Bateau Ivre. The seafood restaurant at Byblos de Neige is a wonder to behold, however few reporters found themselves in this envious price bracket.

On a more mundane scale, Jack's Bar (La Saulire) in the square at 1850 is a resort institution serving modestly priced French food in a warm atmosphere.

Restaurants at **Courchevel 1650** are less Parisian in price. La Poule au Pot is warmly recommended for classic French fare and Le Yeti for fresh seafood. Expect to pay around £25 per head including wine. At **Courchevel 1550**, try the Hotel l'Adret for a quiet provincial French lunch or dinner.

Le Praz (Courchevel 1300) is famed for the outrageously expensive but nevertheless compelling Bistrot du Praz and for Charley, its *bon viveur* host. A *dégustation* of four different types of *foie gras* is the house speciality. Hotel Les Peupliers, the original village inn, is also worth a visit for lunch or dinner and is more modestly priced.

Val Thorens has a limited choice of restaurants. El Gringo's Café in the Péclet shopping centre is the most popular. Le Galoubet is recommended at lunchtime for its dish of the day. Le Choucas, Le Scapin and La P'tite Ferme are also noted by readers.

Les Menuires is no gastronomic delight, but the half-board food in Hotel Les Latitudes in Bruyères is described as 'much more exciting than we could have hoped for'. Better restaurants include La Bouitte in nearby St-Marcel, and La Mascotte and Chalet Necou in St-Martin-de-Belleville.

Self-caterers heading for the Trois Vallées are strongly advised to stock up at the large hypermarket on the outskirts of Moûtiers before beginning the climb up to the main resorts, as prices are markedly cheaper at lower altitude.

Après-ski

In **Méribel**, much of the nightlife revolves around the bustling French

Connection and the Mark Warner Pub. La Taverne, now owned by a British financial consortium, which also owns Dick's T-Bar in Val d'Isère, is a rising contender for the most popular bar in town. Saint-Pères, once the sole disco, now has serious competition from L'Artichaud, which has live bands and a fun atmosphere into the early hours. Le Rond Point is 'very busy and the service is entirely in English'.

In **Courchevel 1850** the Albatross bar has 'good-value beer and snack meals'. La Grange and La Bergerie are outrageously expensive, but nevertheless crowded nightclubs. The real action is at the Dakota Rock Bar.

At **Courchevel 1650** Le Signal is the bar-restaurant where the locals meet. Le Phlouc (it means clown in France or pimple in Scotland) is a small, smoky and busy bar. By night Le Green Club has a modest entry fee, a British DJ and the best music in Courchevel at any altitude. Rocky's Bar is also always busy.

Le Praz is not the place for a raucous nightlife. The Crêperie has 'the best *vin chaud* in the business'. The Bar Brasserie (it bears no other name) is 'the only place with any life'.

Val Thorens has a limited number of night spots. These include Le Lincoln Pub, which is popular with the British and has a good atmosphere. The underground Malaysia Bar has music but is said to be 'expensive', and the Agora disco is small and busy. Both Le Chantaco and the bar in the Temples du Soleil have live music.

Les Menuires has live music most nights at Les Latitudes. La Mousse attracts teenagers, Le Passeport and Le Challenge also have live music. The Piano Bar Pourquoi Pas in St-Martin is also recommended.

Childcare

All the main resorts are well-served with both ski and non-ski kindergarten. However, here in the heartland of French skiing it is important to note that the kind of facilities offered may not be conducive to the enjoyment of your holiday as parents. The Gallic approach to childcare may seem harsh by northern European standards, with a serious emphasis on learning to ski without any accompanying element of enjoyment. The number of children who dig in their heels and tearfully refuse to return to these French establishments on day two of their holiday has led most major tour operators to set up their own more sympathetic crèches and even ski classes.

The ESF runs children's villages in all resorts. The best reports came from Les Menuires, where staff at Les Schtroumpfs are praised for their friendliness and dedication in looking after children from three months to two-and-a-half years old in the nursery and up to seven years in the kindergarten section. The village has a rope-lift for beginners and a longer drag. ESF teachers also take classes out on the mountain and there are good play facilities and a video room for non-skiing children.

Its equivalents in Courchevel 1850 and in 1650 are criticised as being 'too serious' in their approach. We have good reports of the ESF children's ski school in Méribel: 'although the classes were large, the teachers made the lessons fun. This was the first time my son really enjoyed ski school and wanted to go back each day'. In Val Thorens, the ESF runs a non-ski kindergarten for children from three months old. Académie des Neiges is for skiers from three to 16 years old.

Linked or nearby resorts

Two contrastingly different little villages provide alternative bases for skiing the Trois Vallées while avoiding the hustle of the mainstream resorts and their high prices.

St-Martin-de-Belleville 1400m (4,593ft)

This is the 'capital' of the Belleville Valley, a farming community at pastoral counterpoint to the high-tech world of the ski network above it. Reporters praise it as 'quiet and lived-in, unlike the larger towns in the area'. ABT Ski runs the comfortable Chalet Hotel Le Neiger here.

The old cheese-making village has considerable charm and a couple of fine restaurants. L'Etoile de Neige is a lunchtime favourite with ski guides. Les Airelles, on the main road out of the village, is said to offer 'a delicious three-course meal for around 100FF'. La Bouitte in neighbouring Saint Marcel is a serious exercise in gastronomy. The Eterlou Bar is where the locals meet.

St-Martin is connected into the system by a slow triple-chair. Loading has quickened with the addition of a 'moving carpet' conveyor belt. The two runs close to the village are the blue Biolley and the red Jerusalem, which are 'well managed'.

If staying in Méribel don't linger too long over lunch. Allow a full 45 minutes to reach the ridge of the valley on your way home.

TOURIST OFFICE
Tel 33 79 08 93 09
Fax 33 79 08 91 71

La Tania 1350m (4,429ft)

This purpose-built but pleasing village a couple of kilometres away by road from Le Praz is linked by piste to Courchevel 1850 as well as to Méribel via the Col de la Loze. It was constructed as a dormitory satellite for the thousands of extra visitors expected to attend the Albertville Olympics; in the event they stayed at home and watched it on television.

It is a pleasant and reasonably priced base served by a jumbo gondola and, despite its youth, has developed its own village atmosphere. During a heavy snowfall, the tree-lined slopes above it provide some of the most enjoyable powder skiing in the whole of the Trois Vallées area, yet are always under-used.

Hotel Montana has 'clean and comfortable rooms, good food, but not particularly generous portions for hungry skiers'. The resort's supermarket has a limited stock and is said to be 'unimpressive'. One reporter was also unmoved by the nightlife ('the place is a cemetery after dark').

Skiing facts: **Méribel**

TOURIST OFFICE
BP1, F-73551 Méribel, Savoie
Tel 33 79 08 60 01
Fax 33 79 00 59 61

THE RESORT
By road Calais 920km
By rail TGV Moûtiers 18km, regular bus service to resort
By air Chambéry 2 hrs, Geneva 3 hrs, Lyon 2½ hrs
Visitor beds 33,000
Transport free ski-bus with lift pass

THE SKIING
Linked or nearby resorts La Tania (l), Courchevel (l), Val Thorens (l), Les Menuires (l), St-Martin-de-Belleville (l)
Longest run Campagnol (Mont Vallon), 3.6km (red)
Number of lifts 57 in Méribel, 200 in Trois Vallées
Total of trails/pistes 105km (58% easy, 28% intermediate, 14% difficult), 600km in Trois Vallées
Nursery slopes 7 lifts
Summer skiing at Val Thorens
Snowmaking 18.3km covered

LIFT PASSES
Area pass Trois Vallées 1,035FF, Méribel Valley 845FF, both for 6 days
Day pass Méribel Valley 176FF, Trois Vallées 215FF
Beginners 1 free lift at Le Rond Point and 1 in Méribel Mottaret (special beginners' pass also available)
Pensioners reductions for 60 yrs and over
Credit cards accepted yes

SKI SCHOOLS
Adults ESF 185FF per day, 950FF for 6 days. Ski Cocktail, 600FF for 6 mornings. ESI, 177FF per day, 888FF for 6 days. Magic in Motion, details on request
Private lessons 277FF for 1½ hrs, 1,450FF per day
Snowboarding beginners (10am-1pm), intermediates (1.45-4.45pm), 720FF for 5 half-days
Cross-country ESF, prices as regular ski school. Loipe 33km
Other courses slalom, telemark, moguls, off-piste
Guiding companies through ski schools

CHILDREN
Lift pass 6-16 yrs, Trois Vallées 776FF, Méribel Valley 591FF, both for 6 days, free for 5 yrs and under
Ski kindergarten Les P'tits Loups (at Méribel and Méribel Mottaret), 3-5 yrs, 9.15am-5pm, 804FF for 6 days
Ski school ESF, 4-8 yrs, 1,233FF for 6 days not including lunch
Non-ski kindergarten Club Saturnin, 18 mths and over, 9am-5pm, 1,207FF for 6 days including lunch

FOOD AND DRINK PRICES
Coffee 10FF, glass of wine 12-15FF, small beer 10FF, dish of the day 65-75FF

TOURIST OFFICE
Tel 33 79 08 40 40
Fax 33 79 08 54 71

Skiing facts: **Courchevel**

TOURIST OFFICE
BP37, La Croisette, F-73122 Courchevel, Savoie
Tel 33 79 08 00 29
Fax 33 79 08 15 63

THE RESORT
By road Calais 925km
By rail TGV Moûtiers 25km, frequent buses
By air Chambéry 2 hrs, Geneva 3 hrs, Lyon 2½ hrs
Visitor beds 32,000
Transport free ski-bus with lift pass

THE SKIING
Linked or nearby resorts La Tania (I), Méribel (I), Val Thorens (I), Les Menuires (I), St-Martin-de-Belleville (I)
Longest run Les Creux, 4.2km (red)
Number of lifts 68 in Courchevel, 200 in Trois Vallées
Total of trails/pistes 180km in Courchevel, 600km in Trois Vallées
Nursery slopes 26 slopes
Summer skiing at Val Thorens
Snowmaking 474 snow-cannon

LIFT PASSES
Area pass Trois Vallées 1,035FF for 6 days, Courchevel 845FF for 6 days
Day pass Courchevel 176FF, Trois Vallées 215FF
Beginners 12 free lifts
Pensioners 60 yrs and over, Courchevel 591FF and Trois Vallées 776FF, both for 6 days
Credit cards accepted yes

SKI SCHOOLS
Adults ESF: (1850) 935FF, (1650) 840FF, (1550) 500FF, all for 6 days. Ski Academy, 650-750FF for 6 days. Ski Masterclass, details on request
Private lessons (1850) and (1650) 1,300-1,400FF, (1550) 1,200-1,300FF, Ski Academy 1,500FF, all per day (7 hrs)
Snowboarding ESF 1850, 9.30am-midday and 2.30-5pm, 1,350FF for 6 days
Cross-country all ski schools, times and prices on request. Loipe 50km
Other courses slalom, ski-touring, telemark, monoski, competition
Guiding companies through ski schools

CHILDREN
Lift pass 6-16 yrs, Courchevel 591FF and Trois Vallées 776FF, both for 6 days, free for 5 yrs and under
Ski kindergarten (1850) ESF Village des Enfants, 3-12 yrs, 9am-5pm, 1,155FF for 6 days including lunch. (1650) ESF, 3-5 yrs, prices and times as ski school. Vacances des Petites, 1,100FF for 6 days including lunch. (1550) ESF, 3-6 yrs, 9.30am-4.30pm, 900FF for 6 days not including lunch
Ski school (1850) ESF Village des Enfants, 3-12 yrs, 9am-5pm, 1,155FF for 6 days including lunch. (1650) ESF, Vacances des Petites, 3-5 yrs, 1,100FF for 6 days including lunch
Non-ski kindergarten (1850) Village des Enfants, 2 yrs and over, 9am-5pm, 235FF per day including lunch. Courchevel 1650, Vacances des Petites, 2-7 yrs, 9am-5pm, 1,155FF for 6 days including lunch

FOOD AND DRINK PRICES
Coffee 10FF, glass of wine 12-15FF, small beer 10-13FF, dish of the day 70-75FF

Skiing facts: **Val Thorens**

TOURIST OFFICE
F-73440 Val Thorens, Savoie
Tel 33 79 00 08 08
Fax 33 79 00 00 04

THE RESORT
By road Calais 928km
By rail Moûtiers 34km, frequent buses to resort
By air Chambéry 2 hrs, Geneva 3 hrs, Lyon 2½ hrs
Visitor beds 19,000
Transport free ski-bus

THE SKIING
Linked or nearby resorts La Tania (l), Méribel (l), Les Menuires (l), Courchevel (l), St-Martin-de-Belleville (l)
Longest run Boulevard Cumin, 3.6km (blue)
Number of lifts 27 in Val Thorens, 200 in Trois Vallées
Total of trails/pistes 120km in Val Thorens (40% easy, 50% intermediate, 10% difficult), 600km in Trois Vallées
Nursery slopes 2 lifts
Summer skiing 4 lifts and 4 runs on Péclet Glacier
Snowmaking 72 snow-cannon

LIFT PASSES
Area pass Trois Vallées 1,035FF, Val Thorens 770FF, both for 6 days
Day pass Val Thorens 176FF, Trois Vallées 215FF
Beginners 2 free lifts
Pensioners 60 yrs and over: Val Thorens 540FF, Trois Vallées 776FF, both for 6 days.

50% reduction for 65 yrs and over, 70 yrs and over free in Val Thorens and half-price for Trois Vallées, 80 yrs and over ski free in whole Trois Vallées
Credit cards accepted yes

SKI SCHOOLS
Adults ESF, 675FF for 6 half-days. ESI Ski Cool, 600FF for 5 half-days
Private lessons ESF 170FF per hr, ESI Ski Cool 190FF per hr
Snowboarding ESF and ESI Ski Cool, 600FF for 5 days (3 hrs per day)
Cross-country ESF, 140FF per half-day, 580FF for 6 half-days. Loipe 3km
Other courses telemark, moguls, skwal
Guiding companies through ESF

CHILDREN
Lift pass 6-15 yrs, Val Thorens 540FF, Trois Vallées 776FF, both for 6 days, free for 5 yrs and under
Ski kindergarten ESF Miniclub, 3-12 yrs, 9am-5.30pm, 1,200FF for 6 days including lunch. Bambi ski courses, 2½-4 yrs, 1,350FF for 6 days
Ski school ESF, 2½-12 yrs, 735FF for 5 days (5 hrs), ESI Ski Cool, 2½-12 yrs, 1,100FF for 5 days including lunch. ESF Stage Etoile, 5-12 yrs, 9am-5pm, 1,350FF for 6 days including lunch and 2 hrs play time
Non-ski kindergarten ESF, 3 mths-3 yrs, 1,315FF for 6 days including lunch

FOOD AND DRINK PRICES
Coffee 10FF, glass of wine 10FF, small beer 10FF, dish of the day 65FF

Skiing facts: **Les Menuires**

TOURIST OFFICE
BP22, Les Menuires, F-73440
St-Martin-de-Belleville, Savoie
Tel 33 79 00 73 00
Fax 33 79 00 75 06

THE RESORT
By road Calais 960km
By rail TGV Moûtiers 28km
By air Geneva 3 hrs, Lyon 2½ hrs,
Chambéry 2 hrs
Visitor beds 22,000
Transport free ski-bus around resort

THE SKIING
Linked or nearby resorts Méribel (I),
Courchevel (I), Val Thorens (I), La Tania (I),
St-Martin-de-Belleville (I)
Longest run La Masse, 3.5km (red)
Number of lifts 48 in Les Menuires and St-
Martin, 200 in Trois Vallées
Total of trails/pistes 120km in Les
Menuires, 600km in Trois Vallées
Nursery slopes 6 green and 12 blue runs
Summer skiing in Val Thorens
Snowmaking 70 hectares covered in Les
Menuires and St-Martin

LIFT PASSES
Area pass Les Menuires 850FF, Belleville
Valley 965FF, Trois Vallées 1,035FF, all for
6 days
Day pass Les Menuires 176FF, Trois

Vallées 215FF
Beginners 6 free lifts and Réseau Redruit
beginners area with 11 lifts (100FF per day)
Pensioners 60 yrs and over as children
Credit cards accepted yes

SKI SCHOOLS
Adults ESF 895FF for 6 days, ESI 850FF for
6 days, both 5½ hrs per day
Private lessons ESF 170FF per hr, ESI
175FF per hr
Snowboarding prices as regular ski school
Cross-country ESF, 895FF for 6 days (5½
hrs per day). Loipe 28km
Guiding companies through ESF and ESI

CHILDREN
Lift pass 6-16 yrs: Les Menuires 618FF,
Belleville Valley 745FF, Trois Vallées 760FF,
all for 6 days, free for 5 yrs and under
Ski kindergarten Village des Schtroumpfs,
3 mths-7 yrs, 772FF for 6 days
Ski school ESF 790-1,080FF for 6 days. ESI
745FF for 6 days
Non-ski kindergarten Village des
Schtroumpfs, 3 mths-4 yrs, 9am-4.30pm,
1,390FF for 6 days including lunch. Les
Marmottons, 2½-6 yrs, 1,390FF for 6 days
including lunch

FOOD AND DRINK PRICES
Coffee 6FF, glass of wine 8FF, small beer
10FF, dish of the day 50-60FF

Val d'Isère/Tignes

ALTITUDE Val d'Isère 1850m (6,068ft), Tignes 2100m (6,888ft)

Whenever two or three skiers are gathered together anywhere in the world the conversation will inevitably turn towards Val d'Isère and its linked sister resort, Tignes. Early in December — if snow permits — the self-crowned capital of modern European skiing traditionally hosts the first World Cup men's downhill. Between then and the May Bank Holiday, more British skiers come to this remote and rather unprepossessing resort at the head of the Tarentaise Valley than anywhere else.

It is a destination for serious enthusiasts, which somehow manages to blend a cocktail of high ski-tech and mass-market tourism with a smooth topping of sophistication. It is a social melting pot, and although it may not attract as many millionaires as Courchevel, those that it does can usually ski like a dream.

The ski area is directly linked to neighbouring Tignes and is jointly marketed as **L'Espace Killy**, after its most revered son who swept the board of gold at the 1968 Winter Olympics. The fact that Jean-Claude Killy actually comes from lowland Alsace and his elite clothing empire is now British-owned bothers no one at all.

The quality of the skiing, both on- and off-piste, is so varied and demanding that it has raised a whole genre of international experts (many of them British) who ski here at least twice a year and never anywhere else. A huge vertical drop of 1890m, coupled with 102 lifts including two high-speed underground railways, six gondolas and four cable cars, form the hardcore infrastructure. But for the expert the real joy lies in the unlimited off-piste opportunities to be found in this wild region on the edge of the Vanoise National Park.

VAL D'ISERE
■ GOOD POINTS

Large ski area, variety of intermediate and expert skiing, plenty of off-piste skiing, early- and late-season skiing, reliable snow record, extensive lift system, lively après-ski, tough runs

■ BAD POINTS

Strung-out village, limited for beginners, restricted choice of mountain restaurants, few activities for non-skiers, lack of skiing convenience

On the mountain
top 3439m (11,279ft) bottom 1550m (5,084ft)

Val d'Isère alone has eight major mountain-access points, which means that queues hardly exist at all, even at peak holiday times. The long valley floor is covered by an efficient ski-bus service mysteriously known as the *train rouge*, and a little experience means you can avoid even the smallest of rush-hour lift lines.

L'Espace Killy divides naturally into six separate ski sectors. On the Val d'Isère side there are **Col de l'Iseran/Pisaillas**, **Solaise** and **Bellevarde**, which are strung in a row along the curving road from the satellites of **Le Fornet** to **La Daille**. The first two sectors are linked by lift at altitude, with Solaise and Bellevarde linked only at valley level just beside the main resort. Bellevarde links with Tignes via the Tovière ridge.

TIGNES
■ GOOD POINTS

Large ski area, variety of intermediate skiing, plenty of off-piste skiing, year-round skiing, reliable snow record, skiing convenience, tough runs

■ BAD POINTS

Ugly resort architecture, lack of ambience, limited for non-skiers, lack of tree-level runs, limited après-ski, restricted choice of mountain restaurants

The skiing at Tignes divides itself into three areas: **Tovière**, **Grande Motte** (going up to the glacier), and **Palet/Aiguille Percée**. Tignes has a state-of-the-art underground railway which, after a prolonged and fraught gestation, has proved to be worth waiting for. Passengers are whisked at high speed up through the rock and permafrost from **Val Claret** at 2100m to the Panoramic restaurant at 3030m in just six minutes.

An alternative network of lifts takes you from **Tignes-Le-Lac** up towards the dramatic rock formation of L'Aiguille Percée in one direction or towards the greater demands of the Val d'Isère ski area in the other. A new lift has greatly eased the bottleneck caused by the volume of skiers moving between the two. In the depth of winter Tignes offers more skiing down to the lower lying hamlets of **Les Boisses** at 1850m and **Les Brevières** at 1550m.

Once up the mountain, it is the dispersal of skiers that is so clever. The lie of the terrain encourages you further into the mountain range, rather than immediately returning towards the valley, with the result that you rarely find yourself wanting to ski the same run twice. The choice of where to go and what to ski is enormous.

If the skiing in both resorts has a drawback it is that the authorities have a frank disregard for the needs of timid skiers. There seems little point in adopting the system of four grades of piste-colouring — green (beginner), blue (easy), red (intermediate), black (difficult) — when some of those listed as green are steep enough to become mogul fields. The reason is that the classification system in ski resorts is usually based on the average gradient of the run. If your level of proficiency suggests that you will be happiest on a green run, you do not want to encounter a single frozen bump, let alone a whole pasture of them at La Daille.

Piste-grooming has dramatically improved, thanks largely to the investment in equipment for the 1992 Olympics. However, the complexity and severity of the terrain make it prone to avalanches, and after a big dump visitors are often disappointed to discover that most lifts remain closed for a day. Those in the know take a day out on the protected pistes of Sainte-Foy. However, in windy conditions both resorts

La Grande Casse 3852m

La Grande Motte 3656m

Ptc Du Montet 3488m

Signal de L'Iseran 3241 m

L'Aiguille Percée

Col du Palet

Tignes Les Brévières 1550m

Tignes-Les-Boisses 1850m

VAL CLARET

Tignes-le-Lac

TIGNES 2100m

Grande Motte Funicular

Le Lavachet

Pte du Lavachet

Col de Fresse

Rocher de Bellevarde 2827m

Funival

La Daille 1785m

Tête de Solaise 2560m

VAL D'ISÈRE 1850m

Le Laisinant

Gorges de Malpasset

Le Fornet 1930m

benefit enormously from their underground railways. The Funival at La Daille gives guaranteed access to the Rocher de Bellevarde and some of the best runs in the resort.

Both Val d'Isère and Tignes are resorts for serious skiers. You do not have to be an expert, but it certainly helps. You do, however, have to be keen. If your idea of a skiing holiday is to eat, drink and dance, with just the occasional potter down the slopes between meals, then these are not the resorts for you. According to some dubious French statistics, the average skier in Courchevel skis for one hour a day; his or her counterpart in Val d'Isère and Tignes skis for more than five hours.

Beginners

Val d'Isère is unfairly denigrated as a resort for beginners. In fact, it has acceptable nursery slopes right in the centre of the village and a wide choice of ski schools. The problem stems from the fact that the resort is suitable for absolute novices only, not for wobbly second-weekers. Once you have graduated on to the main mountain, most of the slopes are too steep to build the confidence of lower intermediates.

The nursery slopes are free of charge, but the big problem is where to go next. Do not trust the piste map. Some of the runs marked green could frighten the daylights out of you. The Col de l'Iseran sector has some gentle runs, but as in other parts of the resort, it is too difficult to ski back to the valley. Tignes has a good choice of blue runs on the glacier, but it is a cold place in which to be falling about.

Intermediates

Piste-grading is not Val's strongest point and colour coding is on the dark side; some blues would be reds elsewhere, and you may find the odd red that is positively black by lowland Tyrolean standards. The Bellevarde sector provides plenty of variety. The Solaise Bumps down the front face of the 2560m Tête de Solaise are classic; never be persuaded to join the weekly torchlight descent here: the moguls can be the size of 2CVs.

The OK run around the shoulder of the Rocher de Bellevarde is the World Cup downhill course; when unprepared for racing it provides an excellent cruise. Orange, from the same starting point, is also superb.

Advanced

The Face de Bellevarde, reached by the Funival funicular railway, became the men's downhill course for the Albertville Olympics in 1992. It was sculptured by veteran Swiss racer Bernhard Russi at a reputed cost of £2 million (he even changed the route during construction to preserve the habitat of a rare wild flower). In February 1992 Austrian victor Patrick Ortlieb announced rather churlishly from the rostrum that he thought the course was terrible, and in all probability it will never be raced again. However, the legacy is a superb black run, which takes you back to Val in rather more than 2.2 minutes.

Sache, a superb long black, starts from the blue Corniche run below

L'Aiguille Percée and takes you almost down to Tignes-Les-Brevières where it merges with the red Pavot. The run down through the trees from the top of Le Fornet can be the best in the resort in the right snow conditions.

Off-piste

The starting points for some of the most challenging itineraries are ill-advisedly marked on the piste map. Once you begin you are on your own and it is easy to get lost or worse. It is imperative to have a local guide who can read the snow conditions and knows which routes are safe.

In fresh powder the Tour Charvet is a particular favourite. The Signal de l'Iseran/Glacier de Pisaillas sector has some of the most dramatic runs, but the beauty of Val and Tignes is the accessibility of good off-piste throughout the region.

Snowboarding

L'Espace Killy is in the forefront of the snowboarding movement. Hors Limites Surf School runs free introductory lessons, with equipment included, on the nursery slopes on Sunday afternoons. The school takes riders from five years old, in classes of 6 to 8. Most of the 12 ski schools also offer lessons.

Ski schools and guiding

To get the best out of this extraordinary ski area you need some expert help: the two resorts now have 12 ski schools and 800 instructors at peak times. Back in 1976 the French Ski School (ESF) had the monopoly throughout the country on instruction; Patrick and Jean Zimmer, two young ex-racers from Alsace, took on the ESF in true David and Goliath fashion — all the way to the French high court — and won the right to open their own ski school in Val d'Isère. Since their precedent, alternative schools have sprung up in almost every resort, but the Zimmer brothers' Top Ski has a cult following. The secret of its success is that it has remained small. Patrick and Jean take groups of six skiers off-piste in the mornings and guarantee to find them the best snow in the resort. They also give instruction on piste technique in the afternoons and arrange ski-tours and heli-skiing.

Other alternative ski schools include Snow Fun, Alpine Experience and Evolution 2. The ESF operates in both resorts, but Anglo-Saxons tend to favour the alternatives, which are linguistically and emotionally more geared towards to the needs of the calibre of skier who wants to spend his days in the powder off the beaten track.

We have continuing good reports of Snow Fun ('both instructors were personable, spoke fluent English and made the effort to learn the names of their pupils'). 'We were highly impressed by their organisation and emphasis on group grading,' said another reporter.

Mountain restaurants

Good mountain restaurants are both sparse and expensive. It costs about as much to build a new loo up a mountain as it does to install a lift, and L'Espace Killy concentrates on the latter. The better establishments are on the Val side, and include Trifollet, which is halfway down La Daille, and La Folie Douce, at the top of La Daille bubble. Upstairs at Le Signal, at the top of the Fornet cable car, maintains a consistently high standard. The top of Tovière is the place for a fine *steak frites* and a great view.

Wise skiers return to the valley at lunchtime, where restaurants are as busy as they are by night. The family-run Crech'Ouna near the Funival station is the favourite among reporters. Try its *fondue savoyarde*. A change of family management resulted in a temporary slip in standards, but reporters agree that it was back on stream last season. Clochetons is also praised for its 'reasonably priced *table d'hôte* lunch', which is 'beautifully cooked and served'. The Bouida, by the gondola at Les Brevières, is said to be good value.

The little restaurant at the Col du Palet is described as 'very welcoming'. La Savouna, near Palafour above Tignes-Le-Lac, is also popular.

Off the mountain

Apart from its eleventh-century church, precious little remains of the old village of Val d'Isère, which used to be called L'Aval de Tignes and housed the hunting lodges of the Dukes of Savoie, before becoming a winter-sports resort in 1932. Today, it has grown into a hotch-potch of a ski town, which sprawls from the apartment blocks of **La Daille** at one end to **Le Fornet** at the other. Until the mid-1980s the centre was an ill-defined area where the petrol stations, concrete *résidences* and the occasional more pleasing chalet gave way to a row of shops and bars on either side of the wide and busy main road.

However, a cluster of 'old' stone buildings (created for the 1992 Olympics), house the smarter boutiques and restaurants, and provide a pleasant village focal point, which the resort previously lacked. Attempts to limit the traffic, which tends to clog this long drawn-out resort, have been partially successful. Anyone who does not use the underground car-park or the parking lots on the edge of town risks a hefty fine.

The *train rouge*, the frequent and efficient free ski-bus service, provides the main form of transport. So conscious is the resort of its traffic pollution problem that it now runs the buses on a cocktail of diesel and vegetable oil. The result is brown exhaust fumes rather than blue — and the smell of a deep fat chip fryer supplants the scent of raw diesel.

The town centre houses a number of expensive boutiques and delicatessen, as well as the usual sports shops. The overall impression is of greater shopping opportunities than there actually are. The weekly market is good for bargains.

The old village of Tignes disappeared beneath the waters of the Lac du Chevril when the valley was dammed in 1952. Its replacements, a series of high-rise housing estates at varying altitudes around the 2000m mark, represent some of the most ghastly excesses of French alpine architecture of the 1960s.

The 'hamlets' of **Val Claret**, **Tignes-Le-Lac**, **Le Lavachet**, and even the much lower community of **Tignes-Les-Boisses**, would all benefit aesthetically from a compulsory demolition order. Only the valley farming community of **Tignes-Les-Brevières** should be reprieved. Demolition has never been an option; instead, serious but unsustained attempts have been made to reclad the worst of the untreated concrete with pine. New buildings are constructed in a far more sympathetic mountain-style. Under a heavy dump of snow anywhere can look presentable, but dedicated students of the period that also brought us the tower blocks of the 1960s should pay a visit here on a summer's day to catch its full concrete glory.

Skiing is year-round in Tignes. Permanent winter conditions on the Grande Motte Glacier allow racers and dedicated recreational skiers to practice on its wide and open slopes even in July and August. In winter at least, the ugliness of the resort itself is completely counterbalanced by the glory of the skiing.

Even in a winter of poor, early snow-cover such as in 1994–5, the run down to the village was open from November; while other resorts struggled to open enough rock-strewn runs for Christmas, visitors here were wallowing in powder.

Buses between the two resorts are neither frequent nor cheap, and taxis can be extortionate. However, a reporter notes that the bus system within Tignes is efficient. If you have your own car and want a change of scenery, day trips to Les Arcs, La Plagne, La Rosière and Sainte-Foy are possible.

Accommodation

In **Val d'Isère** a cluster of four-stars head a choice of 39 hotels; the Blizzard and the Christiania are the most comfortable. The Savoyarde and the Tsanteleina have a strong British following.

Most skiers stay in chalets or in self-catering apartments. The Ski Company has a collection of the most sumptuous designer chalets in what has become its own Millionaire's Row, up above Club Med. YSE, the largest specialist chalet operator here, runs Mountain Lodges, a seventeenth-century farmhouse divided into two units,

> ■ **OTHER SPORTS**
>
> **Val d'Isère:** parapente, snow-shoeing, ice-driving, dog-sledding, snowmobiling, curling, swimming
> **Tignes:** ice-driving, skating, indoor tennis and squash, parapente, hang-gliding, indoor climbing walls, husky sleigh-rides

which provides a similar hedonistic level of accommodation. The Maeva Le Rond Point apartments are said to be cramped ('the five-beds are smaller than the four-beds I have experienced in other resorts') but sufficiently equipped. Résidence Squaw Valley, tucked behind the piste near the old church, contains large and beautifully furnished apartments.

In **Tignes** most of the accommodation is in self-catering apartments, which vary dramatically in quality in direct relation to their age. The newer developments are much more spacious, and it is important to

Skiing facts: **Val d'Isère**

TOURIST OFFICE
BP 228, F-73150 Val d'Isère, Savoie
Tel 33 79 06 06 60
Fax 33 79 06 04 56

THE RESORT
By road Calais 960km
By rail Bourg-St-Maurice 32km
By air Geneva 3 hrs, Lyon 3 hrs, Chambéry 2½ hrs
Visitor beds 26,480
Transport *train rouge* free ski-bus

THE SKIING
Linked or nearby resorts Tignes (l), Sainte-Foy (n)
Longest run OK, 4.8km (red)
Number of lifts 51 in Val d'Isère, 102 in L'Espace Killy
Total of trails/pistes 300km in L'Espace Killy (59% easy, 33% intermediate, 8% difficult)
Nursery slopes 7 lifts
Summer skiing at Grande Motte, and limited on Glacier Grand Pisaillas
Snowmaking 125 snow-cannon in Val d'Isère, 225 in L'Espace Killy

LIFT PASSES
Area pass L'Espace Killy, 960FF for 6 days
Day pass L'Espace Killy 209FF
Beginners 7 free lifts
Pensioners 60 yrs and over 810FF for 6 days, free for 80 yrs and over
Credit cards accepted yes

SKI SCHOOLS
Adults ESF 1,030FF and Snow Fun 1,020-1,030FF, both for 6 days
Private lessons ESF, 9.30am-5pm, 1,420FF per day
Snowboarding ESF, 550FF for 6 half-days. Off-piste snowboarding 590FF for 5 days (3 hrs per day). Snow Fun group and private lessons, times and prices on request
Cross-country ESF private lessons, 400FF for 2½ hrs. Loipe 44km in L'Espace Killy
Other courses telemark, ski-touring, off-piste, slalom
Guiding companies Top Ski and through ESF

CHILDREN
Lift pass 6-12 yrs, 675FF for 6 days, free for 5 yrs and under
Ski kindergarten Snow Fun Club Nounours, 3-6 yrs, 9.30pm-5pm, 130FF for 3 hrs. Snow Fun, 5-12 yrs, 9.30am-5pm, 1,100FF for 6 days including lunch. ESF, 4-6 yrs, 9.30am-5pm, 1,100FF for 6 days including lunch
Ski school ESF and Snow Fun, as ski kindergarten
Non-ski kindergarten Garderie Isabelle, 2½-8 yrs, 210FF per day. Petits Poucets, 3-8 yrs, 8.30-5.30pm, 210FF per day

FOOD AND DRINK PRICES
Coffee 8-15FF, glass of wine 10-14FF, small beer 10-14FF, dish of the day 60-70FF

question your tour operator closely before booking. The Club Med building at Val Claret is said to be in serious need of refurbishment. Of the handful of hotels reporters strongly recommend the two-star Hotel de la Vanoise ('convenient, with an excellent breakfast and five-course dinner, fine room with bathroom and large balcony').

Eating in and out

In **Val d'Isère** the Grande Ourse is always dependable. La Solaise is the smartest restaurant in town (the kind of place where two people help you on with your coat) but is worth going for a treat. Perdrix Blanche is unpretentious and renowned for its fresh seafood.

Hotel fare in French ski resorts is often some of the best. The restaurants in the Savoyarde and Tsanteleina are excellent for dinner, and Sur Le Toit at the Sofitel is outstanding. Bananas is an old favourite among reporters. Try also the Brasserie des Sports and the Belle Etoile next to the swimming-pool. Crêpe Val, close to the post office, is recommended for regional specialities as well as crêpes. Le Pré d'Aval is also popular with reporters both at lunchtime and in the evening.

At **Tignes**, L'Osteria in Le Lavachet is recommended for raclette and *pierrade*. The Wobbly Rabbit in Val Claret serves Mexican food and fondue. The Codec supermarket in Val Claret is expensive but has a wide range of goods for self-caterers.

Après-ski

Val d'Isère positively buzzes with a fun-seeking après-ski crowd unparalleled elsewhere in France. 'Have An Affair in Val d'Isère' proclaimed the T-shirt of the 1980s as it gyrated sensually in the strobe-lighting of Dick's T-Bar. The T-shirt's creator is now a happily married London-based mother of four, but the T-Bar's still there — and so, too, is Dick. He sold it at the end of 1994 to a British financial consortium, but we are promised that what is the most famous bar and disco in the Alps will continue unchanged with Dick at the helm. Other bars come and go. Café Face and Couleur Café are riding high. Aventure is for the French, and Playbach has turned slightly sleazy. G Jay's has cheap beer, sausages and beans, chalet girls and a crush of homesick ex-pat ski bums.

'What après-ski?' said one reporter of **Tignes**. Certainly it is limited in comparison to that of its smoother and more sophisticated neighbour over the mountain. Harri's Bar and the predominantly British-frequented Cavern Bar in Le Lavachet have a strong following. The Cave du Lac in Tignes-Le-Lac has a small disco floor. 'When the lifts close skiers just melt back to their apartments without stopping off for one or two drinks before dinner,' was how one reporter summarised it. Later on, the Playboy Club is the liveliest spot and it also attracts the locals.

Childcare

Facilities for small children in Val d'Isère have improved but are still limited. If you want to take your under-eights on holiday, there are far

Skiing facts: **Tignes**

TOURIST OFFICE
BP 51, F-73321 Tignes, Savoie
Tel 33 79 06 15 55
Fax 33 79 06 45 44

THE RESORT
By road Calais 960km
By rail Bourg-St-Maurice 25km
By air Geneva 3 hrs, Lyon 3 hrs or
Chambéry 2½ hrs
Visitor beds 28,000
Transport free ski-bus between Les
Boisses and Val Claret

THE SKIING
Linked or nearby resorts Val d'Isère (l),
Sainte-Foy (n)
Longest run Double M, 1.4km (red)
Number of lifts 49 in Tignes, 102 in
L'Espace Killy
Total of trails/pistes 300km in L'Espace
Killy (59% easy 33% intermediate, 8%
difficult)
Nursery slopes 3 lifts
Summer skiing 13 pistes and 23 lifts on
Grand Motte Glacier
Snowmaking 100 snow-cannon in Tignes,
225 in L'Espace Killy

LIFT PASSES
Area pass L'Espace Killy, 960FF for 6 days
Day pass L'Espace Killy 209FF
Beginners 3 free lifts
Pensioners 60 yrs and over 810FF for 6
days, free for 80 yrs and over
Credit cards accepted yes

SKI SCHOOLS
Adults ESF, 900FF for 5 days. ESI, 590FF
for 5 half-days. Evolution 2 and Ski Action,
times and prices on request
Private lessons ESF and ESI, 170FF per hr,
1,450FF per day
Snowboarding ESF 595FF for 5 half-days.
Beginners 145FF per half-day. Snow Fun,
Kebra Surfing, Evolution 2, times and prices
on request
Cross-country ESF, 595FF for 5 half-days,
beginners 145FF per half-day. Loipe 44km
in L'Espace Killy
Other courses off-piste, slalom, race
training, moguls
Guiding companies Bureau des Guides,
Association 9 Valleys

CHILDREN
Lift pass 6-12 yrs, 675FF for 6 days, free
for 5 yrs and under
Ski kindergarten Les Marmottons,
8.30am-5pm, 2-10 yrs, 1,450FF for 6 days
including lunch
Ski school ESF, 840FF for 5 days, ESI
490FF for 5 half-days, both 4 yrs
and over
Non-ski kindergarten Les Petits Lutins,
crèche for 3 mths and over, day nursery for
3 yrs and over at Le Lac and Val Claret, both
1,450FF for 6 days including lunch

FOOD AND DRINK PRICES
Coffee 8-15FF, glass of wine 10-14FF,
small beer 10-14FF, dish of the day
60-70FF

better-equipped and more convenient resorts in which to do so. The resort's charm is an adult one.

In Tignes the Val Claret nursery slopes are strongly criticised: 'Skiers from the main runs ski through the area with total disregard; there is no reason at all why it cannot be roped off.'

Linked or nearby resorts

Sainte-Foy 1550m (5,084ft)

Sainte-Foy is an unremarkable old hamlet on the road up from Bourg-St-Maurice to Tignes and Val d'Isère. However, just above it and reached by a side road lies the ski resort of the same name. To call it a resort is, in fact, an exaggeration; the lift ticket office, ski shop and bar provide the only main base facilities of what is a raw and exciting ski area still wonderfully unknown and usually free of crowds, even at peak times.

This is where the locals come to enjoy untracked powder after a fresh fall. When high winds or unstable conditions shut down the main components of L'Espace Killy, Sainte-Foy is the place to spend the day.

Three chair-lifts take you up to the **Col de l'Aiguille** (at a respectable 2620m), which is the starting point for 600 vertical metres of challenging piste. Experts can ski off the back with a guide. Intermediates will find plenty of satisfying runs on the lower half of the mountain. At the moment, Sainte-Foy remains remarkably unspoilt. Plans to extend the lift system and to build accommodation may change all that. At present the only place to stay is the simple, but pleasant, Hotel Monal in the old village.

TOURIST OFFICE
Tel 33 79 06 91 70
Fax 33 79 06 95 09

Valmorel

ALTITUDE 1400m (4,592ft)

Valmorel has considerably more charm than any other purpose-built resort in France. Indeed, the first-time visitor may be surprised to discover that it is purpose-built. The cosy high street has an air of long-established permanency, which belies the fact that the resort is only in its second decade.

It is a prime example of the second wave of French purpose-built resorts, designed to contradict their ghastly forerunners in Tignes, Flaine and early La Plagne. As the first grumbles of a collective European 'green' conscience were making themselves heard, this resort was to blend seamlessly into the Savoie mountain scenery.

The planners took a couple of old farm buildings in a beautiful valley, only 15km from Moutiers; this foresight was completely unexpected from French architects in the 1970s. Using local wood, stone and slate they manufactured a 'traditional' resort. As an experiment it was an enormous success. It is not in fact one resort, but a series of satellites that the French call *hameaux;* they are not hamlets at all, but clusters of chalet-style apartments assembled at intervals around the home piste. These *hameaux* are all self-contained units, with their own reception area, perched higgledy-piggledy on different contours of the mountain. However, they are all focused upon one central and surprisingly picturesque shopping street.

The ski area in itself is modest by major resort standards, with 54 pistes served by 31 lifts, but it is connected to the neighbouring village of **St-François-Longchamp** in the Maurienne Valley. This easily negotiated link adds a further 31 pistes and 18 lifts to form a highly respectable ski area of 163km, which is known as **Le Grand Domaine**.

St-François-Longchamp's slopes are sunny, wide and gentle, while the Valmorel side holds the snow better and is both more extensive and more challenging. It is an ingeniously laid out resort which, even by the exalted standards of the Tarentaise and the best piste-skiing in the world, has remarkably few faults. Reporters continue to complain that the pistes are seriously undergraded. Anyone judging the area by the local piste map might think it lacking in any challenge for serious skiers. However, it is important to note that for reasons best known to Valmorel the local map flies in the face of accepted European colour-coding, with green described as easy, blue as moderate, red as difficult and black as very difficult.

■ GOOD POINTS

Minimal queues, ideal for family skiing, extensive nursery slopes, varied off-piste skiing, skiing convenience, traffic-free, resort friendliness

■ BAD POINTS

Lack of facilities for non-skiers, high night-time noise level (in Bourg-Morel), lack of tough runs

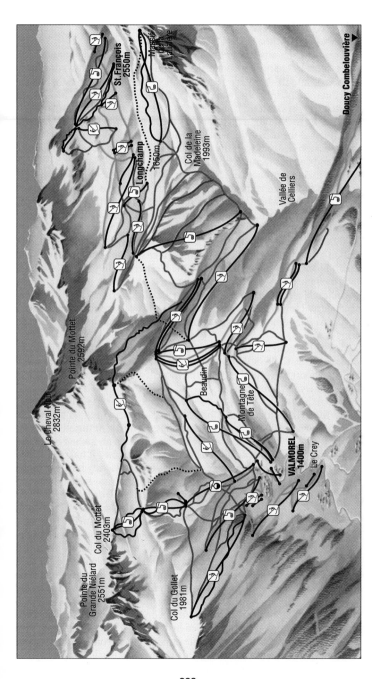

On the mountain
top 2550m (8,364ft) bottom 1250m (4,100ft)

The resort itself sits at the head of an enclosed valley surrounded on three sides by sparsely wooded slopes and wide, undulating snowfields above. Although there are tenuous links, the skiing above the village splits naturally into the two main sectors of **Beaudin** and **Col du Mottet/Col du Gollet**. The Mottet sector faces mainly north and the skiing goes up to 2400m; it therefore has the best snow. Lifts from Hameau du Mottet at the top of Valmorel give access to the 1981m Col du Gollet at the eastern extremity of the lift system. The skiing here is open, quite steep and catches the afternoon sun.

The main mountain access is via the Pierrafort gondola, which starts from the top of the village; this serves a broad slope where the runs are all graded blue, which according to the local lift map correctly means moderate. In other resorts some of them would be graded distinctly red in any snow conditions.

The Riondet drag-lift used to act as the only on-mountain method of crossing from the Mottet to Baudin ski areas. As the run from here is a harsh black, which dips down into the **Celliers Valley**, the majority of intermediate skiers were forced to return to the resort, thereby creating considerable traffic and a queue for the Beaudin and shorter Planchamp chair-lifts. However, the new Morel drag-lift now provides alternative access to Beaudin without returning to the village and has greatly eased congestion.

From Beaudin a series of drag-lifts serve long, easy runs. The blues down into the Celliers Valley are again undergraded. These slopes catch the afternoon sun and therefore the moguls here can be intimidatingly hard and icy in the mornings.

From the Celliers Valley a two-speed, three-seater chair-lift takes you up to the broad ridge above the road pass of the Col de la Madeleine (closed in winter). One reporter describes this lift as 'infuriating, rather than ingenious. It has two gaps in its line of chairs and when no-one is getting on or off it speeds up. The net result is queues. If half your party catch the lift and the other half do not, this means waiting for them at the top'. The two red runs back down have pitches of nearly 30 degrees and would be graded black elsewhere. There are, however, easier alternatives.

On the sunny side of the ridge the runs down to Longchamp are open and gentle. A combination of schuss and plod takes you from the top of the chair to the col, and beyond it to the Lauzière quad-chair; this goes up to the highest point of the ski area at 2550m on the Longchamp side of the road pass, although it is still covered by the local Valmorel ski pass. This chair is under-used and the off-piste opportunities from here are exceptional. The black run down from this chair is not particularly steep but faces south and is often slushy by mid-afternoon.

There are several ways back to Valmorel; one of them, via the Côte 2305m drag-lift to the top of the Madeleine chair, involves a particularly nasty stretch of blue run that should be graded red/black. The broad west-facing slopes above the road linking St-François and Longchamp are little-used by Valmorel-based skiers. They include some intermediate pistes through light woods above the road and down to the village. It is good confidence-building territory and even the blacks are not particularly intimidating.

Annoyingly, the main lift map marks the Longchamp pistes by numbers but fails to provide any key as to their names. One reporter complains that when you actually get to them, the runs are marked by name only: 'this makes navigation interesting; you can get a map with a key from the restaurant in Longchamp — if you can work out how to get there.' The main home-piste to Valmorel is floodlit and open for night-skiing until 10pm on Thursdays.

Beginners

Valmorel has good nursery slopes with three lifts away from the main pistes. Many reporters complain that reaching the nursery area from some of the accommodation involves a serious and tedious uphill hike. Good green runs above the resort are ideal for the next stage of learning. Second-weekers should be aware that a number of the blue runs here would be graded red elsewhere and may be beyond their capabilities.

Intermediates

This is ideal cruising terrain with enough serious challenges to keep most intermediates happy for a full two weeks. The long runs down into the Celliers Valley and the steeper options off the Col du Gollet provide classic skiing; this is a resort where you always feel you are actually going somewhere, rather than repeating the same, or similar, runs down the same bowl.

Advanced

A good choice of black runs is evenly distributed around the ski area. The Mottet chair, above the Pierrafort gondola, gives access to some testing pistes. The wide mogul field under the top part of the chair is quite genuinely black and a good 33 degrees in places, but after an awkward start it is usually not too intimidating because of the quality of the snow.

Off-piste

Skiers who like a challenge will be delighted to discover Valmorel's best-kept secret: outstanding off-piste, which, because of the family image of the resort, is unknown to ski-bums and therefore deserted. The Col du Gollet is the start of the Nine Valleys tour. You can ski off-piste from here into the **Vallée de Belleville** and link (with a short taxi ride) into the Trois Vallées ski area at **Les Menuires**.

Snowboarding

Valmorel has a new snowboard stadium and half-pipe, L'Harmonium Papouasia, which is situated in the Arnouillaz sector. The French Ski School (ESF) organises snowboarding classes.

Ski schools and guiding

The ESF has a rare monopoly here, and as a result standards might be lax. The number of pupils in a class, we are told, can also be uncomfortably high. However, overall reports are favourable ('special courses like powder-skiing were only available in high season, but the instruction was good'). Another reader comments: 'The instructors adapt their classes to the nerve and ability of the clientèle and all concerned seemed to be pleased'. However, some readers complain that the school found it hard to cope with the number of skiers wanting lessons during half-term weeks ('if you can avoid these peak times, you are going to have a much better holiday').

Mountain restaurants

Mountain eating-places continue to improve here and are of a reasonable standard. They vary from 'respectable' to 'excellent'. Le Prairiond, beneath the gondola, is lively and 'a good last-minute stop before the final run of the day'. Refuge 2000, a family-run establishment at the Col de la Madeleine, serves excellent salads and is described as 'very informal' but has 'only one smelly toilet with a huge queue'. Altipiano is said to be 'the best; it has a decent loo, but is probably the most expensive restaurant'.

Les 2 Mazots has the best *croûte du fromage*, but service is said to be slow. Le Grenier, next to the ski school, is extremely popular, while L'Alpage is 'big and characterless'. Le Cheval Noir in Longchamp is good for pizzas but criticised for its slow service, and Le Slalom, opposite the St-François nursery slopes, 'serves excellent food and beers from around the world'.

Off the mountain

The heart of Valmorel is **Bourg-Morel**, a colourful, arcaded pedestrian street full of restaurants, interesting shops, bars and pavement cafés. One reporter aptly describes it as 'Disney-cute'. It is all modern but by no means lacking in alpine charm. A car is not necessary as local buses travel the 15km to Moutiers four times a day during the week and eight times at weekends. There are 20km of cross-country loipes in the area, and non-skiers will find several kilometres of cleared and signposted walks at the top of Beaudin and Lanchettes.

■ **OTHER SPORTS**

Parapente, snow-shoeing, dog-sledding, tobogganing, winter walks

The free Télébourg gondola connects Bourg-Morel with the upper *hameaux* until 11.30pm. It is efficient but prone to queues at lunch-time, and one reporter comments that it should not be relied upon if you want to get to ski school on time.

Accommodation

Most of the accommodation is in apartments, all of which are 'compact' in the French style with 'apartment for four' meaning 'just bearable for two'. However, the Planchamp and Fontaine apartments appear to be of a slightly superior standard. Location is not particularly important. However, most reporters prefer being close to the main street despite the fact that we have continuing reports of late-night revelry disturbing those who wish to sleep. Hotel du Bourg is 'comfortable and clean', although the rooms are 'claustrophobically small'. Hotel Planchamp is slightly smarter but not as centrally placed. Skiers with cars can stay in the hamlet of Les Avanchers in the simple but pleasant Cheval Noir.

Eating in and out

For what is by no means a large purpose-built resort, the variety of restaurants comes as a surprise. Bookings are essential for much of the season. Reporters recommend Chez Albert ('fantastic — the best pizzas ever'). Pizzeria du Bourg receives equally ecstatic commendations, La Galette is good for *pierrade* ('the only place where we didn't feel rushed'). Au Petit Savoyard and La Cordée beside it have fine fondue and raclette. Le Creuset has 'stupendous' grills. Le Petit Prince is said to be 'overpriced with an unexciting menu'. Reservations are necessary in most of the restaurants at peak times. One reporter points out that families with small children tend to eat early and it is easier to find a table after 9pm.

The supermarkets are praised by reporters for their 'good selection of high-quality fruit and vegetables' as well as delicious spit-roasted chickens. The take-away pizzas from Chez Albert are also recommended. Au Caprice delivers croissants to apartments at breakfast-time.

Après-ski

The nightlife is muted and confined to a few bars, which stay open late. The Ski-Roc has live music most nights and is highly recommended. Café de la Gare is 'trendy but empty until 10pm', and Perce-Neige is 'very friendly and attracts the late crowd'. Au Petit Savoyard has 'a good French atmosphere, busy all day and night. Why move?'. Le Pub in the Hotel du Bourg has a 9 to 10pm happy-hour. Le Grenier is 'better at midday and for postcard writing, but is unexciting in the evenings'.

Childcare

The quality, or rather the user-friendliness, of some of its nursery facilities, on which much of the resort's reputation is founded, are now seriously questioned. Saperlipopette is the Valmorel kindergarten that has in the past been hailed as the model for all other such establishments. We have, however, had some contrary reports. In our own experience we have been put off by the rigidity of the hours. If, as a parent you fail to

Skiing facts: **Valmorel**

TOURIST OFFICE
La Maison de Valmorel, Bourg-Morel,
F-73260 Valmorel, Savoie
Tel 33 79 09 85 55
Fax 33 79 09 85 29

THE RESORT
By road Calais 910km
By rail Moûtiers 15km, regular bus service
to resort
By air Geneva 3½ hrs
Visitor beds 8,500
Transport traffic-free village centre, free
Télébourg gondola between village sectors

THE SKIING
Linked or nearby resorts St-François-
Longchamp (l)
Longest run La Madeleine, 3.5km (blue)
Number of lifts 49 in Grand Domaine area
Total of trails/pistes 163km in area (70%
easy, 20% intermediate, 10% difficult)
Nursery slopes 4
Summer skiing none
Snowmaking 30 hectares covered

LIFT PASSES
Area pass Grand Domaine (covers Valmorel
and St-François-Longchamp), 658FF for 6
days. Valmorel 632FF for 6 days
Day pass Valmorel 118-148FF, Grand
Domaine 122-154FF

Beginners no free lifts
Pensioners 60 yrs and over, as children
Credit cards accepted yes

SKI SCHOOLS
Adults ESF, 550FF for 6 half-days.
Beginners course 1,054FF for 6 full days
including lift pass
Private lessons ESF, 240FF for 1½ hrs
Snowboarding 550FF for 6 half-days
Cross-country 550FF for 6 half-days, pri-
vate lessons 240FF for 1½ hrs. Loipe 20km
Other courses monoski, off-piste, race
training
Guiding companies through ESF

CHILDREN
Lift pass Valmorel, 528-668FF for 6 days.
Grand Domaine, 558-711FF for 6 days
Ski kindergarten Saperlipopette, 3-7 yrs,
8.30am-5pm, 782-846FF for 6 days, extra
60FF per day for lunch
Ski school ESF, 4-13 yrs, 510FF for 6 half-
days including lift pass. Beginners courses,
966FF for 6 half-days
Non-ski kindergarten Saperlipopette,
6 mths-7 yrs, 782-846FF for 6 days, extra
60FF per day for lunch

FOOD AND DRINK PRICES
Coffee 7-10FF, glass of wine 12FF, small
beer 12-13FF, dish of the day 38-50FF

deliver your children on time before 9am they will not be admitted until the afternoon, thus ruining your day's skiing. We found the claim that 'all our instructors speak English' is simply not true. It is, however, very well-equipped and takes babies from six months old. One reporter speaks of serious understaffing levels: 'Our admittedly demanding and clingy children hated it, the four-year-old cried incessantly from day one and the two-year-old from day three. At times the children were taught skiing with one staff member to 13 children'.

It would be unfair to judge the Saperlipopette kindergarten wholly on these reports. However, it does seem that the over-serious and not out-wardly friendly Gallic attitude towards small children, which we have found more markedly elsewhere in France, highlights our respective cultural differences.

Linked or nearby resorts

St-François-Longchamp 1650m (5,412ft)

Valmorel's neighbour is a sequence of hamlets below the Col de la Madeleine, linked by a free bus service. These are no-frills resorts that attract mainly French families. The top hamlet, Longchamp, is an ugly group of A-frame buildings built in the early 1960s, surrounded by gentle slopes. The skiing is ideal for both beginners and intermediates. All the hotels are graded two-star. Longchamp has a kindergarten, skating rink, several restaurants and crêperies, a disco, piano bar, supermarkets and some good specialist food shops. St-François is a group of simple old hotels and hostels at 1450m.

TOURIST OFFICE
Tel 33 79 59 10 56
Fax 33 79 59 13 67

Round-up

RESORTS COVERED Isola 2000, Pra-Loup, Valloire

Isola 2000
top 2610m (8,561ft) bottom 1800m (5,904ft)

Isola is a purpose-built resort and the most southerly ski area in France. In reasonable weather conditions it is 90 minutes from Nice up the dramatic road beside the Tinée Ravines. The resort was built by a British property company in the 1960s; it was created with families in mind and has a convenient complex of shops, bars, economically designed apartments and hotels next to the lift station, and a large, sunny nursery area. Isola is not accessible from the north, which in part accounts for why so few tour operators offer it in their brochures. British skiers do, however, make up a big slice of the winter business and many of them have bought their own apartments here.

The original building, the ugly Front de Neige, is right on the slopes. In an attempt to dress up the soulless centre, the more attractive, wood-clad additions of Le Bristol, Le Hameau and Les Ardets were built behind Front de Neige. These are less convenient but contain bigger and better apartments and a luxurious hillside hotel. This has greatly helped the overall look of Isola, dissipating some of its claustrophobic atmosphere.

The ski area is limited, but varied enough for beginners, families with small children and intermediates. There are 46 pistes covered by 24 lifts with 32 hectares of snowmaking. The resort guarantees sun and offers self-caterers a free week's accommodation at another time if the resort's heliograph registers no sun for more than three consecutive days in a week. The nearby resorts are **Auron** and **Valberg**, both of which are within easy reach for a day's skiing.

TOURIST OFFICE
Tel 33 93 23 15 15
Fax 33 93 23 14 25

Pra-Loup
top 2500m (8,200ft) bottom 1600m (5,248ft)

This small resort in the Hautes Alpes has a surprisingly extensive range of beginner and intermediate skiing although it is limited for advanced skiers. The 160km of piste is shared with neighbouring **La Foux d'Allos**. Named after the wolves that once frequented these pine forests Pra Loup is a collection of hotels and apartments built in the 1960s, along with some older chalets. The restaurants and bars are lower priced than in better-known French resorts and there is one disco, the Marmotel.

The skiing takes place on two main mountains, with access by cable car from the top of the village. Intermediates will find open-bowl skiing and good tree-line runs with spectacular scenery. There is extensive off-piste skiing (for which you will need a guide) but only five black (difficult) runs.

TOURIST OFFICE
Tel 33 92 84 10 04
Fax 33 92 84 02 93

Valloire
top 2600m (8,528ft) bottom 1430m (4,690ft)

Valloire is an attractive, reasonably large village set above the Maurienne Valley in an isolated bowl. It is still very much a traditional French farming community, and the odd whiff of manure mingling with the aroma of freshly baked bread is all part of the morning walk to the lifts. It is a reasonably priced resort, friendly and uncrowded except in peak season. However, its proximity to the Italian border means that when the resort is busy it can be very noisy.

The 150km of pisted skiing comprises 89 runs, which are mostly at intermediate level. The skiing takes place in two main areas: La Sétaz and Le Crey du Quart, on two adjacent mountains reached by lifts starting a few minutes from the village centre and going up to 2500m. The terrain is varied, and some of the runs are as long as 1000 vertical metres. The skiing is not difficult; even the black runs would be red (intermediate) by the standards of many resorts.

Mountain access to La Sétaz is by a six-person gondola from the village up to Thimel, followed by a chair- and a drag-lift to the summit. From here the main route down to the village is an enjoyable red run. Served by artificial snow-cannon and groomed to a high standard, the area provides a choice of runs from the wide but sometimes icy red to the gently meandering blue (easy) runs towards Les Verneys or Valloire. An alternative finish is to catch the end of the green (beginner) path of Les Myosotis, which takes you to the centre of the village. You can also fork right below the Thimel quad-chair and follow Les Myosotis all the way down as it curves gently through the trees. Several reporters point out that in sunny weather conditions Les Myosotis quickly becomes badly worn, rutted and rocky.

Access to Le Crey du Quart ski area is either by the Montissot and Colerieux chair-lifts via the green Les Myosotis, or directly from Valloire on two long chairs. Once you are there, skiing is mainly of the red motorway variety, with the gentler slopes going down towards Valloire.

Valmeinier 1500 is a small and traditional village with a satellite at 1800m. Plans to link the latter with **Valfréjus** and with **Bardonecchia** across the Italian border have yet to materialise.

TOURIST OFFICE
Tel 33 79 59 03 96
Fax 33 79 59 09 66

Italy

For the past two years Italy has been one of the most sought after of all ski destinations. An extremely favourable exchange rate combined with good snow cover has attracted skiers who might otherwise have been drawn to Austria, Switzerland and even France. A mountain-restaurant barbecue with all you can eat and drink for less than £8 in simple Sauze d'Oulx or a gourmet dinner with wine for £15 in smart Cortina d'Ampezzo does wonders for the holiday budget.

The skiing in the Dolomites is some of the most charming and extensive anywhere, and the upgrading of Verona and Venice airports has greatly improved access. The country's share of the British market has shot from 5 per cent to 20 per cent (a ceiling dictated by the number of tourist beds that tour operators have managed to maintain).

However, Italy is no newcomer to skiing. Winter tourists first appeared in Cortina d'Ampezzo as long ago as 1902, and the resort hosted the Winter Olympics in 1956. Through the boom years of the 1960s Italy ranked alongside Austria, Switzerland and newly emergent France as an equal alpine partner in ski tourism.

Its position was washed away in the meltwater of economic uncertainty, which followed the 1970s OPEC oil crisis. British travel firms moved their operations to less hazardous parts of the Alps, and the Dolomite resorts lost their share of the international market.

The lean years that followed were marked by a disastrous snow record. However, as Italy's economy was restructured, so too were its ski resorts. Multi-million pound lift systems replaced the rickety drags and second-hand chair-lifts and some of the most sophisticated snow-cannon networks in Europe were installed.

However, it took an international currency crisis for today's generation of British skiers to begin to rediscover it. When the lira and sterling both fell through the floor of the Exchange Rate Mechanism in November 1992, hugely favourable exchange rates relaunched the forgotten resorts of Europe as suddenly sought-after ski destinations. Ironically, increasing uncertainties once again over Italy's economic stability have returned, seriously worrying tour operators who are considering further investment.

First-time visitors will be delighted by the Italian zest for enjoyment both on and off the slopes, and mountain eating is an art form. Long before midday delicious scents from every wayside hut in resorts like Courmayeur are enough to tempt you in for a lunch that can last far into the afternoon. The Italian penchant for partying extends to après-ski, which starts early and carries on late into the night.

Although the Italians are well-known for their love of children, the major resorts are mysteriously lacking in childcare facilities. Exceptions to the rule include Cortina d'Ampezzo and Courmayeur.

Bormio

ALTITUDE 1225m (4,018ft)

Bormio's history dates from Roman times when its location at a cross-roads in the Valtellina in the mountains of Lombardy made it a natural staging post for trans-Alpine traffic. Attracted by hot springs and spectacular views over what is now the **Stelvio National Park**, the Romans built a town and thermal bath complex at the foot of the pass. The town prospered during the Middle Ages and its ancient cobbled streets date from that time. In subsequent centuries it was sidelined by history, but the post-war tourist boom has restored some of its former vitality. Today its ugly suburbs spread over the broad valley floor, but without impinging on the charm of the pedestrianised centre.

Bormio shares a lift pass, but not a lift link, with the neighbouring village of **Santa Caterina** and with the small **Valdidentro** ski area above the village of Oga on the opposite side of the valley. The lift pass is also valid for **Livigno**, an hour's drive away over a pass to the west. **St Moritz**, across the Swiss border in the Engadine, is another option for a day excursion.

> **■ GOOD POINTS**
>
> Long runs, fast intermediate cruising, empty slopes, family skiing, late-season skiing, attractive medieval town centre, good restaurants on and off the mountain, activities for non-skiers
>
> **■ BAD POINTS**
>
> Long airport transfer, lack of challenging runs, short season for resort-level snow

On the mountain
top 3012m (9,879ft) bottom 1225m (4,018ft)

Bormio's first lifts opened in the 1960s, but the resort came of age in 1985 when it hosted the Alpine World Championships. The slopes rise steeply on a single broad mountain served by two base-stations, both within a few minutes' walk of the town centre. The main one is the starting point for the two-stage cable car to the Cima Bianca via **Bormio 2000**, a substantial mid-station with a large family hotel and a small shopping mall. This can also be reached by car in most conditions. The alternative is the six-seater gondola to **Ciuk**, a lower mid-station, which also has accommodation and restaurants.

The top third of the mountain is above the tree-line, with a network of chair-lifts providing a variety of choices. Currently this area is being made more user-friendly by a newly acquired grinding machine that reduces stones to sand. Lower down the skiing is in glades cut from the forest, ensuring good visibility when the weather closes in, and outstanding skiing after a fresh snowfall.

Beginners

The only nursery slopes are at Bormio 2000, a mixed blessing in that everyone has to buy a lift pass from day one. On a more positive note, it means that everyone learns halfway up the mountain, which gives more of a feeling of what skiing is all about. After a few days' mastering the basic manoeuvres, beginners will find plenty of easy pistes in the wooded area down to Ciuk. By the end of the week, many will be skiing the blue (easy) runs from the top of the cable car.

Intermediates

For the two-week-plus brigade, Bormio's slopes are to die for, with no particularly steep sections and lots of high-speed cruising. The 14km descent from the Cima Bianca to the town is just one of many exhilarating options. Work is currently underway to widen the bottom section of the Bosco Basso piste to provide an alternative route back to the gondola station. There are plans to replace the slow Nicoletta drag lift above Bormio 2000 with a double-chair in time for the 1995–6 season.

Advanced

Advanced piste skiers may be frustrated by the lack of challenge as the two short runs that are graded black (difficult) might well be red (intermediate) in a steeper resort. The Stelvio FIS course, which runs from just above La Rocca past Ciuk to the bottom of the gondola, is one of the less demanding choices on the occasional World Cup circuit.

Off-piste

The powder opportunities off the **Cima Bianca** more than compensate for the shortage of black bump runs. To the west of the main piste there is a steep, open bowl leading down to some shallow gradient tree-line skiing. Those who plan to go below the right-hand turn off to Bormio 2000 should first check that the Ornella drag-lift is running. To the east of the pistes, a wider choice of terrain gives access to a more heavily wooded area. A long trail leads back to the Praimont chair. An alternative is to ski down the flattering run to Santa Caterina. Those who are prepared to hire a guide and climb on skins will find magnificent terrain in both winter and summer on the **Stelvio Glacier**.

Snowboarding

The three main ski schools, Alta Valtellina, Nazionale and Bormio 2000, have group classes when there is sufficient demand. The off-piste opportunities are extensive but there are no specialist on-mountain facilities for surfers. For those who want to experiment, boards can be rented by the hour or half-day at Bormio 2000.

Ski schools and guiding

Of the six competing ski schools in Bormio, the Alta Valtellina,

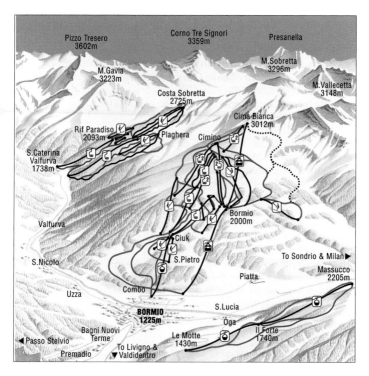

based near the nursery slopes at Bormio 2000, is highly recommended for its young and friendly, English-speaking instructors. The more traditional alternatives include the Nazionale and Bormio 2000. The Sertorelli and the Capitani specialise in summer ski-touring, retaining only a skeleton winter-staff for valued clients.

Mountain restaurants

The favoured stopping-off point for lunch or mid-ski refreshments is La Rocca, an old-fashioned hut on the main trail from the top of the mountain to **Bormio 2000**. It has two rooms, each with a wood-burning stove, and friendly service. It also hosts dinner followed by a torchlight descent whenever there is sufficient demand. The Girasole hotel and the self-service cafeteria at Bormio 2000 are equally convenient, though less traditional, alternatives.

Off the mountain

Bormio is the most Italian of resorts, with a strong sense of style in its immaculate shops and restaurants. In the early evening, chattering crowds stroll down the narrow cobbled streets and fill the bars and cafés on the historic Via Roma, the centre of activity in the old town. The new town, with its modern hotels and high-rise apartment blocks, makes a stark contrast.

Bormio's nearest airports are Bergamo and Milan, both three-and-a-half hours away. The drive from Milan includes a dramatically beautiful section along the shore of Lake Como. Work is currently in progress on a four-lane highway up the Valtellina, which is expected to cut the journey time from Milan when it opens in the late 1990s.

Accommodation

The modernised four-star Posta, on a pedestrianised street in the old town, offers luxurious accommodation, plus a swimming-pool and fitness centre. The alternative four-star recommendations are the Rezia and the Palace. Those who prefer to be near the lifts should consider one of the modern three-star options, the Derby, the Nevada or the Funivia. In the two-star category, the family-run Dante and the atmospheric Gufo offer exceptional value in central locations.

As the town of Bormio is only ski-in ski-out when snow conditions are good in January and February, there is an excellent case to be made for staying in the three-star Girasole at **Bormio 2000**. This is especially true for holidays over the Easter period when the main resort begins to wind down. The hotel is run with a strong emphasis on family entertainment by the hospitable Alfredo Cantoni and his English wife, Elizabeth.

Eating in and out

Although *pizzocheri*, a rather gritty indigenous pasta, is something of an acquired taste, the Valtellina has an interesting range of specialities including charcuterie, mushrooms and locally produced wines. The best places to try them are the Rasiga, a beautifully converted sawmill, the Vecchia Combo and the Taulà. The Al Cambrin is a welcome recent addition to Bormio's gastronomy. All four restaurants will prepare multi-course gourmet feasts at modest all-inclusive rates provided they are reserved in advance. Bormio also has five pizzerias and a spaghetteria.

■ OTHER SPORTS

Swimming, squash, parapente, snow-mobiling, helicopter rides, indoor tennis, tobogganing, skating, thermal baths, climbing wall

Self-catering is not the norm in a resort which has such a wide choice of inexpensive eating places. However, the specialist groceries on the Via Roma certainly stock all the necessary ingredients for home cooking on a magnificent scale.

Après-ski

The Bagna Vecchi, a few miles out of town, has a natural sauna and curative hot baths in a cave in the hillside. These are part of a very atmospheric turn-of-the-century spa complex offering a range of treatments for weary skiers. In town, the natural hot water has been put to good use in the large public swimming-pool. The Gorky on the Via Roma and the Vagabond in the church square are the current favourite pubs, after both

Skiing facts: **Bormio**

TOURIST OFFICE
Via Roma 131/B, I-23032 Bormio, Lombardy
Tel 39 342 903300
Fax 39 342 904696

THE RESORT
By road Calais 1146km
By rail Tirano 39km
By air Milan $3\frac{1}{2}$ hrs
Visitor beds 6,035
Transport free ski-bus with lift pass

THE SKIING
Linked or nearby resorts Livigno (n), Santa Caterina (n), San Colombano (n)
Longest run Pista Stelvio, 14km (red)
Number of lifts 16
Total of trails/pistes 25km Bormio only (23% easy, 68% intermediate, 9% difficult)
Nursery slopes 4 on the mountain at Ciuk and Bormio 2000
Summer skiing 20km on Stelvio Pass between May and November
Snowmaking 7km covered

LIFT PASSES
Area pass (covers Bormio, Livigno, Santa Caterina, San Colombano) L180,000-205,000 for 6 days
Day pass (Bormio only) L40,000-44,000
Beginners no free lifts

Pensioners 65 yrs and over as children
Credit cards accepted yes

SKI SCHOOLS
Adults Alta Valtellina, 9-11am or 11am-1pm, L95,000 for 6 x 2 hr lessons. Nazionale 10am-12.30pm or 2-4.30pm, L120,000 for 6 x $2\frac{1}{2}$ hr lessons. Also Anzi, Bormio 2000, Capitani and Sertorelli ski schools
Private lessons L40,000-45,000 per hr
Snowboarding all ski schools, times and prices on request
Cross-country Scuola Sci Fondo, prices on application. Loipe 12.5km
Other courses off-piste, telemark
Guiding companies Casa delle Guide Alpine Bormio, Associazione Guide Alpine Alta Valtellina

CHILDREN
Liftpass 13 yrs and under, L125,000-140,000 for 6 days
Ski kindergarten none
Ski school Alta Valtellina, 10am-1pm, L180,000-200,000 for 6 days
Non-ski kindergarten none

FOOD AND DRINK PRICES
Coffee L1,200-1,400, glass of wine L1,200, small beer L3,000, dish of the day L7,000-10,000

skiing and dinner, with the Bar Roma as a more local alternative. Late nightlife focuses on the King's Club and the Shangri-la discos, both open until 3am, with the piano bar at the Aurora hotel a less frenetic option.

Childcare
The Alta Valtellina ski school provides excellent English-language group lessons for children of four years old and over. There is no formal crèche service, but the Girasole hotel arranges local babysitters during the day and in the evening.

Linked or nearby resorts

Santa Caterina 1737m (5,697ft)

Santa Caterina, or San Cat as it is known, is a quiet, attractive village 30 minutes away by bus up a mountain road that is a dead-end in winter when the Gavia Pass is closed. It usually has better snow than its larger neighbour, Bormio, with which it shares a lift pass. Local skiing is on the north-east facing slopes of the 3296m **Sobretta**. The higher slopes are fairly steep and graded black. There are also some winding intermediate trails down between the trees.

Santa Caterina's ski school receives mixed, but generally favourable, reviews. There is good cross-country skiing (10km loipe) beyond the resort, and skating on a natural rink.

The San Matteo Hotel is recommended for comfort and food. Self-caterers have a choice of two well-stocked supermarkets. Nightlife is limited, with one fairly large disco and a number of cosy bars, which remain open until after midnight.

TOURIST OFFICE
Tel 39 342 935598

Cervinia

ALTITUDE 2050m (6,724ft)

Cervinia may not be either the most attractive or the most challenging of ski resorts but its growing band of loyal followers view its shortcomings through rose-tinted goggles. It is connected, on skis, to **Zermatt** but there the similarity ends. While the Swiss resort is rich in alpine charm and var-ied skiing, the Italian side of the Matterhorn is sunnier but positively bland in comparison. Once it was the showpiece of Italian ski resorts, a gleaming contemporary development set high above the tree-line in a sunny south-facing valley.

Mussolini changed its name from Breuil to Cervinia, after the Italian name for the Matterhorn. Cable cars swept skiers up to unprecedented heights, and Italy's élite flocked to enjoy the novelty. Then they moved on. Other, better, resorts developed elsewhere while poor old Cervinia's lift system lapsed into disrepair and its grand but utilitarian architecture was eclipsed by more environmentally sympathetic villages.

> **■ GOOD POINTS**
>
> Wide and easy pistes, extensive nursery slopes, reliable resort-level snow, early- and late-season skiing, summer skiing, wide choice of hotels, short airport transfer
>
> **■ BAD POINTS**
>
> Little challenging skiing, lack of tree-level skiing, high-season queues, weekend traffic, limited facilities for non-skiers, poor piste preparation, lack of resort charm

Today there are positive signs that Cervinia is climbing out of its time-warp, and the resort, in recent years, has undergone a major facelift both on- and off-piste. In particular, the addition of one of the biggest cable cars in the world has done much to reduce the queues for access to **Plateau Rosa**. What one reporter described as 'hideous examples of neo-brutalist concrete' have given way to wood and stone, and some of the main hotels in the central square have been reclad. However, regard-less of cosmetics, nothing can change the basic face of the mountain, which lacks challenge to anyone above the average intermediate level.

Cervinia is extremely popular with beginners or near-beginners and has a faithful following of older intermediates who enjoy the open and long pistes, which present no hidden horrors. 'Just what the doctor ordered' said one reporter, 'I cannot stress enough how enjoyable Cervinia skiing is'. Another commented: 'A complete beginner, I have been bragging about the speed of my progress ever since, and my ego had to come back as excess baggage.' Without doubt there are few resorts where beginners might, by the end of the week, find themselves capable of skiing from the Plateau Rosa right down to Cervinia, a lengthy 8km through 1500m vertical, with a confidence that will stay with them.

The resort's second strongest attribute is its snow record. Because of its high altitude village-level skiing can be relied upon as early as November and well into April.

As historical rivals there was no love lost between Cervinia and Zermatt, but both resorts have now finally realised that working together has its advantages. Although the resorts are directly linked, the distances involved mean that day visitors from either area can enjoy no more than a taste of the other's skiing.

One experienced reporter writes that Cervinia 'suits anyone who can cope for a week without the challenges of difficult blacks and dramatic mogul fields'.

On the mountain
top 3490m (11,447ft) bottom 1524m (4,999ft)

The main mountain access is via a six-seater gondola or an ancient 75-person cable car, which takes you up Plan Maison at 2555m. Reporters complain that the climb on foot up to the base-station is hard work and tedious, not helped by cars trying to push through the crowds during the morning rush-hour. The alternative is to make your way slowly up the mountain via the more conveniently reached Cretaz drag-lifts, which start from the lower end of the village in what is a huge nursery area lined with rows of deckchairs for sunbathers.

■ WHAT'S NEW

Additional chair-lift and snowmaking at Plan Maison

From here a range of lifts fan out across this wide, open mountainside, including a modern 12-person jumbo gondola that takes you on up to Laghi Cime Bianche at 2812m. A 140-person cable car completes the journey to the summer ski area at Plateau Rosa and the link with Zermatt. The whole lift system is erratic, and reporters complain that, for no apparent reason, any one link is liable to close without warning. While the gondola from the village runs all the time, the parallel cable car may not function during low season. Similarly, the Plan Maison-Plateau Rosa cable cars via Cime Bianche may be taken out of service from day to day.

The cable car from Plan Maison to Furggen (3492m) has fallen into disuse and there are no plans to replace it. This sadly robs Cervinia of its best black (difficult) run and a number of important off-piste variants. Piste preparation is not of a high standard, and runs tend to remain closed longer than necessary after a major snowfall.

The main run down from Plateau Rosa is the famous Ventina, an uninterrupted 8km of easy family skiing for the most part, despite its red (intermediate) grading. It is easy to repeat the middle section of the run via the Lago Goillet triple-chair. From the top of this (or from Plateau Rosa) a long run with a number of variations takes you all the way down to **Valtournenche** at 1524m.

Beginners

Cervinia has a large nursery area at the bottom of the mountain and at

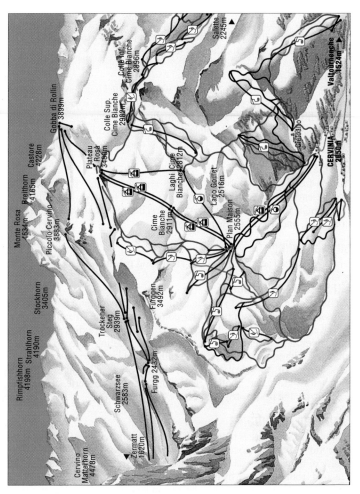

Plan Maison. The best place for absolute novices is the Baby La Vielle lift ('L' on the local map), which has a green (beginner) run on one side and a blue (easy) on the other. Both are described by reporters as 'easy and safe as well as being close to the comforts of Plan Maison'. The short green run next to the Baby Cretaz lift ('D') is 'only suitable for toddlers and the very, very scared'. Within a few days beginners should be able to progress to the blue number 5 run from Plan Maison, which is described as 'long, wide, fairly quiet, but somehow still thrilling'.

Intermediates

This is an ideal resort for confidence building and perfecting technique. None of the skiing is difficult, and most of the wide pistes here are of a similar easy gradient, which is ideal for fast cruising. The skiing here is all above the tree-line, and orientation can be difficult in a white-out. The long Ventina run is one of the best in the resort.

Advanced
This is not a resort for expert skiers, who will quickly tire of the lack of variety. However, the short black number 12 from the top of the Cretaz 1 drag-lift is more testing than it initially looks. One veteran reporter comments: 'If Cervinia's skiing lacks challenge, then I am not as good a skier as I thought. I found it steep, narrow and impossibly mogulled'.

Off-piste
After a fresh fall of snow the pisteurs are always slow to prepare the slopes, leaving some runs untouched by machine for days. Enjoyable off-piste can be found along the Swiss border, but this glacial area is heavily crevassed, and a local guide is essential.

Snowboarding
The Cervino ski school gives both group and private lessons.

Ski schools and guiding
We have received mixed reports of both the Cervino and Cieloalto ski schools. The Cervino in particular comes in for some strong criticism: 'We were left on 4 out of 12 occasions. Groups were disbanded, then regrouped and given different instructors. Meeting places and times changed without warning; attitude rather than language was the problem. We spent a total of ten hours during one week waiting for our instructor.' However, another reader described her experience with the Cervino as 'the best instruction I have ever had'.

Mountain restaurants
Italian mountain fare is better than in most countries, and Cervinia is no exception, although prices are high. Reporters were unanimous in their praise of Baita Cretaz da Mario on the blue run home from Plan Maison, reached from the village by the Cretaz I drag-lift. Reports were of a 'wide and imaginative menu' and 'the best plain food in town at not unreasonable prices'.

The restaurant at Plan Maison is to be avoided at peak times, but 'you can hire a deck-chair and take your own picnic; it is a bit like being on a beach'. Reporters were shocked by the standard of the hole-in-the-ground type of loos in some establishments. However, the Chalet Etoile, reached from Blue 26 or Blue 6 has 'spotless sit-down loos and a wholesome selection of meals'. Lo Stambecco was praised for its food and efficient service ('but terrible stand-up toilets').

One reporter found the best *polenta* he had ever tasted at the Lombard restaurant at the top of Blue 6 on the way down from Plateau Rosa. La Dailhu is also recommended for its 'fresh table linen, good food and friendly service'.

Off the mountain

The centre of the resort is a pedestrian zone. Roads on the outskirts tend to become clogged with traffic, especially during high-season weekends. Cervinia is essentially a small and compact village with one main street lined with bars, shops and restaurants.

Above the cable car station, buildings (mostly the more expensive hotels) stretch on up the hill towards the Carosello lifts. There is no need for a car here, and the more remote hotels

■ **OTHER SPORTS**

Skating, snowmobiling, tobogganing, swimming

tend to operate courtesy mini-buses. The shopping is 'generally good quality', with a smattering of upmarket boutiques and sports shops interspersed with supermarkets and souvenir shops.

Accommodation

Cervinia boasts a wide range of hotels and some quite new apartments. Hotel Compagnoni is strongly recommended. It is said to be 'well situated, but suffers from the noise of Saturday-night revellers'. Hotel Joli is 'in an unbeatable location and is pleasantly furnished'. However, another reporter complained at the noise-level of the karaoke emanating from the adjoining Dragon Bar. Hotel Astoria, next to the cable car station, has 'reasonable food, is very clean, but could do with redecorating'.

Hotel Jumeaux continues to receive glowing recommendations ('the ideal Italian resort hotel'). The neighbouring Bucaneve is also praised for its comfort and high standard of cuisine. Hotel Marmore is described as 'basic, but adequate', and the Hotel Cristallo is lavishly recommended with 'everything one could expect of a four-star hotel in a country that does not have fives'. The four-star Punta Maquignaz receives a similar billing, and The Edelweiss is 'quite small, but smart'.

Eating in and out

The Matterhorn has 'a friendly atmosphere and pleasant food', and Lino's, beside the skating rink, has 'a friendly atmosphere and is ideal for children'. The *tagliatelle* with *pesto* sauce in the Copa Pan is recommended. Le Petit Monde has been replaced by the extremely popular Al Solito Posto (reservations essential), and La Bamba is now the Restaurant du Mont Cervin ('splendid pizzas with plenty of good Chardonnay for £10 a head'). Mario's Baita Cretaz, just above the village near the end of Blue 5, is said to be the best restaurant in the resort and is reached by a free snowmobile ride ('the menu included jugged hare, wild boar and baked trout').

Après-ski

Most reporters are disappointed with the lack of après-ski in Cervinia, which was not at all what they expected. 'The bars lacked atmosphere' according to one reporter. In fact, there is nightlife here but it starts extremely late, with most bars having their happy-hour between 9 and 10pm. The Dragon Pub in the Hotel Pelissier is the focal point along with

Skiing facts: **Cervinia**

TOURIST OFFICE
Via Carrel 29, I-11021 Breuil-Cervinia,
Aosta
Tel 39 166 949136
Fax 39 166 949731

THE RESORT
By road Calais 1001km
By rail Châtillon 27km, regular buses to
resort
By air Turin or Geneva 2½ hrs
Visitor beds 5,700
Transport free bus from Camper's Square
to the church

THE SKIING
Linked or nearby resorts Zermatt (I),
Valtournenche (I)
Longest run Ventina, 8km (red)
Number of lifts 73 with Zermatt
Total of trails/pistes 80km in Cervinia
(34% easy, 53% intermediate, 13%
difficult). 230km with Zermatt
Nursery slopes 2 lifts
Summer skiing on Plateau Rosa, 8 lifts and
a cable car
Snowmaking 7 hectares covered

LIFT PASSES
Area pass (covers Cervinia and

Valtournenche) L225,000 for 6 days
Day pass L45,000
Beginners points tickets
Pensioners no reduction
Credit cards accepted yes

SKI SCHOOLS
Adults Cervino and Cieloalto ski schools,
10am-1pm, L170,000 for 6 days
Private lessons both ski schools, L45,000
per hr
Snowboarding Cervino Ski School, 10am-
1pm, L170,000 for 6 days, private lessons
L45,000 per hr
Cross-country Cervino Ski School, details
on request. Loipe 5km on edge of village
Other courses off-piste, telemark
Guiding companies Guide Del Cervino

CHILDREN
Lift pass 6 yrs and over as adults, free for 5
yrs and under
Ski kindergarten none
Ski school both ski schools, 5 yrs and over,
10am-1pm, L240,000 for 6 days
Non-ski kindergarten none

FOOD AND DRINK PRICES
Coffee L1,300, glass of wine L1,500, small
beer L2,000, dish of the day L25,000

Lino's, Yeti and the Gran Becca.
There are two main discos: La Chimera and Blow-Up; the latter is out
of the centre but operates a courtesy bus.

Childcare
Cervinia does not have a non-ski kindergarten, although babysitting can
be arranged privately through the tourist office. Skiing children of five
years and over are cared for either by the Cieloalto or the Cervino ski
school. The nursery slopes are right in the village at the foot of the main
runs and so are extremely convenient for families.

Cortina d' Ampezzo

ALTITUDE 1224m (4,015ft)

Cortina d'Ampezzo has at long last been allowed to resume its old role as Italy's premier *Gran Turismo* resort. It sits in isolated and stately splendour in the Ampezzo Valley, a two-hour journey from Venice. Unlike its neighbours in the German-speaking Sud Tirol, Cortina is outrageously Italian and largely devoid of German and Austrian tourists. Some 90 per cent of its visitors are Italian.

The resort was extensively developed for the 1956 Winter Olympics and ranks with St Moritz and Chamonix as one of the world's few all-round winter-sports resorts. Cortina's downhill skiing includes some of the best nursery slopes anywhere and long, challenging runs for intermediate to accomplished skiers; all of this takes place amid stunningly beautiful scenery.

Cortina has an upmarket reputation, which can put off those skiers who see Italy as the destination for

> ### ■ GOOD POINTS
> Extensive nursery slopes, variety of restaurants, long intermediate runs, many activities for non-skiers, beautiful scenery, skiing for all standards, extensive cross-country, tree-level skiing, attractive town, lively après-ski
>
> ### ■ BAD POINTS
> Distance between main ski areas and town centre, limited for late-season holidays, traffic outside pedestrian area, weekend skiers

cheap and cheerful holidays, but it is not an exclusive or overtly expensive resort. There are plenty of pleasant, reasonably priced family-run hotels, as well as simple bars, which are full of character.

On the mountain
top 2948m (9,669ft) bottom 1224m (4,015ft)

The skiing is divided between the main **Tofana-Socrepes** area to the west of town, which is reached via the *Freccia nel Cielo* (arrow in the sky) cable car, and **Staunies-Faloria** on the other side of town, which is made up of two sectors separated by a minor road.

A scattering of smaller ski areas along the Passo Falzarego road still belong to individual farmers. One of them, **Cinque Torri**, reached by an isolated two-stage chair-lift, is a small area of intermediate runs and breathtaking scenery. **Passo Falzarego**, further down the road and a total 20 minutes from the town centre, links with the Sella Ronda ski area.

The disparate nature of the skiing and the inconvenience of travel between the separate areas are two of the resort's most irritating points and they detract from its appeal. A free and oversubscribed ski-bus service runs between the two cable car stations (Tofana and Faloria). 'The ski buses were erratic', said a reporter, 'They behaved like ketchup: none would come and then a lot came at once'. Less frequent buses travel to and from the more distant ski areas.

Both Tofana and Faloria can be reached on foot from most accommodation, if you are prepared for a long slog in ski boots. Morning queues for the Tofana cable car are not a problem due to the late rising-time of the average Cortina skier. Cortina's morning rush-hour is never before 10.30am. The top section of Tofana is designated for sunbathers and sightseers only.

Beginners
A long serpentine blue (easy) piste takes you down from Tofana's mid-station to link with Socrepes, a huge undulating area of blue runs above the road at Pocol, which is served by easy drag-lifts and covered by snow-cannon. This delightful area, strangely reminiscent of a sloping Kensington Gardens, is ideal novice terrain. **Pierosà-Miétres** is an equally gentle sector, but is rather isolated.

Intermediates
The majority of Cortina's skiing is of intermediate standard, with long runs in both the main ski areas. Between the resort and Col Druscié the Tofana cable car travels over gentle tree-lined terrain and open fields with wide and easy trails, which cross rough roads without much warning for either skiers or drivers. Snow conditions often make these runs testing, hence their red (intermediate) and black (difficult) gradings. The second stage of the cable car climbs the sheer, rocky mountainside to Ra Valles, in the middle of a pleasant bowl.

A day trip into the **Sella Ronda** ski area should not be missed. This starts from Passo Falzarego, where a cable car soars a dramatic 640 vertical metres up a cliff-face to Lagazuoi, linking into the area via a beautiful 11km red run past a shimmering turquoise ice-fall and several welcoming huts to **Armentarola** and **San Cassiano** beyond.

Advanced
Higher up at Tofana, the **Ra Valles** sector at 3000m offers the best snow in the resort. Near the bottom of the Tofana bowl, a gap in the rock gives access to a narrow black trail, which has a fairly steep south-facing stretch in the middle. The run ends up at the Pomedes chair-lifts, an area which itself offers some excellent runs, including a couple of good blacks and the spectacular Cannellone downhill racecourse.

From the foot of Monte Cristallo at Faloria, where the great Olympic champion Alberto Tomba can sometimes be seen honing his gate technique, a two-stage chair-lift climbs to Forcella Staunies, one of the best couloirs in the area. The top section of the descent necessitates

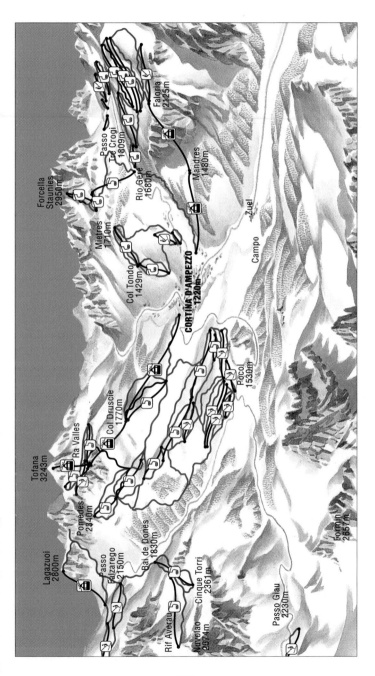

Faloria
2125m

Passo
Tre Croci
1809m

Rio Gere
1680m

Mandres
1480m

Forcella
Staunies
2950m

Zuel

Mietres
1710m

Campo

Col Tondo
1429m

CORTINA D'AMPEZZO
1220m

Pocol
1530m

Tofana
3243m

Ra Valles

Col Druscie
1770m

Pomedes
2440m

Lagazuoi
2800m

Passo
Falzarego
2150m

Bai de Dones
1830m

Cinque Torri
2361 m

Fornin
2657m

Rif Averau

Nuvolao
2574m

Passo Giau
2230m

some good sharp turns, as it is both narrow and very steep.

Off-piste
After a fresh snowfall, Forcella Staunies becomes an appealing off-piste area, as do the higher reaches of Tofana. Gruppo Guide Alpine, the resort's ski guiding organisation, can arrange everything from day ski-tours to special high-altitude weeks.

Snowboarding
Both group and private lessons are available through the Scuola Sci Cortina.

Cross-country
Long and varied cross-country trails include one extended loipe that follows the old railway track to **Dobbiaco**. Another takes you all the way to Villach in Austria. The annual Dobbiaco-Cortina international Langlauf race is classic entertainment.

Ski schools and guiding
The main Cortina Ski School has an office in the town centre and meeting places at Socrepes, Pocol and Pierosà. The standards appeared to be mixed, with some favourable reports. However, one reporter said: 'The instructor skied beautifully but his English was weak. He picked one single fault in the pair of us and identified it for three hours. It was a waste of money.' The Azzurra Ski School is smaller with an office at the foot of the Faloria cable car. Special courses include off-piste skiing and race training.

Mountain restaurants
Eating is a memorable experience in Cortina, and the choice of restaurants is extensive in the main ski areas. Col Drusciè and Rifugio Duca d'Aosta are both recommended, as is Rifugio Berghaus Pomedes, which has hand-carved furniture and a varied menu. Duca d'Aosta has wood-panelled walls and heart-warming local dishes. If you want to continue skiing after lunch it would be wise to avoid the *Kanederli*; consumption of these heavy dumplings filled with ham, bread, cheese and other kitchen leftovers is not conducive to afternoon athleticism on the slopes. Reporters praise El Farel at the foot of Socrepes and Col Taron, in the same area, which serves 'really delicious pasta'.

Next stage down the mountain from the Duca d'Aosta is Baita Pie Tofana, a relaxed eating place with a good sun terrace and attractive interior. Rifugio Averau at Cinque Torri is worth a visit, if only for its stunning views. The fresh pasta and *gnocchi* are particularly recommended. Rifugio Lagazuoi is situated a steep but worthwhile walk from the top of the Falzarego cable car.

Expensive places for serious lunching include El Camineto at the bottom of the Olympic piste. This is the most important of all lunchtime venues, where skiers join their fur-coated friends for exotic fare served in silver-domed dishes by a battalion of white-coated waiters.

Rifugio Scotoni on the long run down to **Armentarola** is highly recommended for mid-morning refreshment or lunch for late starters.

Off the mountain

Cortina is a large, attractive town, centred on the main shopping street of Corso Italia and the Piazza Venezia with its green and white bell tower. The large, frescoed buildings have an air of faded grandeur, and the views of the pink rock faces of Monte Cristallo are some of the most sensational in the Dolomites. More recent architectural additions are in a sympathetic Italian alpine style in keeping with the town's dramatic surroundings. The centre is mercifully traffic-free, with cars confined to a busy one-way perimeter road.

Accommodation

Hotels range from the large international variety to the simple, family-run establishments. There is also a large number of private apartments and chalets. The resort's smartest hotel, the Miramonti Majestic, is 2km out of town. The Cristallo is the other five-star.

The 15 four-stars include the attractive Hotel de la Poste, which is situated in the heart of Cortina and especially known for its food. Also well-located and comfortable is the Ancora on the Corso Italia, run by the eccentric Flavia Bertozzi. The Parc Hotel Victoria is well-placed and furnished with antiques. However, the half-board menu there has not always been to our reporters' tastes. One commented: 'Dinner was clear evidence of a kitchen that fed its punters, rather than cared about the food it produced'. On three successive nights the vegetarian option was: 'Tuna omelette, followed by scrambled eggs with tomato, followed by eggs Florentine. The following night they had run out of eggs and the veggie option was liver and onions. Lucky veggies!'

Two small, attractive three-star hotels within walking distance of the main cable car are the Capannina, with a good restaurant, and the inexpensive Barisetti. The Italia is a popular two-star hotel with good food and a loyal following. Although inconveniently positioned, the Menardi is recommended for its good food and reasonable prices. The Montana and

> ### ■ OTHER SPORTS
> Skating, hockey, curling, indoor tennis, swimming, ski-jumping, polo and horse shows on the frozen lake, snow rafting, tobogganing, bob-sleigh, dog-sledding, snow-shoeing, parapente, hang-gliding

the friendly and informal Olimpia are among the cheapest and most central bed-and-breakfast establishments.

Eating in and out

Dining is a serious part of the evening in Cortina. More than 80 restaurants cater for all tastes from simple pizzas to gourmet dining. El Camineto, popular with skiers at lunchtime, is also open in the evenings. It has two dining-rooms and the head waiter prefers to discuss the food and drink with you rather than show you a menu. Tivoli on the edge of town has a warm atmosphere with delicious and often unusual cooking. El Toulà is a converted hayloft with a good atmosphere. Il Meloncino on the road to **Passo Falzarego** has the freshest home-made pasta around. The Croda Caffé, Il Ponte and the Cinque Torri are all good for pizzas. Lunch at the Hotel Poste is 'brilliant, delicious and expensive'.

Après-ski

At around 5pm the early evening *passeggiata* along the **Corso Italia** heralds the start of the après-ski. The street becomes alive with promenading, fur-clad Italians admiring the elegant shop windows and each other. Cortina's shopping is absorbing and varied and includes an art gallery, antique and jewellery shops, sportswear and designer boutiques, enticing delicatessen, the good-value Cooperativa department store and even a Porsche dealership. As one reporter commented: 'As the old ladies swish by in their fur coats, mobile phones ringing in the mountain air, you can contemplate whether to buy the 911 Turbo or the Cabriolet.'

After dinner the action starts at the crowded Enoteca bar and Jerry's Wine Bar, then moves on to the throbbing Hyppo, Area and VIP discos. The entrance fee asked by the nightclubs does not subsidise the drink prices as it does in some comparably smart resorts. Partying is, consequently, an expensive occupation here.

An ice disco on the Olympic rink and the bobsleigh practice are both popular attractions, and big league ice hockey matches make interesting viewing. For non-skiers there is a cinema and three museums.

Childcare

There are two non-ski kindergarten, including Natural...Mente, a flexible operation, which picks children up in the morning and returns them after skiing. Staff also provide a babysitting service.

Linked or nearby resorts

Cortina links, in one direction only, into the Sella Ronda circuit at Lagazuoi, and shares the Superski Dolomiti lift pass. You need to start early in the day in order to achieve any distance on skis. Taxis wait at Armentarola to take skiers back to Lagazuoi, but a bus service brings you back to Falzarego.

Kronplatz 900m (2,953ft)

This resort on the Italian-Austrian border and covered by the **Superski Dolomiti** pass is virtually unknown outside Italy, yet it is an easy day trip just 60km from Cortina. Reporters comment on its excellent lifts and good variety of runs that go up to 2275m.

TOURIST OFFICE
Tel 39 474 555447
Fax 39 474 555544

Skiing facts: **Cortina d'Ampezzo**

TOURIST OFFICE
Piazzetta San Francesco 8, I-32043 Cortina d'Ampezzo, Belluno
Tel 39 436 3231
Fax 39 436 3235

THE RESORT
By road Calais 1200km
By rail Calalzo-Pieve di Cadore 35km
By air Venice 2½ hrs
Visitor beds 22,700
Transport free bus connects the town centre with the main lifts

THE SKIING
Linked or nearby resorts Armentarola (I), San Cassiano (I), San Vito di Cadore (n), Kronplatz (n)
Longest run Son Forca-Rio Gere, 9km (black/red)
Number of lifts 53 in area
Total of trails/pistes 140km in area (44% easy, 49% intermediate, 7% difficult)
Nursery slopes 5 runs, 3 lifts
Summer skiing none
Snowmaking 51km covered

LIFT PASSES
Area pass Cortina only L201,000-231,000 for 6 days. Superski Dolomiti (covers 450 lifts), L212,000-243,000 for 6 days
Day pass Cortina L42,000-47,000, Superski Dolomiti L44,000-49,000
Beginners coupons available
Pensioners 20% reduction for over 60s
Credit cards accepted no

SKI SCHOOLS
Adults Scuola Sci Cortina, 9.30am-midday, L240,000 for 6 days. Scuola Sci Azzurra, 9.15am-1pm, L420,000 for 6 days
Private lessons Cortina L52,000 per hr, Azzurra L56,000 per hr
Snowboarding Scuola Sci Cortina, 9.30am-midday, L350,000 for 6 days, or midday-2pm L230,000 for 6 days. Private lessons L20,000 per hr
Cross-country Scuola Italiana Sci Fondo, private lessons L47,000 per hr. Loipe 74km in the valley north of Cortina
Other courses race training, off-piste, tele-mark, ski-touring
Guiding companies Gruppo Guide Alpine Cortina

CHILDREN
Lift pass 30% reduction for under 14 yrs
Ski kindergarten Scuola Sci Cortina and Scuola Sci Azzurra, 2 yrs and over, times and prices as children's ski school
Ski school Scuola Sci Cortina, 9.30am-midday, L370,000. Scuola Sci Azzurra Cortina, 15 yrs and under, 9.15am-1pm, L420,000 for 6 days
Non-ski kindergarten Natural... Mente, nursery for 1-3 yrs, recreational and sporting activities 1-14 yrs, from 7.45am. Mini Club, 2-8 yrs, 8am-8pm, prices on request

FOOD AND DRINK PRICES
Coffee L1,400-1,500, glass of wine L1,500-1,800, small beer L2,800-3,000, dish of the day L10,000

Courmayeur

ALTITUDE 1230m (4,034ft)

Courmayeur is an attractive cobbled-stone village reached through the 11.6km Mont Blanc Tunnel from **Chamonix**. It is the nearest Italian resort by road from Britain and equally accessible by air from Turin and Geneva. The ski area offers stunning views of Mont Blanc. Off-piste opportunities include the Vallée Blanche and spectacular powder runs from the 2755m Cresta d'Arp. Its mountain restaurants are some of the best in Europe, and the village itself is a network of narrow streets with high-quality shops and a wide selection of restaurants, all within easy walking distance of the centre.

This is the favourite resort of the Milanese, a clientèle for whom lunch is frequently a greater priority than skiing. Weekenders provide a fashion parade of fur coats and the latest Italian *haute couture*.

■ **GOOD POINTS**

Beautiful scenery, excellent mountain restaurants, alpine charm, easy road access, short airport transfer, varied off-piste skiing, big vertical drop, tree-level skiing, extensive snowmaking

■ **BAD POINTS**

Lack of skiing convenience, limited nursery slopes, few tough runs

On the mountain
top 3470m (11,382ft) bottom 1370m (4,494ft)

The main mountain access is via a cable car across the river gorge and the arterial Mont Blanc Tunnel road. This takes you up to **Plan Checrouit**, a sunny plateau from where, annoyingly, you have to plod on up to the foot of the lifts. The mountain can also be reached by cable car from **Val Veny**, which is just as inconvenient. Queues at the bottom of the Plan Checrouit cable car can be a problem at peak times but this does not detract from the overall appeal of Courmayeur as a ski resort.

Reporters consistently remark on the friendliness of the locals, which is a startling contrast to the dour Gallic attitude of those on the other side of the tunnel. Extensive investment in snow-cannon has done much to improve skiing on the lower slopes down to Plan Checrouit and, over the mountain, down to Val Veny. However, the skiing is not satisfactory for everyone; the pisted runs are mainly short and lack challenge.

Advanced skiers will be more interested in the separate shared ski area with Chamonix, reached by the three-stage Mont Blanc cable car at **La Pallud** near the village of **Entrèves** on the tunnel side of Courmayeur. This ancient lift was closed for much of last season to the chagrin of expert skiers who use it to access some of the best powder skiing in the Mont Blanc massif.

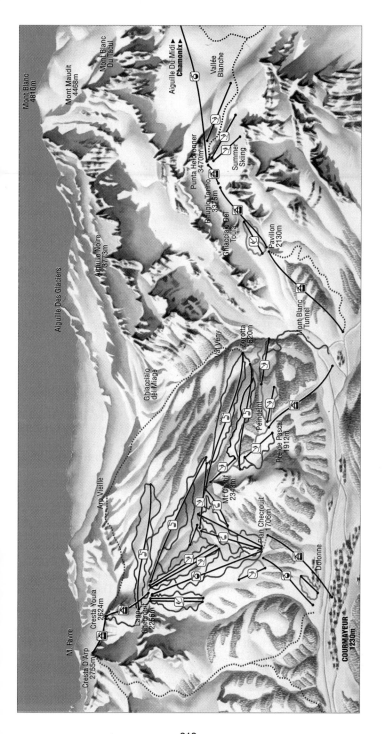

Mont Blanc
4810m

Mont Maudit
4468m

Mont Blanc
Du Taoul

Aiguille Du Midi ►
Chamonix ►

Vallée
Blanche

Aiguille Noire
3773m

Punta Helbronner
3470m

Summer
Skiing

Aiguille Des Glaciers

Rifugio Torino
3335m

Ghiacciaio Del
Toula

Pavillon
2130m

Ghiacciaio
del Miage

Mont Blanc
Tunnel

M. Favre

Val Vény

Zerotta
1620m

Cresta D'Arp
2755m

Cresta Youla
2624m

Arp Vieille

Peindelm

Pte de Pascal
1912m

Mt Chétif
2344m

Lago
Checrouit
2256m

Plan Checrouit
1706m

Dolonne

COURMAYEUR
1230m

313

Beginners

The nursery slopes are somewhat hazardous, with those at Plan Checrouit cramped by crowds of skiers descending from the main pistes. The baby slopes at the top of Val Veny and **Dolonne** are quieter.

Intermediates

The east-facing Checrouit Bowl has many quite short intermediate runs served by a variety of lifts, including a six-seater gondola. The pistes are often crowded, especially at the bottom where they merge. There are some surprisingly steep and narrow passages, even on some of the blue (easy) runs. The wooded north-facing Val Veny side of the mountain is linked in a couple of places with the Checrouit Bowl; it has longer and more varied pistes, with two red (intermediate) runs and a black (difficult) trail following the fall-line through the trees. Queuing for the Plan Checrouit and Mont Blanc ski areas is much worse at weekends when the crowds arrive from Turin and Milan. Quad-chairs at La Gabba and Zerotta have eased some of the other bottlenecks on the mountain, but the Youla cable car can still be a problem.

■ WHAT'S NEW

Three additional hotels: Gallia Gran Baità, La Baità and Ottoz

Advanced

The pistes served by the Gabba chair, at the top of the ski area and to the west of Lago Checrouit, are reported to keep their snow well, and the off-piste run underneath them is testing. The Youla cable car above Lago Checrouit opens up a deep and sheltered bowl, which serves a single uncomplicated red run with plenty of space for short off-piste excursions. It is also possible to ski (with a guide) the long itinerary run off the back of Youla down into Val Veny.

Off-piste

The serious off-piste begins at the top of the short cable car to Cresta d'Arp. The main route of 1500 vertical metres is down a beautiful and secluded valley; it is a long and varied run with some steep and difficult tree-line skiing on the lower stages, which finally emerges near the base-station of the Dolonne gondola or on the river bank near **Pré-St-Didier**. There is also a good run from the top, which takes you southwards through the Vallon de Youla to **La Balme** near La Thuile. There are no pistes from Arp.

The Mont Blanc cable car rises over 2000m to Punta Helbronner, giving easy access to the Vallée Blanche without the dreaded ice steps (see *Chamonix*). There is an afternoon bus back from Chamonix. The off-piste run down the Italian side of the massif is steep at the top and involves a clamber along a fixed rope and the hair-raising negotiation of a long, exposed and awkward staircase. However, the bottom stage of the cable car from Pavillon has a long, uncomplicated red piste that is rarely skied.

Snowboarding

Private lessons and some group lessons are available at the Scuola di Sci Monte Bianco. The off-piste at Cresta D'Arp makes for some excellent snowboarding, and for the less advanced Plan Checrouit has plenty of intermediate runs around the main ski area. Beginners will need to go to the nursery slopes at Val Veny.

Ski schools and guiding

Reports of the ski school are mixed, with criticism of poorly spoken English. The general verdict is that private instructors and guides are excellent value, but that group instructors often appeared jaded: 'Our instructor gave us the impression that he wasn't interested in our skiing at all. He was never enthusiastic or encouraging.' Special courses are available for off-piste, ski-touring, ski mountaineering, monoskiing and slalom.

Mountain restaurants

Eating on the mountain is one of the greatest pleasures of Italy, and Courmayeur takes it to new heights. One reporter comments: 'Delicious food at reasonable prices. Very easy to sit all afternoon when the weather is bad, with wonderful aromas wafting around your nose at all times.' There are too many restaurants to list, including welcoming chalets and charismatic converted cow-sheds. Plan Checrouit has a number of bars and restaurants. The Château Branlant serves full meals with waiter-service and 'heavenly desserts'. The Christiania (downstairs) and La Baità are also recommended. La Grolla at Peindeint on the Val Veny side is described as outstanding and 'expensive, but worth it and difficult to find, thank goodness'.

Other recommendations are the Petit Mont Blanc at **Zerotta**, Chiecco and Le Vieux Grenier for pasta, and 2000 at the altiport for sun-worshippers. On the Mont Blanc side there are bars at each lift stage. The Rifugio Pavillon at the top of the first stage of the cable car is reportedly excellent and has a sun-terrace. Rifugio Torino, at the next stage, is also said to be good. Rifugio Maison Vielle at L'Aiguille Noir, which has a large wood-burning stove, and Rifugio Monte Bianco between the Zerotta and Peindeint chairs, have pasta, *polenta*, sausages and a long wine list.

Off the mountain

The heart of the old village is a delightful maze of cobbled alleys (partly reserved for pedestrians), which are full of attractive shops selling fashion, as well as the inevitable ski shops. There are more bars, cafés and restaurants than could ever seem necessary, but they have a lively clientèle. The village has expanded, and the built-up area has now almost engulfed the neighbouring hamlets of **Verrand**, **Villair** and **La Saxe**; all of them are quiet and prosperous second-home areas with some beautiful rough-stone buildings. For a change of scenery and culture,

Skiing facts: **Courmayeur**

TOURIST OFFICE
Piazzale Monte Bianco, I-11013
Courmayeur, Aosta
Tel 39 165 842060
Fax 39 165 842072

THE RESORT
By road Calais 921km
By rail Pré-St-Didier 5km, regular buses
from station
By air Geneva 2 hrs, Turin 3 hrs
Visitor beds 20,722
Transport ski-bus, not included in lift pass

THE SKIING
Linked or nearby resorts Cervinia (n),
Champoluc (n), Chamonix (l), Gressoney-
la-Trinité (n), Pila (n), La Thuile (n)
Longest run Internazionale, 4.5km (red)
Number of lifts 32
Total of trails/pistes 100km (44% easy,
52% intermediate, 4% difficult)
Nursery slopes 1 at Dolonne and at Plan
Checrouit
Summer skiing 4km of slopes at Colle del
Flambeau and Colle del Gigante
Snowmaking 14km covered

LIFT PASSES
Area pass (Courmayeur Mont Blanc) L190-
220,000 for 6 days
Day pass L44,000 (Courmayeur only)
Beginners 3 free lifts

Pensioners no reduction
Credit cards accepted yes

SKI SCHOOLS
Adults Scuola di Sci Monte Bianco, 10am-
3pm, L170,000 for 6 days
Private lessons L47,000 per hr
Snowboarding through ski school
Cross-country through ski school. Loipe
35km in Val Ferret
Other courses monoski, off-piste, slalom,
ski-touring, heli-skiing
Guiding companies Società delle Guide di
Courmayeur

CHILDREN
Lift pass L190-220,000 for 6 days. 50%
reduction for 1.3m tall and under, free for
under 1m. (Courmayeur cable car and Val
Veny lift free for children under 1.1m with
parent)
Ski kindergarten Kinderheim and Scuola di
Sci Monte Bianco, 9am-4pm, both
L360,000 for 6 days including lunch
Ski school Scuola di Sci Monte Bianco,
10am-1pm, L170,000 for 6 days
Non-ski kindergarten Kinderheim, 6 mths
and over, 9am-4pm, L24,000 for 6 days

FOOD AND DRINK PRICES
Coffee L1,300-1,500, glass of wine L1,500,
small beer L3,500, dish of the day
L25-30,000

Chamonix is on the other side of the tunnel; there is an infrequent bus
link.

Accommodation
Few of the great variety of hotels, apartments and chalets are well-
situated for the main cable car. Several reporters stress the undesirability
of hotels located on the main road, which is used by countless lorries on
their way to the Mont Blanc Tunnel (not to be confused with the main
street through the village). The four-star Grand Hotel Gallia is expensive

but highly recommended. The Pavillon is well-situated opposite the cable car; it is comfortable and expensive, with a good swimming-pool and sauna. Hotel Courmayeur is 'friendly, with a roaring log-fire in the sitting area'. The Edelweiss and the two-star Berthod are good value for money. The Bouton d'Or is located just off the main square, and the Cristallo is attractive and comfortable.

Other recommendations include the Royal ('smart and expensive') and the Roma ('simple and cheap'). The Télécabine in Dolonne has its own crèche and is endorsed by a number of reporters.

Eating in and out

Restaurants are varied, plentiful and lively. The Turistica in Via Donzelli is a favourite; it is good value and serves large helpings. Pierre Alexis has great antipasta, an extensive menu and is reasonably priced. The Coquelicot is recommended for its grills. Le Bistroquet offers 'wonderfully prepared regional dishes'. La Palud is known for its fresh fish. Courmayeur also has plenty of pizzerias, including Mont Frety, which also serves regional dishes, and La Terrazza. Chalet Proment in Val Veny (if you have a car) serves good wholesome food. La Maison de Filippo at **Entrèves** is an exercise in unparalleled gluttony; it offers a fixed-price menu of at least 30 courses. Self-caterers are advised to shop at the Desparu supermarket on the Via Regionale directly above the cable-car station as there are no supermarkets in town and the few market shops are pricey.

Après-ski

Après-ski becomes more of a hanging-out situation, with certain times for certain bars, and often more than one in a night or a return visit after dinner. This is centred around the many bars in and around the Via Roma. The Bar Roma, with its comfortable sofas and armchairs, fills up early, and is especially good if you are tired after skiing. Steve's Privé has become an institution where regulars

■ OTHER SPORTS

Parapente, skating, ski-jumping, hang-gliding, indoor tennis, dog-sledding, climbing wall

of good standing can run up a tab for most of their holiday. The American Bar has good cocktails, and Ziggi's is more beer-orientated. Cadran Solaire is where the sophisticated Milanese go. The Abat-Jour and Le Clochard are the discos. The swimming-pool at **Pré St-Didier** is 5km away and is open from 3.30 to 8pm, and the floodlit skating rink is open every evening until midnight, complete with disco music.

Childcare

The Kinderheim at Plan Checrouit looks after children from six months old. The Scuola di Sci Monte Bianco has private and group lessons for children, with lunch included. The non-ski kindergarten is for children six months and over.

Livigno

ALTITUDE 1820m (5,970ft)

Livigno is one of the cheapest and consequently most popular ski resorts in Europe. It is eminently suitable for the 18 to 30s age group who are looking for beginner to intermediate skiing and a lively, afford-able nightlife that is greatly enhanced by the resort's duty-free status.

The great disadvantage is Livigno's remoteness, the five-hour drive from Milan or Zurich is one that reporters find particularly irksome at both the start and the end of their holiday.

The high and wide slopes along both sides of the valley above the resort provide a lot of uncomplicated inter-mediate skiing. The season here is a long one, with almost guaranteed resort-level snow throughout. On a fine day 'Piccolo Tibet', as Livigno is known locally, is extremely welcoming.

> ■ **GOOD POINTS**
>
> Easy runs, extensive nursery slopes, resort-level snow, late-season holidays, duty-free shopping
>
> ■ **BAD POINTS**
>
> Long airport transfer, few tough runs, difficult road access, heavy traffic, limited for non-skiers, lack of children's facilities

However, when the weather closes in few resorts are as bleak. The ski areas are separate, although they are linked by a fast and efficient bus service for those who do not want to walk. The lift system has been seri-ously upgraded in recent years, and the only queues are usually on the nursery slope lifts during high-season weeks.

Thanks to the road tunnel from Switzerland, it is possible to reach Livigno from Zurich, thus avoiding the risk of being fog-bound at Milan. A number of our reporters chose to drive 'an easy 11 hours from Ostend' and said that having a car was an advantage for visiting Bormio and Santa Caterina; both are covered on the area lift pass.

On the mountain
top 2797m (9,174ft) bottom 1816m (5,956ft)

The skiing takes place in two separate areas on both sides of the valley. The two-stage **Carosello** 3000 gondola takes you up from the southern end of town over wide, open, south-east-facing mountainside to 2797m. All the runs back down are graded red (intermediate), but none is severe, at least not until the final descent through the trees to the base. Poor snow cover and somewhat inadequate piste-marking can make these pitches more difficult. Behind the top-station is a quiet area of short runs beside the Federia drag-lifts, where the snow is usually at its best.

The less extensive slopes of **Mottolino** on the other side are reached by a 12-person gondola from outside the town. Other access points

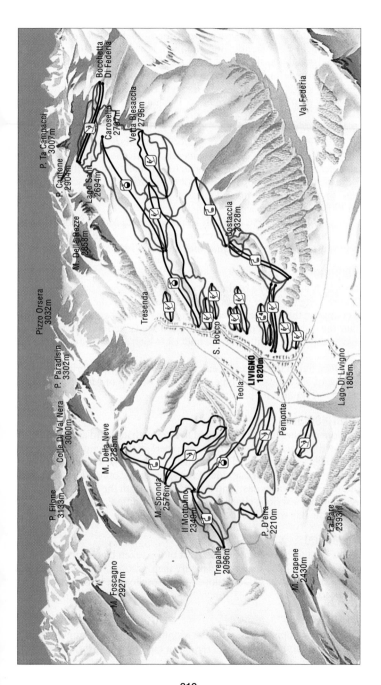

along the Bormio road serve a spectrum of intermediate runs complicated only by poor signposting and by the road itself, which cuts awkwardly through the ski area. A long, satisfying blue (easy) run takes you from **Monte della Neve** via **Monte Sponda** and Mottolino all the way down to the bottom of the gondola.

The majority of the skiing is above the tree-line, and when the weather closes in both sides of the valley are inhospitable places in which to find oneself, particularly as the local lift map bears no close relation to the actual installations on the mountain ('the piste map is so hopeless it is not even obvious which way the pistes run. Signposting is awful and most of my party just gave up on the map and followed their noses').

The old lifts are systematically being upgraded: Monte Sponda is now reached by a high-speed quad-chair. Blesaccia II, on the other side of the valley, is also a high-speed quad and Blesaccia I is now a triple-chair.

Beginners

Livigno is essentially a beginner's resort with a dozen novice lifts spread evenly along the lower slopes of the Carosello side of the valley, as well as a couple on the far side. Indeed, so great is the number of beginners here that the only queues on either mountain are to be found in the novice areas, especially at lifts 17, 18, and 19, which are favoured by the ski schools.

Once out of the nursery area, there are wide slopes offering an ample choice of easy runs. The blue pistes from the top of Monte della Neve down to **Trepalle** are particularly satisfying.

Intermediates

The open skiing here is best suited to intermediates who are not looking for anything radical, but are content to perfect their technique in what is essentially a rather limited area, which is annoyingly disjointed by having to take a bus from one side of the valley to the other. The wide slope above Trepalle faces east, and the red run beneath the chair-lift can represent quite a serious challenge in certain conditions, particularly at the end of the day when it is icy.

Advanced

This is not a resort for experts. Most of the token black (difficult) runs shown on the piste map barely justify their grading. Delle Streghe and Zuelli on the lower wooded sloped of Carosello can, however, be tricky in icy conditions.

Off-piste

The off-piste opportunities off the Monte della Neve are numerous, but most of the longer itineraries require a bus- or a taxi-ride back to the resort.

Snowboarding

All four ski schools give both group and private lessons. One reader describes Livigno as 'the ideal resort in which to learn, especially because the cost of lessons is so low'.

Ski schools and guiding

Livigno has four ski schools; the most popular with British clients is the Scuola Italiana Sci Livigno, which generally receives good reports, although class sizes of up to 13 are considered acceptable. All instructors speak good English and are a mixture of nationalities ('when we were there they included three English, two Argentinians and a Dane'). Another reader commented: 'the top class was first class, we received good instruction, covered a lot of ground and dramatically improved in the week.'

Mountain restaurants

The Costaccia with its outside barbecue is good, but expensive. Both Mottolino and Carosello are said to offer sound value-for-money. Ristoro Tea Borch, situated between the bottom and the mid-station of the Carosello 3000 cable car, is an old farmhouse with a lot of character ('warm and welcoming with good toilets'). Tea del Vidal at Mottolino and Tea del Plan (Costaccia) are as popular as ever ('excellent and full of character'). The Gatto Nero at Trepalle is highly recommended.

Off the mountain

A reader aptly describes Livigno as 'a beautiful, curious mixture of olde worlde charm and tacky bars'. The resort is centred around a square with chalet-style buildings and a modicum of alpine ambience. It has developed so much in 30 years that it is hard to remember that it was once a remote farming community cut-off from the outside world throughout the long winter months. The four communities of **Santa Maria**, **San Antonio**, **San Rocco** and **Trepallo** combine together to market themselves as a single resort. The result is a strung-out series of villages spread out along the floor of this remote valley, an unbroken 5km straggle of hotels, bars, garages, duty-free shops and supermarkets. These commercial enterprises are irregularly interspersed with old barns, working farms, and the occasional fine chalet.

■ **OTHER SPORTS**

Skating, ice-driving, sleigh rides, parapente, snowmobiling, winter walks

Part of the centre is now pedestrianised, but elsewhere traffic remains a hazard. The free ski-buses receive much praise from reporters for their regularity: 'We never waited more than ten minutes for a bus and although some were very full, journeys are tolerable and short.' However, once the ski-buses stop after 6pm, the evening bus service seems to be less reliable. Taxis are cheap and easily obtainable, and there are also buses to Bormio and to St Moritz. Livigno's *raison d'être* is

Skiing facts: **Livigno**

TOURIST OFFICE
Via dala Gesa 65, I-23030 Livigno, Sondrio
Tel 39 342 996379
Fax 39 342 996884

THE RESORT
By road Calais 1,107km
By rail Tirano 2½ hrs
By air Milan or Zurich 5 hrs, Bergamo 4 hrs
Visitor beds 7,989
Transport free ski-bus around resort

THE SKIING
Linked or nearby resorts Bormio (n), St Moritz (n), Valdisotto (n), Valdidentro (n), Santa Caterina (n)
Longest run Blesaceia, 2.6km (red/blue)
Number of lifts 31 in Livigno, 37 in linked area
Total of trails/pistes 100km (44% easy, 45% intermediate, 11% difficult)
Nursery slopes 12 lifts and 5km of runs
Summer skiing at Stelvio Pass/Diavolezza
Snowmaking 12km covered in Livigno

LIFT PASSES
Area pass (covers Bormio, Santa Caterina, Valdidentro, Valdisotto and 1 day in St Moritz) L205,000 for 6 days
Day pass L42,000 (Livigno only)

Beginners no free lifts
Pensioners 65 yrs and over, as children
Credit cards accepted yes

SKI SCHOOLS
Adults 4 ski schools: Scuola Italiana Sci Livigno Inverno-Estate, Sci Azzurra Livigno, Sci Livigno Italy, Sci Livigno Soc Coop, all L100,000 for 6 days (2 hrs per day)
Private lessons all 4 ski schools, L40,000 per lesson
Snowboarding all 4 ski schools, prices and times on request
Cross-country Scuola Italiana Sci Fondo Livigno, L95,000 for 6 days, private lessons L39,000 per hr. Loipe 50km
Other courses monoski, telemark
Guiding companies Lodovico Cusini

CHILDREN
Lift pass L36,000 for 6 days
Ski kindergarten none
Ski school all 4 schools, 4 yrs and over, L95,000 for 6 days (2 hrs per day)
Non-ski kindergarten none

FOOD AND DRINK PRICES
Coffee L1,300-1,500, glass of wine L1,000-1,500, small beer L2,500-3,000, dish of the day L10-12,000

shopping, with prices for spirits and tobacco reportedly half those on the cross-channel ferry.

Accommodation
Most hotels and apartments are strung along the resort's single axis from Santa Maria to San Rocco. The three-star Hotel Astoria is recommended both for its four-course dinners and its position in San Rocco near the Carosello 3000 gondola. Hotel Sankt Anton, at the other end of town, is described as 'clean and simple'. Camana Veglia is 'small, convenient, family-run, with bags of character'. Hotel Pastorella received unfavourable comments. A regular visitor continues to praise the family-run Silvestri. The Golf Hotel Parc and the Intermonti are the two luxury

category hotels, and there is a wide choice of three-stars. The Fausto apartments at the bottom of the Carosello 3000 gondola are recommended ('three big shower rooms for six of us').

Eating in and out

There is an excellent choice of restaurants, ranging from those serving pizzas and pasta to local dishes such as venison and *bresaola*. The Bellavista is strongly recommended for its 'fabulous' pizza as well as soups and local specialities. The Vecchia Lanterna and Mario's Pub are both popular. The Pesce d'Oro is a good fish restaurant, which is unusual in a resort so far from any sea. Foxi's is praised for its 'great burgers and low prices', and The Ambassador has 'the best pizzas in Livigno and good service'. Other recommended eating places are New Snack and the Ski Grill, Marco's Video Bar is recommended for its eggs-on-toast breakfasts and its bacon sandwiches, and the fondue in the Hotel Astoria is also praised.

Après-ski

Marco's Video Bar is for 'loud music, dancing, and friendly bar staff'. The Igloo Bar is what it says it is and is 'obviously cold, but a good place to go when you have your ski gear on'. Neither The Kokodi or Il Cielo, which attracts a wealthy Italian set, warm up until midnight. The action begins at the Bar Scuola Sci, headquarters of the main ski school, and the British tend to gather at Galli's bar in San Rocco. Other favoured nightspots include Foxi's in San Antonio, while the Underground Bar is popular though too noisy for some reporters' tastes.

Childcare

Like many other Italian resorts Livigno does not cater for small children; there is neither a ski nor a non-ski kindergarten. All four schools give lessons for children from four years of age.

The Milky Way

ALTITUDE Montgenèvre 1850m (6,068ft), Sauze d'Oulx 1500m (4,920ft), Sestriere 2035m (6,675ft)

The Milky Way is one of the most attractive and unsung of the giant ski circuits in Europe, marred unjustly in reputation by the infamy of Sauze d'Oulx as an alpine haunt of lager-louts on which the fun never sets. It straddles the French/Italian border and is more easily reached from Turin than from Grenoble. Its southerly location is compensated for by the height of the main resorts and snow cover is surprisingly sound. However, spring arrives a month earlier here than in the Haute Savoie and this should be taken into account in choosing when to visit.

The three major centres all have markedly different characters. **Montgenèvre**, the only French resort on the circuit, is an old stone-built village perched on the pass into Italy. It has been developed for tourism in a pleasant enough manner and retains considerable charm despite the busy international arterial road through its centre.

■ GOOD POINTS

Large ski area, easy runs, skiing convenience, extensive tree-level skiing, varied off-piste skiing, low prices, lively après-ski (Sauze d'Oulx), reliable snow cover (Sestriere)

■ BAD POINTS

Lack of activities for non-skiers, unreliable late-season snow, lack of mountain restaurants, lack of tough runs, lack of alpine charm, heavy traffic (Montgenèvre)

Sauze d'Oulx (pronounced Sow-zee Doo) has tried to clean up its act by heading upmarket, a feat at which it cannot succeed until more luxurious hotels are built to cater for a more sophisticated class of clientèle. In contrast, **Sestriere**, just a few kilometres away as the mountain chough flies, is one of the two smartest and most fashionable resorts in Italy (Cortina d'Ampezzo is the other).

The Milky Way (*Voie Lactée* or *Via Lattea*) is bounded by Montgenèvre at one end and by Sauze d'Oulx at the other. In between lie the villages of **Sestriere**, **Clavière**, **Cesana Torinese** and **Sansicario**, as well as a handful of small hamlets that are little more than ski-lift access points. The area is very spread out; it takes a long time to work one's way from one sector of the circuit to another, so a car is useful.

On the mountain
top 2820m (9,250ft) bottom 1350m (4,428ft)

Montgenèvre's slopes are on both sides of the pass. The south-facing side, Chalvet, is slightly higher with runs up to 2600m and is usually less crowded than the north-facing pistes, which create the main link with the

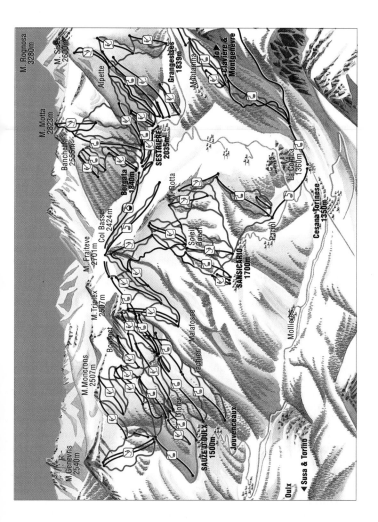

Italian Milky Way resorts. On the other side of the pass, mountain access is by gondola from the Briançon end of the village, as well as by drag-lifts and a chair from the centre. These serve easy runs through woods, opening into wide nursery slopes above the road.

From the top of the gondola there is a choice of three small ski areas. The wide, sheltered bowl of Le Querelay/Les Anges has ruined fortress buildings around the crest and some red (intermediate) and black (difficult) runs beneath them, but no challenging skiing overall.

The Milky Way link from Montgenèvre starts with a poorly signed traverse around the mountain, which is easy to miss in bad light. Otherwise, it is not a difficult link and leads to a long run, which starts as red and becomes blue (easy) past the Gimont drag-lifts and down to Clavière. The north-facing slopes of Monti della Luna, above Clavière and Cesana Torinese, offer plenty of challenge including some vast trails through the woods and good off-piste.

Reporters are unanimous in their opinion that the best skiing in the Milky Way is above **Sestriere**. Lifts are being systematically upgraded in preparation for the 1997 Alpine World Championships, and the whole resort does not suffer from the lack of investment apparent elsewhere in the Milky Way. The bulk of the skiing around Sestriere is on mainly north- and west-facing slopes on two mountains, Sises and Banchetta, separated by a deep valley.

The **Sauze d'Oulx** slopes face west and north and the majority of them are below the tree-line. The lifts are positively old-fashioned in comparison with those of Sauze's smart neighbour, even though they are run by the same company. A quad-chair takes you up to the centre of the skiing at **Sportinia**, a sunny woodland clearing with a few hotels, a small busy nursery area and a variety of restaurants. Above it there is some wide, open intermediate skiing served by several drags, one of which gives access to Col Basset and the run down to Sestriere. The other goes up a shaded mogul slope to the shoulder of Monte Fraiteve.

Below Sportinia there are wide runs back through the woods graded red and black; these are quite steep in places although never really demanding. There are also blue and black runs down to **Jouvenceaux**.

Queues in Montgenèvre are bad only at weekends and when snow in the nearby resorts is poor. The main queue problems at the Italian end of the Milky Way are on the Sauze side of the mountain, which a reporter who was there during an Italian bank holiday describes as 'horrendous'. The local lift map has been improved, but it is still difficult at times to work out exactly where you are. Reporters describe trail-marking as virtually non-existent, which adds to the problems of orientation.

Beginners

A dozen nursery slopes are scattered around the different resorts of the Milky Way on both sides of the border and the area is good learner territory. The main nursery slope for Sauze is at **Sportinia**, open and sunny, but often very crowded. There are also nursery slopes at Belvedere on the **Genevris** side, as well as in the village when there is snow. Sauze d'Oulx and Montgenèvre in particular are geared towards international clients. The Montgenèvre end of the circuit has the best choice of easy blue runs.

Intermediates

The long red runs down to Sansicario from **Monte Fraiteve** are satisfyingly varied and some of the best on the circuit. Red run 29, back

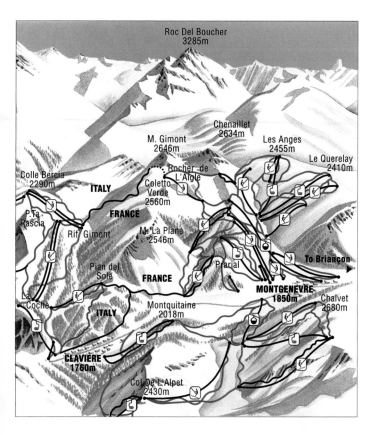

through the trees to Sauze, is the favourite of several reporters. Old hands to the area say that high-season crowds are a problem throughout the Milky Way, but particularly around Sestriere. The secret is to ski the remote **Genevris/Moncrons/Bourget** sector on Saturdays and Sundays ('a pleasure to ski and no queues at all here').

Advanced
An assortment of difficult runs scattered throughout the Milky Way makes this an underrated playground for advanced skiers who will find plenty of challenge. The Sauze sector quite wrongly has a novice label attached to it because of the predominance of beginner and early inter-mediate skiers that it attracts. In fact, some of the reds here could easily be graded black in other resorts, and a few of the blacks (notably runs 33 and 21) are seriously challenging in difficult snow conditions. The best of the skiing is found above Sansicario and Sestriere, although this may not be apparent from the local map.

The steep Motta drag-lift and chair serve the highest and toughest of

Sestriere's skiing and reach the top point of the Milky Way at 2823m. Here the slopes beside the drag can have gradients of up to 30 degrees and are often mogulled.

Off-piste
Monte Fraiteve is an exposed crest with impressive views of the French mountains, where the ski areas of Sauze d'Oulx, Sestriere and Sansicario converge. It is also the start of the famous Rio Nero off-piste run, a long descent that follows a river gully down to the Oulx-Cesana road, 1600m below. An infrequent bus-service takes you back to the lifts at Cesana.

The long dog-leg drag, La Crête, goes through magnificent rocky scenery to Rocher de l'Aigle and the start of an outstanding off-piste bowl and an alternative steep couloir. Anyone attempting the latter draws admiring glances from those on the piste below.

Snowboarding
The French Ski School (ESF) at Montgenèvre has group and private lessons, Sestriere Ski School offers private ones, and Sauze's three ski schools all provide tuition.

Ski schools and guiding
Recent reports speak well of the ESF at Montgenèvre ('friendly and helpful instructors, with good English') for all grades of skier and for private lessons. The Sauze d'Oulx Ski School has two rivals, Sauze Project and Sauze Sportinia. We have mixed reports of the Sauze d'Oulx ('too much follow-my-leader, and the grading on the first day took an eternity, with 200 people lined up in knee-deep snow'). However, the overall standard of instruction is said to be 'extremely high' and most instructors speak fluent English.

Mountain restaurants
Montgenèvre is seriously short of mountain restaurants. However, the excellent and inexpensive bars and restaurants above Clavière (particularly La Coche) help make up for this shortfall.

The five restaurants at Sportinia include the Capanna, which is said to be 'the busiest but not the best.' La Capannina, 100m away, is 'cosier and with a more authentic feel to it'. Monte Triplex has 'a good choice of food, friendly and efficient service, and is not too crowded.'

At Sansicario, Bar Soleil Boeuf is described as 'elegant and traditionally furnished.' Chalet Genevris at Genevris is renowned for its barbecue with all you can eat or drink for around £8 ('very friendly with an excellent atmosphere of camaraderie at lunchtimes, which often stretched well into afternoons').

Sestriere's Bar Chisonetto, halfway down Red 8 on Banchetta, is recommended for its hamburgers. Bar Conchinetto is a traditional wood-and-stone restaurant renowned for its *polenta*, and La Gargote has plenty of atmosphere but is more expensive.

Off the mountain

The first impression of **Montgenèvre** is of a rather untidy and higgledy-piggledy collection of bars, restaurants, shops and hotels lining an extremely busy main road where skiers joust with pantechnicons. The real village is tucked away on the northern side and has plenty of atmosphere, despite the traffic. Shopping facilities are limited, but the weekly open-air market adds considerable colour and the occasional bargain. Prices are markedly lower than in most other French resorts. Italy begins at the border post on the outskirts of town and both currencies are in circulation here.

In its prime, the main street of **Sauze d'Oulx** was at its noisiest at 3am. Raucous revellers, still in their ski boots and awash with cheap lager and tequila slammers, staggered homewards from the infamous Andy Capp bar to a dozen shabby two-star hotels for a few hours of further recreation before hitting the slopes once more. To the 2,000 young British skiers (50 per cent of the resort's customers) who flocked to this corner of Piedmont each winter in search of snow, sex and mind-shattering amounts of alcohol, it was known as 'Suzy does it'.

Suzy, it seems, has matured beyond the abandoned follies of her youth and after a decade in the doldrums is enjoying a more classy comeback. If she still does it, she has at least drawn the curtains and turned down the lights. At the height of recession the number of weekly British visitors slumped into the hundreds, but it has climbed gradually back without the extreme yobbo element, which has moved on to fresh grazing elsewhere.

The local tourist board aims to transform Sauze into an upmarket family resort and in no uncertain terms has told tour operators to provide a better class of visitor. To achieve its aim, however, the resort first needs to provide better accommodation.

Recently reporters have been pleasantly surprised to find the village far from boisterous, with more of an Italian ambience to it than in the past. While British influence is still prevalent — many of the locals speak English and some ski shops price equipment in sterling — the majority of visitors are Italian. The old village retains its charm, but the more recent development that contains most of the accommodation and restaurants is an unappealing hotchpotch of mainly ugly, modern buildings.

Sestriere was Europe's original purpose-built ski resort, a joint operation between Mussolini and Agnelli (of Fiat fame). After years of negligence, it has now torn down its rusty cable cars and invested heavily in snow-cannon and new lifts. This, together with its high altitude of around 2000m, makes Sestriere one of the more snow-sure resorts at this end of the Alps. Although it has the reputation of attracting rich Italians from Turin, it does not wear its mantle of affluence with any great show of style — a collection of unappealing modern edifices spread across a high, windy pass that generates a rather soul-less atmosphere.

The landmarks are the tall, round towers of the old Duchi d'Aosta Hotel, now occupied by Club Med, and the Gothic turrets of the restored Principi de Piemonte Hotel. This is some way from the resort centre, but it has its own lift access to the Sises ski area. Buses run to and from **Borgata**, **Grangesises** and the end of the Rio Nero run (on the Oulx–Cesana road).

The more shrewd Italians have now swapped Sestriere for nearby Sansicario, a smaller, more sophisticated and modern development with its own ski area, linked to Sestriere and Sauze on the one side and Cesana Torinese on the other.

Accommodation

Montgenèvre's accommodation is mostly in apartments scattered along the road, in the old village and on the lower south-facing slopes; there are also a few catered chalets. Access to the skiing is easy from most places, but the Italian end of the village is more convenient. The pick of Montgenèvre's half-a-dozen less than luxurious hotels are the Napoléon, convenient but basic, and the more attractive Valérie, near the church. Others include the Chalvet and simple La Grange.

Accommodation in **Sauze** is mostly in cheap hotels, which reporters generally find adequate. The best location is around the bottom of Clotes. The hotels in this area are the Hermitage, Stella Alpina and the Sauze. The Sauze is about 100m from the Clotes lift and is described as 'very clean and spacious'. The Gran Baità, next to the church, is recommended as 'excellent — very clean, the staff are pleasant and the hotel is five minutes' walk from everything'. San Giorgio is far from luxurious and badly placed, but friendly and inexpensive.

The Chaberton is a simple bed-and-breakfast place and the Savoia overlooks the Clotes piste and is close to the lifts. The Palace is the biggest and most expensive hotel, however, it is not particularly stylish. Il Capricorno at Clotes is expensive and attractive. You can be first on the nursery slopes by staying at the Monte Triplex or the Capanna at Sportinia. The Ciao Pais above Clotes also offers cheap and simple accommodation.

Sestriere's accommodation is in hotels, apartments in large new complexes and at Club Med. Apart from the Principi, the most luxurious hotel is the modern low-rise Sestriere. The Savoy Edelweiss is simple and central. The Grand Hotel is in the resort centre and five minutes' walk from the lifts.

The Miramonti is not very well situated, but friendly, attractive and good value. The Biancaneve is just outside town and has its own mini-bus service to the slopes.

Eating in and out

In **Sauze**, La Griglia is strongly recommended. Del Falco is praised for its relaxed and friendly service ('food great and certainly not expensive'). Sugo's specialises in pasta. Albertino's is more of a café than a restaurant, with prices to match. Del Borgo is famed for its *tiramisù*. Il Lampione has 'good pub-grub to please the English pie-and-chips brigade'. Kaly and Villa Daniella are also recommended.

In **Montgenèvre**, there are more than a dozen eating places including Les Chalmettes, Le Pichounet, L'Estable, Pizzeria La Tourmente, the smart Le Jamy and Chez Pierrot for pizzas and grills.

Eating-places in **Sestriere** range from pizzerias to smart international restaurants. The Last Tango is for grills and the Fraiteve in the Grand Hotel specialises in local Piedmont cuisine.

Après-ski

Après-ski activity in **Montgenèvre** is extremely limited, but there is a good choice of inexpensive bar-restaurants in which to make merry, and three of them have disco-nightclubs. The Ca del Sol is a popular bar in the centre and La Graal has satellite television. The Blue Night and Play Boy are the two discos. There is little for non-skiers to do, although the village has a good skating rink.

In **Sauze**, the infamous Andy Capp and the New Scotch Bar near the bottom of the home run catch the early evening crowd and are awash with pints of Tartan long before dark. Later on the action moves to the Cotton Club, Hotel Derby Bar and Moncrons. Max's Bar shows British sport on satellite TV. Osteria da Gigi and The Village Gossip both have live music six nights a week. The Shuss, New Life and Rimini Nord discos 'keep you dancing as long as you want'. One reporter notes that entry to all clubs is free, a pleasant contrast to France.

Sestriere's après-ski is fairly lively and stylish when the Italians are in residence at weekends and in holiday periods, although at other times it is quieter. The Black Sun and Tabata discos are popular at weekends. An ice-driving course can be included in the hotel/lift-pass formula, but there is little else for non-skiers here.

Childcare

Montgenèvre has a non-ski kindergarten, which takes children from 12 months to four years. The ESF takes three- to five-year-olds in its ski kindergarten. Italy is not renowned for its childcare facilities but the Milky Way is an important exception. Sauze's Pro Loco kindergarten takes infants from six months to six years of age with ski tuition for the older ones; the ski schools take children from five years old. Sestriere has no public crèche, but Club Med looks after its smallest members from four years of age, as does the ski school.

Linked or nearby resorts

Bardonecchia 1312m (4,303ft)

This is a large and traditional market town set in a sunny valley and surrounded by beautiful scenery. Although it is not part of the Milky Way circuit, it lies close to both Montgenèvre and Sestriere. It is popular with

Italians who swarm in from Turin at weekends and holidays. The skiing is spread over three areas, linked by free ski-bus, with a total of 140km of piste and offers a surprising amount of challenge. The nightlife is limited to a couple of rather dull bars and a disco.

Hotels include La Bettula (close to the shopping centre), the Tabor (near the ski-bus stop) and the Larici (250m from the heart of the resort). There are no facilities for small children.

TOURIST OFFICE
Tel 39 122 99032
Fax 39 122 980612

Borgata 1840m (6,035ft)

This is a small resort five minutes by road from Sestriere; a bus runs between them every half hour. Hotel Hermitage is recommended ('nice rooms, but the food was not up to much'). Reporters who stayed in the Nube d'Argenta self-catering apartments praised them as 'clean, modern and convenient for the lifts'. There have been complaints about the ski school ('very poor, with limited spoken English; little progress was offered in the lessons, but the teachers were pleasant enough'). The après-ski is almost non-existent ('a couple of sleepy bars with miserable staff and no, or few, customers'). As another reporter put it: 'When the sun goes down, it is time to eat and go to bed.'

TOURIST OFFICE
as Sestriere

Cesana Torinese 1350m (4,428ft)

Cesana is an attractively shabby old village dating back to the twelfth century, set on a busy road junction at the foot of the Italian approach to the Montgenèvre Pass. It is rather confined and shaded, and accommodation is mainly in apartments and a few hotels. The chair-lifts up to the skiing above Clavière and Sansicario are a long walk from the centre and the place can be safely recommended only to those with a car for access to other resorts. The Chaberton is a three-star hotel and there are half-a-dozen small one-stars. Restaurant La Selvaggia specialises in regional specialities, La Noblerot serves French cuisine and the smart Fraiteve is for truffles; the Brusachoeur is a popular pizzeria. Après-ski spots include the Pussy-Cat pub and the Cremeria Rinaldo e Luciana bar.

TOURIST OFFICE
Tel 39 122 89202
Fax 39 122 811315

Clavière 1760m (5,773ft)

Clavière is a small border town in the northern Valle di Susa, with the customs post in the middle. During the eighteenth century it was part of Montgenèvre. The village consists of a few hotels and a row of shops (including several good supermarkets) on the Italian side, specialising in food and cheap local alcohol, with prices in both francs and lire.

Reporters say the village has a pleasant, relaxed atmosphere and is ideal for families; it is tightly enclosed by wooded slopes and the nursery area is small and steep. Lifts give access to the skiing above Montgenèvre and Cesana, with easy runs back from both. Queuing is not usually a problem, although it does tend to become slightly busier at weekends. Mountain eating-places close to the village are the Località Gimont and La Coche. There is a cross-country trail up to Montgenèvre and back. The ski school has some English-speaking instructors and, outside high season, mainly English-speaking pupils. At weekends there is heavy through-traffic.

There are eight hotels along the road. The two-star Hotel Roma, close to the main chair-lift, is recommended ('good value, plenty of food, and comfortable rooms'). Others include the Passero Pellegrino, Pian del Sole and the Savoia. The restaurants are mainly in hotels, and others include the Bar Ristorante Ski-Lodge, the Sandy and the Gran Bouc crêperie. Clavière is 'not a place for those interested in a hectic après-ski'. It has half-a-dozen bars including the Bar Caffé Torino and the Pub Kilt, plus Disco La Scacchiera.

TOURIST OFFICE
Tel 39 122 878856
Fax 39 122 878888

Sansicario 1710m (5,609ft)

The village is in a sunny position halfway up a west-facing mountainside and is well placed for exploring the Milky Way. It is purpose-built, consisting mainly of apartment buildings linked to a neat commercial precinct by shuttle-lift. Facilities are generally good for beginners, and especially for children. There is a good ski- and non-ski kindergarten (the Junior Club) providing daycare, including lunch, for 3- to 11-year-olds. Sansicario has its own ski school.

There is little variety among the après-ski facilities, just a disco, three restaurants, three bars and few other sporting activities. Accommodation is of a generally high standard, mostly in apartments, but with a few comfortable, expensive hotels. The most attractive of these is the Rio Envers, a short walk from the centre. Others include the four-star Monti della Luna and the simpler San Sicario.

TOURIST OFFICE
Tel 39 122 831596
Fax 39 122 831880

Skiing facts: **Montgenèvre**

TOURIST OFFICE
F-05100 Montgenèvre, Hautes-Alpes
Tel 33 92 21 90 22
Fax 33 92 21 22 45

THE RESORT
By road Calais 978km
By rail Briançon 10km
By air Turin 2 hrs, Grenoble 3 hrs
Visitor beds 8,000
Transport bus service throughout the resort
and to Briançon

THE SKIING
Linked or nearby resorts Bardonecchia
(n), Borgata (l), Clavière (l), Cesana
Torinese (l), Grangesises (l), Jouvenceaux
(l), Sansicario (l), Sauze d'Oulx (l), Sestriere
(l), Sportinia (l)
Longest run Le Chalvet, 2.5km (red)
Number of lifts 24 in Montgenèvre, 101 in
Milky Way
Total of trails/pistes 65km in Montgenèvre
(49% easy, 32% intermediate, 19%
difficult), 400km in Milky Way
Nursery slopes 1 free drag-lift
Summer skiing none
Snowmaking 15% of runs covered

LIFT PASSES
Area pass Montgenèvre 610FF for 6 days,
extension pass for Milky Way (Voie Lactée)
Day pass Montgenèvre 115FF, Milky Way

170FF
Beginners Petit Réseau Pass for beginners
(covers 7 lifts) 80FF a day for adults, 60FF
for children
Pensioners 60-69 yrs, 480FF for 6 days,
free for 70 yrs and over
Credit cards accepted yes

SKI SCHOOLS
Adults ESF, 745-770FF for 6 days (5 hrs
per day)
Private lessons ESF, 160FF per hr
Snowboarding ESF, prices and times as
regular ski school
Cross-country ESF, 485FF for 6 half-days.
Loipe 50km on either side of the pass and at
Les Alberts, 7km away
Other courses off-piste, moguls, slalom
Guiding companies through ski schools

CHILDREN
Lift pass 5-12 yrs, 480FF for 6 days, free
for 4 yrs and under
Ski kindergarten Jardin d'enfants, 3-5 yrs,
100FF per half-day
Ski school ESF, 3-5 yrs, 695FF for 6 days
Non-ski kindergarten Haute Garderie, 12
mths-4 yrs, 9am-5.30pm, 550FF for 6 days
not including lunch

FOOD AND DRINK PRICES
Coffee 6-7FF, glass of wine 9-12FF, small
beer 10-12FF, dish of the day 60-70FF

Skiing facts: **Sauze d'Oulx**

TOURIST OFFICE
Piazza Assietta 18, I-10050 Sauze d'Oulx, Piedmont
Tel 39 122 858009
Fax 39 122 850497

THE RESORT
By road Calais 998km
By rail Oulx 5km, frequent buses to resort
By air Turin 2 hrs
Visitor beds 4,350
Transport free ski-bus runs from 8am-6pm daily

THE SKIING
Linked or nearby resorts Bardonecchia (n), Borgata (I), Clavière (I), Cesana Torinese (I), Grangesises (I), Jouvenceaux (I), Montgenèvre (I), Sansicario (I), Sestriere (I), Sportinia (I)
Longest run Gran Pista Number 12, 12km (red)
Number of lifts 25 in Sauze d'Oulx, 101 in Milky Way
Total of trails/pistes 120km in Sauze d'Oulx (27% easy, 61% intermediate, 12% difficult), 400km in Milky Way
Nursery slopes 3 lifts in Sauze d'Oulx
Summer skiing none
Snowmaking 5km in Sauze d'Oulx

LIFT PASSES
Area pass Milky Way (includes all lifts in Sauze d'Oulx, Sestriere, Sansicario, Cesana and Clavière), L210-230,000 for 6 days
Day pass L44,000 (Milky Way)
Beginners points tickets
Pensioners 60 yrs and over, L175-195,000 for 6 days
Credit cards accepted no

SKI SCHOOLS
Adults Sauze d'Oulx, Sauze Project and Sauze Sportinia, 10am-1pm, L160,000 for 6 days (3 hrs per day)
Private lessons all ski schools L42-46,000 per hr
Snowboarding group and private lessons through ski schools
Cross-country very limited. Loipe 3km
Other courses heli-skiing from Sestriere
Guiding companies through ski schools

CHILDREN
Lift pass 8-12 yrs, L185,000, free for 7 yrs and under
Ski kindergarten The Village Kindergarten, 6 mths-6 yrs, 9am-5pm, L250,000 for 6 days
Ski school all ski schools, 4-6 yrs, 10am-1pm, L172,000 for 6 days
Non-ski kindergarten Pro Loco, 18 mths-6 yrs, 9am-5pm, L250,000 for 6 days

FOOD AND DRINK PRICES
Coffee L1,300, glass of wine L1,000, small beer L3,000, dish of the day L20,000

Skiing facts: **Sestriere**

TOURIST OFFICE
Piazza Agnell, I-10058 Sestriere, Piedmont
Tel 39 122 755444
Fax 39 122 755171

THE RESORT
By road Calais 1020km
By rail Oulx 22km, buses to resort
By air Turin 2 hrs
Visitor beds 16,846
Transport ski-bus L2,500 per day

THE SKIING
Linked or nearby resorts Bardonecchia
(n), Borgata (I), Clavière (I), Cesana
Torinese (I), Grangesises (I), Jouvenceaux
(I), Montgenèvre (I), Sansicario (I), Sauze
d'Oulx (I), Sportinia (I)
Longest run Rio Nero, 7km (black)
Number of lifts 25 in Sestriere, 101 in
Milky Way
Total of trails/pistes 120km in Sestriere
(39% easy, 42% intermediate, 19%
difficult), 400km in Milky Way
Nursery slopes several areas
Summer skiing none
Snowmaking 65km covered

LIFT PASSES
Area pass Milky Way (includes all lifts in
Sauze d'Oulx, Sestriere, Sansicario, Cesana
Torinese and Clavière) L210-230,000 for 6
days
Day pass L44,000 (Milky Way)
Beginners L12-23,000 per day
Pensioners reductions for 60 yrs and over
Credit cards accepted no

SKI SCHOOLS
Adults Sestriere Ski School, 10am-1pm,
L42,000 per day, L160,000 for 6 days
Private lessons L42,000 per hr
Cross-country private lessons through ski
school, details on request. 2 loipes covering
15km
Snowboarding private lessons through ski
school, details on request
Other courses heli-skiing
Guiding companies through ski school

CHILDREN
Lift pass 8-12 yrs, L185,000, free for 7 yrs
and under
Ski kindergarten Sestriere Ski School, 4
yrs and over, 10am-1pm, L42,000 per hr,
L160,000 for 6 days
Ski school as ski kindergarten
Non-ski kindergarten Neve Sole, 3-11 yrs,
9am-5pm, L10,000 per hr, L35,000 per day
including lunch

FOOD AND DRINK PRICES
Coffee L1,300, glass of wine L1,000-1,500,
small beer L3,000, dish of the day L20,000

Sella Ronda

ALTITUDE Selva 1550m (5,084ft), Canazei 1440m (4,724ft)

The largest ski area in the world is set in the most dramatic and beautiful mountain range in Europe. For palettes jaded by the stolid commercial realities of holidays in the French Alps and in Austria, this is the much-needed and refreshing sorbet to European skiing. It comprises an astonishing 464 lifts serving 1100km of largely intermediate skiing set against a backdrop of craggy peaks and dramatic granite cliffs, which turn a distinctive and glorious shade of rose pink in the light of the setting sun.

By no means are all of these runs linked, but nearly all are included in the Superski Dolomiti lift pass, which at around £90 per week in low season and £100 at peak times, represents the best value in the northern hemisphere.

At the core of the Dolomites lies the **Sella Ronda**, a celebrated circuit of four valleys involving 90 minutes of lifts, 120 minutes of downhill skiing and an always undetermined Joker factor of queuing time. Miss the crucial lift home owing to deteriorating weather or volume of people and you are in for an expensive taxi ride.

The best-known, but by no means the most important, of these valleys, is **Val Gardena**, scene in 1981 of Britain's best-ever World Cup downhill result. Konrad Bartelski claimed second place, a feat so surprising that TV commentator David Vine at first thought the clock was wrong. **Selva**, or Wolkenstein as it is also known in this bilingual border area of Italy, is the actual name of the resort, and is barely more than a small village strung along the main valley road.

The second most popular is **Canazei**, in the Italian-speaking Val di Fassa. This large and bustling village acts as one of the main holiday bases for skiing in the region and is the best for those in search of non-skiing activities and a good nightlife.

On the periphery of the Sella Ronda circuit lies a whole range of resorts from established international ski towns like chic **Cortina d'Ampezzo** to the sleepy and essentially Italian villages of **San Martino di Castrozza** and **Vigo di Fassa**. You cannot hope to ski it all in a week, or even in a season.

Vastly improved services to the upgraded airports at Venice and Verona, coupled with two-and-a-half-hour motorway transfers to most

> ## SELVA
> ### ■ GOOD POINTS
> Enormous intermediate ski area, outstanding scenery, variety of mountain restaurants, extensive ski-touring opportunities, many activities for non-skiers, comprehensive beginners' and children's facilities
>
> ### ■ BAD POINTS
> Unreliable snow record, heavy traffic, lack of village centre

Dolomite resorts, have opened up what is an unspoilt corner of the European ski map.

As one veteran visitor to the area puts it: 'What you find here is a lack of the complacency in comparison to Italy's alpine neighbours. They don't turn on the snow-cannon at the start of the season, they turn them on a month earlier to ensure conditions will be perfect from the word go.

Gone are the days of dangling your legs off ancient lifts, which closed at lunchtime while the operator went off for a plate of pasta and a bottle of wine; they have been replaced with modern gondolas and detachable quads. Combine this professionalism with excellent prices, good food and wine, and the current popularity of everything Italian and you have the formula for success.'

> **CANAZEI**
> **■ GOOD POINTS**
>
> Superb intermediate skiing, outstanding scenery, wide choice of shops, variety of mountain restaurants
>
> **■ BAD POINTS**
>
> Large sprawling resort, heavy traffic, uncertain resort-level snow

The layout of the Sella Ronda and the whole Superski Dolomiti region is not as confusing as it sounds and you will soon get your bearings, provided you invest in the Ordnance Survey-style map of the region, called Sellaronda E Valli Ladine Carta Sciistica, which costs about £3 from any newsagent. It shows all the lifts and the standard of each run. The local tourist board piste maps raise more questions than they answer.

On the mountain
top 2950m (9,676ft) bottom 1225m (4,018ft)

With its mainly blue (easy) and unproblematic red (intermediate) runs, the Sella Ronda is more a way of seeing some wonderful scenery than of trying some really challenging skiing. Although the peaks of these mountains are high, the skiing is virtually all lower down; this is the main cause of the variable snow record of the Dolomites, a handicap that has been offset by heavy investment in modern snowmaking techniques.

The only real problems with poor snow conditions are when the south-facing slopes in particular become very worn and unpleasant. One reporter recounted having to remove her skis and walk certain sections of the circuit during a mild spell; indeed, short walks between lifts are not uncommon, even when conditions are good.

The Sella Ronda can be skied in either direction with all kinds of variations, but it is wise to stick to the basic circuit until you have worked out how long it takes to complete the homeward section.

Clockwise mountain access from Selva is via the Dantercëpies gondola to the start of a long and mainly red cruise through 730 vertical metres all the way to **Colfosco**. From here a chair-lift takes you to Corvara and a cable car brings you to Boè and the Crep de Munt for a short red run down to Campolungo. You can take a drag-lift up to the Rifugio Bec de Roces, which is the start of a pleasant red (intermediate)

and blue (easy) run with dramatic backdrops down into **Arabba**. A chair-lift is the most direct, but not necessarily the quickest, onward route. The cable car to Belvedere involves more skiing and a much more challenging piste, which allows you to rejoin the blue route before Pont de Vauz.

Two slow chairs, which can produce an unpleasant bottleneck, bring you to Sas Becè and the red run down to Lupo Bianco. A short red takes you off the circuit into Canazei or you continue with two chairs up to Col Salei. From here, a short red and a long blue cruise through 700 vertical metres return to Selva.

Beginners

The best of the novice skiing is found in the **Alta Badia** sector bordered by **Armentarola** in the east, **Corvara** in the west and **La Villa** in the north. The gentle wooded meadows here are reminiscent of the Austrian Tyrol. At the other end of the circuit, try the long blue that starts above the Passo Sella at 2400m and takes you gently down to Selva at 1570m.

Intermediates

The whole of the Sella Ronda is ideally suited to cruisers who really want to put some mileage beneath their skis each day in this outstanding setting. Where to base yourself is a matter of personal choice. The Selva-Canazei end of the circuit has some of the better long runs, a statement with which fans of Corvara and Colfosco would strongly disagree.

Advanced

Arabba is the Argentière of Italy and the place to base yourself for the toughest skiing in the area. Anyone who imagines that the Dolomites consist solely of scenic blue cruising runs is in for a wicked shock here. From the edge of the village a two-stage jumbo gondola and a cable car take you up nearly 900m over the granite cliffs off the Soura Sass to the start of what is, by any standard, some serious expert skiing. The choice of black (difficult) runs down the front face are testing in the extreme.

Alternatively, from the halfway stage of the gondola you can ski off the Sella Ronda on a wonderful 20km journey down usually deserted pistes to the town of **Malga Ciapela**. From here you pay a £10 supplement to your lift pass for the long cable car to the top of the 3269m **Marmolada**, revered by mountaineers in the same breath as the Matterhorn, the Eiger and Mont Blanc. The lift opens only in February, and once you have admired the views from the top, a mighty 12km red run takes you to within one drag-lift of the home run back down to Arabba. Powderhounds can also enjoy moderately priced heli-skiing on the Marmolada.

Off-piste

Passo Pordoi, between Arabba and Canazei, is the base-station of the Sas Pordoi cable car, which takes you up to the Rifugio Maria at 2958m. Piste-grooming machines have never made it up here and all the skiing is left as nature intended it. The long run down the Val de Mesdi is one of the most taxing in the Dolomites and should not be attempted without a guide. The front face of Sas Pordoi is a shorter, difficult challenge with a steep and usually icy entrance guaranteed to get one's adrenalin pumping; falling is not advised.

Snowboarding

All three Val Gardena ski schools offer private snowboarding tuition. Boards are available for hire through the ski school at **Ortisei**. The Canazei Marmolada Ski School also gives snowboarding lessons.

Ski schools and guiding

The Selva Ski School receives as usual excellent reports, and tuition appears to be of a high standard ('good teaching and no silly end-of-week races'). The only drawback in Selva and indeed in all the Sella Ronda resorts, is the instructors' often limited knowledge of English. Santa Cristina and Ortisei are the other two ski schools in the Val Gardena area, but we have no reports of them. The Canazei Marmolada Ski School offers group and private tuition.

Mountain restaurants

The Dolomites abound with mountain eateries, but the standard varies markedly between the Italian and German-speaking regions, with the better food found in the former. Pizzeria El Table in Arabba is strongly recommended. Plan Boé above the village is popular for traditional Austro-Italian fare. Trapper's Bar, on the Passo Campolungo between Corvara and Arabba, has a sun terrace and live music. Rifugio Crep de Mont, above Corvara, also has a terrace and a warm welcome. Try Mesules — its position on the edge of the road and the piste between Selva and Colfosco means it can be reached by skiers and non-skiers alike.

Rifugio Scotoni is a welcome wayside warming hut on the run down from Lagazuoi, if you can't make it to the even cosier Alpina 2km further on. You need some refreshment before the next lift — a horse-drawn tow. A more gastronomic lunch can be found at the Hotel Grand Angel on the edge of the Armentarola cross-country track. Baità del Gigio, on the nursery slopes above Malga Ciapela, is worth the long run down and is exceptionally good value.

Chez Anna on the run from Secada to Ortisei is said to be worth a visit for spectacular ham-and-eggs. Baità Frederola, near Belvedere, is recommended for its pizzas. Way off the beaten track is the Ospizio di Santa Croce, reached via a ski-bus from La Villa to **Pedraces** and two lifts up to the Abbey of the Holy Cross. Ristorante Lé, at the top of chair, is renowned for the best *Gulaschsuppe* in the Sud Tirol.

Off the mountain

Selva is an unassuming village, which sprawls in suburban style up the Val Gardena. Traffic is heavy, and weary skiers are more at risk crossing the road than they are on piste. For all that, the village maintains a quiet, unsophisticated charm, which makes it popular with families. Examples of the local wood-carving industry colourfully adorn houses and even lamp-posts.

Canazei is a large, attractive and lively village on a busy main road in the Italian-speaking Val di Fassa. It is the best place to stay for those in search of non-skiing activities and a good nightlife. The village itself is a tangle of narrow streets, with a mixture of old rural buildings, new hotels and some delightful shops. Such is the scramble for beds in the **Val di Fassa** that tour operators offer hotels in outlying villages as far away as **Pera**, **Pozza**, **Vigo di Fassa** and even **Moena**. These little Italian communities have their own tiny ski areas, which are fine for beginners and slalom specialists only — Olympic champion Alberto Tomba stays at the extremely comfortable Parc Corona in Vigo. If you don't meet Tomba, you will see at least his equally beefy dog, who winters at the hotel. However, the valley ski-bus is slow, irregular and over-subscribed. If you want to ski Canazei and the Sella Ronda from here you need a car.

Accommodation
In **Selva** Hotel Gran Baità is the pick of the four-stars, together with the Aaritz and the Alpinroyal. Hotel Laurin is a favourite amongst visitors and is renowned for its good food. Accommodation is based mainly around small hotels, most of which are very comfortable. We have good reports of the Hotel Solaia and, in particular, its buffet breakfast. The centrally situated Hotel Antares is also praised, as is the simple Stella. Inexpensive bed-and-breakfast hotels include the Eden, the Somont and the more comfortable Savoy, which also has a restaurant. Several British tour operators run chalets, which are generally of a high standard.

In **Canazei** the Croce Bianca is the best hotel in town, with hand-painted pine furniture in abundance. The Dolomiti is built in Grand Hotel style, while the newly upgraded four-star Astoria has the friendliest atmosphere. Hotel Bellevue is well-placed for the skiing, which is inconvenient from many of the village hotels.

Eating in and out
In Selva two of the best restaurants are the Salfeur Pizzeria and Pizzeria Rino. A wider selection of dishes can be found at Café Mozart and the restaurant of the Hotel Laurin. Other eating-places include Armin, Lo Sciattolo, La Freina, the restaurant in the Hotel Gran Baità, and La Plaza and Dosses in Santa Cristina. Canazei abounds with modestly priced restaurants. Try Al Vecchio Mulino for local Italian dishes. Rosticceria Melester also has a warm atmosphere.

Après-ski
At first sight Selva does not appear to have much of a nightlife. Half-a-dozen cafés serve homemade cakes and pastries, but the resort is quiet in the evening, with few lights, seemingly little activity and without the buzz of a serious party resort. In fact, behind the shutters there is a thriv-

ing après-ski scene and a good choice of nightspots, but light sleepers are unlikely to have their slumber disturbed.

The De Luisl is the most popular haunt after skiing ('only place with any real life between skiing and dinner, but check your change carefully'). The challenge of drinking a line of glasses of the local *grappa* is an activity fondly, if vaguely, remembered by one of our reporters. Bar La Stua has twice-weekly folk music evenings. Also recommended are the Hotel Laurin bar, La Frainela and the Monica and Mozart bars. The Dali and Stella Club discos throb through the night. The Savoy nightclub has live music and is said to be 'very expensive'. In nearby Santa Cristina, Yeti's Ombrella Bar is popular, and others include the Calés and I Tublà bars.

In Canazei The Montanara Bar is *the* place to meet after skiing, as is the Frogs Pub a few kilometres up the valley road in **Alba**. Nightlife centres largely around the numerous bars, the busy Gatto Negro disco in Canazei and Veruschka in Alba.

Childcare

Selva is an excellent area for children of all ages to learn to ski. The nursery slopes are based below the Dantercëpies gondola at the northern edge of the village. There is a kindergarten at the bottom of the Biancaneve drag-lift where toddlers and small children are taught the

> ■ **OTHER SPORTS**
>
> Selva: skating, curling, indoor shooting range, sleigh-rides, helicopter rides, parapente, indoor tennis and squash, swimming, tobogganing
> Canazei: parapente, tobogganing winter walks, swimming

rudiments of skiing among cartoon characters. Instructors are plentiful and patient, and there seemed to be none of the 'here is an entire generation to be put off skiing' attitude that you encounter in some French resorts. The surrounding area is ideal for older children to learn or improve their skiing.

Linked or nearby resorts

Arabba 1600m (5,248ft)

This small, unspoilt village is tucked away in a fold of the land and is surrounded by the most challenging skiing in the area. The village itself is hopeless for non-skiers, and facilities for babies and toddlers are non-existent. The language here is Italian, although Arabba is only a couple of kilometres south of the Sud-Tirol border. The Sport is the smartest hotel, but the Porto Vescovo is more lively and houses the Stübe Bar, which along with Peter's Bar just about sums up the nightlife. Ski Beach Villas, the only tour operator here, has a choice of four catered chalets. The Rue de Mans (very Italian despite its name) is an excellent restaurant just outside the village.

TOURIST OFFICE
Tel 39 437 940083

Fax 39 437 940073

Campitello 1440m (4,723ft)

A small collection of old buildings make up this quiet village set beside a stream, well back from the main road. The Col Rodella cable car (45-minute queues reported) goes up to the ski area and there is no piste back down again. The village is, however, ideal for complete beginners as some of the area's best nursery slopes are right on its doorstep. Hotels include the Fedora, next to the lift station, and the Medil, a modern hotel built in traditional alpine style with its own fitness centre and bar with music. Hotel Sella Ronda is an alpine-style hotel owned by a priest. It is comfortable, although a reporter recommends avoiding the upper rooms ('due to a massive beam, headroom at one end of the rooms is no more than a metre'). Hotel Rubino has a swimming-pool and piano bar among its many facilities.

TOURIST OFFICE
Tel 39 462 61137
Fax 39 462 62771

Colfosco 1650m (5,412ft)

Colfosco has easy access to both Selva and Corvara's skiing, although the village also has a small ski area of its own with good nursery slopes. Recommended hotels are the Kolfuschgerhof and the Centrale. Speckstube Peter, Stria, Matthiaskeller and Tabladel are the most popular eating places. Black Hill Nevada is a pub serving food, and the Capella is the smartest eating place.

TOURIST OFFICE
Tel 39 471 846176
Fax 39 471 847277

Corvara 1550m (5,084ft)

This pleasant Sella Ronda resort fails to attract any British tour operators, but it is strategically placed for some of the best skiing in the region. Hotel Posta-Zirm, the old post house at the bottom of the Col Alto chairlift, is the place to stay. The building dates from 1808 and has been carefully renovated; the hotel also keeps alive the tradition of the tea dance. The Pensione Ladina nearby is a less expensive alternative and is renowned for its home-made blueberry *grappa*. There is cross-country skiing and a skating rink in the village. The ski school has a kindergarten for children from three years of age, but English is not widely spoken.

TOURIST OFFICE
as Colfosco

Ortisei 1240m (4,067ft)

This is the major town of the Val Gardena, although not a good base for

Skiing facts: **Selva**

TOURIST OFFICE
Strada Meisules 213, I-39048 Selva
Gardena
Tel 39 471 795122
Fax 39 471 794245

THE RESORT
By road Calais 1226km
By rail bus service from Bressanone
(35km), Bolzano 40km, Chiusa 27km
By air Munich 4 hrs, Verona 3 hrs, Milan 4
hrs, Innsbruck 1½ hrs
Visitor beds 17,000 in Val Gardena area
Transport free ski-bus between Ortisei and
Val Gardena

THE SKIING
Linked or nearby resorts Arabba (I),
Armentarola (I), Campitello (I), Canazei (I),
Colfosco (I), Cortina d'Ampezzo (I), Corvara
(I), La Villa (I), Ortisei (I), Pedraces (I), San
Cassiano (I), Santa Cristina (I)
Longest run Seceda-Ortisei, 9km (red)
Number of lifts 464 in region
Total of trails/pistes 1100km in region
(30% easy, 62% intermediate, 8% difficult)
Nursery slopes 10 runs
Summer skiing none
Snowmaking 78km covered in Val
Gardena-Alpe di Suisi

LIFT PASSES
Area pass Superski Dolomiti (covers 450
lifts), L233,000-268,000 for 6 days
Day pass Superski Dolomiti L47,000-
54,000

Beginners points tickets
Pensioners 20% discount for 60 yrs and
over
Credit cards accepted yes

SKI SCHOOLS
Adults Val Gardena ski schools, L190,000-
200,000 for 6 days (4 hrs per day)
Private lessons Val Gardena ski schools,
L45,000-47,000 per hr
Snowboarding Val Gardena ski schools,
private lessons L45,000-47,000 per hr
Cross-country Val Gardena ski schools,
10am-4pm, L133,000-150,000 for 3 days.
Loipe 98km
Other courses freestyle, off-piste, race
training, slalom
Guiding companies guides available
through ski schools, L175,000-190,000 for
3 days

CHILDREN
Lift pass 6-14 yrs, Superski Dolomiti
L148,000-170,000 for 6 days, free for 5 yrs
and under
Ski kindergarten Mini Ski Club, 2½-4 yrs,
L190,000 for 5 days including lunch
Ski school Val Gardena ski schools, 5-12
yrs, L145,000-200,000 for 6 days
Non-ski kindergarten Val Gardena ski
schools, from 12 mths, L340,000-360,000
for 6 days (6 hrs per day)

FOOD AND DRINK PRICES
Coffee L2,500, glass of wine L2,000, small
beer L3,500, dish of the day L18,000

Skiing facts: **Canazei**

TOURIST OFFICE
APT Val di Fassa, Via Costa, I-38030 Alba di Canazei
Tel 39 462 602466
Fax 39 462 602502

THE RESORT
By road Calais 1240km
By rail Bolzano 40km and Chuisa 27km
By air Munich 4 hrs, Verona 3 hrs, Milan 4 hrs, Innsbruck 1½ hrs
Visitor beds 44,300 in Val di Fassa
Transport free ski-bus

THE SKIING
Linked or nearby resorts Arabba (I), Armentarola (I), Campitello (I), Colfosco (I), Cortina d'Ampezzo (I), Corvara (I), La Villa (I), Ortisei (I), Pedraces (I), San Cassiano (I), Santa Cristina (I), Selva (I)
Longest run Pista del Bosco, 6.5km (red)
Number of lifts 464 in region
Total of trails/pistes 1100km in region (30% easy, 62% intermediate, 8% difficult)
Nursery slopes 10 runs
Summer skiing none
Snowmaking 54km covered in Val di Fassa

LIFT PASSES
Area pass Superski Dolomiti (covers 450 lifts), L233,000-268,000 for 6 days
Day pass Superski Dolomiti L47,000-54,000
Beginners points tickets
Pensioners 20% discount for 60 yrs and over
Credit cards accepted yes

SKI SCHOOLS
Adults Canazei Marmolada, L145,000 for 5 days (3 hrs per day)
Private lessons Canazei Marmolada L40,000 per hr
Snowboarding as regular ski school
Cross-country Scuola Fondo Fassa-Canazei, times and prices on request. Loipe 25km
Other courses monoski, off-piste, competition
Guiding companies Guide Alpine Val di Fassa

CHILDREN
Lift pass 6-14 yrs, Superski Dolomiti, L148,000-170,000 for 6 days, free for 5 yrs and under
Ski kindergarten Canazei Ski School, 4 yrs and over, L58,000 per day, L270,000 for 6 days (2½ hrs per day)
Ski school as ski kindergarten
Non-ski kindergarten as ski kindergarten

FOOD AND DRINK PRICES
Coffee L2,000, glass of wine L2,000, small beer L3,500, dish of the day L18,000

skiers. The centre is bypassed by the main valley road, but the busy highway still has to be crossed on foot to reach the cable car. Staying in Ortisei, as in Selva, means a lot of walking. The Adler is the resort's four-star hotel, with the Posta an old establishment and the Snalterhof a simple and inexpensive hostelry. The nightlife is not as lively as Selva's, but there are some good bars such as Corso's, Purgler's and Siglu, and restaurants include the Adler, Concordia and Waldheim. The discos are Dancing Mauriz and the Cianél.

TOURIST OFFICE
Tel 39 471 796328
Fax 39 471 796749

San Cassiano 1537m (5,041ft)

A small, roadside village with mainly new Dolomite-style buildings, San Cassiano has some excellent skiing for beginners and early intermediates who want to avoid challenges. Long, easy runs go into the village from Pralongia and Piz Sorega. Reporters mention the lack of English in a resort that attracts mainly wealthy Italians. The down side of this is being the sole English speaker in a ski school class where lessons become 'laborious, with everything spoken in German and Italian'.

The Rosa Alpina is a large and comfortable hotel in the village centre and is also the focal point for après-ski with a live band. The Ski Bar is recommended for good, cheap pizzas and the Capanna Alpina, Saré, Sas Dlacia and Tirol are all busy restaurants. La Siriola, Rosa Alpina, Fanes and the restaurant in Hotel Diamant are the more expensive eating places. There is bowling at the Diamant, but otherwise the village tends to be on the quiet side. Armentarola, with its own hotels and restaurants, is a kilometre away.

TOURIST OFFICE
as Colfosco

La Thuile/La Rosière

ALTITUDE La Thuile 1441m (4,726ft), La Rosière 1850m (6,068ft)

This joint ski area spans the border between Italy and France, linking the resorts of La Thuile in the Aosta Valley with La Rosière in the Tarentaise. The road over the Petit-St-Bernard Pass, which separates the two, is closed in winter as Hannibal most probably discovered in 218BC when he lost half his army and his elephants here. Of all the alpine routes the Carthaginian general is thought to have taken on his journey from Spain to Rome, this is the most likely.

The skiing today takes place mainly on the exposed slopes above the pass at a top altitude of 2642m on the Italian side and 2400m on the French **Col de la Traversette**. The tenuously linked 135km ski area is equally divided, but certainly the best part of it belongs to Italy, with long intermediate runs, some steeper black (difficult) runs through the trees and a reputation for severely cold temperatures. La Rosière's skiing consists of open, sunny and mainly easy slopes on the south-facing side of Tarentaise, above Bourg-St-Maurice and opposite Les Arcs and L'Aiguille Rouge. There are also a few steeper runs through the woods below the resort. It is a quiet and friendly village, which is ideal for families and cheap by local standards.

La Thuile itself is less appealing than its skiing: a purpose-built resort centred around a giant hotel and conference centre, cavernous apartment blocks and a car-park near the site of what used to be an old mining village. The development has attracted considerable investment, which is certainly justified by the skiing on offer. It has the ski-in ski-out convenience and a lack of atmosphere that you would expect of a purpose-built resort of this nature.

On the mountain
top 2642m (8,666ft) bottom 1150m (3,772ft)

La Thuile's ski area consists of steep, tree-lined slopes above the resort, a wide and gentle east-facing mountain above the trees and steeper north-facing slopes from the top lifts towards the Petit-St-Bernard road. On both sides of the mountain the steeper slopes are surrounded by long intermediate runs, giving a good variety of pistes back to the resort. **La**

LA THUILE
■ GOOD POINTS

Compact village, large intermediate ski area, tree-level skiing, extensive nursery slopes, varied off-piste, skiing convenience, low prices

■ BAD POINTS

No childcare facilities, lack of alpine charm, limited for non-skiers, limited après-ski

---

348

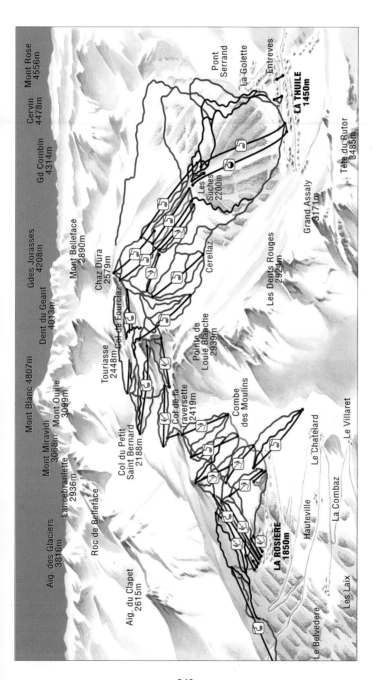

Rosière's area is a wide, mainly south-facing mountain criss-crossed by easy intermediate runs.

The main mountain access is by a fast jumbo gondola and a chair-lift, which climb steeply from the edge of La Thuile to **Les Suches** at 2200m (a cluster of buildings above the woods where the mountain flattens out). Three black runs drop back down through the woods; they are steep and in the shade. Red (intermediate) La Tour provides an easier way back to the resort. The views from the higher slopes are wonderful. On the easterly side of the ski area is a very long and little-skied run down to the resort, again through the woods.

LA ROSIERE
■ **GOOD POINTS**
Large intermediate ski area, ideal for beginners and families, low prices
■ **BAD POINTS**
Lack of tough runs, lack of skiing convenience, limited après-ski

The link to France is reached either via the San Bernardo chair from the top of the pass or from the Belvedere chair. A 50m walk from Belvedere takes you to the border and a long schuss into the Bellecombe Valley to the Chardonnet quad-chair; this climbs steeply over a cliff face to the Col de la Traversette, a gap in the rocky terrain crowning La Rosière's ski fields, complete with Napoleonic fortifications commanding the pass. The start of the red L'Ours run from the top of the San Bernardo also leads down into the **Bellecombe Valley**.

Return from La Rosière is only possible via the narrow red Bouquetin piste (less confident skiers can download via the Chardonnet chair), followed by the two Bellecombe drags back up to Belvedere.

Queues in both resorts are rare, except at weekends when linking lifts can become serious bottlenecks. There is artificial snow covering 10km of north-facing piste down to La Thuile via Les Suches. La Rosière has one mobile snow-cannon on the main slope above the village.

Beginners

La Thuile has a small area of nursery slopes near the main lift station and a more extensive area on the easy slopes above Les Suches. La Rosière has excellent nursery slopes directly above the resort and around the altiport, served by a number of easy lifts. Directly above La Rosière is a wide blue slope (served by a long chair and a drag-lift), which is good for beginners and popular with ski-school classes.

Intermediates

The vast no-man's land between France and Italy is excellent for intermediates. Above Les Suches an area of easy wide runs opens into an even wider bowl of intermediate skiing under the rocky peaks of Belvedere and Chaz Dura. Most of the runs under the Belvedere and Cerellaz chairs are wide and gentle, but slightly steeper on the slopes of Chaz Dura. The wide mogul field under the Chaz Dura chair is about the only run that is not constantly groomed.

Advanced

Experts will be pleasantly surprised by the challenge of some of the terrain here. Some of La Thuile's best skiing is on the rocky north-facing slopes above the Petit-St-Bernard Pass, served by the Fourclaz and the San Bernardo chair and accessible from both Chaz Dura and Belvedere.

The pistes on the pass side of La Rosière, immediately above the treeline and on down through the woods, are the best runs here, although experts will prefer the skiing at La Thuile.

Off-piste

In fresh snow the Italian side of the mountain offers good powder skiing (with a guide) from Chaz Doura. However, experts will be far more interested in the heli-skiing opportunities on the **Ruitor Glacier** and elsewhere in the Aosta Valley.

Snowboarding

Both La Thuile's ski school and the French Ski School (ESF) in La Rosière offer six-day beginners courses.

Ski schools and guiding

Reports of La Thuile ski school are all positive ('sympathetic instruction in reasonable English'). The ESF in La Rosière is said to offer 'excellent value, excellent instruction' and has greatly improved in recent years.

Mountain restaurants

■ WHAT'S NEW
La Rosière to open a planetarium

There are several eating-places on the Italian side, the largest being a characterless self-service at Les Suches serving home-made pasta and soups. Le Foyer, in the middle of the upper La Thuile bowl, has a terrace, a good restaurant and a large bar with an open fire. The Off Shore at the Belvedere chair ('best toasted sandwiches') and the Roxi Bar at the Fourclaz chair are recommended. The Altitude Bar is 'the best stopping place on the mountain'. The Plan Repos is the only mountain restaurant above La Rosière.

Off the mountain

La Thuile stands in a rather austere and enclosed setting 10km from Pré-St-Didier and a further 6km from Courmayeur and the Mont Blanc Tunnel. The ski resort is entirely purpose-built with a huge hotel, apartment buildings, a sports centre and a range of shops. Aside from the sports centre, non-skiers are not well catered for.

La Rosière is little more than a collection of traditional-style buildings lining the hairpin bends of the road up towards the Petit-St-Bernard Pass. It has, as one reporter describes it, 'a hint of a real village'. There are several old farming hamlets scattered around the sunny slopes nearby. In winter the road ends with a snow bank at the top of the village beside a pen containing a few sun-bathing St Bernards that pose professionally at the sight of a camera. Access to the skiing is from the roadside at the top of the village, where the first lift was installed in 1962 behind the Relais du Petit-St-Bernard.

Accommodation

La Thuile's accommodation is mainly in the Planibel Complex of modern apartments and the large and comfortable four-star Hotel Planibel, which houses two swimming-pools and is convenient for the shops. The apartments are built around a courtyard near the main gondola and are recommended as 'spacious, chalet-style studios'. The Chalet Alpina is set in woodland 500m from the resort with a bus-stop outside. Hotel Edelweiss is 'very basic, but OK'.

> ### ■ OTHER SPORTS
> **La Thuile**: parapente, indoor tennis and squash, swimming
> **La Rosière**: parapente, winter walks, dog-sledding, snow-shoeing, tobogganing

La Rosière's accommodation has developed over the years below the Relais du Petit-St-Bernard, but the expansion of the late 1960s and 1970s, which transformed the other Tarentaise resorts, largely passed by this little backwater. A number of reasonably sympathetic apartment blocks have sprung up in recent years, but most of the resort's visitors stay in private chalets hidden in the trees at Le Gollet below the main street.

A regular free bus-service connects **Le Gollet** and the outlying hamlet of **Les Eucherts** to the main ski area. The buses cease running soon after the lifts close, and après-ski excursions from Le Gollet involve strenuous hikes up one of the 'short-cuts' to the main road. A number of simple, convenient hotels provide accommodation nearer the ski area. These include the Plein Soleil and the original Relais, which also has a popular bar. The family-run Hotel Le Solaret is popular with reporters. Le Vanoise is also recommended for families, as the kindergarten is housed in the same building. The Terrasses apartments are 300m from the lifts and are warmly recommended.

Eating in and out

La Thuile has an acceptable choice of restaurants. Recommendations include Les Marmottes ('an excellent evening out') and La Bricole, a converted barn between the old and new parts of the resort. Lo Creton and La Grotta pizzerias are both cheap and cheerful. The raclette in the Planibel Complex is said to be 'very reasonable'. The restaurant in the Planibel hotel is said to be 'smart and expensive'. Others favoured by reporters are La Maison de Laurent and La Tufeja. The Gelateria by the gondola station is justly famous for its ice-cream and cakes.

In **La Rosière**, recommended restaurants include La Montagnette and L'Ancolie. La Montagne is a 'small, inexpensive crêperie'. The Terrasse du Yéti ('the greatest pizzas'), La Pitchounette and the Relais du Petit-St-Bernard are all praised. Le Christophi is known for its fondue and raclette. La Chaumière is an old restored Savoyard farmhouse, 7km away in the village of **Montvalezan**.

Skiing facts: **La Thuile**

TOURIST OFFICE
I-11016 La Thuile, Aosta
Tel 39 165 884179
Fax 39 165 885196

THE RESORT
By road Calais 938km
By rail Pré-Saint-Didier 10km
By air Geneva 2½ hrs, Turin 3 hrs
Visitor beds 3,123
Transport free bus service in the village

THE SKIING
Linked or nearby resorts Pila (n), La
Rosière (l), Courmayeur (n)
Longest run San Bernardo, 11km (red)
Number of lifts 15 in La Thuile, 33 in linked
area (with La Rosière)

Total of trails/pistes 85km (48% easy,
31% intermediate, 21% difficult), 140km in
linked area
Nursery slopes 3 lifts
Summer skiing none
Snowmaking 12km covered

LIFT PASSES
Area pass Aosta Valley (covers La Thuile,
La Rosière, Pila and Courmayeur) L240,000
for 6 days. La Thuile/La Rosière L175-

202,000 for 6 days
Day pass L43,000
Beginners 1 free baby lift
Pensioners no reductions
Credit cards accepted yes

SKI SCHOOLS
Adults La Thuile, 10am-12.30pm,
L147,000 for 6 days
Private lessons La Thuile, L47,000 per hr
Snowboarding through ski school, prices
and times as regular ski lessons
Cross-country through ski school. Loipe
16km
Other courses slalom, off-piste, racing,
heli-skiing on the Ruitor Glacier
Guiding companies through ski school

CHILDREN
Lift pass 50% reduction for 5-10 yrs, free
for 4 yrs and under
Ski kindergarten none
Ski school La Thuile, 5 yrs and over, 10am-
12.30pm, L1478,000 for 6 days
Non-ski kindergarten none

FOOD AND DRINK PRICES
Coffee L1,301,500, glass of wine
L1,500, small beer L3,500, dish of the day
L18,000

Several reporters comment on the good choice of food at reasonable
prices in the supermarket at La Rosière.

Après-ski

Après-ski entertainment is not La Thuile's strong point and there is little
to do apart from tour the bars. La Crèmerie, Bar Bricolette and La
Brasserie are all crowded when the lifts close. The action later moves to
Le Rendez-vous pub and later still to the Fantasia disco.

La Rosière's après-ski usually begins directly after the lifts close at the
Relais bar (also known as Toni's). On fine evenings the balcony is
packed with people enjoying the view, the *vin chaud* and the pizzas.
Arpin's bar in front of the tourist office and Le Dahu, which has a games

Skiing facts: **La Rosière**

TOURIST OFFICE
F-73700 La Rosière Montvalezan, Savoie
Tel 33 79 06 80 51
Fax 33 79 06 83 20

THE RESORT
By road Calais 940km
By rail Bourg-St-Maurice 23km
By air Chambery $1\frac{1}{2}$ hrs, Lyon 3 hrs, Geneva $2\frac{1}{2}$ hrs
Visitor beds 7,119
Transport free ski-bus runs every 15-30 mins, 8am-6pm

THE SKIING
Linked or nearby resorts Les Arcs (n), La Thuile (l)
Longest run Choucas, 4.1km (blue)
Number of lifts 18 in La Rosière, 33 in area
Total of trails/pistes 55km in La Rosière (15% beginner, 36% easy, 34% intermediate, 15% difficult), 140km in area
Nursery slopes 2 free lifts
Summer skiing none
Snowmaking 2 hectares covered

LIFT PASSES
Area pass Domaine International (covers La Rosière and La Thuile) 786FF for 6 days including 1 free day in Les Arcs. La Rosière only 642FF for 6 days
Day pass La Rosière 125FF, Domaine International 160FF
Beginners 2 free lifts

Pensioners 60 yrs and over: La Rosière 417FF, Domaine International 519FF, both for 6 days
Credit cards accepted yes

SKI SCHOOLS
Adults ESF, 9.15-11.45am and 1.30-5pm, 620FF for 6 days
Private lessons ESF, 142FF per hr, Nouvelles Traces, 150FF per hr
Snowboarding ESF, private lessons 142FF per hr (group lessons also available)
Cross-country 142FF per hr. Loipe 12km
Other courses monoski, telemark, off-piste, heli-skiing on Ruitor Glacier
Guiding companies ESF and Nouvelles Traces

CHILDREN
Lift pass 12 yrs and under, La Rosière 417FF for 6 days, Domaine International 519FF for 6 days
Ski kindergarten Le Village des Enfants, 1-10 yrs, 170FF per day (including ski lesson)
Ski school ESF, 4 yrs and over, times as adults, 590FF for 6 days
Non-ski kindergarten Le Village des Enfants, 1-10 yrs, 9am-5.30pm, 970FF for 6 days including lunch

FOOD AND DRINK PRICES
Coffee 7FF, glass of wine 10-12FF, small beer 12FF, dish of the day 60-70FF

room, are also both popular.

Childcare
La Thuile has no special childcare facilities, and the ski school does not accept children under five years old. In La Rosière, Le Village des Enfants has a good reputation and cares for children from 12 months old between 9am and 5.30pm.

Round-up

Champoluc
top 3370m (11,054ft) bottom 1570m (5,150ft)

Surrounded by the towering Monte Rosa range in a secluded wooded valley, Champoluc is an attractive, unspoilt village. The chalets and houses are made mostly of wood and stone with traditional slate roofs. The ski area connects with Gressoney-La-Trinité and there are un-limited off-piste excursions. The area boasts a number of good-value eating-places (there are 27 mountain restaurants in the Monte Rosa area), and the nightlife centres around a few bars, which usually empty out quite early.

Spectacular views dominate the skiing, which is primarily intermedi-ate, with beginner slopes at the top of the Crest gondola where there is a wide open bowl. Advanced skiers are the least catered for; there are only a few black (difficult) runs in Champoluc.

Accomplished skiers will want to concentrate on the moguls of Sarezza and some steep skiing off the back of the main ski area, as well as the long runs to Stafal. Off-piste skiers will find that this is an un-limited area to explore, with excursions to Alagna or Cervinia possible.

TOURIST OFFICE
Tel 39 125 307113
Fax 39 125 307785

Gressoney-La-Trinité
top 3370m (11,054ft) bottom 1640m (5,379ft)

Just 90 minutes from Turin, after a scenic drive through tiny medieval towns, is the attractive Gressoney Valley. Gressoney-La-Trinité remains unspoilt, with a collection of old wooden chalets and a few hotels. A pic-turesque church dominates the small town, and a network of cobbled streets and alleyways surround it. There are a number of good restau-rants and a few bars, but the nightlife is subdued. One bar offers karaoke but it is not usually busy, as one reporter commented: 'I found myself singing to an audience of one — my ex-boyfriend.'

In the shadow of the Monte Rosa the three connecting valleys were first settled by the 'Walsers' in the Middle Ages. The isolated geographi-cal position meant this area was cut off from other villages, and many locals still speak a dialect derived from the language of their ancestors.

The skiing takes place in three areas: **St Jean**, **La Trinité** and **Stafal**. It is extensive, mostly intermediate but with good beginner slopes and excellent off-piste for advanced skiers (particularly in the Alagna Valley). It is also possible to ski to Champoluc from the Colle Bettaforca. The lift system is antiquated, but improvements are underway, with several new lifts already operating and a number of additions and replacements planned over the next few years. In all there are 30 lifts servicing 70km of piste with some 12km of snowmaking. The Monte Rosa area has 45 lifts covering 150km of piste.

TOURIST OFFICE
Tel 39 125 355185
Fax 39 125 355895

Madesimo
top 2884m (9,459ft) bottom 1530m (5,018ft)

This small, attractive resort centred around an old church is a $2\frac{1}{2}$-hour drive north of Bergamo. Right on the Swiss border, it is close enough for a shopping spree in St Moritz. The old town has narrow streets and a few shops and some old converted farm houses, as well as some unattractive modern concrete buildings. Its appeal is that it is cheaper than other better-known resorts and is excellent value for money.

The skiing is mostly intermediate and concentrated on the slopes of the 2984m Piz Groppera, with long runs leading down into the neighbouring **Valle de Lei**. There are 23 lifts serving 43km of mostly red (intermediate) pistes, with some challenging blacks and good nursery slopes. The lower slopes have snow-cannon, and the ski school is reputed to be good, with small classes.

TOURIST OFFICE
Tel 39 342 53015
Fax 39 342 53782

Madonna di Campiglio
top 2579m (8,459ft) bottom 1520m (4,986ft)

Set in a wooded valley in the spectacular Brenta Dolomites, Madonna di Campiglio is a two-hour drive from Verona. The village has a good choice of hotels and more than 20 restaurants, varying from cheap pizzerias to attractive cafés, and several lively bars. Most of the clientèle is Italian, and the boutiques are upmarket. The village centre is based around a frozen lake, which is used for skating. The resort is close enough for day trips to Venice, Lake Garda, Verona and Innsbruck.

The skiing centres around **Madonna** and the neighbouring resorts of **Folgarida** and **Marilleva**. There is a total of 150km of pistes, 26 lifts and 13 mountain restaurants. Most of the runs are quite short, with the longest being 4km.

TOURIST OFFICE
Tel 39 465 42000
Fax 39 465 40404

Switzerland

Modern skiing began in Switzerland and while it may well be a complete exaggeration to suggest that British winter holidaymakers introduced the sport, they certainly helped to promote it in the Parsenn, the Bernese Oberland and the Engadine. In November 1883 the editor of a Davos newspaper wrote: 'As you probably know, skis are a kind of elongated snowshoe with which you can travel very quickly in deep snow, both up and down mountains. Why should these "skis" not replace the ungainly snowshoes, which are commonplace around here?'

Six years later a certain English lady Miss Katherine Symonds took to skis in the Parsenn, and in 1894 Sir Arthur Conan Doyle wrote passionately of a ski-tour to Arosa. It is, therefore, a great sadness that few of their countrymen today can afford to visit Switzerland. The combination of a prohibitive rate of exchange against sterling, the imposition of across-the-board 6.5 per cent VAT and rising prices because of domestic inflation have even forced affluent tourists to seek fresh pastures.

It is hoped that this situation is merely a bare patch on the piste of time, and that British skiers will once again return in numbers to what are some of the most colourful resorts and beautiful mountains in the world.

Ecological pressure to preserve the natural mountain environment has largely prevented the overdevelopment of Swiss ski villages. The 1960s–70s concept of the giant linked ski area was never fully realised here; even the Portes du Soleil only really brushes into Switzerland via the Illiez Valley. As a result, most resorts remain traditional villages, still largely unspoilt by the demands of mass tourism. The downside of this has been a lack of investment in uphill transport and lift systems, which still rely on ancient cog-railways, outdated cable cars, double chair-lifts and the ubiquitous T-bar.

In spite or because of this, the skiing remains delightfully unhomogenised, with natural rather than man-made runs against outstanding alpine backdrops. Mountain restaurants, for those who enjoy and can afford the relaxed ski lunch, are among the best in Europe, and the standard of hotels and apartments is consistently high. Almost all Swiss resorts can be reached by train from Geneva and Zurich airports.

Switzerland has two types of rail pass, which can be purchased in advance at advantageous rates from the Swiss Centre in London before leaving home. These vouchers allow either airport transfers to and from your resort or 'rover' facilities for the duration of your stay.

As expected in Switzerland, trains run to the strictest of timetables and you are strongly advised to send your luggage in advance whenever possible. The Swiss themselves rarely travel with more than hand luggage. Trolleys are consequently scarce, with little provision for suitcases on trains.

Crans Montana

ALTITUDE 1500m (4,920ft)

Crans Montana is a classic Swiss resort, which has evolved from its early days as a health spa into an interlinked skiing complex above the three agglomerations of **Crans**, **Montana** and **Aminona**; the official umbrella name for the resort is Crans Montana.

Two hours from Geneva airport, by motorway for the most part, Crans Montana sits on what is claimed to be the sunniest plateau in the Alps, dotted with larches and lakes. The views of the Matterhorn, Mont Blanc and the Rhône Valley were described by Sir Arnold Lunn as among the finest in Europe. A funicular, built in 1911, runs to Montana from Sierre.

Crans Montana is a destination that cultivates an elite clientèle (mostly middle-aged), half of whom are Swiss, with the French, Germans and Italians each accounting for about ten per cent. Its shopping, in chic boutiques, is advertised as the finest in the Alps. An official publication describes Crans Montana as a 'fancy resort'. The skiing is irretrievably intermediate.

Although the first hotel was built in 1893, a ski lift did not appear until 1936. The new 30-person Funitel cable car system, the second in Switzerland, is expected to triple the capacity of the queue-prone cable car, which used to run up to the glacier on **Plaine-Morte** at 3000m from Violettes. Most visitors are content with making a few casual runs in the sunshine each day on the 160km of groomed piste served by 40 lifts; two are modern high-speed quad-chairs, although more than half are antiquated drag-lifts.

Aminona, little more than two tower blocks and a few chalets, is more an appendage than a satellite. It has its own shops and the only lift queue in the Alps that passes right across the floorspace of a restaurant.

Many reporters complain about heavy traffic and plain architecture: 'Both resorts are choked with traffic and exhaust fumes and have little atmosphere. They are tolerable when the sun is out, but very unattractive on overcast days.' It is sometimes hard to remember that Crans and Montana which started life separately and grew together over 20 years ago owe their existence to the once pure mountain air so beneficial to convalescents from tuberculosis.

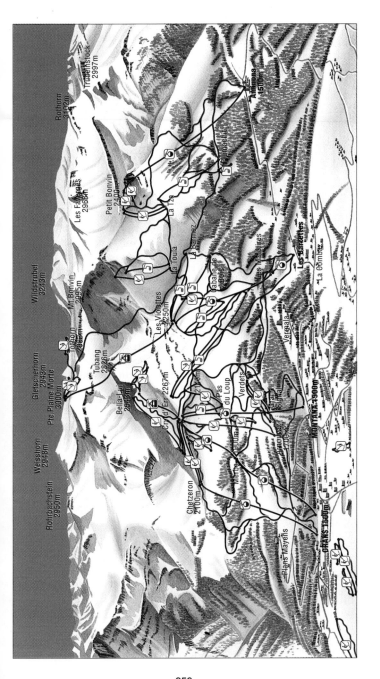

On the mountain
top 3000m (9,840ft) bottom 1500m (4,920ft)

Crans Montana is an intermediate's resort with good beginner-terrain. All the pistes are easier than the rating suggests. The off-piste skiing is limited, and powder potential seriously hampered by south-facing exposure and sunshine; snowmaking is scant. Mountain access is via five points spread from west to east across the base of the mountains from Crans to Montana to Aminona.

Queuing is not a serious problem here. The red (intermediate) run from Cry d'Err towards Pas du Loup is, according to reporters 'the only area that could occasionally be described as congested'. However, another mentions queues of up to half-an-hour for the Plaine-Morte Glacier.

A single gondola from Montana and the Chetseron and Cry d'Err gondolas at Crans lead up through the woods to **Cry d'Err**, where a cable car and chair-lift continue to the 2600m summit of the sector. Between Montana and Aminona, the glacier skiing at 3000m on Plaine-Morte is reached by a new Funitel gondola system continuing upwards from the Violettes gondolas, which start from the outskirts of Montana at Barzettes. The resort's longest run is the 1500-vertical-metre drop from the glacier to town-level at Barzettes. From Crans Montana a bus takes skiers to Aminona, where a gondola rises to **Petit Bonvin** at 2400m. All sectors, except the glacier, are mutually accessible, but not without traversing multiple lifts.

Piste-marking is described by reporters as being 'not too brilliant; it was not easy to relate the sign posts to the piste map' and 'pistes are not numbered or named, and signposts refer to lifts, not runs, which can be confusing'.

■ WHAT'S NEW

TGV snow train from Paris cuts train travel time to Crans Montana to 7 hrs (Saturdays only)

Cable car to Plaine-Morte replaced by 30-person Funitel

Reduced lift pass prices planned, with supplement for the Funitel

Hotel Royal renovated

Aquamust Spa constructed at Crans

Beginners

Starting at the top, beginners have three short but easy runs on the Plaine-Morte Glacier, where good snow is guaranteed. The nursery slopes down by the golf course in Crans are even easier but susceptible to sun. Cry d'Err has the most beginner runs, a handful accessible by no fewer than eight lifts, providing skiing all the way down into Crans or Montana. However, it is impossible to ski back to Aminona entirely on blue (easy) runs.

Intermediates

World Cup pistes like the Nationale are all classified as intermediate. However, despite the generally superior standard of piste-grooming everywhere, passages between rock walls, such as on the 7.5km-long red run from Plaine-Morte, add a genuine thrill. The largest conflux of intermediate pistes is in the Violettes sector, with winding trails through the woods. The Toula chair- and drag-lifts lead to steeper reds. Most exciting are the Nationale and Chetseron, well groomed but with the odd banked drop-off designed to make the stomach flip at high speed. One reporter describes the Nationale as 'an excellent run with some testing sections — a proper red run'.

The Plaine-Morte run is said to be the most avalanche-prone in Switzerland. Although perfectly safe when officially open, its gunbarrel passages and changes in direction require a high level of commitment from even the most adept skier.

Advanced

The only officially graded black (difficult) run in the entire resort is a bumpy fall-line pitch on the ridge under the Toula chair-lift ('no more than a red really'), which is often groomed impeccably on the lower section. Two short sections in the middle of red pistes are also marked black; one is the women's downhill racecourse on Chetseron, the other is an innocuous link between the Violettes mid-station and the long red coming down from the glacier.

Off-piste

Crans Montana has no death-defying couloirs, but there are three unmarked itineraries, which require guides. From the Plaine-Morte Glacier it is possible to ski across open slopes and through three bands of rock down to the lake at Zeuzier. Walking through tunnels (torches required) and skiing a summer roadway leads to the ski lifts in the neighbouring resort of **Anzère**. Another route from the glacier guarantees fresh tracks in powder straight down into the Vallon d'Ertenze. The only way out at the bottom is by helicopter.

Each weekend around 200 skiers attack the Faverges itinerary from Plaine-Morte down to Aminona, a route which is deserted on weekdays. This is steep, scenic skiing with lots of alternative routes, some through the rocks. In fresh snow, the avalanche danger is considerable, and in spring-snow a fall over the rocks can be fatal. The only way back to the pistes is via a narrow traverse above a river. Inside resort boundaries La Tza sector and wooded terrain under the Aminona and Violettes lifts are ideal for short, ungroomed off-piste skiing.

Snowboarding

Crans Montana is an active snowboarding centre, with parks in Aminona and **Merignou** and a half-pipe at Cry d'Err. Aminona is equipped for snowboarding jumps. Surf Evasion, affiliated with the Montana Ski School, offers group snowboard lessons during holiday periods, private lessons at other times and heli-snowboarding. The Swiss Snowboard School in Crans, part of the Swiss Ski School (ESS), is another learning centre. The Pacific Surf Shop and the Avalanche Pro Shop sell 'surf' fashions and accessories. The local snowboard club, Vague Blanche, has frequent events.

Ski schools and guiding

There are two branches of the ESS, one in Crans and the other in Montana, each of them separately operated. In keeping with the resort's tame skiing, instructors appear in no hurry to prod progress. There is a separate mountain guiding bureau in the Hotel Intergolf, which offers heli-skiing and ski-tours, such as the long run down to **Lenk**.

Mountain restaurants

The Crans Montana clientèle apparently prefers to do its eating in town. The best cuisine on the slopes is down at the Chamois d'Or, set in the woods of the Hauts de Crans hotel. Lift-station eateries at Cry d'Err, Petit Bonvin and Plaine-Morte are adequate but not inspiring. The Cabane des Violettes is an authentic Alpine Club touring hut with simple meals. The recently opened Café de la Cure, alongside the blue run down to Aminona, has character, but the two best inns are Merbe for its *tortellini* and Plumachit for its wild strawberry tart; both are old chalets' with sunny terraces. However, Plumachit is criticised for its service, which is 'generally off-hand and sometimes rude'.

Off the mountain

The resort now boasts 40,000 beds and 55 hotels, with no pretensions to charm, spread out across the three communities. The tower-block Résidence Vermala, sticking out like a sore thumb on a hill above Montana, is arguably the ugliest eyesore in the Alps.

Sprawled as it is, the resort has ample underground parking in town and possibly the best parking facilities at lift bases anywhere in the Alps — all free. Aminona is a ten-minute bus ride from Montana. The main lift complexes are a five-minute walk uphill from their respective town centres.

Gucci, Hermès, Valentino and Vuitton are only some of the designer boutiques in Crans Montana. Alex Sport, with an underground passage connecting its various shops, is the most comprehensive and expensive, but Bouby, Zermatten and Rinaldo Sports also carry chic skiwear. In addition to half-a-dozen cellulite centres and four major medical complexes, the resort has a resident astrologer, Aladin, four foot-reflexologists and three funeral homes.

Accommodation

Hotels in Montana are cheaper than in snooty Crans, where in the early years regulations denied entry to any guest suspected of having tuberculosis, which was the resort's *raison d'être* in the first place. Hotel service is excellent, thanks to apprentice staff from the local hotel school. The five-star Crans-Ambassador and four-star Hauts de Crans forest compound are in Montana.

The Grand Hotel du Golf is the ultimate in Crans, but the three-star Mont Blanc, on a hill above the resort, has the biggest terrace and best views. The rustic Dent Blanche has handpainted wooden beds. The Hostellerie du Pas de l'Ours is a two-season-old luxury hotel, and the five-star Royal has been completely refurbished. Reporters have mixed views of their reception at the family-run Hotel National: 'Madame was not particularly friendly, although several regulars were obviously on very friendly terms with the proprietor and his wife. The dining-room is spoilt by cheap cafeteria-style chairs and the meals were disappointing. The bedrooms, however, are larger than average'.

Self-catered apartments are readily available. One reader comments that his apartment in a block across the road from, and managed by, the Hotel de La Forêt 'looked as if it had been furnished from car-boot sales, with an odd assortment of furniture and cheap crockery'.

Eating in and out

The most celebrated non-hotel gourmet dining is at the Cervin ('rustic ambience, *langoustine cannelloni*), the Rôtiserrie de la Reine ('French chic, *bouillabaisse*') and the Jeanne d'Arc ('wood-and-stone decor, delicious *foie gras*'). The Mont Blanc in the woods above Crans has a marmot zoo for children and serves delicious sea bass. The Crans Ambassador, Pas de l'Ours and St George have varied haute cuisine menus. Dun Huang is Cantonese Chinese, the Diligence serves Lebanese food and wine in a chalet atmosphere, and the Christina has Portuguese specialities such as poached turbot with saffron. Steaks from America and Argentina are grilled at Le Ranch, accompanied by Californian wines. Valaisan-style raclette and fondue are found at the Bergerie du Cervin and Le Chalet. Pizza and pasta are taken seriously at Il Padrino and La Casa della Pizza. For real Italian coffee and *panettone*, try La Casa del Caffe.

Montana has all three of the Swiss discount supermarket chains (Migros, Denner and Coop), and Crans has a Coop. La Source in Montana is said to be one of the cheapest places to shop. Au Petit Chalet in Montana sells 'an amazing variety of cheeses and home-made chocolates, and a breathtaking array of cakes and pastries'.

Après-ski

Floor shows and dancing girls liven up late-night Montana at the Mazot and Noctambule cabarets. Immediately after skiing the younger crowd gathers at Amadeus, which also has weekly theme parties. Le Pub in Crans has darts, video games and pool. A similar clientèle enjoys Studio 7. Teenagers flock to the Number One Club, then on to the Number Two Bar for late drinking. The Absolut disco attracts the under 35s. The Pascha Club, also in Crans, is more for 'show-offs and snobs'. The Memphis in Crans is a comfortable piano bar for the older set, who are also found in the Miedzor, Aida Castel and Crans Ambassador hotels.

Skiing facts: **Crans Montana**

TOURIST OFFICE
CH-3963 Crans, CH-3962 Montana, Valais
Tel Crans: 41 27 413041
Montana: 41 27 412132
Fax Crans: 41 27 411794
Montana: 41 27 417460

THE RESORT
By road Calais 1012km
By rail Sierre 18km
By air Geneva 2 hrs
Visitor beds 40,000
Transport free ski-bus throughout resort

THE SKIING
Linked or nearby resorts Aminona (l),
Anzère (n), Bluche (n)
Longest run Plaine-Morte, 7.5km (red)
Number of lifts 40
Total of trails/pistes 160km (40% easy,
50% intermediate, 10% difficult)
Nursery slopes 5 lifts
Summer skiing July-Aug, 3 lifts on Plaine-
Morte Glacier
Snowmaking 6km covered

LIFT PASSES
Area pass SF215 for 6 days
Day pass SF47
Beginners 1 free lift in Bluches, 2km away
Pensioners women 62 yrs and over and
men 65 yrs and over, as children
Credit cards accepted yes

SKI SCHOOLS
Adults Montana ESS, SF155 for 5 days
($3\frac{1}{2}$ hrs per day). Crans ESS, SF188 for 7
half-days
Private lessons SF50 per hr
Snowboarding ESS in Montana, SF210 for
5 days (12 hrs). ESS in Crans, SF170 for 5
days (10 hrs)
Cross-country Montana ESS, SF155 for 5
days ($3\frac{1}{2}$ hrs per day), private lessons SF50
per hr. Crans ESS, private lessons only,
SF50-70 per hr. Loipe 55km
Other courses telemark, monoski
Guiding companies Bureau des Guides

CHILDREN
Lift pass 6-15 yrs, SF129 for 6 days, free
for 5 yrs and under
Ski kindergarten ESS Jardin des Neiges,
3-6 yrs, 9am-4.45pm, SF300 for 5 days
including lunch
Ski school ESS, as ski kindergarten
Non-ski kindergarten Bibiland, 2 yrs and
over, 9am-midday and 2-6.30pm, SF165
for 5 days not including lunch. Fleurs
des Champs, 2 mths and over, 8am-6pm,
SF215 for 5 days including lunch. Les
Coccinelles, 2 yrs and over, 8am-6pm,
SF230 for 5 days not including lunch

FOOD AND DRINK PRICES
Coffee SF2.70, glass of wine SF2.70, small
beer SF2.70, dish of the day SF18-20

Childcare
Infants from two months old can attend Les Fleurs des Champs kindergarten, next to the hotel Eldorado in Montana. Bibiland, underneath the
tourist office in Crans, takes children from two years old. Les
Coccinelles is situated by the Y'Coor playground next to Lake Grenon.
The Montana Ski School has its own Jardin des Neiges up on the Grand
Signal mid-station. The Crans Ski School also accepts children at its
kindergarten, which is by the golf course. There are also lessons for
advanced child skiers.

Davos/Klosters

ALTITUDE Davos 1560m (5,117ft), Klosters 1130m (3,706ft)

Since January 1971 Davos has each year played host to the World Economic Forum. It was here in 1987 that the German foreign minister, Hans-Dietrich Genscher, persuaded the West to change its views of the Soviet Union and the thaw of the Cold War began. Fortunately, nothing else has been allowed to melt in Davos; the mighty **Parsenn** above Davos and Klosters comprises one of the great ski areas of the world. Its vast and varied terrain of steep snowfields and gentle, long cruising slopes leading down to magnificent runs through the trees and on into sunny pastures will never pall with skiers. Wherever you end up there is always a characterful wooden hut serving wholesome Swiss dishes, plus a station linked into the region's efficient railway network to take you home, or back to a lift point for yet more skiing.

DAVOS
■ GOOD POINTS

Large intermediate ski area, extensive off-piste skiing, variety of restaurants in town, tree-level skiing, many cross-country trails, range of facilities for non-skiers

■ BAD POINTS

Heavy traffic, limited for beginners, sprawling and busy town, short of alpine charm, quiet après-ski, lack of skiing convenience

The history of alpine skiing is irrevocably linked with the Parsenn, and if modern skiing has one birthplace, then this is it. The Parsennbahn railway opened its first stage in 1931 and the Parsenn Derby race has been held here since 1924. The drag-lift was developed here in 1934 (although Alpe d'Huez claimed invention of it just a few weeks earlier). However, apart from sharing the great Parsenn ski area, the large and busy town of Davos and its quieter and undeniably more attractive neighbour Klosters (13km away) do not have much in common.

The first winter visitor came to Klosters in 1904, but the resort has never felt the need to attract the mass-market. Prince Charles' patronage put the village firmly on the map of the Alps; his narrow escape and the death of one of his party in an avalanche in March 1988 made Klosters world famous and publicised the resort in a way no amount of advertising could have equalled.

Since then, the Gotschna cable car has had its first stage rebuilt to reduce the once notorious morning queues, but that apart, the people of Klosters shrugged off the mantle of fame and closed ranks to protect their VIP visitor. The cable car is the only way up into the Parsenn, but the second stage has a much lower capacity than the first; the result is that skiers race each other at the mid-station to avoid missing the cut.

Klosters is divided into two quite separate villages: **Klosters Dorf** and

Klosters Platz. Dorf is a cluster of old farm buildings below the Madrisa ski area. Platz is where the large hotels, most of the shops and restaurants, and the Gotschna cable car up to the Parsenn are situated. Down the railway line, **Davos Dorf** is the centre for hotels and restaurants, while **Davos Platz** is the heart of the resort. The Parsenn is by no means the only ski area here, and a car is helpful for making the most of the region.

Frequent but crowded buses link Davos Dorf and Platz from morning until night, with less frequent services running elsewhere. In Klosters regular buses run between the Gotschna and Madrisa lifts. There are hourly buses from Serneus and regular trains linking all the ski areas except Pischa. With one or two exceptions, all these services are covered by the lift pass.

■ KLOSTERS GOOD POINTS

Large ski area, extensive off-piste skiing, wide range of mountain restaurants, alpine charm, variety of tough runs, tree-level skiing

■ KLOSTERS BAD POINTS

Staid après-ski, lack of skiing convenience, limited for beginners, through-traffic, limited resort-level snow

Reporters are unanimous in their praise of the resort transport: 'The bus service was as reliable as the trains, and the routes in Davos are clearly displayed with timetables at every stop'.

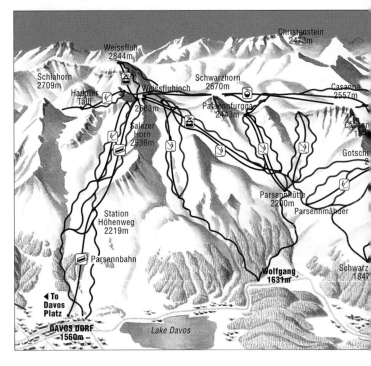

On the mountain
top 2844m (9,328ft) bottom 813m (2,667ft)

Apart from the main Parsenn, the skiing is divided into four separate areas. The **Madrisa**, reached by gondola from Klosters Dorf, provides uncrowded and mainly easy skiing. Similarly **Pischa**, a bus-ride from Davos Dorf, is always uncrowded and has good beginner slopes. **Jakobshorn**, the snowboarders' choice, is accessed by cable car close to Davos Platz station and has some good mogul fields. **Rinerhorn**, reached by gondola from the village of Glaris south of Davos Platz, is a mainly intermediate area with a few long runs. However, the heart of the pistes is the **Parsenn/Weissfluh** above Davos Dorf; this links into the **Strela** area above Davos Platz and the **Gotschna** area above Klosters Platz. Most of the lifts are on the Davos side of the mountain, but Klosters has the north-facing slopes and the best runs. Reporters criticise the area as having 'far too many long T-bars'.

Mountain access from Davos Platz is via the Schatzalpbahn funicular railway. As one reporter put it: 'The lift is a joke; a rackety railway followed by a two-person gondola with doors that have to be locked and unlocked by attendants.' It climbs steeply through the woods to the plateau of Schatzalp at 1861m.

Weekend and high-season lift queues remain a problem throughout

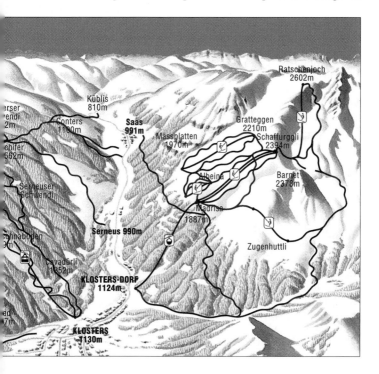

the area. The rebuilding of the Klosters cable car a few years ago has done much to relieve the situation, with reporters during the February half-term week noting that they never waited for more than ten minutes. However, we still have reports of long delays at peak times for the Parsenn railway from Davos Dorf, as well as for the Schatzalpbahn from Davos Platz. Reporters recommend escaping to Pischa at weekends when the main circus becomes clogged in high season. Poor piste-grooming is a complaint of the area, along with inadequate signposting. However, reporters praise the new 'hands-free ski pass'; a credit card is supplied to put in one's wallet and is automatically read by an electronic eye as you pass though the barrier.

Beginners
Neither resort particularly lends itself to beginners. The nursery slopes beside Davos Platz at the bottom of the Jakobshorn are adequate, and Klosters has a good nursery area above the tree-line on the Madrisa at Saaseralp, as well as a few small lifts beside Klosters Dorf. The sunny, south-west-facing Madrisa area is reached via a gondola from Klosters Dorf, but beginners must take the lift down at the end of the day.

Intermediates
Intermediates can explore the extensive, wide, mostly easy motorway-pistes behind the Weissfluhjoch, which is also accessed by the much-enlarged cable car from Parsennhütte and the Klosters side of the mountain. Wolfgang can be reached by a long blue/red run from Parsennhütte, which is easy unless conditions are icy.

You can also embark on tremendously long runs of over 10km to the villages of **Serneus**, **Saas** and **Kublis**. Unless you start from the top of the Weissfluhgipfel, which is reached by another cable car from Weissfluhjoch, none of these is particularly difficult and all are immensely enjoyable. The easiest is a straightforward red run via Cavadürli to Klosters; the trickiest is a slightly more taxing red to Serneus.

There are runs of varying difficulty back down again towards Klosters. Alternatively, a fast and fun red run from the bottom of the Schwarzseealp chair takes you down through the woods past the opulent private chalets to the edge of Klosters itself. At Jakobshorn gentle skiing can be found in the sunny, west-facing bowl above Clavadeler Alp.

Advanced
From the Weissfluhjoch down to Davos Dorf (parallel to the railway line) the runs are gentle to begin with, but below the Höhenweg station the black Standard Ersatz and alternative black Unterer Standard can be extremely icy. Good skiers will enjoy the long run down to the hamlet of **Wolfgang** from the bottom of the Meierhofer Tälli drag-lift. It is steep in places, but well worth the effort for lunch in the village.

Drostobel is a long, steep and seriously challenging black run. The huge moguls on the black run beneath the Schwarzseealp chair provide an interesting challenge for bump-bashers.

Off-piste

The notorious Wang (or to give it is full name, the Gotschnawang) is the direct run down to the Gotschnaboden mid-station. The Wang run is a piste, but is marked on the local piste map by a broken black line. Together with the Swiss Wall above Avoriaz it has the reputation of being awesomely tough, a reputation enhanced by the fatal royal avalanche, which did not in fact happen here at all, but on an adjacent off-piste slope. The reality is that while it is steep in places, it is by no means intimidating and can be wonderfully enjoyable in the right conditions. Because of the danger of avalanches it is not always open. There are, in fact, a variety of routes down the face and you pick the gradient to suit yourself.

> ■ **WHAT'S NEW**
>
> **Davos**: chair-lift replaces gondola on Schatzalp-Strela
> Chair-lift replaces Carjöler lift on Bolgen
> Top Card hands-free ticket system
> **Klosters**: Top Card (as above)

In between the various marked runs and in the woods from the Parsenn down to the hamlets of Küblis, Saas and Serneus is some good and not too difficult off-piste. With a guide you can make a day tour from the Madrisa over to Gargellen in Austria. The return route is via the Gargellen lifts, which are covered by the lift pass, plus a one-hour climb on skins. The best part of the tour is the off-piste run, which follows down to the pretty village of **St Antönien** before taking a bus back to Küblis. Arosa is also easily reached on skis with a guide.

Jakobshorn has great off-piste possibilities, with a highly recommended north-facing descent of nearly 900 vertical metres to Teufl in the Dischmatal, which has an isolated restaurant at the bottom from where you catch the bus back to Davos. Off-piste opportunities are also good behind the Pischahorn and along the shoulder down to the Klosters road at **Laret**.

At Rinerhorn a stiff 20-minute climb gives access to the steep, north-facing side of the Sertigtal, from where it is possible to ski down to the train station at **Frauenkirch**. In good powder conditions the long run down to Glaris, reached from the Nüllisch Grat drag-lift, is entertaining.

Snowboarding

Reporters say that 'snowboarders are everywhere in Davos', particularly on the Jakobshorn. In March 1995 the Jakobshorn hosted the World Snowboarding Championships; consequently, recommended runs for riders are now indicated on the piste maps by a snowboard symbol. The Swiss Ski School (SSS) at Davos organises snowboarding lessons, which are warmly endorsed ('the instructors were very good and spoke fluent English'). There are also two specialist snowboarding schools: the Top Secret and PaarSenn. All offer group or private lessons for both adults and children: 'Two of our children took a snowboarding course with the SSS and learnt a great deal. The instructors were friendly and spoke excellent English.'

Ski schools and guiding

Few of our reporters join group lessons in these upmarket resorts, preferring to take private instruction. The SSS in both Davos and Klosters has the soundest of reputations, and the instructors' standard of English is said to be extremely high. The Saas Ski and Snowboard School in Klosters is run by Prince Charles' ski guide, Bruno Sprecher, and receives highly complimentary reports. The ski schools organise off-piste tours from February onwards. Correspondents who have toured to Arosa and across the Austrian border to Gargellen and back are unanimous in their praise of the guiding and instruction.

Mountain restaurants

The area is dotted with mountain restaurants and delightful little 'Schwendi houses' off the beaten track in the woods down to Klosters and the other smaller villages of the Parsenn. The Conterser Schwendi in particular is recommended for its 'quite outstanding *Bauernrösti*' as is the Serneus Schwendi, which has recently been revamped. The Rinerhorn and the Pischa self-services are also recommended, as is the Alpina at Klosters. The restaurant in the Hotel Kulm at Wolfgang (known as Jakob's) makes the long run down all the more worthwhile. The higher restaurants generally lack character ('the dreadful smell of frying at Parsennhütte and Weissfluhjoch kept us well away').

Off the mountain

Davos is a long, strung-out town of modern Swiss architecture, which lacks alpine charm but is by no means displeasing. Reporters strongly recommend that you either stay near the bus route or hire a car, 'otherwise you will spend a lot of time with your skis wearing a groove in your shoulder', says a reporter. The town is a major health, spa and conference centre, and consequently boasts some of the finest four- and five-star hotels in the Alps with all the amenities to complement it. A reporter notes that 'Weber's Hardware shop is huge and just drips with quality kit for every conceivable task. As Davos attracts the rich, not surprisingly the shopping is wall-to-wall Gucci.' Another says of the resort's excellent medical services: 'If you must have a skiing accident, have it in Davos!'.

> ■ **OTHER SPORTS**
>
> **Davos:** parapente, hang-gliding, skating, curling, indoor tennis and squash, Bavarian curling, winter walks, sleigh rides, climbing wall, tobogganing, swimming
> **Klosters:** parapente, hang-gliding, skating, curling, sleigh rides, tobogganing, swimming

The town's traffic is heavy but it flows well, and away from the main road there are ample pedestrian short-cuts and sedate walks by the river. Non-skiers will find plenty of marked walks as well as Switzerland's largest natural skating rink and a good swimming-pool. Cross-country skiing is also a popular pastime, with 75km of prepared trails in the immediate vicinity.

Klosters Platz remains a charming Swiss village centred around its railway station; it is a cluster of established hotels along with more modern interlopers and a number of smart boutiques and expensive sports shops to cater for the needs of its well-heeled guests. A fine wine and Havana cigar shop just across the street from one of the leading hotels is a telling indication of what Klosters' clients consider essentials. **Klosters Dorf** is a separate sleepy village away from the hub of the resort.

Accommodation

The **Davos** accommodation is mainly in hotels throughout Platz and Dorf, which range from exotic five-stars to the simplest of bed-and-breakfasts. Because Platz has more bars and non-ski facilities than Dorf, it is the most convenient part of town in which to stay, as well as being an easy walk to the lifts for Strela and the Jakobshorn.

The resort's top hotels are the five-star Steigenberger Belvédère in Platz, which has a country-house atmosphere and carved ceilings but is said to have lost some of its style, and the Flüela in Dorf, which is conveniently situated near the Parsennbahn and according to reporters is 'a lovely hotel which merits its five-star rating'. The Alte Post is cheerful and reasonably priced. We have good reports of the budget-priced Hotel Lohner in Platz. The four-star Meierhof in Dorf is recommended. The simple Edelweiss bed-and-breakfast in Dorf is 'clean and comfortable'. The Bünda Hotel in Dorf is a ten-minute walk from the Parsenn station, but the Bunda beginner lift is 'outside your front door, which might be attractive to families and first-timers'.

Many visitors to **Klosters** stay in private chalets in the two villages or in the woods outside, but some of its hotels are as smart and as expensive as their Davos counterparts. Hotel Vereina is one of the oldest hotels in the Alps, with huge public rooms, some recently modernised bedrooms, an in-house crèche and baby-listening service, and a large swimming-pool. However, reporters found the hotel 'disappointing. I would categorise it as a three-star not a four-star; some of its rooms are very tacky', said one reporter. The Alpina is built in a modern chalet-style and is said to be 'very welcoming'. We have mixed reports of the Kaiser: 'friendly staff, food adequate to good and an excellent location next to the cable car', but 'the service was impersonal and there was no room at the hotel car-park for our car'.

The Wynegg, owned by the redoubtable Ruth Guler, is run like a large chalet for its mainly British clients. It has two restaurants: a chalet dining room for residents only, and another, which is open to everyone, including Prince Charles, who is an annual visitor.

Eating in and out

Davos has an enormous choice of restaurants. The Davoserhof, Rössli, Waldhuus and the Flüela-Stübli are all highly recommended. The Bundnerstübli offers regional specialities at affordable prices. A number of reporters found it cheaper and more interesting to eat outside Davos

Skiing facts: **Davos**

TOURIST OFFICE
Promenade 67, CH-7270 Davos Platz
Tel 41 81 4152121
Fax 41 81 4152100

THE RESORT
By road Calais 1000km
By rail Davos Dorf and Davos Platz stations in resort
By air Zurich 2½ hrs
Visitor beds 23,406
Transport free ski-bus with lift pass, free ski-train with Rega Pass

THE SKIING
Linked or nearby resorts Arosa (n), Klosters (l), Wolfgang (l), St Moritz (n), Gargellen (n), Glaris (l)
Longest run Weissfluhgipfel-Küblis, 12km (black/red)
Number of lifts 26 in Davos, 55 in area
Total of trails/pistes 315km in area (30% easy, 40% intermediate, 30% difficult)
Nursery slopes 1 lift on Bünda
Summer skiing none
Snowmaking limited

LIFT PASSES
Area pass Rega Pass (covers all Davos and Klosters lifts, buses and railway), SF259 for 6 days
Day pass Jakobshorn SF46, Parsenn SF52, Pischa SF38, Rinerhorn SF40, Schatzalp SF24
Beginners no free lifts
Pensioners 20% reduction for women 62

yrs and over and men 65 yrs and over
Credit cards accepted yes

SKI SCHOOLS
Adults SSS, 10am-midday and 2-4pm, SF190 for 5 days
Private lessons SF145 per half-day, SF250 per day
Snowboarding Top Secret Snowboarding School, PaarSenn, SSS, all SF160-215 for 5 half-days, private lessons SF130 per half-day
Cross-country SSS, SF190 for 5 days, times as regular ski school. Loipe 75km along the main valley between Glaris and Wolfgang, and in the Flüela, Dischma and Sertig valleys
Other courses off-piste, ski-touring, telemark
Guiding companies Stefan Welz, SSS

CHILDCARE
Lift pass 6-16 yrs, Rega Pass SF155, Gotschna/Strela/Parsenn SF134, both for 6 days. Free for 5 yrs and under
Ski schools SSS, 3-16 yrs, 8.30-11.30am and 2-4.30pm, SF200 for 5 days including lunch
Ski kindergarten as ski school
Non-ski kindergarten Flurina (2.30-4.30pm) and Ursli Schellen (2.15-5pm), both 3-5 yrs, SF5 per hr

FOOD AND DRINK PRICES
Coffee SF3.80, glass of wine SF6-8, small • beer SF4-5, dish of the day SF24

Skiing facts: **Klosters**

TOURIST OFFICE
CH-7250 Klosters, Graubunden
Tel 41 81 4102020
Fax 41 81 4102010

THE RESORT
By road Calais 1000km
By rail Davos Dorf and Davos Platz stations
By air Zurich 2½ hrs
Visitor beds 8,600
Transport free ski-bus with lift pass, free ski-train with Rega Pass

THE SKIING
Linked or nearby resorts Davos (l) Arosa (n), Gargellan (n), Küblis (l), Saas (l), Serneus (l), Wolfgang (l)
Longest run Weissfluhgipfel-Küblis, 12km (black/red)
Number of lifts 29 in Klosters, Gotschna/Parsenn and Madrisa, 55 in area
Total of trails/pistes 315km in area (30% easy, 40% intermediate, 30% difficult)
Nursery slopes 2 lifts in the village and 1 on Madrisa
Summer skiing none
Snowmaking 4.3km (last part of Schwendi-Klosters run) covered, plus 1 mobile snow-cannon in Madrisa area

LIFT PASSES
Area pass Rega Pass (covers all Davos and Klosters lifts, buses and railway), SF259 for 6 days
Day pass Madrisa SF42, Parsenn SF52
Beginners no free lifts
Pensioners 20% reduction for women 62 yrs and over and men 65 yrs and over
Credit cards accepted yes

SKI SCHOOLS
Adults SSS, 10am-midday and 2-4pm, SF200 for 5 days. Saas Ski and Snowboard School, 10am-midday and 1.30-3.30pm, SF295 for 6 days
Private lessons both ski schools, SF250 per day, SF60 per hr
Snowboarding SSS, SF175 for 3 days, Saas Ski and Snowboard School, SF160 for 3 days, private lessons as regular ski prices
Cross-country SSS, SF141 for 6 half-days, private lessons SF55 per hr. Loipe 75km along the main valley between Glaris and Wolfgang, and in the Flüela, Dischma and Sertig valleys
Other courses junior race camps, off-piste, ski-touring, telemark
Guiding companies Bruno Sprecher, Mountain Guide, or through ski schools

CHILDREN
Lift pass 6-16 yrs, Gotschna/Parsenn/Madrisa SF134, Madrisa SF113, Rega Pass SF155, all for 6 days, free for 5 yrs and under
Ski kindergarten as ski school
Ski school SSS, 4-12 yrs, SF170 for 5 days, times as adults. Saas Ski and Snowboard School, 4 yrs and over, 9.30am-3.30pm, SF315 for 6 days including lunch
Non-ski kindergarten Hotel Vereina, 2 yrs and over, 9am-4.30pm, prices on request. Madrisa Kindergarten, 3 yrs and over, 10am-12.30pm and 1.30-4pm, SF5 per hr or SF16 per day including lunch

FOOD AND DRINK PRICES
Coffee SF3.80, glass of wine SF6-8, small beer SF4-5, dish of the day SF24

in the evenings. The Gasthof Landhaus in **Frauenkirch** is recommended, as is the Kulm in **Wolfgang**.

In Klosters, even in low season, it is necessary to book restaurant tables at least a day ahead; the exception to this is the Chesa Grischuna, where you need to reserve at least three days in advance. The Wynegg, with its unofficial royal seal of approval, has reasonable prices and a welcoming atmosphere (press photographers apart). It is renowned for its traditional Swiss cuisine. The Walserhof is expensive but good. The Vereina's pizzeria is popular with guests: 'You could watch the multi-talented Italian chef making pizzas in a special corner and after a while he would emerge and sing *Il Sole Mio* and *Volare* to great applause.'

Après-ski

'Davos', says one reporter, 'is more dinner than disco and more restaurant than bar.' Although there are many early evening activities, including drinking at any of the busy bars near the Parsennbahn after skiing, the resort is quiet later on. There are big-league ice hockey matches in Davos Platz, tea and cakes at Schneider's Café and regular cultural events at the Davos Conference Centre. The piano bar in the Hotel Europe and the Pöstli in the Posthotel Morosani are both popular. Other drinking-places include Carlo's, Ex-Bar and BaarSenn. The Chämi-Bar draws a big crowd throughout the evening. Late-night revellers move on to a choice of the Cabanna Club, Jakobshorn-Bar, Cava Grischa, or Dischma.

In Klosters, reporters complain that there are surprisingly few cafés, and one found the resort 'practically dead'. A Porta's is the popular place for tea and cakes after skiing, and later on the nightlife centres around a handful of bars. The cellar piano bar of the Chesa Grischuna is always busy and you need to book to eat in the main restaurant there. The Aldiana Clubhotel Silvretta disco attracts a young crowd. Sophisticates move on to the Casa Antica and the Robinson Club. The Madrisa Bar in Klosters Dorf is recommended, and the Vereina has two popular bars.

Childcare

The SSS kindergarten in Davos receives mixed reports: 'Excellent facilities for the very young learning to ski, including a baby-lift and indoor facilities for lunch and in poor weather. However, even the good staff forget at times that your child does not speak German.'

Klosters receives mainly unfavourable comments on its suitability for children: 'Definitely not a resort for young children. We had to take our five-year-old to the pony-lift slope in the village and the eight-year-old by bus to the Heidellift — both had to be there by 9.45am.' However, Hotel Vereina in Klosters is a convenient place to stay with small children as it has its own non-ski kindergarten for two- to six-year-olds run by 'an extremely old but very friendly woman with one tooth'. Annoyingly, the ski kindergarten at Madrisa is a bus-ride away from the village centre, and because adult classes are not held, parents cannot ski and meet their children for lunch and then ski again in the afternoon.

Flims

ALTITUDE 1100m (3,608ft)

You would be hard pressed to find a more quintessentially Swiss resort than Flims in any ski brochure. This substantial year-round destination lies in the heart of Graubunden on the road from Chur to Andermatt. Together with its neighbours, **Laax** and **Falera**, it serves the wide south-facing ski area known as the White Arena. Flims itself consists of bustling **Dorf** and tranquil, forested **Waldhaus**. The opening of the 120-bed spa-hotel Kurhaus Waldhaus in 1877 paved the way for nineteenth-century tourism in the region. Today, Waldhaus is the focus of a 60km network of prepared hiking trails, which provide a popular winter alternative to skiing.

> ### ■ GOOD POINTS
> Large ski area, sunny slopes, long runs, efficient lift system, varied mountain restaurants, tree-level skiing, many activities for non-skiers
>
> ### ■ BAD POINTS
> Limited expert challenge, heavy traffic, poor nightlife, no alpine charm, lack of resort-level snow

The old village of Laax, 5km to the west, has a modern satellite base-station at Murschetg and low-cost on-mountain accommodation at **Crap Sogn Gion**. The farming hamlet of Falera provides a rustic alternative.

On the mountain
top 2980m (9,774ft) bottom 1080m (3,542ft)

The **White Arena** stretches over the **Vorab**, **La Siala** and **Cassons** mountains, divided in places by bands of rock and steep wooded gullies, which can create navigational hazards when the weather closes in. The most accessible base-station is Flims Dorf, the start of the two-stage Foppa-Naraus quad and the three-stage Startgels-Nargens gondola. Laax Murschetg offers a choice between a direct cable car and a gondola/chair-lift dogleg through Curnius to the futuristic Crap Sogn Gion mid-station. Falera connects to the main system by a very slow chair to Curnius. Crap Sogn Gion is the gateway to the network of lifts up to the **Vorab Glacier** at 3018m, which is the start of the 14km Weisse Schuss race to Dorf, a team and individual event held annually over the last weekend in January.

Beginners
Class 1 meets on the nursery slope in Flims Waldhaus, but once the learning curve is underway the area has no shortage of gentle practice slopes, both near the base-stations for good visibility in bad weather and higher up to benefit from the long hours of sunshine on clear days. In

Dorf, the Foppa-Naraus chairs open up extensive green (beginner) runs back to the village, and Laax has its own learner slopes below Larnags. For more advanced beginners, the White Arena is a paradise, with huge tracts of blue (easy) cruising on both Vorab and La Siala. Do not miss the long flat Ofen piste from La Siala to **Grauberg**. Reporters comment that the Flims side of the mountain is served almost entirely by drag-lifts, making the uphill journey a long and tiring one for quasi-beginners.

Intermediates
Again there is no shortage of confidence-building motorways in an area where any competent intermediate has the run of the whole mountain, with the exception of unpisted Cassons. Of the red (intermediate) runs, the usually deserted Alp Ruschein on the very edge of the resort below Crap Masegn is highly recommended.

Advanced
The longest black (difficult) run is the FIS downhill from Crap Sogn Gion to Murschetg, but it owes its colouring more to its racecourse status than to its degree of difficulty. The most challenging descents are the short, steeply pitched Platt'Alva from Nagens to Startgels and the Hot Dog and Scansinas trails to **Plaun**, the connecting point between the Vorab and La Siala ski areas.

Off-piste
As is often the case in areas with limited steep skiing, the off-piste potential is unexpectedly good. First, there are not nearly so many contenders for untracked powder as there are in the more radical resorts and second, the size and variety of the terrain gives all-weather cover. In good conditions the wide, evenly pitched descent from **Cassons** to Naraus, reached by a ten-minute walk from the top of the cable car, is perfect for first tracks, though skiers should stick to the marked trail as deviation can lead to the edge of a cliff. On snowy days, the extensive tree runs above Laax allow powderhounds to see as they ski.

Snowboarding
The Swiss Snowboard School (a subsidiary of the Swiss Ski School) has group lessons for a minimum of four people; an alternative is the Swissraft Ski School. There is a new half-pipe at Crap Sogn Gion. Snowboards can be hired at most sport shops, but clients are advised to book in advance.

Ski schools and guiding
Again the choice is between the Swiss Ski School (SSS), which has five-

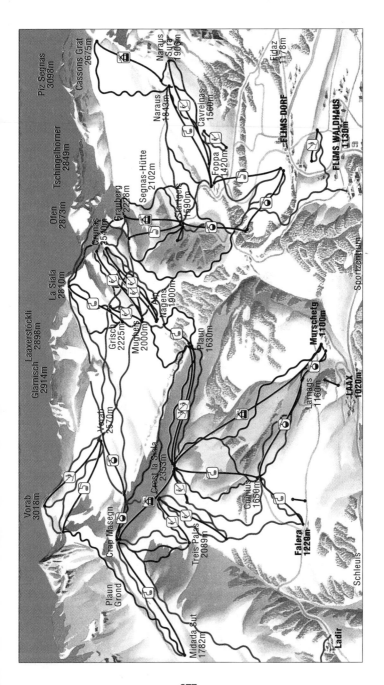

day courses, and the Swissraft Ski School, which also offers cross-country skiing.

Mountain restaurants
The best mountain restaurants in the White Arena are at the lower levels, mostly because they are on hiking trails that attract customers all year round. This also means that they are not on the skiing trails, but the Runca hut below Startgels and the Tegia at Larnags are well worth the detour. Of the alternatives higher up, the Segnes-Hütte is welcoming, while the Plaun self-service cafeteria should be avoided at all costs. The Foppa, an old wooden chalet with a sun terrace, is recommended, as is Nagens, which has a 'huge choice of food and is strong on pasta'. The Berghotel Crap Sogn Gion 'resembles a Klingon battlecruiser perched on a mountain top, but the food is better than the ambience'. The Curnius is another attractive old wooden chalet with self-service food of a high standard. The Elephant restaurant at Crap Masegn is 'small but smart, with excellent food'.

Off the mountain
As **Flims Dorf** and **Waldhaus** are strung out on a series of hilly bends along the congested main highway, it is hard to identify the centre of the resort or indeed to feel that you are in a resort at all. It is generally accepted that Dorf is livelier than Waldhaus, however, the difference is only marginal in a place that dies fairly comprehensively as soon as darkness falls. The Waldhaus hotels may be ideal for cross-country skiers and hikers but are not within easy walking distance of the lifts. The larger ones have a courtesy minibus service to the Dorf base-station. The alternative is the post-bus that plies between Dorf, Murschetg and Laax with occasional extensions to the outposts of Falera, an unspoilt Romansch-speaking village on the edge of the circuit, and Fidaz during daylight hours. Murschetg is a convenient but soulless place to stay, while Laax itself is pleasant but again removed from the lift system.

■ OTHER SPORTS
Snow-shoeing, paragliding, hot air ballooning, winter walks, swimming, skating, curling, indoor tennis, dog-sledding, tobogganing, night-skiing

Accommodation
The five-star Parkhotel Waldhaus, on the site of the original Kurhaus, offers opulent rooms in five buildings connected by underground corridors and covered walkways. This can make for quite a hike to the restaurants and bars in the main building. However, the level of comfort is high, especially in the rooms that offer an environment-friendly spray and dry lavatory facility designed locally to replace loo paper. The hotel has indoor tennis and a bridge club.

The 100-room, four-star Hotel Adula has a more intimate approach to luxury and is recommended for its food, child facilities and the views

Skiing facts: **Flims**

TOURIST OFFICE
CH-7018 Flims-Waldhaus, Graubunden
Tel 41 81 391022
Fax 41 81 394308

THE RESORT
By road Calais 994km
By rail Chur 17km, hourly buses from station
By air Zurich 2 hrs
Visitor beds 5,800
Transport free ski-bus with lift pass

THE SKIING
Linked or nearby resorts Falera (l), Laax (l), Lenzerheide (n)
Longest run White Race (Vorab to Flims Dorf), 14km (blue/red/black)
Number of lifts 12 in Flims, 32 in area
Total of trails/pistes 220km in area (48% easy, 37% intermediate, 15% difficult)
Nursery slopes 2 runs served by 1 lift in village
Summer skiing none
Snowmaking 19 hectares covered in area

LIFT PASSES
Area pass White Arena (covers Flims-Laax-Falera), SF270 for 6 days
Day pass Flims SF35, Flims-Laax-Falera SF45
Beginners SF14 per day for lift on nursery slopes

Pensioners no reduction
Credit cards accepted yes

SKI SCHOOLS
Adults SSS, 9.30-11.30am and 1.30-3.30pm, SF175 for 5 days
Private lessons SSS, SF230 per day
Snowboarding SSS group lessons, SF170 for 3 days, private lessons SF230 per day
Cross-country SSS private lessons, SF65 per hr. Loipe 60km in area
Other courses telemark, ski-touring, heli-skiing (Swissraft)
Guiding companies SSS, Mountain Fantasy, Johny's and Thomy's

CHILDREN
Lift pass 6-16 yrs, SF135 for 6 days, free for 5 yrs and under
Ski kindergarten SSS, 4 yrs and over, 9.30-11.30am and 1.30-3.30pm, SF175 for 5 days. Kinderhort provides supervision for children before and after lessons. Midday supervision in day centre (no lunch provided)
Ski school SSS, 9.30-11.30am and 1.30-3.30pm, SF218 for 5 days including ski lift
Non-ski kindergarten in Hotel Adula, Flims Waldhaus

FOOD AND DRINK PRICES
Coffee SF4, glass of wine SF8-10, small beer SF3.50, dish of the day SF15

from the large picture window. The comfortable Crap Ner is also recommended. In the three-star category, the National, the Grischuna and the Waldeck are particularly popular. The top choice in **Laax** is the Posta Veglia, while the best of the limited options in **Falera** is the modest but well-run two-star Encarna.

Eating in and out
Apart from a sprinkling of pizza parlours, of which the Pizzeria Pomodoro is the best, most eating takes place in hotel restaurants. The

Barga in the Adula is rightly proud of its international cuisine, while the Ristorante la Cena in the Waldhaus concentrates on traditional Swiss and Italian dishes. The fish restaurant in the National is renowned. There were also favourable reports of the Waldeck and the local special- ities in the Posta Veglia in Laax. Few visitors to Flims choose a self-cater- ing holiday, but there are local food shops for those who do.

Après-ski

The all-glass Iglu Bar opposite the Dorf base is the height of Flims chic for après-ski drinks. Later on, such action as there is focuses on the MacGeorge Pub in the Albana, which is described as a 'happening place', and the quieter Segnes Bar, which livens up on the rare occasions when it has live music. There is tea-dancing in the Bellevue and Meiler hotels. In Flims Waldhaus the main bar is the Rock Fabrik, which attracts teenage snowboarders. The new Crap Bar at the foot of the piste in Laax draws skiers at the end of the day.

Childcare

The SSS has classes for children from four years of age and upwards, and there are excellent reports of the ski kindergarten and its enclosed ski area, with its 'strips of red carpet on which children can get the idea of climbing sideways up the hill'. Graduation from enclosure to piste is simple as there is an easy adjacent drag-lift. The Swissraft Ski School offers skiing in its Husky-Land centre as well as babysitting. Both the Parkhotel Waldhaus and the Hotel Adula have crèches, which are open to non-residents. The child-friendly Adula also prepares early suppers for children in its Italian restaurant and can arrange babysitting.

Gstaad

ALTITUDE 1050m (3,444ft)

Gstaad has long been associated with exclusivity, and this reputation remains intact, although the resort is secluded rather than flashy. Its hotels and bars are well-known landmarks of the rich and famous, from the luxurious five-star Palace Hotel to the Olden bar, which has a collection of named mugs for regulars such as Roger Moore and Julie Andrews; yet the village retains the atmosphere of a farming community.

The clientèle is international, and while the first impression of the village is of typical Swiss chalets and delightful scenery, the main street pays homage to the designer label, with Gucci, Cartier, Versace and others vying for the best space. 'Think expensive, then double it,' was one report.

On the mountain
top 3000m (9,840ft) bottom 1000m (3,280ft)

The skiing in Gstaad is neither convenient nor challenging. Experts do not rate it highly, but lesser intermediates will find it uncrowded and varied. It is now collectively marketed with nine smaller villages in the Gstaad-Saanenland area as the Gstaad Super Ski Region — a total of 69 lifts and 250km of piste. The other villages are **St Stephan**, **Zweisimmen**, **Saanenmöser**, **Schönried**, **Lauenen**, **Gsteig**, **Saanen**, **Rougemont** and **Château d'Oex**. The weekly lift pass includes a day's skiing in Adelboden-Lenk and the Vaudoise Alps (Villars, Les Diablerets, Leysin, Gryon and Les Mosses).

Beginners

The nursery slopes nearest to the town centre are at the bottom of **Wispile**, but the snow is often unreliable. There are some easy slopes at the top of Wispile, at Schönried and further afield at Saanenmöser. The best beginner slopes are at **La Braye**; they are covered by the lift pass and reached by train or bus.

Intermediates

The intermediate skiing in the Gstaad area is broken up into three segments: **Eggli**, Wispile and **Wasserngrat**. The Eggli area connects with Rougemont at the top of **La Videmanette**, and you can also ski from Eggli to Saanen on long, varied runs. The Hornberg area is a few kilometres away and is reached by bus or train; it has the most extensive lift network, with 14 lifts reaching St Stephan at the far end of the valley.

Advanced
Advanced skiers should head to the Wasserngrat, which hosts the challenging Tiger Run piste. **Les Diablerets Glacier** is not difficult, but is a long run with a fairly steep start. There are few black (difficult) runs.

Off-piste
From the Wispile there are some challenging off-piste runs from the top of the area down to Feutersoey and to the Chlösterli restaurant.

Snowboarding
There are three snowboarding parks in Gstaad, including one that is weather-dependent on Les Diablerets Glacier. The others are at Saanenmöser and **Rinderberg** and include a half-pipe and other obstacles. Snowboarding is permitted everywhere in the ski area and the ski school offers group and private lessons.

Ski schools and guiding
The English-speaking Gstaad Ski School has a good reputation, with classes for children from four years old. The ski school meets in several ski areas, including Gstaad, Schönried, Saanen, Saanenmöser and Rougemont. The two off-piste guiding companies are Experience Gstaad Saanenland and Mountain Guide Company Gstaad Saanenland.

■ WHAT'S NEW
Ski Data lift pass system for hands-free access to all ski-lifts
New snowboarding parks, including a half-pipe

Mountain restaurants
When it comes to mountain eating the choice is extensive, although it can be expensive. Many of the restaurants have waiter-service. Chemistube above St Stephan is recommended, as is Cabane de la Sarouche at Château d'Oex. Ruble-Rougemont at the bottom of the Gouilles chair-lift is 'half the price of anywhere else' according to one report. Other choices include the Berghaus Wasserngrat ('excellent sun terrace and a good place to spot the ludicrous ski outfits'), and the waiter-service Eggli Hut at the top of the gondola.

Off the mountain
The village of Gstaad is filled with top-quality hotels and a cluster of well-preserved wooden buildings bordering the often busy main road. The centre is dominated by the Palace Hotel, where Peter Sellers in his role as Inspector Clouseau once asked for a 'rhume'. There is little accommodation in less than the three-star category; the cheaper hotels are in the surrounding but not particularly attractive villages of Schönried and Saanenmöser. The most favourable reports are of Rougemont ('a beau-

tiful undiscovered village of traditional chalets') and Château d'Oex (best known for its celebrated balloon festival).

Accommodation

The Palace and Grand Hotel Park are the top five-star hotels. The four-stars include Grand Hotel Alpina, the Christiania, the Bernerhof, the Arc-en-Ciel and Hotel Bellevue Gstaad. Most are set in their own parks, and the latter is famous for its Chez Fritz

■ **OTHER SPORTS**

Parapente, hang-gliding, swimming, helicopter rides, skating, curling, indoor tennis, squash and badminton, climbing wall, hot air ballooning, tobogganing

restaurant. The three-star Olden is family-run and cosy, as is the Posthotel Rössli. Sporthotel Rutti is the cheapest and most basic, but has good food and is said to be good value for money. In Rougemont try the four-star Viva hotel, and in Château d'Oex the three-star Beau Sejour.

Eating in and out

The best restaurants are in the hotels, but these are also the most expensive. La Cave in the Hotel Olden is good and there is also cheaper food in the bar. The sixteenth-century Chlösterli is large but has a great atmosphere. The Alpenrose at Schönried serves more delicate cuisine, the Bären at Gsteig offers traditional Swiss fare. The Chesery receives good marks, as does the Rialto for its pasta.

Après-ski

There is no shortage of nightlife here, although it is considerably busier during high season, particularly at Christmas and New Year. Start off at the Apple-Pie Café, Charly's Tea Room and Pernet for tea and cakes. You can star-gaze at the Olden and step out at the Green Go disco in the Palace or at the Chlösterli. The nightlife starts late, and after lengthy dinners the Gstaad crowd hit Henry's, Richi's and the Rialto. The Taburi at the Sporthotel Viktoria and Rutti's Keller are more rustic dance spots. In Château d'Oex check out Café du Cerf.

Childcare

There are non-ski kindergarten at Gstaad, Saanen, Schönried and Saanenmöser for a limited number of hours each day, and the children's ski school takes four-year-olds and over. Some hotels can arrange babysitting and the Palace has a nursery.

Jungfrau

ALTITUDE Wengen 1274m (4,180ft), Grindelwald 1034m (3,391ft),
Mürren 1650m (5,412ft)

The Jungfrau Region can justly claim to have both the most awe-inspiring scenery and the strongest British influence of any ski area. The great range of Eiger, Mönch and Jungfrau mountains joins with the Schreckhorn and Wetterhorn as a backdrop to **Wengen** and **Grindelwald**. From **Mürren** the plunging chasm of the Lauterbrunnen Valley gives an entirely different perspective to these three mountains: the Maiden guarded by the Monk from the fearsome Ogre.

■ **GOOD POINTS**

Beautiful scenery, variety of slopes, traffic-free villages, English widely spoken

■ **BAD POINTS**

Poorly linked ski areas, limited piste challenges, lower slopes sometimes icy or worn

Thanks largely to the sophisticated network of mountain railways built at the turn of the century (still the foundation of the lift system today), the Jungfrau was one of the real birthplaces of modern alpine skiing. Henry Lunn, a Methodist minister and one-time lawn tennis equipment salesman, is credited with introducing the first-ever ski package holidays here in the winter of 1910–11. To encourage the class-conscious British to come on his tours he founded the Public Schools Alpine Sports Club and somehow managed to persuade the Swiss to continue operating their mountain railways during the winter. His more distinguished son, Sir Arnold, the father of modern skiing, went on to found the Kandahar Ski Club in Mürren where slalom racing was first introduced in 1922.

Over in Wengen British skiers had discovered, to the amazement of local farmers, that it was much easier to take the train up the mountain, rather than to walk on skins. Their activities were considered to be most definitely unsporting; by the standards of the time, to enjoy skiing downhill you should first suffer the pain of climbing up. They called themselves the Downhill Only, and both British ski clubs are alive and functioning in the resorts today. Arnold Lunn lived in Mürren each winter and used it as a cockpit to launch downhill skiing and persuade the world to add downhill and slalom to cross-country and ski jumping on the list of Olympic events.

Wengen, Grindelwald and Mürren are all reached on the Swiss railway network from Interlaken. Both Wengen and Mürren are traffic-free, and a car is of little or no use in the area. The track divides at Zweilutschinen, with the left-hand fork veering through the Lütschental directly to Grindelwald. The right-hand fork goes to **Lauterbrunnen**, which is more of a railway halt than a resort, although it does have a

Jungfrau 4158m

Jungfraujoch 3454m

Mönch 4099m

Eiger 3970m

Schreckhorn 4078m

Wetterhorn 3701m

Lauterbrunnen 796m

WENGEN 1274m

Wengernalp 1873m

Brimps

Innerwengen

Eigergletscher 2320m

Kleine-Scheidegg 2061m

Lauberhorn 2472m

Männlichen 2230m

Saltegg

Tschuggen

Sattelegg

Schluggen

Gumml

Lager

Holenstein

Aspen

Alpiglen 1615m

Brandegg

GRINDELWALD 1034m

Grund 943m

Bodmi

Oberhaus

Grosse Scheidegg 2006m

Bärgelegg

First 2168m

Egg

Bort 1570m

Oberjoch 2486m

number of hotels, and some reporters consider it a convenient and much cheaper base for the area. From here, trains climb steeply up to Mürren on one side of the valley and up to Wengen on the other. The track carries on up above Wengen to the main ski area at Kleine Scheidegg, at the foot of the Eigerwand, before descending into Grindelwald to complete the circuit. The trains stop at wayside halts throughout the area to pick up and set down skiers. They run (as accurately as a Swiss watch) to the timetable printed on the back of the piste map.

This mundane form of transport is painfully slow, and the trains can be as crowded as the London Underground at peak times. However, the network has been augmented by conventional cableways and chairs. The Jungfrau Region is neither so vast in ski area nor so well-knit as the classic French resorts, but nevertheless it provides satisfyingly varied skiing for its faithful clientèle.

On the mountain
Wengen top 2320m (7,610ft) bottom 1274m (4,180ft)
Grindelwald top 2,486m (8,154ft) bottom 943m (3,093ft)
Mürren top 2970m (9,742ft) bottom 796m (2,611ft)

To a great extent the runs, unlike those of many resorts (especially those in the USA), are dictated wholly by the contours of the mountains and the prevailing weather. The pistes are not cut out arbitrarily from forest, nor bulldozed down scarps, but simply follow the best, easiest or most exciting ways down. Slight variations in direction and difficulty are naturally dictated each season by the amount of snow and the direction in which the wind was blowing when it fell.

There is also plenty of satisfying off-piste for those enthusiasts who want to explore.

A circuit of lifts round the Lauberhorn and Tschuggen peaks links the ski areas of Wengen and Grindelwald through the Männlichen and Kleine Scheidegg. From Wengen a cable car rises to the Männlichen, while the train leads up to Kleine Scheidegg and Eigergletscher. From Grindelwald a long gondola rises to the Männlichen and the train also carries on up to Kleine Scheidegg. On the other side of Grindelwald the First area is easily accessible.

Mürren, separated from the other two resorts by the Lauterbrunnen Valley, sits on a shelf facing east. Mürreners are known to look down upon Wengen and remark disparagingly: 'A good place to pick flowers'— whereupon Wengeners respond: 'Strictly for the goats up there.' In fact, the areas are all complementary and one of the pleasures of visiting any of them is to spend days exploring the others. As they all share a lift pass and a good train service, this is easily achieved.

Mürren's skiing is spread across three parallel ridges, the Schiltgrat, Allmendhubel and Maulerhubel, which run roughly north and south above the village. These slopes provide good conditions whatever the weather: powder on the north slopes, spring snow on the south, high bowls for fine weather, trees for shelter and visibility in blizzards.

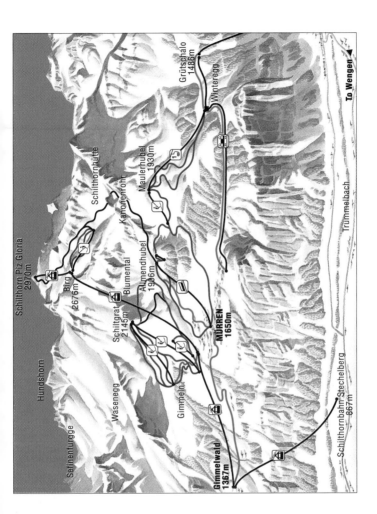

Beginners

Wengen has an excellent nursery area right in the middle of the village. There are also satisfyingly long blue (easy) runs on which even those with little technique can stretch their legs. From Kleine Scheidegg a broad tree-lined road down Schattwald leads to Brandegg. If (instead of the train) you take the Männlichen cable car from Wengen, you arrive at the top of a big sunny scarp, served by several lifts. The easiest route is down under the Männlichen chair.

Grindelwald also has nursery slopes right by the village and others up on the Hohwald and Bargelegg lifts, although beginners will want to return to base in the First gondola. Mürren's nursery slopes are on the

387

upper road behind the Jungfrau Hotel. This is historic ground, where the world's first modern slalom was set. Another small beginners' area lies at the top of the Allmendhubel lift, and is served by a small tow-lift.

Intermediates

Wengen and Grindelwald owe much of their family popularity to their long, medium-difficulty runs. You can take the Männlichen cable car and explore the route under the gondola right down to Grund. From there the train goes up to Kleine Scheidegg, which has a similarly well networked area improved recently by the installation of a detachable quad-chair, on the Lauberhorn. The famous World Cup racecourse, the longest in the world at two-and-a-half kilometres (racers take just two-and-a-half minutes to complete it), forms a good, fairly testing descent at any recreational speed. The nearby Standard run offers an easier way back down.

■ **WHAT'S NEW**

Two additional chairs, with moving carpets, in Mürren's Schilthorn area
Four-seater chair at Oberjoch in Grindelwald
Schreckfeld restaurant in Grindelwald
Three-star Hotel Grindelwalderhof

From Grindelwald the First gondola leads to the Stepfi, a satisfying red (intermediate) run from Oberlager down to the Hotel Wetterhorn. Take a look at the old cable car cabin as you pass the hotel; it was built in 1908 to take summer climbers up to the Gleckstein Hut on the Wetterhorn. The lift was closed in 1914 after being damaged by avalanches, and the cabin was left as a relic. This is a good stop-off before returning by bus to Grindelwald.

At Mürren some very pretty intermediate skiing can be reached by taking the Allmendhubel railway and then a small T-bar to the Hogs Back; turn right towards the Maulerhubel T-bar, up again and then there is a wide area of open slopes leading either back to the bottom of Maulerhubel or off to the halfway station on the main railway. You can return to the village from the bottom of the Maulerhubel on the Palace Run, which was widened last season.

Mürren increased its intermediate skiing in 1994 by opening two new chair-lifts, Muttleren and Kandahar (with moving carpets to help you get on), in the Engetal, which lies halfway up the Schilthorn. This gives good intermediate skiing in a snow-sure bowl. However, the chair that was promised from the bottom of the Muttleren lift to Birg has not been built, so the only way out for those unwilling to face the often icy Kanonenrohr is by a steep and uncomfortable T-bar. This is one of the very few places where queues form in the area.

Advanced

From Wengen the train up to Eigergletscher leads to satisfying black (difficult) runs on Blackrock and Oh God. In sunny weather these are best left until late morning, as they can be hard and icy before the sun reaches them. The Aspen run is the steepest way down from the Männlichen towards Grund. Grindelwald First has a good black piste under the gondola. At Mürren the run from the top of the Schilthorn can be followed by a steep pitch alongside the new Muttleren and then the Kanonenrohr to give an almost continuous black run with plenty of challenge. The Kanonenrohr is particularly steep and narrow.

Off-piste

All three resorts have a great deal of easily accessed off-piste between the beaten trails. In Mürren the Blumental is famous for its powder, Tschingelchrachen off the Schilthornbahn should be treated with care as it is very steep and often closed, Hidden Valley from the summit of the Maulerhubel to Grutsch is a delight. The White Hare, which starts from the foot of the Eigerwand, is a dramatic and exciting powder run. It can be accessed from both Wengen and Grindelwald. Local mountain guides are essential here and Grindelwald's Alpine Centre is one of the most famous guiding establishments in the world. Both ski-touring and heli-skiing can be organised through the centre. Day-tours over to the Lötschental and the Petersgrat can be arranged in good weather.

Snowboarding

All the ski schools offer snowboarding instruction and boards are available for hire. Wengen has half-pipes on the Männlichen and up the Wixi chair.

Ski schools and guiding

The Swiss Ski School (SSS) operates in each village and all three centres have good reputations. Lessons are given daily, except Sunday. Most, but by no means all, instructors speak good English. However, the standard of service provided continues to vary alarmingly. One reader encountered a class of 14 in Grindelwald: 'Our instructor was just interested in skiing madly downhill. It took a sit-in at the ski school office to get the teacher we wanted.' Another praised the ski school in Wengen as a 'well-organised class of eight — I started as a slowish snowplougher and finished the week as a quicker parallel skier'. Another reporter in Mürren complained his mountain guide 'didn't speak English, kept losing people and wouldn't say where he was going'.

Mountain restaurants

Many of the restaurants in the area tend to be large and impersonal, but there are some wonderful exceptions. The Hotel Jungfrau at Wengernalp ('incomparably beautiful views') is renowned for its warm atmosphere and Swiss specialities. The Brandegg restaurant is famed throughout the Alps for its 'quite extraordinarily delicious apple fritters'. The Kleine Scheidegg station buffet is much more interesting than it looks, with a variety of Swiss fare and its own *Röstizza*, a cross between *Rösti* and pizza. The Männlichen restaurant has spectacular views, which are 'very welcome on a bitterly cold day'. The Aspen above Grund has a loyal clientèle. Mary's Café on the home run to Wengen is recommended for its raclette. Café Oberland is a good alternative and is right on the piste. The Victoria Hotel is 'quiet, and conveniently situated near the nursery slopes and the station'. The *Rösti* in the Stübli of the Eiger Hotel is also recommended.

The restaurant at Bort above Grindelwald is said to be 'very pleasant, reasonably priced, but the food is not exceptional'. The big self-service at First boasts 'a glorious hamburger'. The Hotel Wetterhorn on the way down to Grindelwald has a convivial atmosphere and good food.

Above Mürren the Birg restaurant is 'nothing to write home about.' The Gimmeln has 'good raclette and *Apfelküchen*'. We have a whole series of complimentary reports of the revolving Piz Gloria on the summit of the Schilthorn ('not expensive and good value'). One reporter had 'a very good, imaginative salad, and it took a full revolution to demolish it'. Another claimed it to be 'the best and the cheapest menu to be found in Switzerland — what a surprise!' The Schilthornhütte on the descent from here is a mountain refuge serving simple dishes, with a 'fun atmosphere and wonderful views'. Sonnenberg chalet in the valley between the Hogs Back and the top of the Schiltgrat maintains a high standard. Winteregg at the halfway station on the railway is acclaimed for its *Rösti mit Speck*.

Off the mountain

Wengen is almost car-free, although a couple of Range Rovers are allowed to operate as taxis; otherwise, luggage is carried by electric buggy around the resort. Despite expansion it has lost none of its character and appears to have changed surprisingly little since the foundation of the Downhill Only club 70 years ago. Many of its visitors are still British, the same families who return year after year to create their own entertainment. The presence of Club Med at the northern end of town seems incongruous in this otherwise neo-Edwardian setting.

At the heart of it all, on a sunny balcony above the Lauterbrunnen Valley, is the railway. Village life is centred on the comings and goings from the now rebuilt station; it is surrounded by a scattering of largely refurbished hotels built nearly a century ago in the grand manner. The main, indeed only, street stretching southwards from the station is lined with hotels and a modest range of mainly expensive shops and boutiques. The large skating and curling rink beside the nursery slopes forms an integral part of village life.

■ OTHER SPORTS

Skating, tobogganing, ice hockey, parapente, hang-gliding, curling, swimming, indoor climbing wall, indoor tennis, squash

Grindelwald is the original of the three villages. It is a large and busy year-round resort spread along the valley floor between the soaring peaks of the Wetterhorn and the Eiger on the one side and the gentler wooded slopes of its First ski area on the other. There are few more cosmopolitan resorts to be found in the world, with every nationality imaginable listed among its guests, not least the Japanese who come here in numbers to visit the Eiger and the Jungfraujoch, which at 3454m is the highest station in Europe.

The scenery around Grindelwald is spectacular and many reporters consider it the best place to stay in the Jungfrau: 'having seen it all and skied for 22 years, no member of my family would now consider skiing anywhere else.' Its low altitude does, however, mean that snow cover in the village and on the lower mountain is extremely uncertain.

Mürren has few rivals as the prettiest and most unspoilt ski village in Switzerland. Old chalets and hotels line the paths between the railway station at one end and the cable car at the other. The village is on a sunny shelf perched on top of a 500m rock face above Lauterbrunnen. Again, the same British families, nearly all of them members of the Kandahar Club, have been returning here for generations and firm links have been forged with the original villagers.

Accommodation

In **Wengen** the accommodation is split between hotels, apartments and chalets. The resort is quite spread out and distinctly steep. While location is of little importance for the skiing (if staying high up you can ski both down to the train and back to your hotel), a long uphill slog after midnight tends to deter many a holidaymaker from exploring what limited nightlife there is. The Eiger Hotel is central and has long been a favourite among the British. The Falken is variously described as 'delightfully old-fashioned', 'ramshackle' and ' very comfortable' — you take your pick! The Brunner is a simple, but popular hotel with friendly owners. The Hotel Regina is 'spacious, clean and comfortable,' and renowned for its English breakfast.

Hotel Wengener Hof, five minutes' walk from the station, is 'very comfortable' with good food. Hotel Silberhorn is 'excellent, with multinational and very friendly staff, superb and substantial food'. Hotel Alpenrose is said to be of an exceptionally high standard ('we particularly liked the large lounge area with log fire'). Hotel Bernerhof and Hotel Bellevue are also both recommended. Club Med here has a fine reputation, although the presence of large noisy French-led classes on crowded pistes can lead to Agincourt-style confrontations with the more conservative British element.

Grindelwald has the five-star Grand Hotel Regina, which is partly decorated with eighteenth-century antiques and is famous for the ice sculptures in its grounds. A host of four-star hotels include the central 'excellent' Hotel Spinne. Hotel Jungfrau is praised for 'good and plentiful food — we would have paid twice the price for the view from our window'. The Hotel Alpenhof, a few minutes' walk from the village and prettily chalet-shaped, has a sound reputation. Hotel Derby and Hotel Hirschen are both recommended. The Hotel Bodmi, situated on the nursery slopes, is convenient for families and Parkhotel Schoenegg is warmly acclaimed.

In **Mürren** the Hotel Eiger by the railway station opened some luxurious suites last winter to add to its hotel rooms and apartments. The Palace Hotel is central but keeps changing hands. The Alpenruh at the Schilthornbahn end of the village has an excellent restaurant. The

Skiing facts: **Grindelwald**

TOURIST OFFICE
CH-3818 Grindelwald, Bernese Oberland
Tel 41 36 53 12 12
Fax 41 36 53 30 88

THE RESORT
By road Calais 835km
By rail station in resort
By air Zurich 3 hrs
Visitor beds 10,410
Transport ski-bus between Grund, Grindelwald centre and First lift, free with lift pass

THE SKIING
Linked or nearby resorts Wengen (l), Murren (n), Lauterbrunnen (n), Grund (n)
Longest run Lauberhorn-Grund, 13km (red)
Number of lifts 45 in Jungfrau Top Ski region
Total of trails/pistes 200km in Jungfrau Top Ski region (28% easy, 57% intermediate, 15% difficult)
Nursery slopes 2 lifts on Bodmi nursery slopes
Summer skiing none
Snowmaking 20km covered in Grindelwald

LIFT PASSES
Area pass Jungfrau pass (covers Grindelwald, Mürren and Wengen), SF232 for 6 days
Day pass Kleine Scheidegg/Männlichen SF52, First and Mürren SF50

Beginners points tickets
Pensioners no reduction
Credit cards accepted yes

SKI SCHOOLS
Adults SSS, SF192 for 5 days (4 hrs per day)
Private lessons SSS, SF288 per day (5 hrs), SF170 per half-day (2½ hrs)
Snowboarding SSS or Lupo Snowboard School, SF138 for 5 days (2 hrs per day), private lessons SF288 per day, SF170 per half-day
Cross-country SSS, SF192 for 5 days, private lessons SF52 per hr. Loipe 30-35km around the Grindelwald Valley
Other courses telemark, ski-touring, heli-skiing, school for partially sighted, race training
Guiding companies Bergsteigerzentrum Grindelwald

CHILDREN
Lift pass 6-16 yrs, SF116 for 6 days, 17-21 yrs, SF186, free for 5 yrs and under
Ski kindergarten SSS, as below
Ski school SSS, 3-14 yrs, times as adults, SF192 for 5 days
Non-ski kindergarten Children's Club Bodmi, 3 yrs and over, 9.30am-4pm, SF40 per day including lunch

FOOD AND DRINK PRICES
Coffee SF3, glass of wine SF3.60, small beer SF3.50, dish of the day SF14-19

popular Edelweiss is 'convenient, clean, and friendly', the Bellevue-Crystal and the Blumental are both recommended, together with the simpler Belmont.

The village of **Lauterbrunnen** in the valley below is well placed for those who want less expensive accommodation and the chance to try a different area each day, but it does suffer from being hemmed in by cliffs on all sides.

Skiing facts: **Wengen**

TOURIST OFFICE
CH-3823 Wengen, Bernese Oberland
Tel 41 36 55 14 14
Fax 41 36 55 30 60

THE RESORT
By road Calais 835km
By rail station in resort
By air Zurich 3½ hrs
Visitor beds 5,000
Transport traffic-free resort

THE SKIING
Linked or nearby resorts Grindelwald (l),
Grund (l), Lauterbrunnen (n), Mürren (n)
Longest run Mettlen–Grund, 8.5km (blue),
Männlichen, 8.5km (red)
Number of lifts 45 in Jungfrau Top Ski
Region
Total of trails/pistes 200km in Jungfrau
Top Ski region (28% easy, 57% intermedi-
ate, 15% difficult)
Nursery slopes 2 lifts
Summer skiing 1 lift at Jungfraujoch
Snowmaking mobile snow-cannon on
nursery slopes

LIFT PASSES
Area pass Jungfrau pass (covers Wengen,
Grindelwald and Mürren), SF232 for 6 days
Day pass Kleine Scheidegg/Männlichen
SF52

Beginners points tickets
Pensioners no reduction
Credit cards accepted yes

SKI SCHOOLS
Adults SSS, SF234 for 6 days (4 hrs per
day)
Private lessons SSS, SF55 per hr or SF155
per half-day
Snowboarding Swiss Snowboard School,
SF180 for 6 half-days, private lessons SF55
per hr
Cross-country SSS, times and prices on
request. Loipe 17.5km in Lauterbrunnen
Valley
Other courses ski-touring, telemark
Guiding companies through SSS

CHILDREN
Lift pass 50% reduction for 6-16 yrs, 20%
reduction for 17-21 yrs, free for 5 yrs and
under
Ski kindergarten SSS, as below
Ski school SSS, 4-12 yrs, 2 hrs am and pm,
SF330 for 6 days including lunch
Non-ski kindergarten through tourist
office, 3-7 yrs, SF110 for 6 days including
lunch

FOOD AND DRINK PRICES
Coffee SF3.20, glass of wine SF3.20, small
beer SF3.20, dish of the day SF16

Eating in and out

Most restaurants in Wengen are in hotels, but da Mario near Club Med is
strongly recommended for pizzas. Mary's Café offers cheese fondue
accompanied by alp-horn blowing contests. Restaurant Wengen in the
Hotel Hirschen specialises in fondue chinoise. Hotel Victoria-Lauberhorn
has a pizzeria and a crêperie, as well as a more extensive restaurant. The
Felsenkeller in the Hotel Silberhorn is also praised. The Berghaus is
known for its fresh fish and the Bernerhof for fondue and raclette. The
restaurant in the Schonegg Hotel in Wengen is ever popular.

Skiing facts: **Mürren**

TOURIST OFFICE
CH-3825 Mürren, Bernese Oberland
Tel 41 36 55 16 15
Fax 41 36 55 37 69

THE RESORT
By road Calais 940km
By rail station in resort
By air Zurich 3 hrs
Visitor beds 2,000
Transport traffic-free resort

THE SKIING
Linked or nearby resorts Grindelwald (n), Grund (n), Lauterbrunnen (n), Wengen (n)
Longest run Schilthorn–Lauterbrunnen, 15.8km (black/red)
Number of lifts 45 in Jungfrau Top Ski region
Total of trails/pistes 200km in Jungfrau Top Ski region (28% easy, 57% intermediate, 15% difficult)
Nursery slopes 2 runs and 1 lift
Summer skiing none
Snowmaking none

LIFT PASSES
Area pass Jungfrau pass (covers Mürren, Wengen and Grindelwald), SF232 for 6 days
Day pass Mürren SF50
Beginners points tickets

Pensioners no reduction
Credit cards accepted yes

SKI SCHOOLS
Adults SSS, SF123 for 6 half-days
Private lessons SSS, SF110 per half-day
Snowboarding Swiss Snowboard School, SF49 per half-day, private lessons SF110 for 2 hrs
Cross-country lessons not available. Loipe 2km
Other courses heli-skiing, ski-touring
Guiding companies Bergführervermitlung Laüterbrunnen/Wengen/Mürren

CHILDREN
Lift pass 6-16 yrs, SF116 for 6 days, 17-21 yrs, SF186, free for 5 yrs and under
Ski kindergarten none
Ski school SSS, 4 yrs and over, prices and times as adults
Non-ski kindergarten guest kindergarten at the Sports Center, 3 yrs and over, SF32 per day or SF192 for 6 days, both including lunch. 2 yrs old (half-days only), SF16 per half-day or SF192 for 6 half-days, not including lunch

FOOD AND DRINK PRICES
Coffee SF3, glass of wine SF3.60, small beer SF3.60, dish of the day SF15-18

The à la carte Bahnhof restaurant is one of the best places to dine in Grindelwald. Reporters also speak warmly of the Schoenegg and the Schweizerhof. One reader recommends the pizza bar, Chinese and Mexican restaurants in the Hotel Spinne as all having 'great food and fantastic, authentic decor'. The Cava restaurant in the Hotel Derby has 'the best fondue and pasta in town.' The Alte Post by the First lift station has a popular reputation. In Mürren the Eiger Stübli has an excellent, if expensive menu. At the other end of the village, the Alpenruh has a good reputation and the Belmont offers 'excellent value'.

Après-ski

Wengen is not the place for anyone in search of a riotous nightlife, but there is a lot to do during the early evening. The last ski trains are full of families with toboggans going up to Wengernalp for the 4km descent back to the village. Crowds gather in Café Oberland and Mary's Café on the home run, and the ice-bar outside the Hotel Brunner is busy. In the village itself the skating rink is a centre of activity with curling competitions, hockey matches and often dual slalom racing or ski jumping behind the village. Reporters complain that Wengen has no real tea-and-cakes places apart from Café Gruebi, which is 'very cramped'. The Stübli, next to the ski school, is cosy and offers snacks. The Eiger Hotel Stübli is packed out, as is the independent Eiger Bar in the main street. You can swim at the Mountain Beach Club in the Park Hotel Beausite for a small fee.

Younger skiers in Wengen frequent the Tanne bar and the London Pub, with Tiffany's being a rather smarter alternative. Later night entertainment centres around a few bars; Sina's is the most popular (it also has tea-dancing, karaoke and live music). The Carrousel in the Hotel Regina is the best disco in town. In season at weekends, Paradise in the Hotel Belvédère can also be fun.

For such a small village **Mürren** is surprisingly lively after skiing. It has an excellent sports centre with skating, curling, a swimming-pool, sauna and squash courts. The Ballon bar in the Hotel Palace, the Gruebi in the Jungfrau and the Pub in the Belmont are all popular. The Tächi bar in the Hotel Eiger is one of the main meeting places. The Bliemlichäller disco in the Blumental and the Inferno disco in the Palace are packed at weekends and in season.

In **Grindelwald** the Expresso bar draws the young crowd after skiing, while the Gepsi attracts a slightly older clientèle. Later on the Challi bar in the Hotel Kreuz and Post, the Cava in the Derby, and Herby's in the Regina are the most popular. The Plaza Club and the Spyder discos rock on into the small hours.

Childcare

We have pleasing reports of high standards of tuition in all three resorts. Mürren Ski School has come in for considerable criticism for the attitude of its often elderly instructors and outdated methods; all that appears to be in the past under the dynamic leadership of Angélique Feuz. Her teachers apparently speak good English and the standard of instruction is said now to be on a par with the ski schools in both Wengen and Grindelwald. Mürren has little easy skiing and is not suitable for small children. Wengen, on the other hand, has excellent nursery slopes in the centre of the village. The non-ski kindergarten at Wengen is praised. The Mini Club at Club Med is strongly recommended by one reporter: 'My six-year-old daughter loved it and her skiing improved.'

Saas-Fee

Saas-Fee is a compact and charming village in a dead-end valley with the most immediate and stunning glacier views of any resort in the world. Three and a half hours from Geneva, Saas-Fee is a resort unspoilt by weekenders, with a largely Swiss and German clientèle and is well suited to families. It took a bitter debate before the burghers of Saas-Fee agreed to a road from the outside world in 1951. The resort's official history notes: 'No resort can afford not to pay attention to the magical sound of cash.' Now some 57 hotels are mixed among the dark timbers of old chalets and working barns.

■ GOOD POINTS

Car-free resort, breathtaking scenery, alpine charm, extensive ski-touring, good snow record, glacier skiing, excellent nursery slopes

■ BAD POINTS

No public transport, cold and dark for most of winter, limited ski terrain

Still car-free, Saas-Fee has been a pioneer in the development of hi-tech ski lifts. Rejecting the Funitel system, which Verbier and Crans Montana have embraced, Saas-Fee invested instead in a far more sophisticated cableway on the Alpin Express. It also boasts the world's highest underground funicular system, the Metro, among 27 ski lifts serving 100km of pistes. **Saas-Grund** and **Saas-Almagell** are nearby villages with another 11 lifts and 25km of pistes, but not worth the inconvenience of the bus-journey for most skiers. However, if you have your own transport the skiing here adds greatly to what is otherwise a frustratingly limited area.

On the mountain
top 3600m (11,808ft) bottom 1800m (5,904ft)

Saas-Fee is a family resort with excellent nursery slopes, limited but challenging intermediate skiing and exceptional ski-touring possibilities, although expert and off-piste skiing in the resort are constrained by crevasse danger. Mountain access to 3500m is direct from the entry point of the village via Alpin Express and Metro to **Mittelallalin**. From the south of the village the Plattjen gondola rises to the left, and to the right the Spielboden gondola rises to connect with the Längfluh cable car. Despite an hourly capacity of 26,400 skiers in a village of only 9,000 beds, queues have not disappeared.

Alarming as the crevasses of the Fee Glacier appear, skiing is guided along pistes that skirt danger, allowing for none of the wide-ranging cruising found in larger ski arenas. Hannig is a sector of hiking, cross-country and tobogganing pistes served by gondola but banned to skiers.

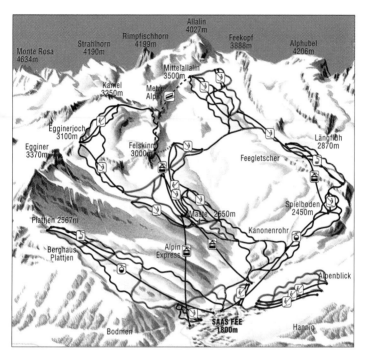

Beginners

Five drag-lifts at the bottom of the mountain make an excellent nursery complex. The Stafelwald and Leeboden lifts are off the path of fast skiers returning to the village. Ambitious beginners will want to try the Weisse Meile, a long blue (easy) run, which cuts across the Feegletscher from 3500m at Mittelallalin over to Längfluh, where the cable car must be taken back to the village. From the Mittaghorn drag, a long blue itinerary with some exciting twists winds right down to the nursery slopes.

Intermediates

There is no solid red (intermediate) run from the top to the bottom of Saas-Fee. Plattjen has only two short, easy reds under the chair-lift. The Egginerjoch piste is more challenging. The Felskinn alongside the Egginer 2 drag-lift is the most direct fall-line skiing. From the top of Saas-Fee at 3500m the Metro piste leads to a series of reds to the bottom of the Kanonenrohr lift, and back to Saas-Fee on blues.

Advanced

The longest sequence of fall-line skiing begins with a steep wall under the Mittelallalin revolving restaurant, following the Alpin, Surprise and Gletscherschuss black (difficult) runs down past the Kanonenrohr lift to the Bach off-piste trail and blue pistes into the village. The Hinterallalin drag-lift is between two steep but short blacks, Chessjen and Hinterallalin, which often offer difficult ice bumps.

Off-piste
Now classified as off-piste, the Weisse Perle, Bach and National are ungroomed runs that are marked on the piste map. More appealing is the climb up the Strahlhorn at 4190m to ski all the way down into Zermatt. It is also possible, without climbing, to cross over the Kamel ridge above the Hinterallalin drag-lift to ski down the Allalingletscher to the lake at Mattmark; a local guide is strongly recommended for this run. Skiing under the ropes to access tempting but crevasse-strewn powder-fields on the Feegletscher will result in confiscation of your lift pass.

■ **WHAT'S NEW**

A second multi-storey car-park

Snowboarding
Paradise Snowboard School is an independent teaching centre, and lessons are also available through the Saas-Fee Ski School. There are two half-pipes, one by the Mittelallalin 1 ski lift, the other near the Maste 4 lift. Powder Tools and Popcorn Snowboardpoint are specialist shops.

Ski schools and guiding
The Swiss Ski School (SSS) in Saas-Fee is a monopoly and suffers from poor organisation and overcrowding in group lessons during peak holiday weeks. Private lessons arc limited to groups of four. The separate mountain guide association, Bergsteigersschule Saastal, has an excellent programme of ski-tours, including ski itineraries down into Zermatt.

Mountain restaurants
The Hannig mountain inn offers Tuesday and Thursday night fondue evenings, which include a toboggan run down a prepared track with the aid of miners' head-lamps. The Britanniahütte is a hike from the pistes but is a classic ski-touring cabin. The rustic Berghaus Plattjen describes its *Rösti* as 'world famous'. The Gletschergrotte has even better 'alpine macaroni'. The world's highest revolving restaurant at Mittelallalin has equally high prices. The views and food over at Längfluh are better.

Off the mountain
The first hotels date from the mid-nineteenth century and traditional chalets remain, hemmed in by glaciers and steep walls, which do not allow much sun in mid-winter. Local families have admitted little outside influence, with the consequence that service is sometimes obdurate and inefficient. Most hotels have been modernised in recent years, giving them a functional look that subtracts from the otherwise cuckoo-clock ambience. There are no buses, electric taxis are not readily available and 'are really becoming dangerous'. It is a 2km walk from the parking area to the ski lifts on the snowfield to the south.

Saas-Fee has received heavy criticism for its 'rip-off factor'. One reporter notes: 'We got that underlying feeling that the main aim of the resort was to part you from your money. There is a car-parking fee, resort tax, everything in the shops is vastly overpriced, and the real howler is the Fee Chatz piste-basher, which conveys you to the Längfluh link with the Metro Alpin for SF6 each time. The ice cave at Mittelallalin would have been nice to see, but again SF6 each deterred us.'

Accommodation
Most hotels are multi-storey with balconies. The leading hotel is the Walliserhof. The Burgener is a small, single-storey, family hotel close to the lifts. Up in the forest is the romantic Landgasthof Hohnegg, which has its own electric taxi service. Apartments in the Allalin, Atlantic and Tobias are bigger than their French counterparts but are a good hike from the lifts. More central is the old palace-style Glacier, now converted into apartments. The Interhome apartments are also recommended.

Eating in and out
The Fletschorn Waldhotel is rated as one of Switzerland's better restaurants. The Hofsaal in the Schweizerhof is recommended for fish and the Cheminée for *flambées*. The Mandarain, which serves Thai food, and El Palatino with its Mexican food, are the only escape from *Rösti*, fondue, raclette and grilled meats. The best of the latter is found at the Belmont, Käse Keller and Schäferstube. Trattoria Mamma-mia and Boccalino have reasonable pizzas.

Après-ski

■ OTHER SPORTS
Skating, curling, ice hockey, indoor tennis, swimming, tobogganing, badminton

The Crazy Night is the hippest techno venue. John's Pub, in the Metropol Hotel, tries for an English ambience, and the VIP Bar (also in the Metropol) goes in for cocktails at higher prices. Rowdy drinking is frequent at Nesti's Ski Bar and the Go-Inn. The Sissy Bar and Pic-Pic are popular and comfortable. The Why-not pub is loud and raucous.

Childcare
The ski school accepts children from five years old. The Bären-Klub in the Hotel Garni Berghof takes children from two-and-a-half years and offers babysitting in the evening. The Alphubel and Schweizerhof hotels organise childminding for their guests, and the Hotel Dom has an unsupervised playroom.

Linked or nearby resorts

Saas-Grund 1559m (5,114ft)
Saas-Grund is a sunny resort strung out along the valley road towards Saas-Almagell, and is a ten-minute ride by free post-bus from Saas-Fee.

Skiing facts: **Saas-Fee**

TOURIST OFFICE
CH-3906 Saas-Fee, Valais
Tel 41 28 57 14 57
Fax 41 28 57 18 60

THE RESORT
By road Calais 1072km
By rail Visp 27km, buses from station
By air Geneva or Zurich, 3½ hrs
Visitor beds 9,000
Transport traffic-free village; ski-bus service SF25 for 6 days, children SF10 for 6 days

THE SKIING
Linked or nearby resorts Saas-Almagell (n), Saas-Balen (n), Saas-Grund (n), Riederalp (n), Zermatt (n), Crans Montana (n)
Longest run Mittelallalin-Felskinn-Saas-Fee, 14km (red)
Number of lifts 27 in Saas-Fee, 38 including Saas-Grund and Saas-Almagell
Total of trails/pistes 100km (50% easy, 25% intermediate, 25% difficult)
Nursery slopes 6 runs and 5 lifts
Summer skiing 20km of runs and 3 lifts on Feegletscher
Snowmaking 60,000m^2 covered by 7 snow-cannon

LIFT PASSES
Area pass SF255 for 6 days
Day pass SF55

Beginners SF90 for 6 days, using 5 village lifts only
Pensioners 10% reduction for 62 yrs and over
Credit cards accepted yes

SKI SCHOOLS
Adults SSS, 9.45-11.45am and 1.30-3.30pm, SF175 for 5 days
Private lessons SF52 per hr
Snowboarding SSS, SF156 for 5 half-days, private lessons SF52 per hr. Also Paradise Snowboard School, details on application
Cross-country SSS, as regular ski lessons. Loipe 26km in Saas Valley
Other courses telemark, ski-touring
Guiding companies Bergsteigersschule Saastal

CHILDREN
Lift pass 6-16 yrs, SF150 for 6 days, free for 5 yrs and under (accompanied by adult)
Ski kindergarten SSS, 5-12 yrs, 9.45am-5pm, SF175 for 5 days
Ski school SSS, 5-12 yrs, 9.45-11.45am and 1.30-3.30pm, SF175 for 5 days
Non-ski kindergarten Hotel Garni Berghof Bären-Klub, 2½-6 yrs, SF60 per day including lunch

FOOD AND DRINK PRICES
Coffee SF3.20 , glass of house wine SF3.20, small beer SF3.60, dish of the day SF26

The skiing, which is mainly suited to intermediates and off-piste enthusiasts, is at **Kreuzboden** at 2400m and is reached by gondola. There is a nursery slope and some gentle runs here, as well as a large mountain restaurant.

Most of the accommodation is in chalets, apartments and small hotels, including the Roby. The village of Saas-Almagell is slightly higher at 1672m and has its own small ski area.

St Moritz

ALTITUDE 1800m (5,904ft)

St Moritz is an urban resort on two levels, above and along the shores of a fir-lined lake in Switzerland's most scenic valley. Four hours from Zurich, St Moritz is where winter holidays were invented — by the British. Twice host to the Winter Olympics, St Moritz sets the world standard for luxury and alpine indulgence. Polo, golf and a number of exotic horse-racing events take place throughout the winter on the frozen lake; the 'season' ends abruptly in February. The Cresta Run, still closed to women, has been the ultimate test of male machismo for more than a hundred years. Among a truly international clientèle, dominated by Germans, the British have all but disappeared in these fraught financial times.

■ GOOD POINTS
Exceptional climate, unparalleled choice of winter sports, wealth of grand hotels and fine dining, good snow record, extensive snowmaking

■ BAD POINTS
Lift queues, skiing sectors widely dispersed, expensive accommodation and dining, lack of architectural charm

St Moritz is a winter-sports resort not just a ski area. Warmed by the Engadine sun and vitalised by the local 'Champagne climate', the first visitors in 1864 took to sledging. Ice-skating, curling, bob-sledding, golf and horse-riding on ice all had their European premiers in St Moritz.

Today, the Engadine regional ski pass covers 60 lifts and 350km of pistes from one end of the valley to the other. **Celerina** and **Pontresina** are outlying villages with ski lifts, as are **Silvaplana** and **Sils Maria**. **Dorf** is the name used for St Moritz proper and **Bad** is down on the lake below.

On the mountain
top 3303m (10,834ft) bottom 1720m (5,642ft)
Not many skiers in St Moritz are fanatics. However, despite its wide range of skiing, it is not the ideal resort in which to learn. There are sunny nursery slopes, abundant red (intermediate) runs and adequate expert and off-piste routes scattered around the dozen lifts rising from the valley floor. The region divides into the sectors of **Corviglia**, **Corvatsch** and **Diavolezza-Lagalp**. From St Moritz itself, the home mountain is Corviglia, accessed by a funicular from the centre of town with skiing up to 3057m at Piz Nair. Celerina and Bad also access the mostly red runs of Corviglia. Corvatsch, on the other side of the valley, has more expert terrain, accessed from Sils Maria and **Surlej**.

Diavolezza and Lagalp, both at nearly 3000m, are much further down the valley and are reached by train or bus. Skiing here is less crowded and more challenging.

Queues of more than an hour at Corvatsch are made more bearable by a system of allocating reservations. A number of lifts, in particular Piz Nair, have queues longer than half an hour. Snowmaking ensures skiing on six Corviglia pistes, to the bottom of Corvatsch at Surlej and from top to bottom of Diavolezza.

Beginners

Crucial for ski-to-lunch addicts is the long, gentle blue (easy) run down from the Marmite on Corviglia through the woods back into St Moritz or all the way across to the cable car at Bad. Every sector has some blue runs. The Furtschellas drag-lifts go up to blue runs at 2800m above Sils Maria, but beginners will have to ride the cable car down.

Intermediates

Corvatsch has the highest skiing and links with even more reds on **Furtschellas**, via the Curtinella drag-lift. South-facing Corviglia has a number of flattering reds, though moving over into the Val Schlattain leads to steeper terrain. The red under the Piz Grisch chair always has excellent snow. However, the best intermediate skiing, with the least crowds, is out of St Moritz, in the Lagalb sector at nearly 3000m.

Advanced

The black (difficult) Hahnensee run from the top of Corvatsch at 3451m winds over open snowfields and into the woods at the edge of Bad; it provides 12km of non-stop skiing down 1600 vertical metres. At Diavolezza, the Schwarzer Hang black piste drops through bands of rock for some good, steep skiing down on to the Bernina black run all the way to the bottom.

Off-piste

The steep face of Piz Nair provides incredible thrills when there is enough powder snow to cover the sheer rock. One of the classic off-piste routes in the Alps is the long glacier itinerary from the top of Diavolezza, around and over crevasses to Morteratsch in the forest.

Snowboarding

Snowboarding is popular in St Moritz, not least because the 1994 Snowboarding World Cup took place here. At Corviglia (accessed by the Munt da San Murezzan chair-lift) there is a snowboard park with a half-pipe and obstacle course. Snowboard School St Moritz offers lessons, as does The Wave, which is part of the ski school at Suvretta.

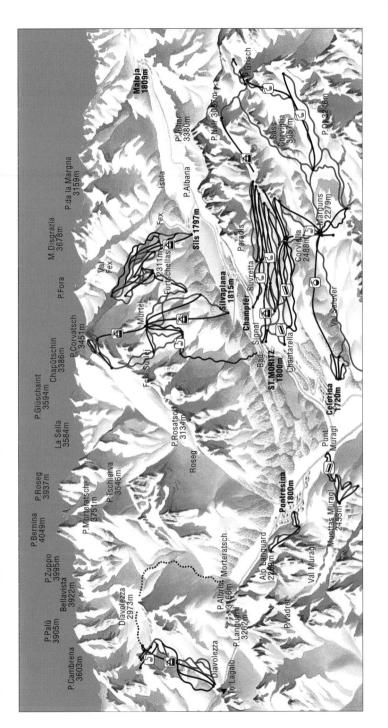

Cross-country

The frozen lakes of St Moritz make this one of the most varied and beautiful cross-country areas in the Alps. Serious Langlaufers would be ideally placed to stay in Bad as this is where the tracks are based. The 42km Engadine Marathon is held here each season and attracts thousands of entrants.

Ski schools and guiding

The St Moritz and Suvretta ski schools are both branches of the SSS. Together they employ a total of 185 instructors, many of whom seem to consider teaching a form of escort service, with paid lunch included. The Palace Hotel has its own school, and an independent grouping, the Privat Ski Lehrers, is now in operation. Off-piste guiding is not widely in demand by the St Moritz clientèle.

Mountain restaurants

Renowned amongst skiers and gourmets alike the Marmite on Corviglia has been radically rebuilt. Reservations must be made, either for the noon or 2pm sitting. Reto Mathis, whose father, Hartly, was the first man to bring haute cuisine to the high mountains, counts caviar and truffles by the kilo. However, his daily specials in the brasserie or self-service sections are always budget priced.

Also on the Corviglia mountain, the Skihütte Alpina is great for pasta and rustic charm. Cheese specialities are best at the Piz Nair.

Off the mountain

Since the beginning of tourism here in 1864 St Moritz has been a hotel town. No other resort has so many luxury hotels — 63 per cent are four- or five-star rated. The urban architecture is bland at best. St Moritz's beauty lies not in the views of the resort itself but in the views from it. The resort is small enough to walk around, although most hotels have shuttle vans, and buses and trains provide adequate public transport to all regions. Designer boutiques are as thick as furs but old-fashioned shops like Ebneter and Biel still sell hand embroidery and silk ties with English hunting motifs.

Accommodation

The Palace Hotel, with its own ski school and grotesque tower, is the most famous of the five-stars. The pastel blocks of the Kulm are preferred by the Cresta Run crowd. Less central, the Suvretta House attracts older, European money. The Carlton has the feel of an old country house. The four-star Schweizerhof and Steffani hotels, both with active après-ski, are downtown and affordable.

Eating in and out

Hanselmann's, in the town centre, is over 100 years old and has coffee, pastries and ice cream to die for. Lunch at the Chesa Veglia, an archi-

Skiing facts: **St Moritz**

TOURIST OFFICE
CH-7500 St Moritz, Graubunden
Tel 41 82 33147
Fax 41 82 32952

THE RESORT
By road Calais 1047km
By rail station in resort
By air Zurich 4 hrs
Visitor beds 13,655
Transport free ski-bus with lift pass

THE SKIING
Linked or nearby resorts Celerina (l),
Champfèr (n), Pontresina (n), Samadan
(n), Sils Maria (l), Silvaplana (l), Surlej (l),
Zuos (n)
Longest run Piz Nair-Celerina, 7km
(black/red)
Number of lifts 23 in St Moritz, 60 in linked
area
Total of trails/pistes 80km in St Moritz
(25% easy, 56% intermediate, 19%
difficult). 350km in linked area
Nursery slopes 4 lifts in St Moritz, 7 in
linked area
Summer skiing June-July on Diavolezza
Glacier
Snowmaking 22 hectares covered

LIFT PASSES
Area pass Upper Engadine (covers St
Moritz, Celerina, Silvaplana, Pontresina,
Sils), SF258 for 6 days including a day's
skiing in Samnaun and Livigno
Day pass Corviglia SF48, linked area
SF51
Beginners points tickets
Pensioners no reductions

Credit cards accepted yes

SKI SCHOOLS
Adults St Moritz, 10am-midday and 1.30-
3.30pm, SF230 for 6 days. Suvretta, 10am-
midday and 2-4pm, SF220 for 5 out of 6
days
Private lessons St Moritz SF80 for $1\frac{1}{4}$ hrs,
Suvretta SF80 per hr
Snowboarding St Moritz Snowboard
School, 10am-midday and 1.30-3.30pm,
SF220 for 5 days, private lessons as regular
ski school. The Wave Snowboard School,
SF220 for 5 days
Cross-country St Moritz, SF125 for 5 half-
days. Loipe 150km in Upper Engadine
Other courses off-piste, competition,
freestyle, slalom, delta, telemark,
heli-skiing
Guiding companies The St Moritz
Experience

CHILDREN
Lift pass Upper Engadine, 6-15 yrs, SF258
for 6 days
Ski kindergarten St Moritz Ski School, 4
yrs and over, 10am-3pm, SF230 for 6 days
Ski school St Moritz Ski School, prices,
times and ages as above. Suvretta Ski
School, SF220 for 6 days. All Activities
Agency, details on request
Non-ski kindergarten Parkhotel Kurhaus
SF29 per day, Hotel Carlton SF22 per day,
Hotel Schweizerhof SF34 per day. All 3 yrs
and over, 9am-5pm including lunch

FOOD AND DRINK PRICES
Coffee, SF3.40-4.50, glass of wine SF5-7,
small beer SF3.60-5.50, dish of the day

tectural museum-piece owned by the Palace, is not expensive compared with dinner. All the top hotel restaurants require suit and tie. Out in Celerina Peter Graber's beef marinated in hay and herbs, served at the Stuvetta Veglia, is a local legend.

■ OTHER SPORTS

Skating, curling, horse-racing, polo, cricket and golf on the frozen lake, swimming, parapente, Cresta Run, Olympic bob-run, hot air ballooning, hang-gliding, winter walks, climbing wall, indoor tennis and squash, tobogganing

Après-ski

At the Kings Club, in the Palace, an orchestra plays until 4am (jacket and tie required). In the Stübli at the Schweizerhof dancing on rough plank tables continues until 2am; after 10pm it is so crowded that you could not possibly fall off the tables. The Stübli across the street in the Steffani is less popular than the Vivai disco in the same hotel. Muli Bar has country and western music. Bobby's Bar is for the under 20s.

Childcare

The kindergarten in the Carlton, Schweizerhof and Park Hotel all accept children over three years old on a daily basis, lunch included. The Park Hotel is down in Bad next to the cross-country track. The Suvretta and St Moritz ski schools accept children over four years and for regular lessons. The St Moritz ski school will collect children from their hotels in the morning.

Linked or nearby resorts

Celerina 1720m (5,643ft)

Village atmosphere, old stone-houses painted with the local *grafitto* designs and ski access to Corviglia make Celerina a quiet alternative. Chesa Rosatsch is a 350-year-old inn now run by a British couple.

TOURIST OFFICE
Tel 41 82 33966
Fax 41 82 38666

Pontresina 1800m (5,904ft)

With no big lifts of its own Pontresina is about mid-way between the out-lying Diavolezza sector and Corviglia. It has good indoor-sports facilities and a loyal clientèle of Italian and German families. Kochendorfer's Albris is an inexpensive hotel with its own bakery and chocolate shop.

TOURIST OFFICE
Tel 41 82 66488
Fax 41 82 67996

Verbier

ALTITUDE 1500m (4,920ft)

Verbier is Switzerland's best resort for range and ruggedness of skiing. Only 90 minutes from Geneva (mostly by motorway) the resort caters primarily for the Swiss (52 per cent) who own holiday apartments or rent them for the winter season. The resort is set on a high plateau with an excellent sunshine record. Its chalets have sprawled unchecked by development restrictions, making for an abundance of self-catered and chalet-party accommodation. Most buildings are wood-clad and few blocks are taller than six storeys. There is no car-free area or evening bus service.

The resort has tried desperately to change its mass-market image, building a vertical golf course on the ski slopes and dropping its 'smiling at the sun' slogan in favour of the unambiguous 'Le Must des vacances' aimed at the Cartier crowd. British visitors have diminished from 18 per cent in 1987 to around 9 per cent and their role as the most important foreign visitors has been taken over by the Germans.

■ GOOD POINTS

Excellent sunshine record, extensive off-piste and snowboarding terrain, generous family lift pass reductions, numerous unspoilt satellites, beautiful mountain views

■ BAD POINTS

Bottleneck queues, poor resort information, overcrowded pistes, inadequate parking, limited snowmaking

Verbier was one of Switzerland's last resorts to be developed. Its first lift was a wooden sledge pulled 200m uphill by a diesel engine. Since 1946, the resort has linked with neighbouring resorts in **Thyon**, **Veysonnaz** and **Nendaz** to form the **Four Valleys** network, with an estimated 400km of piste and 100 lifts on the same ski pass.

In 1987 Switzerland's largest cable car, the 150-person Jumbo, was inaugurated by occasional resident Diana Ross. Last winter (1994–5) Verbier opened the Funispace (30-person hi-tech télécabine system), virtually eliminating queues at the Ruinettes mid-station. However, peak-period queues at the Tortin 'black hole' of one to two hours duration persist. Aside from the satellite resorts in the Four Valleys, Verbier's lift pass extends to the small family areas of **Bruson** and **Champex-Lac**. Vichères, Fouly and even Super St Bernard on the Italian border are also on the pass, with payment of a small supplement. Although Verbier's weekly ski pass is the most expensive in Europe, prices for families with children under 16 are surprisingly moderate.

Verbier has been strongly criticised by the Guide in the past, but there are positive signs that the authorities are taking steps to avoid further market erosion.

On the mountain
top 3330m (10,925ft) bottom 1500m (4,920ft)

Verbier's Four Valleys lift pass is a ticket to a smorgasbord of slopes, some of which are so far-flung that getting back before closing time requires careful planning. With guidance, skiers of every calibre will find suitable blue (easy), red (intermediate) and black (difficult) pistes. It takes an expert, however, to appreciate the resort's vast off-piste potential.

From Verbier itself there are two mountains from which to choose. Savoleyres, towards the top of the village, is a dated four-person gondola, which carries intermediates up to a ridge at 2354m; there is skiing back towards the south on sunny slopes as well as over the top on to better snow down to another gondola station in Tzoumaz.

The **Medran** lift complex, a five-minute walk from the central square, is the main entry point for the Four Valleys and the best skiing. Medran consists of a fast six-person gondola, which ends at the Ruinettes mid-station. There is a chair-lift at Medran, which runs only at peak periods. The old Medran four-person gondola, which runs through from the valley floor at Le Châble, past the mid-station and all the way to **Attelas** at 2727m, is now closed to access from Verbier.

Medran queues, once legendary, are now seldom more than half-an-hour. From the mid-station at Ruinettes skiers have a choice of chair-lifts, or at Ruinettes itself they can board the essentially queue-free 30-person Funispace gondola to access Attelas. From here, the sectors of Lac des Vaux and La Chaux are skiable. Further lifts are required to reach the Mont Gelé, Tortin, Gentianes and Mont-Fort sectors.

Beginners
Verbier has no true beginner runs, though the baby slope at Moulins and the blue at Esserts are easy training grounds for the most inexperienced skier. The Rouge, marked as a blue, really is at least a red, thanks to drop-offs bulldozed on to the formerly easy slope when it was made into a golf course. Beginners with a taste for the big mountain can ski blues down to the Jumbo cable car and ride up to a flat blue piste on the glacier at **Gentianes**.

Intermediates
The main red route down from Attelas to Medran, some 700m of vertical, is densely populated. From the bottom of the Mayentzet chair the only way back to Medran is along a winding road. Pedestrians walking dogs, children on sledges and homeward-bound racers all share this path. The Savoleyres sector offers intermediates more scope, but the easy road back from Savoleyres to Medran via Carrefour is frequently closed because of serious avalanche danger, and there is no pisted route back to the bottom of the Savoleyres lift station.

La Chaux sector, home of the Jumbo, is served by two chair-lifts and offers easy undulating terrain. The spring-snow skiing here is superb, although in the late afternoon the chairs are clogged with skiers returning from Mont-Fort.

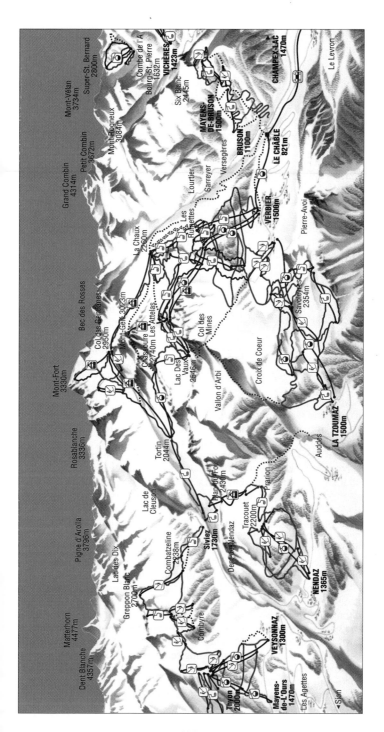

Dent Blanche
4357m

Matterhorn
4477m

Pigne d'Arolla
3796m

Rosablanche
3336m

Mont-Fort
3330m

Bec des Rosses

Grand Combin
4314m

Petit Combin
3672m

Mont-Rogneux
3084m

Mont-Vélan
3734m

Super-St. Bernard
2800m

Combe de l'A

Bourg-St. Pierre
1632m

Six Blanc
2445m

VICHÈRES
1423m

CHAMPEX-LAC
1470m

Le Levron

MAYENS-
DE-BRUSON
1500m

BRUSON
1100m

LE CHÂBLE
821m

Versegères

Lourtier

Sarreyer

VERBIER
1500m

Pierre-Avoi

Les Ruinettes

la Chaux
2260m

Col des Gentianes
2950m

Mont-Gelé 3023m

Chassoure

Les Attelas

Col des
Mines

Mont-Fort
3330m

Lac Des
Vaux
2546m

Croix de Cœur

Savoleyres
2354m

Vallon d'Arbi

Tortin
2044m

LA TZOUMAZ
1500m

Auddes

Lac de
Cleuson

Plan du Fou
2430m

Prarion

Tracouet
2200m

Siviez
1730m

Combatzeline
2438m

Dent-de-Nendaz

Lac des Dix

Greppon Blanc
2700m

Combyre

NENDAZ
1365m

VEYSONNAZ
1300m

Thyon
2000m

Mayens-
de-l'Ours
1470m

Les Agettes

◄ Sion

Bruson and Champex, separate resorts on the Verbier lift ticket, are far less crowded and ideally suited to an intermediate or family day out. The Four Valley resorts contain a wealth of red runs, but it is impossible to reach the **Siviez** starting point without descending either Tortin or Gentianes, both graded beyond black as 'ski itineraries'.

Advanced

Verbier officially marks only a handful of runs as black. The most challenging is the steep bump-run down Mont-Fort. In icy conditions this can be lethal, but usually it is merely irritating. Frightened skiers tend to go across rather than down, turning the bumps into metre-deep trenches. The black from Attelas to Carrefour, once a racecourse, is arguably easier than the reds next to it in so far as it has fewer skiers threatening collisions.

Off-piste

Verbier's off-piste is divided into routes marked on the piste map as itineraries and unmapped areas (like Stairway to Heaven and Hidden Valley), which nonetheless are secrets known to thousands. Mapped itineraries are routinely bombed by avalanche-control teams; they may have cursory markings, but are not patrolled. Many of these routes, like Tortin and Gentianes, are really pistes that have been reclassified from black. Unmapped off-piste routes, like Cleuson, are true *ski sauvage*, but may be trafficked by scores of skiers per weekend.

Tortin is a notorious bump-run, which is glorious in powder. The traverse across the top of Tortin leads to another bowl, Col de Mouche, which is less skied out. Gentianes is a heavily travelled bowl under the eponymous cable car, negotiable by most intermediates: spring snow to the right, bumps in the middle. The Vallon d'Arbi and Col des Mines are both reached by a traverse at the bottom of Lac des Vaux. When the warning rope is down it means that a bulldozer has made this traverse into a roadway with high walls. Otherwise, it can be a dangerously narrow ledge of ice. Arbi is an entire valley without pistes or lifts, which usually retains powder in the trees on the skier's left.

The front face of Mont Gelé, under the cable car, is awkward to access. After side-stepping over rocks, however, the shaded powder in a choice of couloirs is worthwhile. The best and longest route in Verbier is the back of Mont-Fort, down to the Cleuson dam and through trees to Siviez. It would be unwise to explore here without a local guide.

Verbier falsely advertises a skiing range from 3330m to 800m at Le Châble. In fact, this route is very rarely advisable. Wire fences, stone terraces and water standpipes are only some of the hazards. One reporter skied into a fountain and another broke his skis. There is almost never enough snow all the way to the bottom.

Snowboarding

Verbier is a boarder's dream, and shredders are often the first off-piste. However, the snowboard park at La Chaux has lost its half-pipe, and the jumps there are lacklustre. In summer there is a snowboard camp at Mont-Fort. The best range of boards for hire is at Xtreme. No Bounds is another speciality shop, affiliated with the Swiss Snowboard School, the only place to go for lessons.

Ski schools and guiding

The Swiss Ski School (ESS) is a lottery. Teaching expertise and concern for the class vary erratically. More than half the school's 170 red jackets are worn by 'auxiliary' teachers. These are students or ski bums with no qualifications, who work on a temporary basis. Private lessons are better. The rival Ecole de Ski Fantastique specialises in off-piste teaching and guiding. Half of its 40 members are qualified mountain guides and conduct all off-piste parties. Both schools offer heli-skiing and ski-touring. Fantastique also offers ice-waterfall climbing.

Mountain restaurants

Chez Dany is the favourite lounging and lunching spot; it is reached on skis down a narrow trail from the bottom of the Fontanays chair on an officially classified off-piste itinerary. Cabin Mont-Fort, one of the Haute Route waystations, has a more limited menu but better views and higher ski credibility. The Marmotte, on Savoleyres, has its own rope-tow, but access back to Verbier is often closed by avalanche risk.

The cafeteria at Ruinettes has Verbier's best pastries, and a good waiter-service restaurant upstairs. The two Attelas lift station eateries have little but locale to offer. The worst place of all to eat is at La Chaux, where orders are blared out incessantly over a loudspeaker. The ramshackle wood cafeteria at Gentianes does a good sausage and *frites*. Watch out everywhere on Verbier terraces for Swedish and other ski bums 'grazing' leftovers.

Off the mountain

Driving in Verbier is difficult and parking is impossible. The roundabout in the central square is highly hazardous, since no one seems to understand who has right of way. Parking at the main Medran lift station adds another £5 per day to a lift ticket. The free buses are overcrowded and prone to delays caused by other traffic. Walking from the main square to Medran, pedestrians are forced on to the roadway, both by illegally parked cars and by the absence of any sidewalk.

Thanks to its hardcore clientèle, Verbier has the best ski shops in the Alps. British-owned Mountain Air is headquarters for off-piste, telemark and the latest boot fitting technology. Number One has the best ski tuning.

Accommodation

Visitors to Verbier stay mainly in chalets and self-catered apartments.

There are only 1,500 hotel beds for peak-season crowds of 30,000 skiers. The majority of visitors, the Swiss, actually own apartments or rent them for the season. There is no five-star hotel in Verbier. The Rosalp, below the Medran lift station, is Verbier's poshest hotel and only serious restaurant, but some of its new rooms and suites are said to be 'rather over-the-top'. The Vanessa is the brightest of the four-stars. The Hotel Verbier in the main square is spartan in style but popular with long-time visitors. The most appealing hotel is the Rois Mages, five floors of light pine tucked away down a residential side street not far from the church.

■ **OTHER SPORTS**

Swimming, squash, climbing wall, indoor tennis and golf, hang-gliding, ice-climbing, parapente, skating, winter walks

Eating in and out

Aside from the Rosalp, with its kitchens presided over by celebrity chef Roland Pierroz, Verbier's restaurants seem more interested in collecting cash than dishing out decent food. The Vieux Verbier by the Medran lifts is popular, but two reporters were ill after eating the salmon pasta. The Caveau cheese den, next to the tourist office, served one correspondent a *croûte champignon*, which 'looked and tasted like sliced cheese and tinned mushrooms on burnt toast'.

The Verluisant at Savoleyres has an honest bourgeois menu. The Relais de Neige at Medran is the best in Verbier for inexpensive eating. For pizzas the Borsalino and Fer à Cheval both beat Al Capone. For fast food, Harold's has burgers. Jesse's Juice Bar has an exotic mix of Californian-Mediterranean sandwiches. Verbier's 'in' place to meet at breakfast (English and served all day) is the Offshore, right next to the Medran lifts and decorated with surf boards and a pink VW Beetle.

Après-ski

The Farm Club, once frequented nightly by Fergie before her marriage, is still the most sophisticated and expensive nightclub in town. However, it is not as popular as in its heyday, and now has serious competition. The Tara is more fashionable with the in-crowd and Marshall's attracts a younger clientèle. The still younger frequent Big Ben and the older generation lounge contentedly in Jacky's Bar in the Grand Combin. Disco-goers on a budget flock to the Scotch.

The Pub Mont-Fort, behind Medran, is where ski bums line up for a 'cement mixer', a shot of aquavit from the freezer before the bartender issues a helmet and smashes your head against the wall. Right after skiing the Farinet features a live rock band. The Fer à Cheval is an important rendezvous spot at all hours.

Childcare

The Schtroumpfs non-ski kindergarten accepts youngsters between five months and three years old for a whole or half-day, lunch included. The Kids Club, run by the ESS, has now moved to the Moulins nursery area. We have good reports of the Club, which takes children from 3 to 10 years old and has its own lift. We have mixed reports of Tip Top underneath the tourist office, which takes children from 2 to 5 years old.

Linked or nearby resorts

Bruson 1100m (3,609ft)

No accommodation, but Bruson has off-piste tree-line skiing, which rates alongside Canadian helicopter terrain. It is reached within 15 minutes by free buses from Le Châble train station. Bruson rarely has even the shortest queue on its shaded north-facing steeps when Verbier is broiling in weekending Genevans fighting for a thin line of powder.

Bruson provides adequate piste-skiing on reds and blues, but the challenges are limited. Verbier's piste map shows several proposed lifts in Bruson, including a gondola from the valley. However, ecologists argue convincingly that none of these will ever be built.

TOURIST OFFICE
Tel *as Verbier*

Champex-Lac 1470m (4,823ft)

Champex is a retreat from resort hassles and is the most scenic of Verbier's satellites. An hour's drive by car or an awkward train and bus journey from Le Châble, Champex is lushly forested and graced by a small frozen lake. Two chair-lifts access very easy skiing along a forest road from the top, inexplicably marked as intermediate terrain. Experts will adore the steep face, with powder and bumps, right down the open fall-line. Weeks after Verbier is tracked out, powder remains untouched in Champex. The Belvedere restaurant, 100m off to the right of the village entrance, offers much more in haute cuisine, at a third of the price, than anywhere in Verbier.

TOURIST OFFICE
Tel *as Verbier*

Nendaz 1365m (4,478ft)

This ugly and inconvenient resort is at a dead-end of the Four Valleys. Most skiers, anxious to get to the Verbier sector, opt to take the bus to Siviez (formerly Haute Nendaz) to connect with the region's only high-speed quad-chair and on through Tortin to Gentianes and Mont-Fort.

TOURIST OFFICE
Tel 41 27 881444
Fax 41 27 883900

Siviez 1730m (5,676ft)

This sunny resort is nothing more than a serviceable cluster of new concrete apartments, a complex of shops and a swimming-pool. Germans

Skiing facts: **Verbier**

TOURIST OFFICE
CH-1936 Verbier, Valais
Tel 41 26 316222
Fax 41 26 313272

THE RESORT
By road Calais 998km
By rail Le Châble 15 mins
By air Geneva 1½ hrs
Visitor beds 25,000
Transport free ski-bus

THE SKIING
Linked or nearby resorts Bruson (n),
Champex-Lac (n), Fouly (n), Nendaz (l),
Super St Bernard (n), La Tzoumaz (l), Thyon
(l), Veysonnaz (l), Vichères (n)
Longest run Mont-Fort to Verbier, 8km
(red/blue)
Number of lifts 100 in area
Total of trails/pistes 400km in area
(39% easy, 43% intermediate,
18% difficult)
Nursery slopes 3 slopes with 3 lifts
Summer skiing 2 lifts, open from end of
June to mid-August
Snowmaking 30km covered in area

LIFT PASSES
Area pass (covers 4 Valleys) SF297 for
6 days
Day pass SF59
Beginners no free lifts

Pensioners 65 yrs and over, SF178
Credit cards accepted yes

SKI SCHOOLS
Adults ESS, 9.15-11.45am and 2.10-
4.30pm, SF297 for 6 days
Private lessons ESS, SF55 per hr, Ecole de
Ski Fantastique, SF160 for a half-day,
SF300 per day
Snowboarding ESS, 9.45am-12pm, SF27
Cross-country ESS and Ecole du Ski
Fantastique, prices and times on request.
Loipe 9km in Verbier, 43km in 4 Valleys
Other courses off-piste, telemark,
heli-skiing, ski safari
Guiding companies ESS and Ecole du Ski
Fantastique

CHILDREN
Lift pass 5 yrs and under SF89, 6-16 yrs
SF178 for 6 days
Ski kindergarten ESS Kids Club, 3-10 yrs,
8.30am-5pm, SF275 for 6 days including
lunch
Ski school ESS Kids Club (see above)
Non-ski kindergarten Chez les
Schtroumpfs, 7 yrs and under, SF248 for 6
days (54 hrs). Tip Top, 2-5 yrs, SF300 for 6
days (51 hrs), both including lunch

FOOD AND DRINK PRICES
Coffee SF3, glass of wine, SF2.8, small
beer, SF3.50-4, dish of the day SF15-20

looking to cut down Verbier prices have made it a home of their own.
Tactically, there is no faster way to the Four Valleys highspot, Mont-
Fort, than the jump-start from Siviez's quad-chair. However, after 11am
mind-numbing queues at Tortin, caused by skiers coming from Verbier,
shut down any advantage.

TOURIST OFFICE
Tel as Nendaz

Villars-sur-Ollon

ALTITUDE 1300m (4,264ft)

Villars has always been considered a quiet and traditional family ski-resort, and has had a strong international following even before the railway wound its way up in 1901 to what is a sunny balcony above the Ollon Valley. So many Anglo-Saxon visitors have come over the years to this mountain retreat that in 1883 they even built their own English church. It is still the Sunday focal point for members of the extensive British community who have holiday or retirement homes here.

Many of them have taken advantage of the local cantonal regulation allowing foreigners to buy property only in this part of Switzerland. The church's original wooded setting was first dwarfed by the Edwardian magnificence of the Palace Hotel. Then, sadly, the owners of this once great alpine hostelry sold out to the mass market in the ski boom of the 1960s. Today's worshippers pass through a porchway fronted by the giant kitchen waste-bins of what became a giant Club Med.

> ■ **GOOD POINTS**
>
> Attractive scenery, short airport transfer, facilities for family skiing, wide and sunny slopes, easy resort access
>
> ■ **BAD POINTS**
>
> Lack of tough runs, no artificial snowmaking, limited après-ski

The village is set on a through-road with chalets and hotels scattered along it. The modern additions blend in well with the older buildings and there are a number of chalets of ornate and original design.

Villars has an impressive amount of intermediate skiing through pine forests and over undulating summer pastures, which provide a variety of terrain. It is linked directly to the neighbouring glacial resort of **Les Diablerets** over the 1949m Tête du Meilleret, but the connection is sometimes closed owing to bad weather or lack of snow. Together, the two areas provide 120km of terrain served by 45 lifts, which is best suited to parallel skiers who prefer the individuality of a small resort with manageable skiing rather than an endless, impersonal ski circus. A car is a mixed blessing: Les Diablerets can be reached by road when the skiable connection is closed, as can **Gstaad** and **Verbier**; however, local parking restrictions make movements around town difficult.

On the mountain
top 2120m (6,954ft) bottom 1128m (3,700ft)

The quickest access to **Bretaye**, the hub of the ski area at 1800m, is by the Roc d'Orsay gondola, which is a long walk or a short bus-ride from the centre of town. Alternatively, you can take the painfully slow but wonderfully scenic railway from the main station. Another gondola from the nearby village of **Barboleusaz** also feeds into the system. Bretaye is the major crossroads for the lifts and runs, which makes for some congestion. It does, however, have the advantage of being the main meeting point for skiers of all standards and the ski schools.

The pistes from Roc d'Orsay and Bretaye go down to the village, the latter linking with the wide and sunny slopes to La Rasse at 1350m. The chair from here to Chaux de Conches opens up some good blue (easy) and red (intermediate) runs from its mid-station, and a black (difficult) mogul field on the upper part. The drag-lifts from La Rasse link with the separate, intermediate-level skiing on Les Chaux. The sunny run from Les Chaux to the tiny village of **Les Fracherets** loses its snow early, as does the run down to the bottom of the gondola at Barboleusaz.

The Chaux des Conches chair provides the sometimes elusive link to Les Diablerets. The run is graded black because of the steep and ungroomed mogul field near the top. However, most of it is easy blue motorway; indeed the majority of the Villars-Les Diablerets pistes vary between blue and red and are all on north-facing slopes through the trees.

Les Diablerets Glacier is actually part of Gstaad's ski area, although it can be approached either on the Col du Pillon gondola in the **Isenau** area or by cable car from **Reusch**. The glacier can be crowded when the snow is poor in Villars and Gstaad. The runs are wide and easy, with the highlight being the long run down the Combe d'Audon. A drag-lift from here goes to **Oldenegg**, opening up a run to Reusch. A post-bus returns you to the various lift stations along the valley.

Isenau, Les Diablerets' separate ski area, is approached by gondola from the far side of the village. The skiing here is on gentle but limited slopes. It is worth noting that with a supplement to your lift pass you can ski on towards Gstaad. However, the distances involved and the time spent on lifts makes this impractical if you want to return before nightfall.

Beginners
Novices take the train up to Bretaye, where the ski schools meet. The nursery slope is ideally situated and of a gentle gradient. A wide choice of blue runs are reached by chair- and drag-lift from here.

Intermediates
This is ideal intermediate terrain. The one criticism reporters have is that the pistes tend to be short. The east-facing runs from Grand and Petit Chamossaire are graded red, and are very exposed at the summit and moderately steep. Grand Chamossaire, which can be approached from the Roc d'Orsay gondola, can also be reached by a drag from Bretaye. It has a couple of good runs served by a short drag on the back of the hill. The long blue run from Grand Chamossaire down to Col de Soud is recommended. The west-facing runs from Chaux Ronde to Bretaye cover

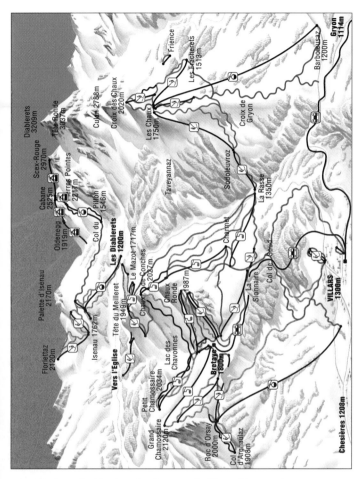

an open slope that is steep in places and offers a blue route.

Advanced

This is not a resort for advanced skiers, but the size of the area means that there is sufficient entertainment to keep you busy for a few days. Experts visiting Villars for a family holiday can easily arrange day trips to Verbier and other nearby resorts, which offer greater challenges.

Off-piste

After a fresh snowfall, the powder remains untracked for far longer than in resorts with more expert terrain, and there is plenty of opportunity for short but steep and exciting runs off Petit and Grand Chamossaire, as well as through the trees below Roc d'Orsay. Some gentle off-piste can be found on the slopes around La Rasse and Charmet.

Snowboarding

Both the Swiss Ski School (ESS) and the Ecole de Ski Moderne (ESM) offer group and private snowboard lessons. Two new snow parks have been prepared for the 1995–6 season.

Ski schools and guiding

The two ski schools have their offices in the village centre and at Bretaye. The ESS is well spoken of and has friendly instructors. The ESM uses the *ski évolutif* method of teaching beginners and specialises in snowboarding and parapente; it also offers lessons for the disabled (including parapente for the blind). Club Med has its own ski school in Villars.

Mountain restaurants

The main restaurant at Bretaye is conveniently placed but lacks charm and is expensive, although it has 'great hot-dogs'. The Lac des Chavonnes serves dishes containing mushrooms, which are gathered each autumn by the owners. It is one of the great alpine restaurants, tucked away in a delightful lakeside setting; a snowmobile acts as a drag-lift to take skiers back to the piste after lunch. The Buffet Col de Soud is an attractive chalet with a large sun-terrace giving superb views of the Diablerets Glacier.

> ### ■ OTHER SPORTS
> Parapente, lugeing, hang-gliding, skating, curling, indoor tennis and squash, swimming, climbing wall, sleigh rides

The Refuge de la Rasse, also known as Chez Mic's, is a rustic mountain eating-place where you grill your own sausages.

Off the mountain

The village sprawls along the main road from the satellites of **Chesières** at one end to **Arveyes** at the other. The actual centre is small, with a limited choice of shops and restaurants. An efficient free bus-service links the outlying areas and provides regular transport to the rail and gondola stations. Its low altitude means that the resort is free of snow for much of the season and Villars would have considerably more charm if it were traffic-free; exhaust fumes detract strongly from what limited ambience there is.

Accommodation

The Hotel Bristol has a comfortable and modern interior, although some reporters found it too formal. Hotel du Cerf is family run with 'lots of home-style cooking'. The large, modern Eurotel is something of an eyesore, but its apartments are 'spacious, clean, and the staff excellent'. The three-star Hotel du Golf opposite the train station is strongly recommended ('very convenient, large modern rooms and a good restaurant'). Club Med is housed in the old Villars Palace, a leviathan of a hotel. The Hotel Panorama has well-equipped, self-catering apartments but it is a steep walk to the main street from here. The Elite, next to the Roc d'Orsay gondola, has a children's playroom. La Crémaillère in Barboleusaz is a good-value option.

Eating in and out

The choice for dining ranges from fine restaurants and informal Stüblis. Restaurant de la Gare, also known as Chez Jo's, serves fondues, while Le Francis has crêpes and pizza, and the Central Café offers Mexican cuisine. Hotel Bristol is for 'wonderful food in a rather formal atmosphere'. Le Mazarin in the Grand Hotel du Parc, the smartest establishment in town, specialises in dishes cooked with champagne and truffles. Vieux Villars and Café Carnotzet specialise in fondues and raclette.

Self-caterers will find the supermarket Viret has a good range of food and wines, and there are many small delicatessen, cheese shops, butchers and bakers on the high street.

Après-ski

Reporters say the nightlife is disappointing and very quiet: 'Walking around town after 6pm is a lonely experience as it is deserted as soon as the last train of the day has brought skiers down from Bretaye.' What nightlife there is centres mainly on the bars; Charlie's Bar is the liveliest of all. Others include the Blue Coyote and the Mini Pub. The Na Zdorovie and El Gringo discos are busy only at weekends.

Childcare

We have favourable reports of 'sensitively manned lifts', with the operators slowing down the chairs for children to get on. The ESS children's classes are praised by reporters ('children have fun'). Pré Fleur ski kindergarten is said to be 'quite excellent' — children can be picked up from their hotel in the morning and are provided with identical one-piece ski suits; parties are thrown for any birthdays that fall during the holiday.

Linked or nearby resorts

Les Diablerets 1162m (3,811ft)

Les Diablerets is a sprawling village, with mainly chalet accommodation. The few hotels it has are modern and seem out of place, but the overall atmosphere is relaxed and ideal for families. The ski school runs Club Pinocchio at the Hotel des Sources for children from three years old. Hotels include the modern Eurotel, Le Chamois and Hotel Mon Abri ('family-run and cosy'). The resort's après-ski is quiet, with the 200-year-old Auberge de la Poste a good place for an after-skiing drink or evening meal. The Buvette du Pillon is popular for its cheese specialities.

TOURIST OFFICE
Tel 41 25 531358
Fax 41 25 532348

Skiing facts: **Villars-sur-Ollon**

TOURIST OFFICE
Rue Centrale, CH-1884 Villars, Vaud
Tel 41 25 353232
Fax 41 25 352794

THE RESORT
By road Calais 952km
By rail station in village, connects with
Aigle 15km away
By air Geneva 1½ hrs
Visitor beds 9,800
Transport free ski-bus around resort and
bus-service to other resorts

THE SKIING
Linked or nearby resorts Arveyes (n),
Barboleusaz (l), Chesières (n), Gryon (n),
Les Diablerets (l), Gstaad (n)
Longest run Les Bouqetins, 2.5km (black)
Number of lifts 24 in Villars, 45 in area
Total of trails/pistes 120km in Villars
(29% easy, 59% intermediate,
12% difficult), 200km in area
Nursery slopes 3 lifts
Summer skiing on Diablerets Glacier
Snowmaking 3 runs covered

LIFT PASSES
Area pass (covers Villars and Diablerets)
SF210 for 6 days
Day pass Villars SF42, area SF46
Beginners special price of SF8 per day for
beginner lifts

Pensioners reductions for 65 yrs and over
Credit cards accepted yes

SKI SCHOOLS
Adults ESS, 10am-midday, SF100 for 6
half-days, Modern Ski School, 10.30am-
midday, SF115 for 6 half-days
Private lessons both ski schools, SF50
per hr
Snowboarding ESS, 10am-midday, SF100
for 6 half-days, ESM, 10.30am-midday,
SF115 for 6 half-days
Cross-country excursions SF50 per afternoon. Loipe 44km at Bretaye and from the
village up to Col de la Croix
Other courses monoski, slalom,
off-piste, competition, telemark, skwal,
heli-skiing
Guiding companies through ski schools

CHILDREN
Lift pass 6-16 yrs, SF126 for 6 days, free
for 5 yrs and under
Ski kindergarten Pré Fleur, 3 yrs and over,
9am-4pm, SF360 for 6 days
Ski school ESS, 9am-4pm, 3 yrs and over,
SF300 for 6 days
Non-ski kindergarten Pré Fleur, 3 yrs and
over, SF360 for 6 days

FOOD AND DRINK PRICES
Coffee SF2.70-2.80, glass of wine SF3,
small beer SF3, dish of the day SF15

Zermatt

ALTITUDE 1620m (5,314ft)

Zermatt's narrow lanes, lined with old wooden barns and world-class hotels, lie under the angular eminence of the Matterhorn, at the top of a dead-end valley. This is Switzerland's southernmost skiing terrain, four-and-a-half hours from Geneva and five-and-a-half hours from Zurich by train. The resort was an isolated hamlet until it was adopted as a mountain base-camp by British climbers and, later, skiers. The canny burghers began milking the cash cow in earnest during the nineteenth century, committing communal funds to build the Gornergrat railway and passing local legislation forcing every inhabitant of the village to labour on construction of the Zermatterhof Hotel. Surrounded by 30 summits over 4000m, Zermatt today inspires awe among its visitors and envy among its rivals. The older clientèle is split almost equally between Germans and Swiss, with most skiers in the higher income brackets.

> **■ GOOD POINTS**
>
> Superlative scenery and mountain restaurants, high standard of accommodation, alpine charm, excellent après-ski and activities for non-skiers, long runs, extensive ski area, car-free resort, glacier skiing
>
> **■ BAD POINTS**
>
> Inadequate ski school and nursery slopes, awkward access between ski areas and around town, high prices

The lift system dates back to construction of the Gornergrat cog railway in 1898. New express trains can now run twice as fast as the older carriages, which are still in use. However, due to a single track, the express trip is only ten minutes shorter than the standard 40-minute trip, which stops at every station.

A firm favourite with almost everyone who has been here, Zermatt is nonetheless so insecure about its skiing potential that it consistently over-advertises itself. The Zermatt brochures claim 73 ski lifts and 230km of pistes. In fact, a Swiss government document shows that there are only 37 lifts and 150km of pistes in the three sectors covered by the Zermatt lift pass (one of the most expensive in Europe). The other 36 lifts and 80km of pistes are in Italy, where Zermatt skiers are charged a hefty daily supplement for use of the Cervinia network.

On the mountain
top 3899m (12,788ft) bottom 1620m (5,314ft)

Zermatt is a resort for the adept skier with deep pockets and a taste for good living. Zermatt's burghers believe that all good things come to those who wait — and walk. Getting around town and from one lift complex to another is expensive and inconvenient by taxi, sleigh or solar bus. No competent skier will find himself outclassed by any groomed slope in Zermatt, but queues for the Klein Matterhorn cable car and Gornergrat railway — not to mention packed crowds on narrow, icy trails coming down to the village at the end of the day — will keep even the experts on the edge. One reporter notes that Zermatt suits 'bump lovers and people who like skiing on paths'.

An underground funicular begins by the mainline train station and runs up to the **Sunnegga** sector, with sunny slopes continuing up to Blauherd and Rothorn. The Gornergrat mountain railway station, just across from the main railway terminus, is the start of a trip up past Riffelalp and Riffelberg to **Gornergrat**, from where cable cars go onwards to Hohtälli, Rote Nase and Stockhorn. At the Matterhorn edge of Zermatt a cable car and various gondolas head out to Furi. From there, lifts branch left for the Trockener Steg and Klein Matterhorn sectors and right for the **Schwarzsee** area, with Furgg straight up the middle. Among its impressive cable cars, Zermatt retains 18 antiquated drag-lifts.

> ### ■ WHAT'S NEW
>
> 150-person cable car (December 1996) will replace the old Blauherd to Rothorn cabin
>
> High-speed TGV trains from Paris to Brig will cut travel time to Zermatt to 7 hours (Saturdays-only)
>
> Twice-weekly Air Zermatt helicopter day-trips to Verbier

It is possible, in theory, to ski all three Zermatt sectors in one day, and to ski from one to another in both directions, although not without some awkward sections and uphill walking. Surprisingly, the free lift inside the Klein Matterhorn station, which delivers sightseers to the summit view of a 360-degree panorama, is little visited.

Reporters complain of inconsistent piste-grading: 'Some blues seemed more like reds and yet the reds were very straightforward, especially on Trockener Steg, where there were few blues for the children. However, we found wide, quite easy reds here'. One of the major irritations is that, in a resort of this calibre, credit cards are not accepted as payment for lift passes.

Beginners

Zermatt's skiing cannot be recommended for beginners, but it offers a rare chance to ski at exceptionally high altitude. The ski school takes beginners to Blauherd, where the blue (easy) run marked 2A on the piste map returns over flattering terrain to the Sunnegga lift station; but be careful not to turn right on to the National black (difficult) run. At Sunnegga beginners have a short blue called Easy Run. Tuftern, although marked as a blue from Blauherd all the way down to Patrullarve, is actually quite tricky in parts. Gornergrat appears to offer more beginner terrain, but it is important to get off the train at Rotenboden, one stop earlier, to avoid a 'nasty bit' at the top. Guaranteed skiing on the glacier above 3000m is flat and easy on the blues alongside the Gandegg and Theodulpass drag-lifts, going over to

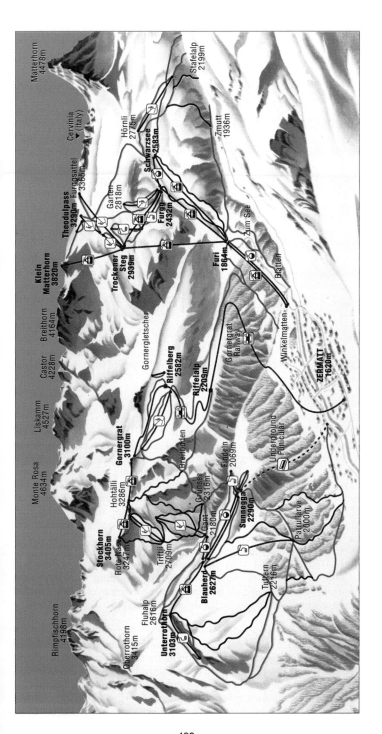

Cervinia from Trockener Steg, as well as on the Plateau Rosa and Testa blues well above 3500m.

Intermediates

Zermatt's red (intermediate) runs often become more than ordinarily testing due to icy conditions and extreme overcrowding on narrow sections down to the village. The highest intermediate skiing, and the easiest, is up in the Klein Matterhorn and Trockener Steg sectors. From the Klein Matterhorn, the long KL red flows alongside blue ice-crevasses down past the Plateau Rosa T-bars to the Führer piste and over to the Testa T-bar. From this area the scenic Matterhornpiste swings over by the Hirli T-bar and down to the Furgg hub, where the black Furgg-Furi run blocks further intermediate access.

Aggressive intermediates will be thrilled by the Kelle run from Gornergrat, passing over a 'scary' ridge to link up at Breitboden with the classic White Hare red, which begins with a narrow, challenging passage up at Hohtälli. Both reds proceed on terrain bordered by woods all the way to Furi, a good 30 minutes on skis without stopping.

Intermediate skiing on the Sunnegga-Blauherd sector is sunnier and smoother and is traditional 'ski to lunch' terrain. The Fluhalp red leads down to the Gant drag-lift, which gives access to the black runs back down from Rote Nase, but also links with the start of the red White Hare and the Furi sector.

Advanced

Triftji is one of the most famous black pistes in the Alps. Unfortunately, this and the other black runs down under the Hohtälli-Rote Nase sector require so much snow to make them skiable that they are often closed until mid-January. Together, the Stockhorn and Grieschumme blacks make an almost perfect fall-line descent from Rote Nase down to Gant, a bone-jarring bump bonanza that only the most rubber-legged will achieve without stopping. Further afield, and invisible to spectators, is Zermatt's least crowded, best black skiing. Sloping sharply down from the Stafel-Hörnli drag-lift into the tree-line, Tiefbach and Momatt are steep runs, which dive towards Zmutt and the borders of the resort. Notorious as a black accident-spot, as well as an expert run, the Furgg to Furi stretch is described by one reporter as being 'like the M25' in late afternoon when it is the main homeward-bound route. But early in the morning, when Furgg-Furi has yet to be scraped clean of snow, it makes an excellent downhill course for the more advanced.

Off-piste

The Schwarzsee sector is cold and uncrowded. The Aroleid trail under the cable car is normally a bump run all the way to Furi. Less skied are the Garten gullies. From the top of the Furgg-Garten drag and to the left of the Garten red run, the two Garten couloirs offer a choice of narrow chutes, very steep for the first 40m but less than life-threatening should you fall. At the bottom there is a favourite 'sky ramp' jump of about 20m,

which has the attractions of a perfect landing and good views for spectators from the Garten lift. Down from Rothorn, on the sunny side of the
mountain, three itineraries (Chamois, Marmotte and Arbzug) become
wide-open powder routes after a good storm.

Zermatt has been described as the biggest heli-skiing centre in the
Alps. In fact, that honour goes to Lacadur Heliskiing in Valgrisenche in
Italy, which has seven times the landing sites at one-third of the price of
Air Zermatt's offering. That said, a day's excursion to Monte Rosa or
Alphubeljoch above Zermatt is a popular way to escape the pistes.

Snowboarding

The Swiss Ski School (SSS) has around 20 snowboard instructors.
Julen Sports houses a new Swiss Snowboard School called Stoked.
There is a half-pipe in the Klein Matterhorn sector, but Zermatt is not
overly adoring of the snowboard ethos.

Ski schools and guiding

Few ski schools have been so heavily criticised. Zermatt's 50-plus mountain guides also have a reputation, even among the Swiss, for aloof indif-
ference. One explanation is that many guides and instructors work as a
hobby, making their real living from local shops or hotels: 'Neither of the
two instructors we experienced bothered to ask the names of the class
members, and many of them did not show any respect for each other; on
several occasions one ski class would cut straight through another'.
Another reporter comments: 'the instructor seemed more concerned
with getting a sun tan than anything else'.

Ski classes are often overpopulated and somewhat chaotic despite a
pool of around 175 teachers: 'The instructor failed to make sufficient
allowances for the weaker skiers, frequently skiing on far ahead and
often going on again before the last members of the class had caught up',
and 'the instructor started off on the first morning by heading down a
steep powder-filled gully without any preliminary check on the standard
of the class'. Another reporter notes: 'No, or very little, tuition is given.
The instructor didn't criticise my skiing because she said I went too fast
for her to see'. However, one reporter says that the 1994–5 season saw
major improvements and 'no major horror stories', although beginners
are still not accepted for group lessons on any day but Monday and many
instructors lack the required Swiss federal certificate: 'We had a young
girl instructor who admitted that she had never tutored a group before',
said a pupil.

Mountain restaurants

Lunching on a wooden terrace follows gazing at the Matterhorn as
Zermatt's main occupation. This is no place to pack a picnic, not when
old wooden barns like Chez Vrony provide crystal glass, starched nap-
kins, sofas on the terrace and intimate nooks and crannies for serious
dining. The Findeln plateau also offers Chez Adler, which some
reporters prefer to Vrony, perhaps because Max, the host, is so genial.

Enzian at Findeln is famous for its salmon dumplings but should not be confused with the legendary Enzo's. In fact, Enzo has gone, the inn has been renamed the Findlerhof and is now run by Heidy and Franz. 'It's still good food', was one laconic report.

The centuries-old hamlet of Zum See houses the inn of the same name, which has a rising reputation as being Zermatt's best; try the curried noodles and king prawns. Higher up in the Furi sector, Simi is the *Rösti* headquarters but also serves delicious salads at reasonable prices. Tony's Grotta has delectable pasta, especially the cannelloni with ricotta and broccoli. Fluhalp, at the top of Rothorn, has pancakes and the best panorama of the Matterhorn. The Gandeg Hütte is very popular: 'the restaurant was so full we ate outside in a blizzard, but they did provide rugs and the atmosphere was still amazing.'

Off the mountain

Zermatt dates as a settlement from the early Middle Ages and inaugurated its first three tourist-beds in 1838. Development has since been constrained by steep valley walls, leaving nothing between the Matterhorn and the village edge but open pasture dotted with wooden barns.

In Zermatt's much vaunted car-free lanes, sheep are still shorn outside centuries-old wooden mazots (ramshackle barns on stilts fitted with stone discs to keep rats at bay), but the conflux of electric taxis and horse-drawn carriages on the main thoroughfare is so frantic that radar traps have been installed.

There are a number of expensive jewellery and souvenir shops but few of the chic boutiques one finds in Crans Montana or St Moritz. 'Expensive for food and wine, otherwise not too bad for ski gear, T-shirts and gifts', comments one reporter, and 'the best shopping experience in any ski resort we have visited' says another. Computers can be rented at Laser-Druck, and software is obtainable at Easy-Hot, a fact which gives a measure of the upward mobility of the clientèle.

Accommodation

Hotel-keepers rule in Zermatt (there are 113 of them), and chalet accommodation is minimal. It is important to choose a hotel close to where you want to ski and spend your evenings. For indulgent romantics nothing compares to the five-star experience of the venerable Zermatterhof, right in the village centre near the sculpted bronze marmots. The five-star Mont Cervin has fewer balconies but has opened sumptuous apartments in a recently built annex; all have private saunas, whirlpools, fireplaces and large kitchens. The four-star Alex Schlosshotel Tenne is a mix of Byzantine and chalet-style architecture. The Monte Rosa, a favourite of Sir Winston Churchill and from where Edward Whymper, the Victorian mountaineer, set off to climb the Matterhorn in 1865, exudes understated opulence. The chalet-style Malteserhaus has generously sized apartments.

Many reporters express satisfaction with the simple Bristol, which is renowned for its cuisine. Hotel Parnass, located close to the Sunnegga Express and with a bus-stop outside the door, is said to have a 'quiet and relaxed atmosphere – not wildly luxurious, but good value for money'. Hotel Bijou, two minutes' walk from the Klein Matterhorn lift, is praised as 'small and friendly, with rooms even better than four-star standard; the food was a culinary delight each evening'.

Eating in and out

Zermatt's restaurants (there are more than 100) have a deservedly high reputation for quality and price. As elsewhere in the Alps, however, world-class cuisine is hard to find. Aside from the Chinese restaurant next to the London Bar and the Fuji Japanese restaurant in the Hotel Albana, meat, cheese and potatoes prevail. Hamburgers and shakes at MacDonald's have injected a youthful flavour into Zermatt cuisine. Le Mazot ('excellent and expensive') is at the top of most lists for haute cuisine, although the Buffet Royal in the Zermatterhof hotel is more sumptu-

■ OTHER SPORTS
Skating, curling, sleigh rides, swimming, tobogganing, winter walks

ous. American-style steaks are grilled at the Viktoria-Centre and Cheminée Steakhouse. Fish, even in fondue, is good at the Coquille Fischstube. Lamb, from the Julen's own flock (watch out for the sheep-dog in the foyer) is excellent at the Schäferstübli. The Whymperstube in the Hotel Monte Rosa has traditional fondue in Edwardian ambience.

Zermatt has around 15 grocery shops. The butcher in the Coop, just across from the railway station, is from Manchester. Migros is the least expensive, followed by PAM. The Gastromatt has a good selection, as does La Source.

Après-ski

Elsie Bar, by the church, is expensive but irresistible for champagne and oysters after skiing or late at night. The Post Hotel complex caters for everybody: its Brown Cow snack bar boasts the best sandwiches in Europe, the Pink Elephant has a high standard of live jazz, Le Broken disco incites dancing on huge beer barrels until 3am. However, the Post's Boathouse wine bar is a tiny haven of cocktail civilisation decorated like the inside of a sloop. For a whale of a time, Moby Dick is open until late and has pool tables. The Alex Hotel's nightclub is sedate but it is the only place where older folk and teens can dance to music that actually allows conversation. Grampi's Pub is a glass-fronted haunt with the cheapest beer in Zermatt. The North Wall is British-run, has excellent pizzas and shows ski videos: 'A worker's bar', says one patron. The Olympia Stübli, on the route down from Sunnegga, has live music into the early hours. The Hotel Post contains a jazz club, two pubs and two discos.

Childcare

The Zermatt Ski School takes children from four to six years old in its well-received new Ski Hasen programme, but only in the afternoons as

Skiing facts: **Zermatt**

TOURIST OFFICE
Train Station Square (Bahnhofplatz), CH-3920 Zermatt, Valais
Tel 41 28 66 11 81
Fax 41 28 66 11 85

THE RESORT
By road Calais 1076km
By rail station in resort, or Visp 36km
By air Geneva 3½ hrs, Zurich 4 hrs
Visitor beds 13,500
Transport ski-bus SF2-3, also electric taxis and horse-drawn sleighs

THE SKIING
Linked or nearby resorts Cervinia (I), Grächen (n), Saas-Fee (n), Riederalp (n), Crans Montana (n)
Longest run Klein Matterhorn to Zermatt, 15km (red/black)
Number of lifts 73 with Cervinia
Total of trails/pistes Zermatt only 150km, 230km including Cervinia (5% beginner, 25% easy, 40% intermediate, 30% difficult)
Nursery slopes 3 nursery slopes
Summer skiing extensive, 25km of trails and 9 lifts on Klein Matterhorn Glacier
Snowmaking 19.5km covered

LIFT PASSES
Area pass SF292 for 6 days
Day pass SF60, or SF91 including Cervinia

Beginners no free lifts
Pensioners 25% reduction for men 65 yrs and over and women 62 yrs and over
Credit cards accepted no

SKI SCHOOLS
Adults SSS, SF215 for 6 days (4 hrs per day)
Private lessons SSS, SF270 per day (4 hrs)
Snowboarding SSS private lessons, SF125 for 3 half-days, group lessons on demand
Cross-country SSS, details on request. Loipe 22km
Other courses race training, moguls, off-piste
Guiding companies Zermatt Mountain Guide Association

CHILDREN
Lift pass 50% reduction for 6-15 yrs, free for 5 yrs and under
Ski kindergarten SSS, 4-6 yrs, 1.15-3.15pm, SF150 for 6 afternoons
Ski school SSS, 6-12 yrs, SF255 for 6 days (4 hrs per day)
Non-ski kindergarten Kindergarten Hotel Nicoletta, 2-8 yrs, 9am-5pm, SF55 per day including lunch. Kinderclub Pumuckel at Hotel La Ginabelle, 2½ yrs and over, 9am-5pm, SF90 per day including lunch

FOOD AND DRINK PRICES
Coffee SF3, glass of wine SF2.8, small beer SF3.50-4, dish of the day SF15-20

the school considers mornings too cold for teaching on Sunnegga. Often there are no more than two children per instructor, although up to six are accepted. Children aged six years and over can be enrolled in the ski school. At the Nicoletta hotel, Seiler's Children Paradise takes kids from two years old. Childminding, with optional ski lessons on a baby slope by the river, is available for the Ginabelle's Kinderclub Pumuckel for children from two years old. The tourist office has a list of English-speaking registered childminders.

Round-up

Andermatt
top 2965m (9,725ft) bottom 1445m (4,740ft)

Andermatt is a retreat for a dedicated skiing minority. Its enormous off-piste opportunities and reputation for generous dumps of snow make it one of Switzerland's lesser-known little gems. It is situated at a major alpine crossroads on the route to the St Gotthard Pass into Italy and was once one of the busiest of the Swiss resorts. Now the Gotthard road and rail tunnels pass under the high Urseren Valley, of which Andermatt is the main village, making it a virtual dead-end in winter.

There are four ski areas along the sides of the Urseren Valley, between the Furka and Oberalp passes. The two main ones lie at either end of Andermatt, and the two smaller and less popular areas lie to the south-west, above the villages of **Hospental** and **Realp**. Descents down the shaded face of Gemsstock, which has 800m of severe vertical and treacherous off-piste skiing in the bowl, should not be tackled without a guide; nor should some of the long off-piste alternatives in other directions from the top-station.

Andermatt has a traditional character including cobbled streets. However, it is one of Switzerland's major centres for the training of alpine troops, and severe barrack buildings are also a feature of the architecture. The heart of the old village receives little sun, hemmed in as it is by mountains, and there is not much traffic and no public transport. Accommodation is in a mixture of hotels and appealing old chalets.

TOURIST OFFICE
Tel 41 44 67454
Fax 41 44 68185

Arosa
top 2653m (8,702ft) bottom 1800m (5,904ft)

In 1883 ski-tourer Dr Otto Herwig-Hold stumbled across the tiny village of **Inner Arosa**, high in the Swiss Graubunden. He climbed to the top of the 2512m Hörnli, looked down at the village and its frozen lake and realised that it was the perfect site for his new tuberculosis sanatorium. The hospital was built and, with its wide range of international patients, soon put Arosa on the map. Today, it remains one of the truly all-round ski resorts of the Alps.

Arosa's skiers are not here to bash the pistes from dawn until dusk. They are in search of a rounded winter-sports experience. The ski area consists of wide, sunny slopes, which are mostly above the tree-line and cover the three peaks of **Hörnli**, **Weisshorn** and **Bruggerhorn**. It is well linked and, although small, with only 16 lifts, there is a total of 70km of piste. Much of this is made up of blue (easy) and red (intermediate) runs over hilly rather than mountainous terrain.

One of the only hazards of Arosa's skiing is the number of pedestrians and tobogganers on the piste. Non-skiers can buy hiking passes covering gondolas and some chair-lifts.

The lift system is, by Swiss standards, modern and efficient. Main mountain access from Obersee is by chair-lift, drag-lift or two-stage cable car. Access from Inner Arosa is by gondola. This is not a resort for expert skiers, although it does have some off-piste for enthusiasts; the top of the Hörnli is the starting point for a variety of off-piste tours involving skins and public transport to neighbouring resorts. The more difficult piste-skiing is reached from the top of the 2653m Weisshorn, a treacherous black (difficult) run that brings you down to the Carmnennahütte, the best of half a dozen mountain restaurants.

Village access is not easy, with 244 bends in the 32km dramatic road from the busy medieval valley town of Chur. Taking the train through stunning scenery is a much better option. In the village the toboggan is an essential form of transport.

TOURIST OFFICE
Tel 41 81 311621
Fax 41 81 313135

Lenzerheide-Valbella
top 2865m (9,397ft) bottom 1500m (4,920ft)

These two resorts used to attract a fair number of British families but in recent years have decreased in popularity. The area has considerable charm, and magnificent cross-country skiing, but alpine skiers may find the terrain limited with a distinct lack of variety.

The villages of Lenzerheide and Valbella lie at either end of a lake in a wide, wooded pass with high mountains on either side. 'Transport is based on a very efficient system of buses travelling clockwise and anticlockwise', was one report, and 'jump on the bus going in the wrong direction and you still arrive at your destination!' was another.

The main street of Lenzerheide has some attractive old buildings. Valbella has less identity; it is no more than a large community of hotels and concrete-box holiday homes crammed on to a hillside, but it is less of a roadside strip and gives direct access to the western ski area.

The skiing is in two separate areas, **Rothorn** and **Danis/Stätzerhorn**, on either side of the inconveniently wide pass. Both have about half woodland and half open-skiing terrain. There are no particularly difficult pistes, although the Rothorn cable car opens up some off-piste skiing.

TOURIST OFFICE
Tel 41 81 343434
Fax 41 81 345383

North America

Every European skier owes it to him/herself to cross the Atlantic and experience the difference of skiing in North America. We are frequently told by readers how even the most famous alpine resorts fail to measure up to the expectations they now have after their visits to the US and Canada.

The first point to strike the European visitor is the size (or rather, lack of it) of the average North American ski area. Anyone used to the networks of up to 200 lifts and hundreds of kilometres of interlinked skiing between villages in France, Austria and Italy is in for a deep shock on this continent where 12 lifts constitute a large resort.

Secondly, with few exceptions, the infrastructure of each North American resort is owned and operated by a single company. The result is a coordinated and sustained standard of service. This uniform attempt to attract and please customers is woefully lacking in too many European resorts, where many staff don't even bother to smile as they take your money.

The skiing, again with some notable exceptions (Jackson Hole and Whistler are two of them) is blander in North America (some would say homogenised), and nearly always consists of man-made trails cut through wooded slopes; their exotic names belie their colour gradings. However, such is the structured layout of most ski areas that families or groups of different standards can ski together, with individuals choosing trails of varying gradients, all of which end at the same lift station.

It is important to note that Americans operate a different form of piste colour-coding: green is easy, blue is intermediate, black or black-diamond is difficult, and double-black-diamond is very difficult. The standard of piste-grooming and trail-marking, fuelled by the threat of skier litigation, is outstanding.

Off-piste, in the European sense, does not really exist. While a few major resorts leave vast tracts of mountainside untouched by machine, going 'under the ropes' and leaving the designated ski area is absolutely forbidden, and you face forfeiting your lift pass — or even arrest.

Accommodation in both hotels and condominiums bears no comparison to the Alps at all. Anyone who has ever experienced the confines of an Avoriaz apartment for six will be delighted to discover that the entire French unit would probably fit into the bathroom of its US or Canadian counterpart.

Such is the sad state of sterling against the Deutschmark and the Swiss and French francs, that the price of skiing in North America is becoming more attractive every year. It is an indictment of European skiing that a winter holiday in North America is considered by many skiers to offer greater value for money as well as being, quite simply, more enjoyable.

Aspen

ALTITUDE 7,945ft (2422m)

Many influences helped shape North America's most famous and fashionable ski resort, but among the most important was the role played by European skiing enthusiasts and the effects of the 10th Mountain Division, Colorado's militiamen on skis. The input of both of these was somehow grafted on to the original Aspen infrastructure that dated back to the early silver-mining days. The brave and sometimes desperate miners who defied vicious weather and marauding Ute Indians to set up a rickety camp in the Roaring Fork Valley in the late 1870s (Ute City), would have been staggered to see how their improvised hovels eventually gave way to America's smartest ski town.

> ■ **GOOD POINTS**
>
> Wide choice of skiing for all standards, excellent children's facilities, fascinating Victorian town with large choice of restaurants, ideal for non-skiers, eclectic nightlife
>
> ■ **BAD POINTS**
>
> No link between 4 mountains, no nursery slopes on Aspen Mountain, expensive lift ticket

The miners struck it rich. During the boom years, Aspen's population reached 12,000 and was served by two railroads, six newspapers, three schools, ten churches and a notorious red-light district. But by 1893 it was all over; the silver market collapsed and the town virtually died. It did not start to recover for almost 50 years.

The forces of change were generated some 5,000 miles away in Europe. During the 1936 Winter Olympics at Garmisch-Partenkirchen, Theodore Ryan, a wealthy American, compared notes with the bobsleigh champion, William Fiske III, about the need for good ski resorts in America. The following summer they were approached by an Aspen mine-owner who was convinced that the snowfields of his home town would make an ideal setting for their plans. War intervened, but when America joined the fighting, the US Army's 10th Mountain Division began to train locally. One of those troops was an Austrian, Friedl Pfeifer, and after the war he and Walter Paepcke, a Chicago industrialist, formed the Aspen Ski Company.

On the mountain

Aspen top 11,212ft (3418m) bottom 7,945ft (2422m)
Snowmass top 12,310ft (3750m) bottom 8,223 ft (2507m)
Aspen Highlands top 11,675ft (3559m) bottom 8,040ft (2451m)
Tiehack top 9,900ft (3018m) bottom 7,870ft (2399m)

Aspen has four completely separate mountains: the one and only **Aspen Mountain**, which is also known as **Ajax**, a name taken from an old

Maroon Peak 14,156ft
Pyramid Peak 14,018ft
Keefe Peak 13,516ft
Hayden Peak 13,559ft
Castle Peak 14,265ft

Olympic Bowl
ASPEN HIGHLANDS
11,800ft
8,000ft

Sundeck 11,210ft
Bonnie's
Grand Junction
ASPEN 7,945ft

433

mining claim; **Aspen Highlands**; **Tiehack**; and **Snowmass**, 12 miles (19km) out of town. They are linked by a free bus service.

Aspen Mountain is strictly the reserve of good skiers and has no beginner slopes. Anyone less than a strong intermediate will struggle to cope with the home-run gradient here, although there are less demanding trails. Tiehack (formerly known as Buttermilk) is ideal beginner and child terrain with no hidden surprises but plenty of variety at a novice level. Snowmass, which has skiing for all levels, is the furthest of the separate ski areas and is a resort in its own right under the same ownership. Aspen Highlands, the newest acquisition, has the toughest, most radical terrain and has greatly added to Aspen's appeal for expert skiers.

> ■ **WHAT'S NEW**
>
> High-speed quad-chair at Elk Camp and at Two Creeks on Snowmass
> Four trails at Two Creeks
> More graduated terrain at Aspen Highlands

Beginners

Tiehack is one of North America's best mountains for beginners, and Snowmass also has excellent novice slopes. The area below Tiehack's West Summit is packed with green (easy) runs like Westward Ho and Homestead Road, and more advanced beginners will thrive on a large network of long blue (intermediate) runs with an impressive vertical drop of more than 1,800ft. The nursery slopes at Snowmass hug the lower slopes and most are accessed by the Fanny Hill high-speed quad. At Aspen Highlands the main nursery slopes are concentrated mid-mountain and reached most quickly by the Exhibition quad-chair. The Skiwee lift at the base also serves a small beginner area.

Intermediates

Of all Aspen's four mountains, Snowmass has the largest intermediate appeal. Almost every run mid-mountain and below provides good cruising, and the region below Elk Camp at the far perimeter of the ski area (with runs like Bull Run, Grey Wolf and Bear Bottom) is another popular haunt. Snowmass is famous for its **Big Burn** area, where a clutch of blue trails separated by a few trees provide almost unlimited cruising. Although the runs have individual names (Whispering Jesse, Timberline, Wineskin, Mick's Gully, etc), the Big Burn is effectively one huge intermediate trail as much as a mile wide in places.

There is plenty of good intermediate skiing with top-to-bottom cruising on Ajax Mountain. Straying by mistake on to more difficult terrain is less likely here than at many resorts; most of the black (difficult) runs tend to be hidden away from the main slopes. The best area for middling skiers at Highlands is near the top of the mountain where the Cloud Nine lift accesses runs such as Scarlett's, Grand Prix and Gunbarrel. Golden Horn and Thunderbowl offer good cruising. All of Tiehack is suitable for intermediates, but the lack of challenging runs means that stronger skiers will quickly become bored.

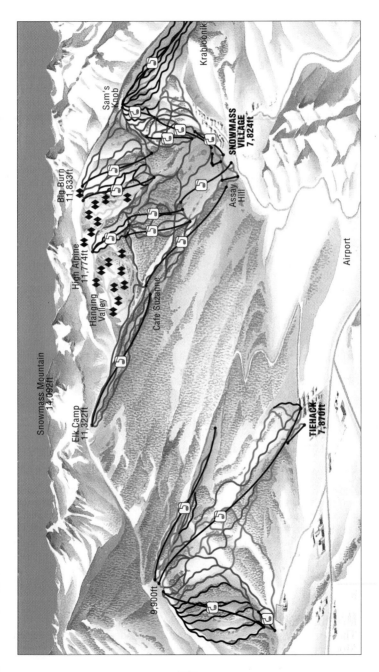

Snowmass Mountain
14,092ft

Elk Camp
11,322ft

Big Burn
11,833ft

High Alpine
11,774ft

Hanging
Valley

Sam's
Knob

Krabloonik

SNOWMASS
VILLAGE
7,824ft

Assay
Hill

Cafe Suzanne

9,900ft

TIEHACK
7,870ft

Airport

Advanced

Aspen Mountain is riddled with short, sharp and quite steep double-black-diamond (very difficult) chutes, including the famous 'dump runs' like Bear Paw, Short Snort and Zaugg Dump, which were created by miners throwing out spoil as they were tunnelling their way into Aspen Mountain. Walsh's is considered the most challenging. Bell Mountain, a peak that juts out from Ajax as if it has been stuck on, provides excellent opportunities for mogul skiers with its variety of individual faces including Face of Bell, Shoulder of Bell and Back of Bell.

Much of the skiing at Aspen Highlands falls into the advanced category. There is a large and challenging gladed area to the left of of the Exhibition quad-chair, including Bob's Glade, Upper Stein and Golden Horn Woods, which are all double-black-diamond trails. At Snowmass there are the largely gladed chutes in the Hanging Valley Wall and Hanging Valley Glades, and The Cirque has even steeper terrain mainly above the tree-line; access to these runs involves a short hike.

Off-piste

Aspen Highlands has some of the most exhilarating off-piste terrain in the valley, much of it accessed by the Lodge Peak quad-chair at the top of the ski area. The chair follows a ridge with steep terrain on both sides. As you ride up, a dramatic area known as Steeplechase opens up on your left; this comprises about half a dozen steep chutes. On your right there is even steeper terrain in Olympic Bowl, although the gradient is not always fully appreciable until you have progressed some way down the slopes. Deception, in particular, is aptly named; it starts off at a fairly moderate pitch, but the further down you ski, the steeper it becomes. There is some good snow cat skiing off the back of Aspen Mountain.

Snowboarding

No snowboarding is permitted at Aspen Mountain, but the other mountains encourage it. Two-hour First Time On Snowboard lessons are available at Aspen Highlands, and Snowmass has snowboard clinics.

Ski schools and guiding

As well as traditional lessons the Aspen Ski School offers Discover Aspen and Snowmass and Master The Mountains courses, which are multi-day ski school weeks that include accommodation, lift tickets and lessons.

Aspen Highlands offers the graduated-length method (GLM), which is similar to the French *ski évolutif* instruction, extreme terrain lessons and telemark and race clinics. Snowmass Ski School offers special bumps, powder, telemark and racing programmes. At Tiehack it is claimed: 'We guarantee you will be able to ski from the top to the bottom by the third day!'

Mountain restaurants

There is a large, busy restaurant at the Sundeck on top of Aspen Mountain, where non-skiers can join skiing friends. Bonnie's, a little way down the mountain just off to the side of the top section of Ruthie's, is smaller and more intimate and prides itself on its *Strudel* and hot apple dumplings. La Baita, at the bottom of Ruthie's and Roch Run, is the old Ruthie's Restaurant, which has been considerably revamped to include a separate waiter-service restaurant specialising in Italian food. At the base of the Silver Queen gondola is the Ajax Tavern (formerly Schlomo's), which serves Mediterranean food. At Snowmass, Up 4 Pizza (home-made) is at the top of the Big Burn lift, and Ullrhof (hearty skiers' break-fast, wood-burning stove, sundeck) is at the bottom. Gwyn's/High Alpine at the top of the Alpine Springs quad is for skiers wanting something more leisurely and sophisticated. Reservations are recommended, but there is also a cafeteria service. Sam's Knob restaurant and cafeteria also features home cooking. The Café Suzanne, at the bottom of the Elk Camp lift, features a southern French menu, and Krabloonik, near the Campground parking lot, specialises in smoked meats and wild game. At Aspen Highlands, the Merry Go Round Restaurant at mid-mountain offers home-made soups, chilli and burgers.

The Highlands Café is another breakfast and lunch spot at the base. There are three mountain restaurants at Tiehack: the Café West near the bottom of Lift 3, which is designed in the style of a French café; Bump's, at the base, includes a *rôtisserie* and grill; the Cliffhouse, at the top of the Summit Express, has food indoors and outdoors along with some of the best scenery on the mountain.

Off the mountain

Skiers making their first visit to Aspen will have heard about the glitz and glamour of this celebrated resort and perhaps be a little over-awed by the prospect: in reality, Aspen is a cheerful, friendly place with a good variety of skiing, an attractive old town with plenty to do in the evenings. You might well bump into the odd celebrity, but Aspen is certainly not teeming with them as some tabloid newspapers like to suggest. And while it might be a little more expensive than the average Rocky Mountain resort, it is still possible to have a moderately priced ski holiday.

Accommodation

In **Aspen** skiers who can afford to live like celebrities should try the Little Nell and the Ritz Carlton, although many people's favourite is the historic Hotel Jerome. For those on limited budgets there are numerous modestly priced lodges such as the Limelite, the Alpine and the Christiania. The Christmas Inn, the Snow Queen and the Innsbruck Inn are all recommended. The Aspen Bed and Breakfast is a little more expensive but is also praised.

Accommodation at **Snowmass** tends to be a little cheaper than in the town of Aspen. Many of the lodges are ski-in ski-out. Top-of-the-range accommodation includes the Silvertree, the Snowmass Lodge and Club, the Chamonix and Crestwood. More moderately priced are the Mountain Chalet, the Stonebridge Inn and Shadowbrooks. For those counting their cents the Pokolodi Lodge and the Snowmass Inn are both close to the slopes, as are the Aspenwood and Laurelwood condominiums. The so-called Inn at Aspen (really at Tiehack) has mid-range prices.

Eating in and out

Aspen has a huge variety of restaurants with almost every type of cuisine imaginable. Bentley's is a Victorian-style pub and restaurant at the Wheeler Opera House featuring American food and a selection of 35 beers from around the world. The Jerome provides excellent fare at its Century Room. The Chart House on East Durant is well known for steaks and seafood. Little Annie's (East Hyman Avenue) has an all-American menu and styles itself 'Aspen's neighbourhood restaurant'.

> ■ **OTHER SPORTS**
>
> Snowmobiling, snow-shoeing, parapente, hang-gliding, swimming, helicopter rides, skating, indoor tennis, climbing wall

Pinons, which achieved an 'Extraordinary to Perfection' rating in a recent US food survey, is one of Aspen's most exclusive restaurants, with prices to match. Entrées (as they call the main course in America) include Colorado pheasant breast with *foie gras*. Farfalla's, on East Main Street, is another fashionable restaurant, which specialises in Italian cuisine. Poppies Bistro Café has 'rustic Victorian charm', while the Red Onion on East Cooper, which dates back more than a century, serves food at more modest prices. Aspen has four Japanese restaurants plus a Japanese take-away (Sushi Ya Go-Go). The Takah Sushi is highly recommended. The Hard Rock Café and Planet Hollywood chains both have restaurants here.

Après-ski

Aspen has wall-to-wall après-ski in dozens of nightspots. The Jerome Bar (better known as the J-Bar), where miners once congregated to celebrate when they struck silver, is always lively. The sundeck at the Ajax Tavern (formerly Shlomo's) gets the crowds at the bottom of Ajax Mountain when the lifts close. Shooters is a Country and Western saloon with live bands. The Howling Wolf is a recently opened late-night coffee bar. Legends of Aspen is a bar featuring memorabilia from prominent local sportsmen and women. The smart Caribou Club is members-only.

Childcare

Aspen has an in-town nursery service and a nursery ski school programme in each resort. At Snowmass Snow Cubs caters for children between 18 months and 3 years. Older children can join the Big Burn Bears. Snowmass also runs a series of Kids Ski Weeks. The Powder Pandas Ski School is at Tiehack. Parents register their children at Aspen Mountain, and the Max the Moose Express brings them to Tiehack, where they can take part in The Brave Good Eagle Great Feather Chase and the Max the Moose Challenge race.

Skiing facts: **Aspen**

TOURIST OFFICE
425 Rio Grande Place, Aspen, CO 81611
Tel 1 970 925 1940
Fax 1 970 920 1173

THE RESORT
By air Eagle County Airport 75 mins, Aspen Airport 10 minutes
Visitor beds 16,000 in area
Transport shuttle-bus between all 4 mountains (free in daytime, small charge in evening)

THE SKIING
Linked or nearby resorts Snowmass (n)
Longest run Big Burn to Fanny Hill at Snowmass, 4.1 miles (7km) - blue
Number of lifts 40 in area
Total of trails/pistes 4,000 acres (1619 hectares) - 16% easy, 40% intermediate, 24% difficult, 20% expert
Nursery slopes 3 slopes and 5 beginner lifts
Summer skiing none
Snowmaking 428 acres (173 hectares) covered

LIFT PASSES
Area pass (covers all 4 mountains) $222-254 for 6 days. Aspen-Vail Premier Passport gives 1 day's free skiing in Vail
Day pass $37-49
Beginners no reduction
Pensioners 65-69 yrs, $186 for 6 days, free for 70 yrs and over
Credit cards accepted yes

SKI SCHOOLS
Adults ski schools at Aspen Mountain, Aspen Highlands, Tiehack and Snowmass, 10.30am-3.30pm, $52 per day or $135 for

3 days
Private lessons $140 for 1$\frac{1}{2}$ hrs
Snowboarding Aspen Highlands, Tiehack and Snowmass, 10.30am-3.30pm, $135 for 3 days. Kevin Delaney Snowbird Camp at Tiehack, prices on request. Snowboard park and half-pipe at Tiehack
Cross-country Aspen Cross-country Center and Snowmass Lodge and Club Touring Center, 8.30am-4.30pm, prices on request. Loipe 80km
Other courses Nastar racing, moguls, off-piste, telemark, dynamic stunts, ski-touring, women's seminars
Guiding companies Aspen Mountain Powder Tours

CHILDREN
Lift pass 7-12 yrs, $162 for 6 days, free for 6 yrs and under
Ski kindergarten Snow Puppies at Highlands, 3$\frac{1}{2}$-6 yrs, 9.30am-3.30pm, $340 for 5 days including lunch. Powder Pandas at Tiehack, 3-6 yrs, 8.30am-4pm, $320 for 5 days including lunch. Big Burn Bears at Snowmass, 4 yrs and over, 8.30am-4pm, $340 for 5 days including lunch
Ski school Highlands, Snowmass and Tiehack, 12 yrs and under, 9.30am-3.15pm, $275 for 5 days including lunch, 13-19 yrs, $240 for 5 days not including lunch
Non-ski kindergarten Kid's Club at Aspen, 12 mths-3 yrs, $285 for 40 hrs, Snow Cubs at Snowmass, 18 mths-3 yrs, 8.30am-4pm, $340 for 5 days including lunch

FOOD AND DRINK PRICES
Coffee $2, glass of wine $3, small beer $2, dish of the day $6

Banff/Lake Louise

ALTITUDE 5,350ft (1631m)

This is a singularly beautiful and wide-ranging ski area, which is made up of three resorts that have nothing much to do with each other except in the minds of marketing people. Lake Louise is by far the most important and, in fact, is 34 miles (58km) from Banff and its local resort of Mystic Ridge/Mount Norquay. It is also 24 miles (39km) from the quite separate destination of Sunshine Village. A free bus-service links the resorts.

Lake Louise could hardly be set in a more breathtaking location. The backdrop to the slopes is formed by some of the finest peaks in the Canadian Rockies. It also makes up the cornerstone of Banff National Park with more than 4,000 square miles (6437km²) of mountains, lakes, rivers, canyons and forests.

■ **GOOD POINTS**

Spectacular scenery, good snow record, long ski-season, ideal for family skiing and mixed-ability groups, extensive children's facilities

■ **BAD POINTS**

Strung-out resorts, low temperatures, lack of accommodation near slopes

On the mountain
top 8,954ft (2730m) bottom 5,350ft (1631m)

Because of the distances involved, there is little point in attempting to ski more than one area in a day. **Lake Louise** itself is the furthest from **Banff** but easily the most varied ski area. From the Mount Whitehorn base at Whiskyjack Lodge, the choice of three chairs includes the Friendly Giant Express quad, which takes skiers to mid-mountain at Whitehorn Lodge. From here another high-speed quad, the Top of The World Express, is the fastest way up and over to the Back Bowls or down to Mount Lipalian's Larch area. The four faces of Whitehorn and Lipalian share some 4,000 acres (1,619 hectares) of terrain, which genuinely cater for every grade of skier.

Sunshine Village is the highest of the three resorts and has predominantly medium-length, moderately steep, intermediate terrain above the tree-line. Despite its name, sunshine is not guaranteed, and it can be a bleak and cold place on a grey day. In the winter months low temperatures can be a serious problem this far north. Goat's Eye Mountain at Sunshine opens this season and is expected to double the size of the existing ski area. **Mount Norquay** is 4 miles (6km) from Banff and used to have both very easy and very steep skiing, with nothing in between. It is now prefixed by **Mystic Ridge**, a primarily intermediate area opened in 1990 to give the resort a broader appeal.

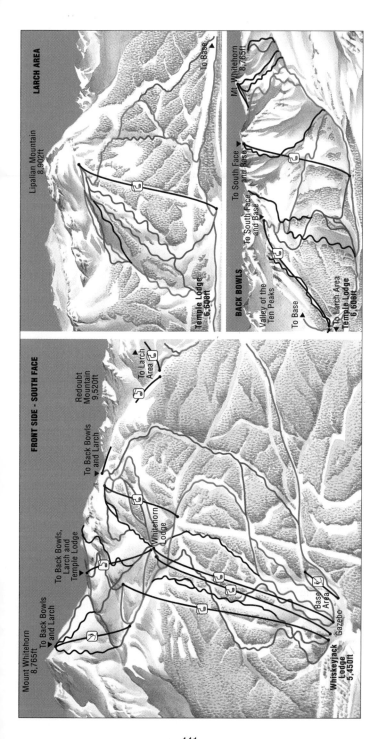

FRONT SIDE - SOUTH FACE

Mount Whitehorn
8,765ft

To Back Bowls
▼ and Larch

To Back Bowls,
Larch and
Temple Lodge

To Back Bowls
and Larch

Redoubt
Mountain
9,520ft

To Larch
Area

Whitehorn
Lodge

Base
Area

Gazebo

Whiskeyjack
Lodge
5,450ft

LARCH AREA

Lipalian Mountain
8,902ft

To Base

Temple Lodge
6,608ft

BACK BOWLS

Mt Whitehorn
8,765ft

To South Face
and Base

To South Face
and Base

To Larch Area
Temple Lodge
6,608ft

To Base

Valley of the
Ten Peaks

Beginners

Because of Lake Louise's policy of ensuring an easy way down from each major lift, novice skiers can share the pleasure of roaming almost at will among the intermediates. Although riding high-speed quads could seem daunting in other resorts, here you can board them confidently and meander down Saddleback and Pika to the Larch chair. This leads to runs like Marmot and Lookout before returning to the main base via Eagle Meadows. If this feels too adventurous, you can warm up on the Sunny T-bar and try skiing the long but gentle Wiwaxy trail.

■ **WHAT'S NEW**

Goat's Eye Mountain expands Sunshine's ski area for 1995–6 season with additional quad chair-lift and new runs

Beginners at Norquay are recommended to ski the runs off the Cascade chair or the Sundance tow. Sunshine has an easy run from the top of Lookout Mountain. There is also some gentle skiing around the Strawberry triple-chair and the Assiniboine T-bar, named after Canada's Matterhorn look-alike.

Intermediates

Intermediates can accomplish huge mileage at Lake Louise over all the terrain, with the possible exception of some of the steeper bowls. Meadowlark, one of the longest runs on the mountain, is an excellent cruising trail. Stronger skiers will want to sample Ridge Run and Whitehorn One on the Back Bowls side. Practically all the runs at Sunshine are within the grasp of intermediates, and nearly all of the 12 new runs at Mystic Ridge were specifically created for recreational skiers of medium experience.

Advanced

At Lake Louise, the Front Face has good men's and women's downhill runs. Other tough runs — Outer Limits, Sunset and Flight Chutes — start higher up. Ptarmigan and Raven are testing glade runs on the Back Bowls side, and Exhibition has the additional challenge of exposing skiers to the gaze of people riding the Ptarmigan chair. Lynx is the one expert trail (the others are off-piste) in the Larch area. Lone Pine, which is fiercely steep and mogulled, is the big challenge at Norquay. At Sunshine, runs like Little Angel, Ecstasy and Big Angel offer steep chute skiing from the top of Lookout Mountain. The new Goat's Eye Mountain at Sunshine offers additional glade skiing for the area, and its runs have an average pitch of 40 degrees.

Off-piste

Large areas of the Back Bowls are permanently closed because of avalanche danger. These are well marked, but sometimes bowls that are normally skiable can be closed too. Paradise Bowl and East Bowl provide good off-piste skiing. Serious powder skiers, who do not mind a hike, claim that Purple Bowl provides the best fresh tracks on the mountain.

Some of the most rewarding tree-line skiing can be found between the upper parts of the Larch chair and the Bobcat run below.

Snowboarding

There are virtually no limits to where snowboarders can go, except at Mystic Ridge/Mount Norquay. Although Norquay hosted the North American Snowboarding Championships in 1988, boarders are not allowed to use the North American chair.

Ski schools and guiding

Lake Louise offers a beginners' special, which includes equipment rental, a beginner-area lift ticket and a half-price ticket valid for all areas for the following day, as well as a ski lesson. A Club Ski Program enables skiers to stay together for four hours a day visiting all three areas with one instructor. All the resorts offer a free piste-guiding service, and Yamnaska Mountain Ski School organises guided off-piste skiing.

Mountain restaurants

Lake Louise's three mountain-lodges have a variety of restaurants, cafés and delicatessen. Whiskyjack at the main base is the location for the Northface Restaurant, a popular après-ski haunt. Other eating places include the Sitzmark bar, a cafeteria with live music most nights in high season, and Cappuccino Corner, which specialises in sandwiches and pizzas. The Whitehorn Lodge has a cafeteria and J Dubb's Deli features soup and sandwiches. Another deli, the Hot Stuff, is at the Temple Lodge on the way to the Larch and Ptarmigan chairs. The Temple Lodge has a bistro called Sawyer's Nook, as well as a cafeteria. Norquay's Cascade Lodge has three restaurants, including the Lone Pine, and a cafeteria. The Eagle's Nest at Sunshine Inn serves soups, salads, pastas, ribs and steak sandwiches. Trapper Bill's offers sandwiches, and the Day Lodge Cafeteria serves chilli, stew, soup and pizzas.

Off the mountain

Banff is a small, attractive community with a frontier-town atmosphere, just 10 miles (16km) into Banff National Park. It attracts hordes of summer visitors — far more than in winter. Apart from the breathtaking scenery the town is famous for its railway history and the wildlife. It is quite common to see elk wandering around, grazing on vegetation protruding through the snow or even rummaging through dustbins. Bighorn sheep can also be spotted. For humans there is a wide variety of shopping and dining opportunities. When Canadian Pacific Railways started bringing tourists here to marvel at the scenery after the park opened in 1885, two neo-Gothic railway hotels were built. The first, the Banff Springs, was completed in 1888. Two years later the magnificent Chateau Lake Louise was finished and today remains the country's most celebrated hotel. This towering fairytale castle is almost cut off from the rest of the world by the magical lake and its glaciers on one side, and lush

Skiing facts: **Banff/Lake Louise**

TOURIST OFFICE
Ski Banff/Lake Louise
PO Box 1085, Banff, Alberta
Tel 1 403 762 4561
Fax 1 403 762 8185

THE RESORT
By rail Banff and Lake Louise stations
By air Calgary Airport 1½ hrs
Visitor beds Banff 9,920, Lake Louise 2,400
Transport ski-buses from hotels to all 3 ski areas

THE SKIING
Linked or nearby resorts Sunshine Village (n), Mystic Ridge/Mount Norquay (n)
Longest run Lake Louise, 5 miles (8km) - blue
Number of lifts Lake Louise 11, Sunshine Village 12, Mystic Ridge/Mount Norquay 5
Total of trails/pistes Lake Louise 62 miles (100km), Sunshine Village 43 miles (70km), Mystic Ridge/Mount Norquay 10.2 miles (16.4km) (area: 25% easy, 45% intermediate, 30% difficult)
Nursery slopes 1 rope-tow at Lake Louise
Summer skiing none
Snowmaking 1,400 acres (567 hectares) at Lake Louise

LIFT PASSES
Area pass CDN$200 for 5 days
Day pass Lake Louise CDN$39.50, Sunshine Village CDN$38, Mystic Ridge/Mount Norquay CDN$29.90
Beginners tow-passes, CDN$15 per day
Pensioners Lake Louise and Sunshine, 65 yrs and over, CDN$35 per day. Mystic Ridge, 55 yrs and over, CDN$25 per day
Credit cards accepted yes

SKI SCHOOLS
Adults Lake Louise, CDN$134 for 3 days, CDN$35 per extra day, times vary between areas
Private lessons CDN$40 per hr
Snowboarding group lessons only available with Club Ski Program, CDN$25 for 2 hrs, private lessons, CDN$39 per hr
Cross-country CDN$20 for 1¼ hrs. Loipe 33 miles (56km)
Other courses heli-skiing, telemark, off-piste, night-skiing, moguls, Club Ski Program in all areas includes instruction, slalom, lift priority, and NASTAR racing
Guiding companies Yamnaska Mountain School

CHILDREN
Lift pass 6-12 yrs, CDN$70 for 5 days, reductions for 13-17 yrs, free for 5 yrs and under
Ski kindergarten Lake Louise, 3-6 yrs, 9am-4pm, CDN$31 per day
Ski school Lake Louise, 7-12 yrs, CDN$38 per day including lunch, Club Ski Program in all areas, 6-12 yrs, prices on request
Non-ski kindergarten Lake Louise, 18 mths-3 yrs, 9am-4pm, CDN$21 per day

FOOD AND DRINK PRICES
Coffee CDN$1, glass of wine CDN$2.25, small beer CDN$2.25, dish of the day CDN$6.50

pine forests on the other. Lake Louise has its own small village.

Accommodation

Unfortunately, not everyone has the budget to stay at the two Canadian Pacific hotels, although winter rates are considerably lower than those in summer. However, there is plenty of choice elsewhere, with almost 40 listed hotels and lodges in **Banff** itself and four more at **Lake Louise Village**. In Banff, The Banff Park Lodge on Lynx Street provides four-star accommodation. On Banff Avenue, Caribou Lodge is almost new, and further into town the Inns of Banff Park is more moderately priced. Bed-and-breakfast establishments and back-country lodges make up the rest of the accommodation. **Norquay** has no lodging of its own, and the only on-mountain accommodation at **Sunshine** is the Sunshine Inn.

> ### ■ OTHER SPORTS
> Snowmobiling, swimming, dog-sledding, sleigh rides, ice-fishing, skating, broomball, snow volleyball

Eating in and out

Many of Banff's wide selection of restaurants are on Banff Avenue. 'If you haven't been to Bumper's, you haven't been to Banff' is the motto of Bumper's Beef House. Joe Btfsplk's Diner looks like a misprint but serves 'meals like Mom used to make', including apple-pie. There are two Japanese restaurants (Shiki Japanese Noodles and Suginoya) and the Silver Dragon serves Cantonese and Peking cuisine. Le Beaujolais serves French dishes, and the three Italian restaurants are Giorgio's, Guido's and the Ristorante Classico at the Rimrock Resort Hotel. The Caboose is a former baggage room at the railway depot, where you can admire the railway memorabilia as you sample lobster, crab and huge steaks.

Après-ski

You can dine and dance at the Rob Roy Room at the Banff Springs Hotel and the Edelweiss or Victoria Dining Room at the Château. Alternatively, let your hair down at various establishments with live music on Banff Avenue: there is rock and roll at Eddy's Back Alley, country-rock at Wild Bill's, blues at The Barbary Coast, live entertainment at Bumper's and live bands at the Silver City Beverage Co. The Caboose Restaurant at the railway depot has karaoke. One of Banff's most popular bars is the Rose and Crown.

Childcare

Chocolate Moose Park at Lake Louise organises ski and play programmes for children up to 12 years of age. The Kinderski programme is geared for three- to six-year-olds. There is also a Kids Ski programme where children are guided round the mountain with instruction along the way. At Mystic Ridge the 'mini-mountain' is exclusively for children to play on. Sunshine has a Kids Kampus Day Care Center for children between 19 months and 6 years of age.

Jackson Hole

ALTITUDE 6,311ft (1924m)

Jackson Hole is set amid some of the most dramatic scenery in America and has some of the steepest and most exciting skiing on the continent, which can be intimidating for those who do not consider themselves advanced skiers. In fact, it is also a suitable resort for beginners, but no one in between the two extremes.

Confusingly, the resort of Jackson Hole is situated in Teton Village, 12 miles (19km) from Jackson, which also has its own resort of Snow King. Skiers stay either in Teton Village at the foot of the slopes or commute for 20 minutes by regular free ski-bus. A car is a distinct advantage.

Jackson is a genuine Wild West town, complete with boardwalks, wooden Victorian shop fronts and tough bars, straight off the set of an authentic Western.

The locals derive their living not just from skiers but also from the summer tourists who stop here en route to Yellowstone National Park, which is 60 miles (97km) away. Working ranches still surround the town, and the horse is the secondary means of transport here behind the four-wheel drive.

The central, attractive square is decorated with arches made of naturally discarded elk antlers from the largest elk reserve in North America, which is a couple of miles out of town. The town was named by a nineteenth-century trapper, Davey Jackson, who hunted in this rugged corner of Wyoming. The Hole is a 50-mile (80km) section of the Snake River, famous for its fishing, which twists its way between the Teton and Gros Ventre mountain ranges.

Jackson Hole is under new ownership, and there are plans to extend Teton Village into a major base-area although whether permission for this will be granted in what is an area of outstanding beauty is debatable. For the moment it consists of a couple of hotels, which offer limited nightlife and après-ski entertainment in comparison with the fleshpots of Jackson.

One criticism of Jackson Hole is that for a resort of such international fame the ski area is quite small and there is little other skiing to be found within driving distance. Snow King, overlooking the town of Jackson, is smaller still. Grand Targhee, 47 miles (76km) away, offers excellent but limited powder skiing and is well worth a day's excursion.

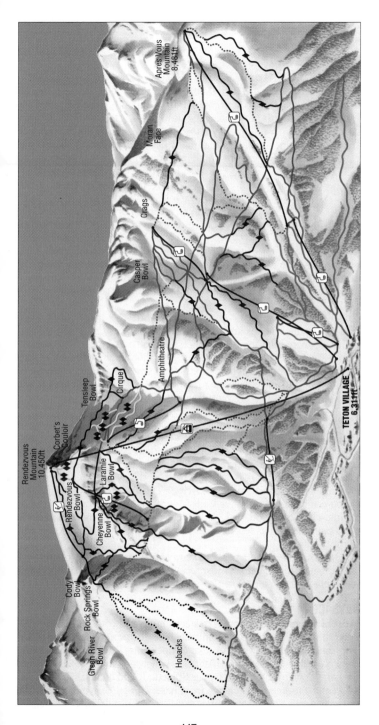

Après Vous Mountain
8,481ft

Moran Face

Crags

Casper Bowl

Amphitheatre

Tensleep Bowl

Cirque

Corbet's Couloir

Rendezvous Mountain
10,450ft

Rendezvous Bowl

Laramie Bowl

Cheyenne Bowl

Cody Bowl

Rock Springs Bowl

Green River Bowl

Hobacks

TETON VILLAGE
6,311ft

On the mountain
top 10,450ft (3186m) bottom 6,311ft (1924m)

The main ski area is on Rendezvous Mountain, which is small by European standards but challenging. It has mostly black (difficult) runs, steep chutes and unlimited off-piste, which is a rarity in the US. Intermediate skiers will find that many of the blue (intermediate) runs can be unpisted. Easier runs are to be found in the Casper Bowl and on neighbouring Apres Vous Mountain.

> ■ **WHAT'S NEW**
>
> Multi-area lift ticket valid at Jackson Hole, Snow King and Grand Targhee

The so-called 'aerial tram', a 30-year-old antiquated cable car, is the main means of uphill transport and the only way up to the peak of Rendezvous Mountain. Despite a refit it is in urgent need of replacement (together with most of the old double chair-lifts) but this has been promised by the new owners of the resort as part of the development plans for the resort over the next few seasons. Queues at peak times can result in an hour's journey to reach the summit.

Beginners
All the beginner slopes are concentrated at the base of Teton Village, which is where both the Kids' Ranch and ski school meet. The nursery slopes are serviced by two short chair-lifts; this allows beginners to start on the easiest slopes and then graduate to steeper gradients. Advanced beginners will find easy blue runs down Apres Vous Mountain and should tackle these before venturing into Casper Bowl.

Intermediates
While much of the terrain provides good, varied intermediate skiing, gradients can change suddenly, and in certain conditions runs that are unpisted are unpredictable and difficult. Like St Anton and Chamonix the colour-grading here is radical. For most skiers 'intermediate' means 'difficult' and 'difficult' means 'extreme'. The most friendly intermediate skiing can be found on Apres Vous Mountain; Casper Bowl, serviced by a triple-chair has good, wide pistes. The runs are well-marked, but you must pay attention as several blues turn into black runs at the lower part of the mountain.

Only the truly confident should stray up the tram. Plenty of mid-skill skiing can be found here in most conditions, but you have to negotiate a harsh black to find any of it.

Advanced
Most of the advanced skiing is in steep chutes and couloirs and on tree-lined runs. The skiing reached initially from the tram is all graded black. The simplest way down is to take Rendezvous Trail, the longest run. Here you can get into the Hobacks, which are ungroomed, or into Laramie Bowl by taking the Upper Sublette Ridge quad-chair. You can also enter the steep Alta chutes from here. Upper Teewinot, under the chair on Apres Vous Mountain, is excellent in fresh powder.

Off-piste

Jackson Hole is one of the few US resorts that has limitless off-piste skiing. The Hobacks (on the lower section of Rendezvous Mountain) are marked as black runs but are, in fact, one large steep snowfield, which is best skied in the morning and is completely unpisted. There are many steep chutes cut through the trees such as Expert Chutes, Alta Chutes and Tower Three Chutes, as well as steep bowls such as Cody, Cheyenne, Rendezvous and Tensleep. On powder days the skiing is excellent.

For those with plenty of nerve there is the notorious Corbet's Couloir off the top of Rendezvous Mountain. This is not as steep as some of the other chutes but it is entered by a 20ft (6m) jump off a cornice, which is enough to deter all but the most suicidal. A short climb accompanied by a local mountain-guide opens up vast tracts of powder on Headwall and Green River, especially in spring.

Snowboarding

Individual and group lessons are available at the ski school. Packages for an hour, half-day and complete courses all include equipment rental. There are two rental shops at the base of Teton Village. Women-only snowboarding camps are also offered.

Ski schools and guiding

The ski school, under the direction of former Olympic medalist Pepi Stiegler, places its emphasis on having fun and being able to tackle simple ski slopes in a short time. Group, private and three-day courses are offered in alpine and nordic skiing. Individual and some group lessons, include video evaluations. The many special clinics include race camps, steep skiing, women's clinics, mountain experience classes, deep powder instruction and a guiding service. All classes meet at Teton Village. The Nordic Center teaches telemark as well as cross-country skiing.

Mountain restaurants

Eating on the mountain is limited, so many skiers head to the oyster bar downstairs at the Mangy Moose or the Alpenhof, a Tyrolean-style restaurant; both are in Teton Village. On the mountain Casper Restaurant serves both hot food and salads, and there are two small snack-bars — one at the base of the Thunder chair-lift and the other at the top of the tram. A basic cafeteria at the bottom of the home run serves the usual sandwiches and salads.

Off the mountain

Jackson is one of the few Western frontier towns turned ski resorts where the past does not clash with the present. Stetsons are as common on the slopes as in the bars. In the summer it is the gateway to Yellowstone National Park, and three million visitors pass through on their way to see moose, buffalo and Old Faithful, the world's largest geyser. In winter it returns to its natural state, a small market-town with an assortment of adventurous shops, restaurants and vast country bars. Here cowboys, who may not be cowboys at all but renegade dentists from Omaha, gulp shots of Wild Turkey, shoot pool and dance to a Wild Frontier rhythm called the Western Swing.

The charismatic town of Jackson is largely made up of single- or double-storied buildings, of which many are renovated saloon-type structures. Teton Village, 20 minutes away by car, is a cluster of hotels and condominiums centred on a picturesque clock tower and the tram. There is a regular bus service between the two, which costs $2 one way. Fervent skiers will stay in Teton Village and avoid the daily commute but will miss out on the overall experience that helps to make Jackson Hole such a unique all-round resort.

Accommodation

If you are looking for a traditional half-board hotel, then the Wort Hotel in Jackson is the one that comes closest to it. The big advantage is its position, right in the centre of town by all the shops and nightlife. Other hotels include the Forty Niner, Rusty Parrot Lodge and the Days Inn. The Lodge at Jackson is on the outskirts of town. Motels include the Parkway Inn, which has a swimming-pool and two hot tubs but no restaurant.

The Inn at Jackson Hole is, in fact, at Teton Village, and is well positioned at the base of the slopes. Self-caterers need to go to Jackson for the supermarkets, which include Albertsons and Foodtown. Further afield on a hill overlooking the valley is Spring Creek Resort, the smartest and most unusual place to stay in the area, but you need a car here.

Eating in and out

Breakfast is a serious business in cowboy country. The real McCoy of 'eggs-over-easy', stacks of pancakes, hash browns and grits are found at Bubba's Bar-B-Que in Jackson or the Mangy Moose in Teton Village. In the evening, the art-deco-style Cadillac Grille in Jackson is a good place for hamburgers, seafood and fresh pasta; it is also fun for children. J.J.'s Silverdollar Bar and Grill in the Wort Hotel has the ubiquitous ribs in various forms. The Blue Lion is a more expensive option, and Stiegler's serves Austrian cuisine. The best pasta is at Nani's. For a more expensive treat go to the Snake River Grill.

Après-ski

Unless you are 21 or over and can prove it you are not going to enjoy yourself outside skiing hours here. Wyoming's licensing laws are so strict that anyone who could be taken for under 40 should carry their identification at all times. The Million Dollar Cowboy Bar, the Silver Dollar Bar and the Rancher in Jackson are where the action is. You can

Skiing facts: **Jackson Hole**

TOURIST OFFICE
PO Box 290, Teton Village, WY 83025
Tel 1 307 733 2292
Fax 1 307 733 2660

THE RESORT
By air Jackson Airport 15 mins from Jackson and 20 mins from Teton Village (reasonably priced airport shuttle-bus to resort)
Visitor beds 12,000
Transport bus service operates day and night between Jackson and Teton Village ($2 each way)

THE SKIING
Linked or nearby resorts Snow King (n), Grand Targhee (n)
Longest run Rendezvous Trail, 7.2 miles (11.5km) - blue
Number of lifts 10 in Jackson Hole
Total of trails/pistes 2,500 acres (1011 hectares) - 10% easy, 40% intermediate, 50% difficult)
Nursery slopes 10% of total slopes
Summer skiing none
Snowmaking 80 acres (32 hectares) covered

LIFT PASSES
Area pass $216 for 6 days ($240 including tram)
Day pass $44 including tram
Beginners no free lifts
Pensioners 65 yrs and over, $20 per day
Credit cards accepted yes

SKI SCHOOLS
Adults Jackson Hole Ski School, $45 per day (4 hrs), or $80 for 3 days (2 hrs each morning)
Private lessons $115 per morning (2 hrs), afternoon extension $90 ($1\frac{3}{4}$ hrs), full day $260 (6 hrs), half-day $170
Snowboarding Jackson Hole Ski School, prices as ski lessons
Cross-country Jackson Hole Nordic Center, $32 per day including lesson, equipment hire and trail pass. Loipe 25km at base of resort
Other courses moguls, disabled skiing, mountain experience (off-piste), race camps, women's ski clinics (Grand Targhee)
Guiding companies Jackson Hole Alpine Guides

CHILDREN
Lift pass 14 yrs and under, $108 for 6 days, $126 including tram. Free for 5 yrs and under on Eagle's Rest
Ski kindergarten Rough Riders, 3-5 yrs, $60 per day including daycare, lunch and 2hr lesson
Ski school Jackson Hole Ski School Skiwee, 6-13 yrs, $210 for 5 days (4 hrs per day) including lunch. Rough Riders for older, more experienced children, $60 per day including lessons, snacks and lift ticket. (Upper mountain skiers need to purchase a $17 lift ticket in addition)
Non-ski kindergarten Tenderfoots Infant Care (2-18 mths), or Wrangler Childcare (18 mths-5 yrs), both 8am-5pm, $52 per day including lunch

FOOD AND DRINK PRICES
Coffee $1.25, glass of wine $2.75-3.50, small beer $2.75, dish of the day $6.50-8.50

dance to live music in all three for most of the season. The Cowboy Bar has the most atmosphere, with real leather saddles as bar stools and a full-sized stuffed grizzly bear silently directing proceedings.

The Mangy Moose at Teton Village is one of the finest après-ski bars in The Rockies. It has live music in the evenings and a video room for those under age. The Wingback Lounge at the Inn is a quieter option, and the Stockman's Lounge at the Sojourner usually has ski videos and free appetisers. If you have hired a car you should drive to Wilson on the road towards the Teton Pass for an authentic Western evening at the Stagecoach Inn, with live music, cowgirls in flounced dresses and good-value food. It is the kind of place where you eat with your hat on and go easy on the eye contact with strangers.

Other après-ski activities include night-skiing at the Snow King resort in Jackson, sleigh-rides through the elk compound, and snowmobiling tours of Yellowstone National Park. Shopping is another important après-ski activity; the Polo Ralph Lauren Factory Store sells end-of-line designer clothes at a fraction of the normal prices.

Childcare

The Kinderschule, which has changed its name to 'Kids Ranch' and is at the base of Teton Village, is one of the better ski kindergarten in the US. Children are taught the 'Edgie Wedgie' technique where ski tips are clipped together with brightly coloured, bendy strips of plastic. This stops the skis from crossing and encourages children to make a wedge or snowplough. Children are taken to and from the nursery slopes in a snowmobile trailer. The non-ski kindergarten is for infants from two months to five years of age.

Linked or nearby resorts

Grand Targhee 8,000ft (2439m)

The small resort is 47 miles (76km) north-west of Jackson and just inside the Wyoming border. It is blessed with an excellent snow record, which is why the main attraction is snow cat skiing in the virgin powder. This is by previous arrangement only, as the cat takes a maximum of ten passengers plus the guide and a patrolman. If you can't get a booking for snow cat skiing, the resort's own 2,500 skiable acres (607 hectares) are varied as well as exciting and are often left ungroomed in fresh snow. The resort has a small shopping centre but limited restaurant choice. Unusual courses available in the resort include 'WomenSki Wholistic Mountain Retreat Weeks.

TOURIST OFFICE
Tel 1 307 353 2304
Tel 1 307 353 8148

Lake Tahoe

Heavenly 6,500ft (1982m) Squaw Valley 6,200ft (1890m)

California is a world unto itself, so it is not surprising that its ski resorts are also unique; **Heavenly** (on the Nevada/California state-line) and Squaw Valley could not be more different. From the top of the Sky Express chair-lift you can turn left to ski in **Nevada** with views of the arid vastness of the Nevada Desert, or turn right to the **California** side, overlooking the lush beauty of Lake Tahoe. This stretch of cobalt blue water lives up to its deserved reputation as the second largest and most magnificent alpine lake in the world after Lake Titicaca in Peru.

Squaw Valley and Heavenly are the largest and best known of the 14 alpine skiing and 7 cross-country resorts set in the mountains above the shores of Lake Tahoe. **Granlibakken** ski area, with its two lifts, is the oldest. Squaw has the toughest skiing, but it is Heavenly that stands out from the pack because of its stunning scenery and unusual nightlife.

Off the slopes, serenity switches to frenzy amid the green baize of the tables and the clunk of one-arm bandits in the 24-hour casinos of **South Lake Tahoe.** These are on the Nevada side of the state-line, where gambling is legal.

Squaw Valley, which hosted the 1960 Winter Olympics, has more challenging slopes above the north shore of the lake (in a corner of the Sierra Nevada), which has a long skiing tradition. As far back as 1856 John 'Snowshoe' Thompson, a Norwegian immigrant, carried the mail on skis between the mining camps in these mountains. Until the railroad was built in 1872, he was the miners' only winter link with the outside world.

On the mountain
Heavenly top 10,100ft (3079m) bottom 7,200ft (2195m)
Squaw Valley top 9,050ft (2759m) bottom 6,200ft (1890m)

Heavenly is one of America's largest ski areas, with almost all of it in the tree-line. It also has one of America's most extensive snowmaking programmes, with 37 miles (59km) of terrain covered by snow-cannon — a total of 66 per cent of the resort's pistes. The skiing is divided between the Nevada and the Californian sides of the mountain. The Nevada face consists mainly of blue (intermediate) runs, with expert skiing in the Mott Canyon area, a north-facing wall with a selection of chutes through the trees and Killebrew Canyon, which has steep unpisted chutes. The green (easy) trails are mostly on the lower and middle slopes. The upper Californian side is mainly fast, cruising, blue terrain. The most difficult skiing on the Californian side is just above the Base Lodge and on the bowl runs. Higher up the mountain there are some black (difficult) runs off Skyline Trail.

The skiing at Squaw Valley takes place on six peaks: Granite Chief, Red Dog, KT-22, Squaw, Emigrant and Broken Arrow. The area is divided into three sectors, with the lifts rather than the runs being colour-graded. All the main lifts on Red Dog, KT-22 and Granite Chief are black, and Squaw and Emigrant's are blue. Intermediates will find a huge amount of skiing, with the highlight a 3-mile (5km) trail from the High Camp area down to the mountain base.

Beginners

There are three beginner areas at Heavenly. The Enchanted Forest at the California base is a secluded area with lifts and simple runs. Another beginners' centre is at Boulder Base Lodge. Mid-way up the mountain on the California side are a number of green (beginner) runs, including a gentle but long slope called Mombo Meadows. Squaw's nursery slopes are in the centre of the ski area up on the mountain.

Intermediates

Intermediates will find they can ski virtually every run on the mountain at Heavenly. The skiing here is 45 per cent intermediate, with much of it long cruising runs bordered by banks of pine trees and there is always a stunning view of the lake. Take the Sky Express chair and try Liz's or Betty's, then head to Nevada and the Big Dipper, Sand Dunes, Perimeter and Galaxy runs. You need to make your way back to the state in which you started by 3.30pm.

Squaw Valley has three main intermediate areas: the runs off Squaw Creek and Red Dog lift, which are best tackled later in the day, the area off Squaw One Express and the bowls on Emigrant Mountain and Shirley Lakes. The runs are groomed but not named on the piste map, which only indicates the lifts.

Advanced

On powder days Heavenly's Milky Way Bowl is a good choice, and in any conditions the most advanced skiing can be found in Mott Canyon and Killebrew Canyon. These are steep, unpisted chutes cut through the trees with runs such as Snake Pit. There are huge areas of tree-line skiing and the odd black run such as Ellie's from the Sky Express and The Face near the California base-lodge. Gunbarrel is a challenging mogul slope.

Squaw is paradise for the advanced skier, with its couloirs, steep gullies and overall fairly steep territory (many ski extreme videos have been filmed here). The most adventurous skiers will find endless terrain with some of the most radical off the KT-22 lift and Olympic Lady. Last season (1994–5) many of the gullies were filled in because of the huge amounts of snow, which made some of the area less steep. Silverado has some sheer chutes, as does Granite Chief.

Off-piste

There is almost unlimited off-piste skiing at Heavenly; many of the trees are packed tightly together and there are some vast untracked areas to discover. The Milky Way, Mott Canyon and Killebrew Canyon are large expanses of off-piste; you need to arrive early on powder days as they are quickly skied-out. Black-diamond runs cut through huge areas of forest, where you can always find untouched snow.

In Squaw Valley the further away from the lifts you travel the more likely you are to find good powder snow. The locals ski by the cliffs behind the cable car, but you need to be accompanied by a local guide in this tricky area. Many skiers opt for Headwall and KT-22, but there is also some excellent skiing off Granite Chief and Silverado.

Snowboarding

Heavenly has a snowboard park on the Nevada side of the mountain. The 'Shred Ready' snowboard school is based at Boulder Lodge and the California Lodge for beginner, group and private lessons.

The Squaw Valley Ski School offers group and private snowboard lessons. At Children's World young skiers between the ages of 7 and 12 can also try snowboarding.

Ski schools and guiding

The ski school at Heavenly offers private, day and group lessons. Special courses include three-hour lessons for first-timers and improvers, Mountain Adventure (off-piste) courses and women's ski seminars.

The Squaw Valley Ski School has programmes for all ages and abilities including Ski Your Pro, which aims to get beginners to intermediate level. Advanced lessons, mogul clinics, cross-country and back-country skiing are also available. At Heavenly, Spooner Lake cross-country ski area has 21 prepared trails and 100km of loipe. At Squaw the prepared cross-country circuit is from Squaw Creek Resort to the base area.

Mountain restaurants

The Monument Peak restaurant, cocktail lounge and cafeteria is at the top of the tram at Heavenly; there is also an outdoor deck here. Sky Meadows has an outdoor barbecue and snack shop. The California Lodge has a cafeteria and a bar. Boulder Lodge has a bar, cafeteria and outdoor deck. Stagecoach Lodge has a cafeteria. East Peak Lodge is the place to go to soak up the sun; it has a barbecue, delicatessen, pizzeria, bar and cafeteria.

At Squaw Valley the highly recommended Resort at Squaw Creek has a daily barbecue. At the base there are several lunch places serving pizza and sandwiches. Gold Coast at the top of the Super Gondola has restaurants and bars on three levels with a big sunny deck. High Camp has five different restaurants and bars, and the main dining-room is open at night.

Off the mountain

The blatant flashing lights, huge neon signs and monstrous casino complexes are such a contrast from the lake front and its simple single-storey homes that it takes a while to digest South Lake Tahoe. One reporter said of the casinos: 'These make interesting sightseeing but if you don't know the rules, the gambling seems pretty daunting'. Après-ski includes taking in a show — some excellent cabaret acts and pop concerts are staged here and feature top artists.

■ OTHER SPORTS

Skating, snowmobiling

There is dancing at Nero's, where the disco may be stopped temporarily for 'The Best Buns' contest, or you can have a flutter at the tables.

Alternatively, you can ignore the tacky glitter and find a small restaurant for an intimate dinner. This is easier to achieve in Tahoe City, a 15-minute drive from Squaw Valley, where there are good restaurants, including several lakeside ones. The drive to Squaw Valley along the lake is spectacular, with a castle on a small inlet, known as Emerald Lake.

Accommodation

The ski area of Heavenly and the town of **South Lake Tahoe** are separate, although Tahoe Seasons Resort hotel-complex is close to the lifts at the California base. Harrah's and the Horizon Casino Resort in South Lake Tahoe are two of the bigger casino hotels, along with Caesar's Tahoe and Harvey's Resort; all have good health spas. Much of the accommodation is in condominiums. On the quieter Californian side, motels are stacked side by side with little to choose between them. Station House Inn and the Timber Cover Lodge are singled out by reporters. There are also condominiums at the Nevada base.

The Resort at Squaw Creek is a large ski-in ski-out complex near the base of **Squaw Valley**, with its own restaurants, bars, fitness centre and skating rink. Squaw Valley Lodge is also close to the base lifts, and the Olympic Village Inn is nearby. The Squaw Valley Inn is opposite the tram (cable car). There are also lodges in and around **Tahoe City**, the livelier place in which to stay.

Eating in and out

The big casino resorts have numerous restaurants, and some of them are excellent. Caesar's has Planet Hollywood with all sorts of movie paraphernalia, including Arnold Schwarzenegger's Robocop outfit. Try the Mexican restaurant at Harvey's or Carlos Murphy's, an Irish/Mexican restaurant. Zachery's and Dixie's specialise in Cajun cooking. The Station House Inn serves reasonably priced meals, and The Chart House is more expensive but has great views. The Cal-Neva Lodge in Crystal Bay has two restaurants and an oyster bar, and The Dory's Oar has good seafood.

At Squaw Valley, the Resort at Squaw Creek has excellent food, Glissandi is a high-priced Italian, Graham's is cosier and midway between the Resort and the Squaw Valley base. The restaurants in Tahoe City and a couple of establishments in **Truckee**, half-an-hour away, are more fun. In Tahoe City, Za's is a cheap and basic Italian, while Christy Hill's is upmarket and overlooks the lake. A couple of boathouse complexes have medium-priced restaurants serving seafood and wholesome American fare.

Après-ski

There is no après-ski at the resort of Heavenly, except for the California Bar at the base. All the post-skiing activities take place in South Lake Tahoe, with bars in all the hotels and most of the motels. Try McP's, which is a lively Irish pub. Turtle's has dancing, and the Christiania Inn, close to the ski area, has a good atmosphere.

The gaming tables attract money, and money attracts the top names in show business. The Tahoe region is renowned for its Vegas-like celebrity shows, although some of the US television names will mean little to Europeans.

At Squaw there is the Plaza Bar and Salsa, and there is dancing at Bar One in the Squaw Valley Mall, Humpty's in Tahoe City and at the Olympic Village Inn at weekends.

Childcare

Heavenly has a number of programmes for children, including Ski Explorers for 4- to 12-year-olds, and first-timer lessons. There is also a mini-clinic and junior ski school. Children's Ski World is at the base of the mountain, where there are a few simple runs for children.

At Squaw the recent addition of the Papoose chair-lift behind the Children's World at Papoose has added to the resort's convenience for families. Parents can deposit their offspring before buying their tickets and proceeding up the mountain on the Papoose chair. Ten Little Indians is a kindergarten for the smallest babies up to three-year-olds. Toddler Care is for children aged two to three years of age. The Fun in the Sun Program is an introduction to skiing for children 13 years and older.

Linked or nearby resorts

Lake Tahoe offers an enormous amount of skiing, so a car is essential to fully appreciate the many different resorts around the lake. The main resorts to visit are Kirkwood, Alpine Meadows and Northstar, but the others in the area are Boreal Ski Area, Diamond Peak at Ski Incline, Granlibakken, Homewood, Mount Rose/Slide Mountain, Sierra Ski Ranch, Sierra Summit, Sugar Bowl, and Tahoe Donner Ski Bowl.

Mammoth Mountain

ALTITUDE 7,953ft (2425m)

If you ask how Mammoth got its name there will be several answers. It is not because the mountain is huge nor because it is shaped like a pre-historic elephant. Some say it was named after the dinosaur bones found in the meadow, others that the mountain owes its name to the Spanish, who dubbed this extinct volcano the 'big mountain'. The real reason stems from mining days when gold was discovered in 1878. The main mining company called itself the Mammoth Mining Company because it was so big, and gradually the geographical features such as the mountain were named Mammoth.

Mammoth Mountain is one of the few top American resorts that is run by its founder instead of an anonymous corporation. Dave McCoy set up a portable rope-tow in 1941 and bought the resort in 1953. Today, he still runs the mountain with his family. Most days he is out on the slopes skiing or checking lift tickets. Mammoth has expanded since those early days and now has 150 named runs and 31 lifts (most are chairs), including two high-speed quads, and there are two gondolas, one drag-lift and one T-bar.

Mammoth Lakes, the closest town, is four miles (7km) away. It is a sprawling little town without much nightlife and is supported by a year-round tourist business. Thirty minutes away is **June Mountain**. The McCoys opened this area in the 1980s and today it has one state-of-the-art large gondola, two detachable quads and five double-chairs. The Mammoth lift ticket covers both ski areas, but if you buy your pass at June Mountain (which costs less) there is an extra daily charge of $5 to ski at Mammoth.

Mammoth and June are popular with southern Californians who head for the Sierra Nevada Mountains on sunny weekends. The ski resorts lie 300 miles (480km) to the north of Los Angeles, a spectacular six-hour drive through the Mojave Desert before the climb into the mountains. Richard Branson rates Mammoth as one of his favourite family-ski destinations, which may in part explain why Virgin flies into Los Angeles. While a car is useful, an efficient shuttle-bus service plies between Mammoth Lakes and the ski area. Taxis are also available. Plans to build a gondola between the two are on the drawing board but have yet to materialise.

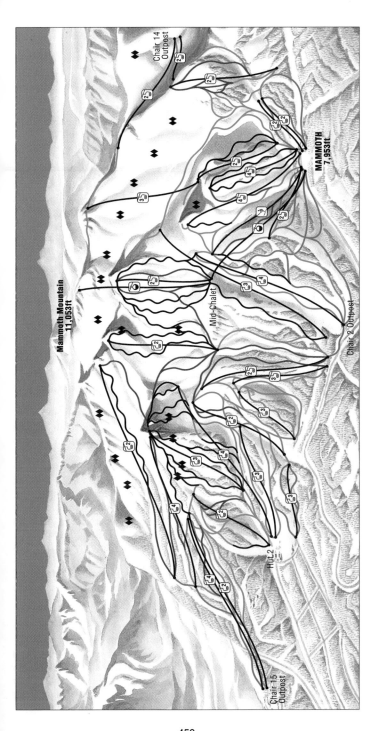

Mammoth Mountain
11,053ft

MAMMOTH
7,953ft

Chair 14
Outpost

Chair 2 Outpost

Mid-Chalet

Hut 2

Chair 15
Outpost

On the mountain
top 11,053ft (3370m) bottom 7,953ft (2425m)

Last season Mammoth had more snow than any other resort in the world. The main street was banked by 15ft (5m) walls as the area wildly exceeded its impressive average annual snowfall of over 27ft (8m). Mammoth has a large skiable area with trees still growing at 9,000ft (2743m). Above the tree-line open bowl-skiing provides a variety of steep black (difficult) runs as well as wide blue (intermediate) trails. Most of the mid-level skiing starts at the tree-line. Above the trees there are five small peaks, accessed by chair-lifts. The rim of an old volcano runs right across the skyline.

■ WHAT'S NEW
Chair 16 upgraded to a high-speed detachable quad
Woollywood Children's Center expanded and improved
New people-mover and replacement Mirror Image chair
Addition of Chair 11b on beginner slopes
Teens' lift ticket introduced

The six-seater Gondola 2 takes you up to the highest point while, a little further to the right as you look up the mountain, the three-person Grizzly chair takes you up to the next highest point. Between the two lifts there are three double-black-diamond (very difficult) trails — Climax, Hangman's Hollow and Drop Out — while for those skiers of a more cautious frame of mind there is a single black-diamond trail, which takes you down a less forbidding gradient into Cornice Bowl.

Even though Mammoth is known for its sunny days and mild temperatures the mountain does not receive its fantastic snowfalls without its share of white-outs and storms. Be prepared to spend days on end in limited visibility during the main winter months.

There are four easy mountain-access points into the lift system, each served by one or other of the shuttles. Mountain 'hosts' help you find your way around. No one should miss the more gentle skiing at June Mountain; both summits here, Rainbow and June itself, are just over 10,000ft (3049m), with trees right up to the top. There are magnificent views of the more jagged peaks in the Sierras. This 500-acre (200-hectare) ski area is a great place to ski at weekends while the Los Angelinos swarm to Mammoth.

A few lean years led Mammoth to expand its snowmaking facilities, which now cover 200 acres (80 hectares) and 22 runs, and can ensure skiing well into July.

Beginners
All the beginner slopes are below the tree-line with most runs concentrated at the main Lodge. This is also where the ski school meets. Most of the runs are green (easy) and can be reached by two chairs. Another novice area is at Warming Hut II. There are a few beginner runs at Chair 15 but these are longer and less accessible. In both easy skiing areas there is a choice of blue runs.

Intermediates

Every area of the mountain has good intermediate skiing, except at the peak, where there are steep black runs. Above the tree-line and the gondola, the top of Chairs 14 and 18 offers good open bowl-skiing. The runs through the trees have been designed to give some tight tree-line skiing as well as some wide, open pistes. The longer runs are accessed from Chair 16 and Chair 10 and from the mid-Chalet. To stay in the good light all day, start at Chair 15 and gradually follow the sun towards Warming Hut II and the Main Lodge, ending up at Chair 13 and 14. The longest run, Road Runner, is 2½ miles (4km); this is a blue that turns into a green before ending at the Main Lodge.

Advanced

One look at the map dotted with double-black-diamond runs will fire up any advanced skier. There are steep chutes, good tree-line skiing, wide open-bowls and plenty of off-piste. On powder days, of which there are many, exhaustion will hit you long before you have explored the mountain. When the snow cover is good the black runs at the top of the mountain are steep but open. Off Chair 22 the trees between Stump Alley and Patrolmen's and Stump and Mambo provide good steep runs. Around the ridge underneath Chairs 13 and 14, where the area is shaded, the snow stays firm until late in the day and has some excellent tree-line skiing.

Off-piste

The large open-bowls above the tree-line provide endless off-piste skiing; it is also easy to find your own route through the trees. If there is fresh powder you should be able to ski it all day, although this is more of a challenge at weekends. The pisteurs start work early in the morning from the Main Lodge and the Warming Hut II. To get to the good snow before they do, head high to Chairs 3, 5, 13 and 14, then 9, 15 and 24. Some of the best first runs of the day include Powder Bowl, Fascination, Stump Alley, Broadway, Mambo and St Anton.

Snowboarding

The ski school offers snowboarding Learn-to-Ski Packages as well as individual and group lessons. Snowboard camps are available for adults as well as children. Six ski shops hire out boards. Riders should try Dragon's Back chute and Hemlock Ridge, which are challenging steep runs. Upper Dry Creek has numerous walls and drop-offs, and you can follow the run into the tree-line until Lower Dry Creek, which is a natural half-pipe. For off-piste boarding, hike up to Hole-in-the-Wall or Sherwin Ridge. For the less advanced there is Meadows Plateau, a 500-acre (200-hectare) ski area, which is excellent for snowboarding. At June Mountain there is a snowboarder's park and a half-pipe.

Ski schools and guiding

Mammoth Mountain Ski School has packages that include group lessons, learn-to-ski specials and two-day weekend courses. Specialist day camps include a women's ski seminar, advanced ski clinics and senior ski clinics. Special courses include bump lessons, race-training, powder skiing and steep skiing clinics. Some courses include video analysis.

Mountain restaurants

Mammoth only has one large restaurant on the mountain at the mid-Chalet. The Outpost restaurants at Chair 14 and 15 are for light snacks, and June Mountain has one on-hill snack bar. The four base areas all have cafeterias. Prices are generally reasonable. The best restaurant is in the Yodler, a Swiss chalet, which was brought over and reconstructed plank by plank in the base area. The Mammoth Mountain Inn is also recommended, as is the Mountainside Grill.

Off the mountain

Keen skiers will want to stay at the Mammoth Mountain Inn at the base, which is a complex containing a bar and restaurant and separate building for sports facilities and a whirlpool.

The town of Mammoth Lakes has no real centre. While there are a number of bars and restaurants there is no feeling of a community. The single main street does have good shopping with numerous sports shops where you can buy ski equipment, tennis shoes and clothing for considerably less than at home. There are six brand-name factory stores, including Polo/Ralph Lauren and Van Heusen; good ski-wear shops include The North Face and Patagonia.

Accommodation

There is a large number of hotels, guest houses, apartments and rooms to be found in Mammoth Lakes, many of them with whirlpools and exercise spas. The Alpenhof is a cheerful place that looks as Tyrolean as its name suggests. Jägerhof Lodge is another recommended hotel, just out of town on the ski-shuttle route. The Austrian influence on the early days of American skiing is reflected in some other more economical establishments such as Holiday Haus and the Kitzbühel Lodge. The newest establishments are Sierra Lodge (a no-smoking hotel), Shilo Inn, and the Quality Inn bed-and-breakfast. The luxury Silver Bear condominiums are within walking distance of the lifts. The Mammoth Mountain Inn, the 1849 and The Bridges condos are at the ski resort base.

■ OTHER SPORTS

Snowmobiling, bob-sleigh, tobogganing, sleigh rides, dog-sledding, hot air ballooning, indoor tennis

Eating in and out

Mammoth Lakes comes into its own here with well over 40 restaurants, delicatessen, ice-cream parlours and pizzerias. There are six steak and seafood establishments, three Mexican restaurants, four Italian, one

Skiing facts: **Mammoth Mountain**

TOURIST OFFICE
1 Minaret Road, Mammoth Lakes,
CA 93546
Tel 1 619 934 2571
Fax 1 619 934 0603

THE RESORT
By air Mammoth/June Lake Airport 40
mins, Los Angeles 6 hrs
Visitor beds 8,200
Transport Mammoth area shuttle-bus provides free transport around the town and to
the Main Lodge, Warming Hut II and Chair
15 areas

THE SKIING
Linked or nearby resorts June Mountain
(n)
Longest run Road Runner, 2½ miles (4km)
- blue
Number of lifts 31
Total of trails/pistes over 3,500 acres
(1,400 hectares) - 30% easy, 40%
intermediate, 30% difficult
Nursery slopes 30% of ski area
Summer skiing none
Snowmaking 200 acres (80 hectares)
covered

LIFT PASSES
Area pass (covers Mammoth and June
Mountain) $175 for 5 days
Day pass $40
Beginners free for those taking ski lessons
Pensioners 65 yrs and over, $20 per day or
$88 for 5 days
Credit cards accepted yes

SKI SCHOOLS
Adults Mammoth Ski School, 10am-midday
and 1.30-3.30pm, $175 for 5 days
Private lessons adults and children, $60
per hr, $180 per half-day, $360 per full day
Snowboarding Snowboard Learn to Ski
package, $68 per day including board and
lifts. Group lessons $38 per day. Private as
ski lessons
Cross-country Tamarack Cross-country
Ski Center or Mammoth Ski School (private
or group lessons on demand), prices on
request. Loipe 35km around the lakes
Other courses powder, moguls, race training, slalom, extreme skiing
Guiding companies through ski school

CHILDREN
Lift pass 7-12 yrs $88 for 5 days, 13-18 yrs
$138 for 5 days, free for 6 yrs and under
Ski kindergarten Small World Day Center,
4-12 yrs, 8am-5pm, $60 per day including
ski lesson, supervision and lunch
Ski school Woollywood Ski Academy, 4-6
yrs, 10am-3.30pm, $58 per day including
lunch. Mammoth Teens Program for
advanced and intermediate skiers, 13-18
yrs, 10am-midday and 1.30-3.30pm,
$38 per day
Non-ski kindergarten Small World
Children's Center, 0-23 mths, 8am-5pm,
$45 per day including lunch. 2-12 yrs, $40
per day including lunch

FOOD AND DRINK PRICES
Coffee $1, glass of wine $3, small beer
$2.75, dish of the day $8.95

Chinese and one Japanese. The Lakefront (nouvelle cuisine in a historic lodge), Natalie's and The Mogul (high-quality steaks) are among the more expensive, while Goats Bar, Las Sierras and the Swiss Café are three of the cheapest. Slocum's Italian and American Grill is a good place for dinner out. The Shogun is the resort's sushi bar, Roberto's offers some of the best Mexican cuisine in town, and The Good Life Café has healthy and wholesome food. Angel's has creative cooking in a cosy atmosphere. Self-caterers can shop at Von's supermarket, which sells a large variety of food, Pioneer Market (a smaller alternative), or the Gourmet Grocer.

Après-ski

Directly after skiing the Yodler offers great cocktails, and the Austria Hof at the base of Hut II has spiced wine and a variety of après-ski drinks. When it comes to late-night drinking, dancing and pool-playing the scene is limited. It is worth looking in on Grumpy's, Annie Rose's, Slocums or Gringo's, but mid-week they can be quite subdued. The Clocktower is where the locals go.

Whiskey Creek offers live entertainment, and Rafters, Ocean Harvest, Kegs and Cue's (for pool) are the other main nightspots. The pace hots up at weekends when the Los Angelinos hit town.

Childcare

There are special learn-to-ski packages for one, two or three days. Prices include lifts, lessons and equipment rental. The expanded Woollywood Ski Academy takes children from four to six years old. Mammoth Teens Program is for intermediate and advanced skiers. Children under seven years old ski free, which is a higher than average age compared with other ski resorts.

Older children of up to 12 years of age can enrol in the Mammoth Explorers programme, which divides into groups of differing abilities. For teenagers up to 17 there are ski clinics with hand-picked instructors who can cope with everyone from first-timers to fast skiers. The very young, from newborn to 23 months, plus 2- to 12-year-olds, can enrol in the Small World Daycare Center at the Mountain Inn.

Park City

ALTITUDE 6,900ft (2104m)

By Utah's strict Mormon standards, Park City is sin city. This means that a degree of polite rowdiness that would be frowned upon in Snowbird is tolerated on Main Street. As the crow flies, it is barely 6 miles (10km) from Snowbird to Park City, yet Utah's two leading resorts could hardly be more different. Where Snowbird is confined in its canyon and trapped in purpose-built glitz, Park City sprawls along a much wider valley with little regard for convenience and none whatsoever for land conservation.

Since mining began here in the mid-nineteenth century, silver to the value of $400 million has been extracted from the hills surrounding Park City. George Hearst, father of William Randolph Hearst, was one

who made his fortune in the 1880s, the era of maximum prosperity. Today Park City has a reputation for being rather more than a ski resort. In recent years its cultural aspirations have been enhanced by the emergence of the Sundance Film Festival. This event, which takes place over the last ten days in January, under the patronage of Robert Redford's Sundance Institute, is now recognised as the premier showcase for American independent films.

On the mountain
top 10,000ft (3049m) bottom 6,900ft (2104m)

Park City's ski area lies on rolling wooded terrain on the slopes of **Jupiter Peak**. Although the US Ski Team has used the resort as its headquarters since 1973, the skiing is much less challenging than that at Snowbird. This is partly because the lower altitude makes for a greater percentage of glade-skiing on trails cut from the forest and partly because the slopes are less steep. Access to the top of the main ski area is by the Silver Queen gondola, which takes 20 minutes from the **Resort Center** (a moderately well-designed complex on three levels, with shops and cafés set around an open-air skating rink) to the Summit House Restaurant. The highest point is **Jupiter Bowl**, which is for experts only and is reached by the two-seater Jupiter chair.

Skiers of all standards will find suitable runs from the summit to the bottom of the Prospector high-speed quad. The easiest is Claimjumper, a broad green (easy) boulevard curving round the mountain towards the Snow Hut restaurant. Night-skiing is on PayDay and First Time.

Beginners

There are two beginner areas, one at the base of the resort area with two lifts and another at the top of the gondola, where runs are concentrated around the Prospector chair. Beginners can profit from a $3\frac{1}{2}$ mile ($5\frac{1}{2}$ km) green descent from the Summit House to the Resort Center via the top of Claimjumper, Bonanza and Sidewinder. This is broad and flat territory, which is perfect for discovering the pleasures of the beautifully groomed snow. The less experienced should avoid it late in the afternoon when it becomes a race-track back to base as the lifts close.

■ **WHAT'S NEW**

First Time triple-chair replaces double-chair, increasing beginner area

Additional snowmaking

Giant slalom run designed for World Cup races

Intermediates

The 89 trails covering 2,200 acres (890 hectares) of terrain are 45 per cent intermediate and cover every area of the mountain except Jupiter Bowl. Confident intermediates will not find themselves unduly tested by Hidden Splendour, Mel's Alley, Powder Keg and Assessment. However, Prospector, Single Jack, Sunnyside and Parley's Park take rather more direct routes down the mountain. Park City has 650 acres (263 hectares) of open bowls; 'overall we found the bowl-skiing excellent,' was one report. The grading of blue (intermediate) runs can be unpredictable ('the variation in the blues is quite alarming for lower intermediates'). Favourite runs include Blue Slip Bowl and 10th Mountain.

Advanced

Advanced skiers have a choice of moderate black (difficult) runs, including The Host, Thaynes, Double Jack, Ford Country and Glory Hole, which all lead into the Thaynes Canyon, a blue cruiser that marks the eastern boundary of the ski area. Halfway down they can take the Motherlode chair-lift back to the Summit House or continue down to the King Consolidated chair-lift, which is the access point for ten short blue runs leading into Broadway and Hot Spot.

Off-piste

Those in search of adventure should take the Jupiter Access trail from the Summit House to the Jupiter chair-lift. This goes up to the top of the resort, a wind-blown ridge with a variety of ungroomed options. Shadow Ridge and Fortune Teller go straight down under the chair through sparsely wooded snowfields, but a ten-minute walk along the ridge to the east brings skiers to the top of Scott's Bowl. Further along Portuguese Gap is a narrow, often heavily mogulled, field between the trees. A 20-minute walk along the ridge to the west leads to Jupiter Peak. Here there

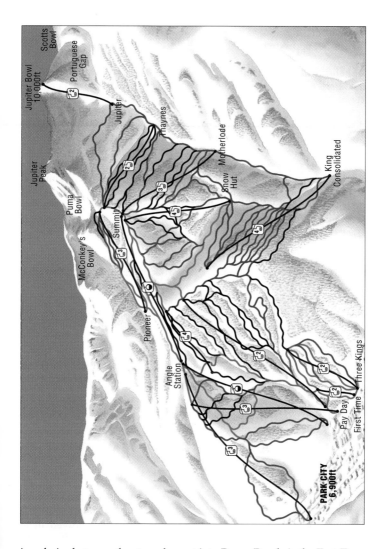

is a choice between the steep descent into **Puma Bowl** via the East Face or back to the chair-lift via the West Face. Expert skiing in Park City is dependent on the Jupiter chair-lift being open.

When the wind gets up, as it frequently does, or the cloud closes in the options are drastically reduced. The black alternatives to the west of the resort are six parallel descents through aspen trees and they are also prone to closure because of poor snow conditions. A guided programme called Ski Utah Interconnect, which takes a whole day, is an off-piste adventure that covers five ski areas.

Snowboarding

This is not permitted in Park City.

Ski schools and guiding

The Park City Ski School uses the American Teaching System as pre-scribed by the Professional Ski Instructors of America (PSIA). There are full- and half-day adult group lessons for visitors aged 14 years and over. The Mountain Experience programme takes good intermediate to advanced skiers into the high bowls on Jupiter Peak. Private lessons are also available.

Beginners and low intermediate 'wedge turners' meet at the bottom of the mountain, and intermediate to advanced at the Summit Ski School area at the top of the Prospector high-speed quad. Special courses include moguls, freestyle, slalom, off-piste, race clinics and women's ski performance workshops. There are 19km of cross-country tracks, and lessons are available at the White Pine Touring Center.

Mountain restaurants

The Mid-Mountain restaurant, a low wooden cabin built to serve the miners in 1898 (and moved to its present site in 1987) offers high-qual-ity fast food ('simply heaven on a sunny day — at weekends they even have a live band'). It is only open at lunchtime whereas its rivals, the Summit House at the top of the gondola and the Snow Hut at the bot-tom of the Prospector high-speed quad, serve breakfast as well. Steeps, a ski-in ski-out bar at the bottom of the main run back to the Resort Center, has table service at lunch-time. It is also an essential après-ski stop, with live music, happy-hour prices and a party atmosphere.

Off the mountain

Park City, like many of its Colorado rivals, has artfully converted a min-ing past into a colourful touristic present. There is a museum with real-istic exhibits of its mining history and a video made for its recently celebrated centennial. Its focus is Main Street, home to the Wasatch Brewery, the Egyptian Theater and a host of art gal-leries and boutiques. Between them there are numerous bars, coffee shops and restaurants.

■ **OTHER SPORTS**

Ice-driving, snowmobiling, snow-shoeing, parapente, aeroclub, hang-gliding, swimming, helicopter rides, skating, curling, indoor tennis and racket-ball, climbing wall, hot air ballooning, sleigh rides, snow cat skiing, ski jumping, nature treks, night-skiing

A less cosmopolitan area is Prospector Square, where you can find Albertsons the supermarket, a video shop and one of Park City's two liquor stores (the other is on Main Street), which are the only places, besides the bars and discos, where you can buy alcohol. Other Main Street shops specialise in pottery and Native American artifacts. The Factory Stores at Park West, 4 miles (6km) away (near the Best Western Landmark

Inn) is a large shopping centre selling end-of-the-line designer clothing.

A car is useful for exploring the area and the nearby resorts of **Snowbird**, **Alta**, **Solitude**, **Brighton**, **Wolf Mountain**, **Park West**, **Sundance** and **Deer Valley**. All of them are less than 45 minutes' drive from Park City.

Accommodation

Much of the accommodation is condominiums, many of which are on the ski slopes. One of the most convenient places to stay is the Silver King Aparthotel, a complex offering 85 units ranging from studios to penthouses. Most of the hotels, including The Radisson Inn and Yarrow Hotel, are a few miles from Park City on the free-bus route. The Chamonix Lodge is at the slopes, and The Prospector Square Hotel, which is about 15 minutes away by free shuttle-bus, resembles a collection of Nissen huts and is priced accordingly. It also has a superb athletics club with an Olympic-sized indoor swimming-pool, four racket-ball courts and an impressive mechanised gym. The Best Western Landmark Inn is located 4 miles (6km) away but is good value and has its own sports complex.

Eating in and out

An evening on Main Street could have no more traditional start than dinner at The Claimjumper, an all-American establishment serving portions of 'surf-and-turf' and buffalo so huge that a 'wolfie bag' is the only way to clear your plate. Finer dining is available at Alex's, another popular Main Street haunt where the menu includes decidedly non-American ingredients such as frogs' legs and sweetbreads. They tend to be oversauced to conceal what many clients might see as dubious origins, but a request for sauce on the side reveals that both the raw material and the cooking are good. The Ichiban Sushi and Japanese Cuisine, opposite the Claimjumper, has a wide selection of fresh fish.

Après-ski

Main Street, which looks deceptively full of knick-knack shops and empty restaurants in the day, comes to life at night. There is a variety of bars to suit all tastes, from café society to low life. The latter crowd is catered for at the Alamo, a dive that serves as the headquarters for the Park City Rugby Club. Its memorabilia share the walls with stuffed moose and elk heads, which are those omnipresent symbols of the Great American West.

The Alamo has pool, table football, darts and occasional live music. Although it is a private club (often a prerequisite in the state of Utah because of the tough drinking laws) it has a relaxed approach towards sponsorship. This means that strangers ask the barman if he can find them a sponsor, and he turns to the nearest drinker and asks him to oblige; he nods, you buy him a drink and you and your party are members for the evening.

Cisero's Club, further up Main Street on the opposite side, is owned by a pair of musicians who use their expertise to maintain high standards for their nightly live music sessions. It, too, is a private club, so again sponsors must be found. Exceptions to this rule include Park City Billiards, a new pool hall near the Resort Center, The Shaft and the Wasatch Brew Pub at the top of Main Street. By 1.30am Main Street is as quiet as Bond Street on Christmas Day.

Childcare

The Park City Ski School divides its programme into Youth (7 to 12 years) and Kinderschule (3 to 6 years). The Youth programme offers group lessons on the same terms as the adult programme, but the Kinderschule package includes lunch and indoor supervision. The Kinderschule Mountain Adventure is for children aged 3 to 6 who are capable of Stem Christies or better.

Linked or nearby resorts

Deer Valley 7,200ft (2195m)

Unashamedly luxurious, Deer Valley is 3 miles (5km) north-east of Park City up a winding mountain road lined with multi-million-dollar homes. It is a place where grooming counts, both on slopes that are meticulously pisted ('the best grooming I have ever seen') and with its clientèle, who are a walking advertisement for designer clothing. 'It is worth a visit for two or three days', says one reporter, 'if only to observe the outfits!'

The skiing is on three different mountains served by 13 lifts and is constantly being expanded. Last season saw the addition of eight new runs, a double chair-lift, more snowmaking and six extra snow cats, so inspite of its exclusive image Deer Valley appears to be growing in popularity amongst those who are not quite so well-heeled. However, reporters found the lift pass here to be 'the most expensive in the US, at $44 per day'.

The Deer Valley Ski School offers group and private lessons, and special ski courses including black-diamond workshops, parallel breakthrough, style clinics, ladies-only clinics, mountain extreme and teen equipe (for 13- to 18-year-olds). No snowboarding is allowed at Deer Valley.

Children aged 2 months to 12 years are looked after by Deer Valley Child Care, and Deer Valley Children's Ski School takes children from $4\frac{1}{2}$ to 12 years of age.

The resort is a short, free bus-ride from Park City. There is no town as such, but there are several large condominiums and a few small hotels including the Stein Eriksen Lodge. Restaurants include The Mariposa, and The Lounge is a popular bar.

TOURIST OFFICE
Tel 1 801 649 1000
Fax 1 801 649 1910

Ski the Summit

ALTITUDE 9,300ft (2835m)—9,594ft (2925m)

Ski The Summit refers to four jointly marketed resorts, which incorporate a total of ten mountains within a 30-mile radius in Summit County, Colorado. The area, in particular Breckenridge, attracts more British skiers than any other in the United States. Some 12,000 skiers spent a holiday here last winter. Since **Keystone**, which already owned **Arapahoe Basin** five miles up the road, bought **Breckenridge** from its Japanese owners in 1993, **Copper Mountain** has become the odd resort out and is not included on the regular joint lift pass. The area has good all-round family skiing with no frills and there is ample scope for stronger skiers on some mountains.

Only the old mining town of Breckenridge has a historic centre and any ambience. Arapahoe Basin, or A-Basin as it is known locally, is an older ski area with not much of a resort. Keystone and Copper Mountain are both purpose-built; Keystone has the most extensive night-skiing operation in the USA. The Summit County resorts are all close to each other and are easily reached by free shuttle-bus or car.

> ### ■ GOOD POINTS
> Choice of ten mountains, short airport transfer, ideal for family skiing and mixed-ability groups, excellent night-skiing, extensive snowmaking
>
> ### ■ BAD POINTS
> Extremely high altitude can cause health problems, busy at weekends, lift queues during high season

On the mountain
top 13,050ft (3978m) bottom 9,300ft (2835m)

Breckenridge has four linked mountains, part of the Ten Mile Range, which are prosaically given numbers rather than names. The town sits at the foot of Peaks 7, 8, 9 and 10, and the skiing takes place on mainly north-east facing slopes. Peak 7 has no lifts or grooming and involves a 40-minute walk. Each of the other mountains has at least one high-speed quad-chair (on Peak 10, the Falcon quad is the only lift). Peak 8 provides the most varied of skiing. Peak 9 is gentler, with only about 10 per cent of the runs in the expert category. Peak 10 is the toughest: two-thirds of the trails are difficult and most of the others are intermediate. Any reasonably strong intermediate should be able to attack Breckenridge's skiing with gusto. One repeated criticism from European skiers is that the runs are annoyingly short.

Keystone, often the first American resort to open each season, once had a reputation for bland skiing. Despite its long cruising trails, advanced skiers tended to ski at Keystone's funky old satellite, A-Basin.

Then came North Peak, with its predominantly intermediate and advanced terrain. Hardly had these new runs opened when a third mountain, the Outback, was on the drawing board. This joined the lift system four years ago with a mix of open bowls, chutes and tree-line skiing.

Copper Mountain likes to describe its ski area as one of the best-designed in the country. There is a natural tendency for the tree-lined trails to become more difficult as you move east (left on the lift map). Thus experts tend to stick to the main face of Copper Peak, and beginners will find little beyond their capabilities on Union Peak. In between the two peaks, the terrain is mainly intermediate.

■ **WHAT'S NEW**

Keystone is planning a new resort centre called The Village at River Run

At Keystone, the Skyway Gondola base will be moved across the Snake River to the new centre

At Copper Mountain, an additional lift in Copper Bowl

At Breckenridge, additional chutes on Peak 9 for 1995–6 season

Beginners

About one-third of the runs on **Breckenridge**'s Peak 9 are green (easy). Sawmill runs gently down the gulch, separating Peaks 8 and 9, to the Peak 9 base. Much of Peak 9's face is a network of green trails, notably Silverthorne, Lower American and Sundown. On Peak 8 the nursery slopes such as Freeway, Powerline and Park Lane are mainly confined to a wooded ridge close to the base. Beginners will find little for them on Peak 10.

Similarly, there is little point in beginners at **Keystone** attempting to venture beyond Keystone Mountain, where a third of the trails are in the 'easiest' category. For complete beginners Energiser and Bunny Slope are right at the base with their own drag-lift. For adventurous novices a long green run called Schoolmarm runs from the top of the Skyway gondola to the base, linking with other easy runs such as Silver Spoon, Gassy Thompson, Gold Rush Alley and Last Chance.

At **A-Basin** Dercum's Gulch accesses the only long beginner-trails of Wrangler, Sundance and Chisholm, but there is also a small nursery area at the base. The best among the substantial network of novice skiing is Easy Feelin', below Union Peak at Copper Mountain. Those who have logged a few days of skiing can ride the long high-speed American Flyer quad-chair to the top.

Intermediates

Intermediates will have a field-day working their way around the trails spread across the Ski The Summit slopes. They will have no trouble with the terrain on Peaks 8 and 9 at Breckenridge, except for a few short, sharp, black-diamond (difficult) chutes. On **Keystone Mountain** you can wander at will. From the top of the Lenawee and Norway lifts at **A-Basin** almost every run down the middle is intermediate or beginner terrain. In spite of **Copper Mountain**'s notion that the skiing is packaged into easily separated advanced, intermediate and beginner terrain, there is little here on the groomed trails to intimidate a parallel skier.

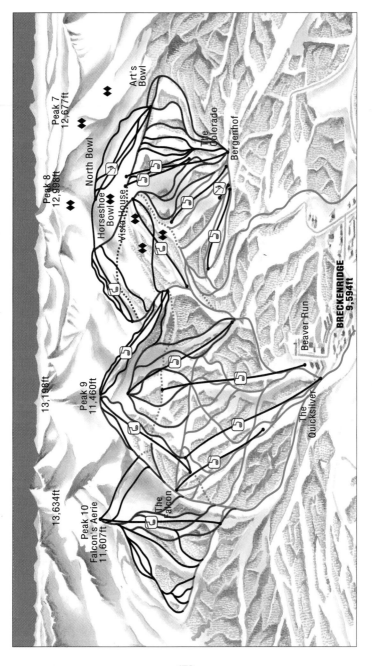

Art's Bowl

Peak 7
12,677ft

The Colorado

Bergenhof

Peak 8
12,998ft

North Bowl

Horseshoe Bowl

Vista House

13,198ft

Peak 9
11,460ft

BRECKENRIDGE
9,594ft

Beaver Run

The Quicksilver

13,634ft

The Falcon

Peak 10
Falcon's Aerie
11,607ft

Advanced

The principal lift-served expert terrain at **Breckenridge** is a string of chutes between Peaks 8 and 9, with emotive names like Psychopath, Adios and Lobo. The extreme flank of Peak 10 also includes some harsh runs like Black Hawk, Dark Rider and Mustang. Some of the mogulled chutes on the otherwise benign Peak 9, such as Mineshaft and Devil's Crotch, are fierce and challenging.

Keystone's North Peak has black-diamond trails like Ambush, Black Hawk and Cat Dancer, plus the Black Forest runs of Timberwolf, Bushwacker, Badger or the Grizz in The Outback.

A-Basin has the highest lift-served skiing at 12,450ft (3795m), and Palivacinni is one of the longest bump runs in North America.

Off-piste

Peak 7 Bowl and Art's Bowle, off the recently opened Peak 7, are the areas that off-piste skiers will want to try at **Breckenridge** – plus the other bowls off neighbouring Peak 8: Imperial, Horseshoe, Contest and Cucumber. Horseshoe Bowl is accessed by a T-bar (an oddity in America). The Burn area of Peak 10 provides good tree-line skiing.

The bowls at Keystone's **Outback** are challenging but short. **A-Basin** has good ungroomed terrain in the Alleys and off the East Wall.

Copper Mountain offers 'out of bounds' (off-piste) skiing in **Copper Bowl**. The resort is opening a new lift for the 1995–6 season between the back of Union and Copper Peaks and Tucker Mountain, however, snow cat tours will still continue nearby. There is also excellent ungroomed terrain on the flanks of Copper Peak off both sides of the Storm King lift, in Spaulding Bowl and Enchanted Forest, which links with Hallelujah Bowl, Looking Glass and Cache Glades.

Snowboarding

Breckenridge has a snowboard park and half-pipe and permits the sport on all four mountains. It is not permitted at Keystone, but riders are welcome at nearby A-Basin. Copper Mountain has an annual snowboard race series and its own half-pipe.

Ski schools and guiding

The highly rated **Breckenridge** Ski School offers special courses and ski clinics. One reporter echoed the thoughts of many others: 'Organisation, from beginning to end, was superb. The tuition was professional, friendly, and effective. I wish that this could be matched in Europe.' We have fair reports of the Ambassador Guiding operation. **Keystone**'s ski school has small classes of up to eight pupils. **Copper Mountain**'s ski school offers group and private lessons, as well as bumps and powder workshops and beginner packages.

Mountain restaurants

In **Breckenridge** the Bergenhof Restaurant is at the base of Peak 8, while the Vista House with its home-made specialities is at the top of the

Colorado Super Chair. Peak 9 has the Copper Top and Maggie at its base, as well as the uninspiringly named Peak 9 Restaurant on the slopes. Falcon's Aerie, at the top of the Falcon Super Chair on Peak 10, is good for snacks. Peak 8 is generally quieter than Peak 9, but one reporter comments that such is the demand for seats that lunch after 1pm can result in a cold hot-dog.

In the US they rather over-use the phrase 'fine-dining' but at **Keystone** they have the genuine article. The Alpenglow Stube is the ultimate American version of a mountain restaurant with European overtones. Perched at 11,444ft (3490m) at the Outpost on top of North Peak, the attractive restaurant offers four-or-more-course gourmet lunches. These are enhanced by magnificent scenery and a splendid crackling fire. Unbooted feet relax in the moccasins that are provided. Quicker, cheaper fare at the Outpost can be found at the Timber Ridge Cafeteria ('beautifully situated with marvellous views'). At the top of the main mountain is Taco's On, a separate cafeteria and a barbecue in good weather. At the base area Gassy's is a popular lunch spot, while the Mountain House Cafeteria is good for a quick pit-stop. Ernie's Pizzeria is also recommended.

A-Basin has a cafeteria and bar at the base and a barbecue mid-mountain. At the top of the American Flyer quad-chair in **Copper**, Flyers features 'gourmet sandwiches' and 'patio-dining at its best'. Solitude Station, at the summit of the American Eagle quad-chair, has an outdoor grill. At the base is O-Shea's and the Copper Commons Day Lodge. In the Mountain Plaza building at the base, Pesce Fresco offers excellent fresh fish and home-made pasta. The Clubhouse and the Union Creek Day Lodge both have barbecues.

Off the mountain

All visitors should take serious heed of the high altitude, which takes several days of acclimatisation. Those anxious to sell you holidays here are not always keen to point out that the top lift station is the best part of two miles above sea-level. At 9,596ft (2925m) temperatures can sometimes be extremely low. The town is 2,051ft (625m) higher than Val Thorens in France. Alcohol intake should be reduced at the start of your holiday and plenty of water is essential. If you ski at all on the first day, take it very easy indeed.

Breckenridge has seen it all: the old mining town went from boom and bonanza to bust ghost town and then found new life and prosperity as one of America's most famous ski resorts. Because of surveying errors, Breckenridge was accidentally left off the map of America until 1936. However, today the Breckenridge formula of four linked mountains plus an old but cleverly spruced-up main street awash with Victorian buildings, is a pleasing formula for success. A horse-drawn sleigh, driven not by an Austrian in Tyrolean jacket and shaving-brush hat but by a cowboy in stetson and floor-length duster, incongruously plies for hire in streets heavy with traffic.

Keystone started life as an old railhead. It was not until the 1960s that a group of developers created this lakeside mountain resort. **Copper Mountain**, purpose-built on the site of an old lumber and mining town (Wheeler Junction), is rather drab, with copper-brown being the dominant colour. More recent development has broken away from this concept, providing a brighter and more cheerful ambience.

Accommodation

Breckenridge describes itself as 'the motherlode' of lodging, boasting more slope-side accommodation than any other Colorado ski resort. There is certainly a wide range of hotels (including a Hilton), lodges, condominiums and bed-and-breakfast accommodation. The Village At Breckenridge Resort has its own sports centre as well as 40 shops and restaurants. The Beaver Run Resort is handy for the slopes. Breckenridge Mountain Lodge ('outdoor hot tubs, comfortable rooms, good breakfasts') offers good, cheap accommodation near the town centre, and the Powderhorn Apartments, Pine Ridge and Liftside Condominiums are also recommended. The Lodge at Breckenridge is a spa outside the resort, but has its own shuttle-bus. Williams House is a restored gold-miner's home offering bed-and-breakfast with en-suite bedrooms furnished with antiques.

Keystone and **Copper** predominantly have condominiums and A-Basin has no lodging at all. Keystone's accommodation includes the lakeside Keystone Lodge, which has a swimming-pool, restaurant and fitness centre, and the luxurious slopeside Chateaux d'Mont condos. Just outside the main village there is accommodation at the delightful Ski Tip Lodge, which was a stagecoach inn during the 1860s, and the Inn at Keystone is another pleasant country lodge.

Eating in and out

Breckenridge has an international choice of restaurants, but we have consistent complaints of unacceptable queues for tables between 6.30 and 8pm; reporters spoke of estimated 45-minute waits lasting twice as long. Le Bon Fondue is singled out for consistently good crêpes and pasta ('served with Austrian beer') along with Pierre's Terrace for 'fine French fare'. Fa-Heatas Bar and Grill offers Mexican food. Mi-Casa, another Mexican restaurant, received mixed comments; 'brilliant', said one reporter, 'a long wait, awful cold meal and the toilets were disgusting', said another. The Breckenridge Brewery offers good-value food and 'brilliant beer'. The Whale's Tail has 'excellent food and service'. The Hearthstone is highly recommended for its 'unbelievably good jalepeño prawns'. Fatty's and Downstairs at Eric's are both recommended for pizzas. The Snow Goose serves 'an astounding breakfast'.

The resort is adequately served with food shops, and one supermarket, a mile out of town, is open from 6am to midnight. Down the road in **Frisco**, the Blue Spruce Inn is recommended.

The restored **Keystone** Ranch serves six-course dinners. The Bighorn Steak House in the Keystone Lodge is known for its fresh seafood. The

Ski Tip Lodge serves candlelit four-course dinners in an intimate, wood-beamed dining-room. The Alpenglow Stube stays open for late-night diners using the resort's gondolas, and Der Fondue Chessel opens for Swiss-style fondue and raclette. You can also try the 'progressive dinner', which involves taking each course in a different restaurant with a stage-coach for transport.

At **Copper Mountain**, the Racquet and Athletic Club offers above-average dining, and Farley's, in the Snowflake building, is also popular. The B-Lift pub is another favourite. The Imperial Palace offers Chinese food in the Village Square, where other restaurants include That Soup Place. The Corner Grocery provides a reasonable choice for self-caterers.

The Chateaux d'Mont at Keystone provides guests with a 'welcome pack' of groceries. Grocery shopping is not easy at the Keystone Condominiums as you have to cross the main road to get to the shops.

> **■ OTHER SPORTS**
> Swimming, snowmobiling, racket-ball, skating, indoor tennis, sleigh rides, snow-shoeing, climbing wall

Après-ski

At **Breckenridge** the Gold Pan Saloon has a smoky, olde-worlde atmosphere and dancing. An equally lively evening can be spent sampling the local brew at the Breckenridge Brewery and Pub. Jake T Pounder (allegedly named after a dog) has cowboy music. Other popular night haunts include the Whale's Tail and Shamus O'Toole's Roadhouse Saloon. Downstairs At Eric's, and Joshua's at the bottom of Peak 9, both provide loud music. Tiffany's in the Beaver Run Resort has live music as the lifts close ('very funny, with lots of audience participation'). Tiger Run Tours' guided snowmobiling into the backwoods finishes up at an abandoned mining camp for dinner. It is alcohol-free because you have to drive back again.

At **Keystone**, the Bandito's has live entertainment and pool tables. The Snake River Saloon in **Dillon** is a lively spot, and Montezuma's in Keystone village has a large dance floor.

The **Copper Mountain** Racquet and Athletic Club has excellent facilities including a swimming-pool, indoor tennis and racquet-ball courts. Visiting international ski-racers make good use of the weight-training gymnasium. Skating on West Lake is free from midday until 10pm. In Copper Mountain the liveliest haunts include the B-Lift Pub, Farley's and O'Shea's.

Childcare

Children especially can suffer from dehydration caused by the altitude at these resorts. In **Breckenridge**, Kid's Castle at the base of Peak 8 incorporates a Children's Center. The equivalent at the base of Peak 9 takes children from three years old for skiing or play. The Cuddly Bear Toddlers' Center at the Hilton looks after one- to three-year-olds.

The Children's Center at **Keystone Mountain Base** accepts infants as young as two months old, and the nursery at **A-Basin** from 18 months.

Skiing facts: **Breckenridge**

TOURIST OFFICE
PO Box 1058, Breckenridge, CO 80424
Tel 1 970 453 5000
Fax 1 970 453 3202

THE RESORT
By air Denver International Airport 2 hrs
Visitor beds 26,000
Transport free bus and trolley system runs throughout resort

THE SKIING
Linked or nearby resorts Arapahoe Basin (n), Copper Mountain (n), Keystone (n)
Longest run Four O' Clock, $3\frac{1}{2}$ miles (5.6km) - blue/green
Number of lifts 17
Total of trails/pistes 2,000 acres (809 hectares) -18% easy, 27% intermediate, 55% difficult
Nursery slopes 3 children's areas with lifts: the Village Center, Beaver Run and Peak 8 Children's Center
Summer skiing none
Snowmaking 450 acres (182 hectares) covered

LIFT PASSES
Area pass Ski the Summit (covers Breckenridge, Keystone and A-Basin), $192 for 6 days
Day pass $42 (Breckenridge only)
Beginners no free lifts
Pensioners 60-69 yrs $19 per day, free for 70 yrs and over

Credit cards accepted yes

SKI SCHOOLS
Adults Breckenridge Ski School (Peak 8/Peak 9/Village), 9.45am-4pm, $228 for 6 days
Private lessons $70 per hr
Snowboarding as regular ski lessons
Cross-country Breckenridge Nordic Center, times and prices on request. Loipe 38km, $\frac{1}{2}$ mile from Peak 8 base
Other courses moguls, race training, women's seminars
Guiding companies Ambassador Guiding

CHILDREN
Lift pass 6-12 yrs, $12 per day
Ski kindergarten Peak 8 and Peak 9 Children's Centers: 3-12 yrs, 8.30am-4.30pm, $50 per day including lunch; 4-5 yrs, 8.30am-4.30pm, $56 per day including lunch, or $265 for 5 days
Ski school Breckenridge Ski School, 6-12 yrs, 9.45am-4pm, $135 for 6 days including lunch
Non-ski kindergarten Snow Play at Peak 8 (2-5 yrs) and Peak 9 (3-5 yrs), 8.30am-4.30pm, $50 per day including lunch. Infant care at Peak 8 Children's Center, 2 mths-1 yr, 8.30am-4.30pm, $50 per day

FOOD AND DRINK PRICES
Coffee $1, glass of wine $4, small beer $2.50, dish of the day $10-15

Keystone Nursery is a non-ski kindergarten for infants and upwards. Mini-Minors is a ski kindergarten for three-to four-year-olds, and Minor's Camp is for children from five years.

At **Copper**, the Belly Button Babies accepts children from two months to two years old, and its stable-mate, the Belly Button Bakery, caters for children over two and skiers over three. Copper Mountain has Junior and Senior Ranch ski programmes for children.

Snowbird

ALTITUDE 8,100ft (2468m)

In the state of Utah, which proclaims it has the greatest snow on earth, Snowbird is generally considered a prime example of where this fortunate phenomenon can be best experienced. Like **Alta**, its neighbour up the road in the steep-sided Little Cottonwood Canyon, Snowbird receives some of the deepest and driest snow in North America. The skiing terrain is prettier than in many Utah resorts, but the architecture is uglier. The resort, which is situated less than 30 miles (48km) from Salt Lake City International Airport, is dominated by the Cliff Lodge, a huge 11-storey building of concrete and glass.

On the mountain
top 11,000ft (3352m) bottom 8,100ft (2468m)

Snowbird has one of America's few cable cars, or 'aerial trams' as they are called in the US. This whisks 125 skiers almost 3,000ft (914m) to the top of Hidden Peak in eight minutes. There is only one moderate run down: Chip's, a 3 mile (5km) trail back to the base area. Elsewhere the higher skiing is dominated by bowls, chutes and gullies — an exciting arena for advanced skiers who enjoy powering through steep, ungroomed snow. There is a shortage of real novice skiing, but intermediate needs are well-catered for.

Beginners

Novice skiers should stay away from the top of Hidden Peak unless they really feel they can cope with Chip's Run, which is a very long blue (intermediate) trail. If they only have the stamina for part of it, the Peruvian lift goes almost halfway. Complete beginners might want to ski off the Chickadee lift down by the **Cliff Lodge**. Otherwise the Mid Gad Lift (with a midway unloading station) and the Wilbere lift serve some of Snowbird's least intimidating terrain. This includes Big Emma, named after an old mining claim, which is one of the widest green (easy) trails in the Rocky Mountains.

Intermediates

The area offers plenty of well-groomed trails best suited to confident parallel skiers. Bassackwards, Election, Bananas and Lunch Run are all straightforward cruising runs. Intermediates should be able to ski most of Snowbird's groomed trails without difficulty.

Advanced

Strong skiers are spoilt for choice, with everything from fairly easy open-bowl skiing to very difficult bump chutes. Most of the runs off Hidden Peak are classified as either single- or double-black-diamond (difficult or very difficult). There are also challenging black runs through spruce and lodgepole pine such as Gadzooks and Tiger Tail, reached from Gad 2 lift. The Road To Provo traverse from Hidden Peak — also reached by the Little Cloud lift — leads to other challenging runs like Black Forest and Organ Grinder.

Off-piste

Snowbird's off-piste terrain is superb and the Cirque Traverse from Hidden Peak is the key to it. From this narrow ridge skiers can drop off both sides into a big selection of chutes and gullies. Some are sandwiched between pines twisted and stunted by blizzards, others are guarded by imposing outcrops of granite. You can choose from quite steep to worryingly steep.

> ■ **WHAT'S NEW**
>
> Snowmaking in beginners' area Baby Thunder double-chair will expand beginner and intermediate terrain

Plunges into Silver Fox, Great Scott and Upper Cirque on one side and Wilbere Chute, Wilbere Bowl, Barry Barry Steep and Gad on the other can be exhilarating in fresh, deep snow and quite frightening in difficult conditions. There is also some challenging back-country skiing below Twin Peaks in **Gad Valley**.

Snowboarding

Snowboarders are allowed on most of the mountain but are banned from the Gad 2 chair-lift. Speciality snowboard workshops are available.

Ski schools and guiding

As well as normal lessons, the ski school operates speciality workshops for style, bumps-and-diamonds and racing. There is also a Mountain Experience clinic as well as twice-daily free guided tours.

Mountain restaurants

There is only one real restaurant at Mid-Gad. The Snowbird trail map describes it as a 'fuel stop', which is exactly what it is. The Peak Express warming hut on Hidden Peak serves coffee and light snacks.

Off the mountain

Snowbird is no beauty. When Dick Bass, a Texan oilman, built Snowbird almost 30 years ago he apparently fell under the wicked spell of the latest concrete additions in the Alps. Officially, the heart of the resort is the **Snowbird Center**, the departure point for the aerial tram,

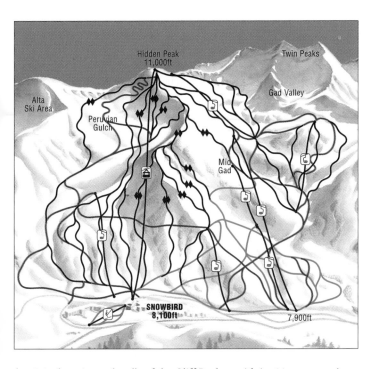

but it is the mirrored walls of the Cliff Lodge, with its 11-storey atrium, which dominate the long, narrow sprawl of contemporary buildings and car-parking facilities. The Center consists of the Plaza Deck and open space surrounded by limited shops on three levels. Outlying buildings house condominiums, and the overall impression is of a single-function resort with few alternatives for non-skiers.

Accommodation

Most people stay either at the Cliff Lodge or one of the three other condominium lodges nearby: The Lodge at Snowbird, The Inn and the Iron Blosam Lodge.

Eating in and out

Dinner choices of 12 restaurants include the Aerie, enclosed by glass at the top of the Cliff Lodge, which offers continental cuisine and a sushi bar, and the Keyhole Junction (also in the Cliff Lodge) featuring south-western food. At the Snowbird Center, Pier 49 features gourmet pizza, and the Steakpit, also recommended, offers steak, lobster, salmon, chicken and its speciality of king crab. The Wildflower Ristorante at the Iron Blosam Lodge specialises in Italian food. Several reporters commented on the lack of anywhere suitable to take children for tea.

Après-ski

Under Utah's licensing laws, all Snowbird's bars are designated private clubs, and those who wish to drink in them must buy a resort membership card for $5 for two weeks. Each member may be accompanied by four friends. This is more a bureaucratic nonsense than a deterrent, but

> ### ■ OTHER SPORTS
> Climbing wall, squash, indoor tennis, racket-ball

Snowbird's bars are few in number and formal enough to deter all but the most enthusiastic nightlifers. When the lifts close, skiers gravitate towards the Forklift, just across the plaza from the Tram and the Wildflower Lodge. Later on the Aerie often has a pianist, but sitting here until closing time is not particularly exciting. If the roads are clear and no storms are imminent, you could try a night-out in **Salt Lake City**, 25 miles (40km) away.

Childcare

Day care for children of two months and upwards is available at the Camp Snowbird Children's Center at the Cliff Lodge. The ski school offers programmes combining ski instruction with daycare.

Linked or nearby resorts

Alta 8,550ft (2606m)

An old-fashioned, unpretentious resort, which is revered by powder skiers, ski bums and skiers in search of a cheap lift ticket and powder that can sometimes better Snowbird's. Alta, just a mile up the hill, was here some 30 years before Snowbird and likes to remind you of that fact. It has rather more beginner/lower intermediate terrain, but also phenomenal chutes and secret powder caches reached only by back-country hiking. Devotees refuse to accept that Snowbird is in the same class. Realists count their blessings that two outstanding powder resorts are so close together; many believe that eventually the two will be linked. They already form the most challenging section of the back country Interconnect circuit, which includes Park City, Solitude and Brighton, in an attempt to reproduce the alpine concept of skiing from one resort to another.

TOURIST OFFICE
Tel 1 801 742 3333
Fax 1 801 742 3333-411

Steamboat

ALTITUDE 6,900ft (2104m)

This northern Colorado resort, known for its abundant dumps of snow, is more down-to-earth than its glitzy neighbours, Vail and Aspen, and is ideal for family skiing. Like many US ski areas the resort is designed to be functional rather than charismatic. The original town of **Steamboat Springs**, 3 miles (5km) away from the lifts, is much more attractive, with lively après-ski bars and restaurants. It is a favourite resort for genuine cowboys, particularly from Texas; in January you can expect to share the gondola with a ranch-hand in stetson and chaps training for the annual Cowboy Downhill, which is held here.

The resort began operating on 12 January 1963, with one double-chair on Storm Mountain. The following year Billy Kidd won America's first-ever silver medal at the Innsbruck Olympics and returned to become Steamboat's Director of Skiing. The resort claims to have produced more Olympic skiers than any other US town.

During the intervening three decades, the resort has kept on expanding. It now has 21 lifts and a total of 107 trails. A substantial 390 acres (158 hectares) of trails are covered by artificial snowmaking. Steamboat is three-and-a-half hours by road from Denver, just far enough to avoid weekend skiers, which means that lift queues are rare.

■ GOOD POINTS
Reliable snow cover, good facilities for family skiing, efficient lift system, lack of queues, extensive snowmaking, tree-level skiing, wide choice of restaurants

■ BAD POINTS
Limited for advanced skiing, small ski area, lack of resort charm

On the mountain
top 10,568ft (3222m) bottom 6,900ft (2104m)

Four mountains (**Sunshine Peak**, **Storm Peak**, **Christie Peak** and **Thunderhead Peak**) make up the ski area. Most of the skiing is intermediate with wide, cruising pistes. Steamboat is also known for its tree-level skiing, which is both extensive and varied. Experts can practice skiing between the widely spread fir trees at the top, while the more tightly spaced aspens lower down provide a real challenge.

Beginners
The beginner slopes are at the gondola base, where lift attendants diligently slow the chairs for nervous skiers or snowboarders. There are more green (easy) runs off the Christie lifts and a few runs on the upper slopes. The pistes are gentle and well prepared.

Intermediates

Nearly every area offers challenges to intermediates, whether it is for tree-level skiing, bump runs, or clocking up the miles on the long and uncrowded pistes. Tomahawk, Quickdraw and High Noon are gentle but fast runs off the Sunshine chair. Storm Peak has even wider runs.

Advanced

The steepest runs are the chutes off Storm Peak and Christmas Tree Bowl. To reach the chutes you head as far left as possible off the Storm Peak chair. For bump skiing try Olympic medallist and bump instructor Nelson Carmichael's stomping ground: Two O'Clock and Three O'Clock. There are a couple of black-diamond (difficult) runs next to Bashor, as well as Concentration, Oops and Vertigo.

> ### ■ WHAT'S NEW
>
> Ski area expanded at top of Storm Peak-Morningside Park and Pioneer Ridge
> Upgraded children's facilities
> Additional snowmaking
> Thunderhead lift replaced with high-speed quad
> Burgess Creek double-chair replaced with triple-chair

Off-piste

On powder days, of which there are many, you should be able to find untracked snow on the trails and between the trees. The best off-piste is from Storm Peak chair and involves a ten-minute hike at **Mount Werner**, which is a steep and unpisted area leading to the chutes.

Snowboarding

Last season, due to popular demand, Steamboat's ski school doubled the number of snowboard instructors it employed. There are daily group lessons (half-day or all day), as well as individual lessons. Ski-patrol and mountain hosts are also to be seen on snowboards. The Dude Ranch snowboard park has quarter-pipes and obstacles.

Ski schools and guiding

The Steamboat Ski School has over 230 instructors. As well as private and group lessons, there are speciality classes in powder, bumps, racing, telemark and cross-country, and women's ski seminars.

Mountain restaurants

Steamboat has better-than-average mountain restaurants for the US, with a distinct lack of crowds ('we rarely had to queue and there was always plenty of space to sit down'). There are three eating centres, which contain a number of restaurants: at Rendezvous Saddle, at the top of the Thunderhead gondola and at the Four Points Hut. Hazie's, at the top of Thunderhead, is waiter-service with a great view; Remington's at the base in the Sheraton serves steak, pasta and fish. Ragnar's at Rendezvous Saddle offers a wholesome lunch in atmospheric surroundings. Western BBQ at Thunderhead features an all-you-can-eat buffet.

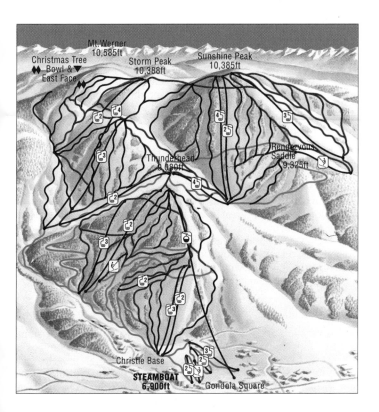

Off the mountain

The old town of Steamboat, reached by shuttle-bus, is full of atmosphere and does not have the usual rows of T-shirt shops. There are bars and restaurants, a cinema and supermarkets that do not charge the typically high resort-prices. The newer ski-in ski-out resort is 'a mixture of ugly central concrete blocks, with wooden chalet-style buildings on the out-skirts'. Only a few hotels have been built at the ski area, but the condo-miniums are much cosier; some have swimming-pools and whirlpools.

The natural hot springs at **Strawberry Park**, 4 miles (6km) from the old town, are worth a visit or you can try ice-driving at French rally driver Jean-Paul Luc's winter driving school. Howelsen Hill, in Steamboat Springs, has an Olympic ski jump with a jumping evening held every Wednesday. Shopping for fashion, jewellery and souvenirs is recom-mended here: 'We found everything to be particularly good value'.

Accommodation

Reporters recommend staying in the old town: 'Downtown has much more charm, better shops, and better restaurants and bars.' Here, the

Harbor Hotel is furnished in an elaborate Victorian style, and the Alpiner Lodge is 'fairly basic, just rooms and a lobby, but definitely good value'. There are several comfortable motels. The resort's most upmarket hotel is the Sheraton but it is large and impersonal. Smaller, and also on the slopes, is the Ptarmigan Inn. The Holiday Inn is medium-priced and located about a mile from the ski area, and the Bearclaw ski-in ski-out condominiums have a swimming-pool and whirlpool.

Eating in and out

Cipriani's, in Thunderhead Lounge, has good Italian food, and Hazie's, reached by the gondola, also serves dinner. Downtown try Antares, Mattie Silks for puddings, the Old Town Pub, the Smokehouse, L'Apogee for expensive French or The Ore House for steaks. Rancheros is recommended for breakfast, the Cantina for Mexican cuisine and Anderson Friends for 'great salads'. The Brewery at the ski area has 'an interesting menu and home-brewed beer'. The Sheraton has Remington's. Reporters enjoyed the evening snowmobiling through Rabbit Ears Pass: 'We would definitely recommend the dinner tour, watching the sun go down and then back to a remote log cabin for dinner.' Self-caterers found the supermarkets 'excellent, with normal prices'.

■ OTHER SPORTS

Snow cat skiing, snowmobiling, ice-driving, hot air ballooning, bungee-jumping, bob-sleigh, dog-sledding, ice-fishing, skating, indoor tennis, handball, racket-ball, hot-springs pool

Après-ski

Après-ski begins at the base in Buddy's Run at the Sheraton when it is sunny or with margaritas at Dos Amigos or home-brewed beer at the Heavenly Daze Brew Pub. At the Inferno the price of beer, which can be as low as 24 cents, is determined by a big wheel that spins and stops at the price for the next hour. There are also Western-type bars, such as the Tugboat Saloon, where there is no shortage of cowboy hats and the staff will check your ID (drinking age is 21). For late-nights try the Old Town Pub, Harwigs and the Steamboat Brewery. For live music there is BW3 and Murphy's Exchange. Reporters recommended the hot springs at the local sports centre as well as the water slide and massage. There is also a large indoor tennis centre.

Childcare

The Kiddie Corral Nursery is a non-ski kindergarten for children between six months and six years old. Buckaroos takes children from two to three-and-a-half years old; a one-hour private lesson (even for the youngest) is included in the daily package ('very good mix of day-care and on-snow support'). Mavericks Sundance Kids is for skiing children three-and-a-half to six years of age. Rough Riders is the ski school for children aged 6 to 15. The beginners' area has a 'magic carpet' lift. Other programmes on offer include special classes for teenagers, learn-to-ski weekends, race-training and powder lessons.

Vail/Beaver Creek

ALTITUDE Vail: 8,200ft (2,500m) Beaver Creek: 8,100ft (2470m)

Vail is consistently voted top resort in the US and it is easy to see why. This picturesque, pedestrianised village, modelled in Tyrolean style, is one of the biggest ski areas in North America. It has perfectly groomed slopes, serviced by an efficient lift-system, which provide good skiing for all standards. Colorado boasts 300 days of sunshine a year, and while the Rockies may not provide the dramatic peaks, couloirs and glaciers of the Alps, guaranteed sun and consistent light powder weigh heavily in its favour.

By European standards Vail's 25 lifts seem a small number, especially when compared to the Trois Vallées, which have over 200. However, the eager visitor can get as much skiing in Vail as in Europe by consistently riding the high-speed quads.

Unlike some of the Wild West resorts that have developed from a history of mining, Vail is a new town, which first opened as a resort in 1962. In the 1800s the Vail Valley was inhabited by the Ute Indians who hunted for the plentiful elk and deer. Immigrants began to settle towards the end of the nineteenth century, gradually forcing the native Americans off the land. Legend has it that they retaliated by setting the mountainside alight, killing the huge areas of forest, which have now become Vail's famous **Back Bowls**.

The mountain was developed by Pete Siebert, a 10th Mountain Division ski trooper who, together with local resident Earl Eaton, opened the slopes on 15 December 1962 with three lifts and eight instructors. Today Vail and its sister resort, **Beaver Creek**, has one of the largest ski schools in the world, with 1,100 instructors and more than two million skiers a season.

Whereas Aspen attracts the Hollywood crowd, Vail tends to play host to Wall Street bankers. As a result the restaurants and shops are largely upmarket. In high season Vail can compete with Cortina d'Ampezzo in Italy for the number of fur coats, while the shops heave with glitzy ski-suits. However, there are nooks and crannies where you can get a cappuccino for under $3 and a reasonably priced lunch.

The outward growth of Vail has been limited by the ever present I-70 freeway, which borders the 3-mile (5km) stretch of conurbation from

---

■ GOOD POINTS

Favourable snow record, terrain to suit all standards, separate children's ski area, recommended ski school, good off-piste skiing, wide choice of restaurants and après-ski

■ BAD POINTS

Little steep skiing, limited activities for non-skiers, lack of characterful mountain restaurants, high-priced accommodation and restaurants, homogenised après-ski bars

East Vail to Cascade Village. East Vail, a free bus-ride away from the slopes, is where much of the chalet accommodation is located. **Lionshead** is at the west base of the Vail ski area. The only advantage of its motorway location is that it is possible to ski other resorts such as Copper Mountain, Breckenridge, Aspen and Steamboat for the day and be back in Vail for the evening.

Vail, Beaver Creek and **Arrowhead** are owned entirely by Vail Associates. Vail's successful bid to host the 1999 World Alpine Championships means that the next five years will see substantial capital expenditure on new lifts, restaurants, snowmaking and piste development.

Ten miles west of Vail lies Beaver Creek, one of the most luxurious ski resorts in America and it is included on the Vail ski pass. Many visitors to Vail ski Beaver Creek for a day out of curiosity and then wish they had more time to ski it again. Its long winding trails, lack of crowds and family-orientated facilities are fast helping to develop its reputation as a rival to Vail. On powder days when the hounds head to the Back Bowls, the locals hit Beaver Creek's **Grouse Mountain**. The base area that is now steeped in exclusive condominiums and five-star hotels was once a mining village. In 1880 gold was struck by two miners who were prospecting in the waterfalls at Eagle River. The two miners named the nearby stream Beaver Creek and the name has proved to be more durable than the mine. Beaver Creek is the first ski area to be designed by a computer programme, and plans have had to satisfy a growing hard-core of Colorado environmentalists. The islands of trees in the middle of pistes are not for the benefit of skiers but are to make elk feel less threatened when crossing open spaces.

In 1994 Vail Associates bought neighbouring Arrowhead Mountain, increasing skiable terrain in this area by 40 per cent; a high-speed chair-lift will eventually provide the link between these two areas.

On the mountain
top 11,450ft (3491m) bottom 8,200ft (2500m)
The limited ski-in ski-out access to Vail is compensated for by the free bus system, which drops off skiers five minutes from the main high-speed chair-lift, the Vista Bahn. This is often congested at morning peak-times but there are three other access points: **Golden Peak**, near the beginner slopes on the east side of the mountain, Lionshead, with its gondola and high-speed quad and **Cascade Village**, outside the Westin Resort on the west side.

The three main areas on the front face of the mountain have mostly pisted runs on north-facing slopes. On the back side are the Back Bowls, which are not pisted except for the occasional blue (intermediate) run.

For skiers who have battled against icy conditions, breakable crust and poor snow-cover in Europe, typical Colorado conditions will come as a great delight to the ego. The light, fluffy snow is easy to ski and described as velvet or corduroy — so named because of the stripes left from the piste-bashers. State-of-the-art snowmaking, which ensures

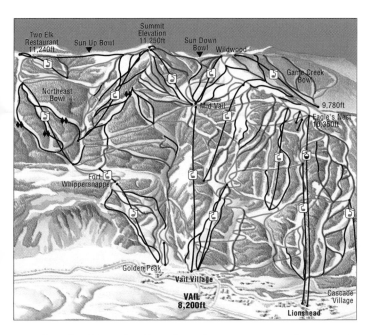

cover from late November throughout the season, means the mountain is always in decent condition; ice is unusual in The Rockies. In a country where the development of skiing has been dictated by costly law suits, the result is immaculate and consistent grooming, well-posted signs and eager and constant patrolling. The courtesy of the local people is much commented on: 'Being helped on to chair-lifts made a pleasant change from Europe — in fact, everyone seemed to try harder to make things work.'

The 4,014 acres (1624 hectares) of skiing includes 121 trails. The variety of pistes ranges from challenging mogul runs to long, easy cruises. The tree-line goes up to 11,000ft (3353m) and has many areas to explore that are not marked on the map. Getting around the mountain is easy enough to enable beginners and experts, parents and children to meet at one of the mountain restaurants or base areas for lunch.

Readers experienced high-season waits of up to 30 minutes on the Orient Express lift, which serves 15 runs, however, 'the signboards at the top of the mountain indicating whether a lift was clear or had a wait of at least 20 minutes were very useful, usually making it possible to find some skiing without too long a delay'.

The skiing at Beaver Creek covers three areas: **Spruce Saddle**, Grouse Mountain and **Strawberry Park**. Most of it is intermediate, with several double-black-diamond (very difficult) runs on Grouse Mountain. There are 81 runs covering a ski area of 1,125 acres (455 hectares), 11 lifts, and the longest run, Centennial, is 2.75 miles (4km).

A free mountain tour, which takes three hours for intermediate skiers, departs daily at 9am from the Guest Information Centers in Vail Village and Lionshead. There is a similar tour at Beaver Creek.

Beginners

Most of the beginner slopes are located at Golden Peak, where there are a variety of runs and short lifts to suit most standards. The children's ski area is reached via the Golden Peak lift, where there is an enclosed area called Fort Whippersnapper, which is a model of an old frontier fort.

Beginner ski school classes meet here or at Lionshead, which is the other main beginner area. Golden Peak is a quieter area off the beaten track from the main pistes, whereas Lionshead is a major thoroughfare, especially at lunchtime and at the end of the day. For second-week skiers there are many runs on all parts of the mountain. The beginner slopes (greens on the piste map) are wide and flat with no sudden steep pitches and they are always pisted. There are novice slopes off all the main lifts and from all mountain restaurants.

At Beaver Creek the beginner area is at the base of the Centennial Express lift, and there is a park for children at Spruce Saddle. There are a number of green (easy) runs suitable for confident beginners off the top of Stump Park lift.

> ### ■ WHAT'S NEW
> At Vail the Hunky Dory lift replaced by a high-speed quad
> Additional snowmaking at Golden Peak, Vail Village, Lionshead and Game Creek Bowl
> Chair-lift at Beaver Creek
> Extension of Bitterroot adding 30 acres (12 hectares) to Beaver Creek
> Beginner and intermediate snowboarding trails at Stickline Park
> Tater's Restaurant at top of Strawberry Express
> Additional snowmaking on Arrowhead Mountain

Intermediates

It takes about two runs for intermediate skiers to become instant converts to American skiing. Those who have never skied powder or bump runs will find Vail Mountain the perfect training ground. Others who want to clock up vertical feet may need new legs at the end of the day. The main skiing area is reached by taking the Vista Bahn to Mid-Vail, where many of the runs funnel into an area served by two high-speed quads. The Mountaintop Express lift goes to the summit from where you can access the Back Bowls, take long winding runs back to mid-Vail or ski blue or black (difficult) runs to the Northwoods chair.

Game Creek Bowl can be accessed by challenging black runs, including Ouzo and Faro, that lead through the trees (keep an eye out for porcupines) or by the medium-gradient runs such as The Woods and Dealers Choice, which usually have some bumps. Don't be put off by the Back Bowls; while recommended for advanced skiers, they are not steep. Test out the terrain in China Bowl and you can always bale out on to the Poppyseeds blue run.

At Beaver Creek intermediates can enjoy limitless runs on usually

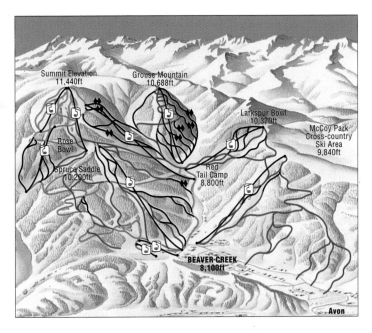

uncrowded slopes in beautiful surroundings. From the Centennial
Express lift some runs start as blacks (mostly because there are a few
moguls) and then turn into long blues such as Latigo and Centennial.
From the Strawberry Express lift runs such as Bitteroot, Stacker and
Pitchfork will soon help to clock up a few miles.

Advanced

Most good skiers head to the Back Bowls area, which on powder days is
Utopia. Both the Sun Bowls and China Bowl are skied-out quickly.
However, it is possible to ski powder all day by heading over to the
Mongolia Bowls, accessed by a short drag-lift, and also as far as you can
go along Game Creek Bowl. The bowls are south-facing so head over in
the morning. Don't miss the Underwear Tree as you ride up the High
Noon lift. This unusual sight is a constantly growing rack of men's and
women's underwear, which skiers add to throughout the season.

The front side of the mountain has equally challenging skiing and
often better snow. For steep skiing there is a cliff area off the
Mountaintop Express lift; recommended entry points are marked on the
map, but you can also take your own line down with caution.
Immediately off the Northwoods there are some steep drops along the
North and South rim; the steepest skiing is almost directly under the
chair-lift. For moguls head to Highline, Roger's Run and Blue Ox. Vail
has excellent tree-line skiing and it is easy to find untracked powder. Try
Ouzo Woods, just past Ouzo Glade, which has evenly spaced trees.

Kangaroo Cornice and Look Ma are good, steep tree-line runs.

Grouse Mountain at Beaver Creek is an expert's mountain with plenty of double-black-diamonds and some mogul runs such as Bald Eagle and Falcon Park. There are some difficult runs off the Centennial Express lift, but the basic black classification here often means that only one or two short pitches are truly testing.

Off-piste
Most of the off-piste is in the Back Bowls. If conditions are good the Minturn Mile is a long run off the back side of the mountain that ends in Minturn; you will need a guide for this. For back-country sking there is a hut system, but this involves a day's hike and overnight stay to access the limitless off-piste.

Snowboarding
The growing sport is well catered for here, with an increasing number of exclusive snowboarding shops offering equipment for hire. A half-pipe on Golden Peak draws crowds of spectators as well as participators. The ski school offers private and group lessons at Golden Peak, Lionshead and Beaver Creek.

In 1994–5 Beaver Creek opened Stickline snowboard park. This season additional trails have been added for beginners and intermediates. Also available are the Delaney snowboard camps, which are taught by Brian Delaney, the US and Australia snowboarding champion, at Beaver Creek.

Ski schools and guiding
The Vail/Beaver Creek ski school has a justified worldwide reputation for excellence. In Vail the adult ski school has three base locations: Golden Peak, Lionshead and Vail Village. It also has three on-mountain offices at Two Elk, Mid-Vail and Eagle's Nest. Several readers comment favourably on the private lessons. The Beaver Creek locations are at Village Hall and on the mountain at Spruce Saddle. Arrowhead has its own ski school with special programmes for children under 16 years and snowboarding lessons.

Cross-country
Vail has two cross-country centres: one at Golden Peak and the other at the Nordic Center at the golf course. The Beaver Creek Cross-Country Center is at Strawberry Park at the base of Chair 12. McCoy Park, at the top of Chair 12, has a cross-country track system including 32km of groomed double-set track and a skating lane. Another cross-country centre is at Cordillera, 15 miles (24km) west of Beaver Creek.

Mountain restaurants
Volume rather than intimacy seems to be the priority at most mountain restaurants. Beautifully designed but overpoweringly large is the all-wood Elk Two Restaurant (referred to as 'Too Elkspensive' by locals).

This luxurious cafeteria serves pasta, grills, pizzas, and salads. At the smaller Wildwood Smokehouse you can get a *Bratwurst* for $5.75. At mid-Vail the Cook Shack has two cafeterias and waiter-service. The Wine Stube at the top of Lionshead has self-service and waiter-service. Eagle's Nest has a cafeteria. Buffalo's, at Chair 4, is an outdoor establishment, and Wok 'n' Roll at the bottom of the Orient Express lift has *Teriyaki*-style sandwiches. The members-only Game Creek Club, off the Ouzo ski trail, opens this year.

At Beaver Creek Beano's cabin in Larkspur Bowl is as close to an alpine Stube (although substantially larger) as you will get. It is a private members' club at lunchtime and open to the public at night. At Spruce Saddle there is a cafeteria and waiter-service at Rafters. Red Tail Camp has an open-air barbecue. McCoy's Bar and Restaurant is cafeteria style. Tater's is a new small ski-and-snack venue due to open this season at the top of the Strawberry Park Express lift.

Off the mountain

The Vail Valley is deceptively large, and while most skiers will find themselves limited to areas covered by the free bus-route, East Vail, Vail Village, Lionshead and West Vail, there is far more to the area than meets the eye. However, unless you have a car it is unlikely you will visit more than Vail and Beaver Creek. In between the two lies the small town of **Minturn**, which has a few good restaurants including the Saloon, the unofficial end of The Minturn Mile. It is decorated with autographed photos of celebrities, including John Wayne,

■ OTHER SPORTS

Snowmobiling, snow-shoeing, bob-sleigh, hot air ballooning, ice hockey, dog-sledding, skating, sleigh rides, snow cat tours, indoor squash and tennis, climbing wall.

who has his own memorial booth. In the valley town of **Avon** try Cassidy's Hole in the Wall Saloon, which is a bar and restaurant with live music and is decorated with moose heads. In Edwards, the next town along, go to the Gashouse for cheap succulent steaks or Fietas' Café and Cantina for Mexican cuisine. For unsurpassed luxury try lunch or visit the spa at Cordillera, 25 minutes from Vail. This stunning 28-room lodge has one of the most spectacular views in the valley. The shopping is reasonable, by ski resort standards, ranging from 'the more utilitarian to the definitely glamorous; nothing was very cheap, but most of it was good quality'. Readers of *Snow Country* magazine voted Kenny's Double Diamond in Vail one of the top six ski shops in The Rockies and among the top 50 in the US.

Accommodation

Vail, Beaver Creek, Arrowhead and Avon have a total of 41,305 beds, mostly in condominiums and hotels. The smartest hotels in **Vail Village** are the Sonnenalp Hotel and The Lodge at Vail, which is owned by Orient Express Hotels. Also centrally located, but cheaper, are the Vail

Village Inn and Holiday Inn's Chateau Vail. The Marriott has two hotels, one in Lionshead and one in **West Vail**. Best Western has the Vailglo Lodge in **Lionshead**. Most of the budget chalets are in East Vail and these tend to be of a far higher quality than their equivalents in Europe. En-suite bedrooms, modern decor and outdoor whirlpools are standard.

In **Beaver Creek** luxury knows no bounds: from the exclusive Saddleridge to suites at the St James, the Hyatt Regency or the remoteness of Trappers Cabin up the mountain. The Poste Montane is a small, more intimate hotel. Beaver Creek Lodge only has suite acccommodation. Christie Lodge, in **Avon**, is good value.

Eating in and out

Whatever your mood, you will be able to choose somewhere to suit you from the endless list of eating places, although most are expensive. La Tour, the Left Bank, Wildflower in The Lodge and Mirabelle in Beaver Creek have the best French cuisine. Sweet Basil and Terra Bistro in the Vail Athletics Club are Californian style, The Swiss Chalet in the Sonnenalp has cheese fondue and other Swiss specialities. The Siamese Orchid serves Thai food, and Nozawa in the West Vail Lodge is Japanese. Up the Creek is 'quite pleasant with good food, but at just over $100 for four people it was more expensive than Blu's or the Red Lion, which were about $70 for four'. The Holiday Inn's Fondue Stube 'provided a memorable meal, with cheese, meat, caramel and chocolate fondue'. For elk and venison try the Tyrolean Inn, for pasta and medium-priced food go to Vendetta's, Blu's or the Bully Ranch in the Sonnenalp. Montauk in Lionshead is good for après-ski seafood. Pazzo's Pizzeria in Vail is low-priced and strongly recommended.

There are two supermarkets: Safeway in West Vail and City Market in Avon. Alfalpha's in Vail Village is an upmarket healthfood shop and delicatessen with many speciality foods. For take-away pizza try Domino's or Chicago Pizza.

Après-ski

There is no shortage of bars but most of them look the same and it is hard to find somewhere with real atmosphere. In Vail check out the sunset with a margarita at Los Amigos, which has been completely rebuilt. The Red Lion and Hong Kong Café are always full, the Ore House has $1.50 margaritas during happy-hour, the Hub is a small brewery. Gartons has live music and Country and Western dancing. Try Pepi's with its *dirndl*-clad waitresses. For a quiet drink try Mickey's Piano Bar in The Lodge or the sofas around the fire in the Sonnenalp.

In Lionshead, Trail End and Bart & Yeti's are popular. Garfinkels has a huge fish-tank on the bar, and the Sundance Saloon is good for pool. In West Vail try the Dancing Bear or Jackalopes for live music. The Westin Resort also has live music, and Booco's Station in Minturn has jazz or blues bands. For late-night dancing Nick's has rock 'n' roll, The Club is popular, and the revamped Sheika attracts the snowboarding crowd. DJ McCadams in Lionshead stays open all night except on

Skiing facts: **Vail**

TOURIST OFFICE
PO Box 7, Vail, CO 81658
Tel 1 970 476 5601
Fax 1 970 845 5728

THE RESORT
By air Eagle Country Airport 45 mins,
Denver Airport 2½ hrs
Visitor beds 41,305
Transport free bus between Vail and
Beaver Creek

THE SKIING
Linked or nearby resorts Arrowhead (n),
Beaver Creek (n)
Longest run Flapjack/Riva, 4½ miles (7km)
- green/blue
Number of lifts 25 in Vail, 11 in Beaver
Creek
Total of trails/pistes 4,014 acres (1624
hectares) in Vail and 1,125 acres (455
hectares) in Beaver Creek (32% easy, 36%
intermediate, 32% difficult)
Nursery slopes 2 areas at Golden Peak and
top of Eagles Nest
Summer skiing none
Snowmaking 332 acres (134 hectares)
covered

LIFT PASSES
Area pass (covers Vail and Beaver Creek)
$162 for 6 days. Aspen-Vail Premier
Passport gives 1 day's free skiing at Aspen
Day pass $46
Beginners no free lifts
Pensioners $37 for 65-69 yrs, free for 70

yrs and over
Credit cards accepted yes

SKI SCHOOLS
Adults Vail Ski School (at Golden Peak, Vail
Village, Lionshead and Beaver Creek) $55
per day
Private lessons $90 per hr, $370 per day
Snowboarding $55 per day, private
lessons $90 per hr or $370 per day
Cross-country $53 per day at Golden Peak
and Beaver Creek. Loipe 32km in McCoy
Park and at Strawberry Park Nordic Skiing
Center
Other courses telemark, women's ski
courses
Guiding companies Paragon Guides or
through ski school

CHILDREN
Lift pass 12 yrs and under, $162 for 6 days
Ski kindergarten Golden Peak, Lionshead
and Beaver Creek, 3-6 yrs, $325 for 5 days
not including lunch
Ski school Golden Peak, Lionshead and
Beaver Creek: 6-12 yrs, $325 for 5 days
including lunch; 3-12 yrs, $325 for 5 days
not including lunch
Non-ski kindergarten Small World
Nursery, 2 mths-2½ yrs, 8am-4.30pm, $55
per day at Golden Peak, Lionshead and
Beaver Creek

FOOD AND DRINK PRICES
Coffee $1, glass of wine $4, small beer
$2.50, dish of the day $10

Mondays.

In Beaver Creek the nightlife is limited, but après-ski begins at the Coyote Café, Beaver Trap Tavern or in the Hyatt, where bartenders are trained to entertain à la Tom Cruise in the film *Cocktail*.

Childcare

The Vail/Beaver Creek Ski School has learn-to-ski programmes for three- to six-year-olds and six- to twelve-year-olds. Small World Play Nursery at Golden Creek, Lionshead and Beaver Creek is a non-ski nursery for babies from 2 mths to $2\frac{1}{2}$ yrs and children from $2\frac{1}{2}$ to 6 years of age. Ski Break is supervised time for tired child skiers at Eagles Nest and Spruce Saddle from 1.30-3.30pm. Arrowhead has learn-to-ski programmes for children from 4 to 16 years. Children and Family programmes include Kid's Night Out Goes Western and The Buckaroo Bonanza Bunch, with Western characters who ski with the children and tell stories of the old Wild West.

Children's ski school centres are at Lionshead and Golden Peak in Vail and at the Village Hall in Beaver Creek.

Whistler/Blackcomb

ALTITUDE 2,214ft (675m)

Although nominally rival resorts, **Whistler Village** and **Blackcomb** (neighbouring peaks in British Columbia's Coastal Mountains, 75 miles (121km) north of Vancouver) are jointly marketed and have captured the imagination of North American skiers and others to the east and west since they were developed a mere 15 years ago.

The area is extremely popular with Japanese skiers, and during Tokyo holiday periods they can account for up to 50 per cent of the clientèle. The sight of so many smiling Orientals clad in samurai-style ski clothing comes as a culture shock to other overseas visitors. Add in European and US imports as well as Australians, New Zealanders and others who have put their ski tips over the Pacific Rim, and you will be hard pressed at times to find a genuine Canadian here.

■ GOOD POINTS
Highest vertical drop in North America, spectacular scenery, wide choice of runs for all standards, modern lift system, long ski-season, extensive off-piste skiing
■ BAD POINTS
Unfriendly maritime climate, short skiing days, weekend queues

Rarely does a ski resort rise to such international fame so soon after being 'invented'. In recent years Whistler and its sister Blackcomb have knocked Vail off its perch as North America's most popular ski area. For the last three years readers of the American *Snow Country* magazine have voted it No 1 in North America. Reporters comment that Whistler's prices last season were 'overall cheaper than the US Rockies and much of mainstream Europe'.

With some 7,000 acres (2,835 hectares) of skiable terrain, the slopes are extensive and test the most finely tuned abilities. What is surprising is Whistler Village's modest altitude of only 2,214ft (675m), which is 280ft (85m) lower than Kitzbühel. This would be worrying if Whistler were not so far north and did not have the largest vertical drop on the continent. Its low altitude and maritime climate mean that much of the almost continuous mid-winter precipitation falls depressingly as rain in the village and as powder higher up. Sunshine days are statistically scarce in comparison to its US Rocky Mountain cousins. Changes in temperature between village and summit can be frostbitingly dramatic.

On the mountain
top 7,429ft (2284m) bottom 2,214ft (675m)
The two mountains of Whistler and Blackcomb stand side by side and share a lift ticket, but they are divided by **Fitzsimmons Creek** and are

only linked at the foot. The eight-person Excalibur gondola up Blackcomb from the Whistler base has dramatically improved communications between the two.

Superficially, the two mountains are not dissimilar: each claims more than a hundred runs and each has good, long cruising trails. However, whereas Whistler is known for its bowls, Blackcomb prides itself on its couloirs and two glaciers.

The recent installations of the Excelerator quad-chair at Blackcomb and the Harmony Express high-speed quad at Whistler have provided the twin resorts with one of the most modern lift systems in the world.

■ WHAT'S NEW

Additional gladed trails cut at Blackcomb

The Holiday Inn Sun Spree Resort in Whistler Village

Beginners

Both areas have easy trails high on the mountain, which means that novices can enjoy the wide-open spaces and a vertical drop usually associated with intermediate ambitions. At Whistler you can ride all the way up on the gondola to the Roundhouse restaurant and ski trails such as Upper Whiskeyjack and Pony Trail (where packhorses once helped to transport lift equipment). Papoose, Bear Cub and Expressway are other options lower down.

At Blackcomb take the Wizard Express quad-chair and switch to the Solar Coaster Express, which takes you to the easy Expressway link with the 7th Heaven Express quad and Xhiggy's Meadow (a black (difficult) run, but also the top of the easy Green Line trail). From here novices can also ski from the top of the Crystal Traverse, which leads to the Jersey Cream and Glacier Express quads, both of which give access to easy beginner-trails. There are also nursery slopes around Whistler gondola's Olympic Station and at Blackcomb's base area.

Intermediates

Whistler and Blackcomb both offer exhilarating top-to-bottom skiing, much of it in the tree-line. More than half of the runs on both mountains are graded intermediate. Both the Blackcomb and Horstman Glaciers have some excellent skiing, and even some of Whistler's bowl-skiing need not be confined to experts.

The Peak Chair leads to the bowls and has a mid-station, which provides access to the Last Chance blue (intermediate) run down to two T-bars. These take skiers to a predominantly intermediate area, where the Ridge Run (just above Pika's and the Roundhouse) links with long blue trails such as Ego Bowl, Jolly Green Giant and Ratfink. The Green Express quad-chair is the fastest way back up to the Roundhouse area. Franz's run offers cruising all the way from mid-mountain to Whistler Creek.

At Blackcomb the 7th Heaven Express and Showcase T-bar to the Blackcomb Glacier serve mainly intermediate terrain at the top of the mountain. The mid-mountain area beneath the Solar Coaster Express

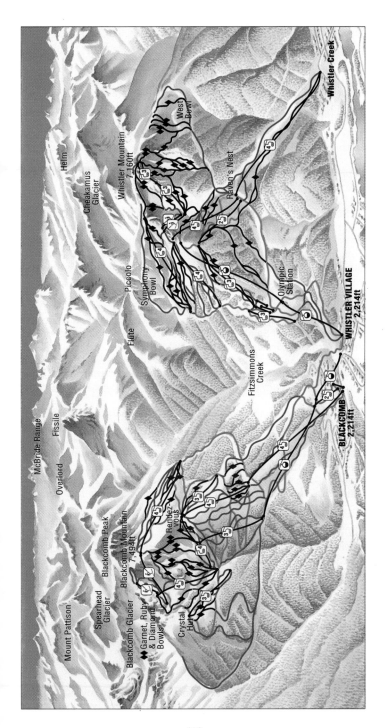

Mount Pattison

Spearhead Glacier

McBride Range

Overlord

Fissile

Helm

Cheakamus Glacier

Blackcomb Peak

Blackcomb Glacier

Blackcomb Mountain 7,494ft

Garnet, Ruby & Diamond Bowls

Crystal Hut

Rendez-vous

Fitzsimmons Creek

Whistler Mountain 7,160ft

West Bowl

Piccolo

Flute

Symphony Bowl

Raven's Nest

Olympic Station

WHISTLER VILLAGE 2,214ft

BLACKCOMB 2,214ft

Whistler Creek

499

quad-chair is dominated by a large number of intermediate runs, including the long Springboard trail. Zig Zag and Cruiser are also popular pistes.

Advanced

At Whistler much depends on whether the Peak Chair or the brand new Harmony Express quad are open. If not, there is some good expert terrain around Chunky's Choice and GS. Lower down, off the Black Chair, Seppo's and Raven provide black-diamond (difficult) skiing, and the Orange Chair accesses the long Dave Murray Downhill and two expert cut-offs: Bear Paw and Tokum.

Some of Blackcomb's best expert runs are in the trees, in a broad triangle between the lower sections of the Glacier Express and Crystal Chair, which means you can inspect them before you ski them; Trapline, Straight Shot, Rock 'n Roll and Overbite are the Crystal Chair's featured runs, and The Bite, Staircase and Blowdown are on your right as you board the Glacier Express.

Off-piste

Blackcomb's couloirs and Whistler's bowls are the main areas of interest for off-piste skiers. Saudain Couloir, now renamed Couloir Extreme, is the one that separates the advanced skier from the expert. It is the unlikely location for an annual extreme ski-race in which more than a hundred competitors, both professional and amateur, compete for honours and prize money in a contest described as '2,500 feet of thigh-burning hell'.

Pakalolo is another couloir that attracts good skiers. It has a fearsome reputation but is not quite in the same league as Couloir Extreme. The **Blackcomb** and **Horstman Glaciers** usually provide excellent intermediate off-piste conditions. Whistler's five bowls — Symphony, Glacier, Whistler, Harmony and West Bowls — offer a wide spectrum of off-piste challenges. Two local companies run daily heli-skiing excursions, which should not be compared with traditional Canadian heli-skiing in the Bugaboo, Monashee or Cariboo mountain ranges.

Snowboarding

Blackcomb has a new snowboard park where 'bordercross' (a snowboarding version of autocross) meetings are held. The resort has two half-pipes, and some ski-patrol members use boards rather than skis to make riders feel they have equal status on the mountain. Blackcomb offers a beginner snowboard-package, which includes a group lesson, lift ticket for the Magic Chair at the base area and equipment hire. There is also a summer training camp for snowboarders, which is run by Craig Kelley, five-times world champion. The resort estimates that 50,000 snowboarders visit Whistler each year.

Ski schools and guiding

Each resort runs its own large ski school, and Ski Esprit covers both. We have mixed reports of the Blackcomb School: 'I came here to get away from language problems and got a French-speaking instructor with heavily accented English, which was difficult to understand'. Ski Esprit courses are consistently praised: 'I got lost and missed most of one lesson, but was given another free of charge without asking'.

Whistler's free guiding programme is strongly recommended: 'Grade yourself into Nice and Easy, Cruise The Blues, or Steep and Deep — great fun!' The ski-patrol's Avalanche Awareness Course is described as 'a must for all advanced skiers, but you don't need to be an expert to do it'.

The ski schools in both resorts offer adult workshops in parallel skiing, bumps, powder and racing, as well as ski programmes especially for women.

Mountain restaurants

At Whistler the Roundhouse and Pika's offer a selection of meals from vegetarian fare to outdoor barbecues. The Raven's Nest Café, at the base of Redline Chair, specialises in pasta dishes. Down at Whistler Creek the Quicksilver Café is a good spot for breakfast or a buffet lunch, and Dusty's is another popular lunch location.

At Blackcomb Christine's Restaurant in the Rendezvous Lodge serves a leisurely 'linen and silverware' lunch, while the Rendezvous Bistro offers a more casual fast-food service. The River Rock Grill, upstairs at the new Glacier Creek, is praised for 'a cosmopolitan choice of cuisine with wonderful glacier views'. Downstairs is the Glacier Bite cafeteria. There are also cafeterias at the Horstman Hut and the Crystal Ridge Hut. At the Blackcomb base Merlin's offers pub food.

Off the mountain

Whistler was originally known as Alta Lake, a wild and beautiful area north of Vancouver, accessible only by train or on horseback. The first trails in the valley were cut by Indian hunting-parties, and during the goldmining era the peaks were a landmark on the Cariboo Gold Rush Trail. The first modern commercial ski trails appeared when Whistler — renamed after the cry of the marmot — opened in 1966. Earlier in the 1960s there had been some weekend skiing with the help of petrol-driven drag-lifts.

Whistler Village, built in the late 1970s, provides a good example of

■ OTHER SPORTS
Snow-shoeing, swimming, sleigh rides, indoor tennis, skating, parapente, snowmobiling

how a purpose-built resort can be made attractive. It is a mixture of chalet-style apartments, inns, lodges and condominiums with wood being much more in evidence than concrete. There are no huge tower blocks, and the largest hotel in the region, the Chateau Whistler Resort, is modelled on the neo-gothic style of other big Canadian Pacific hotels. The centre of Whistler is car-free and getting from the village square to Mountain Square at the base of the two gondolas involves a short walk, which is far enough to get soaked in a typical Whistler shower. Whistler

Skiing facts: **Whistler/Blackcomb**

TOURIST OFFICE
4010 Whistler Way, Whistler, BC VON 1B4
Tel 1 604 932 3928
Fax 1 604 932 7231

THE RESORT
By air Vancouver Airport 2 hrs, frequent
coach service to resort
Visitor beds 16,800
Transport free shuttle-bus within the
village loop

THE SKIING
Linked or nearby resorts Whistler
Creek (l)
Longest run Whistler: Burnt Stew,
Sidewinder, Olympic, 7 miles (11km) -
blue/green. Blackcomb: The Green Line,
7 miles (11km)
Number of lifts 26
Total of trails/pistes 6,996 acres (2,833
hectares) - 20% easy, 55% intermediate,
25% difficult
Nursery slopes 2 baby lifts
Summer skiing mid-June to mid-August on
Horstman Glacier at Blackcomb Mountain
Snowmaking 19 snow-cannon at Whistler
covering 1,500 vertical ft (457m), 48 snow-
cannon at Blackcomb covering 4,000 verti-
cal ft (1219m)

LIFT PASSES
Area pass Dual Mountain Pass, CDN$264
for 6 out of 7 days
Day pass CDN$46 one mountain only,
CDN$47 Dual Mountain Pass
Beginners no free lifts
Pensioners reduction for 65 yrs and over
Credit cards accepted yes

SKI SCHOOLS
Adults Whistler Mountain Ski School,
Blackcomb Mountain Ski School, Ski Esprit,
all CDN$199 for 4 days
Private lessons Whistler CDN$65 per hr,
Blackcomb CDN$70 per hr
Snowboarding Whistler 2-day Oxygen
Camp CDN$140, private lessons CDN$68
per hr. Blackcomb 2-day Arc Camp
CDN$150, 10-day Team Divo (13-16 yrs)
CDN$325, private lessons CDN$70
per hr
Cross-country through ski schools.
Loipe 28km around Lost Lake and golf
courses
Other courses Dave Murray Ski Camps,
moguls, women's clinics, slalom, off-piste,
men's mountain masters, heli-skiing
Guiding companies Whistler Alpine Guides
Bureau, Whistler Heli-skiing

CHILDREN
Lift pass Dual Mountain Pass, CDN$42 for
13-18 yrs, CDN$22.50 for 7-12 yrs, free for
6 yrs and under
Ski kindergarten Ski Scamps at Whistler,
2-12 yrs, CDN$175 for 5 days including
lunch and equipment. Kids Kamp at
Blackcomb, 4-12 yrs, CDN$165 for 5 days
(5 hrs per day) including lunch and
equipment
Ski school as ski kindergarten
Non-ski kindergarten childminding at
Blackcomb, 18 mths-3 yrs, CDN$50 per day

FOOD AND DRINK PRICES
Coffee 75c, glass of wine CDN$4.50,
small beer CDN$3.50, dish of the day
CDN$5-15

Village, the much smaller Upper Village (Blackcomb Base) and Village North are also only a five-minute walk apart.

Accommodation
The 13-storey Chateau Whistler Resort dominates the sky-line, has 343 rooms and is the most popular hotel ('top marks for friendliness, help-fulness and general efficiency'). We also have good reports of the Delta Mountain Inn ('next to the mountain and very convenient'). Timberline Lodge is 'comfortable, well-situated and friendly'. For quality lower-budget accommodation the Crystal Lodge (formerly the Nancy Greene Lodge, run by Whistler's celebrated 1968 Olympic gold-medallist) is popular, and the Listel Whistler Hotel has similar rates. Condominiums at the Blackcomb Lodge and Mountainside Lodge are both recom-mended. Carney's Cottage is 'the best bed-and-breakfast in, or rather on the edge of, town'.

Eating in and out
The resorts have more than 30 restaurants. Umberto Menghi, an Italian chef who has a TV show in Canada and restaurants in Vancouver, runs Trattoria di Umberto ('good fun and prices similar to those in London') and Il Caminetto di Umberto. Recently, Umberto's manager in Whistler, Mario Enero, opened his own Blackcomb restaurant, La Rua, which is described as being 'delightful and delicious'. The Wildflower Restaurant in the Chateau Whistler Resort is strongly recommended ('smart dining, not too expensive, and very worthwhile'). Peter's Underground and the Mad Café are 'particularly good value'. Zeuski's Greek restaurant, at the gondola base, is said to have 'soundly priced and tasty meals'. Sushi Village is 'excellent and expensive'. The Rim Rock Café has a strong local following for its fish and steaks. Local supermarkets are expensive, but Nester's, a ten-minute walk away, is said to be cheaper.

Après-ski
The Longhorn Saloon, at the foot of the slopes, catches skiers as they come off the mountain but is much quieter in the evening. Tapley's Pub is 'friendly, cheap and used by the locals'. Garfinkel's, Tommy Africa's and the Savage Beagle are all extremely popular. One reporter writes fondly of the Cinnamon Bear Bar in the Delta Hotel for big-screen sports.

Childcare
Blackcomb Mountain has childminding for children between 18 months and 3 years old, and both mountains offer children's ski programmes. Wee Scamps at Whistler and Wee Wizards at Blackcomb are all-day programmes for two- and three-year-olds. For older children of up to 12 years of age, Blackcomb has a Super Kids Kamp programme ('a bit of a zoo in the mornings, particularly at weekends'), and Whistler has Ski Scamps.

Round -up

Big Sky, Montana
top 11,150ft (3399m) bottom 9,700ft (2957m)

The new aerial tram (cable car) to the top of Lone Mountain now gives Big Sky the highest vertical drop in America of 4,180ft (1274m). On the doorstep of Yellowstone National Park, Montana is in the heart of real cowboy-and-indian country. Custer's last stand was in Bighorn, two hours' drive away, and many of the pioneer routes crossed this state. The scenery is stunning, with wide gurgling rivers, an abundance of wildlife and unspoilt countryside. It is here that *A River Runs Through It* (directed by Robert Redford) was filmed.

As a ski resort, Big Sky has not yet been discovered. You can hire a snowmobile without a guide and go to Yellowstone. However, while the area's appeal lies in its rustic charm, après-ski is a new concept. The Corral is a real cowboy bar, with the skins of grizzlies pinned to the wall, but it is 8 miles (14km) away from the base area, and there are few restaurants. The ski area has no resort as such, and the nearest big supermarket is in **Bozeman**, a 45-minute drive away.

The skiing is suitable for all levels and is spread over two mountains, with 65 miles (110km) of skiing on more than 60 runs. The longest, Morning Star and Mr K, are both 3 miles (5km). Beginners can ski on rolling slopes, intermediates can find good cruising pistes, and advanced skiers have a choice of steep chutes, mogul fields and extensive bowl-skiing. Big Sky is known for its dry, light 'cold smoke' Montana powder.

TOURIST OFFICE
Tel 1 406 995 5000
Fax 1 406 995 5001

Crested Butte, Colorado
top 11,400ft (3476m) bottom 9,100ft (2774m)

This small, historic town is one of the most attractive ski resorts in Colorado. In the old town's Main Street, 40 of the original nineteenth-century buildings have survived to be converted into shops and restaurants and give the place a cosy, Wild West feel to it. The town is overlooked by the 'butte', a mountain that stands alone. Hotels and guesthouses include the Nordic Inn, a family-run ski lodge that is recommended by reporters. The other option is to stay at The Grand Butte Hotel at the base of the slopes 3 miles (5km) away.

Crested Butte is renowned for its steep skiing and hosts ski extreme championships each year. It also has some of the easiest skiing in Colorado. Its 12 lifts serve 82 trails spread over 1,150 acres (460 hectares) of ski terrain. A high 58 per cent of the runs are classed as difficult, 29 per cent intermediate and 13 per cent easy. The **Extreme Limits** area is made up of some 260 acres (104 hectares) of ungroomed extreme skiing, which locals claim is some of the most challenging in Colorado. It includes the renowned North Face.

Irwin Lodge, 12 miles (19km) away and set at 10,700ft (3262m), offers snow cat skiing in 2,400 acres (960 hectares) of ungroomed terrain. The lodge has 23 rooms set on a gallery around a central fireplace and is reached only by snow cat or snowmobile.

TOURIST OFFICE
Tel (freephone) 0800 894085
Fax 1 719 349 2250

Killington, Vermont
top 4,220ft (1287m) bottom 1,045ft (319m)

Killington had modest beginnings as a ski resort. Avid skier, Preston Smith, saw the mountain's potential and spent three years raising enough money to buy it. When the resort opened in December 1958 the original ticket booth was a converted chicken coop.

Today, Killington is the biggest ski resort in Vermont. Combined with neighbouring **Pico** the area offers 8 mountains served by 29 lifts and 204 runs. The major disadvantage is that there is no resort centre; hotels, condominiums, the odd bar, restaurant and shopping centre straggle along the 5-mile (8km) road from the highway. Killington has one of the world's largest snowmaking operations, which covers 44 miles (70km) of runs that are dependent on low temperatures. Indeed, temperatures can be so low here that skiing is extremely unpleasant.

This harsh environment is reflected in the quality of the snow, which is well pisted but often difficult to ski. Ice is common, and the diamond-hard pistes mean you need a particularly high standard of technique. One consolation is that Killington has the only heated gondola in any ski resort. Wide, gentle green (easy) and blue (intermediate) runs are at Rams Head, while the tougher skiing is found on Snowdon, Killington and Skye. Bear Mountain has the awesome mogul run of Outer Limits, and Devil's Fiddle, Wildfire and Bear Claw are all testing.

TOURIST OFFICE
Tel 1 802 422 3333
Fax 1 802 422 4391

Smuggler's Notch, Vermont
top 3,640ft (1109m) bottom 1,030ft (314m)

The name Smuggler's Notch originates from when the pass was used for the illicit passage of goods to and from Canada before the War of Independence. Years later in the 1930s it became a ski resort. Today, it is known as one of the best family skiing resorts in North America. In recent years the resort's childcare and teen programmes have been rated the best in the US. It also has a reputation as a snow-catcher and averages 250 inches a year. The skiing (mainly for beginners and intermediates), is on three interconnected mountains: Madonna, Morse and Sterling. From Sterling you can ski over the back to Stowe. The village has a compact centre comprising condominium buildings and some hotels.

TOURIST OFFICE
Tel (freephone) 0800 897159
Fax 1 802 644 5913

Stowe, Vermont
top 3,650ft (1113m) bottom 1,300ft (396m)

Stowe is the epitome of a New England town. Covered bridges, red barns and small shops selling maple syrup and hand-made quilts dot this quaint 200-year-old village, which is overlooked by a white steepled church. Skiers began to come here from Manhattan and Boston in the late 1930s, and the first lift opened in 1937. Today Stowe has 11 lifts and 45 trails cut through the woods, covering more than 480 acres (194 hectares). The ski area is 7 miles (11km) away from the town, and although there are regular shuttle-buses, a car is a distinct advantage. Boston is three-and-a-half hours away by road.

Stowe is home to Vermont's highest mountain, Mount Mansfield, which is reached by a high-speed gondola. Queues can be bad at weekends. If you can ski the Front Four at Stowe you can ski anywhere. Goat, National, Starr and Liftline are double-black-diamond (very difficult) runs equal to the steepest runs in Europe's top resorts. Skiers have to cope with numbingly low temperatures and the problem of what they call here 'frozen granular patches', and we call ice. Apart from the big four trails, the ski terrain is best suited to intermediate cruising.

TOURIST OFFICE
Tel 1 802 253 7321
Fax 1 802 253 2159

Sun Valley, Idaho
top 9,150ft (2789m) bottom 5,750ft (1753m)

Sun Valley is the oldest US ski resort and has a long history of glamour and style. It was first discovered in 1935 by a dashing Austrian, Count Felix Schaffgotsch, who was sent by Averell Harriman of the Union Pacific Railroad to find the best place for a ski resort. It has long been a favourite of Hollywood stars, and photographs of Greta Garbo, Marilyn Monroe and Clark Gable line the walls of the Sun Valley Lodge.

This corner of Idaho is gloriously sunny and by following the mountain from east to west, you can ski in the sun all day. **Bald Mountain** has most of the runs, while **Dollar** is for beginners. Together they offer 73 runs, 2,067 acres (837 hectares) of skiing and 600 acres (243 hectares) of snowmaking. Most of the skiing is intermediate with many wide cruising runs, and mogul slopes such as Exhibition are legendary.

A lot of money has recently been pumped into Sun Valley, which now has some of the best mountain restaurants in America. Last year the River Run Day Lodge opened as a sister to the luxurious Warm Spring Lodge (complete with marble bathrooms). The stylish yet cosy Sun Valley Lodge and Sun Valley Inn were built in the mid 1930s. Sun Valley and **Ketchum**, the base area for the main skiing, have over 60 restaurants, including Clint Eastwood's favourite, the Pioneer.

TOURIST OFFICE
Tel 1 208 724 3423.
Fax 1 208 726 4533

Taos, New Mexico
top 11,819ft (3603m) bottom 9,207ft (2807m)

This corner of New Mexico has a number of different historical influences. It was first inhabited by Native Americans and then by the Spanish. Small wonder that the Taos Ski Valley has a curious mixture of chalet and cactus, set in arid desert. The ski resort, with its alpine architecture, is in the Carson National Forest, 20 miles (32km) above Taos town with its eclectic collection of authentic sun-dried brick houses, concrete low-rises and neon signs the only break in the desert scenery.

The fact that it was two Europeans who discovered the area near the old mining town of Twinings may explain this dichotomy. Ernie Blake, a German-born Swiss, planted the seeds of a ski resort here in 1955. A year later Jean Mayer, a French racer, set up the ski school and the St Bernard hotel. What they created was an alpine-style village on a mountain top in the middle of the US.

Taos has a reputation for difficult skiing. Al's Run, the steep mogul field beneath the main chair, is not encouraging on first sight. A sign at the bottom of the lift reads: 'Don't panic! You are looking at ⅟₉₀th of Taos Ski Valley. We have many easy runs too.' Indeed, Taos does have slopes for lower levels, although the terrain is rated 51 per cent expert. The tree-line stretches to the top of the mountain; most of the runs are carved out of the woods. From the main ridge there are green (easy) routes back to base, and the groomed blue runs give access to some tougher options. Several black (difficult) trails are left unpisted. Toughest of all are the chutes off the High Traverse.

TOURIST OFFICE
Tel 1 505 776 2291
Fax 1 505 776 8591

Telluride, Colorado
top 12,247ft (3625m) bottom 8,725ft (2660m)

There is a magical feeling to Telluride. This quirky Wild West town has a history of mining, but also seems like a throw-back to the 1960s; what other resort has a Mushroom Festival followed by a Nothing Festival in the summer? Locals complain that now it has been discovered, vast amounts of acres have been bought by its more famous residents, including Tom Cruise, Oprah Winfrey and Christie Brinkley, forcing up the price of land.

Butch Cassidy robbed his first bank here, and the town's name is said to be an abbreviation of 'To Hell You Ride', although a more likely explanation is that it derived from the mineral tellurium. The town is at the end of a remote and beautiful closed canyon, it has good restaurants and bars and operates at a very laid-back pace.

The San Juan Mountains are the most stunning in Colorado, having dramatic jagged peaks, which are quite different from the rounded, tree-covered mountains in the state's northern resorts.

The skiing is steep and deep and a favourite location for ski extreme videos. The area is not huge, with just 10 lifts and 1,050 acres (405 hectares) of piste, of which 47 per cent is intermediate. The mountain access is by two lifts from the town of Telluride, with another access point at Telluride Mountain Village Resort. The easy terrain is off Chair 10. The main skiing is divided between **Gorrono Basin** and **Telluride Face**; The Face is dominated by double-black-diamond (very difficult) runs, such as the Plunge, Spiral and Power Line, but there are also slightly easier ways down.

TOURIST OFFICE
Tel 1 970 728 6900
Fax 1 970 728 6475

Winter Park, Colorado
top 12,057ft (3676m) bottom 8,973ft (2735m)

As the closest resort to Denver, only 67 miles (108km) away, Winter Park has a high number of weekend skiers and would probably disappoint those used to international resorts by its limited accommodation and nightlife. However, the skiing here is excellent, with long and wide runs, challenging mogul fields, few mid-week queues, efficient lifts and perfectly manicured slopes. The skiing is divided into two main areas: Winter Park, which is mostly intermediate, and Mary Jane, which has hard bump skiing as well as tree-line runs and long blues from the Parsenn Bowl. There are 20 chairs covering 1,358 acres (550 hectares). On powder days the Parsenn Bowl has excellent off-piste. The children's area has a 'magic carpet' and a good ski school. There are no mountain restaurants, but there is a choice of cafeteria and waiter-service at both the **Mary Jane** and Winter Park base areas. Other après-ski is in Winter Park resort, a few miles from the ski area.

TOURIST OFFICE
Tel 1 970 726 5514
Fax 1 303 892 5823

Andorra

RESORTS COVERED Pas de la Casa/Grau Roig, Soldeu-El Tarter, Arinsal, Pal, Arcalis

A ndorra has a reputation for 'supermarket skiing', a low-cost, duty-free way for the rowdier end of the British market to don their anoraks, reverse their baseball caps, give the art of snowploughing a try and "'ere we go, 'ere we go" long into the night. However, while the price of a ski trip to Andorra is comparable to one to Eastern Europe, the quality of equipment and facilities is years ahead.

Andorra is bordered by Catalonia in Spain and Les Pyrénées Oriental in France. The closest airports are Barcelona in Spain, Carcassonne, Perpignan and Toulouse in France. The country's population of 55,000 inhabitants lives within an architecturally dreary area of just 464km², and Catalan is the official language.

Much of the country's income is still derived from the summer season when visitors come from all over Europe to take advantage of Andorra's tax-free status. Even this is misleading because, while alcohol, perfumes and tobacco are cheap, other prices are similar to those in Britain. However, bargains can certainly be found, especially in ski wear and equipment, but they are the exception rather than the rule.

Andorra is a good starting point for those new to skiing. Its five ski resorts are cheap, friendly and generally offer a good standard of ski instruction and equipment hire. The food in all resorts can be surprisingly good, with a choice of French or Catalan dishes. Andorra is neither quaint, nor does it provide any testing skiing for experts. However, with a careful choice of resort and an expectation level to match your purse, anyone from a good intermediate downwards (particularly those under 25) can have an enjoyable and rewarding trip.

> ### ■ GOOD POINTS
> Low prices, variety of easy skiing, good facilities for beginners and children, excellent skiing tuition (in most resorts), lively and cheap après-ski
>
> ### ■ BAD POINTS
> Lack of tough runs, limited choice of mountain restaurants, small ski areas, lift queues, lack of resort atmosphere, ugly architecture at Pas de la Casa

Pas de la Casa 2095m (6,872ft)

This is the first resort you reach as you cross the French border. The fundamental impression is of a brash city of giant advertising hoardings, scores of tacky shops, crowds of shoppers and choking traffic fumes. The architecture is both higgledy-piggledy and ugly ('Prince Charles would die'). The village feels like a resort that owes its existence to dime stores not skiing. Supermarket shelves are piled high with cut-price alcohol, much of it produced locally.

The skiing in the Pas de la Casa and linked **Grau Roig** area takes place mainly within two bowls on either side of the 2600m pass, making it the highest resort in Andorra. The 27 lifts serve 42 pistes, which are well covered by snow-cannon.

Main access to the pass is via an efficient but usually oversubscribed quad chair-lift. From the top you can return to the resort via a choice of different coloured runs, which can be either very crowded, very icy or both. Alternatively, you can ski on down gentler but more rewarding pistes to Grau Roig, which is little more than a car-park and a hotel on the floor of the adjoining valley.

The Del Cubil chair-lift gives access to a handful of red (intermediate) and blue (easy) runs; all are fairly short, and the snow tends to disappear quickly here. The better alternative is to catch the drag up to Mont Malus, from where two short but very enjoyable reds or, snow permitting, the black (difficult) Granota (several reporters voted this one of their favourite runs) take you back to Grau Roig.

One major complaint from reporters is that beginners in Pas de la Casa are forced to buy a full area lift pass just to use the two short drag-lifts on the nursery slopes.

TOURIST OFFICE
Tel 33 628 55977
Fax 33 628 55279

Soldeu-El Tarter 1800m (5,904ft)

Readers are unanimous in their praise of Soldeu and its neighbour, **El Tarter**: 'I would recommend Soldeu to anyone. It is especially great for beginners and the ski school is excellent for all levels. The nightlife is cheap and suitable for anyone of any age who wants to let their hair down and who knows how to have a good time. I am hoping to go to Andorra twice next season.'

For many years there has been talk of linking Soldeu and El Tarter with Pas de la Casa, just 15 minutes over the pass, but as yet this has not happened. Soldeu and El Tarter provide a marked contrast to their neighbour, consisting of little more than a ribbon of stone-and-wood buildings alongside the main road. Environmentally sympathetic regulations mean that even the more recent constructions are much more attractive than those in Pas de la Casa.

From Soldeu the ski area is reached by a single-span bridge ('difficult and tiring in ski boots') that would make Indiana Jones think twice. The Edelweiss restaurant is situated between the resort and the bridge for those in need of duty-free Dutch courage along the way. Once that has been negotiated mountain access is via the old Espiolets lift, which takes you slowly up to Pla dels Espiolets and the main skiing area. A chair-lift provides alternative mountain access from El Tarter, 2km down the road. It is an altogether faster and easier way into the lift system, which is euphemistically described on the piste map as 'the most advanced ski

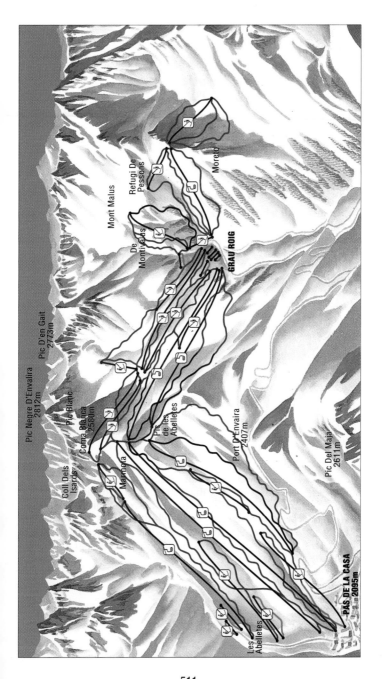

Pic Negre D'Envalira 2812m

Pic D'en Gait 2773m

Coll Dels Isards

Pic Blanc

Coma Blanca 2580m

Marroga

Les Abelletes

Mont Malus

De Montivalls

Refugi De Pessons

Moreto

GRAU ROIG

Pic de les Abelletes

Port D'Envaira 2407m

Pic Del Maia 2611m

PAS DE LA CASA 2095m

lift system in Europe'.

The ski area of Soldeu and El Tarter is made up of mainly long cruising runs, with open terrain going up to the top at 2560m and forest from the mid-mountain downwards. The 22 lifts serve some 60km of varied skiing, which is mainly suitable for intermediates.

TOURIST OFFICE
Tel 33 628 51151
Fax 33 628 51567

Arinsal 1550m (5,084ft)

Arinsal does not look like a ski resort at all, with its small row of shops and bars, and apartment buildings scattered along the road. When snow is scarce in the resort itself the only sign that this is a winter-sports centre is the old double chair-lift, which follows the path of a bubbling stream. This takes you to the start of the main skiing at 1950m, in a bleak and treeless area enclosed between two ridges, and offers the least variety of all Andorra's skiing. Easier access to the main ski area at 1950m is by road. The two main pistes, black La Devesa and blue Les Marrades 1, run from the top of the main Arinsal lift down to the resort and are sometimes closed due to lack of snow. This limits the remainder of the area to beginner and lower-intermediate terrain. As all the runs are channelled into a V-shape that ends on the nursery slopes, even beginners will feel the pressure of the limited runs.

TOURIST OFFICE
Tel 33 628 35693
Fax 33 628 36242

Pal 1780m (5,838ft)

Pal is a small village down the road from Arinsal, with a separate ski area further up a winding road that can be reached by bus. The 15 lifts and 30km of piste are accessed from four different points and share a lift pass with Arinsal. Pal has the smaller but more interestingly laid-out ski area of the two resorts. Of its 24 runs half are graded red.

The skiing at Pal goes up to the highest point of the Pic del Cubil at 2358m. Here you can either come straight down to Coll de la Botella via two red runs or ski over towards Refugi Pla de la Cot at the centre of the ski area on a choice of four red runs. Further to the left of the area is Edifici La Caubella; this is where most of the shorter and easier runs are situated.

TOURIST OFFICE
Tel 33 628 36236
Fax 33 628 35904

Arcalis 1940m (6,363ft)

With runs going up to 2600m, Arcalis is one of the higher resorts with skiing on wide runs above the tree-line. The village of Ordino is 25 minutes from Arcalis and neighbouring **La Massana** and has delightful scenery. The 11 lifts serve 20km of pistes, which suit all standards of skier. Arcalis has the highest percentage of difficult skiing in Andorra, which includes a special slalom piste. Reporters are lavish in their praise: 'The sheer variety of the skiing makes it a great place. No lift queues, one of the best smaller resorts we have been to.'

TOURIST OFFICE
Tel 33 628 64154
Fax 33 628 62540

Snowboarding
All the resorts welcome snowboarders, and Soldeu offers group lessons for three hours each day. Riders can have private tuition in Pas de la Casa, Arinsal and Soldeu.

Ski schools and guiding
Andorra attracts a much higher than average percentage of beginners to its slopes and this is reflected in the high quality of tuition at the ski schools in most resorts. Classes are kept to a maximum of 12 people, and the standard of English spoken is praised by several reporters. This is possibly due to the large amount of BASI-qualified English and Antipodean instructors. **Pas de la Casa**, however, appears to be the exception: 'We counted 30 people in one class', said a couple of reporters.

The ski school in **Soldeu** is lavishly praised. It has 109 downhill instructors who also teach cross-country, telemark, off-piste and competition. Four of the instructors specialise in teaching children. 'The best instructors I have ever had; even they have lessons twice a week', said one reporter, and 'two of our party made tremendous progress through modestly priced private lessons'. Another comments: 'The classes were well organised; the instructors spoke very good English, most as a first language. The class sizes varied between 6 and 12 people'. **Arinsal**'s ski school has 65 instructors who are mainly BASI-trained; special courses here include Golden Ski for mature skiers.

Mountain restaurants
The five mountain eating-places in the **Pas de la Casa/Grau Roig** ski area are mainly cheap and functional and are little more than snack-bars. The Bar El Piolet at the bottom of the Del Clot drag-lift is said to have 'the best baguettes I have ever tasted — especially the hot bacon ones'. However, one reporter comments: 'all the mountain restaurants are rubbish except the Refugi de Pessons, which has a log fire, good food and service.'

The Esqui Calbo restaurant in **Soldeu,** across the bridge from the bottom ski-lift, is recommended for good service and value for money. Xalet Sol I Neu, at the bottom of the mountain at Soldeu, serves 'very tasty chicken curry made with better cuts of chicken breast than I have ever experienced in an English curry house'.

Mountain restaurants in **Arinsal** are, on the whole, 'shabby and over-priced', say reporters, although there are one or two exceptions. At the bottom of the Arinsal chair-lift Asteric's serves local dishes ('a warm and friendly place with delicious food, especially the Catalan sausages'), as does its sister establishment Obelic's, at the Bambi chair-lift. For such a small place Arinsal is well supplied with good off-slope restaurants and bars. The pick of the resort is the Red Rock, which has a good ambience after the bleakness of the skiing. Thrifty reporters noted that they were able to buy an entire packed lunch in Andorra's 'extremely cheap' super-markets for 75p each day.

Accommodation

While **Pas de la Casa** cannot in any way be called attractive it does have a large variety of accommodation ranging from the comfortable to the very basic. Much of it is in apartments. One reporter comments: 'Many of the younger people choose the apartments close to the slopes, while families and those seeking a quieter life choose the hotels'. Of the many self-catering apartments Paradis Blanc, next to the slopes, is certainly no paradise, with its limited space, lack of cupboards and paper-thin walls. Reporters who mistakenly booked here do not recommend it for families: 'Drunken and even violent parties in the corridors kept our children awake into the early hours and my wife was too frightened to go outside our apartment after dark', and 'our studio apartment supposedly slept six, with its one bunk for the children, which was unsafe and had no sides, and a broken double sofa-bed'.

The roadside resort of **Soldeu** has a few well-run hotels, including the El Duc, a comfortable chalet-style hotel in the village centre opposite the ski slopes. Beside it is the comfortable and traditional Sport Hotel with its own sauna, gym and games room. The hotel also has its own physio-therapist. Aparthotel Edelweiss and the Cabo apartments both share the Sport Hotel's facilities. The Naudi is a small family-run hotel with a friendly bar. At the foot of the slopes in El Tarter is the conveniently placed Hotel Llop Gris, which has a swimming-pool, whirlpool, saunas and three squash courts, and satellite TV in every room. Further down the road is Parador Canaro, which offers yet more comfort.

Reporters who stayed in **Encamp**, 20 minutes from Soldeu, do not recommend it. Although it is an even cheaper alternative to the main resorts, it has no skiing and there is nothing else to do here ('it would have been worth the extra £30-70 to stay in Soldeu simply because of the amount of hassle saved in travelling'). Hotel La Mola is said to be 'a veg-etarian's nightmare. Everything contained meat, usually in great big chunks'.

Arinsal goes in for the cheap but basic accommodation, with the Poblado apartments securing particular praise, and Hotel Rossell receiv-ing criticism for its 'basic food'. Attitude and service at the Hotel Font is not singled out either, and we have mixed views of the Hotel Erts. The

Hotel Daina, 15 minutes from the centre, is a newer addition, while Hotel Janet is a small, family-run place on the outskirts. The large, modern Hotel St Gothard is also one of the village's main nightspots. The Hotel Solana is said to have the resort's best facilities, with an indoor swimming-pool, steam room and sauna, and the more personal Coma Pedrosa has good food.

Eating in and out

The restaurants in **Pas de la Casa** are cheap and good. The food is mainly Spanish, with fresh seafood and the ubiquitous paella, although some concessions have been made to the French. By browsing with care, you can eat well at a reasonable price.

La Braza, Rapid' Pasta and La Gratinada in Pas de la Casa are all recommended by reporters for their friendly atmosphere: 'The restaurants welcomed my small, noisy children in the evenings and let them draw on the paper tablecloths with coloured pencils. There was always suitable food

> **■ OTHER SPORTS**
>
> Skating, swimming, ice-driving, winter walks, night-skiing (Pas de la Casa), heli-skiing, snowmobiling, tobogganing, skating, indoor tennis and squash

for children, such as pizzas, pasta and ice cream'. Les Delicies is recommended as being good value, with three courses for 60FF.

The Esquirol and the Hard Rock Café in **Soldeu** are reporters' favourite restaurants, and the Hotel Bruxelles has good food. The El Pi is said to be good value. Cisco's in **Arinsal** is recommended for Mexican food.

Caldea, the thermal-spring centre at **Escaldes** at the heart of Andorra, has two restaurants: the informal Oasis, with an all-day buffet, and the Aquarius, which is smarter with higher prices. The complex also contains a bar.

Après-ski

Most of the bars in **Pas de la Casa** are cheap, and even the ones with dancing seem to have resisted the urge to charge for entry. Most have fluorescent lighting and deafening music, although the Marseilles bar ('it was often crowded by 5pm when the slopes closed') is somewhere you can both drink and talk at the same time.

The Discoteca Bilboard is a popular disco, which is split into two with 'general nightclub music played in one half and house/garage music in the other. There is no entry fee and you are free to roam between the two halves'. Le Pub has a happy-hour each evening and holds weekly theme nights where you can eat as much pasta, pizza or paella and drink as much sangria as you like for 50FF. Most of the British tour operators organise weekly bar crawls around the resort.

Soldeu's nightlife ('great for such a small resort') centres around the Pussycat, Aspen and El Duc discos. The Piccadilly Pub has 'something going on every night, including an Irish night and karaoke'. The Sport Hotel has a friendly bar.

Caldea, between Soldeu and Arinsal, is a huge thermal spa with futuristic architecture and has an enormous swimming-pool, man-made rock pools to soak in, a gym, a shopping gallery and a variety of health treatments to help you relax. It is open between 10am and 11pm each day and is certainly worth a day trip if the weather is bad.

Skydance at the St Gothard hotel in **Arinsal** is a popular disco, the Red Rock bar has live music and is recommended for its food, and the Solana disco-pub has a good atmosphere. Asteric's has live guitar music in the evenings.

Childcare

The fact that all of the runs in Pas de la Casa end in one area is a big advantage for meeting children after lessons. There are two crèches, one in town and the other on the piste. The Jardi di Neu kindergarten is set in a small wooden hut with its own fenced-off ski and play area with button-lift beside a busy car-park and close to a diesel-driven drag-lift. However, not all our reporters are happy: 'Outside the kindergarten entrance was an icy slope with an unprotected precipice to one side' and 'after the ski lesson, our three-year-old son was left sitting at a table in the sun with other children of his age; there were no toys or games and none of the staff played with the children or made sure they wore hats or sunglasses. As a result my son's scalp and eyes were burned by the sun'.

We have good reports of the nursery slopes in Soldeu, which are 'well prepared and fenced off from the rest of the pistes'. The ski school is also well spoken of, with good children's instruction from English staff, and there are two crèches. Arinsal, Pal and Arcalis also have a crèche each.

Eastern Europe

RESORTS COVERED Bulgaria: Borovets, Pamporovo, Vitosha
Romania: Poiana Brasov, Sinaia
Slovenia: Kranjska Gora, Bled, Bohinj, Bovec, Rogla

The mountains of Bulgaria and Romania and former Yugoslavia all lend themselves to skiing. It seems hard to recall that poor, beleaguered Sarajevo actually hosted the Winter Olympics as recently as 1984. When the slopes there will re-open for business is a question lost in the chaos of civil war. Development has been slow, but as the twenty-first century approaches the mountains of Eastern Europe could represent one of the great future areas for skiers.

While these countries have a struggling domestic ski market, the single biggest advantage for international skiers is the low cost. Skiers on a budget tend to look to **Bulgaria**, **Romania** and what was once part of Yugoslavia, the now independent state of **Slovenia**. Not yet well-known to tourists are **Slovakia** and **Poland**, which to date only attract the more adventurous skiers from abroad, including former East Germans. However, the facilities in these two countries still lag far behind other Eastern European ski resorts.

■ GOOD POINTS
Low prices, excellent beginner skiing, excursions for non-skiers, fascinating cultural experience
■ BAD POINTS
Poor quality food, limited challenging skiing, lack of alpine charm, few consumer goods

Overall, in comparison to the standards expected of Western alpine resorts, accommodation, food, slope preparation and tuition are inferior, but a holiday in Eastern Europe will be cut-price, and the lack of sophistication is compensated for by the generosity, enthusiasm and honesty of the people. These countries provide a fascinating cultural experience that can easily be combined with skiing. For example, in the Romanian resort of **Poiana Brasov** you can ski in the morning and visit Dracula's Castle in the afternoon.

The local people are trying hard to adjust to the rapid changes and particularly to a market economy. The gradual recovery from years of Communist rule means that things do not always run smoothly. There are still shortages, electricity cuts, delays, slow service and sometimes only basic facilities. The majority of reporters have, however, been exceptionally impressed by the friendliness and eager-to-please attitude of eastern Europeans.

We have not given the address or telephone numbers of the local tourist offices as we have done in other countries. We recommend that you travel through a bonded tour operator or via a country's own state travel agency.

BULGARIA

More than other Eastern European destinations, Bulgaria's hotel accommodation, food and internal travel have been steadily improving: 'On my most recent visit to Borovets I noticed a clear overall improvement in the standard of the holiday, without any dramatic difference in price.' Reporters also agree that the skiing experience here bears scant resemblance to skiing in the mainstream alpine countries. The verdict seems to be to enjoy it for what it is: a budget-priced cultural picnic with some skiing thrown in; anyone planning a holiday in Bulgaria should not set off wearing rose-tinted goggles.

A harsh crack-down on the black market has led to fairly uniform exchange rates, but this can still fluctuate during a two-week stay. The rate of inflation is high and most hotels and bars do not accept credit cards. Reports on the quality of food were varied often from the same hotels. A general rule of thumb seemed to be to stay away from miscellaneous soups and stick to simple foods such as roast meat and vegetables. Food for vegetarians is limited more by availability than cooking skills.

Ski lifts are old-fashioned, and the standard of piste maintenance, or rather lack of it, comes in for continued criticism. Similarly, those unfortunate enough to require medical treatment are shocked by the basic hospitals and the lack of facilities, which we in the West take for granted. On the other hand, mountain rescue seems to be efficient, with minor injuries treated speedily and effectively. Simple medications such as aspirin are not readily available. Loo paper on the mountain and in cheaper hotels is scarce.

The quality of hire equipment, once a major problem throughout Eastern Europe, has greatly improved in Bulgaria and a wide choice is available. However, visitors are advised to check the release setting on their bindings for themselves before taking the first lift.

Borovets 1323m (4,339ft)

Borovets' skiing compares favourably with that of many smaller alpine resorts. Spectacularly situated among pine forests high in the **Rila Mountains** the resort is more a spread-out collection of hotels than a village. The skiing is divided into three areas: a variety of wooded runs on the mountain directly above the resort; more wooded intermediate runs reached by gondola to the right of the resort; and open skiing between 2150m and 2540m, above the gondola top-station, served by a series of parallel drag-lifts.

There is a small nursery area at the foot of the main mountain and some long, meandering trails, including one of 6km from the top of the ancient single-chair. The skiing is generally more suited to intermediates, who have the choice of some fairly testing red (intermediate) and black (difficult) runs. There is little in the way of really challenging skiing or off-piste scope for the expert.

Mountain restaurants are few and basic. There is an old café on the 6km blue (easy) run, which is well worth a visit. The gondola is the only means of mountain access to the higher slopes and is prone to serious queuing ('an hour-long wait in the mornings is commonplace'). The quality of piste-grooming is poor, runs are unmarked, and there are few direction signs. Piste maps are hard to come by and may only be found in brochures. The ski school is highly commended by most reporters, and the kindergarten also receives good reports.

Most of the hotels are within five minutes' walking distance of the slopes and lifts. Horse- or donkey-drawn carts circuit the main hotels and are remarkably cheap. The Rila hotel is huge and rather impersonal ('looks like a French apartment block inside and out'). The more recently built Hotel Samakov, which has a swimming-pool, also has better food by Bulgarian standards and is comfortable, but again large and impersonal. It is well placed for the gondola but less so for the chair-lifts. The smaller twin hotels of the Ela and Mura offer comfortable accommodation.

Après-ski takes place in the local bars, where there are discos and floor-shows, with the Rila and Samakov acting as principal entertainment centres. Karaoke and Russian strip-shows are much in evidence. A few small bars, including Jimmy's, are set back from the main road. The hotel Ela has an English bar with prices to match, but also has a cheap pizza bar/café. The Breza bar is recommended, as is Peter's opposite the gondola. Various excursions are available, including trips to the old town of **Plovdiv** and the capital Sofia.

Pamporovo 1620m (5,314ft)

Less popular is Pamporovo (south-west of Borovets), a large resort suited to first-time skiers. The nearest airport, Plovdiv (nearly two hours away), is very basic. Pamporovo's lift system consists entirely of chairs and drags serving mainly easy pistes on the **Snezhanka Mountain** (1925m). There are several good nursery areas and a number of confidence-building pistes through the trees, including one from the top height of 1925m to the lowest point at 1450m. There are two more difficult runs, including the Wall, which is not as steep as it sounds, but is used as a slalom racecourse; advanced skiers would probably find little to maintain their interest after the first two or three days.

Rental equipment is good, and we have favourable reports of the ski school: the instructors take an obvious pride in their English, and instruction is reportedly clear and technically sound ('tuition was outstanding in terms of enjoyment and friendliness'). Pamporovo is the southernmost mountain resort in Eastern Europe, and snow conditions can be unreliable in the latter part of the season. Snack bars on the mountain are numerous but of poor quality. The Pizza Caravan near Stoudnets receives a strong recommendation.

The resort consists of a handful of unattractive modern hotels, lacking atmosphere but offering a surprisingly high standard of accommodation a five-minute free bus-ride from the slopes. The Perelik is adequate though slightly faded. Reporters note that the food is 'not great, but buffets are excellent and the Cabernet Sauvignon is fantastic value'. The hotel's swimming-pool is 'huge, like Hackney municipal baths rather than a leisure pool'.

Après-ski is limited to a few folksy restaurants and hotel discos, although there are nightclubs at the Hotel Perelik and at the Somolyan (a 45-minute bus-ride away). The bar at Molina and the White Hart are reputed to have good food. Also thoroughly recommended are the traditional local evenings laid on for tourists, barbecues at the Cheverme restaurant, 'game' evenings sampling local fare, and 'the instructors even invited us into their homes'.

Vitosha 1800m (5,904ft)

Bulgaria's highest resort is on **Mount Vitosha**, overlooking Sofia. The resort consists of a couple of comfortable hotels, old hunting lodges, a hire shop and lift station on a wooded ledge. Sofia is 20km away by an extremely cheap bus service. The skiing consists of a total of 22km of runs on north-facing slopes above the tree-line served by a small network of lifts, which are apparently closed one day a week for maintenance. It is an ideal resort for beginners and early intermediates. Experts would, however, easily become bored by the extremely limited skiing. There are some cross-country trails in the forest. Vitosha's proximity to the capital means that it is inundated with weekenders, and lift queues can be a problem. The ski school is said to be excellent.

Hotels include the Hunting Lodge, a unique residence set in its own grounds in a forest clearing 700m from the nearest ski lift. The Proster is the largest hotel, with good facilities including a swimming-pool. One reporter comments that 'the view was fabulous, maintenance was appalling, it was very noisy, and the food was poor'. Hotel Moreni is 'basic, with no frills'. The nightlife is said to be minimal apart from the Proster disco.

ROMANIA

Prices in Romania are even lower than in Bulgaria. Tour operators recommend changing £10-20 at a time, and most people found it hard to spend more than £50 a week with a fairly active nightlife. Hire equipment has improved, with the main resorts acquiring last year's equipment from European resorts. English is spoken everywhere. The lifts are old-fashioned, in serious need of upgrading and prone to delays, but the standard of ski tuition is generally high.

Poiana Brasov 1020m (3,346ft)

The best known resort in Romania is Poiana Brasov, three hours north of Bucharest in the attractive **Carpathian Mountains**. It is an unusual purpose-built resort, which was funded by the Ceauşescu administration in the 1950s to promote tourism. A few hotels, restaurants and a large sports centre are set back from the ski area base. It resembles more of an enormous holiday camp than a village. The furthest hotels are about 2km from the ski area, far enough to need a bus, which is free but infrequent.

The main ski area is reached either by gondola (an antiquated open-air bucket where you are provided with blankets) or by two cable cars (do not expect them both to be running at the same time) up to 1775m. The nursery slopes are at the bottom of the mountain, but when there is a lack of snow beginners are taken to a gentle slope at the top of the gondola. Most of the skiing is intermediate with runs roughly following the line of the lifts from top to bottom. There is one black run, which circumnavigates the mountain and ends at the base. It is not difficult, the black rating is because it is not pisted or patrolled, and conditions are unpredictable. Snowmaking has not yet come to Romania, and in bad conditions you could easily be skiing a run and come to a patch with no snow on it at all.

There are a couple of basic mountain restaurants. The best is a wooden chalet at the top of the gondola. The food is simple and cheap, and there is a balcony for sitting in the sun. The Outlaws Hut in the resort is the best restaurant here, according to reporters who found it 'lively, cheap and full of atmosphere'. There is no shortage of ski school instructors who speak excellent English and are keen to show you a good time, 'even if it means buying them all their drinks in the bar at night and then coping with their hangover the next day at class'.

Of the hotels, the Alpin is the best but even this is likely to have threadbare curtains and peeling wallpaper. The Teleferic and Sport are adequate, the Soimul and Cuicas are very basic. Non-skiing activities are limited; other sports include skating, bowling and swimming. The après-ski takes place in the hotels, nearly all of which have discos. The most popular disco is in the Sport Hotel where drinks cost around 50p. There are a few small restaurants, but most tour operators organise dinners at The Outlaws Hut — a lively evening that starts with musicians playing around a log fire — or wine tasting and folklore dinner at The Carpathian Stag in Brasov. The Dacia restaurant has wild boar and gypsy specialities. All the restaurants are cheap.

There are excursions to Dracula's Castle, and there are cheap buses and taxis that can take you into the town of **Brasov**, where there is limited shopping. It is worth spending a day in Bucharest.

The ski school is unanimously recommended: 'Exceptionally good value and the teachers are of an excellent standard'. Reporters speak of the resort's dated feeling; one warned he found it 'full of British yobbos on cheap drunken sprees', but at the same time described his holiday as 'a culturally fascinating experience'.

Sinaia 800m (2,624ft)

Sinaia is where the Romanian Royal Family and entourage used to spend their summers. Each monarch built a summer residence here and, while some of these are now run down, the beautiful Peles Palace is not to be missed. The old Royal Palace is now a hotel and is a short walk from the cable car.

Sinaia's role as a ski resort is relatively minor. A two-stage cable car from the town, its top section duplicated by a chair-lift, serves long intermediate runs down the front of the mountain. These are poorly marked and are consequently quite challenging in poor visibility. The main area is on exposed, treeless slopes behind the mountain and on subsidiary peaks beyond. It consists of short intermediate runs with some variety and plenty of scope for skiing off-piste. The town is quiet and, although there are a few bars and restaurants, après-ski revolves mainly around tour-operator hotels.

SLOVENIA

While Slovenia is an independent state it is still unfairly associated with the continuing civil war in other parts of the country (formerly Yugoslavia). Slovenia in the extreme north-west has some good skiing and those few tour operators who stuck with it protest correctly that their resorts are a long way from the fighting. However, the proximity has been enough to seriously damage the tourist industry.

Like other Eastern European countries Slovenia is reasonably priced. Food, drink and internal travel are about one-third of British prices. Reports of the ski schools are generally favourable, with English widely spoken and the video analysis helpful.

Kranjska Gora 810m (2,657ft)

Set in an attractive valley between craggy wooded mountains, this is one of the best known resorts in the region. It is close to the Italian and Austrian borders and is Austrian in ambience, even down to its domed church. However, its modest hotels are not comparable to cosy Austrian Gasthofs, and its chalets are slightly more severe than their Tyrolean equivalents.

The nursery runs are fairly short, wide, gentle and set right on the edge of the village, and the transition to real pistes is rather abrupt, with the mountains rising quite steeply from the valley floor. One run, from the 1630m Vitranc summit, is particularly testing. There are plenty of drag-lifts serving intermediate pistes on the Vitranc but they go no more than halfway up the small mountain, which means not only limited skiing but also a danger of poor snow cover. A two-stage chair-lift goes further to 1570m, giving a more challenging descent of over 750 vertical metres to the valley.

There are swimming-pools and saunas in several of the slightly institutional hotels, as well as some discos and bars. The bar of the Slavec Hotel is said to have a good local atmosphere. The Hotel Larix is recommended for its location, rooms and facilities. The Garni is equally conveniently situated for the nursery slopes and is clean and spacious. The Prisank has good food but not much variety.

Bled 880m (2,887ft)

While Kranjska Gora is the largest Slovenian ski resort, the attractive old spa town of Bled looks on to a seventeenth-century church on an island in the middle of a lake. Its simple skiing is 8km away at **Zatrnik**, where a total of five lifts serve easy wooded slopes, which are ideal for beginners in good snow conditions but provide little challenge for intermediates. The Golf, a quiet hotel set slightly away from the main centre, is recommended by reporters.

Bohinj 1725m (5,658ft)

Bohinj is a lakeside town with skiing above it at **Mount Vogel**. A cable car takes you to a plateau where seven lifts conveniently connect a handful of easy and intermediate runs among the trees and a small nursery area. If conditions are good you can ski the 8km run all the way down to the lake.

There is accommodation at the base of Mount Vogel in the Zlatorog Hotel near the Vogel cable-car station. It is recommended for skiing convenience, although it is rather isolated in the evenings as it is not really part of the village. The Ski Hotel Vogel, at the top of the cable car, is a good place to stay, as are the hotels Jezero in Bohinj and Kompass, both situated above beautiful Lake Bohinj.

The other skiing area close to Bohinj lake is on **Mount Kobla** and the adjacent **Savnik Mountain**; it consists of a mixture of easy and intermediate runs, entirely below the tree-line between 550m and 1500m. Kobla is quick to become crowded at weekends.

Bovec 520m (1,706ft)

Of the other Slovenian resorts accessible to the British package-holiday skier, Bovec, just south of Kranjska Gora, is the most appealing. It does not have many lifts but what few there are include a three-stage gondola rising to 1750m, which serves some moderately challenging slopes. When there is snow down to the village the run from top to bottom is memorable. Bovec itself was rebuilt after World War II and is a town rather than a resort. Après-ski revolves around hotels and lively local bars. Hotels include the Alp and the Kanin, which are a short distance from the centre.

Rogla 1500m (4,920ft)

This purpose-built resort is 45km from the Austrian border and has a modern lift system, two FIS downhill courses and reliable snow conditions. The Hotel Planja, overlooking the ski area, is recommended and has its own sports hall.

Norway

RESORTS COVERED Geilo, Hemsedal, Lillehammer, Oppdal, Trysil, Voss

Thanks mainly to the Olympic torch, which burnt throughout the 1994 Winter Games in Lillehammer, the flames of British skiers' love affair with Norway are being rekindled after almost three decades. That, at least, is what the Norwegians would like to believe, and an increased number of overseas visitors last winter gave some support to it. However, it must be clearly stated that while the experience of alpine skiing here may be less pressurised and at least as enjoyable, it bears no genuine comparison to the Alps.

■ GOOD POINTS

Extensive beginner/intermediate slopes, good family skiing, few queues, good-value equipment rental and lift tickets, English widely spoken

■ BAD POINTS

Low mountains, lack of challenging skiing, few long runs, expensive alcohol

British skiers have of course remained loyal to Norway, but many began to desert the country's slopes with the advent of regular package holidays to the Alps in the 1960s. By the 1970s only the staunchest of supporters remained. But what will the others find should they return today?

First, Norway will seem cheaper than they remember. This is because prices in the Alps have risen faster in the interim period than in Scandinavia. Ski rental and lift tickets are now about one-third of the price of their alpine counterparts. On the other hand, food and drink are still expensive, especially alcohol.

Second, some of the old lifts have been upgraded. Although the T-bar is still prominent, the high-speed quad-chair has found its way to some resorts, notably Hemsedal. Third and most important, Norway's snow record is not subject to the peaks and troughs experienced in more southerly latitudes.

Traditionally, British skiers travelling to Norway tend to be beginners, intermediates and cross-country enthusiasts. It is fair to say that Norway is not the best destination for experts, even though there is some good off-piste. Although the country has almost 200 locations where skiing is possible, including scores of cross-country centres and some very small ski hills. Norway's mountains are not huge, with vertical drops of 300 to 750m. Only about a dozen ski areas can truly be called resorts.

Night-skiing is popular, English is widely spoken and the Norwegians are well-disposed towards British skiers. There is little serious queuing. Some resorts offer a Winterlandet card, which allows you to ski more than one resort. For example Gol, Geilo, Hallingskarvet, Hemsedal, Uvdal and Al are on the same lift pass, offering a total of 71 runs and 44 lifts.

Geilo 800m (2,624ft)

This is a traditional British favourite, especially for cross-country skiing. The downhill skiing, which comprises 32 runs served by 18 lifts, is excellent for beginners and intermediates. Although there are seven notional 'black' (difficult) runs and some fun tree-level skiing, experts will quickly become bored here. However, several novice and intermediate reporters described the terrain as 'perfect'.

The skiing is divided into two areas on opposite sides of town. The only way to get from one to the other is by snow-taxi, which offers a special rate to skiers of 15Kr per person (about £1.50). As many resent this payment, the resort is looking at ways to remove the charge — possibly by laying on a free ski-bus service.

The **Vestlia** area, with a vertical drop of around 244m, has the easiest skiing but is well worth a visit. The highlight is Bjornloypa, a popular long green (beginner) run. The main area has a much wider selection of pistes, including some quite steep terrain and a vertical drop of 378m.

TOURIST OFFICE
Tel 47 320 86300
Fax 47 320 86850

Hemsedal 650m (2,132ft)

Although only an hour's drive from Geilo, in the heart of Norway's **Winterland** region between Oslo and Bergen, Hemsedal's peaks look a lot more mountainous than Geilo's rounded ski hills; psychologically this helps you feel you are in a serious ski resort. In addition, despite the fact that the resort has fewer runs than Geilo, and Oppdal has a larger ski area and more off-piste, Hemsedal has some of the best skiing in Norway, with a healthy vertical drop of 800m and a long season stretching from mid-November to May.

In a country where ski resorts are dominated by the T-bar, Hemsedal also has the most modern lift system, with three quads and three more planned additions to its current total of 15 lifts serving 27 runs. The resort has a couple of genuinely steep black runs and some entertaining advanced skiing.

One snag is that the village is about 3km from the ski area and the free ski-bus service is infrequent (two go from the village in the morning and two return in the afternoon). This means, for example, that guests staying at the Skogstad Hotel (with dinner organised between 6 and 8pm) who wish to take advantage of the much-advertised night-skiing run the risk of missing dinner. One of the planned new lifts will go straight from the village to the ski area.

Hemsedal has some good tree-level skiing, which is known as 'taxi skiing' because you will need to organise transport to get you back to the slopes or to your base. It also has a severe off-piste run called Reidarskaret; this starts with a steep and narrow couloir, usually too dangerous to attempt unless snow conditions are perfect.

TOURIST OFFICE
Tel 47 32 06 01 56
Fax 47 32 06 05 37

Lillehammer 200m (656ft)

Lillehammer resembles an American frontier town with its clapboard houses and single main street. The nearest skiing is based 15km away at **Hafjell**, which has 23km of prepared pistes, 7 lifts and 9 runs. The best are from Hafjelltoppen (1050m) down either the Kringelas or Hafjell runs. Both are graded black and formed part of the 1994 Winter Olympic slalom courses. Night-skiing is also available once a week. **Kvitfjell**, 50km from Lillehammer, was created specifically for the Olympics and is virtually a downhill course and nothing else, making it necessary for its 4km of pistes to be closed to everyone but competitors and officials on race days.

TOURIST OFFICE
Tel 47 61 26 64 43
Fax 47 61 25 65 85

Oppdal 545m (1,788ft)

Oppdal lies 120km south of **Trondheim** and is one of Norway's most northerly downhill resorts. It is also technically its biggest. Although it has only 28 runs (2 fewer than Hemsedal and 4 less than Geilo) and a vertical drop a little lower than Hemsedal, it has extensive areas of off-piste terrain spread between its four ski areas. It offers 78km of piste served by 16 lifts. The most challenging marked trails, Bjorndalsloypa, Hovdenloypa and Bjerkeloypa, were enjoyed by Italian gold medallist Alberto Tomba when he was here for a World Cup race and are on the front face of Hovden, the central ski area.

The Vangslia area also offers a mixture of terrain, while Stolen at the other end of the resort is made up entirely of beginner and intermediate terrain. The fourth area, Adalen, is set in a huge bowl behind Hovden and is dominated by long, mainly blue (easy) cruising runs. At 1pm in Oppdal, for an additional sum of around 70Kr (about £7), snow cats will take up to 50 skiers at a time to the top of the mountain at Blaoret for sightseeing and an additional 240 vertical metres of off-piste skiing.

TOURIST OFFICE
Tel 47 72 42 17 60
Fax 47 72 42 08 88

Trysil 600m (1,969ft)

This is an expanding resort three hours' drive from Oslo. Its 75km of piste served by 22 lifts are spread across the wooded slopes of **Trysilfjellet** at 1132m. It is said to have the most reliable snow cover anywhere in the country. In common with many Norwegian resorts, the lifts are several kilometres from the resort centre. The skiing varies from easy beginner trails to some more challenging red (intermediate) runs, but is often criticised for having too many green runs ('cross-country tracks in disguise').

Accommodation here is mainly hotel- and apartment-based, although mountain cabins, notably the Trysilfjellet, make a pleasant change for hardy self-caterers.

TOURIST OFFICE
Tel 47 62 45 05 11
Fax 47 62 45 11 65

Voss 91m (300ft)

In spite of its low altitude, Voss has a reasonable ski area for beginners and lower intermediates. The 40km of prepared piste includes three black runs, two of which are reasonably challenging, and some off-piste. Several members of Norway's successful Olympic downhill team come from these parts. The nine lifts (almost one for each run) include a cable car, and the longest descent is 3km.

TOURIST OFFICE
Tel 47 56 51 00 51
Fax 47 56 51 17 15

Snowboarding

Snowboarding is still in its infancy in Norway, while telemarking is making a big comeback to its country of origin. However, on Wednesday evenings at the Sletvold Park slope in **Oppdal** there is 'night boarding' on special floodlit courses – complete with rental equipment and a buffet. **Hemsedal** too has a snowboard park offering floodlit boarding and there are snowboarding classes at Geilo and Voss.

Cross-country

Norway is famous as the home of cross-country skiing. Geilo is the traditional Langlauf resort with 175km of loipe on both the valley floor and up on the Hardangevidda Plateau at 1312m. Oppdal also has 150km of trails covering a variety of terrain; five of its tracks are floodlit. Enthusiasts will certainly not be disappointed with Voss and its 63km of prepared trails.

Ski schools and guiding

The Norwegians are justly proud of their ski schools, which are well-organised with English-speaking instructors. There is a keen emphasis on safety, and Norwegians actively encourage the use of ski helmets for children. Many resorts insist on their use and provide free helmet hire and lift passes for children up to eight or nine years old. Children's ski areas are often roped off with netting to stop fast adult skiers hurtling into them at the end of a downhill run.

Oppdal is unusual among Norwegian resorts in having a specialist guiding service (Opplev Oppdal). Guides escort skiers around the area and carry a full kit of safety equipment, including avalanche transceivers (rarely used in Norway), shovels and avalanche probes.

Mountain restaurants

Geilo has six restaurants in its two ski areas. The fast-food restaurant at the top of the main area at Geilohovda is popular, but the splendid Dr Holms Hotel is at the bottom of the slopes, and many skiers choose to congregate here for lunch. Two of Hemsedal's mountain restaurants are near the top of the Hollvinheisen triple-chair. A third, the Skistua, is at the base area and has the option of self- or waitress-service.

Oppdal has six mountain restaurants, one at the bottom of each base area, and two more at the top of the Hovden and Stolen lift complexes. Only the Vangslia lifts are without a mid-mountain restaurant. The semi-circular restaurant at the top of Hovden was originally part of a water-storage structure. The restaurant at the bottom of Stolen, where most of the easiest family skiing takes place, is usually the busiest on the mountain.

Accommodation

Apart from hotels, Norwegian resorts have an abundance of usually expensive cabins and apartments. The sprawling and stately Dr Holms Hotel in **Geilo** is famous throughout Norway and has a fascinating history; during the Second World War German U-boat officers took it over and entertained girls from the Moulin Rouge in Paris in one of the hotel wings. The slopes are only a minute away, and the nearest lift 100m away. You can ski to the three-star Solli Sportell Hotel, and the Highland Hotel is also recommended. In **Oppdal** the recently refurbished Hotel Nor is a sound choice, and guests at the 75-room Hotel Oppdal right by the (not busy) railway station describe it as cosy and quaint, in spite of its size.

Eating in and out

Visitors to Norway are pleasantly surprised by the range and quality of the dishes on offer. Fish lovers are in for a treat, with endless permutations of lax (salmon), sardines and herrings ranging from smoked or fried to marinated or poached, plus seemingly inexhaustable supplies of shrimp. Reindeer is often on the menu too. In **Geilo** the buffet at the Highland Hotel is strongly recommended. For traditional Norwegian food the Hallingstuene is excellent.

The Skogstad Hotel at **Hemsedal** offers a good menu at its bistro and has a good brunch on Sundays. However, some guests eating in the normal dining-room commented on the limited choice and poor quality of the food for what is claimed to be a four-star hotel.

In **Oppdal** it is worth trying the so-called 'Viking evening' (a misnomer), which takes place in a timbered roundhouse in the woods, where local stews, patés and sausages are served in front of a roaring fire with accordion accompaniment.

Après-ski

If you like packed, noisy bars try some of **Hemsedal**'s in-places during a busy weekend. You will be lucky if you can get near the Garasjen (the old bus garage), where it can become so crowded that skiers overflow on to the street. The Skogstad Piano Bar and Hemsedal Café are almost as crowded. You may have more room to breathe at the Kro Bar in the Fanitullen apartment block.

In **Geilo**, the new ski bar at the Dr Holms Hotel is proving to be extremely popular. Other well-patronised bars include the Hos Josn and the Laven at the Vestlia Hotel. Although Oppdal is a fair-sized town, nightlife, apart from a few bars and restaurants, is a little limited.

Buying your own wine in Norway can be a major problem. One British guest in Geilo expressed alarm that the nearest place he could buy a bottle, at an outrageous price, was 50km away.

Childcare

For children of three months and over most resorts have Trollia or Troll Club kindergarten and nurseries for skiing and play, which usually open seven days a week. English is almost invariably spoken. At **Hemsedal** the excellent slope-side babysitting service operates a simple but effective way of telling anxious parents that their toddlers are sleeping soundly at afternoon nap time: if the curtain closest to their infant is closed, all is well, if it is open, the child would appreciate prompt return of parents.

Scotland

RESOLTS COVERED Cairngorm (Aviemore), Glencoe, Glenshee,
The Lecht, Nevis Range (Aonach Mor)

The success of Scotland's ski areas is entirely reliant on the weather and on the type of snow that falls; whether it is followed by a sudden temperature rise bringing a rapid thaw or rain, or whether it is followed by gale-force winds making life on the mountain extremely unpleasant as well as closing vital access lifts. Alternatively, it just might be followed by beautiful sunshine and no wind, with low enough temperatures to keep the snow crisp, but when this happens swarms of enthusiastic Scottish skiers clog up the car-parks, rental shops and ticket counters before creating outlandish lift queues and overcrowded slopes.

■ GOOD POINTS

Friendly atmosphere, wide range of
non-ski activities, late-season skiing,
British Association of Ski Instructors
(BASI) tuition

■ BAD POINTS

Unpredictable weather conditions, lift
queues at peak periods, limited skiing

Because of the weather it is a constant battle for the resort operators to groom slopes effectively and they have to put up chestnut-paling fences everywhere to try to catch and contain drifting snow. Rapid temperature fluctuations make the manufacture of artificial snow difficult.

The five ski centres in the Scottish Highlands are often marketed together. The newest is the Nevis Range on the west coast, 33 miles (55km) away from much-improved Glencoe. Aviemore is in the Spey Valley, in the central Highlands, and the Lecht and Glenshee are on the eastern side.

The achievements of the resort operators and their staff cannot be overstated. Managing to maintain and build their operations against this background of meteorological unpredictability, while persuading public and private institutions to invest the capital needed to expand and improve the centres, shows a dedication that is the reality of Scottish skiing. While many moan about Britain's standing in competitive world skiing, it is Scotland that provides most of the national team members.

It is unrealistic to expect to have the same sort of skiing holiday in Scotland as in the Alps but it is possible to have an excellent time simply by keeping an open mind and being flexible. The Highlands are so used to uncertain weather that the range of alternative outdoor pursuits available puts even the world's top resorts to shame.

There is friendly and healthy rivalry between the ski areas, notably between the Cairngorm (Aviemore) and Nevis Range, which opened in 1989. The fortunes of both the major ski areas are often seen as key to the overall economic picture of the larger communities around them.

In reality, Cairngorm's infrastructural shortcomings were highlighted by the new lifts at Nevis Range, where the gondola generates more tourist income in the summer than in the winter. This money can then be used to reinvest in the ski area. Ambitious plans are now in place for a funicular lift on the Cairngorm slopes, with construction due to commence in the middle of 1996. This would overcome the problem encountered by Nevis Range of wind forcing the gondola (the only access to the slopes) to cease operating. The Nevis Range slopes are 7 miles (11km) away from Fort William, which is closer than Cairngorm's are to Aviemore.

The changeable snow and weather conditions mean that it makes sense to be based at a point where you have access to more than one centre, and not invest in a week's lift ticket for just one resort. Ski Hotline (0891 654654) provides the up-to-date news of conditions.

Aviemore
top 3,608ft (1100m) bottom 1,804ft (550m)

Aviemore is located about 120 miles (192km) north of Edinburgh and Glasgow on the A9 and is the nearest town to the Cairngorm ski area, which lies ten miles to the east. It is served by rail direct from Inverness, and there are daily flights from Heathrow.

As a ski resort the town suffered in the 1980s by having facilities centred around a large 20-year-old concrete development, the Aviemore Centre, which resembled Les Menuires on a bad day and has been in a serious state of decay for the last ten years. Planners have optimistically renamed the area Aviemore Mountain Resort and hope to invest £15 million over the next few years. However, the Centre itself has been left behind by developments on Aviemore's main street and on the outskirts of the town, where high-quality accommodation and leisure attractions have emerged, helping to make Aviemore and the Spey Valley one of Britain's most attractive outdoor holiday destinations.

Parts of the medium-sized ski area are often closed due to poor weather conditions or snow shortage. The 17 lifts serve two distinct sectors, which are accessed from separate bases at Coire Na Ciste and Coire Cas, meeting below the 4,084ft (1245m) Cairngorm peak. Head Wall and West Wall both offer challenging skiing, and White Lady has some excellent moguls.

Trail marking is not a forte, and you need to keep an eye out for half-buried snow fences. One reporter found queues of 45 minutes at the White Lady chair-lift during high season. Reporters found the £12 daily Aviemore lift pass 'excessive, considering the limited skiing'. There are four snack bars: two at the base lodges, one at the mid-mountain Shieling and the fourth is at the panoramic Ptarmigan.

TOURIST OFFICE
Tel (01479) 810363
Fax (01479) 811063

Glencoe
top 3,637ft (1109m) bottom 2,001ft (610m)

The White Corries ski area at Glencoe has attracted a dedicated following for four decades (Britain's first chair-lift opened here in 1961) and the past few seasons have seen considerable investment in infrastructure as the centre is packaged with Nevis Range as 'Ski Lochaber'. There are 6 miles (10km) of piste and 15 runs. A museum of Scottish skiing and mountaineering contains mementos from home and abroad, including Chris Bonnington's ice axe from the 1985 Everest expedition. The centre is the closest to Glasgow, which is 85 miles (136km) south.

■ WHAT'S NEW

Another access road and six-seater gondola for Nevis Range
Cairngorm will have funicular lift (construction due to start mid-1996)

TOURIST OFFICE
Tel (01855) 811303
Fax (01855) 811765

Glenshee
top 3,502ft (1068m) bottom 2,001ft (610m)

Marketed as 'Britain's largest network of ski lifts and tows', and even more optimistically as the UK's 'Three Valleys', Glenshee's vital statistics are impressive, with a total of 26 lifts and 25 miles (40km) of trails. The centre is on a rather desolate pass on the main A93, with the lifts located on both sides of the road. There is a run-of-the-mill café at the base and a better high-altitude restaurant, the Cairnwell.

TOURIST OFFICE
Tel (01250) 875509
Fax (01250) 875733

The Lecht
top 2,600ft (793m) bottom 2,109ft (643m)

The Lecht ski area is made up of a series of lifts along both sides of the A939 between Tomintoul and Ballater, 40 miles (25km) from Cairngorm and 35 miles (22km) from Glenshee. Eleven lifts give access to 20 runs, the longest of which is 2,953ft (900m). Although this is a small ski area with no sizable town nearby the Lecht does have a reputation for friendliness and quality piste-grooming. The centre also has a 656ft (200m) artificial ski slope. The nearest accommodation is at Corgarff, 3 miles (5km) away.

TOURIST OFFICE
Tel (019756) 51440
Fax (019756) 51426

Nevis Range
top 4,006ft (1221m) bottom 2,148ft (655m)

Nevis Range, with its new access-road and modern six-seater Doppelmayr gondola, presents on arrival some of the feeling of an alpine resort. Only when you reach the top station does disillusionment set in. You either have to join a large queue on a slow beginner's drag-lift or slog uphill to reach the bottom of the quad-chair. However, once you make it to the main trails there is plenty to entertain all levels of skier. The 8 lifts and 24 trails are well inte-grated, albeit poorly marked.

Queues for the gondola back down the mountain can be huge when the weather is good. These develop at about 4pm when the Snowgoose restaurant has standing room only.

■ OTHER SPORTS
Climbing, gliding, go-karting, gorge walking, hang-gliding, skating, off-road vehicles, hiking, shooting, squash, swimming, tennis, trekking

Nevis Range opened for the 1989--90 season and was formerly known as Aonach Mor until it was realised that few non-Scots could pronounce the name. Locals continue to call the resort by its former name, finding the new name to be 'scarcely sen-sible, since Ben Nevis is two miles away and separated by a deep rift'. Most of the accommodation is in Fort William, which has a leisure cen-tre and good shopping facilities.

TOURIST OFFICE
Tel (01397) 705825
Fax (01397) 705854

Snowboarding
British interest in snowboarding was pioneered in Scotland in the late 1980s, and riders are now a common sight at all the centres. Most of the local ski schools offer tuition, and the rental shops have boards for hire. Aviemore has a specialist snowboarding shop.

Ski schools and guiding
Scotland boasts an exceptional number of ski schools, many of them based at Cairngorm and in the Spey Valley. Most offer a high standard of tuition under the auspices of the British Association of Ski Instructors (BASI), which is internationally accepted as an excellent teaching method.

Accommodation
The area surrounding the Scottish ski centres offers a wide range of accommodation, from the cheap and cheerful to the luxury of the Inverlochy Castle Hotel, which is frequented by Hollywood stars and the occasional US President and is one of the closest properties to the Nevis Range slopes. It is possible to base yourself in the Spey Valley close to Aviemore and still remain within an hour of the other four resorts. Alternatively, you can stay in Inverness, which is 45 minutes from both

Cairngorm and the Nevis Range. Fort William is the base for Nevis Range and Glencoe; staying near Balmoral places you within 30 minutes of Glenshee and The Lecht.

Between Aviemore and the Cairngorm slopes is the Stakis Coylumbridge Resort, which has a wide range of facilities including a good swimming-pool, a gym and a wide range of children's activities. In nearby Carrbridge, the An Airidh Ski Lodge re-creates the cosy 'open-house' feel of an alpine ski chalet, and in Aviemore itself the Mercury offers good-value accommodation.

Eating in and out
Scotland is still saddled with an unfair reputation for poor dining opportunities. Recently opened Littlejohns restaurant in Aviemore has a friendly atmosphere, with 1930s paraphernalia and copious quantities of American and Mexican food. The Taverna French Bistro has reasonable prices. Aviemore has one supermarket and a small corner shop. In Fort William, the pink lochside Crannog restaurant has a good reputation for its seafood.

Après-ski
In all the ski areas the après-ski is largely hotel-based. Aviemore previously had a reputation for rowdy and sleazy nightlife and little else, but most bars have been refurbished and now there is less of the tough, hard-drinking Scottish pub atmosphere. Activities include a theatre, cinema and indoor sports such as swimming and skating. Reporters generally found the nightlife 'disappointing', with the disco stopping at 11pm.

Fort William is an old lochside town beneath Ben Nevis and has a strong tourist appeal, with a wide variety of hotels, bars and restaurants to suit all tastes. There is also a cinema and a leisure centre with bowling, swimming-pool and a crèche.

Childcare
Nevis Range, Glenshee and The Lecht operate non-ski crèche facilities, which should be booked in advance. The Nevis Range crèche accepts children from three years old.

Spain

Spain is the only country in Europe where the number of skiers is significantly increasing as the sport undergoes a major surge in popularity. In the main French resorts the Spanish are now considered an important section of the tourist trade and it is hard to spend a day in the Trois Vallées or L'Espace Killy without hearing the language spoken.

This increase has also been apparent in Spain, although whether this continues after last season's World Alpine Championships débâcle remains to be seen. The good rate of exchange of the peseta against the pound makes Spanish skiing some of the best value for money in Europe.

■ GOOD POINTS
Efficient lift systems, typically Spanish après-ski, low prices
■ BAD POINTS
Lack of resort charm, mainly limited ski areas, short runs

Spain has no historical connection with skiing and indeed it seems surprising that a country so associated with beaches and summer sunshine should have any skiing at all. It does, in fact, have two quite separate mountain ranges, which both normally receive adequate winter snowfalls, regardless of what is happening in the main alpine countries.

Sierra Nevada, in the mountains of the same name, lies in the far south of the country and was to have hosted the 1995 world championships in February 1995. However, this high and usually snow-sure resort suffered its worst season in 30 years; nature failed to produce sufficient cover and the entire programme had to be postponed.

The resultant publicity has seriously and unfairly damaged the overseas perception of Spanish skiing. Unfair because most of the skiing takes place hundreds of kilometres to the north-east in the Pyrenees, where there was superlative snow cover throughout both the 1993–4 and 1994–5 seasons.

Baqueira-Beret remains the most important of the Pyrenean resorts. It is a small but smart development much loved by the Spanish monarch King Juan Carlos, and one which attracts wealthy skiers from Madrid and Barcelona.

Baqueira-Beret 1500m (4,920ft)

Baqueira-Beret is Spain's answer to Gstaad, a smart and fashionable resort where not all the designer ski-suits you see parading down the main street ever actually make it on to the piste. It lies at the head of the beautiful Val d'Aran, near Viella on the northern side of the Pyrenees; access from France is easy, and the drive from Toulouse takes less than two hours.

The skiing takes place on four wide and well-linked mountains with a vertical drop over varied and often exciting terrain of about 1000m. Most is suited to intermediates but one icy couloir, evocatively called Where Goats Tumble, is a real challenge. Last season saw the opening of the new **Bonaigua** area, which adds to the area's appeal for good skiers.

Plans to expand the already extensive skiing into the next valley and increase this impressive area by 40 per cent are in the final stages of discussion. At present it has 21 lifts with the main mountain-access by quad-chair from the top of the village.

Baqueira is still largely unknown outside Spain, mainly because of the small number of rental beds available. However, it is no newcomer to winter-sports — in December 1994 it celebrated its 30th birthday — and, at a time when even big-name resorts are struggling financially, Baqueira is operating efficiently at a handsome profit.

What makes Baqueira unique in Europe is that the resort has just one owner. The Cerra family from Barcelona is passionate about skiing and happens to have a controlling interest in one of Spain's largest insurance companies. Cerra Occidente owns the land, the lifts, the mountain restaurants and the ski school. It even owned all the real estate in the village, although it has now relinquished a prime building lot in return for a further lift development permit from the regional government.

If all this sounds familiar to transatlantic skiers, so it should. Vail Associates, the hugely successful owner of Vail in Colorado, acted as development consultants to Baqueira. Americans have long since discovered that a single corporate identity in a ski resort is the sure way to improve customer satisfaction and profitability. In concept (mercifully only in concept) Baqueira is a little slice of the US, which has somehow gotten itself into the Pyrenees.

The terrain, right down to the scrubby type of Engelmann spruce which grows here at the lower altitudes, is strongly reminiscent of Squaw Valley in California. But here the resemblance ends. Baqueira is purpose-built in an aesthetically adequate style and is as Spanish as the siesta, which is an essential part of ski survival here. The village lies beside the road up to the very high Bonaigua Pass, which is often but not always closed in winter. Recent sympathetic development has increased its appeal as a base with some good shops, hotels, restaurants and a leisure centre. The atmosphere is relaxed and friendly. **Beret** is the second base-area rather than a separate resort, and consists of little more than a car-park and a cafeteria.

Veteran Olympic skier José Moga, who taught Juan Carlos to ski and who also runs the main ski shop in town, describes it as 'the best-value skiing in a less pretentious atmosphere than you can find anywhere in Europe'.

TOURIST OFFICE
Tel 34 73 644455
Fax 34 73 644488

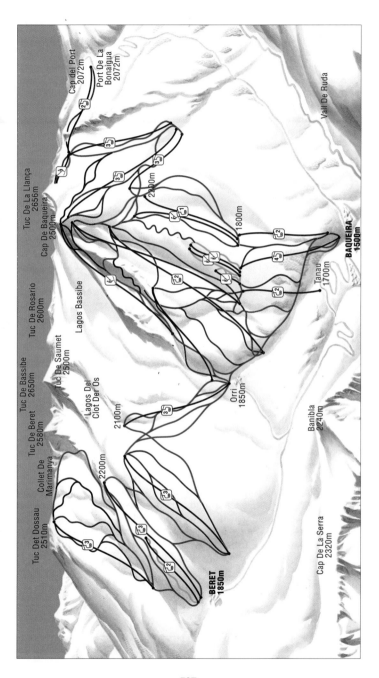

Cap del Port 2072m
Port De La Bonaigua 2072m
Vall De Ruda
Tuc De La Llança 2656m
Cap De Baqueira 2500m
2200m
1800m
BAQUEIRA 1500m
Tuc De Rosario 2600m
Lagos Bassibe
Tanau 1700m
Tuc De Bassibe 2650m
Tuc De Saumet 2500m
Lagos Del Clot Der Os
Orri 1850m
Banibla 2240m
Tuc De Beret 2580m
2100m
Collet De Marimanya
2200m
Tuc Det Dossau 2510m
BERET 1850m
Cap De La Serra 2320m

Sierra Nevada 2100m (6,888ft)

Sierra Nevada lies in Andalusia, 32km from the ancient Moorish city of Granada, and offers Europe's most southerly skiing. Unlike the other Spanish ski resorts, which are nearly all in the Pyrenees in the north-east of Spain, Sierra Nevada is a stark contrast to the surrounding area and nearby resorts of Marbella and Malaga with their yacht clubs and golf courses. The resort used to be marketed under the name of Sol y Nieve (Sun and Snow) and the purpose-built village in which most skiers stay (at 2100m) is known as **Pradollano**.

The ski area is extremely vulnerable to bad weather and the mountain range as a whole is exposed to Atlantic gales. When the weather here is bad everything stops, but when conditions are good the skiing can be excellent and the views stunning. On a clear day you can even see Morocco. However, because of the proximity to Granada and the Costa del Sol, the resort suffers from overcrowding at weekends and on public holidays.

Some £60 million was invested in the resort in preparation for the disastrous world championships and it now has 19 lifts serving 34 mainly intermediate pistes totalling 50km. Access to the main skiing area is via a choice of three lifts (including a gondola).

Most of Pradollano's buildings date from the 1960s and 1970s. It is not an attractive place ('just like Torremolinos with snow and litter'), but the atmosphere is 'quiet, with a Spanish feel to it'.

TOURIST OFFICE
Tel 34 58 249100
Fax 34 58 249131

Formigal 1500m (4,920ft)

The resort of Formigal lies in the Tena Valley in the centre of the Pyrenees, 8km from the French border. It has 20 lifts, including a gondola and six chair-lifts; together they serve some 27 pistes totalling 50km in an open and sunny area rising to Pico Tres Hombres at 2350m. The gentle runs are mainly suited to beginners and intermediates, although there are also a couple of more difficult challenges.

The village itself is modern, with stark concrete-and-wood architecture. Most of the hotels, cafés and bars line a central main street. The Nieve Sol is a large hotel with its own disco, close to the village centre. The Meson Arrigal is a typically Spanish restaurant serving good-value tapas. The resort of **Panticosa**, with its small ski area of 7 lifts and 14 pistes, is a short drive away in the same valley.

TOURIST OFFICE
Tel 34 74 488126

La Molina 1400m (4,592ft)

The resort is 14km from the French border. It connects with neighbouring **Masella** (1600m) via a chair-lift over the peak of Tossa d'Alp. La

Molina has 21 lifts (including one nursery drag-lift), most of which are on the open, intermediate slopes of **Puig Llancada**; Masella has ten lifts and a mixture of runs, including five blacks from the Tossa summit.

The straggling old village of La Molina lacks any real centre and there is a newer purpose-built satellite, **Supermolina**, higher up the mountain at 1700m.

TOURIST OFFICE
Tel 34 72 419419
Fax 34 72 419418

Snowboarding
Spanish youth has endorsed the board with typical noisy enthusiasm and shredders account for around 10 per cent of lift tickets sold in all the main Spanish resorts.

Ski schools and guiding
We have generally unhappy reports about Spanish ski schools, largely because a proportionately low number of instructors speak English in comparison with those at alpine schools, and few British speak Spanish. Reporters in Baqueira complained that the instruction was mainly of the 'follow-my-leader' type.

Mountain restaurants
Baqueira's mountain eating-places serve good food at reasonable prices, but lack atmosphere. One exception is Restaurant 1800 ('wonderful paella for eight, but you must order a day in advance'). Sierra Nevada is rather better served by its choice of restaurants in the main bowl.

Accommodation
Baqueira has only 7,000 beds and many of these are owned or rented for the season by Spaniards who make the journey here every weekend from Barcelona and other cities. The four-star Hotel Montarto is widely praised, as is the less expensive Hotel Tuc Blanc. Many regular visitors prefer to stay in the more traditional hotels further down the valley. There are good *paradors* (inns) in nearby Viella.

In **Sierra Nevada** the accommodation is mainly in hotels. The Melia Sol y Nieve and the four-star Melia Sierra Nevada, both near the main square, are convenient and pleasant. The former has a mini-club for children between 5 and 11 years old. The latter has a swimming-pool, disco and its own shops. The Kenia Nevada is recommended by a reporter as 'a quiet hotel, most guests were Spanish and the service was generally friendly and attentive and the bedrooms comfortable and clean'. The chalet-style Parador, set on its own above Pradollano (accessible by chair-lift and piste), is fairly functional, but has exceptional views. The Albergue Universitani is said to be excellent value and clean.

Eating in and out

The menus in **Baqueira** are truly international and come in three versions: Spanish, Catalan and Aranes (a language peculiar to this corner of the Pyrenees). Fortunately, Baqueira's proximity to the border means that French is also widely understood, if not spoken. This is not a place for vegetarians or the culinary squeamish; Borda Lobato is a lavishly converted cow shed and considered the best restaurant in town ('barbecued rabbit was followed on my second evening by a choice of roast suckling pig or whole baby lamb carved with garden shears'). Other recommended restaurants include La Perdiu Blanca, La Ticolet for *pierrade*, and Tamarro's for tapas. Expect to pay between £10 and £15 a head for a three-course dinner in a fairly smart restaurant. With a bottle of beer costing about a £1 and coffee 50p, prices are among the lowest in any serious ski resort in the northern hemisphere.

In **Sierra Nevada** there is a small range of restaurants serving local, French, Turkish or Italian cuisine. The Borreguiles is one of the most popular eating places.

Après-ski

In Spain partying is an even more serious business than skiing. Wise Anglo-Saxons who stray into this completely alien ski-resort environment either adopt local hours or suffer from what quickly develops into a severe Latin mutation of jetlag. Local skiers hit the slopes at a leisurely 10am and ski furiously until lunch at 2pm. They grab a final hour on the piste before the lifts close at 5pm and then head for the tapas bars before an evening snooze.

The length of the 7pm siesta is largely dependent on the ski energy expended, the size of the paella you ate for lunch, and your intake of *calamares* and Rioja at tea-time. Nobody (not even families with young children) sits down to dinner before 9pm, and restaurants start to get busy at 11pm. Dancing does not begin before 1am and can carry on into daylight hours.

In Baqueira, Tiffany's is the busiest nightclub. Sierra Nevada's late nightspot is Sierra Nevada 53. Early action is centred on a choice of crowded bars. Excursions can be made to Granada, famous for the spectacular Alhambra Palace, as well as for its beautiful renaissance and baroque buildings.

Childcare

Baqueira has three good non-ski and ski kindergarten, which cater for children from three months to eight years old. The Sierra Nevada kindergarten is for children aged three months to four years.

Snowboarding

No matter how much many skiers would like it to, it is not going to go away. Unlike monoski and all the other esoteric forms of *la nouvelle glisse* that we have seen wax and wane over the past couple of decades, snowboarding is now a permanent fixture on the slopes of Europe and North America.

Rivalry, not to mention animosity, between the two types of mountain-user has been nurtured on youth, cultural differences and wholly erroneous misinformation that snowboarders account for a high proportion of collision accidents.

According to slightly dubious figures based on sales of boards, there are already around 1.7 million snowboarders out there, and manufacturers predict that this will rise to 3 million over the next five years. Riders claim they now account for 11.2 per cent of lift tickets sold and expect this figure to rise to 28.6 per cent by the year 2000. Ski industry sceptics don't accept these figures and believe the real current figure in mainstream resorts overall is less than 10 per cent and peaking.

A handful of resorts like Keystone in Colorado and Alpine Meadows in Nevada stubbornly maintain a no-board policy, but it remains to be seen for how long they can commercially afford to marginalise themselves.

Both groups have an equal right to enjoy themselves on the mountain. Snowboarding is slowly coming to maturity and shedding its angry teenage image. Skiers would do well to recall the outrage expressed by telemark purists at the introduction of the fixed ski binding and accept the dramatic change in winter-sports that may provide the boost of new blood, which a large number of European resorts need to survive into the next century.

Joining the board
by Lloyd Rogers, British Snowboard Champion

Once you have tried snowboarding it is easy to understand why it is one of the fastest growing sports in the world. Combining the best of snow skiing, ocean surfing and skateboarding, snowboarding provides an unrivalled sense of freedom, especially in fresh powder conditions.

Snowboarding is available to young and old alike, but the largest participant age group is between 17 and 24 years. Many of these will have never skied before and are attracted instead from surfing or skateboarding backgrounds. Their insurgence is supported by the strong snowboard fashion, culture and attitude, which projects a rebellious image, particularly to the more traditionalist skiers.

The great news about snowboarding for those who have not tried it is that it is relatively easy to learn in comparison with skiing. The first day, which must be spent with a qualified instructor, will almost certainly result in a bruise or two; you will spend much of it sitting on your bottom. However, persevere and the rewards come quickly. Progression from the tremendous feeling of linking the first few turns through to enjoying deep powder snow comes to most within two weeks. Multiply that by at least ten for skiing. Another advantage of snowboarding is that weekly school classes are not necessary. Two or three introductory lessons are all that are needed to enable you to go off and enjoy the sport on your own.

For those who are considering snowboarding, the following is a guide to the main factors to take into account:

Equipment

Board and boots: try or buy?

My advice to the aspiring snowboarder weighing up whether or not to buy equipment is: try it first. The multitude of board types available make it extremely difficult to choose the one that will be right for you, and at around £400 each, a mistake can be an expensive one! Many snowboard and ski shops in Britain offer reasonably priced hire packages with up-to-date equipment and many will deduct the hire price should you decide to buy the board. The disadvantage of hiring before you leave home is that if you are unhappy with the equipment or it breaks, you will have to hire a second board in the resort. If you can be certain of hiring the equipment you need in the resort itself, then it may be better to hire it when you get there.

The choice of board for a beginner, whether hiring or buying, is best left to the snowboard expert in the shop. Your main decision will then be whether you wish to use soft or hard boots. Both are equally good for learning, with hard boots slightly superior in hard-packed snow conditions. Soft boots allow a better performance in soft and fresh snow. In general, skiers crossing the divide will find hard boots easier, whereas newcomers to snow sports will feel more comfortable in 'softs'. If fashion is a factor, then be aware that in Britain soft boots account for around 90 per cent of the market.

What to wear

You can wear your existing ski gear, however, specific snowboard clothing is a good investment. Snowboard clothes are worn much looser than ski clothing to allow for the greater physical mobility required. For their longevity and your comfort, clothing should incorporate waterproof reinforcement at the knees, seat and elbows. These are the impact areas and also those that come into contact with the snow when you are resting in the natural sitting or kneeling positions you adopt on the slopes. Dedicated snowboard gloves are probably the wisest investment of all. Snow is extremely abrasive and even the most expensive skiing gloves will wear out very quickly if used for snowboarding. Look for seam-free, reinforced palms and waterproof materials. Your hands are now your ski poles and outriggers!

Choosing a resort

Snowboarding has already become big business and most ski resorts have not been slow to recognise this. Almost all resorts are open to snowboarders, with some even offering special snowboard-only pistes or 'fun parks'.

The best bet if choosing a resort on the basis of its 'snowboard friendliness' is to think big. Large resorts attract greater numbers of snowboarders and consequently the chances of finding specific snowboard services such as shops and schools will be better. Pick up a copy of one of the specialist snowboard magazines available in newsagents and ski/snowboard shops. These carry resort reports and advertisements offering tailor-made snowboard holidays, including board hire and instruction if required.

Getting started

Instruction is available in most resorts; in fact most countries have their own national snowboard associations and recognised instructors. There is a huge advantage in being taught by a qualified snowboard instructor, rather than by a ski instructor who teaches snowboarding during quiet periods.

As well as learning on snow, it is also possible to employ the services of a British Snowboard Association (BSA) instructor at all good dry-ski-slopes in Britain. Although plastic snow is less forgiving and harsher to fall on than the real thing, a short lesson before you go on holiday will certainly be useful. If you enjoy it you can follow up with more advanced tuition on your return.

By car or train

The opening of the Channel Tunnel and the subsequent price-war with the ferry operators is expected eventually to transform the way in which we travel to the Alps. Anyone who has ever suffered a Saturday at Gatwick in high season will understand why driving or taking a train to the snow is becoming an increasingly popular option. However, neither is as yet cheaper or quicker than the charter flight.

Figures produced by the ferry companies suggest that the DIY cross-Channel ski market has been increasing at a rate of 15 per cent per season as more and more skiers abandon overcrowded airports in favour of their own cars. The result has been the emergence of a new genre of tour operator, the ski-drive specialist, offering holidays inclusive of ferry or tunnel, plus accommodation. More adventurous skiers dial the tourist-office number of their chosen resort and make their own arrangements.

Cars

The continued upgrading of the European motorway network allows easy travel often to within only a few miles of ski resorts, and journey times have not only been greatly reduced but, weather conditions permitting, can be accurately forecast. Both the AA and the RAC offer a personalised route-planning service, which is strongly recommended. You specify your destination, and for a basic fee they supply a computer print-out of your exact route. It is important to note that the hidden extras do add greatly to the cost, although the convenience may outweigh the additional outlay.

Drivers should obtain a Green Card from their insurance company to guarantee adequate cover in the event of an accident. Breakdown insurance is also advisable. It is essential to have your car fully serviced before encountering what may be seriously cold conditions in the Alps. Have the battery checked by a garage before leaving home and replace it if in any doubt as to its efficiency. The level of anti-freeze should be topped up to the manufacturer's handbook recommendation for temperatures down to -30°C. You will also need a stronger solution of winter screenwash. Take with you a torch, a shovel, an old pair of gloves and a tow-rope.

Whatever the month of your holiday you are advised to buy snow chains; if renting a car at Geneva, Zurich or any other gateway airport ensure that the chains supplied match the tyres on the car before you set off. Chains cost from £12 up to £100 and come in three basic types: standard, semi-automatic and automatic. Basically, the more you pay the easier they are to fit. It is extremely important to practise putting them on before you leave home. The most sophisticated type, which takes just a couple of minutes to attach, can be obtained from Rudd Chains of Whitstable or hired from the AA. Make sure you know whether your car is front- or rear-wheel drive and attach the chains to the drive wheels.

French motorway tolls cost between £85 and £100, depending on your destination; Belgian, German and Austrian motorways are toll-free. Switzerland charges a flat fee of around £17 for a windscreen sticker that allows usage of all motorways for a year.

Cars are often frowned upon in resorts, and you are liable to incur heavy weekly parking costs (as high as £70 per week for a covered space) in the most popular resorts. Driving to the Alps is really a viable economic option only for a full car-load of four or more persons.

Trains

The Snowtrain to the French Alps rattles slowly on in the face of all the hype surrounding high-tech improvements to the European rail system. It is inconvenient, uncomfortable, crowded but surprisingly praised by almost every reporter who has tried it. The main reason is that compared with the charter flight it allows you almost eight instead of six days' skiing in a conventional 'one-week' holiday. The disadvantage lies in having to carry luggage on and off ferries, transfer buses, and the train itself. Storage space on the train is limited, the couchettes are cramped, and washing conditions are primitive.

Motorail services run between Calais and Moûtiers on Friday evenings, returning on Saturday nights. This cuts out the tedium of the long drive, while at the same time giving you the flexibility of having your own transport whilst holidaying in the Alps; however, the cost is high.

Eurostar from Waterloo International followed by the TGV from Paris to Moûtiers is at present a comfortable but slow alternative because of inconvenient connections in the French capital. However, it can only be a question of time before express train services direct to the Alps are in operation from London, and this will provide the best possible way of reaching the snow.

Skiing safety

The mountains are like the sea: they give enormous pleasure but they can also be dangerous and should be treated with the utmost respect at all times. Only when you find yourself in an awkward and potentially dangerous situation or witness an accident at first hand do you properly realise what the risks can be. Below are a few useful tips.

Weather and exposure

The weather can change at a moment's notice and vary dramatically at different altitudes. Always dress with this in mind and be prepared for all conditions. Several layers of clothing are best. Never set off without sunglasses or goggles, a hat or headband. It is always preferable to be too hot than too cold and more body heat escapes through the head than anywhere else in the body. In the event of an accident a 'space blanket' can save a life.

All young children should wear safety helmets. Unfortunately, they are not yet compulsory and you will still see more helmets in certain ski countries than others. They can be worn on their own or over a thin balaclava or hat on extremely cold days.

Never ski with a baby or small child in a backpack; even the best skiers can catch an edge, or someone could ski into you.

Exposure to bad weather can result in frostbite or hypothermia. Frostbite is the excessive cooling of small areas of the body, usually of the fingers, toes, nose, cheeks or ears. The affected tissue first turns white and numb. This is called first-degree frostbite and can be dealt with by immediate, gentle re-warming. In cold conditions watch out for signs of frostbite in each other. Hypothermia is a condition resulting from a drop in the whole body's temperature. It is difficult to diagnose: some of the more obvious symptoms are physical or mental lethargy, sluggishness, slurring of speech, spurts of energy and abnormal vision.

Accident procedure

Speed is essential when an accident has occurred:

- Mark the accident site by placing crossed skis about 10m uphill of the casualty
- If the casualty is not breathing, administer artificial respiration (mouth-to-mouth resuscitation). Make sure there is nothing obstructing the mouth or throat
- If the casualty is breathing but unconscious, turn him/her on to their side to minimise the risk of choking. Protect any fractured limb from movement
- If the casualty is bleeding, apply direct pressure to the site of the wound using a clean handkerchief or scarf if possible

- Do not remove the ski boot if there is injury to the lower leg as it acts as a splint
- Keep the casualty warm, comfortable and as cheerful as possible. Alert the ski patrol immediately
- If the casualty appears to be in shock, by going pale, cold and faint, he/she should be encouraged to lie with their head lower than their feet. Do not administer food or drink.

Safety on the piste

A set of rules for skiers is drawn up by the International Ski Federation (FIS). These rules aim to keep skiing accidents to a minimum, and are increasingly forming the basis of legal judgements in both civil and criminal actions in European courts. If you do cause an accident while in breach of these rules, you could be in serious trouble. A list of the rules is printed below:

FIS rules for the conduct of skiers

1   Respect for others: a skier must behave in such a way that he does not endanger or prejudice others.
2   Control of speed and skiing: a skier must ski in control. He must adapt his speed and manner of skiing to his personal ability and to the prevailing conditions of terrain, snow and weather as well as to the density of traffic.
3   Choice of route: a skier coming from behind must choose his route in such a way that he does not endanger skiers ahead.
4   Overtaking: a skier may overtake another skier above or below and to the right or the left, provided that he leaves enough space for the overtaken skier to make any voluntary or involuntary movement.
5   Entering and starting: a skier entering a marked run or starting again after stopping must look up and down the run to make sure that he can do so without endangering himself or others.
6   Stopping on the piste: unless absolutely necessary, a skier must avoid stopping on the piste in narrow places or where visibility is restricted. After a fall in such a place, a skier must move clear of the piste as soon as possible.
7   Climbing and descending on foot: both climbing or descending skiers on foot must keep to the side of the piste.
8   Respect for signs and markings: a skier must respect all signs and markings.
9   Assistance: at accidents, every skier is duty-bound to assist.
10 Identification: every skier and witness, whether a responsible party or not, must exchange names and addresses following an accident.

General comments on the rules

Skiing, like all sport, entails risks. The FIS rules must be considered an ideal pattern of conduct for a responsible and careful skier; their purpose is to avoid accidents on the piste.

The rules apply to all skiers who are obliged to be familiar with them and to respect them. If he fails to do so, his behaviour could expose him to civil and criminal liability in the event of an accident.

Rule 1   Skiers are responsible not only for their own behaviour, but also for their defective equipment. This also applies to those using newly developed equipment.

Rule 2   Collisions usually happen because skiers are travelling too fast, are out of control or have failed to see others. A skier must be able to stop, turn and move within the ability of his own vision. In crowded areas, or in places where visibility is reduced, skiers must ski slowly, especially at the edge of a steep slope, at the bottom of a piste and within areas surrounding ski lifts.

Rule 3   Skiing is a free activity sport where everyone may ski where and as they please, provided that they abide by these rules and adapt their skiing to their own personal ability and to the prevailing conditions on the mountain. The skier in front has priority. The skier behind another in the same direction must keep sufficient distance between himself and the other skier so as to leave the preceding skier enough space to make all his movements freely.

Rule 4   A skier who overtakes another is wholly responsible for completing that manoeuvre in such a way as not to cause a difficulty to the skier being overtaken. This responsibility rests with him until the overtaking manoeuvre has been completed. This rule applies even when overtaking a stationary skier.

Rule 5   Experience proves that entering a piste and starting to ski again after stopping are the cause of accidents. It is absolutely essential that a skier finding himself in this situation enters the piste safely and without causing an obstruction or danger to himself or others. When he has started skiing properly again, even slowly, he has the benefit of Rule 3 against faster skiers coming from above or behind.

Rule 6   Except on wide pistes, stops must be made at the side of the piste. One must not stop in narrow places or where it is difficult to be seen from above.

Rule 7   Moving against the general direction poses unexpected obstacles for the skiers.

Rule 8   The degree of difficulty of a piste is indicated by green (beginner), blue (easy), red (intermediate) or black (difficult) in Europe. However, only Italy and France have green runs. A dotted black line indicates an off-piste itinerary. In North America the degree of difficulty is indicated by green (easy), blue (intermediate), black (difficult), one or two black diamonds denote varying degrees of greater difficulty. A skier is free to choose whichever piste he wants.

The pistes are also marked with other signs, showing direction or giving warnings of danger or closure. A sign closing a piste, like one denoting danger, must be strictly observed. Skiers should be aware that warning signs are posted in their own interests.

Rule 9   It is a cardinal principle for all sportsmen that they should render assistance following an accident, independent of any legal obligation to do so. Immediate first aid should be given, the appropriate authorities alerted and the place of the accident marked to warn other skiers. FIS hopes that a hit-and-run offence in skiing will incur a criminal conviction similar to a hit-and-run offence on the road, and that equivalent penalties will be imposed by all countries where such legislation is not already in force.

Rule 10   Witnesses are of great importance in establishing a full and proper report of an accident; therefore, everybody must consider that it is his duty as a responsible person to provide information as a witness. Reports of the rescue service and of the police as well as photographs, are of considerable assistance in determining civil and criminal liability.

Safety off-piste

No one should ski off-piste without a properly qualified local guide, particularly in glacial terrain where the risk of crevasse is added to that of avalanche. Always wear a recognised avalanche bleeper and take the time to learn how to use it, and carry out a grid search before you set off. The chances of survival after an avalanche deteriorate rapidly after the first five minutes. Listen to your guide, learn basic snowcraft and how to read a slope. However, it is important to remember that the guide is fallible and that you alone remain responsible for decisions concerning your own safety. Remember, you may be many kilometres from a resort or a pisted run with no trail markers to guide you.

In the event of an avalanche, try to ski to the side. If you fall, get rid of your skis, poles and backpack if possible. Swim and fight to stay on the surface.

Tips to remember when skiing off-piste:

- Always ski in a group, never alone
- Always ski in control
- Always stop behind the guide (there may be cliffs or other hazards ahead)
- Carry a map of the area and a compass. Know how to use both
- Be wary of slopes where the run-out is not clearly obvious from the start. Following other skiers' tracks does not necessarily mean the route is safe.

Which tour operator?

Below is a list of bonded ski operators who offer inclusive package holidays from Britain

AA SKI DRIVEAWAY
AA Motoring Holidays, PO Box 128,
Fanum House, Basingstoke,
Hants RG21 2EA
Tel/Fax (01256) 814433
Ski-drive holidays

ABT SKI
Shepperton Marina, Felix Lane,
Shepperton, Middlesex TW17 8NJ
Tel (01932) 252025
Fax (01932) 246140
Chalet holidays in St-Martin-de-Belleville

ACCESSIBLE ISOLATION
Midhurst Walk, West Street, Midhurst,
West Sussex GU29 9NF
Tel (01730) 812535
Fax (01730) 812926
Tailor-made Canadian holidays

ACTIVITY TRAVEL
23 Blair Street, Edinburgh EH1 1QR
Tel 0181-541 5115
Fax 0131-220 4185
Resorts in the Alps and the Rockies

AIRTRACK SNOWBOARDING
16-17 Winder Street, Uxbridge,
Middlesex UB8 1AB
Tel (01895) 810810
Fax (01895) 254088
Snowboarding in Serre Chevalier

ALL CANADA SKI
90 High Street, Lowestoft,
Suffolk NR32 1XN
Tel (01502) 565176
Fax (01502) 500681
Ski holidays in Canada

ALPINE ACTION
10 Kings Road, Lancing,
West Sussex BN15 8EA

Tel (01903) 761986
Fax (01903) 766007
Small operator concentrating on personal service to Trois Vallées

ALPINE OPTIONS
Mont de Lans, F-38860
Les Deux Alpes, France
Tel 33 76 80 19 95
Fax (01202) 877148
Flexible operator with self-drive to France

ALPINE TOURS
54 Northgate, Canterbury, Kent CT1 1BE
Tel (01227) 454777
Fax (01227) 451177
Schools and groups

ALTOURS TRAVEL
41a Church Street, Staveley,
Chesterfield S43 3TL
Tel (01246) 471234
Fax (01246) 471999
Group travel to France, Italy and Austria

AMERICAN CONNECTIONS
7 York Way, Lancaster Road, High
Wycombe, Buckinghamshire HP12 3PY
Tel (01494) 473173
Fax (01494) 473588
A la carte skiing in North America

AUSTRIAN HOLIDAYS
10 Wardour Street, London W1V 4BQ
Tel 0171-434 7399
Fax 0171-434 7393
Specialises in ski holidays to Austria

AUTO PLAN SKI HOLIDAYS
Auto Plan House, Stowe Court, Stowe
Street, Lichfield, Staffordshire WS13 6AQ
Tel (01543) 257777
Fax (01543) 419217
Flexible ski-drive holidays

BALKAN HOLIDAYS
Sofia House, 19 Conduit Street,
London W1R 9TD

Tel 0171-493 8612
Fax 0171-491 7068
Holidays to Bulgaria and Romania

BALKAN TOURS
37 Ann Street, Belfast BT1 4EB
Tel (01232) 246795
Fax (01232) 234581
Holidays to Bulgaria and Romania

BLADON LINES
56/58 Putney High Street,
London SW15 1SF
Tel 0181-780 8800
Fax 0181-789 2592
Major chalet and hotel operator

BORDERLINE
Les Sorbiers, F-65120 Barèges, France
Tel (01963) 250117
Fax (01963) 250508
Holidays to the French Pyrenees

CHALET SNOWBOARD
31 Aldworth Avenue, Wantage,
Oxon OX12 7EJ
Tel/Fax (01235) 767182
Snowboard holidays to France

CHALETS UNLIMITED
50a Friern Barnet Lane, London N11 3NA
Tel 0181-343 7339
Fax 0181-368 1212
Chalet-holiday service

CHALET WORLD
PO Box 260, Shrewsbury,
Shropshire SY1 1WX
Tel (01952) 840462
Fax (01952) 840463
Chalet holidays in France

CHINOOK-IT
30 Samsom Street, London SE5 7RE
Tel 0171-252 5438
Fax 0171-252 5438
Skiing and snowboarding in North America

CLUB EUROPE
Fairway House, 53 Dartmouth Road,
London SE23 3HN
Tel 0181-699 7788
Fax 0181-699 7770
Schools operator

CLUB MED
106 Brompton Road, London SW3 1JJ
Tel 0171-581 1161
Fax 0171-581 4769
Upmarket holiday villages with crèche and own ski school

COLLINEIGE SKI
32 High Street, Frimley, Surrey GU16 5JD
Tel (01276) 24262
Fax (01276) 27282
Small, flexible chalet operator to Chamonix.

CONTIKI
Wells House, 15 Elmfield Road, Bromley,
Kent BR1 1LS
Tel 0181-290 6422
Fax 0181-290 6569
Coach holidays for 18-35s in Hopfgarten,
Austria

CRYSTAL
Crystal House, The Courtyard, Arlington
Road, Surbiton, Surrey KT6 6BW
Tel 0181-399 5144
Fax 0181-390 6378
*Major operator to 113 resorts in
11 countries*

DAWSON AND SANDERSON
60 Middle Street, Consett,
Co Durham DH8 5QE
Tel (01207) 591261
Fax (01207) 591262
Small operator to Norway

EQUITY TOTAL SKI
Dukes Lane House, 47 Middle House,
Brighton, East Sussex BN1 1AL
Tel (01273) 203202
Fax (01273) 203212
*Holidays and group travel to Italy, France
and Austria*

ERNA LOW CONSULTANTS
9 Reece Mews, London SW7 3HE
Tel 0171-584 2841
Fax 0171-589 9531
UK representatives for La Plagne and Flaine

FINLAYS SKIING
The Barn, The Square, Ancrum,
Borders TD8 6XH
Tel (01835) 830562

Fax (01835) 830550
Small specialist operator to Val d'Isère and Courchevel

FIRST CHOICE
First Choice House, London Road,
Crawley, West Sussex RH10 2GX
Tel 0161-745 7000
Fax 0161-745 4622
Major operator to over 60 resorts in 9 countries

FLEXISKI
Crogen Stables, Corwen, Clwyd LL21 0SY
Tel 0171-352 0044
Fax (01490) 440446
Small specialist with weekends and 10-day breaks

LA FRANCE DES VILLAGES SKI
Model Farm, Rattlesden, Bury St
Edmunds, Suffolk IP30 0SY
Tel (01499) 737664
Fax (01499) 737850
Self-drive and self-catering to Champagny-en-Vanoise

FREEDOM HOLIDAYS
30 Brackenbury Road, London W6 0BA
Tel 0181-741 4471
Fax 0181-741 9332
Small, flexible operator

FRENCH IMPRESSIONS
3-5 Crouch End Hill, London N8 8DH
Tel 0181-342 8870
Fax 0181-342 8860
Ski-drive holidays to 20 resorts in France

FRESH TRACKS
Argyll House, All Saints Passage,
London SW18 1EP
Tel 0181-875-9818
Fax 0181-874 8827
Learn to ski powder, off-piste and weekends

FRONTIER SKI
Winge Travel Ltd, 3rd Floor,
Broadmead House, 21 Panton Street,
London SW1Y 4DR
Tel 0171-839 1627
Fax 0171-839 5761
Holidays to Canada

HEADWATER HOLIDAYS
146 London Road, Northwich,
Cheshire CW9 5HH
Tel (01606) 48699
Fax (01606) 48761
Cross-country and alpine skiing in unspoilt places

HUSKI CHALET HOLIDAYS
63A Kensington Church Street,
London W8 4BA
Tel 0171-938 4844
Fax 0171-938 2312
Specialist operator to Chamonix

INGHAMS
10-18 Putney Hill, London SW15 6AX
Tel (Europe) 0181-780 4444
(Canada & US) 0181-780 6600
Fax (Europe) 0181-780 4405
(Canada & US) 0181-780 7705
Major operator to 81 resorts in 9 countries, separate luxury brochure

INNTRAVEL
Hovingham, York YO6 4JZ
Tel (01653) 628811
Fax (01653) 628741
Cross-country specialist

INTERSKI
95 Outram Street, Sutton-in-Ashfield,
Nottinghamshire NG17 4BG
Tel (01623) 551024
Fax (01623) 558941
Specialises in school holidays to Italy, has own ski school

JEAN STANFORD SKI HOLIDAYS
213 Sandcross Lane, Reigate,
Surrey RH2 8LL
Tel (01737) 242074
Fax (01737) 242003
Small operator to France and US,
with free tuition

KINGS SKI CLUB
Castle Mill, Lower Kings Road,
Berkhamsted, Hertfordshire
HP4 2AP
Tel (01442) 876642
Fax (01442) 879968
Established operator to France, Austria and Italy

KUONI
Kuoni House, Dorking, Surrey
RH5 4AZ
Tel (01306) 742500
Fax (01306) 744222
Operator to 20 Swiss resorts

LAGRANGE HOLIDAYS
168 Shepherds Bush Road,
London W6 7PB
Tel 0171-371 6111
Fax 0171-371 2990
*UK branch of French operator
to 88 resorts*

LE SKI
25 Holly Terrace, Huddersfield, West
Yorkshire HD1 6JW
Tel (01484) 548996
Fax (01484) 451909
*Chalet specialists in Courchevel and
Val d'Isère*

LOTUS SUPERTRAVEL
Hobbs Court, Jacob Street,
London SE1 2BT
Tel 0171-962 9933
Fax 0171-962 9965
Holidays to high-altitude resorts

MADE TO MEASURE HOLIDAYS
43 East Street, Chichester,
West Sussex PO19 1HX
Tel (01243) 533333
Fax (01243) 778431
Tailor-made holidays to 110 resorts

MASTERSKI
Thames House, 63-67 Kingston Road,
New Malden, Surrey KT3 3PB
Tel 0181-942 9442
Fax 0181-949 4396
Christian holidays

MARK WARNER
20 Kensington Church Street,
London W8 4EP
Tel 0171-393 3131
Fax 0171-393 0093
Chalet holidays with crèches

MERISKI
The Old School, Great Barrington,
Burford, Oxfordshire OX18 4UR

Tel (01451) 844788
Fax (01451) 844799
Chalet operator to Méribel with crèche

MOGUL SKI
Royal Chambers, Station Parade,
Harrogate, Yorkshire HG1 1EP
Tel (01423) 569512
Fax (01423) 509145
Group holidays to Austria and France

MOSWIN TOURS LTD
Moswin House, 21 Church Street, Oadby,
Leicester LE2 5DB
Tel (01162) 719922
Fax (01162) 716016
Ski holidays to Germany

MOTOURS
Motours House, Old Government
Buildings, Forest Road, Tunbridge Wells,
Kent TN2 5JE
Tel (01892) 518777
Fax (01892) 518666
Ski-drive holidays

**MOUNTAIN AND WILDLIFE
VENTURES**
Compston Road, Ambleside,
Cumbria LA22 9DJ
Tel (015394) 33285
Fax (015394) 34065
Wilderness nordic skiing holidays

NEILSON
71 Houghside Road, Lowtown, Pudsey,
Leeds, West Yorkshire LS28 9BR
Tel (0113) 2394555
Fax (0113) 2393275
Mainstream operator to 51 resorts

NSR TRAVEL
Norway House, 21/24 Cockspur Street,
London SW1Y 5DA
Tel 0171-930 6666
Fax 0171-321 0624
Holidays to Scandinavia

OVER THE HILL
Brierly Place, New London Road,
Chelmsford, Essex CM2 0AP
Tel (01245) 346022
Fax (01245) 354764
Holidays to France for older skiers

PANORAMA SKI
29 Queens Road, Brighton,
East Sussex BN1 3YN
Tel (01273) 206531
Fax (01273) 205338
Budget holidays to Andorra and Italy

PASSAGE TO SOUTH AMERICA
113 Shepherds Bush Road,
London W6 7LP
Tel 0171-602 9889
Fax 0171-602 4251
Holidays to South America

PGL SKI EUROPE
Alton Court, Penyard Lane, Ross-on-Wye,
Herefordshire HR9 5NR
Tel (01989) 768168
Fax (01989) 563162
Schools and groups

PLUS TRAVEL
9 Eccleston Street, London SW1W 9LX
Tel 0171-259 0199
Fax 0171-259 0190
Specialist to Swiss resorts

POLES APART HOLIDAYS
75 Compton Avenue, Plymouth,
Devon PL3 5DD
Tel (01752) 257752
Fax (01752) 229190
Ski and snowboard holidays to France

POWDER BYRNE
4 Alice Court, 116 Putney Bridge Road,
London SW15 2NQ
Tel 0181-871 3300
Fax 0181-871 3322
*Upmarket operator to Switzerland, France,
Italy and Canada*

RAMBLERS
Box 43, Welwyn Garden City,
Hertfordshire AL8 6PQ
Tel (01707) 331133
Fax (01707) 333276
Group cross-country holidays

SIMON BUTLER SKIING
5 Woodbine Cottages, Shalford Common,
Guildford, Surrey GU4 8JX
Tel (01483) 502897
Fax (01483) 452001

Small operator with ski instruction

SILVER SKI
Conifers House, Grove Green Lane,
Maidstone, Kent ME14 5JW
Tel (01622) 735544
Fax (01622) 738550
Catered chalets in Switzerland and France

SIMPLY SKI
Chiswick Gate, 598-608 Chiswick High
Road, London W4 5RT
Tel 0181-742 2541
Fax 0181-995 5346
Small chalet operator with crèche

SKI AIRTOURS
Wavell House, Holcombe Road,
Helmshore, Rossendale,
Lancashire BB54 4NB
Tel (01706) 260000
Fax (01706) 830248
Major operator to 35 resorts

SKI THE AMERICAN DREAM
1/7 Station Chambers, High Street North,
London E6 1JE
Tel 0181-552 1201
Fax 0181-470 1181
US and Canada specialist

SKI AMIS
Alanda, Hornash Lane, Shadoxhurst,
Ashford, Kent TN26 1HT
Tel/Fax (01233) 732769
Self-drive chalet holidays to France

SKI ARDMORE
11-15 High Street, Marlow,
Buckinghamshire SL7 1AU
Tel (01628) 890060
Fax (01628) 898141
*Coach and self-drive holidays for schools
and groups*

SKI BARRETT-BOYCE
14 Hawthorn Road, Wallington,
Surrey SM6 0SX
Tel 0181-647 6934
Fax 0181-647 8620
Holidays to France with ski instruction

SKI BEACH VILLAS
55 Sidney Street, Cambridge CB2 3QR

Tel (01223) 371371
Fax (01223) 68626
Specialist chalet operator to Dolomites

SKI BEAT
57 York Road, Bristol B56 5QD
Tel 0171-955 7361
Fax 0171-941 2099
Chalets in France

SKIBOUND
Olivier House, 18 Marine Parade,
Brighton, East Sussex BN2 1TL
Tel (01273) 677777
Fax (01273) 600999
*Mainstream operator to 40 resorts
in 4 countries*

SKI C&C
Penwood Lodge, Penwood, Burghclere,
nr Newbury RG15 9EX
Tel (01635) 255551
Fax (01635) 255553
Holidays to Canada

SKI CANADA
Cambridge House, Tours Dept,
Third Floor, 8 Cambridge Street,
Glasgow G2 3DZ
Tel 0141-332 1511/
(01345) 090905
Fax 0141-353 0135
Holidays to Canadian Rockies

SKI CHAMOIS
18 Lawn Road, Doncaster DN1 2JF
Tel (01302) 369006
Fax (01302) 326640
Chalet in Morzine

SKI CHOICE
27 High Street, Benson, Wallingford,
Oxfordshire OX10 6RP
Tel (01491) 837607
Fax (01491) 833836
*Individual holidays to France, Austria and
Switzerland*

SKI CLUB OF GREAT BRITAIN
118 Eaton Square,
London SW1W 9YZ
Tel 0171-245 1033
Fax 0171-245 1258
Holidays and courses for all levels

SKI CLUB MEGEVE
213 Sandcross Lane, Reigate,
Surrey RH2 8LL
Tel (01737) 242074
Fax (01737) 242003
Club holidays with free tuition

THE SKI COMPANY
144 Greenwich High Road,
London SE10 8NN
Tel 0171-730 9600
Fax 0171-730 9376
*Luxury chalets in France,
Switzerland and US*

SKI EQUIPE
27 Bramhall Lane South, Bramhall,
Stockport, Cheshire SK7 2DN
Tel 0161-440 0010
Fax 0161-440 0080
*Upmarket chalet and
apartment operator*

SKI ESPRIT
Oaklands, Reading Road North, Fleet,
Hampshire GU13 8AA
Tel (01252) 616789
Fax (01252) 811243
Chalet holidays with crèches and ski tuition

SKI EXPERIENCE
26 College Road, Clifton, Bristol BS8 3HZ
Tel (0117) 9745351
Fax (0117) 9731179
Self-drive holidays to chalets in Méribel

SKI FAMILLE
Unit 9, Chesterton Mill, French's Road,
Cambridge CB4 3NP
Tel (01223) 363777
Fax (01223) 361508
Family holidays with crèches in France

SKI FRANCE
60 Bromley Common, Bromley,
Kent BR2 9PF
Tel 0181-313 0690
Fax 0181-466 0653
Flexible travel to France

SKI GOWER
2 High Street, Studley,
Warwickshire B80 7HJ
Tel (01527) 854822

Fax (01527) 857236
*Schools and groups with British
instructors*

SKI HILLWOOD
2 Field End Road, Pinner,
Middlesex HA5 2QL
Tel 0181-866 9993
Fax 0181-868 0258
*Family holidays with crèches and
junior clubs*

SKI INDEPENDENCE
Broughton Market,
Edinburgh EH3 6NU
Tel 0131-557 8555
Fax 0131-557 1676
Specialist operator to North America

SKI LA VIE
28 Linver Road, London SW6 3RB
Tel 0171-736 5611
Fax 0171-371 8059
*Chalet operator with crèches in
Switzerland and France*

SKI LEOGANG
150 Buckingham Palace Road,
London SW1W 9TR
Tel 0171-730 7234
Fax 0171-730 1180
Operator to Leogang in Austria

SKI LES ALPES
20 Lansdowne Gardens,
London SW8 2EG
Tel 0171-720 7127
Fax 0171-720 7134
Tailor-made holidays

SKI MIQUEL
33 High Street, Uppermill,
Nr Oldham OL3 6HS
Tel (01457) 820200
Fax (01457) 872715
*Long-established operator to Alps
and Spain*

SKI MOOSE
23a High Street, Wealdstone,
Middlesex HA3 5BY
Tel 0181-427 4474/5
Fax 0181-861 4459
Small chalet operator to France

SKI MORGINS
Raughton Head, Carlisle,
Cumbria CA5 7DD
Tel/Fax (016974) 76258
Small operator to Morgins

SKI NORWEST
8 Foxhole Cottages, Foxhole Road,
Horwich, Bolton BL6 6AL
Tel (01204) 668468
Fax (01204) 668568
Holidays to Scotland

SKI OLYMPIC
Pine Lodge, Barnsley Road, Doncaster,
South Yorkshire DN5 8RB
Tel (01302) 390120
Fax (01302) 390787
*Specialist in ski holidays with
crèche to France*

SKI PARTNERS
Friary House, Colston Street,
Bristol BS1 5AP
Tel (0117) 9253545
Fax (0117) 9293697
Operator to Austria, Italy and France

SKI PEAK
The Old Bakery, Dockenfield, Farnham,
Surrey GU10 4HX
Tel (01252) 794941
Fax (01252) 794942
Sole operator to Vaujany with childcare

SKISAFE TRAVEL
Unit 4, Braehead Estate, Old Govan Road,
Renfrew, Scotland PA8 0XJ
Tel 0141-885 1423
Fax 0141-812 1544
*Ski and snowboard in Scotland,
France and Andorra*

SKI SAVOIE
362-364 Sutton Common Road, Sutton,
Surrey SM3 9PL
Tel 0181-715 1122
Fax 0181-644 3068
Specialist operator to Courchevel with crèche

SKI SCOTT DUNN
Fovant Mews, 12 Noyna Road,
London SW17 7PH
Tel 0181-767 0202

Fax 0181-767 2026
*Upmarket operator with crèches, chalets
and heli-skiing*

SKI SOLUTIONS
84 Pembroke Road, London W8 6NX
Tel 0171-602 9900
Fax 0171-602 2882
A la carte hotels and luxury apartments

SKI THOMSON
Greater London House, Hampstead Road,
London NW1 7SD
Tel 0171-707 9000
Fax 0171-387 8451
*Mainstream operator to Europe
and North America*

SKI TOTAL
10 Hill Street, Richmond,
Surrey TW19 1TN
Tel 0181-948 6922
Fax 0181-332 1268
Chalet operator for families

SKI VAL
39a North End Road, London W14 8SZ
Tel 0171-371 4900
Fax 0171-371 4904
*Varied programme to France,
Austria and US*

SKI WEEKEND
2 The Old Barn, Wicklesham
Lodge Farm, Faringdon,
Oxon SN7 7PN
Tel (01367) 241636
Fax (01367) 243833
Weekend breaks with off-piste

SKIWORLD
41 North End Road,
London W14 8SZ
Tel 0171-602 4826
Fax 0171-371 1463
Holidays to France, Andorra and US

SKI WYATT
PO Box 260, Shrewsbury,
Shropshire SY1 1WX
Tel (01952) 840462
Fax (01952) 840463
*Chalet holidays in France,
Switzerland and Austria*

SLOPING OFF
High Street, Handley, Salisbury,
Wiltshire SP5 5NR
Tel (01725) 552247
Fax (01725) 552489
*Coach holidays, schools, groups
and families*

SNOWBIZZ VACANCES
69 High Street, Maxey,
Cambridgeshire PE6 9EE
Tel (01778) 341455
Fax (01778) 347422
*Specialist to Puy St Vincent, crèche and
Kiddies Club*

SNOWCOACH CLUB CANTABRICA
Holiday House, 146-148 London Road, St
Albans, Hertfordshire AL1 1PQ
Tel (01727) 866177
Fax (01727) 843766
Coach holidays to Alps and Pyrenees

SNOWISE HOLIDAYS
The Farmhouse, Nix Hill,
Manea Road, Wimblington, March,
Cambridgeshire OPE15 0PL
Tel (01354) 740493
Fax (01354) 741403
*Personal service for small groups and
families in Châtel*

SNOWLINE HOLIDAYS
Collingbourne House,
Spencer Court, 140-142 High Street,
London SW18 4JJ
Tel 0181-870 4807
Fax 0181-875 9236
*Small operator to France and Switzerland
with crèche*

SNOW STORM SKIING
Courtlands Centre, Kingsbridge, South
Devon TQ7 4BN
Tel (01548) 550227
Fax (01548) 550675
*Small, quality chalet operator to
Chamonix*

SNOWTIME
96 Belsize Lane, London NW3 5BE
Tel 0171-433 3336
Fax 0171-433 1883
Méribel specialist with chalets and crèche

STENA SEALINK HOLIDAYS
Charter House, Park Street, Ashford,
Kent TN24 8EX
Tel (01233) 647033
Fax (01233) 612046
Ski-drive holidays

SUNQUEST BULGARIA
23 Princes Street, London W1R 7RG
Tel 0171-499 9991
Fax 0171-499 9995
Specialist operator to Bulgaria

SUSIE WARD COMPANY
Hurling Burrow, Sevenmilestone, St
Agnes, Cornwall TR5 0PG
Tel (01872) 553055
Fax (01872) 553050
Chalet holidays in France and Switzerland

SWISS TRAVEL SERVICE
Bridge House, 55-59 High Road,
Broxbourne, Hertfordshire EN10 7DT
Tel (01922) 456123
Fax (01922) 448855
*Quality holidays to more than
20 Swiss resorts*

TOP DECK SKI
131-135 Earls Court Road,
London SW5 9RH
Tel 0171-370 4555
Fax 0171-373 6201
Holidays to Alps and Pyrenees

TRAIL ALPINE
68 Mostyn Street, Llandudno,
Gwynedd LL30 2SB
Tel (01492) 871770
Fax (01492) 872437
Ski holidays to France and Canada

TRAVELSCENE SKI DRIVE
11-15 St Ann's Road, Harrow,
Middlesex HA1 1AS
Tel 0181-863 2787
Fax 0181-863 0545
Ski-drive apartment holidays

UCPA/ACTION VACANCES
30 Brackley Road, Stockport,
Cheshire SK4 2RF
Tel/Fax 0161-442 6130
18-40s ski and snowboard packages

VIP
Hyde Park House, Manfred Road,
London SW15 2RS
Tel 0181-875 1957
Fax 0181-875 9236
Exclusively Val d'Isère

VIRGIN SKI
Galleria, Station Road, Crawley,
West Sussex RH10 1WW
Tel (01293) 617181
Fax (01293) 536957
*Operator to California and New
England*

WAYMARK
44 Windsor Road, Slough,
Berkshire SL1 2EJ
Tel (01753) 516477
Fax (01753) 517016
Cross-country specialist

WHITE ROC SKI
69 Westbourne Grove,
London W2 4UJ
Tel/Fax 0171-792 1956
Weekend and tailor-made holidays

WINTERSKI
31 Old Steine, Brighton,
East Sussex BN1 1EL
Tel (01273) 626242
Fax (01273) 620222
*Schools and groups to Italy,
Austria and France*

YSE
The Business Village,
Broomhill Road, London SW18 4JQ
Tel 0181-871 5117
Fax 0181-871 5229
Specialist operator to Val d'Isère

Who goes where?

ANDORRA

Arcalis Snowcoach
Arinsal Crystal, First Choice, Neilson, Panorama, SkiSafe Travel, Ski Thomson
Encamp First Choice, Top Deck
Pal Crystal, Ski Safe Travel, Snowcoach
Pas de la Casa First Choice, Lagrange, Neilson, Panorama, Ski Airtours, Ski Thomson, Top Deck
Soldeu-El Tarter Crystal, First Choice, Neilson, Panorama, Ski Airtours, SkiSafe Travel, Ski Thomson, Skiworld, Top Deck

AUSTRIA

Alpbach Auto Plan Ski Holidays, First Choice, Inghams, Neilson, PGL Ski Europe, Ski Thomson
Altenmarkt Alpine Tours, Mogul Ski
Axamer Lizum PGL Ski Europe, Sloping Off
Badgastein Crystal, First Choice, Inghams, SkiBound, Ski Miquel, Ski Partners
Bad Hofgastein Crystal, First Choice, Made to Measure
Badkleinkirchheim Alpine Tours
Ehrwald Crystal, First Choice
Ellmau Crystal, Inghams, Neilson, Ski Airtours, SkiBound, Ski Thomson
Fieberbrunn SkiBound
Filzmoos Inghams, Made to Measure
Finkenberg Crystal
Flachau Made to Measure
Fügen Ski Partners
Fulpmes Alpine Tours, Crystal
Fuschl Crystal
Galtür Made to Measure
Gargellen Made to Measure
Hopfgarten Contiki, Ski Hillwood, Top Deck
Igls Auto Plan Ski Holidays, First Choice, Inghams, Lagrange, Ski Airtours
Innsbruck Austrian Holidays, Ski Airtours
Ischgl Austrian Holidays, Crystal, Inghams, Made to Measure, Ski Thomson
Itter Crystal
Kaprun Austrian Holidays, Crystal, First Choice, Inghams, Neilson, Ski Airtours
Kirchberg Crystal, First Choice, Neilson, SkiBound, Ski Partners, Stena Sealink, Top Deck, Travelscene Ski Drive
Kirchdorf Crystal
Kitzbühel Austrian Holidays, Crystal, First Choice, Inghams, Kings Ski Club, Lagrange, Neilson, PGL Ski Europe, Ski Airtours, SkiBound, Ski Partners, Ski Thomson, Stena Sealink, Travelscene Ski Drive
Kleinarl Made to Measure
Kolsass Weer Ski Airtours
Kühtai Inghams
Lech Inghams, Made to Measure
Leogang Ski Leogang
Lermoos Crystal, First Choice, Ski Thomson
Mayrhofen Austrian Holidays, Crystal, Equity Total Ski, First Choice, Inghams, PGL Ski Europe, Ski Airtours, Snowcoach, Stena Sealink
Neustift Alpine Tours, Crystal, Inghams
Niederau/Oberau First Choice, Inghams, Lagrange, Neilson, PGL Ski Europe, Ski Thomson
Obergurgl/Hochgurgl Crystal, First Choice, Inghams, Ski Thomson
Obertauern Crystal, Inghams, Neilson, Ski Thomson
Pettneu Crystal
Saalbach/Hinterglemm Crystal, First Choice, Inghams, Kings Ski Club, Mogul Ski, Neilson, PGL Ski Europe, Ski Airtours, SkiBound, Ski Leogang, Ski Partners, Ski Thomson
Scheffau Crystal, First Choice, Ski Thomson
Schladming Crystal, Equity Total Ski, Neilson, PGL Ski Europe, SkiBound, Ski Thomson
Schüttdorf Neilson
Seefeld Austrian Holidays, Crystal, First Choice, Inghams, Ski Thomson
Serfaus Made to Measure
Sölden/Hochsölden Crystal, Inghams, Ski Thomson, Sloping Off
Söll Crystal, First Choice, Inghams, Neilson, PGL Ski Europe, Ski Airtours, SkiBound, Ski Partners, Ski Thomson

St Anton Austrian Holidays, Bladon Lines, Chalets Unlimited, Chalet World, Crystal, First Choice, Inghams, Mark Warner, Neilson, PGL Ski Europe, Ski Equipe, Ski Thomson, Ski Total, Ski Val, Ski Wyatt, Susie Ward
St Johann im Pongau PGL Ski Europe
St Johann in Tirol Crystal, PGL Ski Europe, SkiBound, Ski Partners, Ski Thomson
St Michael Alpine Tours, Ski Partners,
St Wolfgang Crystal, Inghams, Neilson, Ski Airtours, Ski Thomson
Stuben Chalets Unlimited, Ski Total
Waidring Lagrange, Ski Thomson
Wagrain Made to Measure
Westendorf Crystal, First Choice, Inghams, SkiBound, Ski Thomson
Zauchensee Made to Measure, Mogul Ski
Zell am See Crystal, First Choice, Inghams, Lagrange, Neilson, PGL Ski Europe, Ski Airtours, Ski Leogang, Ski Thomson, Travelscene Ski Drive
Zell am Ziller Altours Travel, Equity Total Ski, SkiBound, Stena Sealink, Travelscene Ski Drive
Zürs Made to Measure

BULGARIA
Borovets Balkan Holidays, Balkan Tours, Crystal, Inghams, Ski Ardmore, Sunquest
Pamporovo Balkan Holidays, Balkan Tours, Crystal, Sunquest
Vitosha Balkan Holidays, Sunquest

FRANCE
Alpe d'Huez AA Ski-Driveaway, Alpine Options, Chalets Unlimited, Club Med, Crystal, Equity Total Ski, First Choice, French Impressions, Inghams, Kings Ski Club, Lagrange, Motours, Neilson, PGL Ski Europe, Ski Airtours, SkiBound, Ski Miquel, Ski Partners, Ski Thomson, Skiworld, Stena Sealink, Susie Ward, Travelscene Ski Drive
Les Arcs AA Ski-Driveaway, Club Med, Crystal, Equity Total Ski, First Choice, French Impressions, Inghams, Lagrange, Made to Measure, Masterski, Motours, Neilson, PGL Ski Europe, SkiBound, Ski Thomson, Skiworld, Stena Sealink, Susie Ward, Travelscene Ski Drive, UCPA
Argentière Chalets Unlimited, Crystal, Jean Stanford, Lagrange, Ski Airtours, Ski

Esprit, Snowline, Susie Ward, White Roc
Auris-en-Oisans Lagrange
Avoriaz AA Ski-Driveaway, Chalet Snowboard, Club Med, Crystal, First Choice, French Impressions, Inghams, Kings Ski Club, Lagrange, Made to Measure, Motours, Neilson, Ski Airtours, SkiBound, Ski Thomson, Stena Sealink, Trail Alpine, Travelscene Ski Drive, White Roc
Brides-les-Bains Alpine Options, Crystal, French Impressions, Kings Ski Club, Lagrange, Motours, SkiBound, Stena Sealink, Top Deck
Les Carroz AA Ski-Driveaway, Lagrange, Ski Famille, Winterski
Chamonix AA Ski-Driveaway, Chalets Unlimited, Chinook-It, Club Med, Collineige, Crystal, First Choice, Freedom Holidays, French Impressions, Fresh Tracks, Huski, Inghams, Jean Stanford, Lagrange, Motours, Neilson, Poles Apart, Ski Airtours, The Ski Company, Ski Esprit, Ski Thomson, Snowline, Snow Storm Skiing, Stena Sealink, Susie Ward, Travelscene Ski Drive, White Roc
Champagny-en-Vanoise La France des Villages Ski, French Impressions, Lagrange
Châtel Chalets Unlimited, First Choice, Freedom Holidays, French Impressions, Lagrange, SkiBound, Ski Partners, Ski Weekend, Snowise, Susie Ward, Travelscene Ski Drive
La Clusaz Freedom Holidays, French Impressions, Lagrange, Over the Hill, Silver Ski, Ski Amis, SkiBound, Stena Sealink
Les Coches AA Ski-Driveaway, Chalets Unlimited, French Impressions, Lagrange, Motours, Ski Esprit, Ski Olympic, Travelscene Ski Drive
Les Contamines-Montjoie Chalets Unlimited, Ski Total
Le Corbier Lagrange, Motours
Courchevel AA Ski-Driveaway, Activity Travel, Alpine Action, Bladon Lines, Chalets Unlimited, Chalet World, Crystal, Finlays Skiing Ltd, First Choice, Flexiski, Freedom Holidays, French Impressions, Inghams, Lagrange, Le Ski, Lotus Supertravel, Mark Warner, Motours, PGL Ski Europe, Silver Ski, Ski France, Poles Apart, Powder Byrne, Simply Ski, Ski Airtours, Ski Les Alpes, SkiBound, Ski

Equipe, Ski Esprit, Ski Miquel, Ski Olympic, Ski Savoie, Ski Scott Dunn, Ski Thomson, Ski Val, Ski Weekend, Skiworld, Ski Wyatt, Stena Sealink, Susie Ward, Travelscene Ski Drive, White Roc

Les Deux Alpes Alpine Options, Altours Travel, Bladon Lines, Chalet Snowboard, Chalets Unlimited, Crystal, Equity Total Ski, First Choice, French Impressions, Inghams, Lagrange, Motours, Ski Airtours, SkiBound, Ski Partners, Ski Thomson, Skiworld, Susie Ward, Travelscene Ski Drive, UCPA

Flaine AA Ski-Driveaway, Chalets Unlimited, Crystal, Erna Low Consultants, First Choice, Freedom Holidays, French Impressions, Fresh Tracks, Inghams, Kings Ski Club, Lagrange, Motours, Neilson, Over the Hill, Ski Airtours, SkiSafe Travel, Ski Thomson, Stena Sealink, Travelscene Ski Drive

Les Gets Chalets Unlimited, The Ski Company, Ski Famille, Ski Hillwood, Ski Total, Susie Ward

Le Grand-Bornand Headwater, Lagrange, Stena Sealink

La Grave Fresh Tracks, Neilson, Ski Weekend

Les Houches Chalets Unlimited, Lagrange, Motours

Isola 2000 Made to Measure, Neilson, Travelscene Ski Drive

Megève Chalets Unlimited, Jean Stanford, Lagrange, Ski Ardmore, Ski Barrett-Boyce, Ski Club Megève, Ski Esprit, Ski Weekend, Snowcoach, Travelscene Ski Drive, White Roc

Les Menuires AA Ski-Driveaway, Alpine Action, Club Med, Crystal, Inghams, Lagrange, Motours, PGL Ski Europe, Poles Apart, Ski Airtours, SkiBound, Travelscene Ski Drive

Méribel AA Ski-Driveaway, Activity Travel, Alpine Action, Alpine Options, Bladon Lines, Chalets Unlimited, Chalet World, Club Med, Crystal, Equity Total Ski, First Choice, Flexiski, Freedom Holidays, French Impressions, Inghams, Kings Ski Club, Lagrange, Lotus Supertravel, Mark Warner, Meriski, Motours, Neilson, Over the Hill, PGL Ski Europe, Poles Apart, Silver Ski, Simply Ski, Ski Airtours, The Ski Company, Ski Experience, Ski France, Ski la Vie, Ski Moose, Ski Partners, Ski

Scott Dunn, Skiworld, Ski Wyatt, Snowcoach, Snowtime, Stena Sealink, Susie Ward, Travelscene Ski Drive, White Roc

Montalbert Ski Amis

Montchavin Chalets Unlimited, Lagrange, Simply Ski, Ski Esprit

Montgenèvre Equity Total Ski, First Choice, Lagrange, Ski Ardmore, SkiBound, Ski Thomson

Morgins Ski Morgins

Morillon Lagrange, Mogul Ski, Winterski

Morzine Chalets Unlimited, Chalet Snowboard, Crystal, First Choice, Freedom Holidays, Lagrange, Neilson, SkiBound, Ski Chamois, The Ski Company, Ski Esprit, Ski Moose, Ski Thomson, Snowline, Susie Ward, Trail Alpine, White Roc

Les Orres SkiBound

La Plagne AA Ski-Driveaway, Alpine Options, Altours Travel, Chalets Unlimited, Chalet World, Club Med, Crystal, Erna Low Consultants, First Choice, French Impressions, Inghams, Lagrange, Made to Measure, Mark Warner, Motours, Neilson, PGL Ski Europe, Silver Ski, Simply Ski, Ski Airtours, Ski Amis, Ski Beat, SkiBound, Ski Partners, Ski Thomson, Skiworld, Ski Wyatt, Stena Sealink, Susie Ward, Travel Ski Drive, UCPA

Pra Loup Kings Ski Club, Lagrange, Ski Thomson, Snowcoach

Puy-St-Vincent Alpine Tours, Snowbizz Vacances

Risoul/Vars Crystal, First Choice, Inghams, Lagrange, Neilson, Ski Airtours, Ski Ardmore, SkiBound, Ski Thomson

La Rosière Ski Olympic

Samoëns Lagrange

Serre Chevalier/Briançon Airtrack Snowboarding, Alpine Options, Alpine Tours, Altours Travel, Bladon Lines, Crystal, Equity Total Ski, First Choice, Inghams, Kings Ski Club, Lagrange, Motours, Neilson, PGL Ski Europe, Ski Airtours, Ski Ardmore, SkiBound, Ski Miquel, Ski Partners, Ski Thomson, Stena Sealink

St-Gervais Alpine Tours, Lagrange, PGL Ski Europe, Ski Barrett-Boyce, Snowcoach

St-Martin-de-Belleville ABT Ski, Chalets Unlimited, Ski Total, Stena Sealink

La Tania Alpine Action, Crystal, French

Impressions, Inghams, Lagrange, Neilson, Stena Sealink

Tignes AA Ski-Driveaway, Alpine Options, Altours Travel, Bladon Lines, Chalets Unlimited, Club Med, Crystal, First Choice, Freedom Holidays, Inghams, Kings Ski Club, Lagrange, Motours, Neilson, PGL Ski Europe, Ski Beat, SkiBound, Ski France, Ski Olympic, Ski Thomson, Skiworld, Stena Sealink, Susie Ward, Travelscene Ski Drive, UCPA

La Toussuire First Choice, Motours

Val Cenis Action Vacances, Lagrange, SkiBound, UCPA

Val d'Isère AA Ski-Driveaway, Alpine Options, Bladon Lines, Chalets Unlimited, Chalet World, Club Med, Crystal, Finlays Skiing, First Choice, Freedom Holidays, French Impressions, Inghams, Kings Ski Club, Lagrange, Le Ski, Lotus Supertravel, Mark Warner, Motours, Neilson, Silver Ski, Ski Les Alpes, SkiBound, Ski France, Ski Olympic, Ski Scott Dunn, Ski Thomson, Ski Val, Ski Weekend, Skiworld, Ski Wyatt, Stena Sealink, Susie Ward, Trail Alpine, Travelscene Ski Drive, UCPA, VIP, White Roc, YSE

Valfréjus Lagrange, Motours, Neilson

Valloire/Valmeinier First Choice, Lagrange, Snowcoach

Valmorel/St-François-Longchamp AA Ski-Driveaway, Altours Travel, Chalets Unlimited, Crystal, Equity Total Ski, French Impressions, Inghams,Lagrange, Motours, Neilson. Simply Ski, SkiBound, Ski Thomson, Stena Sealink, Susie Ward, Travelscene Ski Drive

Val Thorens AA Ski-Driveaway, Alpine Action, Alpine Options, Crystal, Equity Total Ski, First Choice, Freedom Holidays, French Impressions, Inghams, Lagrange, Motours, PGL Ski Europe, SkiBound, Ski France, Poles Apart, Ski Airtours, Ski Thomson, Stena Sealink, Susie Ward, Travelscene Ski Drive, UCPA, White Roc

Vaujany Ski Peak

ITALY

Alba Crystal, Simply Ski

Andalo Equity Total Ski, PGL Ski Europe, Winterski

Arabba Ski Beach Villas

Bardonecchia Crystal, Equity Total Ski,

Neilson, Ski Airtours, Ski Ardmore

Bormio Altours Travel, Crystal, First Choice, Ski Airtours, Ski Thomson

Campitello First Choice, Inghams

Canazei Crystal, First Choice, Inghams, Simply Ski

Cavalese First Choice

Cervinia Crystal, First Choice, Inghams, Ski Airtours, Ski Thomson

Cesana Torinese PGL Ski Europe, SkiBound

Champoluc Crystal

Chiesa First Choice

Clavière Equity Total Ski, Neilson, SkiBound

Cortina d'Ampezzo Crystal, Powder Byrne, Winterski

Courmayeur Bladon Lines, Crystal, First Choice, Inghams, Interski, Mark Warner, Ski Airtours, Ski Thomson, Ski Weekend, Stena Sealink, White Roc, Winterski

Foppolo Crystal, Equity Total Ski, SkiBound, Ski Partners, Winterski

Gressoney Crystal

Livigno Crystal, First Choice, Inghams, Panorama Ski, Ski Airtours, Ski Thomson

Macugnaga Crystal, Neilson

Madesimo Altours Travel, Crystal, Inghams, Ski Airtours, SkiBound, Ski Partners, Ski Thomson

Madonna di Campiglio Crystal, Inghams, Ski Airtours, Winterski

Marilleva Equity Total Ski, Winterski

Passo Tonale Altours Travel, Crystal, Equity Total Ski, First Choice, PGL Ski Europe, Ski Airtours, Winterski

Piancavallo PGL Ski Europe

Pila Interski

Pozza di Fassa Crystal, Winterski

San Cassiano First Choice

Sansicario Equity Total Ski, Stena Sealink

Santa Caterina Crystal, First Choice, Ski Airtours, Ski Thomson

Sauze d'Oulx Crystal, First Choice, Inghams, Neilson, Panorama Ski, Ski Airtours, SkiBound, Ski Partners, Ski Thomson, Winterski

Selva Bladon Lines, Crystal, First Choice, Inghams

Sestriere Club Med, Crystal, Equity Total Ski, Neilson

La Thuile Bladon Lines, Crystal, First Choice, Interski, Neilson, Ski Thomson

Vigo di Fassa Crystal

La Villa Ski Beach Villas

NORTH AMERICA

Aspen/Snowmass Activity Travel, Crystal, Ski The American Dream, Ski Independence, Skiworld

Banff/Lake Louise Accessible Isolation, Activity Travel, All Canada Ski, Chinook-It, Crystal, Frontier Ski, Inghams, Lotus Supertravel, Made to Measure, Neilson, Powder Byrne, Ski Airtours, Ski The American Dream, Ski Airtours, SkiBound, Ski Canada, Ski C&C, Ski Gower, Ski Independence, Ski Thomson, Skiworld

Beaver Creek Crystal, Flexiski, Inghams, Ski The American Dream, Ski Thomson, Skiworld

Big Sky Crystal

Blue Mountain All Canada Ski

Breckenridge Activity Travel, Chalet World, Crystal, Equity Total Ski, First Choice, Inghams, Jean Stanford, Neilson, Ski Airtours, Ski The American Dream, Ski Gower, Ski Independence, Ski Thomson, Skiworld, Ski Val

Copper Mountain Club Med, Ski Airtours

Crested Butte Activity Travel, Ski The American Dream, Ski Independence, Skiworld

Deer Valley Virgin Ski

Frisco Equity Total Ski, Ski Airtours

Heavenly Inghams, Skiworld, Ski The American Dream, Virgin Ski

Jackson Hole Activity Travel, Crystal, Lotus Supertravel, Ski The American Dream, Ski Independence, Ski Scott Dunn, Skiworld

Jasper All Canada Ski, Crystal, Frontier Ski, Inghams, Ski The American Dream, Ski Independence, Ski Thomson

Keystone Crystal, Ski Airtours, Ski The American Dream, Ski Independence, Skiworld

Killington Activity Travel, Crystal, Ski The American Dream, Ski Independence, Virgin Ski

Lake Tahoe Activity Travel, Crystal, Virgin Ski

Mammoth Mountain Activity Travel, Crystal, Inghams, Skiworld, Ski The American Dream, Virgin Ski

Mont Tremblant All Canada Ski, Crystal, Inghams

Panorama All Canada Ski, Frontier Ski,
Ski Gower

Park City Activity Travel, Crystal, Ski The American Dream, Ski Independence, Skiworld, Virgin Ski

Smuggler's Notch Ski The American Dream

Silver Star All Canada Ski, Accessible Isolation, Frontier Ski, Ski The American Dream, Ski Canada

Snowbird Crystal, Ski The American Dream, Virgin Ski

Squaw Valley Skiworld, Ski The American Dream, Virgin Ski

Steamboat Activity Travel, Crystal, First Choice, Lotus Supertravel, Ski The American Dream, Ski Independence, Skiworld

Stowe Crystal, Ski The American Dream, Ski Independence, Virgin Ski

Sun Valley Activity Travel, Ski The American Dream, Ski Independence

Taos Crystal, Ski The American Dream, Ski Independence, Skiworld

Telluride Ski The American Dream, Ski Independence, Skiworld

Vail Activity Travel, Crystal, First Choice, Inghams, Lotus Supertravel, Ski The American Dream, The Ski Company, Ski Independence, Ski Thomson, Ski Val, Skiworld

Whistler/Blackcomb Accessible Isolation, Chinook-It, Crystal, Frontier Ski, Inghams, Lotus Supertravel, Neilson, Powder Byrne, Ski The American Dream, SkiBound, Ski Canada, Ski C&C, Ski Independence, Ski Miquel, Ski Thomson, Skiworld, Trail Alpine

White Fish Chinook-It

Winter Park Crystal, Ski The American Dream, Ski Independence, Ski Thomson

NORWAY

Geilo Auto Plan Ski Holidays, Crystal, Dawson and Sanderson, NSR, Waymark

Hemsedal Crystal, NSR, Waymark

Lillehammer NSR, Ramblers

Voss Crystal, Dawson and Sanderson, NSR

THE PYRENEES

Barèges Borderline, Ski Thomson

Cauterets Lagrange, Ski Thomson

Font-Romeu Lagrange

La Mongie Lagrange
St-Lary Lagrange
Superbagnères Club Med

ROMANIA
Poiana Brasov Balkan Holidays, Balkan Tours, Crystal, First Choice, Inghams, Sunquest
Sinaia Crystal

SCOTLAND
Aviemore Ski Norwest, SkiSafe Travel
Glenshee Ski Norwest, SkiSafe Travel
Nevis Range Ski Norwest, SkiSafe Travel

SLOVENIA
Bled Alpine Tours
Bohinj Alpine Tours
Kransjska Gora Alpine Tours, Inghams.

SPAIN
Baqueira-Beret Ski Miquel
Formigal Ski Thomson
Sierra Nevada First Choice, Ski Thomson

SWEDEN
Are Crystal

SWITZERLAND
Adelboden Auto Plan Ski Holidays, Inghams, Kuoni, Plus Travel
Andermatt Made to Measure
Anzère Lagrange, Made to Measure
Arosa Inghams, Kuoni, Plus Travel, Ski Gower, Swiss Travel Service
Champéry Chalets Unlimited, Freedom Holidays, Kuoni, Ski La Vie, Ski Weekend, Snowline
Champoussin Snowline
Château d'Oex Kuoni, Ski Airtours
Crans Montana Inghams, Kuoni, Lagrange, PGL Ski Europe, Plus Travel, Travelscene Ski Drive
Les Diablerets Lagrange, Ski Gower
Davos Inghams, Kuoni, Plus Travel, Ski Gower, Ski Weekend, Swiss Travel Service, White Roc
Engelberg Auto Plan Ski Holidays, Kuoni, Plus Travel, Ski Gower, Ski Weekend
Flims/Laax Plus Travel, Powder Byrne, Ski Choice, Ski Weekend, Swiss Travel Service
Grächen Ski Choice
Grindelwald Inghams, Kuoni, Plus Travel, Powder Byrne, Ski Gower, Ski Thomson, Swiss Travel Service
Gstaad Made to Measure, Ski Gower
Interlaken Auto Plan Ski Holidays, Kuoni
Kandersteg Kuoni, Waymark
Klosters Kuoni, Plus Travel, Powder Byrne, The Ski Company, Ski Gower, Ski Weekend, Swiss Travel Service
Lauterbrunnen Ski Miquel, Top Deck
Lenzerheide/Valbella Club Med, Inghams, Kuoni, Ski Gower
Leysin Lagrange
Morgins Chalets Unlimited
Mürren Chalets Unlimited, Inghams, Kuoni, Made to Measure, Plus Travel, Ski Gower, Swiss Travel Service
Nendaz Travelscene Ski Drive
Ovronnaz Lagrange
Pontresina Club Med, Ski Gower, Swiss Travel Service
Saas-Fee Crystal, Inghams, Kuoni, Lagrange, Plus Travel, Ski Gower, Ski Thomson, Swiss Travel Service
Saas-Grund Lagrange, PGL Ski Europe
St Moritz Club Med, Inghams, Kuoni, Ski Gower, Swiss Travel Service
Verbier Activity Travel, Bladon Lines, Chalets Unlimited, Chalet World, Crystal, First Choice, Flexiski, Fresh Tracks, Inghams, Kuoni, Mark Warner, Neilson, Plus Travel, Silver Ski, Simply Ski, Ski Equipe, Ski Esprit, Ski Thomson, Ski Weekend, Ski Wyatt, Susie Ward, Swiss Travel Service, White Roc
Villars-sur-Ollon Chalets Unlimited, Club Med, Kuoni, Ski Esprit, Ski Weekend, Stena Sealink, Swiss Travel Service, Travelscene Ski Drive
Wengen Club Med, Crystal, Inghams, Kuoni, PGL Ski Europe, Plus Travel, Ski Gower, Ski Thomson, Swiss Travel Service
Zermatt Bladon Lines, Chalets Unlimited, Crystal, Inghams, Kuoni, Lotus Supertravel, Plus Travel, Powder Byrne, Ski Les Alpes, Ski Gower, Ski Scott Dunn, Ski Thomson, Ski Total, Susie Ward, Swiss Travel Service
Zinal Club Med

Skiing by numbers

Travel to ski

NATIONAL TOURIST OFFICES
The tourist offices listed below are for countries with recognised ski resorts.

Andorran Delegation
63 Westover Road, London SW18 2RF
Tel 0181-874 4806 (no fax)

Austrian National Tourist Office
30 St George Street, London W1R 0AL
Tel 0171-629 0461 **Fax** 0171-499 6038

Balkan Holidays (for Bulgaria)
Sofia House, 19 Conduit Street, London W1R 9TD
Tel 0171-491 4499 **Fax** 0171-491 7068
Snowline (0839) 400 409

Canadian High Commission
The Visit Canada Centre, 62-65 Trafalgar Square, London WC2N 5DY
Tel 0171-839 2299 **Fax** 0171-389 1149

Cedok (Czech Republic and Slovakia)
49 Southwark Street,
London SE1 1RU
Tel 0171-378 6009 **Fax** 0171-403 2321

French Government Tourist Office
178 Piccadilly, London W1V OAL
Tel (08912) 44123 (no fax)

Italian State Tourist Office
1 Princes Street, London W1R 8AY
Tel 0171-408 1254 **Fax** 0171-493 6695

Norwegian Tourist Board
Charles House, 5-11 Lower Regent Street, London SW1Y 4LR
Tel 0171-839 6255 **Fax** 0171-839 6014

Romanian National Tourist Office
83a Marylebone High Street, London W1M 3DE
Tel/Fax 0171-224 3692

Scottish Tourist Board
23 Ravelston Terrace, Edinburgh, Lothian EH4 3EU
Tel 0131-332 2433 **Fax** 0131-343 1513

Slovenian Tourist Office
2 Canfield Place, London NW6 3BT
Tel 0171-372 3767 **Fax** 0171-372 3763

Spanish Tourist Office
57 St James's Street, London SW1A 1LD
Tel 0171-499 0901 **Fax** 0171-629 4257

Swedish Tourist Board
73 Welbeck Street, London W1M 8AN
Tel 0171-935 9784 **Fax** 0171-935 5853

Swiss National Tourist Office
Swiss Centre, New Coventry Street, London W1V 8EE
Tel 0171-734 1921 **Fax** 0171-437 4577

United States Travel and Tourism
PO Box 1EN, London W1A 1EN
Tel 0171-495 4466 **Fax** 0171-495 4377

SKI TRAVEL AGENTS AND CONSULTANTS
Alpine Answers
The Business Village, 3-9 Broomhill Road, London SW18 4JQ
Tel 0181-871 5100 **Fax** 0181-871 9676

Erna Low Consultants
9 Reece Mews, London SW7 3HE
Tel 0171-584 2841/7820 **Fax** 0171-589 9531

Ski Solutions
84 Pembroke Road, London W8 6NX
Tel 0171-602 9900 **Fax** 0171-602 2882

Ski and Surf
37 Priory Field Drive, Edgware, Middlesex HA8 9PT
Tel 0181-958 2418 **Fax** 0181-905 4146

Ski Travel Centre
1100 Pollokshaws Road, Shawlands,

Glasgow, Strathclyde G41 3NJ
Tel 0141-649 9696 **Fax** 0141-649 2273
Skiers Travel Bureau
Marco Polo Travel, 79 Street Lane,
Roundhay, Leeds LS8 1AP
Tel (0113) 2666876 **Fax** (0113) 2693305

Snowline
1 Angel Court, High Street, Market
Harborough, Leicestershire LE16 7NL
Tel (01858) 433633 **Fax** (01858) 433266

Susie Ward Company
Hurling Burrow, Sevenmilestone,
St Agnes, Cornwall TR5 0PG
Tel (01872) 553055 **Fax** (01872) 553050

HELI-SKI COMPANIES
ITALY
ETI 2000
Quart, Aosta
Tel 39 165 765417
Fax 39 165 765418
Courmayeur, Valgrisenche and Cervinia

Lacadur Heli-Ski
I-11010 Valgrisenche, Aosta
Tel 33.50 54 08 40 (Chamonix)
Tel/Fax 39 165 97138 (Valgrisenche)
Three-day packages in Aosta Valley area

SWITZERLAND
Air Glaciers Trans-Heli SA
Box 236, CH-1868 Colombey
Tel 41 25 712626 **Fax** 41 25 719453

Bohag
3814 Gsteigwiler
Tel 41 36 229230 **Fax** 41 36 220972
Bernese Oberland

CANADA
Canadian Mountain Holidays (UK agent)
61 Doneraile Street, London SW6 6EW
Tel 0171-736 8191 **Fax** 0171-384 2592
*Nine locations in British Columbia.
Packages include accommodation*

Mike Wiegele Helicopter Skiing
Box 249, Banff, Alberta, Canada
Tel 1 403 762 5548 **Fax** 1 403 762 5846
*Blue River in British Columbia. Packages
include luxury accommodation*

Fresh Tracks (UK agents for Mike
Wiegele)
Argyll House, All Saints Passage, London
SW18 1EP
Tel 0181-875 9818 **Fax** 0181-874 8827

Ski Scott Dunn (UK agents for Mike
Wiegele)
Fovant Mews, 12 Noyna Road, London
SW17 7PH
Tel 0181-767 0202 **Fax** 0181-767 2026

GUIDED SKI COURSES
The names listed below specialise in ski
clinic holidays and do not appear in the tour
operators list. Note, several of the tour
operators in the main list also offer ski
clinic-type courses.

Ali Ross
Ski Solutions, 84 Pembroke Road, London
W8 6NX
Tel 0171-602 9900 **Fax** 0171-602 2882
*Specialist intermediate and advanced
courses in Tignes*

Alpine McAnnix
(contact Ski and Surf)
37 Priory Field Drive, Edgware, Middlesex
HA8 9PT
Tel 0181-958 2418 **Fax** 0181-905 4146
*Andi McCann's personal performance
courses in Soldeu and Vail*

BEST
Tel (01803) 859075
*British European Ski Teachers is a co-oper-
ative of BASI-qualified instructors based
and licensed to teach in the Alps*

British Alpine Ski School
*British instructors licensed to teach in
France who have set up their own ski school*

(Avoriaz)
7 Orleigh Court, Buckland Brewer,
Bideford, Devon EX39 5EH
Tel/Fax (01237) 451099

(Morzine/Les Gets)
4 Chilvers Place, Heacham, Norfolk
PE31 7JT
Tel (01485) 572596 or 33 50 79 86 58

Fred Foxon
The Old Vicarage, Merton, Bicester
OX6 ONF
Tel/Fax (01865) 331621
*Personal performance weeks in
Val d'Isère*

Fun Ski
43 East Street, Chichester, West Sussex
PO19 1HX
Tel (01243) 533333 **Fax** (01243) 778431
*Personalised ski development courses in
Altenmarkt, Austria*

McGarry The Ski System
5 Barnhill Road, Dalkey, Co Dublin,
Ireland
Tel (353) 1 285 9139 **Fax** (353) 1 284
9932
Ski clinics in Châtel, Portes du Soleil

Mountain Experience
The Cottage, Whitehough Head, Chinley,
Stockport, Cheshire SK12 6BX
Tel/Fax (01663) 750160
*Guiding and ski-touring in Chamonix. Also
Haute Route and Bernese Oberland*

Optimum Ski Courses
Chalet Tarentaise, Le Pré, Villaroger,
F-73640 Sainte-Foy, France
Tel 33 79 06 91 26/(01992) 561085
*Ski clinics in Les Arcs and Tignes with BASI
trainer*

Ski Club of Great Britain
118 Eaton Square, London SW1W 9AF
Tel 0171-245 1033 **Fax** 0171-245 1258
*Ski courses for all standards, off-piste and
ski safaris*

Ski Masterclass
Birchview, Railway Terrace, Aviemore,
Scotland PH22 1SA
Tel (01479) 810814/33 79 08 22 00
Fax (01479) 811659/33 79 08 39 91
*English-speaking classes with BASI
instructors in Courchevel*

Ski Principles
19 Church Street, Brixham, Devon TQ5
8HG
Tel (01803) 852185
Personal performance courses in Méribel

The Ski Company
13 Squires Close, Bishop's Park,
Bishop's Stortford, Hertfordshire
CM23 4DB
Tel (01279) 653746 **Fax** (01279) 654705
*Special ski weeks in Tignes. Also mogul and
slalom clinics*

Roland Stieger
Route de Taconnaz, F-74310 Les
Houches, France
Tel 33 50 54 43 53 **Fax** 33 50 54 46 26
*Chamonix-based courses and mountain
guiding*

Top Ski
Galerie des Cimes, BP 41, F-73150
Val d'Isère, France
Tel 33 79 06 14 80 **Fax** 33 79 06 28 42
*Leading alternative ski school. Off-piste,
summer skiing and piste clinics*

SKI INSURANCE COMPANIES
American Express
Sussex House, Civic Way, Burgess Hill,
West Sussex RH15 9AQ
Tel (01444) 239900 Fax (01444) 235257

Douglas Cox Tyrie Ltd
Central House, High Street, London
E15 2PF
Tel 0181-534 9595 **Fax** 0181-519 8780

Endsleigh Insurance Services Ltd
97-107 Southampton Row,
London WC1B 4AG
Tel 0171-436 4451 **Fax** 0171-637 3132

Europ Assistance
Sussex House, Perrymount Road,
Haywards Heath, West Sussex
RH16 1DN
Tel (01444) 442211 **Fax** (01444) 459292

Fogg Travel Insurance Ltd
Fullerton Lodge, Crow Hill Drive,
Mansfield, Nottinghamshire NG19 7AE
Tel (01623) 631331/5 **Fax** (01623) 420450

Hamilton Barr
Bridge Mews, Bridge Street, Godalming,
Surrey GU7 1HZ
Tel (01483) 426600 **Fax** (01483) 426382

SKIING ORGANISATIONS

Artificial Ski Slope Instructors (ASSI)
The English Ski Council, The Area Library Building, Queensway Mall, The Cornbow, Halesowen, West Midlands B63 4AJ
Tel 0121-501 2314 **Fax** 0121-585 6448

British Association of Ski Instructors (BASI)
Grampian Road, Aviemore, Scotland PH22 1RL
Tel (01479) 810407 **Fax** (01479) 811222

British Ski Federation
258 Main Street, East Calder, West Lothian, Scotland EH53 0EE
Tel (01506) 884343 **Fax** (01506) 882952

British Snowboarding Association
c/o Steve Davis, 5 Cressex Road, High Wycombe, Buckinghamshire HP12 4PG
Tel (01494) 462225

SKI COUNCILS

These bodies govern the sport as a whole, taking responsibility for promoting and developing skiing and skiers' interests with the aid of grants from the Sports Council.

English Ski Council
Area Library Building, Queensway Mall, The Cornbow, Halesowen, West Midlands B63 4AJ
Tel 0121-501 2314 **Fax** 0121-585 6448

Scottish National Ski Council
Caledonia House, South Gyle, Edinburgh EH12 9DQ
Tel 0131-317 7280 **Fax** 0131-339 8602

Ski Council of Wales
240 Whitchurch Road, Cardiff CF4 3ND
Tel (01222) 619637 **Fax** (01222) 522178

SKI CLUBS

Alpbach Visitors Club
Barhaus, A-6236 Alpbach, Tyrol, Austria
Tel 43 5336 5282

British Alpine Racing Ski Clubs (BARSC)
c/o J Hewitt, Suite 45, IMEX Business

Park, Shobnall Road, Burton-on-Trent, Staffordshire DE14 2AU
Tel (01283) 515521 **Fax** (01283) 515841

British Ski Club for the Disabled
Springmount, Berwick St John, Shaftesbury, Wiltshire SP7 0HQ
Tel (01747) 828515

Downhill Only
c/o Jenny Alban Davies, Troutbeck, Otford, Sevenoaks, Kent TN14 5PH
Tel (01959) 525439
Based in Wengen, Switzerland

Kandahar Ski Club
c/o Mrs J Holmes, Woodside, Benenden, Cranbrook, Kent TN17 4EZ
Tel (01580) 240606 **Fax** (01580) 241684
Based in Mürren, Switzerland

Ladies Ski Club
c/o J Glasson, 40 Aynhoe Road, London W14 0QD
Tel 0171-603 7464

Mardens
c/o S Ingram, Southridge House, Streatly, nr Reading, Berkshire RG8 9SJ
Tel (01491) 872710
Based in Klosters, Switzerland

Scottish Ski Club
Mayview, Ardagie, By Forgandenny, Perthshire PH2 9DG
Tel/Fax (01738) 812180

Ski Club of Manchester
210 Bramhall Moor Lane, Hazel Grove, Stockport SK7 5JJ
Tel 0161-483 3139

The Uphill Ski Club of Great Britain
12 Park Crescent, London W1N 4EQ
Tel 0171-636 1989 **Fax** 0171-436 2601
Organisation for disabled skiers

Ski Club of Great Britain
118 Eaton Square, London SW1W 9AF
Tel 0171-245 1033 **Fax** 0171-245 1258

Now the dominant club for British skiers, the SCGB was formed in 1903 by a group of 11 pioneers of downhill skiing 'to encourage the sport of skiing, assist novices, give information to members and bring together persons interested in the sport'. In the Club's early days, the organisation of ski racing formed a significant part of its activities (the first World Championships in alpine downhill and slalom racing were organised by the Club at Mürren in 1931). Although the club retains its original aims, it concentrates these days on recreational skiing, and offers its members an impressive range of services and benefits to help them get the most out of their skiing holidays.

The aspect of the Club best known to non-members is its gathering of information about skiing conditions: its snow reports are widely published during the skiing season. These reports come from the Club's representatives who are present in over 30 major resorts (listed below) throughout the season to help visiting members. The reps organise weekly programmes, as part of which they lead groups of different standards around the slopes, on- and off-piste. Members who like the idea of skiing for the whole of their holiday in a compatible group led by a qualified person, perhaps with the intention of improving a particular aspect of their skiing, are catered for by the Club's programme of organised skiing parties.

The Club also administers the British Ski Tests, designed to provide skiers with a measure of their skiing competence, and runs an Information Department at its London headquarters, staffed by experienced skiers with access to extensive files of detailed information on resorts and on other aspects of skiing including, for example, equipment stockists.

The clubhouse is also a social centre, with a popular bar serving snacks. There is a year-round programme of events (social and ski-related) here and around the country. The Club has a network of regional and local representatives, and links with many dry ski slopes. As well as an annual Members' Handbook, members receive five issues of *Ski Survey*, Britain's original skiing magazine. Among other benefits for members are discounts (commonly 5 or 10 per cent) on the cost of ski holidays and equipment from a wide range of suppliers, in the Alps as well as Britain.

Resorts expected to have SCGB representatives in the 1995–6 season include:

Andorra
Soldeu

Austria
Igls ● Kitzbühel ● Mayrhofen ● Obergurgl ● St Anton ● Schladming ● Söll

France
Alpe d'Huez ● Avoriaz ● Chamonix/Argentière ● Courchevel ● Flaine ● Isola 2000 ● La Plagne ● Megève ● Serre Chevalier ● Tignes ● Val d'Isère ● Val Thorens

Italy
Cervinia

Switzerland
Arosa ● Crans Montana ● Gstaad ● Klosters ● Mürren● St Moritz ● Verbier ● Villars ● Wengen ● Zermatt

GETTING THERE

GOING BY AIR
Main airlines in the UK
Those listed below offer international scheduled flights to airports close to the ski areas.

American Airlines
Tel 0181-572 5555
Austrian Airlines
Tel 0171-434 7300
Air Canada
Tel 0181-759 2636
Air France
Tel 0181-742 6600
Alitalia
Tel 0171-602 7111

British Airways
Tel 0181-897 4000
Continental Airlines
Tel (01293) 776464
Delta Airlines
Tel (0800) 414767
Lauda Air
Tel 0171-630 5924
Northwest Airlines
Tel (01293) 561000
Swissair
Tel 0171-439 4144
United Airlines
Tel (0800) 888 555
Virgin Atlantic Airways
Tel (01293) 747747

GOING BY RAIL
Going by rail to the Alps is often easier for families, financially and luggage-wise, and the added bonus is an extra day's skiing. A group of tour operators offer the Snow Train option to France and Austria, leaving Calais on Friday evenings and arriving in time for skiing the following morning.

Below are a few useful telephone numbers if travelling by rail.

British Rail International
Tel 0171-834 2345
French Railways
Passenger information Tel (0891) 515477
Motorail Tel 0171-409 3518
Swiss Rail
Tel 0171-734 1921

GOING BY CAR
For further information on driving out see page 544

Brittany Ferries (Portsmouth-Caen)
Tel (01705) 827701
Hoverspeed (Dover-Calais, Folkestone-Boulogne)

Tel (01304) 240241
Le Shuttle
Tel (0990) 353535
North Sea Ferries (Hull-Zeebrugge, Hull-Rotterdam)
Tel (01482) 377177
P & O European Ferries (Portsmouth-Le Havre, Dover-Calais, Felixstowe-Zeebrugge, Portsmouth-Cherbourg)
Tel (01304) 203388
Sally Lines (Ramsgate-Dunkerque, Ramsgate-Ostend)
Tel (01843) 595522
Stena Sealink Line (Dover-Calais, Harwich-Hook, Newhaven-Dieppe, Southampton-Cherbourg)
Tel (01233) 647047

BREAKDOWN INSURANCE
AA Five Star Services
Tel (0345) 555577
Autohome Ltd
Tel (01604) 232334
Europ Assistance
Tel (01444) 442211
Green Flag
National Breakdown
Tel (0800) 800600
Mondial Assistance
Tel 0181-681 2525
RAC Travel Services
Tel (0800) 550055

CAR RENTAL COMPANIES
Alamo Rent-A-Car
Tel (01895) 443355
Avis
Tel 0181-848 8733
Budget Rent-a-Car
Tel (0800) 181181
Europcar Inter Rent
Tel (0113) 2422233
Hertz
Tel 0181-679 1799
Holiday Autos
Tel 0171-491 1111

Reporting on the resorts

Reporters to the Guide stand a good chance of winning a free copy of the next edition. Resort reports should use the structure set out below and be sent to: Dept CD, Consumers' Association, FREEPOST, 2 Marylebone Road, London NW1 4DF. No stamp is needed.

Please write as clearly as you can, or if at all possible, type your resort reports. Use separate sheets for different resorts, however short your reports.

Please keep sending us your reports, they are an invaluable contribution to the essence of the book. You can now contact us via electronic mail.

E-mail address: guidereports@which.co.uk

Resort report checklist:

BASICS
Your name and address
Your skiing background (experience, competence)
Resort name/country
Date of visit
Tour operator used
Hotel/chalet/apartment block stayed in

VERDICTS
Your reaction to our 'good points' and 'bad points' verdicts on the resort.

OPERATION OF LIFTS
New lifts, upgraded lifts, lift queues, lift passes (and where they cover) and other payment systems.

OPERATION OF RUNS
Remarks on piste-marking, piste-grooming, piste closure, artificial snow, accuracy of resort piste map. Name any favourite runs and interesting off-piste descents.

MOUNTAIN RESTAURANTS
General comments, specific named recommendations.

SKI SCHOOLS
Remarks on organisation, tuition, language, use of time, allocation of pupils to classes, group size etc. Cover private lessons, guiding and special courses if you tried them. It is essential to specify which ski school you used.

CHILDREN'S FACILITIES

Remarks on ski and/or non-ski kindergarten: facilities, staff competence and attitude, language, approach to ski tuition, meals, hours, cost etc. Specify which kindergarten or ski school.

LOCAL TRANSPORT

Transport within the resort, where you can get to, and where you cannot, frequency, reliability, convenience, cost, crowding, value of having a car.

ACCIDENT/MEDICAL FACILITIES

Your experience of any mountain rescue and subsequent hospital treatment.

SHOPPING

Range of everyday (food/supermarket) shops, including quality, service and prices. Range of other (clothing/jewellery/gift) shops.

NON-SKIING FACILITIES

Range, quality, convenience, price of sporting and other non-skiing facilities in the resort; excursion possibilities.

EATING OUT

Range and type of restaurant, general comments; specific recommendations essential.

APRES-SKI

Range and style of bars, restaurants, discos, clubs; what happens in the resort after skiing, from tea-time until the small hours; specific recommendations essential.

Resort index

Untergurgl	87	Vaujany	158	Waidring	139
Vail	487	Venosc	197	Wengen	384
Val di Fassa	337	Vent	87	Westendorf	125
Val d'Isère	271	Verbier	407	Whistler Creek	502
Val Gardena	337	Veysonnaz	407	Whistler	497
Val Thorens	254	Vichères	414	Winter Park	508
Valbella	430	Vigo di Fassa	337	Wirl	55
Valberg	290	La Villa	340	Wolfgang	368
Valdidentro	322	Villard-Reculas	159	Zauchensee	150
Valdisotto	322	Villaroger	161	Zell am See	141
Vallandry	166	Villars-sur-Ollon	415	Zell am Ziller	79
Vallée Blanche	179	Villeneuve	248	Zermatt	421
Valloire	291	La Villette	159	Zug	66
Valmeinier	291	Vitosha	520	Zürs	72
Valmorel	282	Vorderlanesbach	79	Zweisimmen	381
Valtournenche	300	Voss	527	Zwieselstein	118
Vars	246	Wagrain	150		